MASS MEDIA RESEARCH

From the Wadsworth Series in Mass Communication and Journalism

■■

General Mass Communication

Biagi, *Media/Impact: An Introduction to Mass Media*, Enhanced Tenth Edition

Fellow, *American Media History*, Third Edition

Hilmes, *Connections: A Broadcast History Reader*

Hilmes, *Only Connect: A Cultural History of Broadcasting in the United States*, Third Edition

Lester, *Visual Communication: Images with Messages*, Sixth Edition

Overbeck, *Major Principles of Media Law*, 2013 Edition

Straubhaar/LaRose/Davenport, *Media Now: Understanding Media, Culture, and Technology*, Eighth Edition

Zelezny, *Cases in Communications Law*, Sixth Edition

Zelezny, *Communications Law: Liberties, Restraints, and the Modern Media*, Sixth Edition

Journalism

Bowles/Borden, *Creative Editing*, Sixth Edition

Davis/Davis, *Think Like an Editor: 50 Strategies for the Print and Digital World*, Second Edition

Hilliard, *Writing for Television, Radio, and New Media*, Tenth Edition

Kessler/McDonald, *When Words Collide: A Media Writer's Guide to Grammar and Style*, Eighth Edition

Kessler/McDonald, *Cengage Advantage Books: When Words Collide: A Media Writer's Guide to Grammar and Style + Exercise Book*, Eighth Edition

Rich, *Writing and Reporting News: A Coaching Method*, Seventh Edition

Public Relations and Advertising

Diggs-Brown, *Strategic Public Relations: Audience Focused Approach*

Diggs-Brown, *The PR Styleguide: Formats for Public Relations Practice*, Third Edition

Drewniany/Jewler, *Creative Strategy in Advertising*, Eleventh Edition

Hendrix, *Public Relations Cases*, Ninth Edition

Newsom/Haynes, *Public Relations Writing: Form and Style*, Tenth Edition

Newsom/Turk/Kruckeberg, *Cengage Advantage Books: This is PR: The Realities of Public Relations*, Eleventh Edition

Sivulka, *Soap, Sex, and Cigarettes: A Cultural History of American Advertising*, Second Edition

Research and Theory

Baran/Davis, *Mass Communication Theory: Foundations, Ferment, and Future*, Sixth Edition

Sparks, *Media Effects Research: A Basic Overview*, Fourth Edition

Wimmer/Dominick, *Mass Media Research: An Introduction*, Tenth Edition

Tenth Edition

MASS MEDIA RESEARCH
An Introduction

ROGER D. WIMMER
Wimmer Research

JOSEPH R. DOMINICK
University of Georgia

WADSWORTH
CENGAGE Learning·

Australia • Brazil • Japan • Korea • Mexico • Singapore • Spain • United Kingdom • United States

WADSWORTH
CENGAGE Learning

Mass Media Research: An Introduction,
Tenth Edition
Roger D. Wimmer and Joseph R. Dominick

Publisher: Michael Rosenberg

Editor-in-Chief: Lyn Uhl

Assistant Editor: Erin Bosco

Editorial Assistant: Rebecca Donahue

Media Editor: Jessica Badiner

Brand Manager: Ben Rivera

Marketing Development Manager:
Kara Parsons (Kindstrom)

Rights Acquisitions Specialist: Mandy Groszko

Manufacturing Planner: Doug Bertke

Art and Design Direction, Production
Management, and Composition: PreMediaGlobal

Cover Image: Cover painting by Jeremy S.
Wimmer, Littleton, CO. The colors in the
painting are the colors of the covers for
editions 1 to 9 of this text

For product information and technology assistance, contact us at
Cengage Learning Customer & Sales Support, 1-800-354-9706.
For permission to use material from this text or product,
submit all requests online at **www.cengage.com/permissions**.
Further permissions questions can be emailed to
permissionrequest@cengage.com.

Library of Congress Control Number: 2012949261

ISBN-13: 978-1-133-30733-4

ISBN-10: 1-133-30733-7

Wadsworth
20 Channel Center Street
Boston, MA 02210
USA

Cengage Learning is a leading provider of customized learning solutions with office locations around the globe, including Singapore, the United Kingdom, Australia, Mexico, Brazil and Japan. Locate your local office at **international.cengage.com/region**.

Cengage Learning products are represented in Canada by Nelson Education, Ltd.

For your course and learning solutions, visit **www.cengage.com**.

Purchase any of our products at your local college store or at our preferred online store **www.cengagebrain.com**.

Instructors: Please visit **login.cengage.com** and log in to access instructor-specific resources.

Printed in the United States of America
8 9 10 11 12 13 14 23 22 21 20 19

Our families have supported us through some or all of the ten editions of this book, and we would like to thank all of them.

Roger Wimmer: Darnell, Shad, Jeremy, and Leigh

Joe Dominick: Carole and Meaghan

Finally, we thank all the teachers and students who have used Mass Media Research: An Introduction *in the past and those who will use it in the future.*

Roger Wimmer
Joseph Dominick

BRIEF CONTENTS

CONTENTS

PREFACE

Please read this preface. The information is important to help make your experience with this book more rewarding.

Introduction

When we began teaching mass media research in the late 1970s, there were no texts devoted to the topic and we were forced to use research texts from psychology and sociology. As you might expect, it didn't take us very long to realize that journalism and mass media students did not relate well to research examples using rats running in a maze and other such non-media discussions. In the early 1980s, we decided to write the first mass media research text, and over the years we have maintained and expanded that focus as new technologies have reshaped the mass media.

As we have stated in previous editions, things change constantly in all areas of life, and it is sometimes difficult to keep up with all the changes. In every edition of this text, we have faced several new technologies and research approaches that didn't exist in previous editions. It has been interesting to watch the development of such things as satellite television and radio, CDs, the Internet, MP3 players, DVDs, and Blu-ray. But the technological leaps of the past few years have been staggering, particularly smartphones, smart TVs, and computer tablets. Each new technology offers a wealth of new research topics and opportunities, and it has been fun to observe how mass communication has changed.

As mass media teachers and professional researchers, we want to provide you with the most detailed and most current information possible. Accomplishing that task with a textbook is difficult, however, because changes in mass media research happen frequently. Our best alternative, therefore, is to provide basic information and help you find the most current information about the topics we discuss in this text. As in our previous editions, the text is designed for undergraduate students taking their first course in research and for media professionals who need a basic reference book to guide them in conducting or interpreting research.

Therefore, throughout this text we provide many Internet searches to help you find more information about the topics we discuss in the book; we urge you to use these search suggestions. We use a specific format for the searches we suggest. Enter the search exactly as we suggest, and feel free to go beyond the searches we provide.

The format we use for Internet searches is *italics*. That is, whenever we suggest an Internet search, the search is shown in italics. If you see quotation marks with the search, be sure to include those: they are important in refining the search and eliminating useless information. For example, if we recommend that you search the Internet for more information about this text and suggest *"mass media research" Wimmer Dominick*, then input your search exactly as written, including the quotation marks.

If you are new to using Internet search engines, please go to our book's website at *www.wimmerdominick.com* and read the article about using search engines in the "Readings" section.

Approach and Organization

As in the previous editions, our goal is to provide you with the tools you need to use mass media research in the professional world through simplified explanations of goals, procedures, and uses of information in mass media research. We want you to be comfortable with research and to recognize its unlimited value, so we use extensive practical applications to illustrate its use in the world today.

The book is divided into four parts. In Part One, we begin with an overview of mass communication research, including elements, ethics, and sampling. Part Two explores each major approach to research, including qualitative research, content analysis, survey research, longitudinal research, and experimental research. In Part Three, we continue with a section on data analysis, covering statistics and hypothesis testing. Part Four concludes the book with a forward-looking section on research applications—including those for newspapers and magazines, electronic media, advertising, and public relations—that provide additional information and enhance learning and understanding of concepts.

Each chapter opens with a chapter outline and ends with a list of key terms, questions for discussion, suggested Internet exercises and references. A comprehensive glossary is also included.

New to This Edition

We have made substantial changes to most of the chapters in this edition. The changes were made based on comments from teachers, students, and media professionals who have used our book, as well as in response to changes in the media industries. The Internet and social media have greatly affected mass media research, and we have tried to document their impact in the appropriate chapters. Specific changes and additions include:

- Chapter 1 (Science and Research) includes a new definition of mass media with a new subcategory of mass media (smart media) and new discussions of the new mass media.
- Chapter 2 (Elements of Research) includes updated examples and updated discussions of various measurement instruments.
- Chapter 3 (Research Ethics) now contains updated information on federal rules concerning the use of human subjects as well as a discussion about the ethics of doing research involving social media such as Facebook and Twitter.
- Chapter 4 (Sampling) includes updates to most of the types of sampling methods and problems that can occur with sampling.
- Chapter 5 (Qualitative Research Methods) includes new sections on the mixed methods technique and on "netnography."
- Chapter 6 (Content Analysis) now includes a section on framing analysis.
- Chapter 7 (Survey Research) includes updates in most discussions of the types of survey research, with expanded sections on Internet (online) research and identifying outliers in all types of research.
- Chapter 9 (Experimental Research) contains a new discussion of how to minimize dropouts in online experiments.
- Chapter 11 (Hypothesis Testing) includes updated examples and discussions.

- Chapter 12 (Basic Statistical Procedures) includes a new definition for *degrees of freedom* that eliminates the usual confusion with the concept.
- Chapter 13 (Newspaper and Magazine Research) looks at current research concerning the impact of tablet computers (such as the iPad) on newspaper and magazine readership.
- Chapter 14 (Research in the Electronic Media) includes new information about Arbitron's Portable People Meter and other new research considerations related to audience ratings, and an expanded discussion on respondent verification for all research methods.
- Chapter 15 (Research in Advertising) includes an expanded and updated discussion about new advertising channels, such as search engines and social media.
- Chapter 16 (Research in Public Relations) now contains a section on social media message analytics, a group of measures becoming more important in public relations research.
- Finally, this tenth edition contains many new or expanded boxed inserts labeled "A Closer Look" that highlight topics in the text. References and examples have also been updated.

In addition to the sixteen chapters in the tenth edition, you will find two chapters on the text's companion website: "Research in Media Effects" and "Writing Reports." The website also now includes the sample ratings book pages from Arbitron and Nielsen that were used in the eighth edition.

Additional Resources

Please make use of the website we constructed as a companion for our text (*www.wimmerdominick.com*). The website includes a variety of information, including Supplemental Information, Readings, Chapter Questions & Exercises, Research Ideas, Information Sources, Statistics Sources, Student Resources prepared by Cengage, sampling calculators, and a link to *The Research Doctor Archive* (Roger Wimmer's column on AllAccess.com).

We update the website whenever we find something of interest to mass media researchers, so visit often. If you have any suggestions for additional content on the site, please contact one of us.

In addition, Cengage Learning has a book companion website that offers a variety of information to help in learning about and teaching mass media research. Students can prepare for quizzes and exams with chapter-level tutorial quizzes, an online version of the glossary, flashcards, and Internet exercises. A helpful, password-protected Online Instructor's Manual includes chapter overviews, class-tested activities and exercises, technology resources, test items, and assessment tests. Each chapter includes an overview and a test bank. The website can be found at *www.cengagebrain.com* (a link is on our text website).

Acknowledgments

We would like to express our gratitude to the many individuals who have provided assistance to us over the years. For this edition in particular, we would like to thank the team at Cengage Learning for their work on our behalf: Michael Rosenberg, Publisher, Humanities; Erin Bosco, Assistant Editor; Rebecca Donahue, Editorial Assistant; and Preetha Sreekanth, PreMediaGlobal Project Manager.

Finally, we are especially grateful to the following reviewers whose experience with the previous edition and expert feedback helped shape the new edition: James D. Ivory, Virginia Tech; Ann Liao, Buffalo

State College; and Daniel G. McDonald, Ohio State University.

Your Feedback

As we have stated in the previous nine editions: If you find a serious problem in the text or the website, please contact one of us. Each of us will steadfastly blame the other for the problem and will be happy to give you his home telephone number (or forward any email). Have fun with the book and the website. The mass media research field is still a great place to be!

Roger Wimmer
Denver, Colorado
roger@rogerwimmer.com

Joseph Dominick
Ponte Vedra, Florida
joedom@uga.edu

CHAPTER 1

SCIENCE AND RESEARCH

CHAPTER OUTLINE

INTRODUCTION

When hearing the words *mass media research* for the first time, many people ask two questions: (1) What are the mass media? and (2) What types of things do mass media researchers investigate? Let's address these questions before getting to the specifics of research.

What are the mass media? In order to answer this question, we must first back up and define **mass communication,** which is *any form of communication transmitted through a medium (channel) that simultaneously reaches a large number of people.* Mass media are the channels that carry mass communication. However, categorizing what a mass medium is has become complicated during the past several years. Our previous definition of the mass media has been *any communication channel used to simultaneously reach a large number of people, including radio, TV, newspapers, magazines, billboards, films, recordings, books, and the Internet.*

Our traditional definition of mass media is no longer applicable to the new high-tech communication channels, and we now add a new category to the list. We call the new category **smart mass media,** which include **smartphones, smart TVs,** and **tablets**—three media that are essentially computers. As stand-alone devices, each of these media can function as an individual mass medium. For example, using these smart media, one person or one organization can now communicate simultaneously with hundreds of thousands or even millions of people via tweets, text messages, social media posts, and email. However, smart media can access the Internet and additionally serve the function of all other mass media. For example, a person can watch TV and movies; listen to radio and recordings; or read a magazine, book, or newspaper, all using a smart media device. In short, smart media represent yet another form of mass communication,

and our revised definition of mass media is therefore *any communication channel used to simultaneously reach a large number of people, including radio, TV, newspapers, magazines, billboards, films, recordings, books, the Internet, and smart media.*

What types of things do mass media researchers investigate? Here are a few examples:

- Which format should a radio station adopt?
- Which songs should a radio station play?
- What type of hosts do listeners want on a radio station's morning show?
- How do viewers evaluate a pilot for a new TV show?
- What do viewers like most and like least about their favorite local TV news program?
- How effective is advertising on TV, radio, the Internet, and in all types of print?
- Which ads do readers see most often in their local newspaper?
- How many people regularly read newspapers?
- How are cell phones affecting people's use of the other mass media?
- Who should be the spokesperson for a new consumer product?
- Who should be the host of a new TV game show?
- Are there more violent acts on TV now than five years ago?
- What are the characteristics of successful websites?
- Is there a way to predict the success of a smartphone app before it is released?
- How many employees read their company's internal newspaper or newsletter?
- What kinds of people watch TV online?
- Why do some people prefer Internet radio stations to broadcast radio stations?

The types of questions investigated in mass media research are virtually unlimited. However, even this short list demonstrates why it's necessary to understand mass media research—because literally every area of the mass media uses research, and anyone who works in the media (or plans to) will be exposed to or will be involved in research.

Our goal in this book is to introduce you to mass media research and dispel many of the negative thoughts people may have about research, especially a fear of having to use math and statistics. You will find that you do not have to be a math or statistics wizard. The only thing you need is an inquiring mind.

WHAT IS RESEARCH?

Regardless of how the word *research* is used, it essentially means one thing: *an attempt to discover something.* We all do this every day. This book discusses many of the different approaches used to discover something in the mass media.

Research can be very informal, with only a few (or no) specific plans or steps, or it can be formal, where a researcher follows highly defined and exacting procedures. The lack of exacting procedures in informal research does not mean the approach is incorrect, and the use of exacting procedures does not guarantee that formal research is correct. Both procedures can be good or bad—it depends on how the research is conducted. The important thing for all researchers to understand is the correct methods to follow to ensure the best results.

Most people who conduct research are not paid for their efforts. Although the research industry is an excellent field to enter, our approach in this book is to assume that most readers will not become (or are not now) paid professional researchers. We assume that most of you will work for, or are

already working for, companies and businesses that use research, or that you are simply interested in finding out more about the field. With these ideas in mind, our approach is to explain what research is all about—to show you how to use it to discover something. We also hope our discussions will make your life easier when a research report is put on your desk for you to read or when you face a question that needs to be answered.

Now, back to the idea that all of us are researchers and conduct research every day, remember that we define research as an attempt to discover something. Every day we all conduct numerous "research projects." We're not being facetious here. Just consider the number of things you must analyze, test, or evaluate, to perform daily tasks:

1. Set the water temperature in the shower so you do not freeze or burn.

2. Decide which clothes to put on that are appropriate for the day's activities.

3. Select something to eat for breakfast that will stay with you until lunchtime.

4. Decide when to leave the house to reach your destination on time.

5. Figure out the easiest way to accomplish a task.

6. Decide when to move to the side of the road if you hear an emergency siren.

7. Determine how loudly to talk to someone.

8. Estimate how fast you need to walk to get across the street so you won't be hit.

9. Evaluate the best way to tell a friend about a problem you have.

10. Determine when it's time to go home.

The list may seem mundane and boring, but the fact is that when we make any of these decisions, we have to conduct a countless number of tests or rely on information from previous tests. We all make many attempts to discover things to reach a decision about any event. In essence, we are all researchers from a very young age.

The simplicity of research begs the question: Why read this book? The reason is that there are good ways to attempt to discover something and there are not-so-good ways to attempt to discover something. This book discusses both the good and the bad so that you will be able to distinguish between the two. Even if you do not plan to become a professional researcher, it is important to learn the best way to collect information and analyze it because research results are so widely used in all areas of life.

The underlying theme presented in this book highlights the Three-Step Philosophy of Success followed by the senior author of this book for the past 35+ years as a paid professional researcher. There are three basic steps to success in business and, for that matter, almost every facet of life:

1. Find out what the target audience wants (one or more customers, friends, family, colleagues, etc.).
2. Give it to them.
3. Tell them that you gave it to them.

Failure is virtually impossible if you follow this three-step philosophy. How can you fail when you give people what they ask for? The way to find out what people want is through research, and that is what this book is all about.

GETTING STARTED

Keep in mind that the focus of this book is to discuss attempts to discover something in the mass media. Although it would be valuable to address other fields of endeavor, this chapter contains discussions of the development of mass media research during the past several decades and the methods used to collect and analyze information. It also includes a discussion of the scientific method of research. The purpose of this chapter is to provide a foundation for the topics discussed in detail in later chapters.

Two basic questions a beginning researcher must learn to answer are (1) how to use research methods and statistical procedures and (2) when to use research methods and statistical procedures. Although developing methods and procedures is a valuable task, the focus for most researchers should be on applications.

This book supports the tasks and responsibilities of the *applied data analyst* (researcher), not the statistician; it does not concentrate on the role of the statistician because the "real world" of mass media research usually does not require an extensive knowledge of statistics. Instead, the real world requires an understanding of what the statistics produce, how to interpret results, and how to use the results in decision making. After conducting thousands of mass media research studies for many years, we have concluded that those who wish to become mass media researchers should spend time learning *what* to do with the research methods, not *how* they work.

Both statisticians and researchers are involved in producing research results, but their functions are quite different, even though one person may sometimes serve in both capacities. What do statisticians do? Among other complex activities, they generate statistical procedures, or formulas, called **algorithms**. Researchers use these algorithms to investigate **research questions** and **hypotheses**. The results of this cooperative effort are used to advance our understanding of the mass media.

For example, users of radio and television ratings, produced by Arbitron and A. C.

A CLOSER LOOK

Searching the Internet

Throughout this book, we suggest a variety of Internet searches to help you find more information about specific topics. The searches we suggest often include quote marks, such as *"mass media research"* examples. When you conduct your search, type the search exactly as shown, including the quote marks, because the search looks for those words in that specific order. For more information about Internet searching, go to *www.wimmerdominick.com*.

Nielsen, continually analyze the instability of ratings information. The audience information (ratings and shares) for radio and television stations in a given market sometimes vary dramatically from one survey period to the next without any logical explanation (see Chapter 14). Users of media ratings frequently ask statisticians and the ratings companies to help determine why this problem occurs and to offer suggestions for making syndicated media audience information more reliable, a demonstration of how statisticians and researchers can work together.

During the early part of the twentieth century, there was no interest in the size of a media audience or in the types of people who make up the audience. Since then, mass media operators have come to rely on research results for nearly every major decision they make. The increased demand for information has created a need for more researchers, both public and private. In addition, within the research field are many specializations. Research directors plan and supervise studies and act as liaisons to management, methodological specialists provide statistical support, research analysts design and interpret studies, and computer specialists provide hardware and software support in data analysis.

Research in mass media is used to verify or refute opinions or intuitions for decision makers. Although common sense is sometimes accurate, media decision makers need additional objective information to evaluate problems, especially when they make decisions that involve large sums of money. The past 50 years have witnessed the evolution of a decision-making approach that combines research and intuition to produce a higher probability of success.

Research is not limited only to decision-making situations. It is also widely used in theoretical areas to attempt to describe the media, to analyze media effects on consumers, to understand audience behavior, and so on. Every day there are references in the media to audience surveys, public opinion polls, growth projections, status reports of one medium or another, or advertising or public relations campaigns. As philosopher Suzanne Langer (1967) said, "Most new discoveries are suddenly-seen things that were always there." Mass media researchers have a great deal to see, and virtually everyone is exposed to this information every day.

Finally, there are two additional points before we get into media research. First, media research and the need for qualified researchers will continue to grow, but it is difficult to find qualified researchers who can work in the public and private sectors. Second, we urge you to search the Internet for additional information on every topic discussed in this book. We have identified some areas for further investigation, but do not limit your searching to only our suggestions. Internet searches are not good for primary research, but they are useful as a starting point for information gathering.

THE DEVELOPMENT OF MASS MEDIA RESEARCH

Mass media research has evolved in definable steps, and similar patterns have been followed in each medium's needs for research (see Figure 1.1). As you read the following paragraphs about the development of mass media research, consider the smart media (the newest mass media) as examples. In Phase 1 of the research, there is an interest in the medium itself. What is it? How does it work? What technology does it involve? How is it similar to or different from what is already available? What functions or services does it provide? Who will have access to the new medium? How much will it cost?

Phase 2 research begins once the medium is developed. In this phase, specific information is accumulated about the uses and the users of the medium. How do people use the medium in real life? Do they use it for information only, to save time, for entertainment, or for some other reason? Do children use it? Do adults use it? Why? What gratifications does the new medium provide? What other types of information and entertainment does the new medium replace? Were original projections about the use of the medium correct? What uses are evident other than those that were predicted from initial research?

Phase 3 includes investigations of the social, psychological, and physical effects of the medium. How much time do people spend with the medium? Does it change people's perspectives about anything? What do the users of the medium want and expect to hear or see? Are there any harmful effects related to using the medium? In what way, if any, does the medium help people? Can the medium be combined with other media or technology to make it even more useful?

In Phase 4, research is conducted to determine how the medium can be improved, either in its use or through technological developments. Can the medium provide information or entertainment to more types of people? How can new technology be used to perfect or enhance the sight and/or sound of the medium? Is there a way to change the content to be more valuable or entertaining?

The design of Figure 1.1 is not intended to suggest that the research phases are

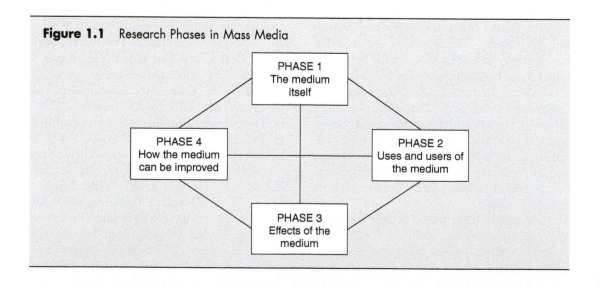

Figure 1.1   Research Phases in Mass Media

linear—that when a phase is over, it is never considered again. In reality, once a medium is developed and established, research may be conducted simultaneously in all four phases. For example, although television has been around for decades, researchers continue to investigate the medium itself (satellite or online-delivered digital audio and video), the uses of TV (pay-per-view programming, TV on computers and handheld devices), effects (violent programming), and improvements (3DTV).

Research is a never-ending process. In most instances, a research project designed to answer one series of questions produces a new set of questions no one thought of before. This failure to reach closure may be troublesome to some people, but it is the essential nature of research.

Figure 1.1 depicts four phases of research. However, in some instances, as in private sector research, an additional element permeates every phase: How can the medium make money? The largest percentage of research conducted in the private sector relates in some way to money—how to save it, make more of it, or take it away from others. This may not "sit well" with people who view the media as products of artistic endeavor, but this is how the real world operates.

At least four major events or social forces encouraged the growth of mass media research. The first was World War I, which prompted a need to understand the nature of propaganda. Researchers working from a *stimulus–response* point of view attempted to uncover the effects of the media on people (Lasswell, 1927). The media at that time were thought to exert a powerful influence over their audiences, and several assumptions were made about what the media could and could not do. One theory of mass media, later named the **hypodermic needle** model of communication, suggested that mass communicators need only "shoot"

messages at an audience and those messages would produce preplanned and almost universal effects. The belief then was that all people behave in similar ways when they encounter media messages. We know now that individual differences among people rule out this overly simplistic view. As DeFleur and Ball-Rokeach (1989) note:

> These assumptions may not have been explicitly formulated at the time, but they were drawn from fairly elaborate theories of human nature, as well as the nature of the social order…. It was these theories that guided the thinking of those who saw the media as powerful.

A second contributor to the development of mass media research was the realization by advertisers in the 1950s and 1960s that research data are useful in developing ways to persuade potential customers to buy products and services. Consequently, advertisers encouraged studies of message effectiveness, audience demographics and size, placement of advertising to achieve the highest level of exposure (efficiency), frequency of advertising necessary to persuade potential customers, and selection of the medium that offered the best chance of reaching the target audience.

A third contributing social force was the increasing interest of citizens in the effects of the media on the public, especially on children. The direct result was an interest in research related to violence and sexual content in television programs and in commercials aired during children's programs. Researchers have expanded their focus to include the positive (prosocial) as well as the negative (antisocial) effects of television. Investigating violence on television is still an important endeavor, and new research is published every year.

Increased competition among the media for advertising dollars was a fourth contributor to the growth of research. Most media managers are now sophisticated and use long-range plans, management by objectives, and an increasing dependency on data to support the decisions they make. Even program producers seek relevant research data, a task usually assigned to the creative side of program development. In addition, the mass media now focus on audience fragmentation, which means that the mass of people is divided into small groups, or niches (technically referred to as the "demassification" of the mass media). Researchers need information about these smaller groups of people.

The competition among the media for audiences and advertising dollars continues to reach new levels of complexity. The media "survival kit" today includes information about consumers' changing values and tastes, shifts in demographic patterns, and developing trends in lifestyles. Audience fragmentation increases the need for trend studies (fads, new behavior patterns), image studies (people's perceptions of the media and their environment), and segmentation studies (explanations of behavior by types or groups of people). Large research organizations, consultants, and media owners and operators conduct research that was previously considered the sole property of the marketing, psychology, and sociology disciplines. With the advent of increased competition and audience fragmentation, media managers more frequently use marketing strategies in an attempt to discover their position in the marketplace. When this position is identified, the medium is packaged as an *image* rather than a product. Similarly, the producers of consumer goods such as soap and toothpaste try to sell the image of these products because the products themselves are similar, if not the same, from company to company.

The packaging strategy involves determining what the members of the audience think, how they use language, how they spend their spare time, and so on. Information on these ideas and behaviors is then used in the merchandising effort to make the medium seem to be part of the audience. Positioning thus involves taking information from the audience and interpreting the data to use in marketing the medium. For more information about positioning companies and products in the business and consumer worlds, search the Internet for *corporate imaging, corporate positioning,* and *product branding.*

Much of the media research before the early 1960s originated in psychology and sociology departments at colleges and universities. Researchers with backgrounds in the media were rare because the mass media were young, but this situation changed. Media departments in colleges and universities grew rapidly in the 1960s and 1970s, and media researchers entered the scene. Today mass media researchers dominate the mass media research field, and now the trend is to encourage cross-disciplinary studies in which media researchers invite participation from researchers in sociology, psychology, political science, and others. Because of the pervasiveness of the mass media, researchers from all areas of science are now actively involved in attempting to answer media-related questions.

Modern mass media research includes a variety of psychological and sociological investigations, such as physiological and emotional responses to television programs, commercials, or music played on radio stations. In addition, computer modeling and other sophisticated computer analyses are now commonplace in media research to determine such things as the potential success of television programs (local, network, or syndicated). Once considered eccentric by some, mass media research is now a legitimate and esteemed field.

MEDIA RESEARCH AND THE SCIENTIFIC METHOD

Scientific research is an *organized, objective, controlled, qualitative or quantitative empirical analysis of one or more variables*. The terms that define the scientific research method describe a procedure that has been accepted for centuries. In the sixteenth century, for example, Tycho Brahe (pronounced TEE-koh BRAH-hee) conducted years of organized and controlled observation to refute many of Aristotle's theories of the solar system and the universe.

As mentioned earlier, we all conduct research every day. We do this whenever we test a question about anything. Children conduct "research studies" to determine which items are hot and which are cold, how to ride a bicycle or a skateboard, and which persuasive methods work best with parents. Teenagers "test" ideas about driving, dating, and working; adults "test" ideas about family, finance, and survival.

All research, whether formal or informal, begins with a basic question or proposition about a specific phenomenon. For example, why do viewers select one television program over another? Which sections of the newspaper do people read most often? Which types of magazine covers attract the most readers? What type of radio format will attract the largest number of listeners? Which websites attract the most visitors? Which types of advertising are most effective in communicating messages to consumers? These questions can be answered to some degree with well-designed research studies. However, the task is to determine which data collection method can most appropriately provide answers to specific questions.

THE METHODS OF KNOWING

There are several possible approaches to answering research questions. Kerlinger and Lee (2000), using definitions provided nearly a century ago by C. S. Peirce, discuss four approaches to finding answers, or **methods of knowing**: tenacity, intuition, authority, and science. To this list, we add self-discovery.

A user of the *method of tenacity* follows the logic that something is true because it has always been true. An example is the store-owner who says, "I don't advertise because my parents did not believe in advertising." The idea is that nothing changes—what was good, bad, or successful before will continue to be so in the future.

In the *method of intuition,* or the a priori approach, a person assumes that something is true because it is "self-evident" or "stands to reason." Some creative people in advertising agencies resist efforts to test their advertising methods because they believe they know what will attract customers. To these people, scientific research is a waste of time, and their advertising effectiveness usually suffers as a consequence.

The *method of authority* promotes a belief in something because a trusted source, such as a parent, a news correspondent, or a teacher, says it is true. The emphasis is on the source, not on the methods the source may have used to gain the information. For example, the claim that "consumers will spend money to receive news updates via fax machine because producers of the information say so" is based on the method of authority. During the late 1990s, this was shown *not* to be true. Only a handful of consumers signed up to receive the new product, and research was conducted to find out what failed. The research indicated that very few people had fax machines at home, and they were not interested in the material being sent to their workplace—a simple answer that wasn't perceived by the product's producers.

The *self-discovery* method refers to things we learn and know without intervention from an outside source. While we may use information gathered from other sources to provide an answer to a question or problem, self-discovery is evident when a person synthesizes a variety of information to come to a decision about something, or maybe even to invent a new product or service. Self-discovery involves using one or more of the other methods of knowing, but the difference is that the discovery was made alone. In essence, the method of self-discovery is similar to the scientific method, without the characteristic of being public, and it may be considered a subset of the method of authority, where a person becomes his or her own authority based on knowledge gained from personal experience.

The *scientific method* approaches learning as a series of small steps, and unlike the other methods of knowing, it has several definable characteristics. These are discussed in the next section.

CHARACTERISTICS OF THE SCIENTIFIC METHOD

Six basic characteristics, or tenets, distinguish the scientific method from other methods of knowing. A research approach that does not follow each of these tenets is not a scientific approach.

1. *Scientific research is public.* Advances in science require freely available information. Researchers (especially in the academic sector) cannot plead private knowledge, methods, or data in arguing for the accuracy of their findings; scientific research information must be freely communicated from one researcher to another. As Nunnally and Bernstein (1994) note:

> Science is a highly public enterprise in which efficient communication among scientists is essential. Each scientist builds on what has been learned in the past; day-by-day his or her findings must be compared with those of other scientists working on the same types of problems.... The rate of scientific progress in a particular area is limited by the efficiency and fidelity with which scientists can communicate their results to one another.

Researchers, therefore, must take great care in their published reports to include information on sampling methods, measurements, and data-gathering procedures. Such information allows other researchers to independently verify a given study and support or refute the initial research findings. This process of replication allows for correction and verification of previous research findings. Though not related to media research, the importance of replication in scientific research was highlighted in two areas, one where physicists were unable to duplicate the fantastic claim made by two University of Utah chemists who said they had produced fusion at room temperature, and the second involving the discrediting of research in 2009 about the link between autism and vaccinations by British physician Dr. Andrew Wakefield. (See "Writing a Research Report" in the Readings section on *www.wimmerdominick.com*.)

Researchers need to save their descriptions of observations (data) and their research materials so that information not included in a formal report is available to other researchers on request. Nunnally and Bernstein (1994) say, "A key principle of science is that any statement of fact made by one scientist should be independently verifiable by other scientists." Researchers can verify results only if they have access to the original data. It is common practice to keep all raw research materials for at least five years, and in many cases, the materials are kept forever. The materials are usually provided free as a courtesy to other researchers, or for a nominal fee if copying or additional materials are required.

2. *Science is objective.* Science tries to rule out eccentricities of judgment by researchers.

When a study is conducted, explicit rules and procedures are developed and the researcher is bound to follow them, letting the chips fall where they may. Rules for classifying behavior are used so that two or more independent observers can classify behavior patterns or other elements in the same manner. For example, to measure the appeal of a television commercial, researchers might count the number of times a viewer changes channels during a commercial. This is an objective measure because any competent observer would report a channel change. On the other hand, to measure appeal by observing how many viewers make negative facial expressions during a commercial would be a subjective approach because different observers may have different ideas of what constitutes a negative expression. An explicit operational definition of "negative facial expression" would reduce or eliminate potential coding errors.

Objectivity also requires that scientific research deal with facts rather than interpretations of facts. Science rejects its own authorities if statements conflict with direct observation. As the noted psychologist B. F. Skinner (1953) wrote, "Research projects do not always come out as one expects, but the facts must stand and the expectations fall. The subject matter, not the scientist, knows best." Mass media researchers have often encountered situations where media decision makers reject the results of a research project because the study did not produce the anticipated results. (In these cases, we wonder why the research was conducted.)

3. *Science is empirical.* Researchers are concerned with a world that is knowable and potentially measurable. (Empiricism comes from the Greek word for "experience.") Researchers must be able to perceive and classify what they study and reject metaphysical and nonsensical explanations of events. For example, scientists would reject a newspaper publisher's claim that a decline in the number of subscribers is "God's will" because such a statement cannot be perceived, classified, or measured. (People whose areas of research rely on superstition and other nonscientific methods of knowing, such as astrology, are said to practice "bad science.") This *does not* mean that scientists avoid abstract ideas and notions; they encounter them every day. However, they recognize that concepts must be strictly defined to allow for objective observation and measurement. Scientists must link abstract concepts to the empirical world through observations, which may be made either directly or indirectly via various measurement instruments. Typically, this linkage is accomplished by framing an operational definition.

Operational definitions are important in science, and a brief introduction requires some backtracking. There are two basic kinds of definitions. A **constitutive definition** *defines a word by substituting other words or concepts for it.* For example, here is a constitutive definition of the concept "artichoke": An artichoke is a green leafy vegetable, a tall composite herb of the *Cynara scolymus* family. In contrast, an **operational definition** *specifies procedures that allow one to experience or measure a concept.* For example: Go to the grocery store and find the produce aisle; look for a sign that says "Artichokes"; what's underneath the sign is an artichoke. Although an operational definition assures precision, it does not guarantee validity; a stock clerk may mistakenly stack lettuce under the artichoke sign. This possibility for error underscores the importance of considering both the constitutive definition and the operational definition of a concept to evaluate the trustworthiness of any measurement. Carefully examining the constitutive definition of artichoke indicates that the operational definition might be faulty.

Operational definitions can help dispel some of the strange questions raised in philosophical discussions. For instance, if you have taken a philosophy course, you may have encountered the question, "How many angels can stand on the head of a pin?" The debate ends quickly when the retort is, "Give me an operational definition of an angel, and I'll give you the answer." Any question can be answered as long as there are operational definitions for the independent or dependent variables. For further discussions of operational definitions, see *Psychometric Theory* (Nunnally & Bernstein, 1994) and *The Practice of Social Research* (Babbie, 2010), and search the Internet for "*operational definition.*"

4. *Science is systematic and cumulative.* No single research study stands alone, nor does it rise or fall by itself. Astute researchers always use previous studies as building blocks for their own work. One of the first steps in conducting research is to review the available scientific literature on the topic so that the current study will draw on the heritage of past research. This review is valuable for identifying problem areas and important factors that might be relevant to the current study. (Please read Timothy Ferris's preface in *The Whole Shebang*, 1998.)

In addition, scientists attempt to search for order and consistency among their findings. In its ideal form, scientific research begins with a single carefully observed event and progresses ultimately to the formulation of theories and laws. A **theory** is *a set of related propositions that presents a systematic view of phenomena by specifying relationships among concepts.* Researchers develop theories by searching for patterns of uniformity to explain their data. When relationships among variables are invariant under given conditions, researchers may formulate a law. A **law** is *a statement of fact meant to explain, in concise terms, an action or set of actions that is generally accepted to be true and universal.* Both theories and laws help researchers search for and explain

consistency in behavior, situations, and phenomena.

5. *Science is predictive.* Science is concerned with relating the present to the future. In fact, scientists strive to develop theories because, among other reasons, they are useful in predicting behavior. A theory's adequacy lies in its ability to predict a phenomenon or event successfully. A theory that offers predictions that are not borne out by data analysis must be carefully reexamined and perhaps discarded. Conversely, a theory that generates predictions that are supported by the data can be used to make predictions in other situations.

6. *Science is self-correcting.* As mentioned earlier, the scientific method approaches learning in a series of small steps. That is, one study or one source provides only an indication of what may or may not be true; the "truth" is found only through a series of objective analyses. This means that the scientific method is self-correcting in that changes in thoughts, theories, or laws are appropriate when errors in previous research are uncovered. A non-media example is when in 1984 Barry Marshall, a medical resident in Perth, Australia, identified a bacterium (*Helicobacter pylori*) as the cause of stomach ulcers (not an increase in stomach acid due to stress or anxiety). After several years, hundreds of independent studies proved that Marshall was correct, and in 1996 the U.S. Food and Drug Administration (FDA) approved a combination of drugs to fight ulcers—an antacid and an antibiotic.

Another example of how the scientific method is self-correcting was the preliminary finding in late 2011 that neutrinos travel faster than the speed of light. However, in early 2012 the initial results were found to have been created by a loose cable (measurement error), and further analysis verified that neutrinos do not travel faster than the speed of light.

In communications, researchers discovered that the early ideas of the power of the media

A CLOSER LOOK

Scientific Research

Although the Internet is a valuable information source, it is also a source for misunderstanding, incorrect information, and perpetuation of falsehoods and urban legends. Look at some of the information passed along on the Internet by conducting a search for *urban legends*. Why do you think these legends are so popular? In which method of knowing do these urban legends belong?

(the hypodermic needle theory) were incorrect and after numerous studies concluded that behavior and ideas are changed by a combination of communication sources and that people react differently to the same message. Isaac Asimov (1990) said, "One of the glories of scientific endeavor is that any scientific belief, however firmly established, is constantly being tested to see if it is truly universally valid." However, the scientific method may be inappropriate in many areas of life—for instance, in evaluating works of art, choosing a religion, or forming friendships—but it has been valuable in producing accurate and useful data in mass media research. The next section provides a more detailed look at this method of knowing.

RESEARCH PROCEDURES

The purpose of the scientific method of research is to provide an objective, unbiased collection and evaluation of data. To investigate research questions and hypotheses systematically, both academic and private-sector researchers follow a basic eight-step procedure. However, simply following the eight research steps does not guarantee that the research is good, valid, reliable, or useful. An almost countless number of intervening variables (influences) can destroy even the best-planned research project. The situation is similar to someone assuming he or she can bake a cake by just following the recipe. The cake may be ruined by an oven that doesn't work properly, spoiled ingredients, altitude, or numerous other variables. The typical research process consists of these eight steps:

1. Select a problem.
2. Review existing research and theory (when relevant).
3. Develop hypotheses or research questions.
4. Determine an appropriate methodology/research design.
5. Collect relevant data.
6. Analyze and interpret the results.
7. Present the results in an appropriate form.
8. Replicate the study (when necessary).

Step 4 includes deciding whether to use **qualitative research,** such as focus groups or one-on-one interviews that usually use small samples, or **quantitative research,** such as telephone interviews, where large samples are usually used to allow results to be generalized to the population under study (see Chapter 5 for a discussion of qualitative research).

Steps 2 and 8 are optional in the private sector, where some research is conducted to answer a specific and unique question related to a future decision, such as whether to invest a large sum of money in a developing medium. In this type of project, there generally is no previous research to consult, and there seldom is a reason to replicate the study because a decision is made based on the first analysis. However, if the research produces inconclusive results, the study is revised and replicated.

Each step in the eight-step process depends on all the others to produce a maximally efficient research study. For example, before a literature search is possible, the researcher must have a clearly stated research problem; to design the most efficient method of investigating a problem, the researcher must know what types of studies have been conducted; and so on. In addition, all the steps are interactive—a literature search may refine and even alter the initial research problem, or a study conducted previously by another company or business in the private sector might expedite (or complicate) the current research effort.

TWO SECTORS OF RESEARCH: ACADEMIC AND PRIVATE

Research is divided into two major sectors, *academic* and *private*, which are sometimes called "basic" and "applied," respectively, although we do not use these terms in this text because research in both sectors can be basic or applied. The two sectors are equally important and in many cases work together to answer mass media questions.

Scholars from colleges and universities conduct public sector research. Generally, this research has a theoretical or scholarly approach; that is, the results are intended to help explain the mass media and their effects on individuals. Some popular research topics in the theoretical area are the use of media and various media-related items, such as smartphones and multiple-channel cable systems, differences in consumer lifestyles, effects of media "overload" on consumers, and effects of various types of programming on children.

Nongovernmental companies or their research consultants conduct **private-sector research**. It is generally applied research; that is, the results are intended to facilitate decision making. Typical research topics in the private sector include media content and consumer preferences, acquisitions of additional businesses or facilities, analysis of on-air talent, advertising and promotional campaigns, public relations approaches to solving specific informational problems, sales forecasting, and image studies of the properties owned by the company. Private-sector research has recently become more important as media companies cope with shrinking audiences and declining advertising revenue.

There are other differences between **academic research** and private-sector research. For instance, academic research is public. Any other researcher or research organization that wishes to use the information gathered by academic researchers should be able to do so by asking the original researcher for the raw data. Most private sector research, on the other hand, generates proprietary data that are the sole property of the sponsoring agency and usually cannot be obtained by other researchers. Some private-sector research is released to the public soon after it has been conducted, such as public opinion polls and projections concerning the future of the media. Other studies may be released only after several years, although this practice is the exception rather than the rule.

Another difference between academic research and private-sector research involves the amount of time allowed to conduct the work. Academic researchers generally do not have specific deadlines for their research projects (except when they receive research grants). Academicians usually conduct their research at a pace that accommodates their teaching schedules. Private-sector researchers nearly always operate under some type of deadline. The time frame may be imposed by management or by an outside agency or a client that needs to make a decision.

Academic research is generally less expensive to conduct than research in the private sector. This is not to say that academic research is "cheap," because in many cases it is not. But academicians usually do not need to cover overhead costs for office rent, equipment, facilities, computer analysis, subcontractors, and personnel. Private-sector research must consider such expenses, regardless of whether the research is conducted within the company or with a research supplier. The lower cost of academic researchers sometimes motivates large media companies and groups to use them rather than professional research firms.

Despite these differences, beginning researchers must understand that academic research and private-sector research are not independent of each other. Academicians perform many studies for industry, and private-sector groups conduct research that can be classified as theoretical. (For example, the television networks have departments that conduct social research.) Similarly, many college and university professors act as consultants to, and often conduct private sector research for, the media industry.

It is important for all researchers to refrain from attaching to academic or private-sector research stereotypical labels such as "unrealistic," "pedantic," and "limited in scope." Research in both sectors, though occasionally differing in cost and scope, uses similar methodologies and statistical analyses. In addition, the two sectors have common research goals: to understand problems and/or predict the future. When conducting a study according to the scientific method, researchers must have a clear understanding of what they are investigating, how the phenomenon can be measured or observed, and what procedures are required to test the observations or measurements.

Answering a research question or hypothesis requires a conceptualization of the research problem and a logical development of the procedural steps. These steps are discussed in greater detail in the following sections of this chapter.

RESEARCH PROCEDURES

The scientific evaluation of any problem must follow a sequence of steps to increase the probability that it will produce relevant data. Researchers who do not follow a prescribed set of steps do not subscribe to the scientific method of inquiry and simply increase the amount of error present in a study. This chapter describes the process of scientific research—from identifying and developing a topic for investigation to replicating the results. The first section briefly introduces the steps in the development of a research topic.

Objective, rigorous observation and analysis characterize the scientific method. To meet this goal, researchers must follow the prescribed steps shown in Figure 1.2. This research model is appropriate to all areas of scientific research.

Selecting a Research Topic

Not all researchers are concerned with selecting a topic to study; some are able to choose and concentrate on a research area that is interesting to them. Many researchers come to be identified with studies of specific types, such as those concerning children and media violence, newspaper readership, advertising, or communications law. These researchers investigate small pieces of a puzzle to obtain a broad picture of their research area. In addition, some researchers become identified with specific *approaches* to research, such as focus groups or historical analysis. In the private sector, researchers generally do not have the flexibility to select topics or questions to investigate. Instead, they conduct studies to

Figure 1.2   Steps in the Development of a Research Project

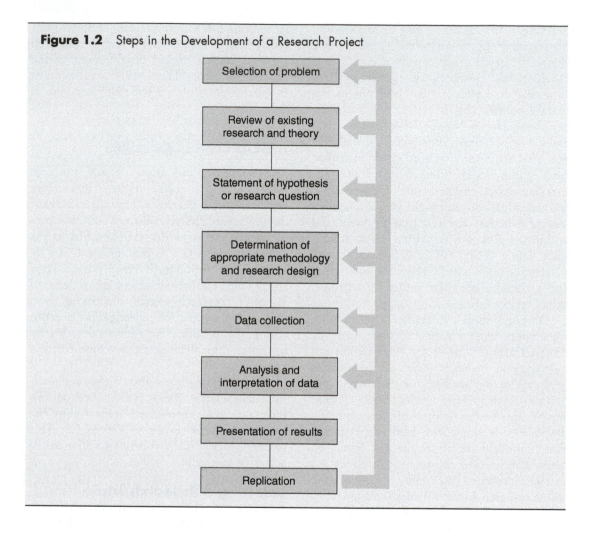

answer questions raised by management, or they address the problems and questions for which they are hired, as is the case with full-service research companies.

Although some private-sector researchers are occasionally limited in selecting a topic, they are usually given total control over how the question should be addressed (that is, which methodology should be used). The goal of private-sector researchers in every research study is to develop a method that is fast, inexpensive, reliable, and valid. If all these criteria are met, the researcher has performed a valuable task.

Selecting a topic is a concern for many beginning researchers, especially those writing term papers, theses, and dissertations. The problem is knowing where to start. Fortunately, many sources are available for research topics; academic journals, periodicals, newsweeklies, and everyday encounters provide a wealth of ideas. This section highlights some primary sources.

Professional Journals

Academic communication journals, such as the *Journal of Broadcasting & Electronic Media, Journalism & Mass Communication*

Quarterly, and others listed in this section, are excellent sources of information. Although academic journals tend to publish research that is 12 to 24 months old (due to review procedures and the backlog of articles), the articles may provide ideas for research topics. Most authors conclude their research by discussing problems they encountered during the study and suggesting topics that need further investigation. In addition, some journal editors build issues around specific research themes, which often can help in formulating research plans. Many high-quality journals cover various aspects of research; some specialize in mass media, and others include media research occasionally. The journals listed here provide a starting point in using academic journals for research ideas.

In addition to academic journals, professional trade publications offer a wealth of information relevant to mass media research. These include *Broadcasting & Cable, Advertising Age, Media Week,* and *Editor & Publisher.* Other excellent sources for identifying current topics in mass media are weekly newsletters such as *MinOnline* and many others that can be found via a search for *"media newsletters."*

Most college and university libraries offer access to research literature databases. These listings provide the full text or summaries of research articles and can be valuable sources for research topics. Some of the most useful for mass media researchers are Academic Search Complete, Communication and Mass Media Complete, Lexis/Nexis Academic, and Sociological Collection.

Magazines and Periodicals

Although some educators feel that publications other than professional journals contain only "watered-down" articles written for the public, these articles tend to eliminate tedious technical jargon and are often good sources for identifying problems and hypotheses. In addition, more and more articles

written by highly trained communications professionals appear in weekly and monthly publications such as *Time* and *Newsweek*. These sources often provide interesting perspectives on complex problems in communication and raise interesting questions that media researchers can pursue. For a current list of mass media journals, search the Internet for *"media journals."*

Research Summaries

Professional research organizations periodically publish summaries that provide a close look at the major research areas in various fields. These summaries are often useful for obtaining information about research topics because they survey a wide variety of studies. Good examples of summary research (also known as "meta-research") in communication are *Television and Human Behavior* by George Comstock and others (1978); *Media Effects and Society* by Perse (2001); *Milestones in Mass Communication Research* by Shearon, Lowery, and Melvin DeFleur (1995); *Media Effects Research: A Basic Overview* by Sparks (2009); and *Media Effects: Advances in Theory and Research* by Bryant and Oliver (2008).

The Internet

The Internet brings the world to a researcher's fingertips and must be considered whenever the goal is to find a topic to investigate. Search engines make it easy to find information on almost any topic. For example, assume that you have an interest in 3DTV. A search for that term on Google produces several million matches, although not all may be relevant to your specific research. That's a lot of material to consider, but suppose you wonder about mobile 3DTV. A search for "mobile 3DTV" produces far fewer items, many of which provide interesting information about the new technology.

A great exercise on the Internet is to search for broad categories. For example, to see the variety of questions that can be answered, search for "*What was the first*," "*How is*," "*How does*," "*Why is*," or "*Why does*." In addition, conduct a search for "*research topic ideas*." You'll find an incredible list of items to use for preliminary information.

Everyday Situations

Each day, people are confronted with various types of communication via radio, television, newspapers, magazines, movies, personal discussions, and so on. These are excellent sources for researchers who take an active role in analyzing them. With this in mind, consider the following questions:

- How do smartphones change people's use of the media?

- Why do advertisers use specific types of messages in the mass media?

- Why are *Entertainment Tonight, Jeopardy*, and *Wheel of Fortune* so popular?

- Why do so many TV commercials use only video to deliver a message when many people don't always watch TV—they just listen?

- How effective are billboards in communicating information about products and services?

- What types of people listen to radio talk shows?

- How many commercials in a row can people watch on television or hear on the radio before the commercials lose their effect?

- Why do commercials on radio and television always sound louder than the regular programming? (Search the Internet for "*Calm Act*.")

- What is the appeal of "reality" programs on TV?

- How many people listen to the music channels on cable or satellite TV?

- Why are Facebook and Twitter so popular?

- Does anyone really watch the Weather Channel?

These and other questions may become a research idea. Significant studies based on questions arising from everyday encounters with the media and other forms of mass communication have covered investigations of television violence, the layout of newspaper advertisements, advisory warnings on television programs, and approaches to public relations campaigns. Pay attention to things around you and to conversations with others because these contacts can produce a wealth of questions to investigate.

Archive Data

Data archives, such as the Inter-University Consortium for Political and Social Research (ICPSR) at the University of Michigan, the Simmons Target Group Index (TGI), the Gallup and Roper organizations, and the collections of Arbitron and Nielsen ratings data (see Chapter 15), are valuable sources of ideas for researchers. Historical data may be used to investigate questions different from those that the data were originally intended to address. For example, ratings books provide information about audience size and composition for a particular period in time, but other researchers may use the data for historical tracking, prediction of audiences in the future, changes in the popularity of types of stations and programs, and the relationship between audience ratings and advertising revenue generated by individual stations or an entire market. This process, known as **secondary analysis**, is a marvelous research approach because it saves time and resources.

Secondary analysis provides an opportunity for researchers to evaluate otherwise unavailable data. Becker (1981, p. 240) defines secondary analysis as:

[the] reuse of social science data after they have been put aside by the researcher who

gathered them. The reuse of the data can be by the original researcher or someone uninvolved in any way in the initial research project. The research questions examined in the secondary analysis can be related to the original research endeavor or quite distinct from it.

Advantages of Secondary Analysis

Ideally, every researcher should conduct a research project of some magnitude to learn about design, data collection, and analysis. Unfortunately, this ideal situation does not exist—research is too expensive. In addition, because survey methodology has become so complex, it is rare to find one researcher who is an expert in all phases of large studies.

Secondary analysis is one research alternative that overcomes some of these problems. Using available data is inexpensive. There are no questionnaires or measurement instruments to construct and validate, interviewers and other personnel do not need to be paid, and there no costs for subjects and special equipment. The only expenses entailed in secondary analysis are those for duplicating materials (some organizations provide their data free of charge) and usually some fee to cover postage and handling. Data archives are valuable sources for empirical data. In many cases, archive data provide researchers with information that can be used to address significant media problems and questions.

Although novice researchers can learn much from developing questionnaires and conducting a research project using a small and often unrepresentative sample of subjects, this type of analysis rarely produces results that are externally valid. (External validity is discussed later in this chapter.) Instead of conducting a small study that has limited value to other situations, these people can benefit from using previously collected data. Researchers then have more time to understand and analyze the data (Tukey,

1969). All too often, researchers collect data that are quickly analyzed for publication or reported to management and never touched again. It is difficult to completely analyze all data from any research study in just one analysis, yet researchers in both the academic and private sectors are guilty of ignoring data gathered earlier.

Many years ago, Tukey (1969, p. 89) argued for data reanalysis, especially for graduate students, but his statement applies to all researchers:

> There is merit in having a Ph.D. thesis encompass all the admitted steps of the research process. Once we recognize that research is a continuing, more or less cyclic process, however, we see that we can segment it in many places. Why should not at least a fair proportion of theses start with a careful analysis of previously collected and presumably already lightly analyzed data, a process usefully spread out over considerable time? Instant data analysis is—and will remain—an illusion.

Arguments for secondary analysis come from a variety of researchers (Glenn, 1972; Hinds, Vogel, & Clarke-Steffen, 1997; Hyman, 1972; Tukey, 1969). While secondary analysis provides excellent opportunities to produce valuable knowledge, the procedure is not universally accepted—an unfortunate myopic perspective that limits the advancement of knowledge.

Disadvantages of Secondary Analysis

Researchers who use secondary analysis are limited in the types of hypotheses or research questions that can be investigated. The data already exist, and because there is no way to go back for more information, researchers must keep their analyses within the boundaries of the data originally collected.

In addition, there is no guarantee that the data are good. It may be that the data were poorly collected, inaccurate, fabricated, or flawed. Many studies do not include information about research design, sampling procedures, weighting of subjects' responses, or other peculiarities. Although individual researchers in mass media have made their data more readily available, not all follow adequate scientific procedures. This drawback may seriously affect a secondary analysis.

Despite the criticisms of using secondary analysis, the methodology is an acceptable research approach, and detailed justifications for using it should no longer be required.

DETERMINING TOPIC RELEVANCE

Once a basic research idea has been chosen or assigned, the next step is to ensure that the topic has merit. This is accomplished by answering eight basic questions.

Question 1: Is the Topic Too Broad?

Most research studies concentrate on one small area of a field; researchers do not attempt to analyze an entire field in one study. However, beginning researchers frequently choose topics that are too broad to cover in one study—for example, "the effects of television violence on children" or "the effects of mass media information on voters in a presidential election." To avoid this problem, researchers usually write down their proposed title as a visual starting point and attempt to dissect the topic into a series of questions.

For example, a University of Colorado master's degree student was interested in why viewers like the television shows they watch and how viewers' analyses of programs compare to analyses by paid TV critics. This is a broad topic. First of all, what types of programs will be analyzed? After a great deal of thought about the questions involved, the student settled on the topic of "program element importance" in

television soap operas. She asked viewers to identify what is important to them when they watch a soap opera, and she developed a "model" for a successful program.

Question 2: Can the Problem Really Be Investigated?

Aside from being too broad, a topic might prove unsuitable for investigation simply because the question being asked has no answer or at least cannot be answered with the facilities and information available. For example, a researcher who wants to know how people who have no television set react to everyday interpersonal communication situations must consider the problem of finding subjects without a TV set in the home. A few such subjects may exist in remote parts of the country, but the question is virtually unanswerable due to the current market saturation of television. Thus, the researcher must attempt to reanalyze the original idea to conform with practical considerations. A. S. Tan (1977) solved this particular dilemma by choosing to investigate what people do when their television sets are turned off for a period of time. He persuaded subjects not to watch television for one week and to record their use of other media, their interactions with their family and friends, and so on. (Subjects involved in these types of media-deprivation studies usually cheat and use the medium before the end of the project.)

Another point to consider is whether all the terms of the proposed study can be defined. Remember that all measured variables must have operational definitions. A researcher interested in examining youngsters' use of the media must develop a working definition of the word *youngsters* to avoid confusion.

Problems can be eliminated if an operational definition is stated: "Youngsters are children between the ages of three and seven years." One final consideration is to review available literature to determine whether the topic has been previously investigated. Were there any problems in previous studies? What methods were used to answer the research questions? What conclusions were drawn?

Question 3: Can the Data Be Analyzed?

A topic does not lend itself to productive research if it requires collecting data that cannot be measured in a reliable and valid fashion. In other words, a researcher who wants to measure the effects of not watching television should consider whether the information about the subjects' behavior will be adequate and reliable, whether the subjects will answer truthfully, what value the data will have once gathered, and so forth. Researchers also need to have enough data to make the study worthwhile. It would be unacceptable to analyze only 10 subjects in the "television turn-off" example because the results could not be generalized to the entire population. (A sample of 10 may be used for a **pilot study**—a test of the research procedures.)

Another consideration is the researcher's previous experience with the statistical method selected to analyze the data: that is, does the researcher really understand the proposed statistical analysis? Researchers need to know how the statistics work and how to interpret the results. All too often, researchers design studies that involve advanced statistical procedures they have never used. This tactic usually creates errors in computation and interpretation. Research methods and statistics should not be selected because they happen to be popular or because a research director suggests a given method but because they are appropriate for a given study and are understood by the person conducting the analysis. A common error made by beginning researchers—selecting a statistical method without understanding what the method produces—is called the **law of the instrument**.

It is much wiser to use simple frequencies and percentages and understand the results than to try to use a misunderstood high-level statistic and end up confused.

Question 4: Is the Problem Significant?

It is important to determine whether a study has merit *before the research is started*; that is, to determine whether the study has practical or theoretical value. The first question to ask is this: Will the results add knowledge to information already available in the field? The goal of research is to help further the understanding of the problems and questions in a field of study. If a study does not do this, it has little value beyond the experience the researcher acquires from conducting it. Of course, not all research has to produce earth-shattering results. Many researchers waste valuable time trying to address monumental questions when in fact the smaller problems or questions are more important.

A second question is: What is the real purpose of the study? This question is important because it helps focus ideas. Is the study intended for a class paper, a thesis, a journal article, or a management decision? Each of these projects requires different amounts of background information, levels of explanation, and details about the results generated. For example, applied researchers must consider whether any useful action based on the data will be possible, as well as whether the study will answer the question(s) posed by management.

Question 5: Can the Results of the Study Be Generalized?

If a research project is to have practical value beyond the immediate analysis, it must have **external validity**; that is, it must be possible to generalize the results to other situations. For example, a study of the effects of a small-town public relations campaign might be appropriate if plans are made to analyze

Occam or Ockham?

In previous editions of this book, the authors used the spelling "Occam" as the name of the fourteenth-century English philosopher. However, following the self-correcting aspect of the scientific method, the authors investigated the question. After learning that William was from the town in England spelled "Ockham," it was decided to use the spelling of his birthplace and no longer use "Occam."

such effects in several small towns, or if it is a case study not intended for generalization; however, such an analysis has little external validity and cannot be related to other situations.

Question 6: What Costs and Time Are Involved in the Analysis?

In many cases, the cost of a research study alone determines whether the study is feasible. A researcher may have an excellent idea, but if costs would be prohibitive, the project is abandoned. A cost analysis must be completed early on. It does not make sense to develop the specific designs and the data-gathering instrument for a project that will be canceled because of lack of funds. Sophisticated research is particularly expensive; the cost of one project can easily exceed $50,000.

A carefully itemized list of all materials, equipment, and other facilities required is necessary before beginning a research project. If the costs seem prohibitive, the researcher must determine whether the same goal can be achieved if costs are shaved in some areas. Another possibility to consider is financial aid from graduate schools, funding agencies, local governments, or other groups that subsidize research projects. In general, private-sector researchers are not severely constrained by expenses; however, they must adhere to budget specifications set by management.

Time is also an important consideration in research planning. Research studies must be designed so that they can be completed in the time available. Many studies fail because the researchers do not allot enough time for each research step, and in many cases, the pressure of deadlines creates problems in producing reliable and valid results (for example, failure to provide alternatives if the correct sample of people cannot be found).

Question 7: Is the Planned Approach Appropriate to the Project?

The best research idea may be needlessly hindered by a poorly planned approach. For example, a researcher might want to measure changes in television viewing habits that may accompany an increase in time spent on the Internet. The researcher could mail questionnaires to a large sample to determine how their television habits have changed during the past several months. However, the costs of printing and mailing questionnaires, plus follow-up letters and possibly phone calls to increase the response rate, might prove prohibitive.

Could the study be planned differently to eliminate some of the expense? Possibly, depending on its purpose and the types of questions planned. For example, the researcher could collect the data by telephone interviews or even via email to eliminate printing and postage costs.

Although some questions might need reworking to fit the telephone or email

A CLOSER LOOK

Ockham's Razor

Although Ockham's razor is mentioned only briefly here, it is an enormously important concept to remember and is mentioned many times in this book. It is important in research and in every facet of people's lives. If you are stumped with a sampling problem, a questionnaire design problem, a data analysis problem, or a report problem, always ask yourself, "Is this the easiest way to approach the problem?" In most cases, you'll find the difficulty is that you're making the problem too complex. The same situation often occurs in your everyday life. Always look for the simplest approach to any problem you encounter. It will always be the best approach to follow.

methods, the essential information could be collected. A close look at every study is required to plan the best approach. Every procedure in a research study should be considered from the standpoint of the **parsimony principle,** or **Ockham's razor.** The principle, attributed to fourteenth-century philosopher William of Ockham, states that a person should not increase beyond what is necessary the number of entities required to explain anything or make more assumptions than the minimum needed. Applying this principle to media research says that *the simplest research approach is always the best.*

Question 8: Is There Any Potential Harm to the Subjects?

Researchers must carefully analyze whether their project may cause physical or psychological harm to the subjects under evaluation. Will respondents be frightened in any way? Will they be required to answer embarrassing questions or perform embarrassing acts that may create adverse reactions? Is there a chance that exposure to the research conditions will have lasting effects? Before the start of most public-sector research projects involving humans, subjects are given detailed statements explaining the exact procedures involved in the research to ensure that they will not be injured in any way. These statements protect unsuspecting subjects from exposure to harmful research methods.

Underlying the eight steps in the research topic selection process is the necessity for validity (discussed later in this chapter). In other words, are all the steps (from the initial idea to data analysis and interpretation) the correct ones to follow in trying to answer the question(s)?

Suppose that after you carefully select a research project and convince yourself that it is something you want to do, someone confronts you with this reaction: "It's a good idea, but it can't be done. The topic is too broad, the problem cannot really be investigated, the data cannot be analyzed, the problem is not significant, the results cannot be generalized, it will cost too much, and the approach is wrong." How should you respond? First, consider the criticisms carefully to make sure that you have not overlooked anything. If you are convinced you're on the right track and no harm will come to any subject or respondent, go ahead with the project. It is better to do the study and find nothing than to back off because of someone's misguided criticism.

Literature Review

Researchers who conduct studies under the guidelines of scientific research never begin a research project without first consulting available literature to learn what has been done, how it was done, and what results were found. Experienced researchers consider the literature review to be one of the most important steps in the research process. It allows them to learn from (and eventually add to) previous research and saves time, effort, and money. Failing to conduct a literature review is as detrimental to a project as failing to address any of the other steps in the research process.

Before they attempt any project, researchers should ask these questions:

- What type of research has been done in the area?
- What has been found in previous studies?
- What suggestions do other researchers make for further study?
- What has not been investigated?
- How can the proposed study add to our knowledge of the area?
- What research methods were used in previous studies?

Answers to these questions will usually help define a specific hypothesis or research question.

STATING A HYPOTHESIS OR RESEARCH QUESTION

After identifying a general research area and reviewing the existing literature, the researcher must state the problem as a workable hypothesis or research question. A **hypothesis** is *a formal statement regarding the relationship between variables and is tested directly.* The predicted relationship between the variables is either true or false. On the other hand, a **research question** is *a formally stated question intended to provide indications about something; it is not limited to investigating relationships between variables.* Research questions are appropriate when a researcher is unsure

about the nature of the problem under investigation. Although the intent is merely to gather preliminary data, testable hypotheses are often developed from information gathered during the research question phase of a study.

Singer and Singer (1981) provide an example of how a topic is narrowed, developed, and stated in simple terms. Interested in whether television material enhances or inhibits a child's capacity for symbolic behavior, Singer and Singer reviewed available literature and then narrowed their study to three basic research questions:

1. Does television content enrich a child's imaginative capacities by offering materials and ideas for make-believe play?
2. Does television lead to distortions of reality for children?
3. Can intervention and mediation by an adult while a child views a program, or immediately afterward, evoke changes in make-believe play or stimulate make-believe play?

The information collected from this type of study could provide data to create testable hypotheses. For example, Singer and Singer might have collected enough valuable information from their preliminary study to test these hypotheses:

1. The amount of time a child spends in make-believe play is directly related to the amount of time spent viewing make-believe play on television.
2. A child's level of distortion of reality is directly related to the amount and types of television programs the child views.
3. Parental discussions with children about make-believe play before, during, and after a child watches television programs involving make-believe play increase the child's time involved in make-believe play.

The difference between the two sets of statements is that the research questions pose only general areas of investigation, whereas the hypotheses are testable statements about the relationship(s) between the variables. The only intent in the research question phase is to gather information to help the researchers define and test hypotheses in later projects.

DATA ANALYSIS AND INTERPRETATION

The time and effort required for data analysis and interpretation depend on the study's purpose and the methodology used. Analysis and interpretation may take from several days to several months. In many private-sector research studies involving only a single question, data analysis and interpretation may be completed in a few minutes. For example, a radio station may be interested in finding out its listeners' perceptions of the morning show team. After a survey is conducted, that question may be answered by summarizing only one or two items on the questionnaire. The summary may then determine the fate of the morning show team.

Every research study must be carefully planned and performed according to specific guidelines. When the analysis is completed, the researcher must step back and consider what has been discovered. The researcher must ask two questions: Are the results internally and externally valid? Are the results accurate?

For example, here is an excerpt from the conclusion drawn by Singer and Singer (1981, p. 385):

Television by its very nature is a medium that emphasizes those very elements that are generally found in imagination: visual fluidity, time and space flexibility and make-believe.... Very little effort has emerged from producers or educators to develop age-specific programming.... It is evident that more research for the development of programming and adult mediation is urgently needed.

Researchers must determine through analysis whether their work is both internally and externally valid. This chapter has touched briefly on the concept of external validity: An externally valid study is one whose results can be generalized to the population. To assess **internal validity**, on the other hand, one asks: Does the study really investigate the proposed research question?

INTERNAL VALIDITY

Control over research conditions is necessary to enable researchers *to rule out plausible but incorrect explanations of results*. For example, if a researcher is interested in verifying that "y is a function of x," or $y = f(x)$, control over the research conditions is necessary to eliminate the possibility of finding that $y = f(b)$, where b is an **extraneous variable**. Any such variable that creates a possible but incorrect explanation of results is called an **artifact** (also referred to as a **confounding variable**). The presence of an artifact indicates a lack of internal validity; that is, the study has failed to investigate its hypothesis.

For example, suppose that researchers discover through a study that children who view television for extended periods have lower grade point averages in school than children who watch only a limited amount of television. Could an artifact have created this finding? It may be that children who view fewer hours of television also receive parental help with their schoolwork; parental help (the artifact), not hours of television viewed, may be the reason for the difference in grade point averages between the two groups.

Artifacts in research may arise from several sources. Those most frequently encountered are described next. Researchers should be familiar with these sources to achieve internal validity in the experiments they conduct (Campbell & Stanley, 1963; Cook & Campbell, 1979).

1. *History.* Various events that occur during a study may affect the subjects' attitudes, opinions, and behavior. For example, to analyze an oil company's public relations campaign for a new product, researchers first pretest subjects' attitudes toward the company. The subjects are next exposed to an experimental promotional campaign (the experimental treatment); then a posttest is administered to determine whether changes in attitude occur because of the campaign. Suppose the results indicate that the public relations campaign was a complete failure, that the subjects display a poor perception of the oil company in the posttest. Before the results are reported, the researchers must determine whether an intervening variable could have caused the poor perception. An investigation discloses that during the period between tests, subjects learned from a television news story that a tanker owned by the oil company spilled millions of gallons of crude oil into the North Atlantic. News of the oil spill—not the public relations campaign—may have acted as an artifact to create the poor perception. The potential to confound a study is compounded as the time increases between a pretest and a posttest.

The effects of history in a study can be devastating, as was shown during the late 1970s and early 1980s when several broadcast companies and other private businesses perceived a need to develop subscription television (STV) in various markets throughout the country where cable television penetration was thought to be very low. An STV service allows a household, using a special antenna, to receive pay television services similar to Home Box Office or Showtime. Several cities became prime targets for STV

because both Arbitron and A. C. Nielsen reported low cable penetration. Research conducted in these cities supported the Arbitron and Nielsen data. In addition, the research found that people who did not have access to cable television were receptive to the idea of STV. However, it was discovered later that even as some studies were being conducted, cable companies in the target areas were expanding rapidly and had wired many previously nonwired neighborhoods. What were once prime targets for STV soon became accessible to cable television. The major problem was that researchers attempting to determine the feasibility of STV failed to consider historical changes (wiring of the cities) that could affect the results of their research. The result was that many companies lost millions of dollars and STV quickly faded away.

2. *Maturation.* Subjects' biological and psychological characteristics change during the course of a study. Growing hungry or tired or becoming older may influence how subjects respond in a research study. An example of how maturation can affect a research project was seen in the early 1980s, when radio stations around the country began to test their music playlist in auditorium sessions (see Chapter 14). Some unskilled research companies tested as many as 800 songs in one session and wondered why the songs after about 600 tested differently from the others. With only a few studies, it was discovered that the respondents were physically and emotionally drained once they reached 600 songs (about 100 minutes of testing time), and they merely wrote down any number just to complete the project.

Technology and experience have changed the approach in auditorium music testing. In several studies during 2001, the senior author of this book tested a variety of auditorium music testing methods and found that, among other things, if a professional production company is used to produce consistent hooks (song segments) and sufficient breaks are given for the respondents, it is possible to test as many as 600 songs in one session without compromising the data.

3. *Testing.* Testing itself may be an artifact, particularly when subjects are given similar pretests and posttests. A pretest may sensitize subjects to the material and improve their posttest scores regardless of the type of experimental treatment given. This is especially true when the same test is used for both situations. Subjects learn how to answer questions and to anticipate researchers' demands. To guard against the effects of testing, different pretests and posttests are required. Or, instead of administering a pretest, subjects can be tested for similarity (homogeneity) by means of a variable or set of variables that differs from the experimental variable. The pretest is not the only way to establish a **point of prior equivalency** (the point at which the groups were equal before the experiment) between groups—it also can be accomplished through sampling (randomization and matching). For further discussion on controlling confounding variables within the context of an experiment, see Chapter 9.

4. *Instrumentation.* Also known as **instrument decay**, this term refers to the deterioration of research instruments or methods over the course of a study. Equipment may wear out, observers may become more casual in recording their observations, and interviewers who memorize frequently asked questions might fail to present them in the proper order. Some college entrance tests, such as the SAT and ACT, are targets of debate by many researchers and statisticians. The complaints mainly address the concern that the current tests do not adequately measure knowledge of today, but rather what was once considered necessary and important.

5. *Statistical regression.* Subjects who achieve either very high or very low scores on a test tend to regress to (move toward) the sample or population mean during subsequent testing sessions. Often *outliers* (subjects whose pretest scores are far from the mean) are selected for further testing or evaluation. Suppose, for example, that researchers develop a series of television programs designed to teach simple mathematical concepts, and they select only subjects who score very low on a mathematical aptitude pretest. An experimental treatment is designed to expose these subjects to the new television series, and a posttest is given to determine whether the programs increased the subjects' knowledge of simple math concepts. The experimental study may show that, indeed, after only one or two exposures to the new programs, math scores increased. But the higher scores on the posttest may not be due to the television programs. They may be a function of learning from the pretest, or they may be a function of **statistical regression** (or regression toward the mean). That is, regardless of whether the subjects viewed the programs, the scores in the sample may have increased merely because of statistical regression. (Statistical regression is a phenomenon that may occur in situations where subjects or elements are tested more than once. In subsequent testing, subjects or elements that scored high or low in the first test may score lower or higher in a subsequent test, and this causes the subjects or elements to move closer to the mean of the group or items tested or measured.)

With regard to the TV math programs, the programs should be tested with a variety of subjects, not just those who score low on a pretest.

6. *Experimental mortality.* All research studies face the possibility that subjects will drop out for one reason or another. Especially in long-term studies, subjects may refuse to continue with the project, become ill, move away, drop out of school, or quit work. This **mortality**, or loss of subjects, is

A CLOSER LOOK

Data Analysis—The Wimmer-Dominick Data Analysis Principle

One thing beginning researchers always find interesting is the ability of seasoned researchers to look at data and say something like, "This looks wrong." The beginners wonder how the veteran knows that. The reason the veteran researcher knows that something is wrong is based on experience, a process we refer to as the Wimmer-Dominick Data Analysis Principle, which states: *If something looks wrong in a research study, it probably is.*

Here's a real example. In a research study using rating scales from 1 to 10, a few responses had mean scores above 10. The data looked wrong and, of course, they were because it's impossible to have a mean greater than 10 on a 1–10 scale. Experience in research will allow you to locate these types of errors. Trust your judgment—if something looks wrong, it probably is.

sure to have an effect on the results of a study because most research methods and statistical analyses make assumptions about the number of subjects used. It is always better to select more subjects than are actually required—within the budget limits of the study. It is common to lose 50% or more of the subjects from one testing period to another (Wimmer, 1995).

7. *Sample selection.* Most research designs compare two or more groups of subjects to determine whether differences exist on the dependent measurement. These groups must be selected randomly and tested for homogeneity to ensure that results are not due to the type of sample used (see Chapter 4).

8. *Demand characteristics.* The term **demand characteristics** is used to describe subjects' reactions to experimental situations. Orne (1969) suggests that under some circumstances subjects' awareness of the experimental purpose may be the sole determinant of how they behave; that is, subjects who recognize the purpose of a study may produce only "good" data for researchers.

Novice researchers quickly learn about the many variations of demand characteristics. For example, research studies seeking to find out about respondents' listening and viewing habits always find subjects who report high levels of NPR and PBS listening and viewing. However, when the same subjects are asked to name their favorite NPR or PBS programs, many cannot recall even one. (In other words, the respondents are not telling the truth.)

Cross-validating questions is often necessary to verify subjects' responses; by giving subjects the opportunity to answer the same question phrased in different ways, the researcher can spot discrepancies, which are generally error-producing responses. In addition, researchers can help control demand characteristics by disguising the real purpose of the study; however, special attention is necessary when using this technique (see Chapter 4).

Finally, most respondents who participate in research projects are eager to provide the information the researcher requests and are flattered to be asked for their opinions. Unfortunately, this means that they will answer any type of question, even if the question is ambiguous, misleading, vague, or uninterpretable. For example, this book's senior author once conducted a telephone study with respondents in area code 717 in

Pennsylvania. An interviewer mistakenly called area code 714 (Orange County, California). For nearly 20 minutes, the respondent in California answered questions about radio stations with *W* call letters—stations impossible for her to receive on any normal radio. The problem was discovered during questionnaire validation.

9. *Experimenter bias.* Rosenthal (1969) discusses a variety of ways in which a researcher may influence the results of a study. Bias can enter through mistakes made in observation, data recording, mathematical computations, and interpretation. Whether experimenter errors are intentional or unintentional, they usually support the researcher's hypothesis and are biased (Walizer & Wienir, 1978).

Experimenter bias can also enter into any phase of a project if the researcher becomes swayed by a client's wishes for a project's results. Such a situation can cause significant problems for researchers if they do not remain totally objective throughout the entire project, especially when they are hired by individuals or companies to "prove a point" or to provide "supporting information" for a decision (this is usually unknown to the researcher). For example, the news director at a local television station may dislike a particular news anchor and want information to justify the dislike (to fire the anchor). A researcher is hired under the guise of finding out whether the audience likes or dislikes the anchor. In this case, it is easy for the news director to intentionally or unintentionally influence the results through conversations with the researcher in the planning stages of the study. It is possible for a researcher, either intentionally or unintentionally, to interpret the results in a way that supports the program director's desire to eliminate the anchor. The researcher may have like/dislike numbers that are very close but may give the "edge" to dislike because of the news director's influence.

Experimenter bias is a potential problem in all phases of research, and researchers must be aware of problems caused by outside influences. Several procedures can help to reduce experimenter bias. For example, individuals who provide instructions to subjects and make observations should not be informed of the purpose of the study. Experimenters and others involved in the research should not know whether subjects belong to the experimental group or the control group (called a **double-blind experiment**), and prerecorded audio or video information should be used whenever possible to provide uniform instructions to subjects.

Researchers can also ask clients not to discuss the intent of a research project beyond what type of information is desired. In the news anchor example, the program director should say only that information is desired about the like/dislike of the program and should not discuss what decisions will be made following the research. In cases where researchers must be told about the purpose of the project, or where the researcher is conducting the study independently, experimenter bias must be repressed at every phase.

10. *Evaluation apprehension.* Rosenberg's (1965) concept of evaluation apprehension is similar to demand characteristics, but it emphasizes that subjects are essentially afraid of being measured or tested. They are interested in receiving only positive evaluations from the researcher and from the other subjects involved in the study. Most people are hesitant to exhibit behavior that differs from the norm and tend to follow the group even though they may totally disagree with the others. The researcher's task is to try to eliminate this passivity by letting subjects know that their individual responses are important.

11. *Causal time order.* The organization of an experiment may create problems with data collection and interpretation. It may be that an experiment's results are due not to the stimulus (independent) variable but

rather to the effect of the dependent variable. For example, respondents in an experiment that is attempting to determine how magazine advertising layouts influence their purchasing behavior may change their opinions when they read or complete a questionnaire after viewing several ads.

12. *Diffusion or imitation of treatments.* In situations where respondents participate at different times during one day or over several days, or where groups of respondents are studied one after another, respondents may have the opportunity to discuss the project with someone from another session and contaminate the research project. This is a special problem with focus groups when one group leaves the focus room at the same time a new group enters. (Professional field services and experienced researchers prevent this situation.)

13. *Compensation.* Sometimes individuals who work with a control group (the one that receives no experimental treatment) may unknowingly treat the group differently because the group is "deprived" of something. In this case, the control group is no longer legitimate.

14. *Compensatory rivalry.* Occasionally, subjects who know they are in a control group may work harder or perform differently to outperform the experimental group.

15. *Demoralization.* Control group subjects may literally lose interest in a project because they are not experimental subjects. These people may give up or fail to perform normally because they may feel demoralized or angry that they are not in the experimental group.

The sources of internal invalidity are complex and may arise in all phases of research. For this reason, it is easy to see why the results from a single study cannot be used to refute or support a theory or hypothesis. In attempting to control these artifacts, researchers use a variety of experimental designs and try to keep strict control over the research process so that subjects and researchers do not intentionally or unintentionally influence the results. As Hyman (1954) recognized:

> All scientific inquiry is subject to error, and it is far better to be aware of this, to study the sources in an attempt to reduce it, and to estimate the magnitude of such errors in our findings, than to be ignorant of the errors concealed in our data.

EXTERNAL VALIDITY

External validity refers to how well the results of a study can be generalized across populations, settings, and time (Cook & Campbell, 1979). The external validity of a study can be severely affected by the interaction in an analysis of variables such as subject selection, instrumentation, and experimental conditions (Campbell & Stanley, 1963). A study that lacks external validity cannot be projected to other situations; it is valid only for the sample tested.

Most procedures used to guard against external invalidity relate to sample selection. Cook and Campbell (1979) make three suggestions:

1. Use random samples.
2. Use heterogeneous samples and replicate (repeat) the study several times.
3. Select a sample that is representative of the group to which the results will be generalized.

Using random samples rather than convenience or available samples allows researchers to gather information from a variety of subjects rather than from those who may share similar attitudes, opinions, and lifestyles. As discussed in Chapter 4, a random sample means that *everyone (within the guidelines of the project) has an equal chance of being selected for the research study.*

Several replicated research projects using samples with a variety of characteristics (heterogeneous) allow researchers to test hypotheses and research questions and not worry that the results will apply to only one type of subject. Selecting a sample that is representative of the group to which the results will be generalized is basic common sense. For example, the results from a study of a group of high school students cannot be generalized to a group of college students.

A fourth way to increase external validity is to conduct research over a long period of time. Mass media research is often designed as short-term projects that expose subjects to an experimental treatment and then immediately test or measure them. In many cases, however, the immediate effects of a treatment are negligible. In advertising, for example, research studies designed to measure brand awareness are generally based on only one exposure to a commercial or advertisement. It is well known that persuasion and attitude change rarely take place after only one exposure; they require multiple exposures over time. Logically, then, such measurements should be made over weeks or months to take into account the "sleeper" effect—that attitude change may be minimal or nonexistent in the short run and still prove significant in the end.

PRESENTING RESULTS

The format used to present results depends on the purpose of the study. Research intended for publication in academic journals follows a format prescribed by each journal; research conducted for management in the private sector tends to be reported in simpler terms, often excluding detailed explanations of sampling, methodology, and review of literature. However, all results must be presented in a clear and concise manner appropriate to both the research question and the individuals who will read

the report. (See "Writing a Research Report" in the **Readings** section of *www.wimmer dominick.com*.)

Replication

One important point mentioned throughout this book is that the results of any single study are, by themselves, only indications of what might exist. A study provides information that says, in effect, "This is what may be the case." For others to be relatively certain of the results of any study, the research must be replicated, or repeated. Too often, researchers conduct one study and report the results as if they are providing the basis for a theory or a law. The information presented in this chapter, and in other chapters that deal with internal and external validity, argues that this cannot be true.

A research question or hypothesis must be investigated from many different perspectives before any significance can be attributed to the results of one study. Research methods and designs must be altered to eliminate **design-specific results**—results based on, and hence specific to, the design used. Similarly, subjects with a variety of characteristics should be studied from many angles to eliminate **sample-specific results**, and statistical analyses need to be varied to eliminate **method-specific results**. In other words, every effort must be made to ensure that the results of any single study are not created by or dependent on a methodological factor; studies must be replicated.

Researchers overwhelmingly advocate the use of **replication** to establish scientific fact. Lykken (1968) and Kelly, Chase, and Tucker (1979) identify four basic types of replication that can be used to help validate a scientific test:

1. **Literal replication** involves the exact duplication of a previous analysis, including the sampling procedures, experimental conditions, measuring

techniques, and methods of data analysis.

2. **Operational replication** attempts to duplicate only the sampling and experimental procedures of a previous analysis, to test whether the procedures will produce similar results.

3. **Instrumental replication** attempts to duplicate the dependent measures used in a previous study and to vary the experimental conditions of the original study.

4. **Constructive replication** tests the validity of methods used previously by deliberately not imitating the earlier study; both the manipulations and the measures differ from those used in the first study. The researcher simply begins with a statement of empirical "fact" uncovered in a previous study and attempts to find the same "fact."

Despite the obvious need to replicate research, mass media researchers generally ignore this important step, probably because many feel that replications are not as glamorous or important as original research. The wise researcher recognizes that even though replications may lack glamour, they most certainly do not lack importance.

RESEARCH SUPPLIERS AND FIELD SERVICES

Most media researchers do not conduct every phase of every project they supervise. Although they usually design research projects, determine the sample to study, and prepare the measurement instruments, researchers generally do not actually make telephone calls or interview respondents in on-site locations. Instead, the researchers contract with a research supplier or a field service to perform these tasks.

Research suppliers provide a variety of services. A full-service supplier participates in the design of a study, supervises data collection, tabulates the data, and analyzes the results. The company may work in any field (such as mass media, medical and hospital, or banking) or specialize in only one type of research work. In addition, some companies can execute any type of research method—telephone surveys, one-on-one interviews, shopping center interviews (intercepts), or focus groups—whereas others concentrate on only one method.

Field services usually specialize in conducting telephone interviews, mall intercepts, and one-on-one interviews and in recruiting respondents for group administration (**central location testing**, or CLT) projects and focus groups. The latter projects are called **prerecruits** (the company prerecruits respondents to attend a research session). Although some field services offer help in questionnaire design and data tabulation, most concentrate on telephone interviews, mall interviews, and prerecruiting.

Field services usually have focus group rooms available (with one-way mirrors to allow clients to view the session) and test kitchens for projects involving food and cooking. Although some field service facilities are gorgeous and elaborate, others look as though the company just filed for bankruptcy protection. Many field services lease space, or lease the right to conduct research, in shopping malls to conduct intercepts. Some field services are actually based in shopping malls.

Hiring a research supplier or field service is a simple process. The researcher calls the company, explains the project, and is given a price quote. A contract or project confirmation letter is usually signed. In some cases, the price quote is a flat fee for the total project, or a fee plus or minus about 10%, depending on the difficulty of the project.

Sometimes costs are based on the cost per interview (CPI), which is discussed shortly.

One term that plays an important role in the research process is **incidence**, which describes how easy it is to find qualified respondents or subjects for a research project. Incidence is expressed as a percentage of 100—the lower the incidence, the more difficult it is to find a qualified respondent or group of respondents. **Gross incidence** is the percentage of qualified respondents reached of all contacts made (such as telephone calls), and **net incidence** is the number of respondents or subjects who actually participate in a project.

For example, assume that a telephone research study requires 100 female respondents between the ages of 18 and 49 who listen to the radio at least 1 hour per day. The estimated gross incidence is 10%. (Radio and television incidence figures can be estimated by using Arbitron and Nielsen ratings books; in many cases, however, an incidence is merely a guess on the part of the researcher.) A total of about 1,818 calls will have to be made to recruit the 100 females, not 1,000 calls, as some people may think. The number of calls required is not computed as the target sample size (100 in this example) divided by the incidence (.10), or 1,000. The number of calls computed for gross incidence (1,000) must then be divided by the **acceptance rate**, or the percentage of the target sample that agrees to participate in the study.

The total number of calls required is 1,000 divided by .55 (a generally used acceptance rate), or 1,818. Of the 1,818 telephone calls made, 10% (182) will qualify for the interview, but only 55% of those (100) will actually agree to complete the interview (net incidence).

Field services and research suppliers base their charges on net incidence, not gross incidence. Many novice researchers fail to consider this when they plan the financial budget for a project.

There is no "average" incidence rate in research. The actual rate depends on the complexity of the sample desired, the length of the research project, the time of year the study is conducted, and a variety of other factors. The lower the incidence, the higher the cost of a research project. In addition, prices quoted by field services and research suppliers are based on an estimated incidence rate. Costs are adjusted after the project is completed and the actual incidence rate is known. As mentioned earlier, a quote from a field service is usually given with a plus or minus 10% "warning." Some people may think that understanding how a CPI is computed is unnecessary, but the concept is vitally important to any researcher who subcontracts work to a field service or research supplier.

Returning to the CPI discussion, let's assume that a researcher wants to conduct a 400-person telephone study with adults who are between the ages of 18 and 49. A representative of the company first asks for the researcher's estimated incidence and the length of the interview (in minutes). The two figures determine the CPI. Most field services and research suppliers use a chart to compute the CPI, such as the hypothetical one shown in Table 1.1.

The table is easy to use. To find a CPI, first read across the top of the table for the length of the interview and then scan down the left side for the incidence. For example, the CPI for a 20-minute interview with an incidence of 10% is $30. A researcher conducting a 400-person telephone study with these "specs" will owe the field service or research supplier $12,000 (400 × $30) plus any costs for photocopying the questionnaire, mailing, and tabulating the data (if requested). If the company analyzes the data and writes a final report, the

Table 1.1 Hypothetical CPI Chart (shows cost per completed interview or recruit)

	Minutes					
Incidence%	5	10	15	20	25	30
5	44.25	45.50	46.50	47.75	49.00	50.00
6	38.00	39.25	40.50	41.75	42.75	44.00
7	34.00	35.00	36.25	37.50	38.50	39.75
8	30.75	32.00	33.00	34.25	35.50	36.50
9	28.50	29.50	30.75	32.00	33.00	34.25
10	26.50	27.75	29.00	30.00	31.25	32.50
20	14.25	15.50	16.75	17.75	19.00	20.25
30	10.25	11.50	12.50	13.75	15.00	16.25
40	8.25	9.50	10.50	11.75	13.00	14.25
50	7.00	8.25	9.50	10.50	11.75	13.00
60	6.50	7.75	9.00	10.00	11.25	12.50
70	6.00	7.25	8.50	9.50	10.75	11.75
80	5.75	7.00	8.00	9.25	10.50	11.50
90	5.50	6.75	8.00	9.00	10.25	11.00
100	5.00	6.50	7.75	9.00	10.00	10.50

total cost will be between $20,000 and $30,000.

Research projects involving prerecruits, such as focus groups and group administration, involve an additional cost—respondent *co-op* fees, or *incentives*. A telephone study respondent generally receives no payment for answering questions. However, when respondents are asked to leave their homes to participate in a project, they are usually paid between $25 and $100.

Costs rise quickly in a prerecruit project. For example, assume that a researcher wants to conduct a group session with 400 respondents instead of using a telephone approach. Rather than paying a field service or a research supplier a CPI to conduct a telephone interview, the payment is for recruiting respondents to attend a session conducted at a specific location. Although most companies have separate rate cards for prerecruiting (the rates are usually a bit higher than the rates used for telephone interviewing), we will assume that the costs are the same. Recruiting costs, then, are $12,000 (400 × $30 CPI), with another $10,000 (minimum) for respondent co-op (400 × $25). Total costs so far are $22,000, about twice as much as those for a telephone study. In addition, other costs must be added to this figure: a rental fee for the room where the study will be conducted, refreshments for respondents,

A CLOSER LOOK

Incidence and Phone Calls Required

Although the example described shows that about 1,818 calls would be required to complete the study, the actual number of dialings is much higher. The term *dialings* includes wrong numbers, busy signals, fax machines, computer modems, disconnected numbers, and so on. In reality, most telephone studies conducted today require about 40 dialings for each completed survey.

fees for assistants to check in respondents, and travel expenses (another $1,000–$4,000).

Finally, to ensure that 400 people show up (four sessions of 100 each), it is necessary to overrecruit, since not every respondent will show up. In prerecruit projects, field services and research suppliers overrecruit 25% to 100%. In other words, for a 400 "show rate," a company must prerecruit between 500 and 800 people. However, rarely does a prerecruit session hit the target sample size exactly. In many cases, the show rate falls short and a "make-good" session is required (the project is repeated at a later date with another group of respondents to meet the target sample size). In some cases, more respondents than required show for the study, which means that projected research costs may skyrocket over the planned budget.

In most prerecruit projects, field services and research suppliers are paid on a "show basis" only; that is, they receive payment only for respondents who show up, not for the number who are recruited. If the companies were paid on a recruit basis, they could recruit thousands of respondents for each project. The show-basis payment procedure also adds incentive for the companies to ensure that those who are recruited actually show up for the research session.

Although various problems related to hiring and working with research suppliers and field services are discussed in Chapter 4, we present two important points here to help novice researchers when they begin to use these support companies.

1. *All suppliers and field services are not equal.* Regardless of qualifications, any person or group can form a research supply company or field service. There are no formal requirements; no tests to take; and no national, state, or regional licenses to acquire. All that is required are a "shingle on the door," advertising in marketing and research trade publications, and (optional) membership in one or more of the voluntary research organizations. It is thus the sole responsibility of researchers to determine which of the hundreds of suppliers available are capable of conducting a professional, scientifically based research project. Over time, experienced researchers develop a list of qualified, trustworthy companies. This list comes from experience with a company or from the recommendations of other researchers. In any event, it is important to check the credentials of a research supplier or field service. The senior author of this book has encountered several instances of research supplier and field service fraud during the past 35+ years in the industry.

2. *The researcher must maintain close supervision over the project.* This is true even with very good companies, not because their professionalism cannot be trusted but rather to be sure that the project is answering

A CLOSER LOOK

Research Costs

Fees charged by field services and research suppliers are negotiable, and this process becomes much easier once a researcher has a few years of experience. For example, a researcher may conduct a certain type of study and know that the usual CPI is around $30. If a quote is given for the same type of project, that is, say, $50 CPI, the researcher already knows the price is too high. What should the researcher do? It's very simple: Just tell the field service or supplier that the price is too high. The quote will be reduced.

the questions that were posed. Because of security considerations, a research supplier may never completely understand why a particular project is being conducted, and the researcher needs to be sure that the project will provide the exact information required.

Supplement on Incidence Rates and CPI

Incidence is an important concept in research because it determines both the difficulty and the cost of a research project. Table 1.2 illustrates a standard CPI rate chart. The specific

Table 1.2 Computing a CPI

Step		Explanation
1. Gross incidence	1,000	$100 \div .10$
2. Acceptance rate	55%	Standard figure used to determine how many calls are needed
3. Actual contacts necessary	1,818	$1,000 \div .55$
4. Minutes per contact	4	Number of minutes to find correct respondent (bad numbers, busy lines, etc.)
5. Total contact minutes	7,272	$4 \times 1,818$
6. Productive minutes per hour	40	Average number of minutes interviewers usually work in 1 hour (net of breaks, etc.)
7. Total contact hours	182	$7,272 \div 40$
8. Total interview hours	33	$(100 \times 20 \text{ minutes}) \div 60$
9. Total hours	215	Contact hours + interview hours
10. Hourly rate	$15	Industry standard
11. Total cost	$3,225	$215 \times \$15$
12. CPI	$32.25	$\$3,225 \div 100$ interviews

rates shown on the chart are computed through a complicated series of steps. Without exact detail, this supplement explains the general procedure of how each CPI is computed.

As mentioned earlier, CPI is based on the incidence rate and interview length. In pre-recruiting, only incidence is considered, but the CPIs are basically the same as those for telephone interviews. To determine a CPI, let us assume we wish to conduct a 100-person telephone study, with an incidence rate of 10% and an interview length of 20 minutes. The computation and an explanation of each step are shown in Table 1.2. As shown in the table, 1,818 contacts must be made. Of these, 10% will qualify for the interview (182) and 55% of these will accept (100). The total number of hours required to conduct the 100-person survey is 215, with a CPI of $32.25.

SUMMARY

Media research evolved from the fields of psychology and sociology and is now a well-established field in its own right. It is not necessary to be a statistician to be a successful researcher; it is more important to know how to conduct research and what research procedures can do.

In an effort to understand any phenomenon, researchers can follow one of several methods of inquiry. Of the procedures discussed in this chapter, the scientific approach is most applicable to the mass media because it involves a systematic, objective evaluation of information.

Researchers first identify a problem and then investigate it using a prescribed set of procedures known as the scientific method. The scientific method is the only learning approach that allows for self-correction of research findings; one study does not stand alone but must be supported or refuted by others.

The explosion of mass media research is mainly attributable to the rapidly developing technology of the media industry. Because of this growth in research, both applied and theoretical approaches have taken on more significance in the decision-making process of the mass media and in our understanding of the media. At the same time, there continues to be a severe shortage of good researchers in both the academic and private sectors.

This chapter described the processes involved in identifying and developing a topic for research investigation. It was suggested that researchers consider several sources for potential ideas, including a critical analysis of everyday situations. The steps in developing a topic for investigation naturally become easier with experience; the beginning researcher needs to pay particular attention to material already available. He or she should not attempt to tackle broad research questions but should try to isolate a smaller, more practical subtopic for study. The researcher should develop an appropriate method of analysis and then proceed, through data analysis and interpretation, to a clear and concise presentation of results.

The chapter stressed that the results of a single survey or other research approach provide only indications of what may or may not exist. Before the researcher can claim support for a research question or hypothesis, the study must be replicated a number of times to eliminate dependence on extraneous factors.

While conducting research studies, the investigator must be constantly aware of potential sources of error that may create spurious results. Phenomena that affect an experiment in this way are sources of breakdown in internal validity. Only if differing and rival hypotheses are ruled out can researchers validly say that the treatment was influential in creating differences between the experimental group and the control group. A good explanation of research results rules out intervening variables; every plausible alternative explanation should be considered. However, even when this is accomplished, the results of one study can be considered only as an indication of what may or may not exist. Support for a theory or hypothesis is gained only after several other studies produce similar results.

In addition, if a study is to be helpful in understanding mass media, its results must be generalizable to subjects and groups other than those involved in the experiment. External validity can be best achieved through random sampling (see Chapter 4).

Key Terms

Algorithm	Internal validity
Artifact	Law
Causal time order	Law of the instrument
Central location testing	Literal replication
Confounding variable	Maturation
Constitutive definition	Methods of knowing
Constructive replication	Method-specific results
	Mortality
CPI incidence	Net incidence
Cross-validating	Ockham's razor
Data archives	Operational definition
Demand characteristics	Operational replication
Design-specific results	Parsimony principle
Double-blind experiment	Pilot study
	Point of prior equivalency
Eight steps of research	Prerecruits
Empiricism	Private sector research
Evaluation apprehension	Qualitative research
	Quantitative research
Experimenter bias	Replication
External validity	Research question
Extraneous variable	Research suppliers
Field services	Sample-specific results
Gross incidence	Scientific method
Hypodermic needle theory	Smart mass media
	Smartphone
Hypothesis	Smart TV
Incidence	Secondary analysis
Instrument decay	Statistical regression
Instrumental replication	Theory
	Urban legends

 ## Using the Internet

1. Finding information on the Internet is easy with a search engine. See "Search Engine Tips" in the Readings section on *www.wimmerdominick.com* for additional information.

2. Search the Internet for:
   - "research methods" mass media
   - mass media research questions
   - "methods of knowing"
   - "hypodermic needle theory" of communication, validity, and reliability
   - "statisticians" for more information about the tasks these people perform
   - "violence on TV," "violence on television," and "television violence" research examples
   - "research discoveries" science
   - "secondary analysis"

3. For a list of research suppliers, go to *www.greenbook.org*.

4. Visit *www.snopes.com* for research topics and to find out what is true and false about information you hear and see.

Questions and Problems for Further Investigation

1. Obtain a recent issue of a mass media journal and investigate how many articles fit into the research phases depicted in Figure 1.1.

2. In what ways, if any, is the term *research* abused in advertising?

3. Theories are used as springboards to develop bodies of information, yet there are only a few universally recognized theories in mass media research. Why do you think this is true?

4. Some citizens groups have claimed that music lyrics have a significant effect on listeners, especially young listeners. How might these groups collect data to support their claims? Which method of knowing can such groups use to support their claims?

5. Investigate how research is used to support or refute an argument outside the field of mass

media. For example, how do various groups use research to support or refute the idea that motorcycle riders should be required to wear protective helmets? (Refer to publications such as *Motorcycle Consumer News*.)

6. Investigate the world of pseudoscience or "bad science." What common beliefs or perceptions are based on such information?

7. Replication has long been a topic of debate in scientific research, but mass media researchers have not paid much attention to it. Why do you think this is true?

8. An analysis of the effects of television viewing revealed that the fewer hours of television students watched per week, the higher their scores in school. What alternative explanations or artifacts might explain such differences? How could these variables be controlled?

9. The fact that some respondents will answer any type of question, whether it is a legitimate question or not, may surprise some novice researchers until they encounter it firsthand. Try posing the following question to a friend in another class or at a party: What effects do you think the sinking of Greenland into the Labrador Sea will have on the country's fishing industry?

10. Conduct a small study with about 10 respondents (for example, members of a class or organization). Find out how much time they spend using their cell phones during a typical day. How does that compare to their use of the other mass media?

For additional resources go to *www.wimmer dominick.com* and *www.cengagebrain.com*.

References and Suggested Readings

Achenbach, J., & Thompson, R. (1993). *Why things are: The big picture*. New York, NY: Ballantine Books.

Agostino, D. (1980). Cable television's impact on the audience of public television. *Journal of Broadcasting, 24*(3), 347–366.

Anderson, J. A. (1987). *Communication research: Issues and methods*. New York, NY: McGraw-Hill.

Asimov, I. (1990). Exclusion principle survives another stab at its heart. *Rocky Mountain News,* December 9, p. 42.

Babbie, E. R. (2010). *The practice of social research* (12th ed.). Belmont, CA: Cengage.

Beasant, P. (1992). *1000 facts about space*. New Brunswick, Canada: Kingfisher Books.

Becker, L. B. (1981). Secondary analysis. In G. H. Stempel & B. H. Westley (Eds.), *Research methods in mass communications*. Englewood Cliffs, NJ: Prentice Hall.

Becker, L. B., Beam, R., & Russial, J. (1978). Correlates of daily newspaper performance in New England. *Journalism Quarterly, 55*(1), 100–108.

Berliner, B. (1990). *The book of answers*. New York, NY: Prentice Hall.

Bowers, J. W., & Courtright, J. A. (1984). *Communication research methods*. Glenview, IL: Scott, Foresman.

Brown, J. A. (1980). Selling airtime for controversy: NAB self regulation and Father Coughlin. *Journal of Broadcasting, 24*(2), 199–224.

Bryant, J., & Oliver, M. (2008). *Media effects: Advances in theory and research*. New York, NY: Routledge.

Burnam, T. (1975). *The dictionary of misinformation*. New York, NY: Thomas Crowell.

Burnam, T. (1981). *More misinformation*. New York, NY: Thomas Crowell.

Campbell, D. T., & Stanley, J. C. (1963). *Experimental and quasi-experimental designs for research*. Skokie, IL: Rand McNally.

Carroll, R. L. (1980). The 1948 Truman campaign: The threshold of the modern era. *Journal of Broadcasting, 24*(2), 173–188.

Cohen, J. (1965). Some statistical issues in psychological research. In B. B. Wolman (Ed.), *Handbook of clinical psychology*, 95–121. New York, NY: McGraw-Hill.

Cole, J. (1998). *The UCLA television violence report 1997*. Los Angeles, CA: UCLA Center for Communication Policy.

Comstock, G., Chaffee, S., Katzman, N., McCombs, M., & Roberts, D. (1978). *Television and human behavior*. New York, NY: Columbia University Press.

Cook, T. D., & Campbell, D. T. (1979). *Quasi-experimentation: Designs and analysis for field studies*. Skokie, IL: Rand McNally.

Davis, P. J., & Park, D. (1987). *No way: The nature of the impossible*. New York, NY: W. H. Freeman.

DeFleur, M. L., & Ball-Rokeach, S. (1989). *Theories of mass communication* (5th ed.). New York, NY: Longman.

Feldman, D. (1990). *Why do dogs have wet noses?* New York, NY: HarperCollins Publishers.

Ferris, T. (1988). *Coming of age in the Milky Way.* New York, NY: William Morrow.

Ferris, T. (1998). *The whole shebang.* New York, NY: Touchstone.

Glenn, N. (1972). Archival data on political attitudes: Opportunities and pitfalls. In D. Nimmo & C. Bonjean (Eds.), *Political attitudes and public opinion,* 137–146. New York, NY: David McKay.

Graedon, J., & Graedon, T. (1991). *Graedons' best medicine.* New York, NY: Bantam Books.

Gribben, J., & Rees, M. (1989). *Cosmic coincidences: Dark matter, mankind, and anthropic cosmology.* New York, NY: Bantam Books.

Hall, D. G. Personal correspondence, February 2009.

Haskins, J. B. (1968). *How to evaluate mass communication.* New York, NY: Advertising Research Foundation.

Herzog, H. (1944). What do we really know about daytime serial listeners? In P. Lazarsfeld & F. Stanton (Eds.), *Radio research 1943–44.* New York, NY: Duell, Sloan & Pearce.

Hinds, P. S., Vogel, R. J., & Clarke-Steffen, L. (1997). The possibilities and pitfalls of doing a secondary analysis of a qualitative data set. *Qualitative Health Research,* 7(3), 408–424.

Hirsch, E. D., Kett, J. F., & Trefil, J. (2002). *The new dictionary of cultural literacy: What every American needs to know.* New York, NY: Houghton Mifflin.

Hough, D. L. (1995). Are you hanging it out too far? *Motorcycle Consumer News,* 26(9), 38–41.

Hsia, H. J. (1988). *Mass communication research methods: A step-by-step approach.* Hillsdale, NJ: Lawrence Erlbaum.

Hyman, H. H. (1954). *Interviewing in social research.* Chicago, IL: University of Chicago Press.

Hyman, H. H. (1972). *Secondary analysis of sample surveys.* New York, NY: John Wiley.

Katz, E., & Lazarsfeld, P. F. (1955). *Personal influence.* New York, NY: Free Press.

Kelly, C. W., Chase, L. J., & Tucker, R. K. (1979). Replication in experimental communication research: An analysis. *Human Communication Research,* 5, 338–342.

Kerlinger, F. N., & Lee, H. B. (2000). *Foundations of behavioral research* (4th ed.). New York, NY: Holt, Rinehart & Winston.

Klapper, J. (1960). *The effects of mass communication.* New York, NY: Free Press.

Kraus, S., & Davis, D. (1967). *The effects of mass communication on political behavior.* University Park, PA: Pennsylvania State University Press.

Langer, S. K. (1967). *Philosophy in a new key: A study in the symbolism of reason, rite, and art* (3rd ed.). Cambridge, MA: Harvard University Press.

Lasswell, H. D. (1927). *Propaganda technique in the World War.* New York, NY: Alfred A. Knopf.

Lazarsfeld, P., Berelson, B., & Gaudet, H. (1948). *The people's choice.* New York, NY: Columbia University Press.

Lowery, S. A., & DeFleur, M. L. (1995). *Milestones in mass communication research* (3rd ed.). White Plains, NY: Longman.

Lykken, D. T. (1968). Statistical significance in psychological research. *Psychological Bulletin,* 21, 151–159.

Murphy, J. H., & Amundsen, M. S. (1981). The communication effectiveness of comparative advertising for a new brand on users of the dominant brand. *Journal of Advertising,* 10(1), 14–20.

Nesselroade, J. R., & Cattell, R. B. (Eds.). (1988). *Handbook of multivariate experimental psychology* (2nd ed.). New York, NY: Plenum Press.

Nunnally, J. C., & Bernstein, I. H. (1994). *Psychometric theory* (3rd ed.). New York, NY: McGraw-Hill.

Orne, M. T. (1969). Demand characteristics and the concept of quasi-controls. In R. Rosenthal & R. L. Rosnow (Eds.), *Artifact in behavioral research,* 147–177. New York, NY: Academic Press.

Perse, E. (2001). *Media effects and society.* Hillsdale, NJ: Lawrence Erlbaum Associates.

Poundstone, W. (1989). *Bigger secrets.* New York, NY: Houghton Mifflin.

Reid, L. N., Soley, L. C., & Wimmer, R. D. (1981). Replication in advertising research: 1977, 1978, 1979. *Journal of Advertising,* 10, 3–13.

Rensberger, B. (1986). *How the world works.* New York, NY: Quill.

Ries, A., & Trout, J. (1997). *Marketing warfare.* New York, NY: McGraw-Hill.

Ries, A., & Trout, J. (2001). *Positioning: The battle for your mind* (2nd ed). New York, NY: McGraw-Hill.

Rosenberg, M. J. (1965). When dissonance fails: On eliminating evaluation apprehension from attitude measurement. *Journal of Personality and Social Psychology,* 1, 28–42.

Rosenthal, R. (1969). *Experimenter effects in behavioral research.* New York, NY: Appleton-Century-Crofts.

Rubin, R. B., Rubin, A. M., & Piele, L. J. (2000). *Communication research: Strategies and sources* (5th ed.). Belmont, CA: Wadsworth.

Seeds, M. A. (2005). *Foundations of astronomy* (8th ed). Belmont, CA: Wadsworth.

Sharp, N. W. (1988). *Communications research: The challenge of the information age.* Syracuse, NY: Syracuse University Press.

Singer, D. G., & Singer, J. L. (1981). Television and the developing imagination of the child. *Journal of Broadcasting, 25,* 373–387.

Skinner, B. F. (1953). *Science and human behavior.* New York, NY: Macmillan.

Sparks, G. (2009). *Media effects research: A basic overview.* Boston, MA: Wadsworth.

Sutton, C. (1984). *How did they do that?* New York, NY: Quill.

Sybert, P. J. (1980). MBS and the Dominican Republic. *Journal of Broadcasting, 24*(2), 189–198.

Tan, A. S. (1977). Why TV is missed: A functional analysis. *Journal of Broadcasting, 21,* 371–380.

True, J. A. (1992). *Finding out: Conducting and evaluating social research* (2nd ed.). Belmont, CA: Wadsworth.

Tucker, R. K. (1996). *S.O.B.s: The handbook for handling super difficult people.* Bowling Green, OH: OptimAmerica, Ltd.

Tukey, J. W. (1969). Analyzing data: Sanctification or detective work? *American Psychologist, 24,* 83–91.

Tuleja, T. (1982). *Fabulous fallacies: More than 300 popular beliefs that are not true.* New York, NY: Harmony Books.

Walizer, M. H., & Wienir, P. L. (1978). *Research methods and analysis: Searching for relationships.* New York, NY: Harper & Row.

Weaver, R. M. (1953). *The ethics of rhetoric.* Chicago, IL: Henry Regnery.

Whitcomb, J., & Whitcomb, C. (1987). *Oh say can you see: Unexpected anecdotes about American history.* New York, NY: Quill.

Williams, F. (1988). *Research methods and the new media.* New York, NY: Free Press.

Wimmer, R. D. (1995). *Los Angeles radio listening: A panel study.* Denver, CO: The Eagle Group.

Wimmer, R. D., & Reid, L. N. (1982). Willingness of communication researchers to respond to replication requests. *Journalism Quarterly, 59,* 317–319.

Wimmer Research. (2001). Proprietary research conducted by Roger Wimmer.

Winston, D. (1998). *Digital democracy and the new age of reason.* Internet post of speech presented at the Democracy and Digital Media conference, May 27, 1998.

CHAPTER 2

ELEMENTS OF RESEARCH

CHAPTER OUTLINE

Chapter 1 presented an overview of the research process. In this chapter, we define and discuss four basic elements of this process: concepts and constructs, measurement, variables, and scales. A clear understanding of these elements is essential to conduct precise and meaningful research.

CONCEPTS AND CONSTRUCTS

A **concept** is a term that expresses an abstract idea formed by generalizing from particulars and summarizing related observations. For example, a researcher might observe that a public speaker becomes restless, starts to perspire, and fidgets with a pencil just before giving a speech. The researcher might summarize these observed patterns of behavior and label them "speech anxiety." On a more ordinary level, the word *table* is a concept that represents a wide variety of observable objects, ranging from a plank supported by concrete blocks to a piece of furniture commonly found in dining rooms. Typical concepts in mass media research include terms such as *advertising effectiveness, message length, media usage*, and *readability*.

Concepts are important for at least two reasons. First, they simplify the research process by combining particular characteristics, objects, or people into general categories. For example, a researcher may study families that own computers, modems, MP3 players, cell phones, and DVD or Blu-Ray machines. To make it easier to describe these families, the researcher calls them "Taffies" and categorizes them under the concept of "technologically advanced families." Instead of describing each of the characteristics that make these families unique, the researcher has a general term that is more inclusive and convenient to use.

Second, concepts simplify communication among those who have a shared understanding of them. Researchers use concepts to organize their observations into meaningful summaries and to transmit this information to others. Researchers who use the concept of "agenda setting" to describe a complicated set of audience and media activities find that their colleagues understand what is being discussed. Note that people must share an understanding of a concept for the concept to be useful. For example, when teenagers use the word *emo* to describe a person, most of their peers understand perfectly what is meant by the concept, although adults may not.

A **construct** is a concept that has three distinct characteristics: First, it is an abstract idea that is usually broken down into dimensions represented by lower-level concepts; a construct is a combination of concepts. Second, because of its abstraction, a construct usually cannot be observed directly. Third, a construct is usually designed for a specific research purpose so that its exact meaning relates only to the context in which it is found. For example, the construct "involvement" has been used in many advertising studies (search the Internet for "*advertising involvement*"). Advertising involvement is a construct that is difficult to see directly, and it includes the concepts of attention, interest, and arousal. Researchers can observe only its likely or presumed manifestations. In some contexts, involvement means a subject's involvement with the product; in others, it refers to involvement with the message or even with the medium. Its precise meaning depends on the research context.

Another example in mass communication research is the term *authoritarianism*, which *represents* a construct defined to describe a certain type of personality; it involves nine different concepts, including conventionalism, submission, superstition, and cynicism. Authoritarianism itself cannot be seen, so some type of questionnaire or standardized test is used to determine its presence. The results of such tests indicate what authoritarianism might be and whether it is present under given conditions, but the tests do not provide exact definitions for the construct itself.

The empirical counterpart of a construct or concept is called a **variable**. Variables are important because they link the empirical world with the theoretical; they are the phenomena and events that are measured or manipulated in research. Variables can have more than one value along a continuum. For example, the variable "satisfaction with pay-per-view TV programs" can take on different values—a person can be satisfied a lot, a little, or not at all—reflecting in the empirical world what the concept "satisfaction with pay-per-view TV programs" represents in the theoretical world.

Researchers try to test a number of associated variables to develop an underlying meaning or relationship among them. After suitable analysis, the most important variables are kept and the others are discarded. These important variables are labeled **marker variables** because they tend to define or highlight the construct under study. After additional studies, new marker variables may be added to increase understanding of the construct and to allow for more reliable predictions.

Concepts and constructs are valuable tools in theoretical research, but, as noted in Chapter 1, researchers also function at the observational, or empirical, level. To understand how this is done, it is necessary to understand variables and how they are measured.

INDEPENDENT AND DEPENDENT VARIABLES

Variables are classified in terms of their relationship with one another. It is customary to talk about independent and dependent variables.

Independent variables are systematically varied by the researcher; **dependent variables** are observed, and their values are presumed to depend on the effects (influence) of the independent variables. In other words, the *dependent variable is what the researcher wishes to explain*. For example, assume a researcher is interested in determining how the angle of a camera shot affects an audience's perception of the credibility of a television newscaster. Three versions of a newscast are recorded: one shot from a very low angle, another from a high angle, and a third from eye level. Groups of subjects are randomly assigned to view one of the three versions and complete a questionnaire to measure the newscaster's credibility. In this experiment, the camera angle is the independent variable. The experimenter, who selects only three of the camera angles possible, systematically varies its values. The dependent variable is the perceived credibility of the newscaster as measured by the questionnaire. If the researcher's assumption is correct, the newscaster's credibility will vary according to the camera angle. (The values of the dependent variable are not manipulated; they are simply observed or measured.)

The distinction between types of variables depends on the purposes of the research. An independent variable in one study may be a dependent variable in another. Also, a research task may involve examining the relationship of more than one independent variable to a single dependent variable. For example, the researcher in the previous example could investigate the effects of camera angles and of how the newscaster's manner, or style, in closing the program affects his or her credibility, as perceived by the viewers. In many instances, multiple dependent variables are measured in a single study, which is called a **multivariate analysis**.

Discrete and Continuous Variables

Two forms of variables are used in mass media investigation. A **discrete variable** includes only a finite set of values; it cannot be divided into subparts. For instance, the

Mass Media Variables

Analysis of why people like certain movies, magazines, newspapers, or radio or television shows has historically been difficult because of the number of variables to consider. Even when researchers develop a relatively stable set of variables to measure, assessing popularity of the media is difficult because respondents say something like, "It depends on my mood." As a media researcher, how would you address this problem?

number of children in a family is a discrete variable because the unit is a person. It does not make much sense to talk about a family size of 2.24 because it is hard to conceptualize 0.24 of a person. Political affiliation, population, and gender are other discrete variables.

A **continuous variable** can take on any value, including fractions, and can be meaningfully broken into smaller subsections. Height is a continuous variable. If the measurement tool is sophisticated enough, it is possible to distinguish between one person 72.12 inches tall and another 72.13 inches tall. Time spent watching television is another example; it is perfectly meaningful to say that Person A spent 3.12 hours viewing while Person B watched 3.13 hours. The *average* number of children in a family is a continuous variable; thus, in this context, it may be perfectly meaningful to refer to 0.24 of a person.

When dealing with continuous variables, researchers should keep in mind the distinction between the variable and the measure of the variable. If a child's attitude toward television violence is measured by counting his or her positive responses to six questions, then there are only seven possible scores: 0, 1, 2, 3, 4, 5, and 6. However, it is entirely likely that the underlying variable is continuous even though the measure is discrete. In fact, even if a fractionalized scale were developed, it would still be limited to a finite number of scores. As a generalization, most of the measures in mass media research tend to be discrete approximations of continuous variables.

Variables measured at the nominal level are always discrete variables. Variables measured at the ordinal level are generally discrete, although some underlying continuous measurement dimension may exist. (Nominal and ordinal levels are discussed later in this chapter.) Variables measured at the interval or ratio level can be either discrete (number of magazine subscriptions in a household) or continuous (number of minutes per day spent reading magazines). Both the level of measurement and the type of variable under consideration are important in developing useful measurement scales.

Other Types of Variables

In nonexperimental research, where there is no active manipulation of variables, different terms are sometimes substituted for independent and dependent variables. The variable that is used for predictions or is assumed to be causal (analogous to the independent variable) is sometimes called the **predictor**, or **antecedent, variable**. The variable that is predicted or assumed to be affected (analogous to the dependent variable) is sometimes called the **criterion variable**.

Researchers often wish to control certain variables to eliminate unwanted influences. These **control variables** are used to ensure that the results of the study are due to the independent variables, not to another source.

However, a control variable need not always be used to eliminate an unwanted influence. On occasion, researchers use a control variable such as age, gender, or socioeconomic status to divide subjects into specific, relevant categories. For example, in studying the relationship between newspaper readership and reading ability, researchers know that IQ will affect the relationship and must be controlled; thus, subjects may be selected based on IQ scores or placed in groups with similar IQ scores.

One of the most difficult steps in any type of research is to identify all the variables that may create spurious or misleading results. Some researchers refer to this problem as **noise**. Noise can occur in even simple research projects. For example, a researcher might design a telephone survey to ask respondents to name the local radio station they listened to most during the past week. The researcher uses an open-ended question—that is, provides no specific response choices—and the interviewer writes down each respondent's answer. When the completed surveys are tabulated, the researcher notices that several people mentioned radio station WAAA. However, if the city has a WAAA-AM and a WAAA-FM, which station gets the credit? The researcher cannot arbitrarily assign credit to the AM station or to the FM station, nor can credit be split because this may distort the description of the actual listening habits.

Interviewers could attempt callbacks to everyone who said "WAAA," but this is not suggested for two reasons: (1) the likelihood of reaching all the people who gave that response is low; and (2) even if the first condition is met, some respondents may not recall which station they originally mentioned. The researcher is therefore unable to provide a reliable analysis of the data because not all possible intervening variables were considered. (The researcher should have anticipated this problem and instructed the interviewers to find out in each case whether "WAAA" meant WAAA-AM or WAAA-FM.)

People who unknowingly provide false information create another type of research noise. For example, people who keep diaries for radio and television surveys may err in recording the station or channel they tune in to; that is, they may listen to or watch station KAAA but incorrectly record "KBBB." (This problem is solved by the use of Nielsen's *people meters* and Arbitron's *portable people meters*; see Chapter 14.) In addition, respondents/subjects often answer a multiple-choice or yes/no research question at random (they make up answers) because they do not wish to appear ignorant or uninformed. To minimize this problem, researchers must take great care in constructing measurement instruments. Noise is always present, but a large and representative sample should decrease the effects of some research noise. (In later chapters, noise is referred to as "error.")

With experience, researchers learn to solve many simple problems in their studies. In many situations, however, researchers understand that total control over all aspects of the research is impossible, and they account for the impossibility of achieving perfect control in the interpretation of their results.

Defining Variables Operationally

In Chapter 1, we stated that an operational definition specifies the procedures to be followed to experience or measure a concept. Research depends on observations, and observations cannot be made without a clear statement of what is to be observed. An operational definition is such a statement. Operational definitions are indispensable in scientific research because they enable investigators to measure relevant variables. In any study, it is necessary to provide operational definitions for both independent variables and dependent variables. Table 2.1 lists examples of such definitions taken from research studies in mass communication.

Kerlinger (2010) identifies two types of operational definitions: *measured* and *experimental*. A measured operational definition specifies how to measure a variable. For instance, a researcher investigating dogmatism and media use might operationally define the term *dogmatism* as a subject's score on the *Twenty-Item Short Form Dogmatism Scale*. An experimental operational definition explains how an investigator has manipulated a variable. Obviously, this type of definition is used when the independent variable is defined in a laboratory setting. For example, in a study on the impact of television violence, the researcher might manipulate media violence by constructing two 8-minute films. The first film, labeled "the violent condition," could contain scenes from a boxing match. The second film, labeled "the nonviolent condition," could depict a swimming race. Similarly, source credibility might be manipulated by alternately attributing an article on health to the *New England Journal of Medicine* and to the *National Enquirer*.

Operationally defining a variable forces a researcher to express abstract concepts in concrete terms. Occasionally, after unsuccessfully struggling with the task of making a key variable operational, the researcher may conclude that the variable as originally conceived is too vague or ambiguous and must be redefined. Because operational definitions are expressed so concretely, they can communicate exactly what the terms represent. For instance, a researcher might define "political knowledge" as the number of correct answers on a 20-item true/false test. Although it is possible to argue about the validity (does the test actually measure political knowledge) of the definition, there is no confusion as to what the statement "Women possess more political knowledge than men" actually means.

Finally, there is no single foolproof method for operationally defining a variable.

No operational definition satisfies everybody. The investigator must decide which method is best suited for the research problem at hand. The numerous articles and examples available from an Internet search of "*operational definition*" illustrate the various methods.

Table 2.1 Examples of Operational Definitions

Study	Variable	Operational Definition
Henning and Vorderer (2001)	Need for cognition	Summated scores on a five-point Likert Scale to eight cognition items
Wu (2000)	Press freedom	Scale of press freedom ranging from 1 to 100 taken from yearly evaluations by the Freedom House organization
Angelini (2008)	Arousal	Measure of galvanic skin response
Buijen and Valkenburg (2000)	Children's gift ideas	Children were asked to write down their two most favorite Christmas wishes
Kamhawi and Grabe (2008)	Appreciation of news stories	Semantic differential scale with six bipolar adjective pairs

QUALITATIVE AND QUANTITATIVE RESEARCH

Mass media research, like all research, can be qualitative or quantitative. **Qualitative research** involves several methods of data collection, such as focus groups, field observation, in-depth interviews, and case studies. In all of these methods, the questioning approach is varied. In other words, although the researcher enters the project with a specific set of questions, follow-up questions are developed as needed. The variables in qualitative research may or may not be measured or quantified.

In some cases, qualitative research has certain advantages. The methods allow a researcher to view behavior in a natural setting without the artificiality that sometimes surrounds experimental or survey research. In addition, qualitative techniques can increase a researcher's depth of understanding of the phenomenon under investigation. This is especially true when the phenomenon has not been investigated previously. Finally, qualitative methods are flexible and allow the researcher to pursue new areas of interest. A questionnaire is unlikely to provide data about questions that were not asked, but a person conducting a field observation or focus group might discover facets of a subject that were not considered before the study began.

However, some disadvantages are associated with qualitative methods. First, sample sizes are sometimes too small (sometimes as small as one) to allow the researcher to generalize the data beyond the sample selected for the particular study. For this reason, qualitative research is often the preliminary step to further investigation rather than the final phase of a project. The information collected from qualitative methods is often used to prepare a more elaborate quantitative analysis, although the qualitative data may in fact be all the information needed for a particular study.

Data reliability can also be a problem, since single observers are describing unique events. Because a person conducting qualitative research must become closely involved with the respondents, it is possible to lose objectivity when collecting data. A researcher who becomes too close to the study may lose the necessary professional detachment.

Finally, if qualitative research is not properly planned, the project may produce nothing of value. Qualitative research appears to be easy to conduct, but projects must be carefully designed to ensure that they focus on key issues. Although this book is primarily concerned with quantitative research, we discuss several qualitative methods in Chapter 5.

Quantitative research also involves several methods of data collection, such as telephone surveys, mail surveys, and Internet surveys. In these methods, the questioning is static or standardized—all respondents are asked the same questions and there is no opportunity for follow-up questions.

In the past, some researchers claimed that the difference between qualitative and quantitative research related to only two things:

1. Qualitative research uses smaller samples of subjects or respondents.

2. Because of the small sample size, results from qualitative research could not be generalized to the population from which the samples were drawn.

While these two points may affect some qualitative research, the fact is that sample sizes in both qualitative and quantitative research can be the same.

Quantitative research requires that the variables under consideration be measured. This form of research is concerned with how often a variable is present and generally uses numbers to communicate this amount. Quantitative research has certain advantages.

One is that the use of numbers allows greater precision in reporting results. For example, the Violence Index (Gerbner, Gross, Morgan & Signorielli, 1980), a quantitative measuring device, makes it possible to report the exact increase or decrease in violence from one television season to another, whereas qualitative research could report only whether there was more or less violence.

For the past several years, some friction has existed in the mass media field and in other disciplines between those who favor quantitative methods and those who prefer qualitative methods. Most researchers have now come to realize that both methods are important in understanding any phenomenon. In fact, the term *triangulation*, commonly used by marine navigators, frequently emerges in conversations about communication research. If a ship picks up signals from only one navigational aid, it is impossible to know the vessel's precise location. However, if signals from more than one source are detected, elementary geometry can be used to pinpoint the ship's location. In this book, the term **triangulation** refers to the use of both qualitative methods and quantitative methods to fully understand the nature of a research problem.

Although most of this book is concerned with skills relevant to quantitative research, we do not imply that quantitative research is in any sense better than qualitative research. It is not. Each approach has value, and the decision to use one or the other depends on the goals of the research.

THE NATURE OF MEASUREMENT

The importance of mathematics to mass media research is difficult to overemphasize. As pointed out by measurement expert J. P. Guilford (1954, p. 1):

The progress and maturity of a science are often judged by the extent to which it has succeeded in the use of mathematics.... Mathematics is a universal language that any science or technology may use with great power and convenience. Its vocabulary of terms is unlimited.... Its rules of operation ... are unexcelled for logical precision.

The idea behind **measurement** is simple: A researcher assigns numerals to objects, events, or properties according to certain rules. Examples of measurement are everywhere: "She or he is a 10" or "Unemployment increased by 1%" or "The earthquake measured 5.5 on the Richter scale." Note that the definition contains three central concepts: numerals, assignment, and rules. A numeral is a symbol, such as V, X, C, or 5, 10, 100. A *numeral* has no implicit quantitative meaning. When it is given quantitative meaning, it becomes a number and can be used in mathematical and statistical computations. *Assignment* is the designation of numerals or numbers to certain objects or events. A simple measurement system might entail assigning the numeral 1 to the people who obtain most of their news from television, the numeral 2 to those who get most of their news from a newspaper, and the numeral 3 to those who receive most of their news from some other source.

Rules specify the way that numerals or numbers are to be assigned. Rules are at the heart of any measurement system; if they are faulty, the system will be flawed. In some situations, the rules are obvious and straightforward. To measure reading speed, a stopwatch and a standardized message may be sufficient. In other instances, the rules are not so apparent. Measuring certain psychological traits, such as "source credibility" or "attitude toward violence," calls for carefully explicated measurement techniques.

Additionally, in mass media research and in much of social science research, investigators usually measure indicators of the

A CLOSER LOOK

Qualitative and Quantitative Research

The only difference between qualitative and quantitative research is the style of questioning. Qualitative research uses flexible questioning; quantitative uses standardized questions. Assuming that the sample sizes are large enough and that the samples are properly selected, the results from both methods can be generalized to the population from which the sample was drawn.

properties of individuals or objects rather than the individuals or objects themselves. Concepts such as "authoritarianism" or "motivation for reading the newspaper" cannot be observed directly; they must be inferred from presumed indicators. Thus, if a person endorses statements such as "Orders from a superior should always be followed without question" and "Law and order are the most important things in society," it can be deduced that he or she is more authoritarian than someone who disagrees with the same statements.

Measurement systems strive to be isomorphic to reality. **Isomorphism** means *identity or similarity of form or structure*. In some research areas, such as the physical sciences, isomorphism is not a problem because the objects being measured and the numbers assigned to them usually have a direct relationship. For example, if an electric current travels through Substance A with less resistance than it does through Substance B, it can be deduced that A is a better conductor than B. Testing more substances can lead to a ranking of conductors, where the numbers assigned indicate the degrees of conductivity. The measurement system is isomorphic to reality.

In mass media research, the correspondence is seldom that obvious. For example, imagine that a researcher is trying to develop a scale to measure the "persuasibility" of people in connection with a certain type of advertisement. A test is developed and given to five people. The scores are displayed in Table 2.2. Now imagine that an omniscient being is able to disclose the "true" persuasibility of the same five people. These scores are also shown in Table 2.2. For two people, the test scores correspond exactly to the "true" scores. The other three scores miss the true scores, but there is a correspondence between the rank orders. Also note that the true persuasibility scores range from 0 to 12, and the measurement scale ranges from 1 to 8. To summarize, there is a general correspondence between the test and reality, but the test is far from an exact measure of what actually exists.

Unfortunately, the degree of correspondence between measurement and reality is rarely known in research. In some cases, researchers are not even sure they are actually measuring what they are trying to

Table 2.2 Illustration of Isomorphism

Person	Test Score	"True" Score
A	1	0
B	3	1
C	6	6
D	7	7
E	8	12

measure (**validity**). In any event, researchers must carefully consider the degree of isomorphism between measurement and reality. This topic is discussed in detail later in the chapter.

LEVELS OF MEASUREMENT

Scientists have distinguished four different ways to measure things, or four different levels of measurement, depending on the rules that are used to assign numbers to objects or events. The operations that can be performed with a given set of scores depend on the level of measurement achieved. The four levels of measurement are nominal, ordinal, interval, and ratio.

The **nominal level** is the weakest form of measurement. In nominal measurement, numerals or other symbols are used to classify people, objects, or characteristics. For example, in the physical sciences, rocks can generally be classified into three categories: igneous, sedimentary, and metamorphic. A geologist who assigns a 1 to igneous, a 2 to sedimentary, and a 3 to metamorphic has formed a nominal scale. Note that the numerals are simply labels that stand for the respective categories; they have no mathematical significance. A rock that is placed in Category 3 does not have more "rockness" than those in Categories 1 and 2. Other examples of nominal measurement are the numbers on football jerseys and license plates, and Social Security numbers. An example of nominal measurement in mass media is classifying respondents according to the medium they depend on most for news. Those depending most on TV may be in Category 1, those depending most on the Internet in Category 2, those depending on newspapers in Category 3, and so on.

The nominal level, like all levels, possesses certain formal properties. Its basic property is equivalence. If an object is placed in Category 1, it is considered equal to all other objects in that category. Suppose a researcher is attempting to classify all the advertisements in a magazine according to primary appeal. If an ad has economic appeal, it is placed in Category 1; if it uses an appeal to fear, it is placed in Category 2; and so on. Note that all ads using "fear appeal" are equal even though they may differ on other dimensions such as product type or size, or use of illustrations.

Another property of nominal measurement is that all categories are *exhaustive* and *mutually exclusive*. This means that each measure accounts for every possible option and that each measurement is appropriate to only one category. For instance, in the example of primary appeals in magazine advertisements, all possible appeals need to be included in the analysis (exhaustive): economic, fear, morality, religion, and so on. Each advertisement is placed in one and only one category (mutually exclusive). Nominal measurement is frequently used in mass media research, and several are available on the Internet by searching for "*nominal measurement*" *examples.*

Even a variable measured at the nominal level may be used in higher-order statistics if it is converted into another form. The results of this conversion process are known as **dummy variables.** For example, political party affiliation could be coded as follows:

Republican	1
Democrat	2
Independent	3
Other	4

This measurement scheme could be interpreted incorrectly to imply that a person classified as "Other" is three units "better" than a person classified as a "Republican." To measure political party affiliation and use the data in higher-order statistics, a researcher must convert the variable into a more neutral form.

One way to convert the variable to give equivalent value to each option is to recode it as a dummy variable that creates an "either/ or" situation for each option; in this example, a person is either a "Republican" or something else. For example, a binary coding scheme could be used:

Republican	001
Democrat	010
Independent	100
Other	000

This scheme treats each affiliation equivalently and allows the variable to be used in higher-order statistical procedures. Note that the final category "Other" is coded using all zeros. A complete explanation for this practice is beyond the scope of this book; basically, however, its purpose is to avoid redundancy, because the number of individuals classified as "Other" can be found from the data on the first three options. If, in a sample of 100 subjects, 75 belong in each of the first three options, then it is obvious that there are 25 in the "Other" option.

Objects measured at the **ordinal level** are usually ranked along some dimension, such as from smallest to largest. For example, one might measure the variable "socioeconomic status" by categorizing families according to class: lower, lower middle, middle, upper middle, or upper. A rank of 1 is assigned to lower, 2 to lower middle, 3 to middle, and so forth. In this situation, the numbers have some mathematical meaning: Families in Category 3 have a higher socioeconomic status than families in Category 2. Note that nothing is specified with regard to the distance between any two rankings. Ordinal measurement often has been compared to a horse race without a stopwatch. The order in which the horses finish is relatively easy to determine, but it is difficult to calculate the difference in time between the winner and the runner-up.

An ordinal scale possesses the property of *equivalence*. Thus, in the previous example,

all families placed in a category are treated equally, even though some might have greater incomes than others. It also possesses the property of order among the categories. Any given category can be defined as being higher or lower than any other category. Common examples of ordinal scales are rankings of football or basketball teams, military ranks, restaurant ratings, and beauty pageant results.

Ordinal scales are frequently used in mass communication research, and several can be found on the Internet by searching for "*ordinal scales*" *communication examples*.

When a scale has all the properties of an ordinal scale and the intervals between adjacent points on the scale are of equal value, the scale is at the **interval level**. The most obvious example of an interval scale is temperature. The same amount of heat is required to warm an object from 30 to 40 degrees as to warm it from 50 to 60 degrees. Interval scales incorporate the formal *property of equal differences*; that is, numbers are assigned to the positions of objects on an interval scale in such a way that one may carry out arithmetic operations on the differences between them.

One disadvantage of an interval scale is that it lacks a true zero point, or a condition of nothingness. For example, it is difficult to conceive of a person having zero intelligence or zero personality. The absence of a true zero point means that a researcher cannot make statements of a proportional nature; for example, someone with an IQ of 100 is not twice as smart as someone with an IQ of 50, and a person who scores 30 on a test of aggression is not three times as aggressive as a person who scores 10. Despite this disadvantage, interval scales are frequently used in mass communication research.

Scales at the **ratio level** of measurement have all the properties of interval scales plus one more: the existence of a true zero point. With the introduction of this fixed zero point, ratio judgments can be made. For example, because time and distance are ratio measures, one can say that a car traveling at 50 miles per hour is going twice as fast as a car traveling at 25 miles per hour. Ratio scales are relatively rare in mass media research, although some variables, such as time spent watching television or number of words per story, are ratio measurements.

As discussed in Chapter 12, researchers who use interval or ratio data can use parametric statistics, which are specifically designed for these data. Procedures designed for use with "lower" levels of measurement can also be used with data at a higher level of measurement. Statistical procedures designed for higher-level data, however, are generally more powerful than those designed for use with nominal or ordinal levels of measurement. Thus, if an investigator has achieved the interval level of measurement, parametric statistics should generally be used. Statisticians disagree about the importance of the distinction between ordinal scales and interval scales and about the legitimacy of using interval statistics with data that may in fact be ordinal. Without delving too deeply into these arguments, we suggest that the safest procedure is to assume interval measurement unless there is clear evidence to the contrary, in which case ordinal statistics should be used. For example, ordinal statistics should be used for a research task in which a group of subjects ranks a set of objects. On the other hand, parametric procedures are justified if subjects are given an attitude score constructed by rating responses to various questions.

Most statisticians feel that statistical analysis is performed on the numbers yielded by the measures, not on the measures themselves, and that the properties of interval scales belong to the number system (Nunnally & Bernstein, 1994; Roscoe, 1975). Additionally, there have been several studies in which various types of data have been subjected to different statistical analyses. These studies suggest that the distinction between ordinal data and interval data is not particularly crucial in selecting an analysis method (McNemar, 1969).

MEASUREMENT SCALES

A *scale* represents a *composite measure* of a variable; it is based on more than one item. Scales are generally used with complex variables that do not easily lend themselves to single-item or single-indicator measurements. Some items, such as age, newspaper circulation, or number of radios in the house, can be adequately measured without scaling techniques. Measurement of other variables, such as attitude toward TV news or gratification received from going to a movie theater, generally requires the use of scales. Several scaling techniques have been developed over the years. This section discusses only the better-known methods. Search the Internet for additional information about all types of measurement scales.

Simple Rating Scales

Rating scales are common in mass media research. Researchers frequently ask respondents to rate a list of items such as a list of programming elements that can be included in a radio station's weekday morning show, or to rate how much respondents like radio or TV on-air personalities.

The researcher's decision is to decide which type of scale to use: 1–3? 1–5? 1–7? 1–10? 1–100? Or even a 0–9 scale, which is commonly used by researchers who don't have computer software to accept double-digit numbers (like 10). Selecting a type of scale is largely a matter of personal preference, but there are a few things to consider:

1. *A scale with more points rather than fewer points allows for greater differentiation on the item or items being rated.* For example, assume we are rating the importance of programming

elements contained in a radio station's weekday morning show. Let's say the respondents are told, "The higher the number, the more important the element is to you." Will a 1–3 scale or 1–10 scale provide more information? Obviously, the 1–10 scale provides the broadest differentiation.

Broad differentiation in opinions, perceptions, and feelings is important because it gives the researcher more information. Artificially restricting the range of ratings is called **factor fusion**, which means that opinions, perceptions, and feelings are squeezed into a smaller space. It's better for the respondents and the researcher to have more rating points than fewer rating points. Restricting respondents' responses by using too few scale points always hides the range of potential responses and restricts the potential of any research study.

2. *Our experience shows that males and females of all age groups, races, and nationalities like to use a 1–10 scale.* This is true because the 1–10 scale is universally used, particularly in sporting events such as the Olympics. Virtually everyone understands the 1–10 rating scale. A 10 is best or perfect, a 1 is worst or imperfect. Our experience also shows that researchers should not use a 0–9 or 1–9 rating scale because, quite frankly, respondents do not associate well with a 9 as the highest number.

3. *When using simple rating scales, it is best to tell respondents, "The higher the number, the more you agree," or "The higher the number, the more you like."* Over thousands of research studies, we have found this approach better than telling respondents, "Use a scale of 1–10, where '1' means Dislike and '10' means Like a lot."

Transforming Scales

On occasion, a researcher will conduct a study using one scale and then later want to compare those data to other data using a different rating scale. For example, let's say that a researcher uses a 1–7 rating scale and wants to convert the results to a 1–100 scale. What can be done?

The procedure is always the same: Divide the smaller rating scale into the larger to produce a multiplier to transform the scale. To transform a 1–7 scale to a 1–100 scale, first divide 100 by 7, which is 14.2857, and then multiply this number times each of the 1–7 elements to compute the converted 1–100 scale numbers. The new, transformed (rounded) ratings are:

1 = 14
2 = 29
3 = 43
4 = 57
5 = 71
6 = 86
7 = 100

What about transforming a 5-point scale to a 7-point scale? The procedure is the same: Divide 7 by 5, which produces a multiplier of 1.4. This number is multiplied by each of the numbers in the 5-point scale to produce a transformed scale:

1 = 1.4
2 = 2.8
3 = 4.2
4 = 5.6
5 = 7.0

If you transform scores the other way, such as a 10-point scale to a 5-point scale, simply divide each of the numbers in the scale by the multiplier.

SPECIALIZED RATING SCALES

Thurstone Scales

Thurstone scales are also called *equal-appearing interval scales* because of the technique used to develop them and are typically used to measure the attitude toward a given concept or construct. To develop a Thurstone scale, a researcher first collects a large number of statements (Thurstone recommends at least 100) that relate to the concept or construct to be measured.

Next, judges rate these statements along an 11-category scale in which each category expresses a different degree of favorableness toward the concept. The items are then ranked according to the mean or median ratings assigned by the judges and are used to construct a questionnaire of 20 to 30 items that are chosen more or less evenly from across the range of ratings. The statements are worded so that a person can agree or disagree with them. The scale is then administered to a sample of respondents whose scores are determined by computing the mean or median value of the items agreed with. A person who disagrees with all the items has a score of zero.

One advantage of the Thurstone method is that it is an interval measurement scale. On the downside, this method is time consuming and labor intensive. Thurstone scales are not often used in mass media research, but they are common in psychology and education research.

Guttman Scaling

Guttman scaling, also called *scalogram* analysis, is based on the idea that items can be arranged along a continuum in such a way that a person who agrees with an item or finds an item acceptable will also agree with or find acceptable all other items expressing a less extreme position. For example, here is a hypothetical four-item Guttman scale:

1. Indecent programming on TV is harmful to society.

2. Children should not be allowed to watch indecent TV shows.

3. Television station managers should not allow indecent programs on their stations.

4. The government should ban indecent programming from TV.

Presumably, a person who agrees with Statement 4 will also agree with Statements 1–3. Furthermore, if we assume the scale is valid, a person who agrees with Statement 2 will also agree with Statement 1 but will not necessarily agree with Statements 3 and 4. Because each score represents a unique set of responses, the number of items a person agrees with is the person's total score on a Guttman scale.

A Guttman scale requires a great deal of time and energy to develop. Although they do not appear often in mass media research, Guttman scales are common in political science, sociology, public opinion research, and anthropology.

Likert Scales

Perhaps the most commonly used scale in mass media research is the Likert scale, also called the *summated rating approach*, was developed by psychologist Rensis Likert (LICK-ert) in 1932. A number of statements are developed with respect to a topic, and respondents can strongly agree, agree, be neutral, disagree, or strongly disagree with the statements (see Figure 2.1). Each response option is weighted, and each subject's responses are added to produce a single score on the topic.

The basic procedure for developing a Likert scale is as follows:

1. Compile a large number of statements that relate to a specific dimension. Some statements are positively worded; some are negatively worded.

2. Administer the scale to a randomly selected sample of respondents.

Figure 2.1   Sample of Likert Scale Items

1. Only U.S. citizens should be allowed to own broadcasting stations.

Response	Score Assigned
_____ Strongly agree	5
_____ Agree	4
_____ Neutral	3
_____ Disagree	2
_____ Strongly disagree	1

2. Prohibiting foreign ownership of broadcasting stations is bad for business.

Response	Score Assigned
_____ Strongly agree	1
_____ Agree	2
_____ Neutral	3
_____ Disagree	4
_____ Strongly disagree	5

Note: To maintain attitude measurement consistency, the scores are reversed for a negatively worded item. Question 1 is a positive item; Question 2 is a negative item.

3. Code the responses consistently so that high scores indicate stronger agreement with the attitude in question.

4. Analyze the responses and select for the final scale those statements that most clearly differentiate the highest from the lowest scorers.

Semantic Differential Scales

Another commonly used scaling procedure is the **semantic differential** technique. As originally conceived by Osgood, Suci, and Tannenbaum (1957), this technique is used to measure the meaning an item has for an individual. Research indicated that three general factors—activity, potency, and evaluation—were measured by the semantic differential. Communication researchers were quick to adapt the evaluative dimension of the semantic differential for use as a measure of attitude.

To use the technique, a name or a concept is placed at the top of a series of seven-point scales anchored by bipolar attitudes. Figure 2.2 shows an example of this technique as used to measure attitudes toward *Time* **magazine.**

The bipolar adjectives that typically "anchor" such evaluative scales are *pleasant/unpleasant, valuable/worthless, honest/dishonest, nice/awful, clean/dirty, fair/unfair,* and *good/bad.* However, we recommend that a unique set of anchoring adjectives be developed for each particular measurement situation.

Strictly speaking, the semantic differential technique attempts to place a concept in semantic space using an advanced multivariate statistical procedure called **factor analysis.** When researchers borrow parts of the technique to measure attitudes—images or perceptions of objects, people, or concepts—they are not using the technique as originally

---

Figure 2.2 Sample Form for Applying the Semantic Differential Technique

Time Magazine

Biased	____ : ____ : ____ : ____ : ____ : ____ : ____	Unbiased
Trustworthy	____ : ____ : ____ : ____ : ____ : ____ : ____	Untrustworthy
Valuable	____ : ____ : ____ : ____ : ____ : ____ : ____	Worthless
Unfair	____ : ____ : ____ : ____ : ____ : ____ : ____	Fair

---

developed. Consequently, perhaps a more appropriate name for this technique is bipolar rating scales.

RELIABILITY AND VALIDITY

Using any scale without preliminary testing is poor research. At least one pilot study should be conducted for any newly developed scale to ensure its reliability and validity. To be useful, a measurement must possess these two related qualities. A measure is reliable if it consistently gives the same answer. **Reliability** in measurement is the same as reliability in any other context. For example, a reliable person is one who is dependable, stable, and consistent over time. An unreliable person is unstable and unpredictable and may act one way today and another way tomorrow. Similarly, if measurements are consistent from one session to another, they are reliable and can be believed to some degree.

In understanding measurement reliability, you may think of a measure as containing two components. The first represents an individual's "true" score on the measuring instrument. The second represents random error and does not provide an accurate assessment of what is being measured. Error can slip into the measurement process from several sources. Perhaps a question was worded ambiguously or a person's pencil slipped when completing a measuring instrument.

Whatever the cause, all measurements are subject to some degree of random error, as shown in Figure 2.3. As is evident, Measurement Instrument 1 is highly reliable because

---

Figure 2.3 Illustration of "True" and "Error" Components of a Scale

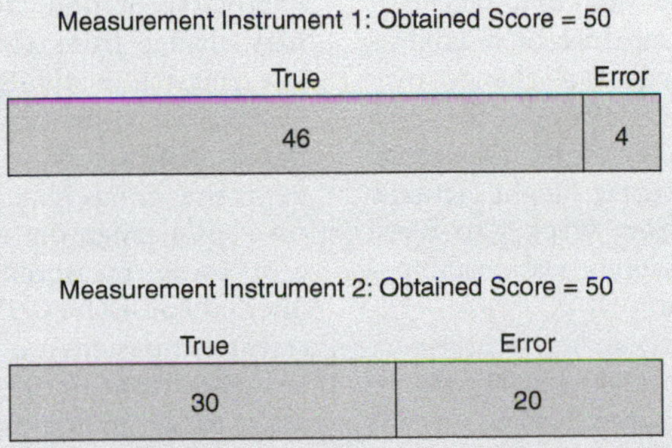

Measurement Instrument 1: Obtained Score = 50

True	Error
46	4

Measurement Instrument 2: Obtained Score = 50

True	Error
30	20

the ratio of the true component of the score to the total score is high. Measurement Instrument 2 is unreliable because the ratio of the true component to the total is low.

A completely unreliable measurement measures nothing at all. If a measure is repeatedly given to individuals and each person's responses at a later session are unrelated to his or her earlier responses, the measure is useless. If the responses are identical or nearly identical each time the measure is given, the measure is reliable; it at least measures something, though not necessarily what the researcher intended. (This problem is discussed later in this chapter.)

The importance of reliability should be obvious now. Unreliable measures cannot be used to detect relationships between variables. When the measurement of a variable is unreliable, it is composed mainly of random error, and random error is seldom related to anything else. Reliability is not a unidimensional concept. It consists of three different components: stability, internal consistency, and equivalency.

Stability refers to *the consistency of a result or of a measure at different points in time.* For example, suppose that a test designed to measure proofreading ability is administered during the first week of an editing class and again during the second week. The test possesses stability if the two results are consistent.

Caution should be exercised whenever stability is used as a measure of reliability, since people and things can change over time. In the proofreading example, it is possible for a person to score higher the second time because some people might actually improve their ability from Week 1 to Week 2. In this case, the measure is not unstable—actual change occurred.

An assessment of reliability is necessary in all mass media research and should be reported along with other facets of the research as an aid in interpretation and evaluation. One commonly used statistic for assessing reliability is the correlation coefficient, denoted as r_{xx}. Chapter 12 provides a more detailed examination of the correlation coefficient.

For now let's say only that r_{xx} is a number ranging from -1.00 to $+1.00$ and is used to gauge the strength of a relationship between two variables. When r_{xx} is a high positive—that is, approaching $+1.00$—the relationship is strong. A negative number indicates a negative relationship (high scores on one variable are associated with low scores on the other), and a positive number indicates a positive relationship (a high score goes with another high score). In measuring reliability, a high positive r_{xx} is desired.

One method that uses correlation coefficients to compute reliability is the test-retest method. This procedure measures the stability component of reliability. The same people are measured at two different points in time, and a coefficient between the two scores is computed. An r_{xx} that approaches $+1.00$ indicates that a person's score at Time A was similar to his or her score at Time B, showing consistency over time. There are two limitations to the test-retest technique. First, the initial administration of the measure might affect scores on the second testing. If the measuring device is a questionnaire, a person might remember responses from session to session, thus falsely inflating reliability. Second, the concept measured may change from Time A to Time B, thus lowering the reliability estimate.

Internal consistency involves examining the consistency of performance among the items that compose a scale. If separate items on a scale assign the same values to the concept being measured, the scale possesses internal consistency. For instance, suppose a researcher designs a 20-item scale to measure attitudes toward newspaper reading. For the scale to be internally consistent, the total score on the first half of the test should correlate highly with the score on the second half of the test. This method of determining reliability is called the **split-half technique.**

Only one administration of the measuring instrument is made, but the test is split into halves and scored separately. For example, if the test is in the form of a questionnaire, the even-numbered items might constitute one half and the odd-numbered items the other half. A correlation coefficient is then computed between the two sets of scores. Since this coefficient is computed from a test that is only half as long as the final form, it is corrected by using the following formula:

$$r_{xx} = \frac{2(r_{oe})}{1 + r_{oe}}$$

where r_{oe} is the correlation between the odd items and the even items.

Another common reliability coefficient is alpha (sometimes referred to as **Cronbach's alpha**), which uses the analysis of variance approach to assess the internal consistency of a measure (see Chapter 12).

The **equivalency** component of reliability, sometimes referred to as **cross-test reliability**, assesses the relative correlation between two parallel forms of a test. Two instruments that use different scale items or different measurement techniques are developed to measure the same concept. The two versions are then administered to the same group of people during a single time period, and the correlation between the scores on the two forms of the test is taken as a measure of the reliability. The major problem with this method, of course, is developing two forms of a scale that are perfectly equivalent. The less parallel the two forms, the lower the reliability.

A special case of the equivalency component occurs when two or more observers judge the same phenomenon, as is the case in content analysis (see Chapter 6). This type of reliability is called **intercoder reliability** and is used to assess the degree to which a result can be achieved or reproduced by other observers. Ideally, two individuals who use the same operational measure and the same measuring instrument should reach the same results. For example, if two researchers try to identify acts of violence in television content based on a given operational definition of violence, the degree to which their results are consistent is a measure of intercoder reliability. Disagreements reflect a difference either in perception or in the way the original definition was interpreted. Special formulas for computing intercoder reliability are discussed in Chapter 6.

In addition to being reliable, a measurement must have *validity* if it is to be of use in studying variables. A valid measuring device measures what it is supposed to measure. Or, to put it another way, determining validity requires an evaluation of the congruence between the operational definition of a variable and its conceptual or constitutive definition. Assessing validity requires some judgment on the part of the researcher. In the following discussion of the major types of measurement validity, note that each one depends at least in part on the judgment of the researcher. Also, validity is almost never an all-or-none proposition; it is usually a matter of degree. A measurement rarely turns out to be totally valid or invalid. Typically it winds up somewhere in the middle.

Concerning measurement, there are four major types of validity, and each has a corresponding technique for evaluating the measurement method: *face validity, predictive validity, concurrent validity,* and *construct validity.*

The simplest and most basic kind of validity, **face validity,** is achieved by examining the measurement device to see whether, on the face of it, it measures what it appears to measure. For example, a test designed to measure proofreading ability could include accounting problems, but this measure would lack face validity. A test that asks people to read and correct certain paragraphs has more face validity as a measure of proof-reading skill. Whether a measure possesses face validity depends to some degree on subjective judgment. To minimize subjectivity, the relevance of a given measurement should be judged independently by several experts.

Checking a measurement instrument against some future outcome assesses **predictive validity**. For example, scores on a test to predict whether a person will vote in an upcoming election can be checked against actual voting behavior. If the test scores allow the researcher to predict, with a high degree of accuracy, which people will actually vote and which will not, then the test has predictive validity. Note that it is possible for a measure to have predictive validity and at the same time lack face validity. The sole factor in determining validity in the predictive method is the measurement's ability to forecast future behavior or events correctly. The concern is not with what is being measured but with whether the measurement instrument can predict something. Thus, a test to determine whether a person will become a successful mass media researcher could conceivably consist of geometry problems. If it predicts the ultimate success of a researcher reasonably well, the test has predictive validity but little face validity. The biggest problem associated with predictive validity is determining the criteria against which test scores are to be checked. What, for example, constitutes a "successful mass media researcher"? One who obtains an advanced degree? One who publishes research articles? One who writes a book?

Concurrent validity is closely related to predictive validity. In this method, however, the measuring instrument is checked against some present criterion. For example, it is possible to validate a test of proofreading ability by administering the test to a group of professional proofreaders and to a group of nonproofreaders. If the test discriminates well between the two groups, it can be said

to have concurrent validity. Similarly, a test of aggression might discriminate between one group of children who are frequently detained after school for fighting and another group, the members of which have never been reprimanded for antisocial behavior.

The fourth type of validity, **construct validity**, is the most complex. In simplified form, construct validity involves relating a measuring instrument to some overall theoretic framework to ensure that the measurement is logically related to other concepts in the framework. Ideally, a researcher should be able to suggest various relationships between the property being measured and the other variables. For construct validity to exist, the researcher must show that these relationships are in fact present. For example, an investigator might expect the frequency with which a person views a particular television newscast to be influenced by his or her attitude toward that program. If the measure of attitudes correlates highly with the frequency of viewing, there is some evidence for the validity of the attitude measure. Similarly, construct validity is present if the measurement instrument under consideration does not relate to other variables when there is no theoretic reason to expect such a relationship. Therefore, if an investigator finds a relationship between a measure and other variables that is predicted by a theory and fails to find other relationships that are not predicted by a theory, there is evidence for construct validity. Figure 2.4 summarizes the four types of validity.

Before closing this discussion, we should point out that reliability and validity are related. Reliability is necessary to establish validity, but it is not a sufficient condition; a reliable measure is not necessarily a valid one. Figure 2.5 shows this relationship. An X represents a test that is both reliable and valid; the scores are consistent from session to session

Figure 2.4   Types of Validity

Judgment-based	Criterion-based	Theory-based
Face validity	Predictive validity Concurrent validity	Construct validity

Figure 2.5   Relationship of Reliability and Validity

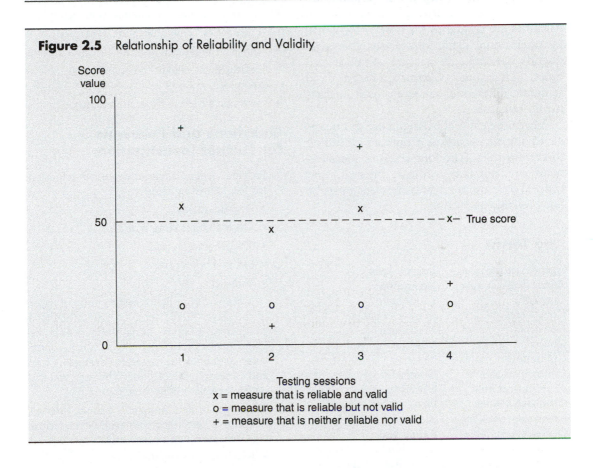

Testing sessions
x = measure that is reliable and valid
o = measure that is reliable but not valid
+ = measure that is neither reliable nor valid

and lie close to the true value. An O represents a measure that is reliable but not valid; the scores are stable from session to session, but they are not close to the true score. A + represents a test that is neither valid nor reliable; scores vary widely from session to session and are not close to the true score.

SUMMARY

Understanding empirical research requires a basic knowledge of concepts, constructs, variables, and measurement. Concepts summarize related observations and express an abstract notion that has been formed by generalizing from particulars. Connections among concepts form propositions that, in turn, are used to build theories. Constructs consist of combinations of concepts and are also useful in building theories.

Variables are phenomena or events that take on one or more different values. Independent variables are manipulated by the researcher, whereas dependent variables are what the researcher attempts to explain. All variables are related to the observable world by operational definitions. Researchers frequently use scales to measure complex variables. Thurstone, Guttman, Likert, and semantic differential scales are used in mass media research.

Measurement is the assignment of numerals to objects, events, or properties according to certain rules. The four levels of measurement are nominal, ordinal, interval, and ratio. To be useful, a measurement must be both reliable and valid.

Key Terms

Agenda setting	Interval level
Antecedent variable	Isomorphism
Concept	Likert scale
Concurrent validity	Marker variable
Construct	Measurement
Construct validity	Multivariate analysis
Continuous variable	Noise
Control variable	Nominal level
Criterion variable	Ordinal level
Cronbach's alpha	Predictive validity
Cross-test reliability	Predictor variable
Dependent variable	Rating scale
Discrete variable	Ratio level
Dummy variable	Reliability
Equivalency	Semantic differential
Face validity	Split-half technique
Factor analysis	Stability
Factor fusion	Thurstone scale
Guttman scale	Triangulation
Independent variable	Validity
Intercoder reliability	Variable
Internal consistency	

 Using the Internet

Search the Internet for:

- operational definition
- rating scales
- reliability
- validity
- dummy variable coding
- "frequency scales" communication examples
- "ratio scales" communication examples
- "split-half reliability"
- "measurement validity" communication examples
- "semantic differential" communication examples

Questions and Problems for Further Investigation

1. Provide conceptual and operational definitions for the following items:

   - Artistic quality
   - Objectionable song lyrics
   - TV program appeal
   - Sexual content
   - Violence

   Compare your definitions to those of others in the class. Would there be any difficulty in conducting a study using these definitions? Have you demonstrated why so much controversy surrounds the topics, for example, of sex and violence on television? What can you find on the Internet about these terms?

2. What type of data (nominal, ordinal, interval, or ratio) is associated with each of the following concepts or measurements?

   - Baseball team standings
   - A test of listening comprehension
   - AC Nielsen's list of the top 10 television programs
   - Frequency of heads versus tails on coin flips
   - Baseball batting averages
   - A scale measuring intensity of attitudes toward violence

- VHF channels 2–13
- A scale for monitoring your weight over time

3. Develop a measurement technique to examine each of these concepts:
   - Newspaper reading
   - Aggressive behavior
   - Brand loyalty in purchasing products
   - Television viewing

4. Assume you are going to conduct a study that requires respondents to rate the importance of programming elements on a radio station. Would you use a semantic differential scale or a 1–10 scale? Why?

5. Provide three examples of variables that could be either an independent or dependent variable in different types of research studies.

For additional resources go to *www.wimmer dominick.com* and *www.cengagebrain.com*.

References and Suggested Readings

Anderson, J. A. (1987). *Communication research: Issues and methods*. New York, NY: McGraw-Hill.

Babbie, E. R. (2010). *The practice of social research* (12th ed.). Belmont, CA: Cengage.

Bae, H. S. (2000). *Product differentiation in national TV newscasts. Journal of Broadcasting & Electronic Media*, 44(1), 62–77.

Buijen, M., & Valkenburg, P. (2000). *The impact of television advertising on children's Christmas wishes. Journal of Broadcasting & Electronic Media*, 44(3), 456–470.

Gerbner, G., Gross, L., Morgan, M., & Signorielli, N. (1980). The mainstreaming of America: Violence profile no. 11. *Journal of Communication, 30*(3), 10–29.

Guilford, J. P. (1954). *Psychometric methods*. New York, NY: McGraw-Hill.

Henning, B., & Vorderer, P. (2001). *Psychological escapism: Predicting the amount of television viewing by need for cognition. Journal of Communication, 51*(1), 100–120.

Hindman, D. B. (2000). *The rural-urban digital divide. Journalism & Mass Communication Quarterly,* 77(3), 549–560.

Huck, S. W. (2011). *Reading statistics and research* (6th ed.). Boston, MA: Addison Wesley Longman.

Kerlinger, F. N. (2000). *Foundations of behavioral research* (4th ed.). New York, NY: Holt, Rinehart & Winston.

Kerlinger, F. N., & Pedhazur, E. (1997). *Multiple regression in behavioral research* (3rd ed.). New York, NY: Holt, Rinehart & Winston.

Mason, E. J., & Bramble, W. J. (1989). *Understanding and conducting research* (2nd ed.). New York, NY: McGraw-Hill.

McNemar, Q. (1969). *Psychological statistics* (4th ed.). New York, NY: John Wiley.

Nunnally, J. C., & Bernstein, I. H. (1994). *Psychometric theory* (4th ed.). New York, NY: McGraw-Hill.

Osgood, C., Suci, G., & Tannenbaum, P. (1957). *The measurement of meaning*. Urbana, IL: University of Illinois Press.

Robinson, J., & Shaver, P. (1973). *Measures of social psychological attitudes* (2nd ed.). Ann Arbor, MI: Institute for Social Research.

Roscoe, J. (1975). *Fundamental research statistics for the behavioral sciences*. New York, NY: Holt, Rinehart & Winston.

Wu, H. D. (2000). *Systemic determinants of international news coverage. Journal of Communication, 50*(2), 110–130.

CHAPTER 3

RESEARCH ETHICS

CHAPTER OUTLINE

ETHICS AND THE RESEARCH PROCESS

Most mass media research involves observations of human beings—asking them questions or examining what they have done. However, in this probing process the researcher must ensure that the rights of the participants are not violated and that the data are analyzed and reported correctly. This concern for rights requires a consideration of **ethics**: distinguishing right from wrong and proper from improper. Unfortunately, there are no universal definitions for these terms. Instead, several guidelines, broad generalizations, and suggestions have been endorsed or at least tacitly accepted by most in the research profession. These guidelines do not provide an answer to every ethical question that may arise, but they can help make researchers more sensitive to the issues.

Before discussing these specific guidelines, let's pose some hypothetical research situations involving ethics.

- A researcher at a large university distributes questionnaires to the students in an introductory mass media course and tells them that if they do not complete the forms, they will lose points toward their grade in the course.

- A researcher is conducting a mail survey about downloading pornography from the Internet. The questionnaire states that the responses will be anonymous. However, unknown to the respondents, each return envelope is marked with a code that enables the researcher to identify the sender.

- A researcher creates a false identity on Facebook and uses it to gather information about the communication behaviors of dozens of college students without the students' knowledge.

- A researcher shows one group of children a violent television show and another group a nonviolent program. Afterward, the children are sent to a public playground, where they are told to play with the children who are already there. The researcher records each instance of violent behavior exhibited by the young subjects.

- Subjects in an experiment are told to submit a sample of their news writing to an executive of a large newspaper and are led to believe that whoever submits the best work will be offered a job at the paper. In fact, the "executive" is a confederate in the experiment and severely criticizes everyone's work. The subjects then rate their own self-esteem. They are never told about the deception.

- A researcher conducting an experiment knowingly assigns subjects likely to support the investigator's hypothesis to the experimental group, while those less likely to support the prediction are assigned to the control group.

Keep in mind these examples of ethically flawed study designs while you read the following guidelines to ethics in mass media research.

WHY BE ETHICAL?

Ethical behavior is the right thing to do. The best reason to behave ethically is the personal knowledge that you have acted in a morally appropriate manner. In addition, there are other cogent reasons that argue for ethical behavior. Unethical behavior may have an adverse effect on research participants. Just one experience with an ethically questionable research project may completely alienate a respondent. A person who was improperly deceived into thinking that he or she was being evaluated for a job at a newspaper when it was all just an experiment might not be so willing to participate in another study. Since mass media research depends on the continued goodwill and cooperation of respondents, it is important to shield them from unethical research practices.

Moreover, unethical research practices reflect poorly on the profession and may result in an increase in negative public opinion. Many readers have probably heard about the infamous Tuskegee syphilis study in which impoverished African American men suffering from syphilis were studied without their consent and left untreated so that researchers could study the progress of the disease (see Jones, 1981, for a complete description). The distrust and suspicion engendered by this experiment in the African American community have yet to subside and have been cited as a factor in the rise of some conspiracy theories about the spread of AIDS (Thomas & Quinn, 1981). It is fortunate that the mass media research community has not had an ethical lapse of this magnitude, but the Tuskegee experiment illustrates the harmful fallout that can result from an unethical research project.

Unethical research usually does not result from some sinister motivation. Instead, it generally comes from pressure on researchers to cut corners in an attempt to publish an article or gain prestige or impress other colleagues. Nonetheless, it is behavior that is potentially serious and little tolerated within the community of mass media scholars.

GENERAL ETHICAL THEORIES

The problem of determining what is right and proper has been examined for hundreds of years. At least three general types of theories have evolved to suggest answers: (1) rule-based or **deontological** theories, (2) balancing or **teleological** theories, and (3) **relativistic** theories. The best-known deontological theory is the one associated with the philosopher Immanuel Kant, who posited moral laws that constituted **categorical imperatives**—principles that define appropriate action in all situations. Following these categorical imperatives represents a moral duty for all humans. To define a categorical imperative, a person should ask whether the behavior in

question is something that he or she would like to see universally implemented. In other words, a person should act in a way that he or she wants all others to act. Note that in many ways, Kant's thinking parallels what we might call the Golden Rule: Do unto others as you would have them do unto you.

A mass media researcher, for example, might develop a categorical imperative about deception. Deception is something that a researcher does not want to see universally practiced by all; nor does the researcher wish to be deceived. Therefore, deception is something that should not be used in research, no matter what the benefits and no matter what the circumstances.

The teleological, or balancing, theory is best exemplified by what philosopher John Stuart Mill called **utilitarianism**. In this theory, the good that may come from an action is weighed against or balanced against the possible harm. The individual then acts in a way that maximizes good and minimizes harm. In other words, the ultimate test for determining the rightness of some behavior depends on the outcomes that result from this behavior. The end may justify the means. As will be noted, most institutional review boards at colleges and universities endorse this principle when they examine research proposals for ethical compliance.

A mass media researcher who follows the utilitarian approach must balance the good that will come from a research project against its possible negative effects. In this situation, a researcher might decide that it is appropriate to use deception in an experiment if the positive benefits of the knowledge obtained outweigh the possible harmful effects of deceiving the subjects. One difficulty with this approach is that it is sometimes difficult, if not impossible, to anticipate all of the harm that might ensue from a given research design. Note that a researcher might use a different course of action depending upon which ethical theory is used as a guide.

Why Be Ethical?

It's the right thing to do.

The **relativism** approach argues that there is no absolute right or wrong way to behave. Instead, ethical decisions are determined by the culture within which a researcher is working. Indeed, behavior that is judged wrong in one culture may be judged ethical in another. One way ethical norms of a culture are established is through the creation of codes of behavior or good conduct that describe what most researchers in the field believe are desirable or undesirable behaviors. A researcher confronted with a particular ethical problem can refer to these codes for guidance.

These three theories help form the basis for the ethical principles discussed next.

ETHICAL PRINCIPLES

General ethical principles are difficult to construct in the research area. However, there are at least four relevant principles. First is the principle of **autonomy**, or self-determination, which has its roots in the categorical imperative. Denying autonomy is not something that a researcher wishes to see universally practiced. Basic to this concept is the demand that the researcher respects the rights, values, and decisions of other people. The reasons for a person's actions should be respected and the actions not interfered with. This principle is exemplified by the use of *informed consent* in the research procedure.

A second ethical principle important to social science research is **nonmaleficence**. In short, it is wrong to intentionally inflict harm on another. A third ethical principle—**beneficence**—is usually considered in tandem with nonmaleficence. Beneficence stipulates a positive obligation to remove existing harms and to confer benefits on others. These two principles operate together, and often the researcher must weigh the harmful risks of research against its possible benefits (for example, increased knowledge or a refined theory). Note how the utilitarian theory relates to these principles.

A fourth ethical principle, the principle of **justice**, is related to both deontological and teleological theories of ethics. At its general level, this principle holds that people who are equal in relevant respects should be treated equally. In the research context, this principle should be applied when new programs or policies are being evaluated. The positive results of such research should be shared with all. For example, it would be unethical to deny the benefit of a new teaching procedure to children because they were originally chosen to be in the control group rather than in the group that received the experimental procedure. Benefits should be shared with all who are qualified.

Frey, Botan, and Kreps (2000) offer the following summary of moral principles commonly advocated by researchers:

1. Provide the people being studied with free choice.

2. Protect their right to privacy.

3. Benefit them rather than harming them.

4. Treat them with respect.

It is clear that mass media researchers must follow some set of rules to meet their ethical obligations to their subjects and respondents. Cook (1976), discussing the laboratory approach, offers one such code of behavior that represents norms in the field:

- Do not involve people in research without their knowledge or consent.
- Do not coerce people to participate.
- Do not withhold from the participant the true nature of the research.

- Do not actively lie to the participant about the nature of the research.
- Do not lead the participant to commit acts that diminish his or her self-respect.
- Do not violate the right to self-determination.
- Do not expose the participant to physical or mental stress.

Research Misconduct and Retractions

Ethical lapses by researchers can lead to serious research misconduct. The most egregious ethical lapses are fabricating data, omitting data that runs counter to a researcher's prediction, or inaccurately describing the research procedures. The Office of Research Integrity, a part of the U.S. Department of Health and Human Services, regularly reports on research misconduct in the medical and biological sciences. According to its most recent summary, the agency found 13 cases of research misconduct in 2008, with 10 cases involving falsification of data.

The results of these ethical failures can be serious, particularly in the life sciences. Administrators at the Mayo Clinic concluded that a researcher had made up data that suggested that a person's own immune system could be used to fight cancer. In addition to raising false hopes among cancer patients, the tainted research led other investigators down a blind alley and wasted both time and money. In another case, a researcher claimed to have discovered an improved drug treatment for high blood pressure. Many doctors prescribed the new treatment for their patients. Further examination revealed doubts about the data collection and that the researcher had failed to

disclose that the investigation didn't use a double blind design (in which the researcher does not know who got the placebo and who got the experimental drug). Thousands of individuals were put at risk by the faulty research.

The scientific journals that published these and other studies that may have falsified data ultimately issued retractions, but the retraction process is a lengthy one, usually taking between 2 and 3 years. Even after a retraction, it's difficult to undo the harm done by the original publication. For example, in 2010, *The Lancet*, a prestigious British medical journal, officially retracted a 1998 study that linked the measles, mumps, and rubella vaccine (MMR) with autism, noting that, among other ethical problems, the author of the study had a financial interest in discrediting the MMR inoculation. Nonetheless, even after the study was discredited, many parents still believe that the MMR vaccine causes autism and do not vaccinate their children.

The results of ethical failures by mass media researchers may not be as serious as those in the medical field, and there have been no recent cases of media journals retracting articles, but media researchers should be mindful of the consequences of poor ethical choices.

- Do not invade the privacy of the participant.
- Do not withhold benefits from participants in control groups.
- Do not fail to treat research participants fairly and to show them consideration and respect.

To this list we add:

- Always treat every respondent or subject with unconditional human regard. (That is, accept and respect a person for what he or she is, and do not criticize the person for what he or she is not.)

Do academic and private sector researchers hold different values or view these core ethical principles differently? Chew (2000) surveyed both groups and found that both valued confidentiality equally, while academic researchers placed a higher value on integrity and beneficence. Private-sector researchers were more sensitive to conflict-of-interest issues.

SPECIFIC ETHICAL PROBLEMS

The following subsections discuss some of the common areas in which mass media researchers might encounter ethical dilemmas.

Voluntary Participation and Informed Consent

An individual is entitled to decline to participate in any research project or to terminate participation at any time. Participation in an experiment, survey, or focus group is always voluntary, and any form of coercion is unacceptable. Researchers who are in a position of authority over subjects (as when a teacher/researcher hands questionnaires to university students) should be especially sensitive to implied coercion: Even though the researcher might tell the class that failure to participate will not affect grades, many students may not believe this. In such a situation, it is better to keep the questionnaires anonymous and for the person in authority to be absent from the room while the survey is administered.

Voluntary participation is not a pressing ethical issue in mail and telephone surveys because respondents are free to hang up the phone or to throw away the questionnaire. Nonetheless, a researcher should not attempt to induce subjects to participate by misrepresenting the organization sponsoring the research or by exaggerating its purpose or importance. For example, telephone interviewers should not be instructed to identify themselves as representatives of the "Department of Information" to mislead people into thinking the survey is government sponsored. Likewise, mail questionnaires should not be constructed to mimic census forms, tax returns, Social Security questionnaires, or other official government forms.

Closely related to voluntary participation is the notion of **informed consent**. For people to volunteer for a research project, they need to know enough about the project to make an intelligent choice. Researchers have the responsibility to inform potential subjects or respondents of all features of the project that can reasonably be expected to influence participation. For example, respondents should understand that an interview may take as long as 45 minutes, that a second interview is required, or that after completing a mail questionnaire they may be singled out for a telephone interview.

In an experiment, informed consent means that potential subjects must be warned of any possible discomfort or unpleasantness that might be involved. Subjects should be told if they are to receive or administer electric shocks, be subjected to unpleasant audio or visual stimuli, or undergo any procedure that might cause concern. Any unusual measurement techniques that may be used must be described. Researchers have an obligation to answer candidly and truthfully, as far as possible, all the participants' questions about the research.

Experiments that involve deception (as described in the next subsection) cause special problems about obtaining informed consent. If deception is absolutely necessary to conduct an experiment, is the experimenter obligated to inform subjects that they may be deceived during the upcoming experiment? Will such a disclosure affect participation in the experiment? Will it also affect the experimental results? Should the researcher compromise the research by telling all potential subjects that deception will be involved for some participants but not for others?

Another problem is deciding how much information about a project a researcher must disclose in seeking informed consent. Is it enough to explain that the experiment involves rating commercials, or is it necessary to add that the experiment is designed to test whether subjects with high IQs prefer different commercials from those with low IQs? Obviously, in some situations the researcher cannot reveal everything about the project for fear of contaminating the results, or in the case of proprietary information. For example, if the goal of the research is to examine the influence of peer pressure on commercial evaluations, alerting the subjects to this facet of the investigation might change their behavior in the experiment.

Problems might occur in research that examines the impact of mass media in nonliterate communities—for example, the research subjects might not comprehend what they were told regarding the proposed investigation. Even in literate societies, many people fail to understand the implications for confidentiality of the storage of survey data on disks. Moreover, an investigator might not have realized in advance that some subjects would find part of an experiment or survey emotionally disturbing.

In 2002, the American Psychological Association's (APA) Council of Representatives adopted a new ethics code that addresses a wide range of ethical issues of relevance to that discipline. Since mass media researchers face many of the same ethical issues faced by psychologists, it seems useful to quote from that document several provisions concerning informed consent. Researchers should disclose:

1. The purpose of the research, expected duration, and procedures
2. The subjects' right to decline to participate and to withdraw from the research once participation has begun
3. The foreseeable consequences of declining or withdrawing
4. Reasonably foreseeable factors that may be expected to influence subjects' willingness to participate, such as potential risks, discomfort, or adverse effects
5. Any prospective research benefits
6. Limits of confidentiality
7. Incentives for participation
8. Whom to contact for questions about the research and research participants' rights

Examine the APA's Code of Conduct at *www.apa.org/ethics/code*.

Research findings provide some indication of what research participants should be told to ensure informed consent. Epstein, Suedefeld, and Silverstein (1973) found that subjects wanted a general description of the experiment and what was expected of them; they wanted to know whether danger was involved, how long the experiment would last, and the experiment's purpose. As for informed consent and survey participation, Sobal (1984) found wide variation among researchers about what to tell respondents in the survey introduction. Almost all introductions identified the research organization and the interviewer by name and described the research topic. Less frequently mentioned in introductions were the sponsor of the research and guarantees of confidentiality or anonymity. Few survey introductions mentioned the length of the survey or that participation was voluntary. Greenberg and Garramone (1989) reported the results of a survey of 201 mass media researchers that disclosed that 96% usually provided guaranteed confidentiality of results, 92% usually named the sponsoring organization, 66% usually told respondents that participation was voluntary, and 61% usually disclosed the length of the questionnaire.

Finally, a researcher must consider the form of the consent to be obtained. Written consent is a requirement in certain government-sponsored research programs and may also be required by many university research review committees, as discussed later in this section. However, in several generally recognized situations, signed forms are regarded as impractical. These include telephone surveys, mail surveys, personal interviews, and cases in which the signed form itself might represent an occasion for breach of confidentiality. For example, a respondent who has been promised anonymity as an inducement to participate in a face-to-face interview might be suspicious if asked to sign a consent form after the interview. In these circumstances, the fact that the respondent agreed to participate is taken as implied consent. The special problems of gaining consent for online research are discussed shortly.

As a general rule, the greater the risks of potential harm to subjects, the greater the need to obtain a consent statement. Figure 3.1 is an example of a typical consent form.

Figure 3.1   Example of a Typical Consent Form

The purpose of this research is to explore possible relationships between watching daytime TV talk shows and perceptions of social reality. You will be asked questions about your general TV viewing, your viewing of daytime talk shows, and your attitudes about interpersonal relationships. This questionnaire will take about 20 minutes to complete. Please answer every question as accurately as possible. Participation is voluntary. Your grades will not be affected if you choose not to participate. Your participation will be anonymous. No discomfort, stress, or risks are anticipated.

I agree to participate in the research entitled "Talk Show Viewing and Social Reality" conducted by _____, in the Department of Mass Communication at the University of _____, (telephone number _____). I understand that this participation is entirely voluntary. I can withdraw my consent at any time without penalty and have the results of this participation, to the extent that they can be identified as mine, returned to me, removed from the research record, or destroyed.

_____   _____

Signature of Researcher (date)   Signature of Participant (date)

Research at the University of _____ that involves human participants is overseen by the Institutional Review Board. Questions or problems regarding your rights as a participant should be addressed to _____, (telephone number _____, email address _____).

Concealment and Deception

Concealment and deception are encountered most frequently in experimental research. **Concealment** is withholding certain information from the subjects; **deception** is deliberately providing false information. Both practices raise ethical problems. The difficulty in obtaining consent has already been mentioned. A second problem derives from the general feeling that it is wrong for experimenters to lie to or otherwise deceive subjects.

Many critics argue that deception transforms a subject from a human being into a manipulated object and is therefore demeaning to the participant. Moreover, once subjects have been deceived, they are likely to expect to be deceived again in other research projects. At least two research studies seem to suggest that this concern is valid. Stricker and Messick (1967) reported finding a high incidence of suspicion among high school–age subjects after they had been deceived. More recently, Jamison, Karlan, and Schechter (2008) found that subjects who were deceived in one experiment were less likely to participate in a second experiment. In addition, when compared to subjects who were not deceived, those individuals who were deceived displayed different behaviors in the subsequent experiment.

On the other hand, some researchers argue that certain studies could not be conducted at all without the use of deception. They use the utilitarian approach to argue that the harm done to those who are deceived is outweighed by the benefits of the research to scientific knowledge. Indeed, Christensen (1988) suggests that it may be immoral to fail to investigate important areas that cannot be investigated without the use of deception. He also argues that much of the sentiment against deception in research exists because deception has been analyzed only from the viewpoint of abstract moral philosophy. The subjects who were "deceived" in many experiments did not perceive what was done to them as deception but viewed it as a necessary element in the research procedure. Christensen illustrates the relativistic approach when he suggests that any decision regarding the use of deception should take into account the context and aim of the deception. Research suggests that subjects are most disturbed when deception violates their privacy or increases their risk of harm. Obviously, deception is not a technique that should be used indiscriminately.

Kelman (1967) suggests that before the investigator settles on deception as an experimental tactic, three questions should be examined:

1. How significant is the proposed study?

2. Are alternative procedures available that would provide the same information?

3. How severe is the deception? (It is one thing to tell subjects that the experimentally constructed message they are reading was taken from the *New York Times*; it is another to falsely report that the test a subject has just completed was designed to measure latent suicidal tendencies.)

Another set of criteria is offered by Elms (1982), who suggests five necessary and sufficient conditions under which deception can be considered ethically justified in social science research:

1. When there is no other feasible way to obtain the desired information

2. When the likely benefits substantially outweigh the likely harm

3. When subjects are given the option to withdraw at any time without penalty

4. When any physical or psychological harm to subjects is temporary

5. When subjects are debriefed about all substantial deception and the research procedures are made available for public review

Pascual, Leone, Singh, and Scoboria (2010) developed a checklist to help new researchers decide whether deception is justified in their research. Some sample items from their list:

(1) Have all reasonably possible costs and benefits been accounted for in considering whether deception may be justified? (Y/N)

(2) Is there any way this study could be done either without or with a lesser degree of deception?

A CLOSER LOOK

Research Ethics and Facebook

The social networking site Facebook is extremely popular among college students. As of 2012, about 900 million people were members of the site, and it regularly shows up among the top 10 most-visited destinations on the Internet. Facebook has also become a gold mine of information for researchers. Social scientists at several universities are using Facebook data to examine such topics as self-esteem, popularity, and personal attraction. Not surprisingly, Facebook has generated a few new ethical issues as well.

To illustrate, researchers at Harvard University studied social relationships by secretly monitoring the Facebook profiles of an entire class of students at a U.S. college. The 1,700 students involved in the project did not know they were being studied, nor had they given their permission to the Harvard research team. The researchers promised that they will take steps to insure the privacy of all the participants. Does such a study violate accepted ethical standards?

Federal human subjects' guidelines were mainly written for an era before Facebook existed and are open to interpretation. As a result, many universities have established their own, sometimes conflicting, policies. For example, the institutional review board at Indiana University will not approve research using data from social networking sites without the site's approval or the consent of those being studied. Other universities seem to rely on the traditional principle that no consent is needed if a researcher is observing public behavior.

But is the information on Facebook public or private? One side of this argument maintains that Facebook members have no expectations of privacy when it comes to posting information on their pages. Indeed, it appears that the prime motivation of Facebook members is to share the information. If users choose not to use the privacy safeguards provided by the site, what they post is fair game.

On the other hand, is the assumption of no privacy expectations accurate? A survey of Facebook members found that most expected that their profiles would be viewed mainly by a small circle of friends—not the world in general. Sharing information in this limited context is not the same as posting something for all to see. Further, even if Facebook members intended that the information be made public, it does not necessarily mean that they consented to the information's being aggregated, coded, analyzed, and distributed. Once the data were published, even if presented only in the aggregate form, it might be possible for someone to identify the subjects involved in the research. (Indeed, once data from the Harvard University study were released, other researchers quickly identified both the college where the research was conducted and the class that was examined.)

Once again, the Internet is forcing researchers to re-examine their traditional assumptions about the ethical dimensions of their research.

(3) Is the deception associated with more than minimal risk?

(4) Are there possible risks that may have been overlooked in the description of this study? (Y/N)

The authors report that a survey of 45 researchers indicated that the checklist was perceived as easy to use and helpful in expediting their University's ethical review process.

The above suggestions offer researchers good advice for the planning stages of investigations.

When an experiment is concluded, especially one involving concealment or deception, it is the responsibility of the investigator to debrief subjects. **Debriefing** means that after the experiment is over the investigator thoroughly describes the purpose of the research, explains the use of deception (if it occurred), and encourages the subject to ask questions about the research. Debriefing should be thorough enough to remove any lasting effects that might have been created by the experimental manipulation or by any other aspect of the experiment. Subjects' questions should be answered and the potential value of the experiment stressed. How common is debriefing among mass media researchers? In the survey cited in Greenberg and Garramone (1989), 71% of the researchers reported they usually debrief subjects, 19% debrief sometimes, and 10% rarely or never debrief subjects. Although it is an ethical requirement of most experiments, the practice of debriefing has yet to be embraced by all investigators.

The APA's 2002 code contains the following provisions concerning deception:

a. Psychologists do not conduct a study involving deception unless they have determined that the use of deceptive techniques is justified by the study's significant prospective scientific, educational, or applied value and

that effective nondeceptive alternative procedures are not feasible.

b. Psychologists do not deceive prospective participants about research that is reasonably expected to cause physical pain or severe emotional distress.

c. Psychologists explain any deception that is an integral feature of the design and conduct of an experiment to participants as early as is feasible, preferably at the conclusion of their participation, but no later than at the conclusion of the data collection, and permit participants to withdraw their data.

The American Sociological Association's guidelines for research contain similar language:

• Sociologists do not use deceptive techniques unless (1) they have obtained the approval of institutional review boards and (2) they have determined that the use of deceptive techniques will not be harmful to research participants; that deception is justified by the study's prospective scientific, educational, or applied value; and that equally effective alternative procedures that do not use deception are not feasible.

• Sociologists never deceive research participants about significant aspects of the research that might affect their willingness to participate, such as physical risks, discomfort, or unpleasant emotional experiences.

• When deception is an integral feature of the design and conduct of research, sociologists attempt to correct any misconception that research participants may have no later than at the conclusion of the research.

No data are available on how often deception is used in mass media research. However, some information is available from other fields. In a study of 23 years of articles published in a leading psychology journal, Sieber (1995) found that 66% of all studies published in 1969 used deception, compared to 47% in 1992. A recent survey of the literature (Hertwig & Ortman, 2008) found that around half of all the studies in social psychology used some form of deception.

Protection of Privacy

The problem of protecting the privacy of participants arises more often in field observation and survey research than in laboratory studies. In field studies, observers may study people in public places without their knowledge (for example, individuals watching TV at an airport lounge). The more public the place, the less a person has an expectation of privacy and the fewer ethical problems are encountered. However, some public situations do present ethical concerns. For example, is it ethical for a researcher to pretend to browse in a video rental store when in fact the researcher is observing who rents pornographic videos? What about eavesdropping on people's dinner conversations to determine how often news topics are discussed? To minimize ethical problems, a researcher should violate privacy only to the minimum degree needed to gather the data.

When they take a survey, respondents have a right to know whether their privacy will be maintained and who will have access to the information they provide. There are two ways to guarantee privacy: by assuring anonymity and by assuring confidentiality. A promise of **anonymity** is a guarantee that a given respondent cannot possibly be linked to any particular response. In many research projects, anonymity is an advantage because it encourages respondents to be honest and candid in their answers. Strictly speaking, personal and telephone interviews cannot be anonymous because the researcher can link a given questionnaire to a specific person, household, or telephone number. In such instances, the researcher should promise **confidentiality**; that is, respondents should be assured that even though they can be identified as individuals, their names would never be publicly associated with the information they provide. A researcher should never use *anonymous* in a way that is or seems to be synonymous with *confidential*.

Additionally, respondents should be told who *will* have access to the information they provide. The researcher's responsibility for assuring confidentiality does not end once the data have been analyzed and the study concluded. Questionnaires that identify people by name should not be stored in public places, nor should other researchers be given permission to examine confidential data unless all identifying marks have been obliterated. The APA's statement does not contain much guidance on issues of privacy and confidentiality. It does say that researchers should inform subjects if they are planning to share or use data that are personally identifiable. The American Sociological Association's guidelines are more detailed. In part they include the following provisions:

- Sociologists take reasonable precautions to protect the confidentiality rights of research participants, students, employees, clients, or others.

- Confidential information provided by research participants, students, employees, clients, or others is treated as such by sociologists even if there is no legal protection or privilege to do so. Sociologists have an obligation to protect confidential information and not allow information gained in confidence to be used in ways that would unfairly compromise research participants, students, employees, clients, or others.

- Sociologists may confront unanticipated circumstances when they become aware of information that is clearly health- or life-threatening to research participants, students, employees, clients, or others. In these cases, sociologists balance the importance of guarantees of confidentiality with other principles in this Code of Ethics, standards of conduct, and applicable law.

- Confidentiality is not required with respect to observations in public places, activities conducted in public, or other settings where no rules of privacy are provided by law or custom. Similarly, confidentiality is not required in the case of information available from public records.

FEDERAL REGULATIONS CONCERNING RESEARCH

In 1971, the Department of Health, Education and Welfare (HEW) drafted rules for obtaining informed consent from research participants including full documentation of informed consent procedures. These rules were eventually codified as the Federal Policy for the Protection of Human Subjects, often referred to as the "Common Rule," and were published as Title 45, part 46, in the *Code of Federal Regulations*. The Common Rule defines research as a "systematic investigation, including research development, testing and evaluation, designed to develop or contribute to generalizable knowledge."

In addition, the government set up a system of **institutional review boards** (IRBs) to safeguard the rights of human subjects. In 2010, there were more than 800 IRBs at medical schools, colleges, universities, hospitals, and other institutions.

IRBs are a continuing source of irritation for many social science researchers, and some seemingly strange IRB decisions have been well publicized. For example, one researcher studying preliterate societies was required by the IRB to have respondents read and sign a consent form before being interviewed. Another IRB tried to block an English professor's essay that used students' personal accounts of encountering violence because the students might be stressed if they read the essay. (See American Association of University Professors, 2006, Research on Human Subjects: Academic Freedom and the Institutional Review Board, available at *www.aaup.org/AAUP/comm/rep/A/ humansubs.htm*, for other examples.) Qualitative researchers were particularly bothered by having to seek IRB approval. They argued that since qualitative research does not have generalizability as a goal, they should not be covered by the Common Rule. (See Chapter 5 for more information on qualitative research.)

At most universities, IRBs have become part of the permanent bureaucracy. They hold regular meetings and have developed standardized forms that must accompany proposals for research that involves human subjects or respondents. For a description of how a typical IRB operates, consult *www.nova.edu/irb/*.

In 1981, the Department of Health and Human Services (HHS, successor to HEW) softened its regulations concerning social science research. The department's Policy for the Protection of Human Research Subjects exempts studies that use existing public data; research in educational settings about new instructional techniques; research involving the use of anonymous education tests; and survey, interview, and observational research in public places, provided that the subjects are not identified and sensitive information is not collected. Signed consent forms are deemed unnecessary if the research presents only a minimal risk of harm to subjects and involves no procedures for which written consent is required outside the research context. This means that signed consent forms are no longer necessary in the interview situation because a person does not usually seek written consent before asking a question.

The Office for Human Research Protections has created a series of intricate decision charts to help researchers decide whether their research needs IRB approval. The 11 charts answer questions related to the following issues:

- Whether an activity is research that must be reviewed by an IRB

- Whether the review may be performed by expedited procedures

- Whether informed consent or its documentation may be waived

The charts may be found at *www.hhs .gov/ohrp/humansubjects/guidance/decision charts.htm.*

Although the new guidelines apparently exempt most nonexperimental social science research from federal regulation, IRBs at some institutions still review all research proposals that involve human subjects, and some IRBs still follow the old HEW standards. In fact, some IRB regulations are even more stringent than the federal guidelines. As a practical matter, a researcher should always build a little more time into the research schedule to accommodate IRB procedures.

As mass media researchers investigate more sensitive topics, such as pornography on the Internet, social networks, coverage of terrorism, and hate speech, their research will be increasingly scrutinized by IRBs. This situation has caused some controversy in the academic community, particularly among journalists who claim IRB review is a potential violation of the First Amendment.

You can read the online version of the HHS's Office for Human Research Protections guidelines at *www.hhs.gov/ohrp/ humansubjects/guidance/45cfr46.htm.*

In July 2011, the HHS proposed to revise the Common Rule for the first time since its enactment. In its notice of proposed rulemaking, the HHS noted that current regulations concerning human subjects were drafted years ago and have not kept pace with many developments, including changes in social and behavioral science research. Although many of the proposed revisions deal with medical and biological science, one proposed change suggests that studies using "educational tests, surveys, interviews and similar procedures" when conducted among competent adults would be excused from IRB review. In addition, HHS asked for comments from researchers to help identify other areas of social and behavioral science methods that could be exempt from IRB review.

Ethics in Data Analysis and Reporting

Researchers are responsible for maintaining professional standards in analyzing and reporting their data. The ethical guidelines in this area are less controversial and more clear-cut. In 2000, the U.S. Office of Science and Technology Policy identified three areas of research misconduct: fabrication, falsification, and plagiarism. One cardinal rule is that researchers have a moral and ethical obligation to refrain from tampering with data: Questionnaire responses and experimental observations may not be fabricated, altered, or discarded. Similarly, researchers are expected to exercise reasonable care in processing the data to guard against needless errors that might affect the results.

Another universal ethical principle is that authors should not plagiarize. The work of someone else should not be reproduced without giving proper credit to the original author.

Only those individuals who contribute significantly to a research project should be given authorship credit. The definition of a "significant contribution" might be fuzzy at times; generally, however, to be listed as an author, a person should play a major role in conceptualizing, analyzing, or writing the final document. Strange (2008) listed potential problems with authorship. Coercive authorship or piggybacking occurs when a subordinate is pressured by someone in authority to include the superior's name on a manuscript even though the superior had little input into the finished product. Honorary authorship occurs when a person adds another author to a research project in order to curry favor with someone. Denial of authorship involves publishing a work without including the names of all those who provided a significant contribution to the project.

Another problem that sometimes occurs involves the order of authorship of an article or a report. If there are two or more researchers involved, who gets listed as first author ("top billing")? Ideally, all those involved should decide on the order of authorship at the beginning of a project, subject to later revision if changes in contribution should happen. Usually, the first author is the one who made the biggest contribution to the work. Finally, special problems are involved when university faculty do research with students. (This topic is discussed later in this chapter.)

Researchers should never conceal information that might influence the interpretation of their findings. For example, if two weeks elapsed between the testing of an experimental group and the testing of a control group, the delay should be reported so that other researchers can discount the effects of history and maturation on the results. Every research report should contain a full and complete description of method, particularly any departure from standard procedures.

Because science is a public activity (see Chapter 1), researchers have an ethical obligation to share their findings and methods with other researchers. All questionnaires, experimental materials, measurement instruments, instructions to subjects, and other relevant items should be made available to those who wish to examine them.

Finally, all investigators are under an ethical obligation to draw conclusions from their data that are consistent with those data. Interpretations should not be stretched or distorted to fit a personal point of view or a favorite theory, or to gain or maintain a client's favor. Nor should researchers attribute greater significance or credibility to their data than is justified. For example, when analyzing correlation coefficients obtained from a large sample, a researcher could achieve statistical significance with an r of only, for example, 0.10. It would be perfectly acceptable to report a statistically significant result in this case, but the investigator should also mention that the predictive utility of the correlation is not large and, specifically, that it explains only 1% of the total variation. In short, researchers should report their results with candor and honesty.

Ethics in the Publication Process

Publishing the results of research in scholarly journals is an important part of the process of scientific inquiry. Science is a public activity, and publication is the most efficient way to share research knowledge. In addition, success in the academic profession is often tied to a successful publication record. Consequently, certain ethical guidelines are usually followed with regard to publication procedures. From the perspective of the researcher seeking to submit an article for publication, the first ethical guideline comes into play when the article is ready to be sent for review. The researcher should submit the proposed article to only one journal at a time because simultaneous submission to several sources is inefficient and wasteful. When an article is submitted for review to an academic

A CLOSER LOOK

Ethics Violations Have Consequences

In early 2009, the Executive Council of the American Association of Public Opinion Research (AAPOR) censured a Johns Hopkins professor for violating the association's ethics policy. The professor, Gilbert Burnham, had published a controversial study in the British medical journal the *Lancet* in which he estimated the number of Iraqi civilian deaths resulting from the U.S. invasion as nearly 650,000, a figure that was several times higher than other estimates.

AAPOR began investigating the study after one of its members questioned the accuracy of Burnham's estimate. During its eight-month investigation, AAPOR asked Burnham for a description of the methodology that he used in the study. Burnham refused to provide all of the information that AAPOR requested.

In its censure statement, AAPOR said that Burnham's refusal to fully cooperate with the probe "violates the fundamental standards of science, seriously undermines open public debate on critical issues and undermines the credibility of all survey and public opinion research."

The AAPOR statement makes no judgment about the accuracy of Burnham's count or about his methodology. The censure was based solely on his refusal to disclose all of the details of his research.

Johns Hopkins officials responded to the AAPOR censure by noting that neither Burnham nor his department are members of AAPOR. Nonetheless, the university announced it was conducting its own investigation into Burnham's methods.

journal, it is usually sent to two, three, or more reviewers for evaluation. Simultaneous submission means that several sets of referees spend their time pointing out the same problems and difficulties that could have been reported by a single set. The duplication of effort is unnecessary and might delay consideration of other articles waiting for review.

A related ethical problem concerns attempts to publish nearly identical or highly similar articles based on the same data set. For example, suppose a researcher has data on the communication patterns in a large organization. The investigator writes one article emphasizing the communication angle for a communication journal and a second article with a management slant for a business journal. Both articles draw on the same database and contain comparable results. Is this practice ethical? This is not

an easy question to answer. Some journal editors apparently do not approve of writing multiple papers from the same data; others suggest that this practice is acceptable, provided submissions are made to journals that do not have overlapping audiences. In addition, there is the sticky question of how different one manuscript has to be from another to be considered a separate entity.

On the other hand, journal editors and reviewers have ethical obligations to those who submit manuscripts for evaluation. Editors and reviewers should not let the decision process take an inordinate amount of time; a prompt and timely decision is owed to all contributors. (Most editors of mass communication journals try to notify contributors of their decision within three months.) Reviewers should try to provide positive and helpful reviews; they should not do "hatchet jobs" on articles submitted to them. Moreover, reviewers should not unjustly squelch manuscripts that argue against one of their pet ideas or that contradict or challenge some of their own research. Each contributor to a journal should receive an objective and impartial review. Neither should reviewers quibble needlessly over minor points in an article or demand unreasonable changes. Reviewers also owe contributors consistency. Authors find it frustrating to revise their manuscripts according to a reviewer's wishes only to find that, on a second reading, the reviewer has a change of mind and prefers the original version.

Fischer (2011) suggests that the best reviews are those that add value to research submitted for publication. He suggests a written code of ethics for reviewers that includes such principles as balance, diplomacy, fair-mindedness, and promptness.

Ryan and Martinson (1999) surveyed nearly 100 scholars whose articles had appeared in two mass communication journals during the mid-1990s. They found that the three biggest complaints of these authors were (1) editors who didn't reach a decision about a manuscript in a reasonable amount of time, (2) editors who blamed delays on reviewers, and (3) reviewers who did not have expertise in the area represented by the manuscript.

ETHICAL PROBLEMS OF STUDENT-FACULTY RESEARCH

Schiff and Ryan (1996) list several ethical dilemmas that can occur in a college setting, including using undergraduate classes for research and claiming joint authorship of articles based on student theses and dissertations. With regard to the first problem, they found that about 36% of a sample of 138 faculty members who had recently chaired a thesis or dissertation committee reported that using a research class to collect data for a

thesis or dissertation was unethical and that 65% thought it was unethical to require undergraduate classes to participate in thesis or dissertation research. (Note that Schiff and Ryan were investigating the ethics involved in using undergraduates for dissertation or thesis research—not research projects conducted by faculty members. Presumably, however, the numbers should be similar.)

Schiff and Ryan found uniform ethical norms concerning authorship of articles stemming from theses and dissertations. About 86% of the respondents stated that requiring students to list a professor as coauthor on any article stemming from the thesis or dissertation as a condition for directing the project was unethical.

The APA's ethics committee provides some guidelines with regard to the joint authorship of articles based on a dissertation or thesis:

- The dissertation adviser may receive only second authorship.
- Secondary authorship for the adviser may be considered obligatory if the adviser supplies the database, designates variables, or makes important interpretive contributions.
- If the adviser suggests the general topic, is significantly involved in the design or instrumentation of the project, or substantially contributes to the writing, then the student may offer the adviser second authorship as a courtesy.
- If the adviser offers only financial aid, facilities, and periodic critiques, then secondary authorship is inappropriate.

However, some researchers argue that a dissertation should comprise original and independent work and that involvement by the researcher sufficient to merit coauthorship may be too much involvement (Audi, 1990).

The Rights of Students as Research Participants

College students provide much of the data in social science research. In psychology, for example, more than 70% of studies use students (Korn, 1988). In fact, it is the rare liberal arts major who has not participated in (or had a request to participate in) social science research. The ethical dimensions of this situation have not been overlooked. Korn (1988) suggests a "bill of rights" for students who agree to be research subjects:

- Participants should know the general purpose of the study and what they will be expected to do. Beyond this, they should be told everything a reasonable person would want to know in order to participate.

- Participants have the right to withdraw from a study at any time after beginning participation in the research.

- Participants should expect to receive benefits that outweigh the costs or risks involved. To achieve the educational benefit, participants have the right to ask questions and to receive clear, honest answers. If they don't receive what was promised, they have the right to remove their data from the study.

- Participants have the right to expect that anything done or said during their participation in a study will remain anonymous or confidential, unless they specifically agree to give up this right.

- Participants have the right to decline to participate in any study and may not be coerced into research. When learning about research is a course requirement, an equivalent alternative to participation should be available.

- Participants have the right to know when they have been deceived in a study and why the deception was used. If the deception seems unreasonable, participants have the right to withhold their data.

- When any of these rights is violated or have objections about a study, they have the right and responsibility to inform the appropriate university officials.

A Professional Code of Ethics

Formalized codes of ethics have yet to be developed by all professional associations involved in mass media research. In 2008, the Association for Education in Journalism and Mass Communication (AEJMC) approved a code of ethics that incorporated a section on ethics in research organized around four core values: accountability, fidelity and truth telling, justice, and caring (AEJMC, 2008). The code states that AEJMC members:

- Never plagiarize or take credit for another individual's work.

- Inform subjects of our status as researchers.

- Do not tailor studies to produce outcomes consistent with interests of funding sponsors or institutions nor ... conceal data or slant the writing of a study to satisfy an outside sponsor or funding agency.

- Protect research participants [and] treat all research participants with respect, fairness, and integrity.... We ensure that participants provide informed consent and that participation in research is not coerced.

ETHICS AND ONLINE RESEARCH

Although much of the research conducted online may not raise questions about ethics, both quantitative and qualitative researchers should be aware that the growing use of the Internet as a research medium has outpaced the efforts of researchers to establish generally accepted ethical principles regarding online research. One problem is that online research can involve a wide variety of settings, including websites, email, chat rooms, instant messages, and social media sites such as Facebook and Twitter, that are not directly addressed in existing ethical guidelines. With that in mind, the following recommendations are general suggestions to guide researchers faced with particular issues in online research.

As a starting point, it is possible to distinguish at least two different types of online research. The first can be labeled *passive research*, where researchers study the content of websites, chat rooms, message boards, social media, or blogs. The researchers may or may not identify themselves to the participants. Much qualitative research and some quantitative content analyses would fall into this area. An example of this might be a researcher who conducts a content analysis of the messages posted on the website of a particular TV show or the content contained in a sample of blogs.

The ethical problem that might arise in this situation is whether the researcher needs consent to analyze and to quote the online material. Obviously, if the site is intended to reach the general public, such as *www.cnn.com*, the material may be freely analyzed and quoted to the degree necessary in the research without consent. This situation would be analogous to analyzing the content of a newspaper or a TV newscast. For example, Greer and Ferguson (2011) content-analyzed the **Twitter** postings of 488 local TV stations.

Let's take a more concrete example. What about analyzing the posts in an online forum such as those administered by Health Boards? One such forum concerns mental health issues. Is it ethical for a researcher to publish quotes from this forum without the consent of the participants? In this situation, the researcher needs to ask: (1) Is the forum open to all? In other words, is it a public or private space? (2) Does it require registration or a password to post? (3) Does the site have a policy against quoting from its content? (4) Do participants have an expectation of privacy concerning their posts?

In this particular example, the forum requires registration, but the site also reminds users that any information posted on its public forums becomes information open for all to see, thus suggesting that it is more of a public space and that participants have little expectation of privacy. In addition, the site has no explicit policy against direct quotes, so that publishing posts without consent would appear to be ethically acceptable.

If a site requires a password or has guidelines that indicate that the members have some expectation of privacy, then a researcher should obtain the consent of the participants. However, the researcher should be aware that posting a message such as "May I record your comments for research purposes?" on a message board may not be met with a warm response. In fact, in many live chat rooms, such a request would be enough to get the researcher kicked out. In addition, if permission is granted, the researcher needs to consider whether the act of recording (and making permanent) comments from the group poses any kind of risk for the participants.

Finally, there is the problem of disguising the identities of participants. Naming the group or forum from which the quotes were taken might enable some people to identify an individual. Further, if a researcher publishes long verbatim quotes, it is possible that a search engine might be able to trace the quotes back to the person who made them. A researcher who promises confidentiality to his or her participants might employ the following safeguards:

- Do not name the group.
- Paraphrase long quotes.

- Disguise some information, such as institutional or organizational names.
- Omit details that might be harmful to individual participants.

What about analyzing the communications on social media sites, such as Twitter, Facebook, and LinkedIn? There seems to be no universal rule to apply in this situation. On the one hand, analyzing the Twitter streams of those who have chosen to make their online comments public seems to raise little ethical concern. In this situation, there seems to be little expectation of privacy, and getting informed consent would seem unnecessary. The situation with Facebook is less clear. There are various privacy settings allowed by the site that make some basic information available to all and some information only available to those who are classified as friends. For example, a person's name and profile picture are available to everyone. A person's status updates may be available only to friends. Sampling a number of Facebook sites and counting the percentage of male and female accounts would pose few ethical problems. On the other hand, as of late 2011, Facebook's privacy policy states that consent must be obtained for the use of any data from a Facebook user's page. Thus, analyzing the types of political messages sent by an individual would require consent. It is possible, however, that analyses that use a Facebook page rather than an individual message as the unit of analysis might not require consent. For example, an analysis of how many Facebook pages include photos of alcohol consumption would not require consent because the research would contain no personally identifiable data. In any case, as a general guideline, all academic researchers should consult the guidelines of their colleges and universities before embarking on a study using data from social media sites. An informal content analysis of recent studies that used individualized data from Facebook indicated that all obtained consent before gathering data. See, for example, Mehdizadeh (2010) and Butler, McCann, and Thomas (2011).

The second type of research can be thought of as *active research*, in which a researcher attempts to gather online information through online surveys, focus groups, or types of experiments. This situation poses even more ethical problems.

First, federal human-subjects rules require that researchers document informed consent from research participants. In addition, the rules also state that this documentation must be a "written form" signed by the subject. This is virtually impossible to do online. Fortunately, this requirement can be waived for research with adults that poses only minimal risks. In this case, the researcher prepares an online version of a consent form, and consent is given online by clicking a button that indicates that respondents have read and understood the form. The following demonstrate a couple of examples to indicate consent:

Please click the appropriate option below. By clicking on the "Yes" option, you are indicating that you are at least 18 years old and are giving your informed consent to be a participant in this study.

- Yes, I am giving my consent. Take me to the survey.
- No, I do not wish to participate.

I voluntarily agree to participate in this project. I understand that I can withdraw from the project at any time and that any information obtained from me during the course of my participation will remain confidential and will be used solely for research purposes. I also affirm that I am at least 18 years old.

- I agree.
- I do not wish to continue.

Some online survey construction sites, such as *surveygizmo.com* and *surveymonkey.com*, have options that allow the researcher to create a questionnaire with a page that includes a method of obtaining informed consent. Figure 3.2 contains a sample consent form for an online survey.

In some situations, it is difficult for a researcher to determine whether the participant truly understands the consent form. Some experts (Kraut et al., 2004) recommend that researchers divide the consent form into logical segments and require participants to check a "click to accept" box for each section. On the other hand, if the research project involves more than minimal risk or is to be done among those under 18, consent should still be obtained by a signature on paper (from the participants or from parents in the case of research involving minors). These consent forms can be sent to the researcher by paper mail or by fax. In addition, an assent form from minors may be required. Of course, respondents may lie about their age, and children can pretend to be their parents. To help guard against this, an investigator might require subjects to provide information that is usually available only to adults (such as a credit card number). If the risk to subjects is high, the researcher might want to consider using more traditional means to collect data.

A second difficulty is debriefing. In a traditional experimental setting, the researcher provides subjects with a full explanation of the research after the subjects have finished the experiment. In addition, if deception was involved, the investigator must explain the deception and why it was necessary. In the online setting, about the best a researcher can do is to provide a link to a debriefing page, but there is no guarantee that the subject will

---

Figure 3.2   Example of Informed Consent Form for an Online Survey

The purpose of this research is to investigate how people watch movies on television. You have been chosen at random from a list of those enrolled in this university to complete this electronic survey. Specifically, you will be asked to report how often you watch movies on TV, how you obtain them, and what devices you use to view them. The potential benefit of this study is a better understanding of the media behaviors of young people. No risks or discomforts are anticipated from taking part in this study. It will take about 10 minutes to complete the survey.

The decision to participate in this research project is voluntary. You do not have to participate, and you can refuse to answer any question. Even if you begin the web-based online survey, you can stop at any time.

Your responses will be automatically compiled in a spreadsheet and cannot be linked to you. All data will be stored in a password-protected electronic format. We will not know your IP address when you respond to the Internet survey. The results of the study will be used for scholarly purposes only. Any reports or publications based on this research will use only group data and will not identify you or any individual as being affiliated with this project.

By clicking on the "start" button below, you acknowledge that you have read this information and agree to participate in this research. You are free to withdraw your participation at any time without penalty. If you have any questions, feel free to contact [insert contact information].

A CLOSER LOOK

Ethics and Broadcast Research

A few years ago, the senior author of this text was contacted by a radio station general manager (GM) who stated, "My morning show host is a pain in the neck, and I want to fire him. I'd like you to conduct a telephone study to back up my opinions." What would you say to the GM? Would you conduct the study?

read it or understand it. In addition, what happens if subjects quit before they finish the experiment? Will they also be sent to a debriefing page?

At the technical level, as Hamilton (1999) points out, the problem of guaranteeing confidentiality becomes more complicated because some web research projects might involve a website run by some individual or organization other than the researcher. Methods for making sure that everyone who has access to the data maintains confidentiality must be worked out. Other technical issues include whether the data are collected only when the research is finished or after every question. Do respondents have the ability to delete all of their data if they change their mind halfway through the research?

Gift certificates, a chance to win an iPod, cash payments, and the like, are common incentives that are frequently used to encourage participation in the study. This creates another problem for online researchers because some means of identification must be used to contact those who receive rewards. To safeguard confidentiality, Barchard and Williams (2008) recommend that such contact information be kept in a separate location from the data collected from the main study, such as in a separate database. Research in a virtual world, such as Second Life, is also subject to ethical considerations. The site's policy requires researchers to identify themselves and get permission from participants before reporting their comments.

Hamilton (1999) suggests an appropriate set of guidelines for online research. He recommends that at a minimum an online researcher should provide the following:

- A way to contact the researcher
- A way to obtain informed consent
- Full disclosure of any risks to confidentiality
- A debriefing page
- A way for participants to obtain the results of the study

SUMMARY

Ethical considerations in conducting research should not be overlooked. Researchers should be familiar with traditional ethical theories because nearly every research study could affect subjects in some way, either psychologically or physically. Researchers who deal with human subjects must ensure that all precautions are taken to avoid any potential harm to subjects. This includes carefully planning a study and debriefing subjects upon completion of a project. Online research raises special problems concerning ethics.

Key Terms

Anonymity
Autonomy
Beneficence

Categorical
  imperatives
Concealment

Confidentiality
Debriefing
Deception
Deontological theories
Ethics
Informed consent
Institutional review
  boards
Justice
Nonmaleficence
Relativism
Relativistic
Teleological
Utilitarianism
Voluntary
  participation

 ## Using the Internet

The Internet is full of articles and discussions of research ethics. For examples and extended discussions of various ethical theories, use search terms such as *"deontological theories," "teleological theories,"* or *"consequential theories."*

Search for codes of conduct in other areas, such as medicine or anthropology. Do these codes have anything in common? What would you do if your study were condemned as unethical?

Search for IRB policies at various colleges and universities (including your own if appropriate). Are some stricter than others?

Questions and Problems for Further Investigation

1. Using the five examples in the first section of this chapter, suggest alternative ways of conducting each study that would be ethically acceptable.

2. In your opinion, what types of media research are unfair to respondents? What types of studies encroach on the guidelines discussed in this chapter?

3. In your opinion, is it wrong for researchers to give respondents the impression that they are being recruited for a particular study when the researchers actually have another purpose in mind? What are the limits to this behavior?

4. What are some other problems that might arise when doing online research? For example, do hackers pose a danger?

For additional resources go to *www.wimmer dominick.com* and *www.cengagebrain.com*.

References and Suggested Readings

AEJMC (2008). Proposed AEJMC Code of Ethics. *AEJMC Newsletter, 41*(4), 12–13.

Audi, R. (1990). The ethics of graduate teaching. In S. M. Cahn (Ed.), *Morality, responsibility and the university*, 119–133. Philadelphia, PA: Temple University Press.

Barchard, K., & Williams, J. (2008). Practical advice for conducting ethical online experiments and questionnaires for United States psychologists. *Behavior Research Methods, 40*(4), 1111–1128.

Beauchamp, T., Faden, R., Wallace, R. J., & Walters, L. (Eds.). (1982). *Ethical issues in social science research*. Baltimore, MD: Johns Hopkins University Press.

Bower, R., & deGasparis, P. (1978). *Ethics in social research*. New York, NY: Praeger.

Butler, E., McCann, E., & Thomas, J. (2011). Privacy setting awareness on Facebook and its effect on user-posted content. *Human Communication, 14*(1), 39–55.

Chew, F. (2000). Cut from the same cloth? Communications researcher ethics. *Journal of Mass Media Ethics, 15*(2), 115–127.

Christensen, L. (1988). Deception in psychological research. *Personality and Social Psychology Bulletin, 14*(4), 664–675.

Cook, S. (1976). Ethical issues in the conduct of research in social relations. In C. Sellitz, L. Wrightsman, & S. Cook (Eds.), *Research methods in social relations*. New York, NY: Holt, Rinehart & Winston.

Elmes, D. G., Kantowitz, B. H., & Roediger, H. L. (1995). *Research methods in psychology* (5th ed.). New York, NY: West Publishing.

Elms, A. (1982). Keeping deception honest. In T. Beauchamp, R. Faden, R. J. Wallace, & L. Walters (Eds.), *Ethical issues in social science research*, 239–242. Baltimore, MD: Johns Hopkins University Press.

Epstein, Y., Suedefeld, P., & Silverstein, S. (1973). The experimental contract. *American Psychologist, 28*, 212–221.

Fischer, C. (2011). A value-added role for reviewers in enhancing the quality of published research. *Journal of Scholarly Publishing, 42*(2), 226–237.

Frey, L. R., Botan, C., & Kreps, G. (2000). *Investigating communication: An introduction to research methods* (2nd ed.). Needham Heights, MA: Allyn & Bacon.

Greenberg, B. S., & Garramone, G. M. (1989). Ethical issues in mass communication research. In G. H. Stempel & B. H. Westley (Eds.), *Research methods in mass communication* (2nd ed.), 262–289. Englewood Cliffs, NJ: Prentice Hall.

Greer, C., & Ferguson, D. (2011). Using Twitter for promotion and branding. *Journal of Broadcasting & Electronic Media, 55*(2), 198–214.

Hamilton, J. (1999, December 3). The ethics of conducting social science research on the Internet. *Chronicle of Higher Education*, B6.

Hertwig, R., & Ortwig A. (2008). Deception in experiments: Revisiting the arguments in its defense. *Ethics and Behavior, 18*(1), 59–92.

Jamison, J., Karlan, D., & Schechter, L. (2008). To deceive or not to deceive. *Journal of Economic Organization & Behavior, 68*(3/4), 477–489.

Jones, J. H. (1981). *Bad blood: The Tuskegee syphilis experiment*. New York, NY: Free Press.

Kelman, H. (1967). Human use of human subjects: The problem of deception in social psychological experiments. *Psychological Bulletin, 67*, 111.

Kelman, H. (1982). Ethical issues in different social science methods. In T. Beauchamp, R. Faden, R. J. Wallace, & L. Walters (Eds.), *Ethical issues in social science research*, 40–98. Baltimore, MD: Johns Hopkins University Press.

Korn, J. H. (1988). Students' roles, rights, and responsibilities as research participants. *Teaching of Psychology, 15*(2), 74–78.

Kraut, R., Olson, J., Banaji, M., Bruckman, A., Cohen, J., & Couper, M. (2004). Psychological research online. *American Psychologist, 59*(2), 105–117.

Mann, T. (1994). Informed consent for psychological research. *Psychological Science, 5*(3), 140–143.

Mehdizadeh, S. (2010). Self-presentation 2.0: Narcissism and self-esteem on Facebook. *CyberPsychology, Behavior & Social Networking, 13*(4), 357–364.

Pascual-Leone, A., Singh, T., & Scorboria, A. (2010). Using deception ethically: Practical research guidelines for researchers and reviewers. *Canadian Psychology, 51*(4), 241–248.

Ryan, M., & Martinson, D. L. (1999). Perceived problems in evaluation of mass communication scholarship. *Journalism and Mass Communication Educator, 54*(1), 69–78.

Saslow, C. (1994). *Basic research methods*. New York, NY: McGraw-Hill.

Schiff, F., & Ryan, M. (1996). Ethical problems in advising theses and dissertations. *Journalism and Mass Communication Educator, 51*(1), 23–35.

Sieber, J. (1992). *Planning ethically responsible research*. Newbury Park, CA: Sage.

Sieber, J. (1995). Deception methods in psychology. *Ethics and Behavior, 5*(1), 67–85.

Sobal, J. (1984). The content of survey introductions and the provision of informed consent. *Public Opinion Quarterly, 48*(4), 788–793.

Strange, K. (2008). Authorship: Why not just toss a coin? *American Journal of Physiology—Cell Physiology, 295*(3), C567–C575

Stricker, L., & Messick, J. (1967). The true deceiver. *Psychological Bulletin, 68*, 1320.

Thomas, S. B., & Quinn, S. C. (1981). The Tuskegee syphilis study. *American Journal of Public Health, 81*(4), 1498–1505.

CHAPTER 4

SAMPLING

CHAPTER OUTLINE

When it comes to research, we live in a world of *small sample* statistics. This chapter describes the basics of the sampling methods used in mass media research. However, because sampling theory has become a distinct discipline in itself, there are some studies, such as national surveys, that require consultation of more technical discussions of sampling.

POPULATION AND SAMPLE

One goal of scientific research is to describe the nature of a **population**—*a group or class of subjects, variables, concepts, or phenomena*. In some cases, an entire class or group is investigated, as in a study of prime-time television programs during the week of September 10–16. The process of examining every member in a population is called a **census**.

In many situations, however, an entire population cannot be examined due to time and resource constraints. Studying every member of a population is also generally cost prohibitive and may, in fact, confound the research because measurements of large numbers of people often affect measurement quality.

The usual procedure in these instances is to take a sample from the population.

A **sample** is *a subset of the population that is representative of the entire population*. An important word in this definition is *representative*. A sample that is not representative of the population, regardless of its size, is inadequate for testing purposes because the results cannot be generalized to the population from which the sample was drawn.

The sample selection process is illustrated using a Venn diagram (Figure 4.1); the population is represented by the larger of the two circles. A census would test or measure every element in the population (A), whereas a sample would measure or test a segment of the population (A1). Although in Figure 4.1 it might seem that the sample is drawn from only one portion of the population, it is actually selected from every portion. If a sample is chosen according to proper guidelines and is representative of the population, then the results from a study using the sample can be generalized to the population. However, the results from any research study must be generalized with some caution because of the error that is inherent in all research.

Whenever a sample is drawn from a population, researchers need a way to estimate the degree to which the sample differs from the population. Since a sample does not provide the exact data that would come from a population,

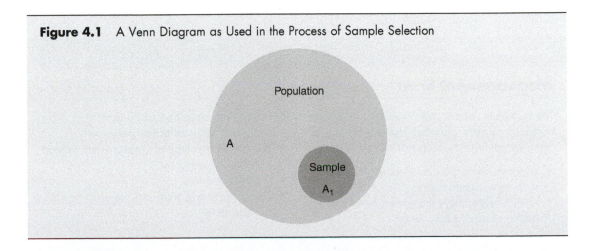

Figure 4.1 A Venn Diagram as Used in the Process of Sample Selection

Population

A

Sample

A_1

error must be taken into account when interpreting research results. Error in research, therefore, is the focus of the next section.

RESEARCH ERROR

All research is riddled with error. Much of the source of error in the behavioral sciences is that research is conducted with human subjects/respondents who constantly change. This is well understood by behavioral researchers, and it is their responsibility to control or eliminate as much error as possible from a research study, knowing that regardless of what steps are taken, some error will always be present. The ever-present error is the basis for virtually all of the tenets of scientific research discussed in Chapter 1.

Our goal in this section of the chapter is to introduce you to the major types of research error. Hopefully, the discussion will highlight the need for researchers to pay close attention to every detail in a research project.

There are two broad types of error present in all research: (1) **sampling error**, or error related to selecting a sample from a population; and (2) **nonsampling error**, which is error created by every other aspect of a research study, such as measurement errors, data analysis errors, the influence of the research situation itself, or even error from an unknown source that can never be identified and controlled or eliminated.

One form of nonsampling error, **measurement error**, is further divided into two categories: **random error** and **systematic error**. Random error relates to problems where measurements and analyses vary inconsistently from one study to another—the results may lean in one direction in one study but then lean in the opposite direction when the study is repeated at a later time. Random errors are caused by unknown and unpredictable variables and may be virtually impossible to detect and correct. On the other hand, systematic error consistently produces incorrect (invalid) results in the same direction, or same context, and is therefore predictable. Unlike random error, researchers may be able to identify the cause of systematic errors and eliminate their influence.

Media reports or discussions about research in every field often include comments such as "The research 'proved' ..." While the search for truth, or true scores, measurements, or observations, is the goal of all research, the fact is that "truth" or "true scores, measurements, or observations" are rarely found. This is because all scores, measurements, and observations include some degree of error. Research

A CLOSER LOOK

Measurement Error

Measurement error can include an almost unlimited number of items. However, some of the most common measurement errors include:

- A poorly designed measurement instrument such as a questionnaire
- Asking respondents the wrong questions or asking questions incorrectly

- Faulty data collection equipment
- Untrained data collection personnel
- Using only one type of measurement instead of multiple measures
- Data input errors
- Using the wrong statistical methodology to analyse data

results are often presented with this simple formula to show "proof" of something:

Observed score/ measurement/ observation	=	True score, measurement or observation

In reality, all research results should be reported and interpreted with this formula:

Observed score/ measurement/ observation	=	True score, measurement or observation + error

A classic example of how error can affect the results of a research study occurred during the 1936 presidential campaign. *Literary Digest* had predicted, based on the results of a sample survey, that Alf Landon would beat Franklin D. Roosevelt (FDR). Although the *Literary Digest* sample included more than a million voters, it was composed mainly of affluent Republicans. Consequently, it inaccurately represented the population of eligible voters in the election. The researchers who conducted the study had failed to consider the population **parameters** (characteristics) before selecting their sample. FDR was reelected in 1936, and it may be no coincidence that *Literary Digest* went out of business shortly thereafter.

The accuracy of presidential election polls has improved during the past few elections. The following summary table shows a selected list of companies and organizations that conducted polls prior to the 2008 contest between Barack Obama (Democrat) and John McCain (Republican).

Source	Obama%	McCain%
Actual Vote	53	46
ABC	53	43
CNN	53	45
CBS News	51	39
Fox News	49	40
Gallup	45	38

ABC and CNN were virtually on target with their numbers, but Gallup, one of the leading research polling companies, missed the actual vote even considering a margin of error of about ±4.0%. We can't expect all of the polls to agree because each company or organization uses its own research methodology. However, the differences among the 2008 polls were probably due to several controversial qualities of both parties' campaigns.

Overall, however, the polling results show that some researchers have become very good at predicting the outcome of elections. Considering the margin of error (about ±4.0%), several polls accurately predicted the 2008 presidential election results. We discuss sampling error in greater detail later in this chapter.

TYPES OF SAMPLING PROCEDURES

Researchers have a variety of sampling methods available to them. This section highlights some of the most commonly used approaches, but keep in mind that many approaches are not discussed here, and it is important for any researcher to pursue additional information about sampling to ensure that the correct sampling method is used for the research study conducted. We first need to discuss the two broad categories of sampling: probability and nonprobability.

Probability and Nonprobability Sampling

Probability sampling uses mathematical guidelines whereby each unit's chance for selection is known. Nonprobability sampling does not follow the guidelines of mathematical probability. However, the most significant characteristic distinguishing the two types of samples is that probability sampling allows researchers to calculate the amount of sampling error present in a research study; nonprobability sampling does not.

There are four issues to consider when deciding whether to use probability or nonprobability sampling:

- *Purpose of the study*. Some research studies are not designed to generalize the results to the population but rather to investigate variable relationships or collect exploratory data to design questionnaires or measurement instruments. Nonprobability sampling is appropriate in these situations.

- *Cost versus value*. A sample should produce the greatest value for the least investment. If the cost of probability sampling is too high in relation to the type and quality of information collected or the purpose of the study, then nonprobability sampling is usually satisfactory.

- *Time constraints*. In many cases, researchers collecting preliminary information operate under time constraints imposed by sponsoring agencies, management directives, or publication guidelines. Because probability sampling is often time consuming, a nonprobability sample may meet the need temporarily.

- *Amount of acceptable error*. In preliminary studies or pilot studies, where error control is not a prime concern, a nonprobability sample is usually adequate.

Although a nonprobability sample has merit in some cases, it is always best to use a probability sample when a study is conducted to support or refute a significant research question or a hypothesis and the results will be generalized to the population.

Probability sampling generally uses some type of systematic selection procedure, such as a table of random numbers, to ensure that each unit has an equal chance of being selected. However, it does not always guarantee a representative sample from the population, even when systematic selection is followed. It is possible to randomly select 50 members of the student body at a university to determine the average number of hours the students spend watching television during a typical week and, by extraordinary coincidence, end up with 50 students who do not own a TV set. Such an event is unlikely but possible, underscoring the need to replicate (repeat) any study.

Research Volunteers

The issue of volunteer respondents/subjects in behavioral research is rarely discussed. In most situations, discussions of research sampling focus on probability and nonprobability sampling, sampling methods, sampling error, and related terms. In this section, we address this extremely important element of behavioral research—research volunteers.

In reality, all behavioral research that uses respondents or subjects uses volunteers. Researchers in the behavioral sciences can only *invite* respondents or subjects to participate in a research project; they cannot force them to answer questions or participate in a research study (nor can researchers force a person to stay involved in a research project until its conclusion). However, there is a significant difference in how such respondents/subjects get into a sample.

In one case, there are no qualifications or restrictions related to who gets into a sample (known as **screener questions** in survey design). This type of sample is a totally self-selected nonprobability sample that we label an **unqualified volunteer sample**. In the second case, probability sampling is followed and the sample consists of systematically selected respondents whose names were chosen using some probability method. These people must qualify (pass) on one or more questions, such as age, sex, use of the media, and so on, to be eligible for the sample. However, even respondents in this type of sample must volunteer to participate in a research project—they cannot be forced to participate. We label this a **qualified volunteer sample**, which is an important aspect of behavioral research sampling, so let's look at the differences between the two approaches.

Unqualified volunteer sample. In this approach, researchers have no control over the respondents or subjects who participate in a research study—virtually anyone can participate. The respondents are self-selected. Unqualified volunteer samples have unfortunately become common in mass media research in the past several years, due mostly to the increased use of the Internet as a data collection tool by trained researchers and people who have no research experience. Even though unqualified volunteer samples are haphazard and produce results that might be invalid and unreliable, the sampling approach is used frequently in mass media research because little or no cost is associated with the method. When many media managers are told that the results from such studies are not scientifically credible, they ignore the warning because the interest in saving money overshadows the need for valid and reliable data.

For example, radio or TV stations invite their audiences to call the station to cast their vote about something happening on the station or perhaps a specific news item ("Call us and tell us if you agree with the mayor's decision on new parking spaces at the arena"). Or radio stations invite listeners to participate in online surveys where the respondents rate the songs the station plays, rate the announcers or DJs, or evaluate other station programming elements. Finally, many newspapers and magazines print annual polls titled something like,"The Best ..." and ask readers to vote for the best restaurant, movie theater, and so on. The data are from unqualified volunteer respondents—there are no controls over who submits the questionnaires—but the results are reported as though they represent a scientifically valid and reliable study.

There is concern in all areas of research that respondents/subjects in an unqualified volunteer sample differ greatly from respondents/subjects in a qualified volunteer sample and may consequently produce erroneous research results. Many years ago, Rosenthal and Rosnow (1969) identified the characteristics of an unqualified volunteer sample based on several studies and found that such subjects, as compared to a qualified volunteer sample, tend to exhibit higher educational levels, higher occupational status, greater need for approval, higher intelligence levels, and lower levels of authoritarianism, and they seem to be more sociable, more "arousal seeking," and more unconventional. These characteristics indicate that the use of unqualified volunteer samples may significantly bias the results of a research study and may lead to inaccurate estimates of various population parameters.

Some researchers say that the difference between unqualified and qualified volunteer respondents is not significant, and they refer to a 2005 study by Stanford University that found few differences among nine different data collection vendors. The problem is that the study did not compare the differences between the two types of volunteer groups but rather the differences between companies that use probability sampling with standard recruiting methods (telephone, etc.) and companies that use probability sampling via the Internet (Stanford University, 2005).

Qualified volunteer sample. Unlike the unqualified volunteer sample, a qualified volunteer sample is selected using probability sampling and employs controls to limit the type of person who is invited to participate in the project. The controls, which constitute a sampling frame, help eliminate spurious results from respondents who should not be involved in the study.

For example, if the management of a radio station that tries to reach men between the ages of 25 and 44 (the radio station's "target" audience, abbreviated as Men 25–44 or M 25–44) wants to conduct research on its programming elements, the research is conducted only with men who are 25–44 years old. Respondents are randomly contacted from some existing list via telephone or other contact and invited to participate. The station manager, or the research company conducting the study, controls the type of respondents who participate in the study and significantly reduces the amount of invalid data.

In addition, probability sampling methods often include procedures to handle instances where a qualified person declines to participate in a research project (known as a "qualified refusal"). If, for example, one household refuses to fill out a survey, the interviewer may be instructed to substitute the house next door. The inferential statistics discussed in later chapters assume some form of probability sampling.

The primary difference between the two types of samples, therefore, relates to the control involved over the type of person who is given the opportunity to voluntarily participate in a research study. Legitimate scientific behavioral research is conducted only with qualified volunteer samples.

Finally, all research reports should include a complete description of the sampling procedures used in the study and indicate whether the respondents/subjects represent an unqualified or qualified sample.

Types of Nonprobability Sampling

Due to one of the four reasons that make the use of nonprobability sampling acceptable (mentioned earlier in this chapter), mass media researchers frequently use nonprobability sampling, particularly in the form of available samples. An **available sample** (also known as a **convenience sample**) is a collection of readily accessible subjects, elements, or events for study, such as a group of students enrolled in an introductory mass media course or shoppers in a mall. Although available samples can be helpful in collecting exploratory information and may produce useful data in some instances, the samples are problematic because they contain unknown quantities of error. Researchers need to consider the positive and negative qualities of available samples before using them in a research study.

A CLOSER LOOK

Sampling

Sampling is an important part of all research, but sampling is often misunderstood by beginning researchers or those who know nothing about research. The usual question is "How can 500 people represent the opinions and attitudes of people in New York (or any other city)?" If you are a beginner, keep this in mind: If sampling is conducted correctly, a sample of adequate size (400–500) will usually represent the characteristics of that population.

The most important part of any sampling procedure is to avoid bias of any kind—each respondent should have an equal chance of being selected. The **sampling design** (scheme used to select respondents) *must* be free from bias.

Available samples are the subject of heated debate in many research fields. Critics argue that regardless of what results they generate, available samples do not represent the population and therefore have no external validity. The respondents are included in a study solely on the basis of their availability. For example, mall intercept studies are criticized because only the people who are at the mall at the time of the study have a chance to participate. No one outside the mall has such an opportunity. However, proponents of using available samples claim that if a phenomenon, characteristic, or trait does exist, it should exist in *any* sample.

In most situations, available samples should be avoided because of the bias introduced by the respondents' proximity to the research situation, but available samples can be useful in pretesting questionnaires or other preliminary (pilot study) work. Available samples often help eliminate potential problems in research procedures, testing, and methodology before the final research study—with an appropriately selected sample—is conducted.

Another type of nonprobability sampling that we have already mentioned is the unqualified volunteer sample, where respondents or subjects voluntarily agree to participate in a research project and are not selected according to any mathematical guidelines.

Although unqualified volunteer samples are inappropriate in scientific research, the media and many websites inappropriately legitimize volunteers through various polls or "studies" conducted for radio and television stations, TV networks, the Internet, newspapers, and magazines. The media almost daily report the results of the most current viewer, listener, or reader poll about some local or national concern.

A CLOSER LOOK

Nonprobability Sampling

One nonprobability sampling method is to select subjects based on appearance or convenience, or because they seem to meet certain requirements— subjects "look" as though they qualify for a study. Haphazard selection involves researcher subjectivity and introduces error—**sampling bias**— because the researcher usually favors selection based on certain characteristics. Some haphazard samples give the illusion of a probability sample, and these must be approached carefully. For example, interviewing every tenth person who walks by in a shopping center is haphazard because not everyone in the population has an equal chance of walking by that particular location. Some people live across town, some shop in other shopping centers, and so on.

Some researchers, research suppliers, and field services try to work around the problems associated with convenience samples in mall intercepts by using a procedure based on what is called the **Law of Large Numbers**. Essentially, the researchers interview thousands of respondents instead of hundreds. The presumption (and the sales approach used on clients) is that the large number of respondents eliminates the problems of convenience sampling and somehow compensates for the fact that the sample is not random. *It does not.* The large number approach is still a *convenience sample*. It is not a simple random sample.

The fact that a sample is large does not guarantee that the sample includes the correct respondents or elements. A huge sample can be as poor, in terms of quality, as a small sample. A large sample does not automatically guarantee a good sample.

Unethical Behavior and Unqualified Volunteer Samples

It is widely known in mass media research, particularly in radio research, that personnel from one radio station often try to sabotage the research of a competing radio station that uses the Internet and unqualified volunteer samples to collect data. How does this happen? Typically, when a radio station asks its listeners to go to the radio station's website and participate in a research study, personnel from competing research stations sign in and provide bogus answers to cause the sponsoring station to make the wrong decisions about the station and its programming. While unethical, it happens often because there is no way to identify the respondents who answer the survey or participate in the research project. Media managers have been told of this type of unethical behavior and the fact that much of the research conducted by the mass media via the Internet is bad science, but most ignore the warnings because Internet data collection costs very little or nothing at all. Cost takes precedence over valid and reliable data, but that is the reality of much of the mass media research conducted in the United States. It will continue until media managers heed the warnings of researchers who understand the problems of data collected via the Internet from unqualified volunteer samples.

Although some media spokespeople occasionally state that the polls are not scientific studies, the results are presented as though they are legitimate. The media are deceiving unwary listeners, viewers, and readers because the results are, at best, only indications, not scientific evidence or proof.

In summary, research using an unqualified volunteer sample is bad science because there is no way to know who participated in the research study. The results from any study using an unqualified volunteer sample should be considered highly questionable.

Another nonprobability sample is the **purposive sample**, which includes respondents, subjects, or elements selected for specific characteristics or qualities and eliminates those who fail to meet these criteria (as demonstrated by the example of the radio station including only men 25–44 years old in its research). In other words, the sample is deliberately selected nonrandomly. Purposive samples are used frequently in mass media studies when researchers select respondents who use a specific medium and are asked specific questions about that medium. A purposive sample is chosen with the knowledge that it is not representative of the general population. In a similar method, the **quota sample**, subjects are selected to meet a predetermined or known percentage. For example, a researcher interested in examining the differences in television use between people who own DVD players and those who do not may know that 40% of a particular population owns a DVD player. The sample the researcher selects would therefore be composed of 40% DVD owners and 60% non-DVD owners (to reflect the population characteristics).

The last nonprobability sampling method in this discussion is a method known as **snowball sampling**. (The term *snowball sampling* is used most often in academic research. In private sector research, this approach is known as *referrals*.) In either case, the method is the same. A researcher (or research company or field service) randomly contacts a few qualified respondents and then asks these people for the names of friends, relatives, or acquaintances they know who may also qualify for the research study. These referrals are then contacted to determine whether they qualify for the research. While this sampling procedure sounds legitimate, the authors of this book do not recommend the procedure for *any* legitimate research because the sample may be completely biased. A researcher may find that the sample consists only of respondents from a particular club, organization, or group.

Types of Probability Samples

The most basic type of probability sampling is the **simple random sample**, where *each subject, element, event, or unit in the population has an equal chance of being selected*. If a subject or unit is drawn from the population and removed from subsequent selections, the procedure is known as random sampling *without replacement*—the most widely used random sampling method. Simple random sampling *with replacement* involves returning the subject, element, or unit to the population so that it has a chance of being chosen another time. Sampling with replacement is often used in more complicated research studies such as nationwide surveys.

Researchers often use a table of random numbers to generate a simple random sample. For example, a researcher who wants to analyze 10 prime-time television programs out of a population of 100 programs to determine how the medium portrays elderly people can take a random sample from the 100 programs by numbering each show from 00 to 99 and then selecting 10 numbers from a table of random numbers, such as the brief listing in Table 4.1. First, a starting point in the table is selected at random. There is no specific way to choose a starting point; it is an arbitrary decision. The researcher then selects the remaining 9 numbers by going up, down, left, or right on the table—or even randomly throughout the table. For example, if the researcher goes down the

table from the starting point of 44 until a sample of 10 has been drawn, the sample would include television programs numbered 44, 85, 46, 71, 17, 50, 66, 56, 03, and 49.

Simple random samples for use in telephone surveys are often obtained by a process called **random digit dialing**, or **RDD**. One RDD method involves randomly selecting four-digit numbers (usually generated by a computer or through the use of a random-numbers table) and adding them to the three-digit exchange prefixes in the city in which the survey is conducted. A single four-digit series may be used once, or it may be added to all the prefixes.

Unfortunately, many of the telephone numbers generated by this method of RDD are invalid because some phones have been disconnected, some numbers have not yet been assigned, and so on. Therefore, it is best to produce at least three times the number of telephone numbers needed; if a sample of 100 is required, then at least 300 numbers should be generated to allow for invalid numbers.

A second RDD method that tends to decrease the occurrence of invalid numbers involves adding from one to three random digits to a telephone number selected from a phone directory or a list of phone numbers. One first selects a number from a list of telephone numbers (a directory or list purchased from a supplier). Assume that the number 448–3047 was selected from the list. The researcher then simply adds a predetermined number, say 6, to produce 448–3053; or a predetermined two-digit number, say 21, to get 448–3068; or even a three-digit number, say 112, to produce 448–3159. Each variation of the method helps to eliminate many of the invalid numbers produced in pure random number generation, because telephone companies tend to distribute telephone numbers in series, or blocks. In this example, the block "30" is in use, and there is a good chance that random add-ons to this block will be residential telephone numbers.

Table 4.1   Random Numbers Table

38	71	81	39	18	24	33	94	56	48	80	95	52	63	01	93	62
27	29	03	62	76	85	37	00	44	11	07	61	17	26	87	63	79
34	24	23	64	18	79	80	33	98	94	56	23	17	05	96	52	94
32	44	31	87	37	41	18	38	01	71	19	42	52	78	80	21	07
41	88	20	11	60	81	02	15	09	49	96	38	27	07	74	20	12
95	65	36	89	80	51	03	64	87	19	06	09	53	69	37	06	85
77	66	74	33	70	97	79	01	19	44	06	64	39	70	63	46	86
54	55	22	17	35	56	66	38	15	50	77	94	08	46	57	70	61
33	95	06	68	60	97	09	45	44	60	60	07	49	98	78	61	88
83	48	36	10	11	70	07	00	66	50	51	93	19	88	45	33	23
34	35	86	77	88	40	03	63	36	35	73	39	44	06	51	48	84
58	35	66	95	48	56	17	04	41	99	79	87	85	01	73	33	65
98	48	03	63	53	58	03	87	97	57	16	38	46	55	96	66	80
83	12	51	88	33	98	68	72	79	69	88	41	71	55	85	50	31
56	66	06	69	40	70	43	49	35	46	98	61	17	63	14	55	74
68	07	59	51	48	87	64	79	19	76	46	68	50	55	01	10	61
20	11	75	63	05	16	96	95	66	00	18	86	66	67	54	68	06
26	56	75	77	75	69	93	54	47	39	67	49	56	96	94	53	68
26	45	74	77	74	55	92	43	37	80	76	31	03	48	40	25	11
73	39	44	06	59	48	48	99	72	90	88	96	49	09	57	45	07
34	36	64	17	21	39	09	97	33	34	40	99	36	12	12	53	77
26	32	06	40	37	02	11	83	79	28	38	49	32	84	94	47	32
04	52	85	62	24	76	53	83	52	05	14	14	49	19	94	62	51
33	93	35	91	24	92	47	57	23	06	33	56	07	94	98	39	27
16	29	97	86	31	45	96	33	83	77	28	14	40	43	59	04	79

A third type of random selection involves not the telephone but rather household addresses. A. C. Nielsen uses a sampling method called **address-based sampling** (ABS) to recruit sample households. The method uses randomly selected addresses rather than telephone numbers to reach the approximately 34% of U.S. households that are not covered by other sampling methods, including cell phone–only households (about 26.6% in the

Simple Random Sampling

Advantages
1. Detailed knowledge of the population is not required.
2. External validity may be statistically inferred.
3. A representative group is easily obtainable.
4. The possibility of classification error is eliminated.

Disadvantages
1. A list of the population must be compiled.
2. A representative sample may not result in all cases.
3. The procedure can be more expensive than other methods.

Systematic Sampling

Advantages
1. Selection is easy.
2. Selection can be more accurate than in a simple random sample.
3. The procedure is generally inexpensive.

Disadvantages
1. A complete list of the population must be obtained.
2. Periodicity (arrangement or order of list) may bias the process.

United States in late 2011) and unlisted land-line telephone households.

There are several methods to develop random numbers or households, but two rules always apply: (1) each unit or subject in the population must have an equal chance of being selected and (2) the selection procedure must be free from subjective intervention by the researcher. The purpose of random sampling is to reduce sampling error; violating random sampling rules only increases the chance of introducing such error into a study.

Similar in some ways to simple random sampling is a procedure called **systematic random sampling,** in which every *n*th subject, unit, or element is selected from a population. For example, to obtain a sample of 20 from a population of 100, or a sampling rate of 1/5,

a researcher randomly selects a starting point and a **sampling interval**. Thus, if the number 11 is chosen as the starting point, the sample will include the 20 subjects or items numbered 11, 16, 21, 26, and so on. To add further randomness to the process, the researcher may randomly select both the starting point and the sampling interval. For example, an interval of 11 with a starting point of 29 generates the numbers 40, 51, 62, 73, and so on.

Systematic samples are used frequently in mass media research. They often save time, resources, and effort when compared to simple random samples. In fact, since the procedure so closely resembles a simple random sample, many researchers consider systematic sampling as effective as the simple random procedure. The method is widely used to select subjects from lists such as telephone directories or directories of organizations or groups.

The accuracy of systematic sampling depends on the adequacy of the **sampling frame,** or the complete list of members in the population. Telephone directories, including those on the Internet, are inadequate sampling frames in most cases because not all phone numbers are listed, some people have only cell phones, and some people do not have telephones at all. However, lists that include all the members of a population have a high degree of precision. Before deciding to use systematic sampling, it is necessary to consider the goals and purpose of a study and the availability of a comprehensive list of the population. If such a list is not available, then systematic sampling is not a good choice.

One major problem associated with systematic sampling is **periodicity**—the arrangement or order of the items in a population list may introduce bias into the selection process. For example, consider the problem mentioned earlier of analyzing television programs to determine how the elderly are portrayed. Quite possibly, every 10th program on the list may have aired on ABC, and the result would be a nonrepresentative sampling of the three major networks.

Periodicity also causes problems when telephone directories are used to select samples. The alphabetical listing does not allow each person or household an equal chance of being selected. One way to solve the problem is to cut each name from the directory, place them all in a "hat," and draw names randomly. Obviously, this would take days to accomplish and is not a real alternative. An easier way to use a directory is to tear the pages loose, mix them up, randomly select pages, and then randomly select names. Although this procedure does not totally solve the problem, it is generally accepted when simple random sampling is impossible. If periodicity is eliminated, systematic sampling can be an excellent sampling methodology.

Although a simple random sample is the usual choice in most research projects, some researchers do not wish to rely on randomness. In some projects, researchers want to guarantee that a specific subsample of the population is adequately represented, and no such guarantee is possible using a simple random sample. A **stratified sample** is the approach used to get adequate representation of a subsample. The characteristics of the subsample (strata or segment) may include almost any variable: age, gender, religion, income level, or even individuals who listen to specific radio stations or read certain magazines. The strata may be defined by an almost unlimited number of characteristics; however, each additional variable or characteristic makes the subsample more difficult to find, and costs to find the sample increase substantially.

Stratified sampling ensures that a sample is drawn from a homogeneous subset of the population—that is, from a population that has shared characteristics. Homogeneity helps researchers to reduce sampling error. For example, consider a research study on subjects' attitudes toward two-way, interactive cable or satellite television. The investigator, knowing that cable and satellite subscribers tend to have higher achievement levels, may wish to stratify the population according to education. Before randomly selecting subjects, the researcher divides the population into three education levels: grade school, high school, and college. Then, if it is determined that 10% of the population completed college, a random sample proportional to the population should contain 10% of the population who meet this standard. As Babbie (2010) notes:

> Stratified sampling ensures the proper representation of the stratification variables to enhance representation of other variables related to them. Taken as a whole, then, a stratified sample is likely to be more representative on a number of variables than a simple random sample.

Stratified Sampling

Advantages
1. Representativeness of relevant variables is ensured.
2. Comparisons can be made to other populations.
3. Selection is made from a homogeneous group.
4. Sampling error is reduced.

Disadvantages
1. Knowledge of the population prior to selection is required.
2. The procedure can be costly and time consuming.
3. It can be difficult to find a sample if incidence is low.
4. Variables that define strata may not be relevant.

Stratified sampling can be applied in two different ways. **Proportionate stratified sampling** includes strata with sizes based on their proportions in the population. If 30% of the population is adults ages 18–24, then 30% of the total sample will be subjects in this age group. This procedure is designed to give each person in the population an equal chance of being selected. Disproportionate stratified sampling is used to oversample or overrepresent a particular stratum. The approach is used because that stratum is considered important for marketing (targeting), advertising, or other similar reasons. For example, a radio station that targets 25–54-year-olds may have ratings problems with the 25–34-year-old group. In a telephone study of 400 respondents, the station management may wish to have the sample represented as follows: 70% in the 25–34 group, 20% in the 35–49 group, and 10% in the 50–54 group. This distribution would allow researchers to break the 25–34 group into smaller subgroups, such as males, females, fans of certain stations, and other subcategories, and still have reasonable sample sizes.

The usual sampling procedure is to select one unit or subject at a time, but this requires the researcher to have a complete list of the population. In some cases, there is no way to obtain such a list. One way to avoid this problem is to select the sample in groups or categories; this procedure is known as **cluster sampling**. For example, analyzing magazine readership habits of people in Wisconsin would be time-consuming and complicated if individual subjects were randomly selected. With cluster sampling, the state can be divided into districts, counties, or ZIP code areas, and groups of people can be selected from each area.

Cluster sampling creates two types of errors: errors in defining the initial clusters and errors in selecting from the clusters. For example, a ZIP code area may contain mostly residents of a low socioeconomic status who are unrepresentative of the rest of the state; if selected for analysis, such a group may create problems with the results. To help control such error, most researchers suggest using small areas or clusters, both to decrease the number of elements in each cluster and to maximize the number of clusters selected.

In many national studies, researchers use a form of cluster sampling called **multistage sampling**, in which individual households or people (not groups) are selected. Figure 4.2 illustrates a four-stage sequence for a

Figure 4.2 Census Tracts

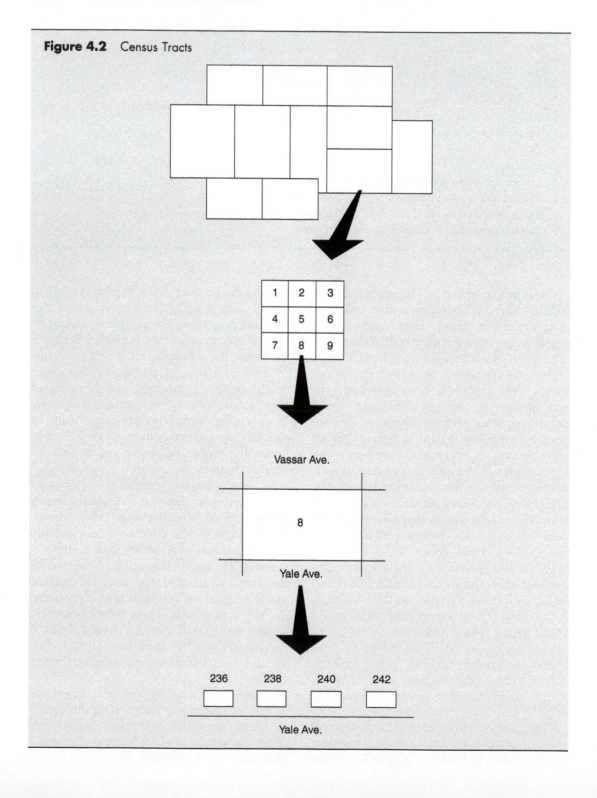

Cluster Sampling

Advantages
1. Only part of the population need be enumerated.
2. Costs are reduced if clusters are well defined.
3. Estimates of cluster parameters are made and compared to the population.

Disadvantages
1. Sampling errors are likely.
2. Clusters may not be representative of the population.
3. Each subject or unit must be assigned to a specific cluster.

nationwide survey. First, a cluster of counties (or another specific geographic area) in the United States is selected. Researchers then narrow this cluster by randomly selecting a county, district, or block group within the principal cluster. Next, individual blocks are selected within each area. Finally, a convention such as "the third household from the northeast corner" is established. Applying the selection formula in the stages just described can thus identify the individual households in the sample.

In many cases, it is also necessary to randomly select an individual in a given household. Researchers usually cannot count on being able to interview the person who happens to answer the telephone. *Demographic quotas* may be established for a research study, which means that a certain percentage of all respondents must be of a certain gender or age. In this type of study, researchers determine which person in the household should answer the questionnaire by using a form of random-numbers table, as illustrated in Table 4.2.

To obtain a random selection of individuals in the selected households, the interviewer simply asks each person who answers the telephone, "How many people are there in your home who are age 18 or older?" If the first respondent answers "Five," the interviewer asks to speak to the

Table 4.2 Example of Matrix for Selecting Respondents at Random

		Number of People in Household						
	1	2	3	4	5	6	7
	1	2	1	3	5	5	7
Person to interview:		1	3	4	3	2	6
		2	2	1	4	1
			1	2	6	4
				4	1	3
				3	2
					5

fifth-oldest person in the home. Each time a call is completed, the interviewer checks off on the table the number representing the person questioned. If the next household called also has five family members, the interviewer moves to the next number in the 5 column and asks to talk to the third-oldest person in the home.

The same table can be used to select respondents by gender; that is, the interviewer could ask, "How many men who are age 18 or older live in your home?" The interviewer could then ask for the *n*th-oldest male, according to the requirements of the survey.

Because the media are complex systems, researchers frequently encounter complicated sampling methods, known as *hybrid situations*. Consider a study that attempts to determine the potential for an interactive channel for a local newspaper on cable or satellite systems, such as the ACTIVE channel on DirecTV. This problem requires investigating readers and nonreaders of the newspaper in addition to cable/satellite subscribers and nonsubscribers. The research therefore requires random sampling from the following four groups:

Group A: Subscribers/Readers

Group B: Subscribers/Nonreaders

Group C: Nonsubscribers/Readers

Group D: Nonsubscribers/Nonreaders

The researcher must identify each subject as belonging to one of these four groups. If three variables are involved, sampling from eight groups is required, and so on. In other words, researchers are often faced with complicated sampling situations that involve numerous steps.

SAMPLE SIZE

Determining an adequate sample size is one of the most controversial aspects of sampling. How large must a sample be to provide the desired level of confidence in the results? Unfortunately, there is no simple answer. Certain sample sizes are suggested for various statistical procedures, but no single sample-size formula or method is available for every research method or statistical procedure. For this reason, we advise you to search the Internet for "*sample size*" *determining* and "*sample size*" *formula*.

The size of the sample required for a study depends on at least one or more of the following seven factors: (1) project type, (2) project purpose, (3) project complexity, (4) amount of error tolerated, (5) time constraints, (6) financial constraints, and (7) previous research in the area. Research designed as a preliminary search for general indications does not usually require a large sample. However, projects intended to answer significant questions (those designed to provide information for decisions involving large sums of money or decisions that may affect people's lives) require high levels of precision and therefore large samples.

A few general principles guide researchers in determining an acceptable sample size. These suggestions are not based on mathematical or statistical theory, but they provide a starting point in most cases.

1. A primary consideration in determining sample size is the research method used. Focus groups (see Chapter 5) use samples of 6–12 people, but the results are not intended to be generalized to the population from which the respondents are selected. Samples with 10–50 subjects are commonly used for pretesting measurement instruments and pilot studies and for conducting studies that will be used only for heuristic value. Keep in mind that it is possible to conduct numerous focus groups and have a sample equal to or greater than another research approach, such as a telephone study.

2. Researchers often use samples of 50, 75, or 100 subjects per group, or cell, such as

A CLOSER LOOK

National Sampling

Most novice researchers believe that conducting a study using a national sample is an impossible task, particularly in reference to obtaining a national sample. On the contrary, national studies are simple to conduct because dozens of survey sampling companies can provide almost any type of national sample. If you're interested in conducting a national study, search the Internet for *"survey sampling" companies*. The only thing you need to do is explain the type of respondent you're interested in interviewing or studying. The company can develop a list for you in a few hours.

adults 18–24 years old. This base figure is used to "back in" to a total sample size. For example, assume a researcher plans to conduct a telephone study with adults 18–54. Using the normal mass media age spans of 18–24, 25–34, 35–44, and 45–54, the researcher would probably consider a total sample of 400 as satisfactory (100 per age group/cell). However, the client may also wish to investigate the differences in opinions and attitudes among men and women separately, which produces a total of eight age cells. In this case, a sample of 800 would be used—100 for each of the cell possibilities. Realistically, not many clients in private-sector research are willing to pay for a study with a sample of 800 respondents (approximately $65,000 for a 20-minute telephone interview). More than likely, the client would accept 50 respondents in each of the eight cells, producing a sample of 400 (8 × 50).

3. Cost and time considerations always control sample size. Although researchers may wish to use a sample of 1,000 for a survey, the economics of such a sample are usually prohibitive. Research with 1,000 respondents can easily cost more than $75,000. Most research is conducted using a sample size that conforms to the project's budget. If a smaller sample is forced on a researcher by someone else (a client or a project manager), the results must be interpreted with caution. However, considering that reducing a sample size from 1,000 to 400 (for example) reduces the sampling error by only a small percentage, researchers may be wise to consider using smaller samples for most projects.

4. Multivariate studies require larger samples than do univariate studies because they involve analyzing multiple response data (several measurements on the same subject). One guideline recommended for multivariate studies is as follows: 50 = very poor; 100 = poor; 200 = fair; 300 = good; 500 = very good; 1,000 = excellent (Comrey & Lee, 1992). Other researchers suggest using a sample of 100 plus 1 subject for each dependent variable in the analysis (Gorsuch, 1983).

5. For panel studies, central location testing, focus groups, and other prerecruit projects, researchers should always select a larger sample than is actually required. The larger sample compensates for those subjects who drop out of research studies for one reason or another, and allowances must be made for this in planning the sample selection. High dropout rates are especially prevalent in panel studies, where the same group of subjects is tested or measured frequently over a long period of time. Researchers can expect 10–25% of the sample to drop out of a study before it is completed, and 50% or more is not uncommon.

6. Use information available in published research. Consulting other research provides a starting point. If a survey is planned and similar research indicates that a representative sample of 400 has been used regularly with reliable results, then a sample larger than 400 may be unnecessary.

7. Generally speaking, the larger the sample, the better. However, a large unrepresentative sample (the Law of Large Numbers) is as meaningless as a small unrepresentative sample, so researchers should not consider large numbers alone. Sample quality is always more important in sample selection than mere size. During our 35-plus years of research, we have found that a sample size of less than 30 in a given cell (such as females 18–24) produces unstable results.

SAMPLING ERROR

Because researchers deal with samples from a population, there must be some way for them to compare the results of (or make inferences about) what was found in the sample to what exists in the target population. However, as mentioned earlier, whenever a sample from a population is studied, the results from the sample (observed measurements) will differ to some degree from what theoretically exists in the population (expected measurements). Computing the error due to sampling provides an estimate of the difference between observed and expected measurements and is the foundation of all research interpretation.

There are two important terms related to computing errors due to sampling: (1) *standard error* (designated as *SE*) and (2) *sampling error*, which is also referred to as margin of error or confidence interval (designated as *se* or *m*, or *CI*). Standard error relates to the population and how samples relate to that population. If a large number of samples are selected from a population, the data (or statistical information) from

those samples will fall into some type of pattern. The standard error of a statistic is the standard deviation (average difference of scores from the population mean) of the sampling distribution of that statistic. Standard error is closely related to sample size—as sample size increases, the standard error decreases.

Sampling error provides an indication of how close the data from a sample are to the population mean. A low sampling error indicates that there is less variability or range in the sampling distribution.

For example, assume we wish to measure attitudes of 18–24-year-old viewers in Denver, Colorado, toward a new television program. Further, assume that all the viewers produce an average score of 6.0 on a 10-point program appeal measurement scale. Some viewers may dislike the program and rate the show 1, 2, or 3; some may find it mediocre and rate it 4, 5, 6, or 7; and the remaining viewers may like the show a lot and rate it 8, 9, or 10. The differences among the 18–24-year-old viewers provide an example of how sampling error may occur. If we asked each viewer to rate the show in a separate study and each one rated the program a 6, then no error exists. However, an error-free sample is highly unlikely.

Respondent differences do exist; some dislike the program and others like it. Although the average program rating is 6.0 in the hypothetical example, it is possible to select a sample from the population that does not match the average rating. A sample could be selected that includes only viewers who dislike the program. This would misrepresent the population because the average appeal score would be lower than the mean score. Computing the percentage of sampling error allows researchers to assess the amount of risk involved in accepting research findings as "real."

Computing sampling error is appropriate *only with probability samples*. Sampling error cannot be computed with research that uses nonprobability samples because not everyone has an equal chance of being selected. This is one reason nonprobability samples are used only in preliminary research or in studies where error is not considered as important.

Sampling error computations are essential in research and are based on the concept of the **central limit theorem**. In its simplest form, the theorem states that the sum of a large number of independent and identically distributed random variables (or **sampling distributions**) has an approximate **normal distribution**. A theoretical sampling distribution is the set of all possible samples of a given size. This distribution of values is described by a bell-shaped curve or **normal curve** (also known as a **Gaussian distribution**, after Karl F. Gauss, a German mathematician and astronomer who used the concept to analyze observational errors). The normal distribution is important in computing sampling error because sampling errors (a sampling distribution) that are made in repeated measurements tend to be normally distributed.

Computing sampling error is a process of determining, with a certain amount of confidence, the difference between a sample and the target population. Error can occur by chance or through some fault of the research procedure. However, when probability sampling is used, the incidence of error can be determined because of the relationship between the sample and the normal curve. A normal curve, as shown in Figure 4.3, is symmetrical about the mean or midpoint, which indicates that an equal number of scores lies on either side of the midpoint.

Confidence Level and Confidence Interval

Sampling error involves two concepts: **confidence level** and **confidence interval**. After a research project is conducted, the researcher estimates the accuracy of the results in terms of a level of confidence that the results lie within a specified interval. The **confidence level** indicates a degree of certainty (as a percentage) that the results of a study fall within a given range of values. Typical confidence levels are 95% and 99%. The **confidence interval** (*margin*

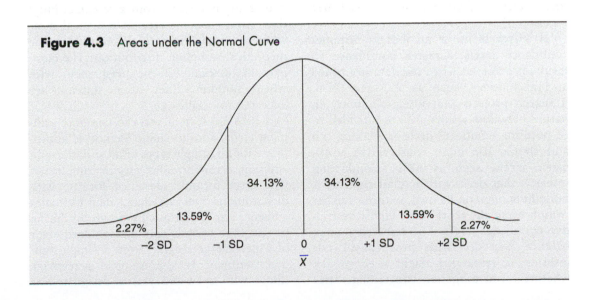

Figure 4.3 Areas under the Normal Curve

of error or *sampling error*) is a plus-or-minus percentage that is a range within the confidence level. For example, if a 5% confidence interval is used and 50% of the sample gives a particular answer for a question, the actual result for that question falls between 45% and 55% (50 ± 5).

When using the confidence level and confidence interval together, researchers using a 95% confidence level with a ±5% confidence interval can say that they are 95% sure their results are accurate within ±5%.

In every normal distribution, the standard deviation defines a standard (or average) unit of distance from the mean of the distribution to the outer limits of the distribution. These standard deviation interval units (z-values) are used in establishing the confidence interval that is accepted in a research project. In addition, the standard deviation units indicate the amount of standard error. For example, using a confidence level of +1 or −1 standard deviation unit—1 standard error—says that the probability is that 68% of the samples selected from the population will produce estimates within that distance from the population value (1 standard deviation unit; see Figure 4.3).

Researchers use a number of different confidence levels. Greater confidence in results is achieved when the data are tested at higher levels, such as 95% or 99%. Research projects that are preliminary in nature or whose results are not intended to be used for significant decision making can and should use more conservative confidence levels, such as 68%. Conducting research that deals with human subjects is difficult enough on its own, without further complicating the work with highly restrictive confidence levels. The researcher must balance necessity with practicality. For instance, a researcher might need to ask whether an investigation concerning tastes and preferences in music should be tested at a confidence level of 95% or 99%. The answer is neither. In fact, the necessity for confidence levels and confidence intervals in behavioral research is under debate. Research is often judged as good or bad depending on whether a study is "statistically significant," not on whether the study contributed anything to the advancement of knowledge. Statistical significance alone does not anoint a research project as scientific; a nonsignificant finding is as important to knowledge as a study that "finds" statistical significance.

The areas under the normal curve in Table 3 of Appendix 1 are used to determine other confidence levels. For example, the 68% confidence level (0.34 on either side of the mean) corresponds to 1.00 standard error; the 95% level corresponds to 1.96 standard errors; and the 99% interval corresponds to 2.576 standard errors. If the statistical data from the sample fall outside the range set by the researcher, the results are considered significant.

Computing Sampling Error

The essence of statistical hypothesis testing is to draw a sample from a target population, compute some type of statistical measurement, and compare the results to the theoretical sampling distribution. The comparison determines the frequency with which sample values of a statistic are expected to occur.

There are several ways to compute sampling error, and no single method is appropriate for all sample types or all situations. In addition, error formulas vary in complexity. One error formula, designed for use with dichotomous (yes/no) data, that estimates audience size for certain TV programs during certain time periods uses the standard error of a percentage derived from a simple random sample. If the sample percentage (those who answered yes) is designated as

p, the size of the sample as N, and the sampling error as se, the formula is:

$$se(p) = \sqrt{\frac{p(100-p)}{N}} \times Z \text{ for associated}$$
$$\text{confidence level}$$

Suppose a sample of 500 households produces a rating (or estimate of the percentage of viewers) of .20 for a particular show. This means that 20% of those households were turned to that channel at that time. At the 95% confidence level, which has an associated z-value of 1.96, the formula can be used to calculate the sampling error of this viewership percentage as follows:

$$se(p) = \sqrt{\frac{20(80)}{500}} \times 1.96 = \pm 3.2\%$$

At the 99% confidence level, the sampling error percentage is:

$$se(p) = \sqrt{\frac{20(80)}{500}} \times 2.57 = \pm 4.6\%$$

This information can be used to calculate confidence intervals at various confidence levels. For example, to calculate the confidence interval at the 0.68 confidence level, simply add and subtract 1 standard error from the percentage (see Table 4.3). (Note that 68% of the normal curve is encompassed by plus and minus one standard error.) Thus, we are 68% confident that the true rating lies somewhere between 18.21 (20 − 1.79) and 21.79 (20 + 1.79).

If we want to have greater confidence in our results, we can calculate the confidence interval at the 0.95 confidence level by multiplying by the associated z-value for 2 standard deviation units, which is 1.96 × $se(p)$. In our example with 500 respondents and a TV rating of 20%, the sampling error at the 95% confidence level would be ±3.50.

As mentioned earlier, sampling error is directly related to sample size. The error figure improves as the sample size is increased, but it does so in relatively small decreasing

Confidence Level %	Associated z-Value to Use in Sample Error Formula
68	1.00
95	1.96
99	2.57

Table 4.3   Finding Error Rate Using a Rating of 20 (68% Confidence Level)

Sample Size	Error	Lower Limit	Upper Limit
600	±1.63	18.37	21.63
700	±1.51	18.49	21.51
800	±1.41	18.59	21.41
900	±1.33	18.67	21.33
1,000	±1.26	18.74	21.26
1,500	±1.03	18.97	21.03

increments. Thus, a small increase in sample size does not provide a huge reduction in error, as illustrated by Table 4.3. As can be seen, even with a sample of 1,500, the standard error is only 0.75 better than with the sample of 500 computed previously. A researcher needs to determine whether the increase in time and expense created by 1,000 additional subjects justifies such a proportionally small increase in precision.

Table 4.4 shows the amount of error at the 95% and 99% confidence level for measurements that contain dichotomous variables (such as yes/no). For example, using a 95% confidence level, with a sample of 1,000 and a 30% "yes" response to a question, the probable error due to sample size alone is ±2.8. This means that we are 95% sure that our values for this particular question fall between 27.2% and 32.8%.

Sampling error is an important concept in all research areas because it provides an indication of the degree of accuracy of the research. Research studies published by large audience measurement firms such as Arbitron and A. C. Nielsen are required by the Media Rating Council (MRC) to include simplified charts to assist in determining sampling error. In addition, each company provides some type of explanation about error, such as the Arbitron statement entitled "Description of Methodology" contained in every ratings publication and in Arbitron's eBook:

> Arbitron estimates are subject to statistical variances associated with all surveys [that] use a sample of the universe…. [T]he accuracy of Arbitron estimates, data and reports and their statistical evaluators cannot be determined to any precise mathematical value or definition.

For its PPM (Portable People Meter) ratings, Arbitron's eBook states:

> PPM ratings are based on audience estimates and are the opinion of Arbitron

and should not be relied on for precise accuracy or precise representativeness of a demographic or radio market.

Statistical error due to sampling is found in all research studies. Researchers must pay specific attention to the potential sources of error in any study. Producing a study riddled with error is tantamount to never having conducted the study at all. If the magnitude of error were subject to accurate assessment, researchers could simply determine the source of error and correct it. Because this is not possible, they must accept error as part of the research process, attempt to reduce its effects to a minimum, and remember always to consider its presence when interpreting their results.

To use these tables, first find the response percentage in a column at the top of the table and find the sample size in the left column—then go across for the appropriate sampling error estimate. For example, if 50% of the respondents in a sample of 400 agree with a particular statement, the estimated amount of error associated with this answer is ±4.9%. That is, the "actual" response ranges from 45.1% to 54.9%. At the 99% confidence level, the estimated amount of error associated with the answer is ±6.4%.

FINITE POPULATION CORRECTION FACTOR

Some researchers contend that if sampling is done without replacement for a small population, it is necessary to adjust the computed sampling error by a factor known as the **Finite Population Correction Factor** (FPCF).

The usual approach is to use FPCF if the sample is more than 5% of the population. The correction factor supposedly accounts for the fact that a parameter can better be estimated from a small population when a large portion of that population's units is sampled.

Table 4.4 Sampling Error at 95% and 99% Confidence Levels

Sampling Error at 95% Confidence Level

Result is:	1% or 99%	5% or 95%	10% or 90%	15% or 85%	20% or 80%	25% or 75%	30% or 70%	35% or 65%	40% or 60%	45% or 55%	50%
Sample Size											
10	6.2	13.5	18.6	22.1	24.8	26.8	28.4	29.6	30.4	30.8	31.0
20	4.4	9.6	13.1	15.6	17.5	19.0	20.1	20.9	21.5	21.8	21.9
30	3.6	7.8	10.7	12.8	14.3	15.5	16.4	17.1	17.5	17.8	17.9
40	3.1	6.8	9.3	11.1	12.4	13.4	14.2	14.8	15.2	15.4	15.5
50	2.8	6.0	8.3	9.9	11.1	12.0	12.7	13.2	13.6	13.8	13.9
75	2.3	4.9	6.8	8.1	9.1	9.8	10.4	10.8	11.1	11.3	11.3
100	2.0	4.3	5.9	7.0	7.8	8.5	9.0	9.3	9.6	9.8	9.8
200	1.4	3.0	4.2	4.9	5.5	6.0	6.4	6.6	6.8	6.9	6.9
300	1.1	2.5	3.4	4.0	4.5	4.9	5.2	5.4	5.5	5.6	5.7
400	.98	2.1	2.9	3.5	3.9	4.2	4.5	4.7	4.8	4.9	4.9
500	.87	1.9	2.6	3.1	3.5	3.8	4.0	4.2	4.3	4.4	4.4
600	.80	1.7	2.4	2.9	3.2	3.5	3.7	3.8	3.9	4.0	4.0
700	.74	1.6	2.2	2.6	3.0	3.2	3.4	3.5	3.6	3.7	3.7
800	.69	1.5	2.1	2.5	2.8	3.0	3.2	3.3	3.4	3.4	3.5
900	.65	1.4	2.0	2.3	2.6	2.8	3.0	3.1	3.2	3.3	3.3
1,000	.62	1.4	1.9	2.2	2.5	2.7	2.8	3.0	3.0	3.1	3.1
1,200	.56	1.2	1.7	2.0	2.3	2.5	2.6	2.7	2.8	2.8	2.8
2,000	.44	.96	1.3	1.6	1.8	1.9	2.0	2.1	2.1	2.2	2.2
3,000	.36	.78	1.1	1.3	1.4	1.5	1.6	1.7	1.8	1.8	1.8
4,000	.31	.68	.93	1.1	1.2	1.3	1.4	1.5	1.5	1.5	1.5
5,000	.28	.60	.83	.99	1.1	1.2	1.3	1.3	1.4	1.4	1.4

(Continued)

Table 4.4 *(Continued)*

Sampling Error at 99% Confidence Level

Result is:	1% or 99%	5% or 95%	10% or 90%	15% or 85%	20% or 80%	25% or 75%	30% or 70%	35% or 65%	40% or 60%	45% or 55%	50%
Sample Size											
10	8.1	17.7	24.4	29.0	32.5	35.2	37.2	38.8	39.8	40.4	40.6
20	5.7	12.5	17.2	20.5	23.0	24.9	26.3	27.4	28.2	28.6	28.7
30	4.7	10.2	14.1	16.8	18.8	20.3	21.5	22.4	23.0	23.3	23.5
40	4.0	8.9	12.2	14.5	16.3	17.6	18.6	19.4	19.9	20.2	20.3
50	3.6	7.9	10.9	13.0	14.5	15.7	16.7	17.3	17.8	18.1	18.2
75	3.0	6.5	8.9	10.6	11.9	12.9	13.6	14.2	14.5	14.8	14.8
100	2.6	5.6	7.7	9.2	10.3	11.1	11.8	12.3	12.6	12.8	12.9
200	1.8	4.0	5.5	6.5	7.3	7.9	8.3	8.7	8.9	9.0	9.1
300	1.5	3.2	4.5	5.3	5.9	6.4	6.8	7.1	7.3	7.4	7.4
400	1.3	2.8	3.9	4.6	5.1	5.6	5.9	6.1	6.3	6.4	6.4
500	1.1	2.5	3.4	4.1	4.6	5.0	5.3	5.5	5.6	5.7	5.7
600	1.0	2.3	3.1	3.7	4.2	4.5	4.8	5.0	5.1	5.2	5.2
700	1.0	2.1	2.9	3.5	3.9	4.2	4.5	4.6	4.8	4.8	4.9
800	.90	2.0	2.7	3.2	3.6	3.9	4.2	4.3	4.5	4.5	4.5
900	.85	1.9	2.6	3.1	3.4	3.7	3.9	4.1	4.2	4.3	4.3
1,000	.81	1.8	2.4	2.9	3.3	3.5	3.7	3.9	4.0	4.0	4.1
2,000	.57	1.3	1.7	2.1	2.3	2.5	2.6	2.7	2.8	2.9	2.9
3,000	.47	1.0	1.4	1.7	1.9	2.0	2.2	2.2	2.3	2.3	2.3
4,000	.40	.89	1.2	1.5	1.6	1.8	1.9	1.9	2.0	2.0	2.0
5,000	.36	.79	1.1	1.3	1.5	1.6	1.7	1.7	1.8	1.8	1.8

FPCF is calculated using this formula (where N = population and n = sample size):

$$FPCF = \sqrt{\frac{N - n}{N - 1}}$$

This number is then multiplied by the sampling error values using the formula shown on page 109.

In 2007, Adam Pieniazek, a student at the University of Massachusetts in Amherst, wrote a lucid description of the value of FPCF:

> When a sample is greater than 5% of the population from which it is being selected and the sample is chosen without replacement, the finite population correction factor should be used. The adjusted z-value would be larger than the normal z-value, meaning that the value is more standard deviations from the middle than in a non-adjusted z-value.
>
> This factor adjusts the z-value to show the extra precision obtained from the sample size being a greater fraction of the population size than normal. Since the standard deviation becomes smaller as the sample size increases, the FPCF shows that a value in a large sample size not at or near the mean is a greater number of standards deviations from the mean than in a small sample size. In other words, it's rarer for a value in a large sample size to be far away from the mean compared to a small sample size.

Sample Weighting

In an ideal study, a researcher has enough respondents or subjects with the required demographic, psychographic (why people behave in specific ways), or lifestyle characteristics. The ideal sample, however, is rare due to the time and budget constraints of most research. Instead of canceling a research project because of sampling inadequacies, most researchers utilize a statistical procedure known as **weighting**, or **sample balancing**.

That is, when the subject totals in given categories do not reach the necessary population percentages, subjects' responses are multiplied (weighted) to allow for the shortfall. A single subject's responses may be multiplied by 1.3, 1.7, 2.0, or any other figure to reach the predetermined required level.

While weighting can be a useful technique in some instances, the procedure remains a highly controversial data manipulation technique, especially in broadcast ratings and some nationally recognized surveys by colleges and universities. The major questions are: (1) Who should be weighted? and (2) How much weighting should be included? Both of these areas can create research that can be considered bad science. Weighting is discussed in greater detail in Chapter 14.

SUMMARY

To make predictions about events, concepts, or phenomena, researchers must perform detailed, objective analyses. One procedure to use in such analyses is a census, in which every member of the population is studied. Conducting a census for each research project is impractical, however, and researchers must resort to alternative methods. The most widely used alternative is to select a random sample from the population, examine it, and make predictions from it that can be generalized to the population. There are several procedures for identifying the units that make up a random sample.

If the scientific procedure is to provide valid and useful results, researchers must pay close attention to the methods they use in selecting a sample. This chapter described several types of samples commonly used in mass media research. Some are elementary and do not require a great deal of time or resources; others entail great expense and time. Researchers must decide what costs and time are justified in relation to the results generated.

Sampling procedures must not be considered lightly in the process of scientific investigation. It makes no sense to develop a research design for testing a valuable hypothesis or research question and then nullify this effort by neglecting correct sampling procedures. These procedures must be continually scrutinized to ensure that the results of an analysis are not sample-specific—that is, that the results are not based on the type of sample used in the study.

Key Terms

Available sample	Purposive sampling
Census	Qualified volunteer
Central limit theorem	sample
Cluster sampling	Quota sample
Confidence interval	Random digit dialing
Confidence level	Random error
Convenience sample	Random sample
Finite Population	Sample
Correction Factor	Sample balancing
Gaussian distribution	Sample weighting
Law of Large	Sampling bias
Numbers	Sampling design
Measurement error	Sampling error
Multistage sampling	Sampling frame
Nonprobability	Sampling interval
sample	Snowball sample
Normal curve	Standard error
Normal distribution	Stratified sampling
Parameters	Systematic random
Periodicity	sampling
Population	Unqualified volunteer
Probability sample	sample
Proportionate	Volunteer sample
stratified sampling	Weighting

Using the Internet

Search the Internet for:

- "research sampling"
- "types of research samples"
- "sample size" recommendations
- "sample size" suggestions
- "random sample"
- "sampling methods" research
- sample weighting

If you need a random-number generator, search for "random number generator." Sampling error and sample size calculators are located at *www.wimmerdominick.com*.

Questions and Problems for Further Investigation

1. Using available samples in research has long been a target for heated debate. Some researchers say that available samples are inaccurate representations of the population; others claim that if a concept or phenomenon exists, it should exist in an available sample as well as in a random sample. Which argument do you support? Explain your answer.

2. Many research studies use small samples. What are the advantages and disadvantages of this practice? Can any gain other than cost savings be realized by using a small sample in a research study?

3. Which sampling technique might be appropriate for the following research projects?

   - A pilot study to test whether people understand the directions to a telephone questionnaire
   - A study to determine who buys DVD or MP3 players
   - A study to determine the demographic makeup of the audience for a local television show
   - A content analysis of commercials aired during Saturday morning children's programs
   - A survey examining the differences between newspaper readership in high-income households and low-income households

4. The average person has little understanding of research procedures, and this is why so many people are persuaded by arguments if the source simply uses the word *research* as an argument to support his or her ideas. To demonstrate this for yourself, conduct your own Jay Leno "Jaywalking" survey and ask 10 or

more people who don't know anything about research this question: If a nationwide study were conducted to find out people's ratings of a new television show, how many people do you think would be necessary to include in the study so that the results could be generalized to the entire nation? How surprised are you with your results?

5. Try to find at least five articles in mass media journals where a sample of subjects or respondents was used. Does the article provide a detailed explanation of how the sample was selected? If an unqualified volunteer sample was used, how is the value of the sample, and therefore the study itself, explained in the article?

6. Search the Internet for the poll results for the 2012 U.S. presidential election. Which polls were close to the actual vote? Which polls were not close? What are the potential problems with conducting national voting polls?

For additional resources, go to *www.wimmer dominick.com* and *www.cengagebrain.com*.

References and Suggested Readings

Note: New books on sampling are published frequently. Search the Internet for *"research sampling books"* and *"research sampling"* to find the most recent additions to the huge list of available materials.

Babbie, E. R. (2010). *The practice of social research* (12th ed.). Belmont, CA: Wadsworth/Cengage Learning.

Comrey, A. L., & Lee, H. B. (1992). *A first course in factor analysis* (2nd ed.). Hillsdale, NJ: Lawrence Erlbaum.

Fletcher, J. E. (Ed.). (1981). *Handbook of radio and TV broadcasting*. New York, NY: Van Nostrand Reinhold.

Gorsuch, R. L. (1983). *Factor analysis* (2nd ed.). Philadelphia, PA: W. B. Saunders.

Nunnally, J. C., & Bernstein, I. H. (1994). *Psychometric theory* (3rd ed.). New York, NY: McGraw-Hill.

Pieniazek, A. (2007). *Finite Population Correction Factor*. Retrieved from *www.adampieniazek.com/statistics/finite-population-correction-factor*

Rosenthal, R., & Rosnow, R. L. (1969). *Artifact in behavioral research*. New York, NY: Academic Press.

Stanford University (2005). *Comparing the results of probability and non-probability sample surveys*. Retrieved from *http://pprg.stanford.edu/current research.html*

Tukey, J. W. (1986). *The collected works of John W. Tukey* (Vols. III and IV). Belmont, CA: Wadsworth and Brooks/Cole.

Walizer, M. H., & Wienir, P. L. (1978). *Research methods and analysis: Searching for relationships*. New York, NY: Harper & Row.

CHAPTER 5

QUALITATIVE RESEARCH METHODS

CHAPTER OUTLINE

Part Two proceeds from a general discussion of research to specific research techniques. Chapter 5 discusses qualitative analysis, which relies mainly on the analysis of visual data (observations) and verbal data (words) that reflect everyday experience. Chapter 6 discusses content analysis, which focuses on words and other message characteristics but is conducted in a more systematic and measured way. Chapter 7 discusses survey research, which relies on greater quantification and greater measurement sophistication than either qualitative research or content analysis. However, this sophistication comes with a price: Increasing quantification narrows the types of research questions that can be addressed. That is, research depth is sacrificed to gain research breadth. Chapter 8 discusses longitudinal research, and, finally, Chapter 9 concludes Part Two with a discussion of experimental methods, which are among the most precise, complex, and intricate of methodologies.

AIMS AND PHILOSOPHY

Discussing the qualitative research approach can be confusing because there is no commonly accepted definition of the term *qualitative*. In fact, some qualitative researchers resist defining the term at all for fear of limiting the technique. The task is further complicated because of the several levels of reference connected with the term. The word *qualitative* has been used to refer to (1) a broad philosophy and approach to research, (2) a research methodology, and (3) a specific set of research techniques. To better understand this area, it is helpful to step back and examine some general considerations related to social science research.

Neuman (1997) and Blaikie (1993) suggest that there are three distinct approaches to social science research: positivist (or objectivist), interpretive, and critical. Each of these represents a model or a **paradigm** for research—*an accepted set of theories,*

procedures, and assumptions about how researchers look at the world. Paradigms are based on axioms, or statements that are universally accepted as true. Paradigms are important because they are related to the selection of research methodologies.

The **positivist paradigm** is the oldest and still the most widely used in mass media research. Derived from the writings of philosophers such as Comte and Mill, positivism is the paradigm most used in the natural sciences. When the social sciences developed, researchers modified this technique for their own purposes. The positivist paradigm involves such concepts as quantification, hypotheses, and objective measures. The positivist paradigm is the one that underlies the approach of this book.

Interpretive social science traces its roots to Max Weber and Wilhelm Dilthey. The aim of the **interpretive paradigm** is to understand how people in everyday natural settings create meaning and interpret the events of their world. This paradigm became popular in mass media research during the 1970s and 1980s and gained added visibility in the 1990s and the new century.

The **critical paradigm** draws on analysis models used in the humanities. Critical researchers are interested in such concepts as the distribution of power in society and political ideology. Though useful in many cases, a consideration of the critical paradigm is beyond the scope of this book. Interested readers should consult Hall (1982). At the risk of oversimplification, in the rest of this section we compare the positivist and interpretive paradigms.

The positivist paradigm differs from the interpretive paradigm along three main dimensions. First, the two approaches have a different philosophy of reality. For the positivist researcher, reality is objective; it exists apart from researchers and can be seen by all. In other words, it is out there. For the interpretive researcher, there is no single reality. Each observer creates reality as part of the research process. It is subjective and exists only in reference to the observer. Perhaps a classic example will help here. If a tree falls in a forest and there is no one there to hear it, does it make a sound? On the one hand, a positivist would answer yes—reality doesn't depend on an observer; it exists independently. On the other hand, an interpretive researcher would say no sound was made—reality exists only in the observer. Furthermore, the positivist researcher believes that reality can be divided into component parts, and knowledge of the whole is gained by looking at the parts. In contrast, the interpretive researcher examines the entire process, believing that reality is holistic and cannot be subdivided.

Second, the two approaches have different views of the individual. The positivist researcher believes that all human beings are basically similar and looks for general categories to summarize their behaviors or feelings. The interpretive researcher believes that human beings are fundamentally different and cannot be pigeonholed.

Third, positivist researchers aim to generate general laws of behavior and explain many things across many settings. In contrast, interpretive researchers attempt to produce a unique explanation about a given situation or individual. Whereas positivist researchers strive for breadth, interpretive researchers strive for depth.

The practical differences between these approaches are perhaps most apparent in the research process. The following five major research areas demonstrate significant differences between the positivist and interpretive approaches:

1. *Role of the researcher.* The positivist researcher strives for objectivity and is separated from the data. The interpretive researcher is an integral part of the data; in fact, without the active participation of the researcher, no data exist.

2. *Design.* For a positivist, the design of a study is determined before it begins. In interpretive research, the design evolves during the research and can be adjusted or changed as the research progresses.

3. *Setting.* The positivist researcher tries to limit contaminating and confounding variables by conducting investigations in controlled settings. The interpretive researcher conducts studies in the field, in natural surroundings, trying to capture the normal flow of events without controlling extraneous variables.

4. *Measurement instruments.* In positivist research, measurement instruments exist apart from the researcher; another party could use the instruments to collect data in the researcher's absence. In interpretive research, the researcher is the instrument; no other individual can substitute.

5. *Theory building.* Where the positivist researcher uses research to test, support, or reject theory, the interpretive researcher develops theories as part of the research process—theory is "data driven" and emerges as part of the research process, evolving from the data as they are collected.

A researcher's paradigm has a great influence on the specific research methods the researcher uses. As Potter (1996) explains, "Two scholars who hold different beliefs [paradigms] … may be interested in examining the same phenomenon but their beliefs will lead them to set up their studies very differently because of their differing views of evidence, analysis and the purpose of the research" (p. 36). The positivist approach is most closely associated with quantitative content analysis, surveys, and experiments, techniques discussed in detail in subsequent chapters. The interpretive approach is most closely connected with the specific research methods discussed in this chapter. Research methods, however, are not conscious of the philosophy that influenced their selection. It is not unusual to find a positivist using focus groups or intensive interviewing, two methods commonly categorized as qualitative, in connection with a quantitative study. Nor is it rare to find an interpretive researcher using numbers from a survey or content analysis. Thus, the guidelines for focus groups discussed in this chapter, or the discussion of survey research in a subsequent chapter, are relevant to both paradigms. Although the methods may be the same, the research goal, the research question, and the way the data are interpreted are quite different.

To use a concrete example, assume that a positivist researcher is interested in testing the hypothesis that viewing negative political ads increases political cynicism. The researcher conducts focus groups to help develop a questionnaire that measures cynicism and exposure to what is defined as *negative advertising*. A statistical analysis is then conducted to determine if these two items are related and if the hypothesis is supported.

An interpretive researcher interested in the same question might also conduct focus groups, but the questions discussed in the groups concentrate on how group members interpret a political ad, what meanings they derive from a negative ad, the context of their viewing, and what makes them feel cynical toward politics. The focus groups stand alone as the source of data for the analysis. The interpretive researcher uses induction to try to find commonalities or general themes in participants' remarks. Thus, both researchers use focus groups, a method traditionally defined as qualitative, but each uses the method somewhat differently.

Despite the differences, many researchers now use a combination of the quantitative and qualitative approaches to understand fully the phenomenon they are studying. As Miles and Huberman (1994) state:

> It is getting harder to find any methodologists solidly encamped in one epistemology or the other. More and more "quantitative" methodologists … are using naturalistic and phenomenological approaches to complement tests, surveys, and structured

A CLOSER LOOK

Methodology and Methods

The words *methodology* and *methods* are sometimes confused. Methodology is the study of methods and the underpinning philosophical assumptions of the research process itself. Different research questions suggest different methodologies. A researcher interested in how the Internet affects copyright laws would probably choose the methodology of legal research. A researcher who wants to trace how radio programming has evolved since the introduction of television would probably choose historical methodology. A study about the effects of television on children might use scientific methodology. In short, methodology deals with the question of "why" to do research in a certain way. It is a guide to what problems are worth investigating and how the research should proceed.

Different methodologies are associated with different paradigms. Quantitative methodology generally adopts the positive paradigm, whereas qualitative researchers promote the critical paradigm. Those who accept the critical paradigm generally follow the methodology of the humanities.

In contrast, a method is a specific technique for gathering information following the assumptions of the chosen methodology. Researchers who choose the positivist paradigm will use such methods as surveys and experiments, whereas those who choose the interpretive paradigm will rely on methods such as focus groups, ethnography, and observation.

interviews. On the other side, an increasing number of ethnographers and qualitative researchers are using predesigned conceptual frameworks and prestructured instrumentation.... Most people now see the world with more ecumenical eyes. (p. 20)

In past years, an occasional "turf war" between the two approaches has erupted (Kover, 2008). In the authors' opinion, framing the debate as the qualitative *versus* the quantitative approach is not productive. It is more useful to look at ways the two methodologies can be integrated. As Neill (2007) puts it, "More good can come of social science researchers developing skills in both realms than debating which method is superior." In fact, recent developments suggest that many researchers have adopted the ecumenical perspective of Miles and Huberman. Although it has yet to become widely used in mass media research, a new approach, called "mixed methods" (see below) has become popular in many of the social sciences.

Although qualitative research can be an excellent way to collect and analyze data, researchers must keep in mind that the results of such studies have interpretational limits if sample sizes are small. Researchers interested in generalizing results should use large samples or consider other methods. However, in most cases qualitative research studies use small samples—respondents or informants that are not necessarily representative of the population from which they are drawn. Like quantitative research, qualitative research is a useful mass media research tool only when its limitations are recognized. All too often, the results from small-sample qualitative projects are interpreted as though they had been collected with large-sample quantitative techniques. This approach can only cause problems.

A CLOSER LOOK

Qualitative Research Definition—A Final Note

Although most qualitative research projects use small samples that eliminate a researcher's ability to generalize the results to the population, the truth is that it is easy to increase sample size to avoid this problem. This is often done in both private- and public-sector research and therefore eliminates the primary argument against using qualitative research. So what's the problem?

If large sample sizes are used, then the difference between qualitative research and quantitative research must relate to something else. It does—it relates to how questions are asked. When all the clouds of controversy are eliminated, the difference between qualitative research and quantitative research boils down to this:

- Qualitative research uses a flexible questioning approach. Although a basic set of questions is designed to start the project, the researcher can change questions or ask follow-up questions at any time.

- Quantitative research uses a static or standardized set of questions. All respondents are asked the same questions. Although follow-up questions (and skips) can be designed into a questionnaire, they must be included in the questionnaire or measurement instrument before the research project begins. Interviewers conducting the interview are not allowed to stray from the questionnaire.

MIXED METHODS RESEARCH

As defined by Creswell (2003), a **mixed methods** approach is one in which the researcher collects, analyzes, and integrates both quantitative and qualitative data in a single study or multiple studies in a sustained program of inquiry. The mixed methods approach draws from the strengths of both qualitative and quantitative techniques. Researchers who advocate this approach are less interested in debating whether quantitative philosophy is compatible with qualitative philosophy and are more interested in using the approach, or combination of approaches, that works best in examining the research question.

There are several models of how mixed methods research may be designed. Figure 5.1, adapted from Creswell (2007), shows three basic approaches. A qualitative approach is abbreviated QUAL, while QUAN denotes a quantitative approach.

In the concurrent design, both qualitative and quantitative data are collected at the same time and both are weighted equally in analysis and interpretation. An example might be a survey questionnaire or interview that contains both closed-ended quantitative items and open-ended qualitative items.

In the sequential designs, one method precedes the other. For example, a researcher might conduct focus groups that generate items to be used in a subsequent survey, or a researcher may follow up a survey by conducting intensive interviews with some of the respondents in order to more fully understand the results.

The mixed methods approach has several advantages. First, the technique can produce stronger evidence for a conclusion through a convergence of findings (akin to the triangulation notion mentioned in Chapter 2). Second, a researcher can answer a broader range of research questions because the research is not confined to a single method. Finally, the technique can provide information and insight that might be missed if only a single method were used.

There are disadvantages, as well. As is obvious, mixed methods research requires more time and effort because the researcher is actually conducting two studies. In addition, the technique requires the researcher to be skilled in both qualitative and quantitative methods. If these skills are lacking, it might require a research team. Lastly, data analysis might be more difficult, particularly if the methods yield conflicting results.

Although still relatively rare in mass media research, studies using the mixed methods approach are beginning to appear in mass communication journals. See, for example, Lieberman, Neuendorf, Denny, Skalski, and Wang (2009); Greenwood (2010); and Gunther, Kautz, and Roth (2011). Those

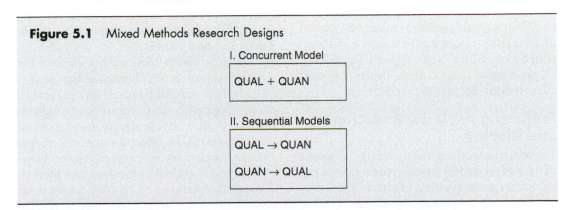

Figure 5.1 Mixed Methods Research Designs

I. Concurrent Model

QUAL + QUAN

II. Sequential Models

QUAL → QUAN

QUAN → QUAL

readers who want to examine more examples should consult the *Journal of Mixed Methods Research* and search the Internet for *"mixed methods research."*

DATA ANALYSIS IN QUALITATIVE RESEARCH

Before examining some specific types of qualitative research, let's discuss qualitative data and methods of analysis in general. Qualitative data come in a variety of forms, such as notes made while observing in the field, interview transcripts, documents, diaries, and journals. In addition, a researcher accumulates a great deal of data during the course of a study. Organizing, analyzing, and making sense of all this information pose special challenges for the researcher using qualitative methods.

Unlike the quantitative approach, in which analysis does not begin until all the numbers are collected, data analysis in qualitative studies is done early in the collection process and continues throughout the project. In addition, quantitative researchers generally follow a deductive model in data analysis: Hypotheses are developed prior to the study, and relevant data are then collected and analyzed to determine whether the hypotheses are confirmed. In contrast, qualitative researchers use an inductive method: Data are collected relevant to some topic and are grouped into appropriate and meaningful categories; explanations emerge from the data. The remainder of this section follows a modified version of the phases of qualitative data analysis suggested by Miles and Huberman (1994): (1) data reduction, (2) data display, (3) conclusion drawing, and (4) verification.

Preparing the Data: Reduction and Display

To facilitate working with the large amounts of data generated by a qualitative analysis, the researcher generally first organizes the information along a temporal dimension. That is,

the data are arranged in chronological order according to the sequence of events that occurred during the investigation. Furthermore, each piece of information is coded to identify the source, and multiple photocopies and computer files of the notes, transcripts, and other documents are mandatory.

The data are then organized into a preliminary category system. These categories might arise from the data or they might be suggested by prior research or theory. Many researchers prefer to do a preliminary run-through of the data and record possible category assignments in the margins. For example, a qualitative study of teenage radio listening might produce many pages of interview transcripts. The researcher would read the comments and might write "peer group pressure" next to one section and "escape" next to another. When the process is finished, a preliminary category system may emerge from the data. Other researchers prefer to make multiple copies of the data, cut them into coherent units of analysis, and physically sort them into as many categories as might be relevant. Finally, some of the toil in qualitative data analysis can be made easier by commercial software programs. Some that are widely used include NVivo, a program that allows users to import, sort, and analyze video and audio files, photos, and text documents and to display results in models and charts; and HyperRESEARCH, a similar program that enables a researcher to code, retrieve, and build models using data from audio, video, and text sources.

Many qualitative researchers like to have a particular room or other space that is specially suited for the analysis of qualitative data. Typically, this room has bulletin boards or other arrangements for the visual display of data. Photocopies of notes, observations written on index cards, large flowcharts, and marginal comments can then be conveniently arrayed to simplify the analysis task. Because it is an efficient way to display

A CLOSER LOOK

Software for Qualitative Data Analysis

Software can help ease the labor-intensive task of analyzing qualitative data. Current programs can provide simple word counts, isolate themes, show interconnections among the data, and produce graphical displays. Many programs also provide the option for the researcher to add comments and marginal notes to the data. Listed below are the names and URLs of some of the more popular qualitative data analysis programs. (This information was current as of late 2011.) Note that the first two on the list are free but have limited capability. The others offer a free trial period.

Weft QDA	http://www.pressure.to/qda/
QDAP	http://www.umass.edu/qdap/
ATLAS	http://www.atlasti.com/
NVivo	http://www.qsrinternational.com/#tab_you
HyperRESEARCH	http://researchware.com/
Ethnograph	http://qualisresearch.com/

the data to several people at once, this "analytical wallpaper" approach is particularly helpful when there are several members of the research team working on the project.

Finally, the researcher is the main instrument in qualitative data collection and analysis and therefore must prepare before beginning the task of investigation. Maykut and Morehouse (1994) describe this preparation as **epoche**, the process by which the researcher tries to remove or at least become aware of prejudices, viewpoints, or assumptions that might interfere with the analysis. Epoche helps the researcher put aside personal viewpoints so that the phenomenon under study may be seen for itself.

Data Analysis: Conclusion Drawing

Qualitative data can be analyzed with many different techniques. This section discusses two of the best known: the constant comparative technique and the analytical induction technique.

The **constant comparative technique** (frequently called Grounded Theory) was first articulated by Glaser and Strauss (1967) and

has subsequently been refined (Lincoln & Guba, 1985). At a general level, the process consists of four steps:

1. Comparatively assigning incidents to categories
2. Elaborating and refining categories
3. Searching for relationships and themes among categories
4. Simplifying and integrating data into a coherent theoretical structure

Comparative assignment of incidents to categories. After the data have been prepared for analysis, the researcher places each unit of analysis into a set of provisional categories. As each new unit is examined, it is compared to the other units previously assigned to that category to see whether its inclusion is appropriate. It is possible that some initial categories may have only one or two incidents assigned to them, whereas others may have a large number. If some units of analysis do not fit any preexisting category, new classifications may have to be created. Units that fit into more than one category should be copied and included where relevant. Throughout the process, the emphasis is on comparing units and finding similarities among the units that fit into the category.

For example, suppose a researcher is conducting a qualitative study about why individuals join social networking sites such as Facebook or Twitter. Interviews are conducted with several people and transcribed. The researcher then defines each individual assertion as the unit of analysis and writes each statement on an index card. The first two cards selected for analysis mention keeping in touch with current friends. The researcher places both of these into a category tentatively labeled "interpersonal connections." The next statement mentions social pressure to belong to a group; it does not seem to belong to the first category and is set aside. The next card mentions finding out about what old high school acquaintances are doing. The researcher decides this reason is similar to the first two and places it in the interpersonal connections category. The next comment talks about not wanting to be left out. The researcher believes that this comment, like the earlier one, reflects social pressure and starts another category called "peer pressure." The process is repeated with every unit of analysis, which can be a long and formidable task. However, at some point during the process, the researcher begins to refine the categories.

Elaboration and refinement of categories. During the category refinement stage, the researcher writes rules or propositions that attempt to describe the underlying meaning that defines the category. Some rules for inclusion might be rewritten and revised throughout the study. These rules help to focus the study and also allow the researcher to start to explore the theoretical dimensions of the emerging category system. The ultimate value of these rules is that they reveal what the researcher learns about a chosen

topic and help determine the research outcome.

After scanning all the data cards in the "interpersonal connections" category, a researcher might write a proposition such as "People subscribe to social networking websites to expand their circle of casual friends." Similar statements are written for the other categories.

Searching for relationships and themes among categories. The third phase of the method involves searching for relationships and common patterns across categories. The researcher examines the propositional statements and looks for meaningful connections. Some propositions are probably strong enough to stand alone; others might be related in several important ways. Whatever the situation, the goal of this phase is to generate assertions that can explain and further clarify the phenomenon under study.

In our online example, the researcher might note that several propositions refer to the notion of expansion. People use social networking sites to expand their circle of friends, or to expand their sources of new music, or to expand the number of groups to which they belong. The analyst then generalizes that the expansion of one's social and cultural space is an essential reason for joining.

Simplifying and integrating data into a coherent theoretical structure. In the final phase of the process, the researcher writes a report that summarizes the research. The results of the foregoing analyses are integrated into some coherent explanation of the phenomenon. The researcher attempts to write a brief explanation, but in sufficient detail to convey an idea of the scope of the project. The goal of this phase of the project is to arrive at an understanding of the people and events being studied.

The **analytic induction strategy** blends hypothesis construction and data analysis. It consists of the following steps (adapted from Stainback & Stainback, 1988):

1. Define a topic of interest and develop a hypothesis.
2. Study a case to see whether the hypothesis works. If it doesn't work, reformulate it.
3. Study other cases until the hypothesis is in refined form.
4. Look for "negative cases" that might disprove the hypothesis. Reformulate again.
5. Continue until the hypothesis is adequately tested.

Note that in this method, an explanation for the phenomenon, in the form of a hypothesis, is generated at the beginning of the study. This process contrasts with the constant comparative technique, in which an explanation is derived as the result of the research.

A simplified example demonstrates how the analytic induction approach works. Suppose that a researcher is interested in explaining why people watch home-shopping channels. Colleagues tell the researcher that the answer is obvious: People watch because they want to buy the merchandise. The researcher is not convinced of this but decides to use the explanation as an initial hypothesis and finds a person who is known to be a heavy viewer of these channels. During the interview, the person says that although she has ordered a couple of things off the air, her primary reason for watching is to find out about new and unusual products.

Armed with this information, the researcher reformulates the hypothesis: People watch the home-shopping channels to buy and find out about new products. Another viewer is interviewed and reports essentially the same reasons, but also adds that he uses the prices advertised on the channel to comparison shop. Once again, the hypothesis is refined. The researcher posits that the home-shopping channels are viewed for practical, consumer-related reasons: finding bargains, learning about products, and comparing prices.

At this point, the researcher tries to find cases that might not fit the new hypothesis. A colleague points out that all the people interviewed so far have been affluent, with substantial disposable income, and that perhaps people who are less well-off economically might watch the home-shopping channels for other reasons. The researcher interviews a viewer from a different economic background and discovers that this person watches because he finds the salespeople entertaining to watch. Once again, the initial hypothesis is modified to take this finding into account.

The researcher then finds other respondents from different economic levels to check the validity of this new hypothesis and continues to gather data until no more cases can be located that do not fit the revised hypothesis.

This process can be exhausting, and it can be difficult for the researcher to determine an exact stopping point. One might always argue that there are still cases in the environment that would not support the hypothesis, but the researcher simply did not find them.

Verification: Reliability and Validity in Qualitative Data

Qualitative researchers must pay attention to several different concerns that may call the credibility of their research into question. First, there is the matter of the completeness of the data. If qualitative researchers do a sloppy job taking notes or otherwise recording what was observed, there is the possibility that incorrect interpretations may be drawn from the data. A second problem concerns selective perception. Qualitative researchers cannot simply dismiss data that do not fit a favored interpretation of the data. They must analyze these cases and offer explanations as to why the data don't seem to fit. Finally, qualitative research often raises the question of **reactivity**—when the act of observing some situation changes the situation itself. Would the same things have occurred if researchers were not there? Reactivity is a difficult problem to overcome, but researchers must try to minimize it whenever possible. Taken together, these three factors suggest that qualitative researchers, much like quantitative researchers, must pay attention to the reliability and validity of their data.

However, the concepts of reliability and validity have different connotations for qualitative data. As we discuss later, quantitative methods use distinct and precise ways to calculate indexes of reliability and several articulated techniques that help establish validity. Yet these concepts do not translate well into the interpretive paradigm. As Lindlof (2002) points out, interpretive research recognizes the changing nature of behavior and perception over time. Nonetheless, though envisioned differently, reliability and validity are no less important in qualitative research. They help readers determine how much confidence can be placed in the results of the study and whether they can believe the researcher's conclusions. Or, as Lindlof (1995) says, "Basically, we want to inspire confidence in readers (and ourselves) that we have achieved right interpretations" (p. 238). Or, as Hammersly (1992) expressed it, validity is achieved when the description of the observed phenomenon accurately depicts what was observed.

Rather than emphasizing reliability and validity, Maykut and Morehouse (1994) address the trustworthiness of a qualitative research project. They summarize four factors that help build credibility:

1. *Multiple methods of data collection.* This factor is similar to the notion of triangulation that was discussed in Chapter 2. The use of interviews along with field observations and analysis of existing documents suggests that the topic was examined from several different perspectives, which helps build confidence in the findings.

2. *Audit trail.* This factor is essentially a permanent record of the original data used for analysis and the researcher's comments and analysis methods. The **audit trail** allows others to examine the thought processes involved in the researcher's work and allows them to assess the accuracy of the conclusions.

3. *Member checks.* In this technique, research participants are asked to read a researcher's notes and conclusions and tell whether the researcher has accurately described what they were told.

4. *Research team.* This method assumes that team members keep each other honest and on target when describing and interpreting data. When appropriate, an outside person is asked to observe the process and raise questions of possible bias or misinterpretation.

Creswell (2007) suggests another method to aid verification—*debriefing*. This consists of having an individual outside the project question the meanings, methods, and interpretations of the researcher. If more detail is needed, Onwuegbuzie and Leech (2006) describe 24 methods for assessing the validity of qualitative research.

Barusch, Gringeri, and George (2011) provide evidence of the relative use of the above verification techniques. They studied 100 articles that used qualitative methods and found that 60% used multiple methods of data collection, 31% used member checks, the same percentage used the research team method, while 9% used an audit trail. Debriefing was the least common at 7%.

IN-PERSON VS. ONLINE

While the Internet has opened new possibilities for qualitative researchers, there are advantages and disadvantages involved. Let's take a broad-spectrum look at the general strengths and weaknesses of online qualitative research and in-person qualitative research. Note that the strength of one approach is usually a weakness in the other. With in-person qualitative research:

- The data are "richer," in that observers can see the physical responses and surroundings of their respondents. Body language and facial expressions can add to understanding.
- Respondents do not need special computer or keyboarding skills.
- Projective tests and product demonstrations are possible.
- Group dynamics can offer clues to analysis and interpretation.
- The researcher is an integral part of the data collection.

With online qualitative research:

- Coverage of wide geographic areas is possible. Neither the respondent nor the researcher has to be in the same spot.
- The online behavior of large groups (for example Facebook users) can be observed.
- Responses may be more thoughtful and contain more information. Recruiting busy respondents is easier since the research can take place at the respondents' convenience.
- There is no bias for or against vocal or outgoing respondents.
- Expenses are often substantially lower than other approaches.

Both approaches have inherent strengths and weaknesses. The choice of which method to use depends primarily on the research question and the objectives of the research. And, of course, it is always possible to combine elements of both approaches. An online focus group might suggest a follow-up participant observation study in real life. The balance of this chapter discusses five common qualitative techniques: field observation, focus groups, intensive interviews, case studies, and ethnography. For each method, we describe the traditional procedures and then examine their online counterparts.

FIELD OBSERVATION

Field observation is useful for collecting data and for generating hypotheses and theories. Like all qualitative techniques, it is concerned more with description and explanation than with measurement and quantification. Figure 5.2 shows that field observations are classified along two major dimensions: (1) the degree to which the researcher participates in the behavior under observation and (2) the degree to which the observation is concealed.

Quadrant 1 in Figure 5.2 represents overt observation. In this situation, the researcher is identified when the study begins, and those under observation are aware that they are being studied. Furthermore, the researcher's role is only to observe, refraining from participation in the process under observation. Quadrant 2 represents overt participation. In this arrangement, those being observed also know the researcher, but unlike the situation represented in Quadrant 1, the researcher goes beyond the observer role and becomes a participant in the situation. Quadrant 3 represents the situation where the researcher's role is limited to that of observer but those under observation are not aware they are being studied. Quadrant 4 represents a study in which the researcher participates in the process under investigation but is not identified as a researcher.

Figure 5.2   Dimensions of Field Observation

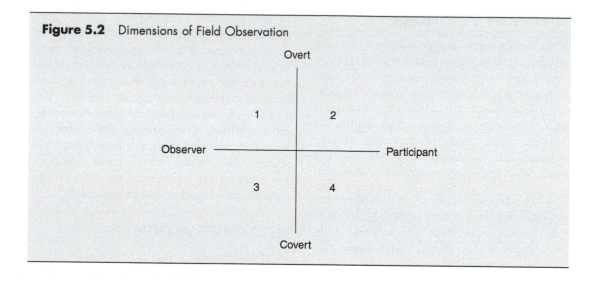

To illustrate the differences among the various approaches, assume that a researcher wants to observe and analyze the dynamics of writing comedy for television. The researcher could choose the covert observer technique and pretend to be doing something else (such as fixing a computer) while actually observing the TV writing team at work. Or the researcher could be introduced as someone doing a study of comedy writing and watch the team in action. If the research question is best answered by active participation, the researcher might be introduced as a researcher, but still participate in the writing process. If the covert participant strategy is used, the researcher might be introduced as a new writer just joining the group (such an arrangement might be made with the head writer, who would be the only person to know the identity of the researcher). The choice of technique depends on the research problem, the degree of cooperation available from the group or individual observed, and ethical considerations. While covert participation may affect subjects' behavior and raise the ethical question of deception, the information gathered may be more valid if subjects are unaware of being scrutinized.

Some examples of field observation studies in mass media research include Gieber's (1956) classic study of gatekeeping (information flow) in the newsroom and Epstein's (1974) description of network news operations. Bielby, Harrington, and Bielby (1999) observed meetings of soap opera fan clubs in their study of the way fans relate to soap opera characters. Smith and Krugman (2010) did in-home observations of how people used their digital video recorders, and Christie (2009) observed how people used new communication technologies in bookstore-cafes.

Advantages of Field Observations

Although field observation is not an appropriate technique for every research question, it does have several unique advantages. For one thing, many mass media problems and questions cannot be studied using any other methodology. Field observation often helps the researcher define basic background information necessary to frame a hypothesis and to isolate independent and dependent variables. For example, a researcher interested in how creative decisions in advertising are made could observe several decision-making sessions to see what happens. Field observations often make excellent pilot studies because they identify important variables and provide useful preliminary information. In addition, because the data are gathered firsthand, observation is not dependent on the subjects' ability or willingness to report their behavior. For example, young children may lack the reading or verbal skills necessary to respond to a questionnaire concerning their TV viewing behavior, but such data are easily gathered by the observational technique.

A field observation is not always used as a preliminary step to other approaches. Sometimes it alone is the only appropriate approach, especially when quantification is difficult. Field observation is particularly suitable for a study of the gatekeeping process in a network television news department because it is difficult to quantify gatekeeping.

Field observation may also provide access to groups that would otherwise be difficult to observe or examine. For example, a questionnaire sent to producers of X-rated movies is not likely to have a high return rate. An observer, however, may be able to establish mutual trust with such a group and persuade them to respond to rigorous questioning.

Field observation is usually inexpensive. In most cases, it requires only writing materials or a small audio or video recorder. Expenses increase if the problem under study requires several observers and extensive travel. Perhaps the most noteworthy advantage of field observation is that the study takes place in the natural setting of the activity being observed and thus can provide data rich in detail and subtlety. Many mass media situations, such as a family watching television, are complex and constantly subjected to intervening influences. Because of the opportunity for careful examination, field observation allows observers to identify these otherwise unknown variables.

Disadvantages of Field Observations

On the negative side, field observation is a poor choice if the researcher is concerned with external validity. Validation is difficult partly because the representativeness of the observations made is potentially questionable and partly because of problems in sampling. Observing the TV viewing behavior of a group of children at a daycare center can provide valuable insights into the social setting of television viewing, but it probably has little correlation with what preschoolers do in other places and under different circumstances. Besides, since field observation relies heavily on a researcher's perceptions and judgments and on preconceived notions about the material under study, experimenter bias may favor specific preconceptions of results, while observations to the contrary are ignored or distorted. Potential bias is why it is rare to use only one observer in a field observation study—observations should be *cross-validated* by second or third observers.

Finally, field observations suffer from the problem of reactivity. The very process of being observed may influence the behavior under study. Of course, reactivity can be a problem with other research methods, but it is most often mentioned as a criticism of field observation (Chadwick, Bahr, & Albrecht, 1984). Lull (1985) provides perspective on observer effects using data taken from an observational study of families' TV viewing behavior. He found that the presence of an observer in the house did have some impact on behavior. About 20% of parents and 25% of children reported that their overall behavior was affected by the presence of an observer. Most of those who were affected thought that they became nicer or more polite and formal because of the observer's presence. As for differences in the key behavior under study, 87% said that the observer's presence had no effect on their TV viewing activity. Additionally, among those who reported an observer effect, there were no systematic differences in the distribution of changes. About the same number said that they watched more because of the observer as said they watched less. Obviously, additional studies of different groups in different settings are needed before this problem is fully understood, but Lull's data suggest that although reactivity is a problem with observational techniques, its impact may not be as drastic as some suggest.

In any case, at least two strategies are available to diminish the impact of selective perception and reactivity. One is to use several observers to cross-validate the results. A second strategy is triangulation, or supplementing observational data with data gathered by other means (for example, questionnaires or existing records). Accuracy is sought by using multiple data collection methods.

Field Observation Techniques

There are at least six stages in a typical field observation study: choosing the research site, gaining access, sampling, collecting data, analyzing data, and exiting.

Choosing the research site.   The nature of the research question or area of inquiry usually suggests a behavior or a phenomenon of interest. Once it is identified, the next step is to select a setting where the behavior or phenomenon occurs with sufficient frequency to make observation worthwhile. The settings also should fit the recording forms and instruments the observer plans to use. For example, video recording usually requires adequate lighting for best results.

Possible research venues can be identified from personal experience, from talking with other researchers, from interviews with people who frequent the site, or from newspaper and magazine stories. Anderson (1987) suggests that researchers select two or three

research sites and then "hang around" (Anderson's terminology) each one to discover their main advantages and disadvantages. He cautions researchers that the site must be permanent and stable enough to permit observations over a period of time. Lindlof (1995) suggests a similar process that he labels "casing the scene." He suggests that researchers gain an understanding of what is possible from a site and make sure that the site holds the potential for fruitful data collection.

Qualitative researchers should avoid choosing sites where they are well known or have some involvement in the area. Studying one's own workplace, for example, is difficult because the researcher's preconceptions may preclude observations that are more objective. Furthermore, at a site where the researcher is a familiar figure, other individuals may find it difficult to relate to a colleague or friend in the role of researcher.

Gaining access.   Once the site is selected, the next step is to establish contact. Williamson, Karp, and Dalphin (1992) note that the degree of difficulty faced by researchers in gaining access to settings depends on two factors: (1) how public the setting is and (2) the willingness of the subjects in the setting to be observed. The easiest setting to enter is one that is open to the public and that gives people little reason to keep their behavior secret (for example, a place where people are watching TV in public—an airport, a bar, a dormitory viewing room). The most difficult setting to enter is one where entry is restricted because participants have good reason to keep their activities confidential (for example, a support group for the victims of abuse).

Observing a formal group (such as a film production crew) often requires permission from management and perhaps union officials. School systems and other bureaucracies usually have a special unit to handle requests from researchers and to help them obtain necessary permissions.

Gaining permission to conduct field observation research requires persistence and public relations skills. Researchers must decide how much to disclose about the nature of the research. Usually it is not necessary to provide a complete explanation of the hypothesis and procedures unless there are objections to sensitive areas. Researchers interested in observing which family member actually controls the television set might explain that they are studying patterns of family communication.

Lindlof (1995) suggests these ways of gaining access:

- Identify the scene's gatekeeper and attempt to persuade him or her of the project's relevance.
- Find a sponsor who can vouch for the usefulness of the project and can help locate participants.
- Negotiate an agreement with participants.

Neuman (1997) illustrates entry and access as an access ladder. The bottom rung represents the easiest situation in which the researcher is looking for public information. The highest rung on the ladder, which requires the most time spent at the field site, involves gaining access to sensitive events and information.

Once access is obtained, the researcher should not expect to immediately begin collecting data. Rapport must first be established with the respondents. Bogdan and Taylor (1998) suggest the following techniques for building rapport: establish common interests with the participants; start relationships slowly; if appropriate, participate in common events and activities; and do not disrupt participants' normal routines. It may take time, perhaps weeks, before those under observation become comfortable with the situation.

Sampling.   Sampling in field observation is more ambiguous than in most other research approaches. First, there is the problem of how many individuals or groups to observe. If the focus of the study is communication in the newsroom, how many newsrooms should be observed? If the topic is family viewing of television, how many families should be included? Unfortunately, there are no guidelines to help answer these questions. The research problem and the goals of the study are indicators of the appropriate sample size; for example, if the results are intended for generalization to a population, studying one subject or group is inadequate. (In most studies, the authors of this text recommend that at least three groups, individuals, or situations be studied. Three observations will eliminate the possibility that one observation is invalid and create a "tie-breaker" if the first observation differs markedly from the second observation.)

Another problem is deciding what behavior episodes or segments to sample. The observer cannot be everywhere and see everything, so what is observed becomes a de facto sample of what is not observed (the Heisenberg Indeterminacy Principle). If an observer views one staff meeting in the newsroom, this meeting represents other unobserved meetings; one conversation at the coffee machine represents all such conversations. Representativeness must be considered even when researchers cannot follow the principles of probability sampling.

Most field observations use purposive sampling, where observers draw on their knowledge of the subject(s) under study and sample only from the relevant behaviors or events. Sometimes previous experience and study of the activity in question suggest what needs to be examined. For example, in a study of newsroom decision making, researchers would want to observe staff meetings because they are an important part of the process. However, restricting the sampling to observations of staff meetings would be a mistake because many decisions are made at the water fountain, at lunch, and in the hallways. Experienced observers tend not to isolate a specific situation but instead to consider even the most insignificant situation for analysis. For most field observations, researchers need to spend some time simply getting the feel of the situation and absorbing the pertinent aspects of the environment before beginning a detailed analysis.

Here are some sampling strategies that might be used (Lindlof, 1995):

- *Maximum variation sampling:* Settings, activities, events, and informants are chosen purposefully to yield as many different and varied situations as possible.
- *Snowball sampling:* A participant refers the researcher to another person who can provide information. This person, in turn, mentions another, and so forth.
- *Typical case sampling:* In contrast to the maximum variation technique, the researcher chooses cases that seem to be most representative of the topic under study.

A more extensive listing of 16 possible sampling strategies is found in Miles and Huberman (1994), including *extreme case sampling*, which looks for highly unusual examples of the phenomenon under study, and *politically important case sampling*, which examines cases that have attracted major attention. Corbin and Strauss (2007) argue for theoretical sampling, a method of data collection based on concepts that emerge from the collected data. Unlike conventional qualitative sampling methods that typically sample locations, people, events, or activities, theoretical sampling selects concepts that are embedded in the data set for further data collection. This method gives researchers the flexibility to explore unexpected ideas that arise as the data are analyzed.

Collecting data. The traditional data collection tools—notebook and pencil—have been supplemented, if not supplanted, by other instruments in recent years. As early as 1972, Bechtel, Achelpohl, and Akers installed television cameras in a small sample of households to document families' TV viewing behavior. Two cameras, automatically activated when the television set was turned on, recorded the scene in front of the set. However, even though a camera can record more information than an observer, Bechtel et al. reported that the project was difficult because of problems in finding consenting families, maintaining the equipment, and interpreting tapes shot at low light levels.

Similarly, Anderson (1987) notes that even though the advantages offered by audio and video recording are tempting, there are five major drawbacks to their use:

- Recording devices take time away from the research process because they need regular calibration and adjustment to work properly.
- The frame of the recording is different from the frame of the observer; a human observer's field of view is about 180°, whereas a camera's is about 60°.
- Recordings have to be cataloged, indexed, and transcribed, adding extra work to the project.
- Recordings take behavior out of context.
- Recordings tend to fragment behavior and distract attention from the overall process.

Video cameras and video recordings have become more portable and easier to use since Anderson first made his observations, but his concerns are still valid. In addition, there are concerns about privacy. Recording individuals as they walk down a public street may not raise any privacy issues, but covertly recording conversations in a sports bar may be a different matter. There are many situations where participants must give consent to be recorded. Consequently, researchers must weigh the pros and cons carefully before deciding to use recording equipment for observations.

Note taking in the covert participant situation requires special attention. Continually scribbling away on a notepad is certain to draw attention and suspicion to the note taker and might expose the study's real purpose. In this type of situation, researchers should make mental notes and transcribe them at the first opportunity. If a researcher's identity is known initially, the problem of note taking is eliminated. Regardless of the situation, it is not wise for a researcher to spend a lot of time taking notes; subjects are already aware of being observed, and note taking can make them uneasy. Brief notes jotted down during natural breaks in a situation attract a minimum of attention and can be expanded later.

Field notes constitute the basic corpus of data in any field study. In these notes, the observers record what happened and what was said, as well as personal impressions, feelings, and interpretations of what was observed. A useful procedure is to separate personal opinions from the descriptive narrative by enclosing the former in brackets.

How much should be recorded? It is always better to record too much information than too little. A seemingly irrelevant observation made during the first viewing session might become significant later in the project. If the material is sensitive or if the researcher does not wish it known that research is taking place, notes may be written in abbreviated form or in code. In addition to firsthand observation, three other data collection techniques are available to field researchers: diary keeping, unobtrusive measures, and document analysis. With the first technique, an investigator routinely supplements his or her field notes by keeping a research diary. This diary consists of personal feelings, sentiments, occasional reflections, and other private thoughts about the research process itself; the writings augment and help interpret the raw data contained in the field notes. Moreover, the researcher may ask the individuals under study to keep a diary for a specified length of time. This enables the researcher to learn about behaviors that take place out of his or her sight and extends the horizontal dimension of the observation. Individuals may be instructed to track certain habits—such as the reading of books or magazines during a specific time of day—or to record general feelings and thoughts—such as the way they felt while watching TV commercials.

One form of diary keeping actually provides researchers with a glimpse of the world as seen through the eyes of the subject(s). The researcher gives the subjects still cameras and asks them to make photographic essays or to keep photographic diaries. Analysis of these photographs might help determine how the subjects perceive reality and what they find important.

A second data collection technique available to the field researcher is unobtrusive measurement. This technique helps overcome the problem of reactivity by searching out naturally occurring phenomena relevant to the research task. The people who provide data through unobtrusive measurement are unaware that they are providing information for a research project. Covert observation, as previously mentioned, is obviously a technique of this type, but there are also other subtle ways to collect data. It might be possible, for example, to determine the popularity of radio stations in a given market by asking auto mechanics to keep track of the dial positions of the radio pushbuttons of cars brought in for repair. Or, in another case, an investigator might use the parking lot at an auto race to discover which brand of tires appears most often on cars owned by people attending the race. Such information might enable tire companies to determine whether their sponsorship of various races has an impact.

Webb, Campbell, Schwartz, and Sechrest (1968) identify two general types of unobtrusive measurements: erosion and accretion. The first type, erosion, estimates wear and tear on a specific object or material. For example, to determine what textbooks are used heavily by students, a researcher might note how many passages in the text are highlighted, how many pages are dog-eared, whether the book's spine is creased, and so on. Accretion, on the other hand, quantifies deposits that have built up over time, such as the amount of dust that has built up on the cover of a textbook.

Accretion and erosion measurement methods do, however, have drawbacks. First, they are passive measures and out of the researcher's control. Second, other factors might influence what is being observed. For example, compulsively neat students might dust their books every day, whether or not they open them, thus providing a misleading accretion measurement. For these reasons, unobtrusive measurements are usually used to support or corroborate findings from other observational methods rather than to draw conclusions from.

Finally, existing documents may represent a fertile source of data for the qualitative researcher. In general terms, two varieties of documents are available for analysis: public and private. Public documents include police reports, newspaper stories, transcripts of TV shows, data archives, and so on. Other items may be less recognizable as public documents, however; messages on Internet bulletin boards, blogs, websites, YouTube videos,

Twitter posts, company newsletters, tombstones, posters, graffiti, and bumper stickers can all fit into this category.

Any of these messages may represent a rich source of data for the qualitative researcher. Shamp (1991), for example, analyzed messages posted on Internet bulletin boards to examine users' perceptions of their communication partners. Priest (1992) used transcripts of *The Phil Donahue Show* to structure in-depth interviews with people who appeared on the TV program.

Private documents, on the other hand, include personal letters, diaries, memos, faxes, emails, home movies and videos, telephone logs, appointment books, reports, and so on. For example, a public relations researcher interested in examining the communication flow among executives in an organization might find copies of memos, faxes, appointments, emails, and telephone logs of special interest.

Much like unobtrusive measurements, document analysis also has occasional disadvantages: missing documents, subjects unwilling to make private documents available, ethical problems with the use of private records such as diaries and letters, and so on. To reduce the possibility of error when working with archival data, Berg (2004) urges researchers to use several data collection methods.

Analyzing data. We have discussed some general considerations of qualitative data analysis. Concerning the specific technique of field observation, data analysis primarily consists of filing the information and analyzing its content. Constructing a filing system is an important step in observation. The purpose of the filing system is to arrange raw field data in an orderly format that is amenable to systematic retrieval later. (The precise filing categories are determined by the data.) From the hypothetical study of decision making in the newsroom, filing categories might include the headings "Relationships," "Interaction—Horizontal," "Interaction—Vertical," and "Disputes." An observation may be placed in more than one category. It is a good idea to make multiple copies of notes; periodic filing of notes during the observation period will save time and confusion later.

Once all the notes have been assigned to their proper files, a rough content analysis is performed to search for consistent patterns. Perhaps, for example, most decisions in the newsroom are made in informal settings such as hallways rather than in formal settings such as conference rooms. Perhaps most decisions are made with little superior–subordinate consultation. At the same time, deviations from the norm should be investigated. Perhaps all reporters except one are typically asked their opinions on the newsworthiness of events; why the exception?

The overall goal of data analysis in field observation is to arrive at a general understanding of the phenomenon under study. In this regard, the observer has the advantage of flexibility. In laboratory and other research approaches, investigators must at some point commit themselves to a particular design or questionnaire. If it subsequently becomes apparent that a crucial variable was left out, little can be done. In field observation, however, the researcher can analyze data during the course of the study and change the research design accordingly.

Exiting. A researcher acting as a participant must have a plan for leaving the setting or the group under study. Of course, if everyone knows the participant, exiting is not a problem. Exiting from a setting that participants regularly enter and leave is also not a problem. Exiting can be difficult, however, when participation is covert. In some instances, the group may have become dependent on the researcher in some way, and the departure may have a negative effect on the group as a whole. In other cases, the sudden revelation that a group has been infiltrated or duped by an outsider might be unpleasant or distressing to some. The researcher has an ethical obligation to do everything possible to prevent psychological, emotional, or physical injury to those being studied. Consequently, leaving the scene must be handled with diplomacy and tact.

Field Observation Online

In the physical world, field observation entails watching people behave in their normal surroundings. In the online world, field observation usually means observing text and images on a computer screen. At one end of the spectrum, the overt participant would join some online group of interest and identify himself or herself as a researcher. The person is an active contributor to the group under study and participates in chat rooms and posts to bulletin boards the same as any other member. At the other end, an overt observer would monitor, record, and analyze the group's messages without taking part in any interactions. (Covert observation raises ethical problems in the online setting. See Chapter 3.)

Data analysis in the online setting requires a different set of skills than those normally used in real-life observation. Traditional observation analyzes what the observer can see or hear: physical behaviors, appearance, facial expressions, movement, objects, spoken words and sentences. In the online world, the data are textual (emails, instant messages, bulletin board posts, chat room conversations, emoticons, etc.) or graphical (website layout, animations, colors, photos, and video clips).

Participant observation takes on a different meaning online when those being observed are not people but their representations or avatars. Anthropologists have used this technique in the virtual world. Williams (2007), for example, reported the results of participant observation of an online graphical social space and offered suggestions on how the method could be adapted to the virtual world.

FOCUS GROUPS

The **focus group**, or group interviewing, is a research strategy for understanding people's attitudes and behavior. Between 6 and 12 people are interviewed simultaneously, with a moderator leading the respondents in a relatively unstructured discussion about the topic under investigation. The focus group technique has four defining characteristics (based on Krueger & Casey, 2000):

- Focus groups involve people (participants).
- The people possess certain characteristics and are recruited to share a quality or characteristic of interest to the researcher. For example, all may be beer drinkers, or Lexus owners, or females 18–34 who listen to certain types of music on the radio.
- Focus groups usually provide qualitative data. Data from focus groups are used to enhance understanding and to reveal a wide range of opinions, some of which the researcher might not expect. In most cases, they are not used to test hypotheses or to generalize to a population. This is accomplished only when several focus groups are conducted to achieve a satisfactory sample size.
- As the name implies, focus groups have a focused discussion. Most of the questions to be asked are predetermined, the sequence of questions is established, and the questions are structured to further the goal of the research. However, the moderator is free to depart from the structure if the participants present relevant information.

A CLOSER LOOK

Ethical Concerns in Qualitative Research

All the ethical principles discussed in Chapter 3 have applications in qualitative research, but the nature of qualitative research raises some additional concerns. With regard to informed consent, it may be necessary for a qualitative researcher to disclose all the details of the project that might make the respondent's life more difficult. A prospective informant for a project using intensive interviewing should be told about the significant time commitment involved if he or she participates in the research. Participation might also mean traveling to the interview site, agreeing to have the interview audio recorded, and possibly being reinterviewed in the future. All these facts should be revealed to the informant to fulfill the obligation of informed consent.

Further, what if covert observation reveals evidence of illegal activity, such as spousal abuse? Is the researcher obligated to share that knowledge with the appropriate authorities? What about promises of confidentiality to the participant? Suppose a researcher is examining the way people watch television in a public place, such as a sports bar. As part of the research, the researcher promises confidentiality and conducts intensive interviews with the staff. The interviews reveal a couple of disgruntled employees. During the project, the sports bar burns down under suspicious circumstances and police suspect arson. The investigators hear about the research project and ask to see the notes and transcripts of the intensive interviews. Should the researcher turn over the notes? (The researcher's notes may be subpoenaed if a lawsuit is filed.) Issues such as these must be considered before the project begins.

A brief guide for conducting focus groups may be found on our website at *www.wimmerdominick.com*. The following discussion of advantages and disadvantages is generally from a positivist perspective. Lunt and Livingstone (1996) provide a discussion of the focus group method with more of an interpretive perspective.

Advantages of Focus Groups

Focus groups allow researchers to collect preliminary information about a topic or a phenomenon. They may be used in pilot studies to detect ideas that will be investigated further using another research method, such as a telephone survey or some other qualitative method. A second important advantage is that focus groups can be conducted quickly. Most of the time is spent recruiting the respondents. A field service that specializes in recruiting focus groups can usually recruit respondents in 7–10 days, depending on the type of participant required.

The cost of focus groups also makes the approach an attractive research method. In the private sector, most sessions can be conducted for about $2,000–$5,000 per group, depending on the type of respondent required, the part of the country in which the group is conducted, and the moderator or company used to conduct the group. When respondents are difficult to recruit or when the topic requires a specially trained moderator, focus groups may cost much more. However, the cost is not excessive if the groups provide valuable data for further research studies. Focus groups used in academic research, of course, cost much less.

Researchers also like focus groups because of the flexibility in question design and follow-up. In conventional surveys, interviewers work from a rigid series of questions and are instructed to follow explicit directions in asking the questions. A moderator in a focus group, however, works from a list of broad questions and more refined probe questions; hence, it is easy to follow up on important points raised by participants in the group. The ability to clear up confusing responses from subjects makes focus groups valuable in the research process.

Most professional focus group moderators use a procedure known as an *extended focus group*, in which respondents are required to complete a written questionnaire before the group session begins. The pre-group questionnaire, which covers the material that will be discussed during the group session, forces respondents to "commit" to a particular answer or position before entering the group. This commitment eliminates one potential problem created by group dynamics—namely, the person who does not wish to offer an opinion because he or she is in a minority.

Finally, focus group responses are often more complete and less inhibited than those from individual interviews. One respondent's remarks tend to stimulate others to pursue lines of thinking that might not have been elicited in a situation involving just one individual. With a competent moderator, the discussion can have a beneficial snowball effect, as one respondent comments on the views of another. A skilled moderator also can detect the opinions and attitudes of those who are less articulate by noting facial expressions and other nonverbal behavior while others are speaking.

Disadvantages of Focus Groups

Focus group research is not free of complications; the approach is far from perfect. Some of the problems are discussed here; others are given at our website.

A self-appointed group leader who monopolizes the conversation and attempts to impose his or her opinion on other participants dominates some groups. Such a person usually draws the resentment of the other participants and may have an adverse effect on the performance of the group. The moderator needs to control such situations tactfully before they get out of hand.

Unless enough groups are conducted, typical focus group research (four to six groups) is inappropriate to gather quantitative data. If quantification is important, it is wise to supplement the focus group with other research tools that permit more specific questions to be addressed to a more representative sample. Many people unfamiliar with focus group research incorrectly assume that the method will answer the question "how many" or "how much." In fact, focus group research is intended to gather qualitative data to answer questions such as "why" or "how." Many times people who hire a person or company to conduct a focus group are disappointed with the results because they expected exact numbers and percentages. Focus groups do not provide such information unless enough groups are conducted.

As suggested earlier, focus groups depend heavily on the skills of the moderator, who must know when to probe for further information, when to stop respondents from discussing irrelevant topics, and how to involve all respondents in the discussion. All these things must be accomplished with professionalism, since one sarcastic or inappropriate comment to a respondent may have a chilling effect on the group's performance. The moderator must remain completely objective.

Looked at from the positivist perspective, focus groups have other drawbacks as well. The small focus group samples may not represent the population from which they were drawn; the recording equipment or other physical characteristics of the location may inhibit respondents; and if the respondents are allowed to stray too far from the topic under consideration, the data produced may not be useful. (Note: All of these problems can be solved by an expert researcher/moderator.)

Uses of Focus Groups

Morgan (1997) suggests that focus groups can be either (1) self-contained, (2) supplementary, or (3) multimethod. A self-contained focus group is one in which the focus group method is the only means of data collection. The results of self-contained groups can stand on their own; the data from the groups provide a sufficient answer to the research question.

A supplementary focus group is one in which the group discussions form a starting point or are a source of follow-up data for a quantitative study. Supplementary focus groups are an example of the mixed methods approach discussed earlier. For example, a researcher planning a survey on why people read online news might develop questionnaire items based on the content of a number of focus groups that discuss that topic. In a related example, a researcher who has conducted a survey on Internet news reading, to gather more in-depth information about the quantitative results, might conduct a number of focus groups to determine the reasons people read the news. In both cases, the focus group method is used to enhance (support or refute) the main data collection instrument.

In the multimethod approach, focus groups are only one of a number of qualitative techniques used to collect data about a topic. The focus group results might be combined with participant observation, case studies, and interviews. In this situation, the focus group is not used to supplement other techniques, but stands as an equal methodology. If the focus group is paired with a quantitative technique, such as a survey or an experiment, the resulting design is another example of the mixed methods technique.

Methodology of Focus Groups

No matter their purpose, there are typically seven basic steps in focus group research:

1. *Define the problem.* This step is similar in all types of scientific research: A well-defined problem is established on the basis of previous investigation or out of curiosity. Some problems that would be appropriate for the focus group method include pilot-testing ideas, plans, or products; discovering factors that influence opinions, attitudes, and behaviors; and generating new thoughts or ideas about a situation, concept, or product. For example, television production companies that produce pilot programs for potential series often conduct numerous focus groups with target viewers to determine the groups' reactions to each concept.

2. *Select a sample.* Because focus groups are small, researchers must define a narrow audience for the study. The type of sample depends on the purpose of the focus group; the sample might consist of adults 18–54 who watch a particular type of television program, men 18–34 who listen to a certain type of music, or teenagers who download more than 20 songs a month.

3. *Determine the number of groups necessary.* To help eliminate part of the problem of selecting a representative group, most researchers conduct three or more focus groups on the same topic. They can then compare results to determine whether any similarities or differences exist, or one group may be used as a basis for comparison with the other group. A focus group study using only one group is rare because there is no way to know whether the results are group-specific or characteristic of a wider audience.

Theoretically speaking, focus group researchers should conduct as many groups as they need to achieve **saturation**. Saturation occurs when the focus groups no longer provide fresh information. In effect, the moderator has heard it all before. It is nearly impossible to predict when the saturation point will occur. It may be after three or four groups, or perhaps after a dozen. There are, of course, practical limits as to how many groups should be conducted. In some situations, the budget or time might run out before saturation is achieved.

4. *Prepare the study mechanics.* We present a more detailed description of the mechanical aspects of focus groups at our

website. Suffice it to say here that this step includes arranging for the recruitment of respondents (by telephone or possibly by shopping center intercept), reserving the facilities at which the groups will be conducted, and deciding what type of recording (audio and/or video) will be used. The moderator must be selected and briefed about the purpose of the group. In addition, the researcher needs to determine the amount of co-op money each respondent will receive for participating. Respondents usually receive between $25 and $100 for attending, although professionals such as doctors and lawyers may require up to $500 or more.

5. *Prepare the focus group materials.* Each aspect of a focus group must be planned in detail; nothing should be left to chance—in particular, the moderator must not be allowed to "wing it." The screener questionnaire is developed to recruit the desired respondents, recordings and other materials the subjects will hear or see are prepared, any questionnaires the subjects will complete are produced (including the presession questionnaire), and a list of questions is developed for the presession questionnaire and the moderator's guide.

Krueger and Casey (2000) offer the following advice when constructing the moderator's guide. Good questions:

- Sound conversational
- Use the vocabulary of the participants
- Are easy to say
- Are clear
- Are usually short
- Ask about only one topic
- Include clear directions (on how to answer)

Generally, a focus group session begins with some type of shared experience so that the individuals have a common base from which to start the discussion. The members may listen to or view a video, examine a new product, or simply be asked how they answered the first question on the presession questionnaire.

One general method that is sometimes followed in sequencing focus group questions is called the **funnel technique**. The moderator starts off with a general question or two then moves to more specific topics. For example, the first couple of questions might be about the participants' travel experiences, the next set might be about what they prefer in a hotel, and the final group of questions might ask them about their feelings toward a particular hotel chain.

The existence of a moderator's guide (see *www.wimmerdominick.com*) does not mean that the moderator cannot ask questions not contained in the guide. Quite the opposite is true. The significant advantage of a focus group is that it allows the moderator to probe respondents' comments during the session. A professional moderator is able to develop a line of questioning that no one thought about before the group began, and the questioning usually provides important information. Professional moderators who have this skill receive substantial fees for conducting focus groups.

6. *Conduct the session.* Focus groups may be conducted in a variety of settings, from professional conference rooms equipped with one-way mirrors to hotel rooms rented for the occasion. In most situations, a professional conference room is used. Hotel and motel rooms are used when a focus facility is not available.

7. *Analyze the data and prepare a summary report.* The written summary of focus group interviews depends on the needs of the study and the amount of time and money available. At one extreme, the moderator/researcher may simply write a brief synopsis of what was said and offer an interpretation of the subjects' responses. For a more elaborate content analysis or a more complete description of what happened, the sessions can be transcribed so that the moderator or researcher can scan the comments and develop a category system, coding each comment into the appropriate category. Focus groups conducted in the private sector rarely go beyond a summary of the groups; clients also have access to the audio and video recordings if they desire.

Online Focus Groups

Not surprisingly, the Internet has become popular as a tool to conduct focus groups. However, there is some controversy as to whether the online version should actually be called a focus group. In any case, there are two variations of this technique: text-only and video.

In the synchronous version of the text-only situation, respondents are recruited to participate at a specific date and time. A password-protected website or other multiple-respondent software service is used to guarantee respondent confidentiality. The moderator poses questions to the group, and all are encouraged to respond. A typical session might last an hour or so. Researchers can see the responses on their own personal computers and can send instant messages to the moderator suggesting new questions as the session progresses. Some argue that this approach cannot be considered an actual focus group because one of the fundamental benefits of focus groups is seeing and hearing the interaction among the participants. This isn't possible with this online approach. Perhaps a more accurate name for this arrangement would be an online chat group.

In the asynchronous version of the text-only situation, the researcher uses a bulletin board setup. The moderator posts a question or questions on a password-protected website, and about 15–25 appropriately selected respondents log on, read the question and any posted replies, and respond at their own convenience.

This technique works best with respondents who are too busy to participate in a live online session. Since respondents have more time to think about and compose their answers, the bulletin board method typically results in longer and more thoughtful responses. Moreover, this technique has been shown to work well with topics that are sensitive or complex. Some of the disadvantages of the bulletin board technique include the lengthy amount of time it takes to gather responses, participants who drop out of the group, and increased cost when compared to online or in-person groups.

A second way of conducting online groups makes use of web cams and streaming video. In this approach, participants are linked together using a special software program that allows real-time responses to questions posed by a moderator who can see all the respondents on his or her monitor. This procedure allows the moderator to see who is actually participating in the group and to monitor if group members are actually paying attention. Many private research companies will arrange web cam focus groups.

The online format does have a few advantages over the face-to-face format:

- An online focus group is typically cheaper.
- An online focus group can be composed of participants from multiple geographic areas, eliminating some of the risks associated with regional bias.
- The influence of group dynamics may be less in the online situation.

Online groups have several shortcomings. In the text-only situation:

- There is no respondent interaction. Face-to-face, interpersonal interactions will always generate more in-depth data than a typed answer from someone in a foreign location.
- The researcher cannot see the nonverbal reactions of the group. In addition, the group does not have the opportunity

to touch and see physical objects, thus limiting the types of topics that can be discussed. A market researcher, for example, would probably not use online focus groups to test a new facial tissue, since the group would not be able to feel how soft it is.

- To participate, respondents must be able to type and read quickly.
- There is no control over the situation. The moderator can never be 100% sure who is typing the answers, and there is no way to control the respondents' environment—the respondents could be watching TV or doing anything else while typing their (supposedly) accurate responses to questions.

In the web cam situation:

- Respondent interaction is still limited and participants might all talk at once, making it harder to transcribe the proceedings and lengthening the time it takes to gather information.
- The moderator needs additional skills to manage the web cam situation.
- Some respondents may not have web cams or are uncomfortable using them.
- The moderator can see only the participants' faces and might miss significant body language information.

Examples of Focus Groups

Goodman (2002) conducted focus groups with Anglo and Latina women about their reactions to women's images in popular magazines. The researcher found that the respondents' culture played a role in how they interpreted the images. Similarly, Pompper, Soto, and Piel (2007) conducted 19 focus groups composed of college males in their study of magazine readership and male body images. They found that readership of certain magazines was related to respondents' feeling ambivalent about their body types. Gunther, Kautz, and Roth (2011) used focus groups to examine the perceptions of female sports broadcasters and found evidence of bias.

INTENSIVE INTERVIEWS

Intensive interviews, or in-depth interviews, are essentially a hybrid of the one-on-one interview approach discussed in Chapter 7.

Intensive interviews are unique for these reasons:

- They generally use smaller samples.
- They provide detailed background about the reasons respondents give specific answers. Elaborate data concerning respondents' opinions, values, motivations, recollections, experiences, and feelings are obtained.
- They allow for lengthy observation of respondents' nonverbal responses.
- They are usually long. Unlike personal interviews used in survey research that may last only a few minutes, an intensive interview may last several hours and may take more than one session.
- They can be customized to individual respondents. In a personal interview, all respondents are usually asked the same questions. Intensive interviews allow interviewers to form questions based on each respondent's answers.
- They can be influenced by the interview climate. To a greater extent than with personal interviews, the success of intensive interviews depends on the rapport established between the interviewer and the respondent.

Advantages and Disadvantages of Intensive Interviews

The most important advantage of the in-depth interview is the wealth of detail that it provides. Furthermore, when compared to more traditional survey methods, intensive interviewing provides more accurate responses on sensitive issues. The rapport between respondent and interviewer makes it easier to approach certain topics that might be taboo in other approaches. In addition, there may be certain groups for which intensive interviewing is the only practical technique. For example, a study of the media habits of U.S. senators would be difficult to conduct as an observational study. Also, it would be difficult to get a sample of senators to take the time to respond to a survey questionnaire. In some cases, however, such people might be willing to talk to an interviewer.

On the negative side, generalizability is sometimes a problem. Intensive interviewing is typically done with a nonrandom sample. Since interviews are usually nonstandardized, each respondent may answer a slightly different version of a question. In fact, it is likely that a particular respondent may answer questions not asked of any other respondent. Another disadvantage of in-depth interviews is that they are especially sensitive to interviewer bias. In a long interview, it is possible for a respondent to learn a good deal of information about the interviewer. Despite practice and training, some interviewers may inadvertently communicate their attitudes through loaded questions, nonverbal cues, or tone of voice. The effect of this on the validity of a respondent's answers is difficult to gauge. Finally, intensive interviewing presents problems in data analysis. A researcher given the same body of data taken from an interview may wind up with interpretations significantly different from those of the original investigator.

Procedures

The problem definition, respondent recruiting, and data collection and analysis procedures for intensive interviews are similar to those used in personal interviews. The primary differences with intensive interviews are these:

- Co-op payments are usually higher, generally $100–$1,000.
- The amount of data collected is tremendous, and analysis may take several weeks to several months.
- Interviewees may become tired and bored. Interviews must be scheduled several hours apart, which lengthens the data collection effort.
- Because of the time required, it is difficult to arrange intensive interviews, particularly for respondents who are professionals.
- Small samples do not allow for generalization to the target population.

Examples of Intensive Interviews

Harrington (2003) conducted intensive interviews with a dozen individuals familiar with the storylines on the soap opera *All My Children* concerning the series' portrayal of homosexuality. Lewis (2008) conducted intensive interviews with eight journalists who had either lost their jobs or were suspended due to plagiarism accusations. He found that part of the problem was the vague way that plagiarism was defined. Winn (2009) interviewed members of 20 families about their viewing of prerecorded video material and found that families members considered this type of viewing to be family social time.

Intensive Interviewing Online

Similar to focus groups, there are two types of online in-depth interviews. Version one is the text-only method that can be done via email, chat room, bulletin board, or even social media such as Facebook. One benefit of this type of online interview is that the interview can take place at the respondent's convenience. The interviewer can post one or more questions, and the respondent can take as long as he or she likes (usually up to a week) to answer. The extra time can allow respondents to reflect about their answers and may provide the researcher with richer content and additional insights. Another benefit is that interviews can be conducted with people over a wide geographic area, without travel expenses. Finally, this method may be helpful in collecting data from people who might be uncomfortable in a face-to-face situation.

However, several weaknesses are associated with this technique. First, it takes longer than a face-to-face session and generates less data. The quality of the data is strongly influenced by the typing and reading skills of the respondent. Further, nonverbal cues are missing and jokes, sarcasm, and inflections are harder to distinguish.

Intensive interviews can also be done in real-time using Skype or video conferencing software. In this situation, the interviewer and respondent can see one another and the researcher can observe nonverbal behaviors that might color the verbal responses. In addition, the interviewer can more easily ask follow-up questions. The researcher also has the option of making both audio and video recordings of the proceedings.

One disadvantage of the real-time technique is that the respondent can more easily terminate the interview than in the face-to-face situation. Also, rapport and trust are more difficult to establish in the live video situation.

A quick search of the web will reveal that there are many private research companies that offer to conduct online intensive interviews.

CASE STUDIES

The case study method is another common qualitative research technique. Simply put, a **case study** uses as many data sources as possible to systematically investigate individuals, groups, organizations, or events. Case studies are conducted when a researcher needs to understand or explain a phenomenon. They are frequently used in medicine, anthropology, clinical psychology, management science, and history. Sigmund Freud wrote case studies of his patients; economists wrote case studies of the cable TV industry for the FCC; and the list goes on and on.

On a more formal level, Yin (2003) defines a case study as an empirical inquiry that uses multiple sources of evidence to investigate a contemporary phenomenon within its real-life context, in which the boundaries between the phenomenon and its context are not clearly evident. This definition highlights how a case study differs from other research strategies. For example, an experiment separates a phenomenon from its real-life context. The laboratory environment controls the context. The survey technique tries to define the phenomenon under study narrowly enough to limit the number of variables to be examined. Case study research includes both single cases and multiple cases. Comparative case study research, frequently used in political science, is an example of the multiple case study technique.

Merriam (1988) lists four essential characteristics of case study research:

1. *Particularistic.* This means that the case study focuses on a particular situation, event, program, or phenomenon, making it a good method for studying practical, real-life problems.
2. *Descriptive.* The final product of a case study is a detailed description of the topic under study.
3. *Heuristic.* A case study helps people to understand what's being studied. New interpretations, new perspectives, new meaning, and fresh insights are all goals of a case study.

4. *Inductive.* Most case studies depend on inductive reasoning. Principles and generalizations emerge from an examination of the data. Many case studies attempt to discover new relationships rather than verify existing hypotheses.

Advantages of Case Studies

The case study method is most valuable when the researcher wants to obtain a wealth of information about the research topic. Case studies provide tremendous detail. Many times researchers want such detail when they do not know exactly what they are looking for. The case study is particularly advantageous to the researcher who is trying to find clues and ideas for further research (Simon, 1985). This is not to suggest, however, that case studies are to be used only at the exploratory stage of research. The method can also be used to gather descriptive and explanatory data.

The case study technique can suggest why something has occurred. For example, in many cities at the beginning of the 21st century, newspaper publishers tried to increase diversity in their newsrooms. Some efforts were more successful than others. To learn why some failed while others succeeded, a multiple case study approach, examining several cities, could have been used. Other research techniques, such as the survey, might not be able to reveal all the possible reasons behind this phenomenon. Ideally, case studies should be used in combination with theory to achieve maximum understanding.

The case study method also affords the researcher the ability to deal with a wide spectrum of evidence. Documents, historical artifacts, systematic interviews, direct observations, and even traditional surveys can all be incorporated into a case study. In fact, the more data sources that can be brought to bear in a case, the more likely it is that the study will be valid.

A CLOSER LOOK

Data Collection and Storage

Just as with all steps in a research project, especially qualitative research, it is necessary to keep duplicates of all information. One mass media researcher, a colleague of the authors of this text, lost three years of qualitative data when his office building burned. Unfortunately, he had not made duplicate copies of his data. Don't make the same mistake.

If you are storing data on your computer, make sure you save a copy to a second internal hard drive or to some external source such as an external hard drive, a USB drive, or a network-attached storage device. Keep in mind that if you save one copy in your documents file and a backup on your desktop, a hard drive crash might wipe out both copies.

Disadvantages of Case Studies

There are three main criticisms of case studies. The first has to do with a general lack of scientific rigor in many case studies. Yin (2003) points out that "too many times, the case study researcher has been sloppy and has allowed equivocal evidence or biased views to influence the … findings and conclusions" (p. 10). It is easy to do a sloppy case study; rigorous case studies require a good deal of time and effort.

The second criticism is that the case study is not amenable to generalization. If the main goal of the researcher is to make statistically based normative statements about the frequency of occurrence of a phenomenon in a defined population, some other method may be more appropriate. This is not to say that the results of all case studies are idiosyncratic and unique. In fact, if generalizing theoretic propositions is the main goal, then the case study method is perfectly suited to the task.

Finally, like participant observation, case studies are often time consuming and may occasionally produce massive quantities of data that are hard to summarize. Consequently, fellow researchers are forced to wait years for the results of the research, which too often are poorly presented.

Conducting a Case Study

The precise method of conducting a case study has not been as well documented as the more traditional techniques of the survey and the experiment. Nonetheless, there appear to be five distinct stages in carrying out a case study: design, pilot study, data collection, data analysis, and report writing.

Design. The first concern in case study design is what to ask. The case study is most appropriate for questions that begin with "how" or "why." A research question that is clear and precise focuses the remainder of the efforts in a case study. A second design concern is what to analyze. What constitutes a "case"? In many instances, a case is an individual, several individuals, or an event or events. If information is gathered about each relevant individual, the results are reported in the single or multiple case study format; in other instances, however, the precise boundaries of the case are harder to pinpoint. A case might be a specific decision, a particular organization at a certain time, a program, or some other discrete event. One rough guide for determining what to use as the unit of analysis is the available research literature. Since researchers want to compare their findings with the results of previous research, it is sometimes a good idea not to stray too far from what was done in past research.

Pilot study.   Before the pilot study is conducted, the case study researcher must construct a study protocol. This document describes the procedures to be used in the study and also includes the data-gathering instrument or instruments. A good case study protocol contains the procedures necessary for gaining access to a particular person or organization and the methods for accessing records. It also contains the schedule for data collection and addresses logistical problems. For example, the protocol should note whether a copy machine is available in the field to duplicate records, whether office space is available to the researchers, and what supplies are needed. The protocol should also list the questions central to the inquiry and the possible sources of information to be tapped in answering these questions. If interviews are to be used in the case study, the protocol should specify the questions to be asked.

Once the protocol has been developed, the researcher is ready to begin the pilot study. A **pilot study** is used to refine both the research design and the field procedures. Variables that were not foreseen during the design phase can emerge during the pilot study, and problems with the protocol or with study logistics can also be uncovered. The pilot study also allows the researchers to try different data-gathering approaches and to observe different activities from several trial perspectives. The results of the pilot study are used to revise and polish the study protocol.

Data collection.   At least four sources of data can be used in case studies. Documents, which represent a rich data source, may take the form of letters, memos, minutes, agendas, historical records, brochures, pamphlets, posters, and so on. A second source is the interview. Some case studies make use of survey

research methods and ask respondents to fill out questionnaires; others may use intensive interviewing.

Observation/participation is the third data collection technique. The general comments made about this technique earlier in this chapter apply to the case study method as well. The fourth source of evidence used in case studies is the physical artifact—a tool, a piece of furniture, or even a computer printout. Although artifacts are commonly used as a data source in anthropology and history, they are seldom used in mass media case study research. (They are, however, frequently used in legal research concerning the media.)

Most case study researchers recommend using multiple sources of data, thus permitting triangulation of the phenomenon under study (Rubin, 1984). In addition, multiple sources help the case study researcher improve the reliability and validity of the study. Not surprisingly, an examination of the case study method found that the ones that used multiple sources of evidence were rated as more convincing than those that relied on a single source (Yin, Bateman, & Moore, 1983).

Data analysis.   Unlike quantitative research techniques, there are no specific formulas or "cookbook" techniques to guide the researcher in analyzing the data. Consequently, this stage is probably the most difficult in the case study method. Although it is impossible to generalize to all case study situations, Yin (2003) suggests three broad analytic strategies: pattern matching, explanation building, and time series.

In the *pattern-matching strategy*, an empirically based pattern is compared with one or more predicted patterns. For instance, suppose a newspaper is about to initiate a new management tool: regular meetings between top management and reporters, excluding editors. Based on organizational theory, a researcher might predict certain outcomes—namely, more stress between editors and reporters, increased productivity, and weakened supervisory links. If analysis of the case study data indicates that these results do in fact occur, some conclusions about the management change can be made. If the predicted pattern does not match the actual one, the initial study propositions have to be questioned.

In the analytic strategy of *explanation building*, the researcher tries to construct an explanation about the case by making statements about the cause or causes of the phenomenon under study. This method can take several forms. Typically, however, an investigator drafts an initial theoretical statement about some process or outcome, compares the findings of an initial case study against the statement, revises the statement, analyzes a second comparable case, and repeats this process as many times as necessary. Note that this technique is similar to the general approach of analytical induction discussed earlier. For example, to explain why some media websites are failing to generate a profit, a researcher might suggest lack of managerial expertise as an initial proposition. But an investigator who examined the situation might find that lack of management expertise is only part of the problem, that inadequate market research is also a factor. Armed with the revised version of the explanatory statement, the researcher next examines the direct broadcast satellite industry to see whether this explanation needs to be further refined, and so on, until a full and satisfactory answer is achieved.

In *time-series analysis*, the investigator tries to compare a series of data points to some theoretical trend that was predicted before the research or to some alternative trend. If, for instance, several cities have experienced newspaper strikes, a case study investigator might generate predictions about the changes in information-seeking behaviors of residents in these communities and conduct a case study to see whether these predictions are supported.

Report writing. The case study report can take several forms. The report can follow the traditional research study format—problem, methods, findings, and discussion—or it can use a nontraditional technique. Some case studies are best suited to a chronological arrangement, whereas comparative case studies can be reported from the comparative perspective. No matter what form is chosen, the researcher must consider the intended audience of the report. A case study report for policy makers is written in a style different from one to be published in a scholarly journal.

Examples of Case Studies

Tovares (2000) examined the development of *Latino USA*, a news program about Latino issues. His case study involved personal interviews with the staff, direct observation, and examination of archival materials. In his study of radio newscasts, Hood (2007) combined data from field observations, intensive interviews, and content analysis to conclude that the meaning of "local" news was hard to distinguish. In her study of net-only radio at Brooklyn College, Baker (2010) interviewed radio station personnel, conducted a survey, and did intensive interviewing of students attending the college.

There is no direct online counterpart to a case study. A traditional case study, however, may have an online component as one or more of its data sources. A researcher might be able to analyze the content of email, blogs, social media, or other online documents as part of a traditional case study.

ETHNOGRAPHY

The term *ethnographic research* is sometimes used as a synonym for *qualitative research* (Lindlof, 1991). **Ethnography**, however, is in fact a special kind of qualitative research. As first practiced by anthropologists and sociologists, ethnography was the process in which researchers spent long periods of time living with and observing other cultures in a natural setting. This immersion in the other culture helped the researcher understand another way of life as seen from the native perspective. Recently, however, the notion of ethnography has been adapted to other areas: political science, education, social work, and communication. These disciplines have been less interested in describing the way of life of an entire culture and more concerned with analyzing smaller units: subgroups, organizations, institutions, professions, audiences, and so on. To reduce confusion, Berg (2004) suggests referring to the traditional study of entire cultures as *macro-ethnography* and to the study of smaller units of analysis as *micro-ethnography*. The latter approach is the one most often used by mass communication researchers.

In addition, Sarantakos (1998) suggests that ethnography can be grouped into two categories: descriptive and critical. Descriptive ethnography is the more conventional approach that is discussed later in this section. In contrast, critical ethnography makes use of the critical paradigm discussed at the beginning of this chapter. It examines such factors as power and hegemony and attempts to uncover hidden agendas and unquestioned assumptions. The goal of critical ethnography is often political and might involve giving a voice to groups who are disempowered in society. For example, a critical ethnographic study of the role of Spanish-language radio in the Hispanic community might reveal that the Hispanic minority does not control much of the media content that plays a role in their culture and provide information that would allow Hispanics to change the existing situation.

Regardless of its focus or approach, ethnography is characterized by four qualities:

- It puts the researcher in the middle of the topic under study; the researcher goes to the data rather than the other way around.

- It emphasizes studying an issue or topic from the participants' frame of reference.

- It involves spending a considerable amount of time in the field.

- It uses a variety of research techniques, including observation, interviewing, diary keeping, analysis of existing documents, photography, video recording, and so on.

The last item seems to distinguish ethnographic research from other forms of qualitative research; indeed, ethnographic research relies upon an assortment of data collection techniques. Although other qualitative research projects can be conducted adequately using only one method, ethnographic research generally uses several of the four common qualitative techniques discussed in this chapter: field observations, intensive interviewing, focus groups, and case studies.

Conducting Ethnographic Research

LeCompte and Schensul (1999) provide a step-by-step procedure for conducting an ethnographic study. Much of this process is similar to other qualitative methods.

The initial stage is to define the problem or phenomenon to be explored. Questions that are most appropriate to ethnography involve examining how a particular group of people views or perceives a certain phenomenon. The ultimate goal of the ethnographer is to try to understand the world as seen by the group under study.

Closely related to the choice of a research question is the choice of a field site, the actual place or places where data will be gathered. In some instances, the research question will be developed first and then an appropriate field site will be selected. In other instances, a researcher might first find an interesting field site and develop a question appropriate to the site.

No matter how the site is identified, the researcher must next gain access and decide what to examine. As is the case in general with field research, an ethnographic researcher will generally use purposive sampling. This sampling can be refined by using **key informants**, long-time members of the group under study who have expert knowledge of the group's routines, activities, and communication patterns. Using the knowledge provided by the informants, the researcher determines what behaviors to observe, where and when to observe them, what individuals to single out for intensive interviews, and what key documents might be relevant to analyze.

Once the sampling strategy has been mapped out, the fieldwork begins. Much of the earlier discussion concerning data collection during field observation also applies to ethnographic research. Researchers should take copious notes. Emerson, Fretz, and Shaw (1995) suggest constructing four types of field notes:

1. Condensed accounts—short descriptions written or recorded in the field that highlight the most important factors that were observed or brought up during an interview. These descriptions are helpful in highlighting what is to be emphasized in later accounts.
2. Expanded accounts—written after the period of observation or after the interview, filling in details not included in the condensed version. These documents should be as complete and thorough as possible. In ethnographic research, it is better to have too much detail than not enough.
3. Fieldwork journal—lists the researcher's personal reactions, impressions, and reflections about the fieldwork or the interview. It contains primarily personal commentary rather than strict reporting.
4. Analysis and interpretation notes—attempts by the researcher to integrate the observational and interview data into some coherent analysis scheme. These are the researcher's first attempts at finding order or patterns in the data.

Data analysis in ethnographic research follows the same patterns as in other forms of qualitative research. The researcher searches for patterns and general themes in the data. Eventually, analytic categories will emerge that are checked back against the data to see whether they provide consistent explanations. At the same time, the researcher is interpreting the data and providing some conceptual bases for a more general understanding of the groups' perceptions and behaviors.

Some qualitative researchers (Daymon & Holloway, 2002) suggest that successful ethnographic research blends together the "outsider" perspective of the researcher with the "insider" perspective of those individuals observed. This approach is sometimes discussed as a blending of the *etic* and the *emic* points of view. The *etic* approach assigns meaning on the basis of general scientific concepts, principles, and theories, whereas the *emic* approach assigns meaning to cultural traits and patterns on the basis of the informants' perspective within the internal meaning system of their culture.

As with other forms of qualitative research, the final phase of ethnographic research is the preparation of a written report. (Somewhat confusingly, the word *ethnography* can refer to both the specific research method and the written report that is derived from using that method.) The report generally starts with a statement of purpose or guiding research question, a description of the method that includes the researcher's personal feelings about the general topic. This is followed by evidence and examples that illustrate the main themes of the data, the researcher's interpretation of the data, and implications for theory and future practice. As is the case with qualitative research reports, an ethnography can be a rather lengthy document.

Mayer (2003) presents example of an ethnographic study that deals with the TV-watching habits of Mexican American females. Her data came from a two-year anthropological study in San Antonio, Texas. In their ethnographic study of news producers and advertisers in Slovenia, Erjavec and Kovacic (2010) spent 1,600 hours in the field at 20 different locations over two years.

Ethnography Online

Virtual (or online) ethnography is a relatively new development in qualitative research. Traditional ethnography involves the immersion of the researcher into the situation, circumstances, and daily lives of his or her subjects. Virtual ethnography extends this notion into cyberspace and involves a variety of techniques. Typically, a targeted sample of respondents might be asked to:

- Keep an online diary of their thoughts and behaviors concerning the study's purpose
- Take pictures relevant to the study and upload them for researchers to analyze
- Participate in online intensive interviewing based on the content of their diaries and photos
- Provide researchers with a web cam virtual "tour" of their surroundings

Another ethnographic approach is online "immersion," a series of exercises and projective tests that give researchers a glimpse into the lives of their respondents. For example, respondents might be asked to describe their ideas of "home" using a photo journal, video clips, and blog entries.

Virtual ethnography is used more by practitioners than by academics, but that situation may change as the technique becomes more popular. Ishmael and Thomas (2006)

provide an example of a virtual ethnography as used in advertising research, and Bortree (2005) used ethnographic techniques in her study of teenage girls' blogs. In her study of the communication behaviors of Estonian students, Kaun (2010) analyzed eight weeks of her participants' online diary and wiki entries. (Netnography, an ethnographic approach using social media, is described below.)

Other Online Techniques

This section will briefly discuss two online techniques developed primarily by market research companies that have no traditional face-to-face counterparts.

An *online research blog* is a personal diary kept by a sample of respondents who have something in common (for example, recently buying a car, applying for a mortgage, or using a moving company). Respondents are asked to record their experiences at every step along the way and to make their blogs available for analysis. The advantages of this method are easy to see. It is quick and inexpensive, and it allows respondents to phrase their responses in their own way, often suggesting perspectives that the researcher might not be aware of. Additionally, a research blog emerges naturally from the respondent rather than being artificially solicited by a moderator in an online focus group. Mass media researchers have yet to make significant use of online research blogs, but their potential is easy to see.

An *online research community* is a targeted group of people who are recruited to a join a private online website to participate in research over a period of time. Research communities are larger than focus groups, sometimes having hundreds of members. They are not as tightly moderated. The community responds to questions posed by the researcher, and a moderator monitors the responses, encourages participation, and poses follow-up questions. The community might take the form of a chat room or an online bulletin board. One disadvantage of this method is that, despite the moderator's encouragement, not everybody will respond. One estimate suggests that only 10–20% of the group will be fully active members, while another 40% will participate occasionally.

Social Media and Qualitative Research

Media researchers are discovering that social media offer new ways to collect qualitative data. For example, **netnography** is a qualitative research method that uses ethnographic research techniques to study communities that are linked together via computer-mediated communication (Kozinets, 2002). Because it relies solely on the Internet as a source of data, it differs from traditional ethnography in a number of ways. First, it is based on published messages rather than direct observation of behavior. Second, it relies on archives. Third, thanks to social media, it examines a form of private interaction that takes place in public space. It is similar to traditional ethnography in that the researcher may choose to be a participant or simply remain an observer.

Nimrod (2011) provides an example of a netnography in his study of seniors' online communities. He identified six leading online communities, such as "50-plus," "cool grandma," and "the over-50 golden group," and analyzed about 50,000 posts to describe seniors' "fun culture." He coded his data using the constant comparison strategy and found distinctive types of topics, behaviors, and interpersonal dynamics represented in the posts.

Qualitative researchers are also using Facebook as a source of data. For example, a market research firm doing research for a client conducted a survey to determine why the client's product wasn't selling well in a particular market. After analyzing the results of the survey, the researchers recruited participants for a specially created Facebook group that allowed individuals to speak freely about the product without sharing their comments with the entire Facebook community. The participants posted photos and remarks and commented on the posts of other members. The resulting data provided insights that might not have been uncovered via traditional qualitative methods ("Facebook for qualitative research," n.d.).

Although social media can be useful in the qualitative approach, researchers should be aware of the disadvantages. First, since many posts are anonymous, commenters may feel free to post inflammatory, mischievous, or off-topic messages that distort the data. Second, not everybody posts comments at the same rate; a few people may account for the majority of messages and skew the results. Finally, if there is a product or service involved, it is possible that people who have a vested interest in the product or service may flood the conversation with positive messages. Conversely, competitors might post negative remarks.

WRITING THE QUALITATIVE RESEARCH REPORT

Writing a quantitative research report is straightforward. Writing the qualitative report, however, is more complicated. In the first place, it is difficult to condense qualitative data into numerical tables and charts. Qualitative data come in the form of sentences, extended quotes, paragraphs of description, and even pictures and diagrams. Second, there is less standardization of the methods used by qualitative researchers. Quantitative researchers generally use techniques such as a telephone survey or an experiment that has methods requiring relatively little description. On the other hand, a qualitative researcher may use a technique that is particular to one given setting or a combination of techniques in varying situations. Indeed, it is possible that

A CLOSER LOOK

Mobile Media and Qualitative Research

About 280 million Americans have mobile phones, and about 98% of these are able to send text messages. Not surprisingly, qualitative researchers, among others, are devising new ways to collect data using this new technology.

In the simplest arrangement, once participants are recruited, the researcher texts questions to them at specific times during the day and the respondents reply via a text. A more sophisticated design might request that the respondents take pictures and/or video clips of certain situations.

Some possible research situations that seem well suited to this technique would include:

- Asking people to explain why they choose to watch a particular TV program or listen to a particular radio station
- Examining the reasons behind buying one product over the competition at the point of purchase
- Obtaining feedback about a specific experience with an event, brand or company

For example, the Country Music Association (CMA) hired a market research firm to gauge fan reaction to its annual four-day CMA Music Festival in Nashville. The firm recruited 100 participants from the event's kickoff parade who had purchased a pass to the entire event. Each morning the company sent a text inquiring what the participants had planned for that day. The researchers then sent 5–6 texts during the day asking things such as which experiences were the most fun, which vendors they liked the most, and what they liked best about the city. The resulting data ran to more than 100 pages and allowed the CMA to experience the festival through the eyes of the attendees.

There are several advantages to gathering data by text messages. First, response time is fast. Since most people carry their phones with them throughout the day, participants tend to reply quickly. Mobile texting gathers immediate data; respondents don't have to remember decisions or behaviors. In addition, data can be gathered from a large sample of participants. Finally, responses can be anonymous, which allows participants to be candid in their responses. On the other hand, text messages are short and provide less detail than other qualitative data-gathering methods. Second, the research design must be kept simple because it is difficult to explain complicated instructions using text messages.

the qualitative researcher might even create entirely new ways of gathering data. As a result, the section of a qualitative report that describes the methods used in the study can be lengthy and complex. Third, qualitative researchers may try to give readers a subjective "feel" for the research setting. There may be lengthy descriptions of the research surroundings, the people involved, and the researcher's subjective thoughts about the project. Finally, whereas quantitative reports are written in an efficient and predictable, albeit unexciting, style, qualitative reports can use more free-form and literary styles. Much qualitative research is written in a loose narrative style that employs many devices used in novels and short stories. Keyton (2001), for example, describes three separate styles that can be adopted by the authors of qualitative reports: realist (a dispassionate third-person point of view), confessional (first-person point of view that reveals much about the author), and impressionist (writer uses metaphors and vivid imagery to get the point across).

As is probably obvious, qualitative reports are generally much longer than their quantitative counterparts. Indeed, it is not surprising to find that many qualitative studies done in an academic setting are published in book form rather than in journal articles.

With that as a preamble, the following is a general format for structuring the qualitative report.

1. *The Introduction.* Similar to its quantitative counterpart, the introduction provides an overview of the project, the precise research question or problem statement, the study's justification, and why the reader should be interested in it. Unlike the quantitative report, the literature review section may not be extensive. In many qualitative studies, there may not be much literature available. In addition, many qualitative researchers prefer not to do an exhaustive literature review for fear of unduly influencing their perceptions of the research situation.

2. *The Method.* This section includes a number of topics that explain what was done in the study:

a. The method or methods used to collect data and an explanation of why a particular method was chosen. For example, the sensitive nature of the data suggested that intensive interviews might be most appropriate.

b. The research setting. The researcher must provide the reader with a context for judging the suitability of the setting and to try to give a "feel" of the study.

c. Sampling. Participants or respondents can be recruited in a variety of ways, and the researcher must describe the recruitment method(s) used. The discussion should also include the sample size and the criteria used for terminating data gathering.

d. Data collection. This section should explain how the data were collected, such as field notes from observation, focus group transcripts, tapes of intensive interviews, or

diaries. The explanation should be detailed so that another researcher could replicate the collection method.

3. *Findings.* This is generally the longest section in the report, as qualitative research generates a lot of data. The biggest challenge is reducing the data to a manageable size. Ideally, the report should not be too thick and ominous; nor should it be too thin and inconsequential. Two guiding principles can help with making the data manageable. First, remember that it is impossible to say everything in a research report. Try to select vignettes, quotes, or examples that most vividly illuminate the findings. Second, choose data that illustrate the variety of information collected, including situations that were uncommon or atypical.

An overall organizational scheme will make the report more understandable. Some possibilities for arranging the findings section might include the following (Chenail, 1995):

- Organize the material chronologically.
- Present the most important findings first.
- Use a dramatic presentation and save the most important points until the end.
- Arrange the data according to some theoretical or conceptual scheme.

The findings section should strike a balance between description and analysis. Detailed quotations or examples should be followed by analysis and generalizations. Qualitative researchers need to guard against the **error of segregation** that occurs when the data are separated so far from the analysis that readers cannot make the connection. One possible arrangement that guards against this problem is as follows:

- Present a summary of the general finding.
- Show an example of the finding.
- Comment on the example.
- Show a second example.
- Comment on the second example.

- When finished with examples, make a transition to next general finding.

4. *Discussion.* This section should include a summary, additional implications of the study that might be explored in future research, and a discussion of the strengths and weaknesses of the study.

SUMMARY

Mass media research can be influenced by the research paradigm that directs the researcher. This chapter discusses the differences between the positivist approach, which generally favors quantitative methods, and the interpretive approach, which favors qualitative methods. We described five main qualitative techniques: field observations, focus groups, intensive interviews, case studies, and ethnography and also provided a description of their online counterparts.

Field observation is the study of a phenomenon in natural settings. The researcher may be a detached observer or a participant in the process under study. The main advantage of this technique is its flexibility; it can be used to develop hypotheses, to gather preliminary data, or to study groups that would otherwise be inaccessible. Its greatest disadvantage is the difficulty in achieving external validity.

The *focus group*, or group interviewing, is used to gather preliminary information for a research study or to gather qualitative data concerning a research question. The advantages of the focus group method are the ease of data collection and the depth of information that can be gathered. Among the disadvantages is that the quality of information gathered during focus groups depends heavily on the group moderator's skill.

Intensive interviewing is used to gather detailed information from a small sample of respondents, the method's primary advantage. However, because intensive interviewing is usually conducted with small, non-random samples, lack of generalizability is sometimes a disadvantage. Interviewer bias can also be a problem.

The *case study* method draws from as many data sources as possible to investigate an event. Case studies are particularly helpful when a researcher desires to explain or understand some phenomenon. Some problems with case studies are that they can lack scientific rigor, they can be time consuming to conduct, and the data they provide can be difficult to generalize from and to summarize.

Ethnographic research has its roots in anthropology and is characterized by long periods of direct observation and fieldwork aimed at allowing the researcher to see a topic from the subject's frame of reference. Netnography studies the behavior of people linked together by social media.

The qualitative research report should include an introductory section, a description of methods, findings, examples, and a discussion.

Key Terms

Analytic induction strategy	Focus group
Audit trail	Funnel technique
Case study	Intensive interview
Constant comparative technique	Interpretive paradigm
Critical paradigm	Key informants
Epoche	Netnography
Error of segregation	Paradigm
Ethnography	Pilot study
Extended focus group	Positivist paradigm
Field observation	Protocol
	Reactivity
	Saturation

 Using the Internet

For more information about the concepts in this chapter, search the Internet for "paradigm," "qualitative research," "field observations," "focus groups," and "ethnography." In addition, there are many useful sites on the web for qualitative researchers:

1. *http://www.qualitativeresearch.uga.edu/QualPage/* is the address of QualPage. This site contains general information about books, discussion forums, electronic journals, papers, conferences, and many other items of interest to a qualitative researcher.

2. *www.focusgroups.com* contains a listing of focus group facilities in metropolitan areas across the United States. There are, for example, two research organizations in South Bend, Indiana, that can arrange focus group research.

3. *www.qsrinternational.com.* QSR International manufactures software that is useful for qualitative analysis of transcripts and other texts. This page describes Nvivo, one of several programs currently available to aid in qualitative data analysis.

Questions and Problems for Further Investigation

1. Develop a research topic that is appropriate for a study by each of these methods:

   - Intensive interview
   - Field observation
   - Focus group
   - Ethnography

2. Suggest three specific research topics that are best studied using the technique of covert participation. Are any ethical problems involved?

3. Select a research topic that is suitable for study using the focus group method, then assemble six or eight of your classmates or friends and conduct a sample interview. Select an appropriate method for analyzing the data.

4. Examine recent journals in mass media research and identify instances where the case study method was used. For each example, specify the sources of data used in the study, how the data were analyzed, and how the study was reported.

5. Generate an example of mixed methods research.

6. What can a positivist researcher learn from an interpretive researcher? What can the interpretive researcher learn from the positivist researcher?

7. Some researchers claim that, excluding data collection, there are no fundamental differences between qualitative and quantitative research. What is your opinion about this perspective?

For additional resources, go to *www.wimmer dominick.com* and *www.cengagebrain.com.*

References and Suggested Readings

Anderson, J. A. (1987). *Communication research: Issues and methods.* New York, NY: McGraw-Hill.

Baker, A. (2010). Reviewing net-only college radio: A case study of Brooklyn College radio. *Journal of Radio & Audio Media, 17*(1), 109–125.

Barusch, A., Gringeri, C., & George, M. (2011). Rigor in qualitative social work research: A review of strategies used in published articles. *Social Work Research, 35*(1), 11–19.

Bechtel, R., Achelpohl, C., & Akers, R. (1972). Correlates between observed behavior and questionnaire responses on television viewing. In E. Rubinstein, G. Comstock, & J. Murray (Eds.), *Television and social behavior* (Vol. IV), 274–344. Washington, DC: U.S. Government Printing Office.

Berg, B. (2004). *Qualitative research methods.* Boston, MA: Allyn & Bacon.

Bickman, L., & Hency, T. (1972). *Beyond the laboratory: Field research in social psychology.* New York, NY: McGraw-Hill.

Bielby, D. D., Harrington, C. L., & Bielby, W. T. (1999). Whose stories are they? *Journal of Broadcasting & Electronic Media, 43*(1), 35–51.

Blaikie, N. W. (1993). *Approaches to social enquiry.* Cambridge, MA: Polity Press.

Bogdan, R., & Taylor, S. (1998). *Introduction to qualitative research methods* (3rd ed.). New York, NY: John Wiley.

Bortree, D. (2005). Presentation of self on the web: An ethnographic study of teenage girls' weblogs. *Education, Communication & Information, 5*(1), 25–39.

Brent, E. E., & Anderson, R. E. (1990). *Computer applications in the social sciences.* Philadelphia, PA: Temple University Press.

Brown, J., Dykers, C., Steele, J., & White, A. (1994). Teenage room culture. *Communication Research, 21*(6), 813–827.

Browne, D. (1983). The international newsroom. *Journal of Broadcasting, 27*(3), 205–231.

Calder, B. J. (1977). Focus groups and the nature of qualitative marketing research. *Journal of Marketing Research, 14,* 353–364.

Chadwick, B., Bahr, H., & Albrecht, S. (1984). *Social science research methods.* Englewood Cliffs, NJ: Prentice Hall.

Chenail, R. J. (1995). Presenting qualitative data. *The Qualitative Report, 2*(3), 1–12.

Christie, E. (2009). A bookstore-cafe: An exploration of the blurring of the public and private spheres. *Kaleidoscope, 8*(1), 1–15.

Corbin, J., & Strauss, A. (2007). *Basics of qualitative research.* Thousand Oaks, CA: Sage.

Cox, K. D., Higginbotham, J. B., & Burton, J. (1976). Applications of focus group interviewing in marketing. *Journal of Marketing, 40,* 77–80.

Creswell, J. (2003). *Research design: Qualitative, quantitative and mixed method approaches.* Thousand Oaks, CA: Sage Publications.

Creswell, J. (2007). *Designing and conducting mixed methods research.* Thousand Oaks, CA: Sage Publications

Creswell, J. W. (2007). *Qualitative inquiry and research design.* Thousand Oaks, CA: Sage.

Daymon, C., & Holloway, I. (2002). *Qualitative research methods in public relations and marketing communications.* New York, NY: Routledge.

Dimmick, J., & Wallschlaeger, M. (1986). Measuring corporate diversification. *Journal of Broadcasting & Electronic Media, 30*(1), 1–14.

Elliot, S. C. (1980). *Focus group research: A workbook for broadcasters.* Washington, DC: National Association of Broadcasters.

Emerson, R., Fretz, R., & Shaw, L. (1995). *Writing ethnographic field notes.* Chicago, IL: University of Chicago Press.

Epstein, E. J. (1974). *News from nowhere.* New York, NY: Vintage.

Erjavec, K., & Kovacic, M. (2010). News producers' pressures on advertisers: Production of paid news in Slovenian television programs. *Journal of Broadcasting & Electronic Media, 54*(3), 357–372.

Erickson, F. (1986). Qualitative methods in research on teaching. In M. C. Wittrock (Ed.), *Handbook of research on teaching.* New York, NY: Macmillan.

Facebook for qualitative research (n.d.). Retrieved from *www.gdc-co.com/work/articles/facebook-qualitative-research.*

Fletcher, A., & Bowers, T. (1991). *Fundamentals of advertising research* (4th ed.). Belmont, CA: Wadsworth.

Gieber, W. (1956). Across the desk: A study of 16 telegraph editors. *Journalism Quarterly, 33,* 423–432.

Glaser, B., & Strauss, A. (1967). *The discovery of grounded theory.* Chicago, IL: Aldine.

Goodman, J. R. (2002). Flabless is fabulous: How Latina and Anglo women read and incorporate the excessively thin body ideal into everyday experiences. *Journalism & Mass Communication Quarterly, 79*(3), 712–728.

Greenwood, D. (2010). Of sad men and dark comedies: Mood and gender effects of entertainment media preferences. *Mass Communication & Society, 13*(3), 232–249.

Gunther, A., Kautz, D., & Roth, A. (2011). The credibility of female sports broadcasters: The perception of gender in a male-dominated profession. *Human Communication, 14*(2), 71–84.

Hall, S. (1982). The rediscovery of ideology. In M. Gurevitch, T. Bennett, J. Curran, & J. Woollacott (Eds.), *Culture, society & the media* (pp. 56–90). New York, NY: Methuen.

Hammersly, M. (1992). *What's wrong with ethnography? Methodological explorations.* London: Routledge.

Harrington, C. L. (2003). Homosexuality on *All My Children. Journal of Broadcasting & Electronic Media, 47*(2), 216–235.

Hood, L. (2007). Radio reverb: The impact of local news reimported to its own community. *Journal of Broadcasting & Electronic Media, 51*(1), 1–19.

Ishamel, G., & Thomas, J. (2006). Worth a thousand words. *Journal of Advertising Research, 46*(3), 274–278.

Kaun, A. (2010). Open-ended online diaries: Capturing life as it is narrated. *International Journal of Qualitative Methods, 9*(2), 133–148.

Keyton, J. (2001). *Communication research.* Mountain View, CA: Mayfield.

Kozinets, R. V. (2002). The field behind the screen: Using netnography for marketing research in online communities. *Journal of Marketing Research, 39*(1), 61–72.

Kover, A. (2008). Qual vs. quant … again. *International Journal of Advertising, 27*(4), 663–666.

Krueger, R. A., & Casey, M. A. (2000). *Focus groups: A practical guide for applied research.* Thousand Oaks, CA: Sage.

LeCompte, M. D., & Schensul, J. J. (1999). *Ethnographer's toolkit.* Walnut Creek, CA: Altamira Press.

Lewis, N. (2008). Plagiarism antecedents and situational influences. *Journalism & Mass Communication Quarterly, 85*(2), 353–370.

Lieberman, E., Neuendorf, K., Denny, J., Skalski, P., & Wang, J. (2009). The language of laughter: A quantitative/qualitative fusion examining television narrative and humor. *Journal of Broadcasting & Electronic Media, 53*(4), 497–514.

Lincoln, Y., & Guba, E. (1985). *Naturalistic inquiry.* Beverly Hills, CA: Sage.

Lindlof, T. R. (1991). The qualitative study of media audiences. *Journal of Broadcasting & Electronic Media, 35*(1), 23–42.

Lindlof, T. R. (2002). *Qualitative communication research methods.* Thousand Oaks, CA: Sage.

Lull, J. (1985). Ethnographic studies of broadcast media audiences. In J. Dominick & J. Fletcher (Eds.), *Broadcasting research methods.* Boston, MA: Allyn & Bacon.

Lunt, P., & Livingstone, S. (1996). Rethinking the focus group in media and communications research. *Journal of Communication, 46*(2), 79–89.

Mayer, V. (2003). Living telenovelas/telenovelizing life. *Journal of Communication, 53*(3), 479–495.

Maykut, P., & Morehouse, R. (1994). *Beginning qualitative research*. Bristol, PA: The Falmer Press.

Merriam, S. B. (1988). *Case study research in education*. San Francisco, CA: Jossey-Bass.

Miles, M. B., & Huberman, A. M. (1994). *Qualitative data analysis* (2nd ed.). Beverly Hills, CA: Sage.

Moriarty, S., & Everett, S. (1994). Commercial breaks: A viewing behavior study. *Journalism Quarterly, 71*(2), 346–355.

Neill, J. (2007). Qualitative versus quantitative research: Key points in a classic debate. Retrieved from *http://wilderdom.com/research/QualitativeVersus QuantitativeResearch.html*

Neuman, W. L. (1997). *Social research methods*. Boston, MA: Allyn & Bacon.

Nimrod, G. (2011). The fun culture in seniors' online communities. *The Gerontologist, 51*(2), 226–237.

Onwuegbuzie, A., & Leech, N. (2006). Validity and qualitative research. *Quality & Quantity, 41*(2), 233–249.

Pompper, D., Soto, J., & Piel, L. (2007). Male body image and magazine standards. *Journalism & Mass Communication Quarterly, 84*(3), 522–545.

Potter, W. J. (1996). *An analysis of thinking and research about qualitative methods*. Mahwah, NJ: Lawrence Erlbaum.

Priest, P. J. (1992). *Self-disclosure on television*. Unpublished doctoral dissertation, University of Georgia, Athens.

Robertson, L., Kelley, A. B., O'Neill, B., Wixom, C. W., Elswirth, R. S., & Haddon, W. (1974). A controlled study of the effect of television messages of safety belt use. *American Journal of Public Health, 64*, 1074–1084.

Rubin, H. (1984). *Applied social research*. Columbus, OH: Charles E. Merrill.

Sarantakos, S. (1998). *Social research*. New York, NY: MacMillan.

Shamp, S. A. (1991). Mechanomorphism in perception of computer communication partners. *Computers in Human Behavior, 17*, 147–161.

Simon, J. (1985). *Basic research methods in social science* (3rd ed.). New York, NY: Random House.

Smith, S., & Krugman, D. (2010). Exploring perceptions and usage patterns of digital video recorder owners. *Journal of Broadcasting & Electronic Media, 54*(2), 248–264.

Stainback, S., & Stainback, W. (1988). *Understanding and conducting qualitative research*. Dubuque, IA: Kendall/Hunt.

Tovares, R. (2000). Latino USA: Constructing a news and public affairs program. *Journal of Broadcasting and Electronic Media, 44*(3), 471–486.

Tull, D., & Hawkins, D. (1990). *Marketing research* (5th ed.). New York, NY: Macmillan.

Webb, E. J., Campbell, D. T., Schwartz, R. D., & Sechrest, L. (1968). *Unobtrusive measures*. Chicago, IL: Rand McNally.

Westley, B. H. (1989). The controlled experiment. In G. H. Stempel & B. H. Westley (Eds.), *Research methods in mass communication* (2nd ed.), 200–220. Englewood Cliffs, NJ: Prentice Hall.

Williams, M. (2007). Avatar watching: Participant observation in graphical online environments. *Qualitative Research, 7*(1), 5–24.

Williamson, J. B., Karp, D. A., & Dalphin, J. R. (1992). *The research craft* (2nd ed.). Boston, MA: Little, Brown.

Winn, J. (2009). Videotime: Selection and structuring family social time with rented commercially prerecorded electronic media. *Journal of Broadcasting & Electronic Media, 53*(2), 227–241.

Wolf, M. (1987). How children negotiate television. In T. R. Lindlof (Ed.), *Natural audiences: Qualitative research of media uses and effects* (pp. 58–94). Norwood, NJ: Ablex.

Woodside, A., & Fleck, R. (1979). The case approach to understanding brand choice. *Journal of Advertising Research, 19*(2), 23–30.

Woodward, B., & Bernstein, C. (1974). *All the president's men*. New York, NY: Simon & Schuster.

Yin, R. (2003). *Case study research* (3rd ed.). Newbury Park, CA: Sage Publications.

Yin, R., Bateman, P., & Moore, G. (1983). *Case studies and organizational innovation*. Washington, DC: Cosmos Corporation.

# CHAPTER 6

CONTENT ANALYSIS

CHAPTER OUTLINE

This chapter discusses content analysis, a specific research approach used frequently in all areas of the media. The method is popular with mass media researchers because it is an efficient way to investigate the content of the media, such as the number and types of commercials or advertisements in broadcasting or the print media. Beginning researchers will find content analysis a valuable tool in answering many mass media questions.

The first example of content analysis was probably an examination of 90 hymns published in Sweden in 1743 (Dovring, 1954). Modern content analysis can be traced back to World War II, when Allied intelligence units painstakingly monitored the number and types of popular songs played on European radio stations. By comparing the music played on German stations with that on other stations in occupied Europe, the Allies were able to measure with some degree of certainty the changes in troop concentration on the continent. In the Pacific theater, communications between Japan and various island bases were carefully tabulated; an increase in message volume to and from a particular base usually indicated some new operation involving that base.

At about the same time, content analysis was used in attempts to verify the authorship of historical documents. These studies were concerned primarily with counting words in documents of questionable authenticity and comparing their frequencies with the same words in documents whose authors were known (Yule, 1944). More recently, this technique was used to attribute the authorship of 12 disputed "Federalist Papers" to James Madison (Martindale & McKenzie, 1995). These literary detective cases demonstrated the usefulness of quantification in content analysis.

After the war, researchers used content analysis to study propaganda in newspapers and radio. In 1952, Bernard Berelson published *Content Analysis in Communication Research*, which signaled that the technique had gained recognition as a tool for media scholars. Since that time, content analysis has become a popular research technique.

Riffe and Freitag (1997) found that about 25% of the 1,977 full-length research articles published in *Journalism and Mass Communication Quarterly* from 1971 to 1995 were content analyses. Kamhawi and Weaver (2003) revealed that content analysis was the most popular data-gathering method reported in major mass communication journals between 1995 and 1999. An informal content analysis of three journals that focus on mass communication research (*Journal of Broadcasting & Electronic Media, Journalism* and *Mass Communication Quarterly,* and *Mass Communication and Society*) from 2009 to 2010 found that content analysis was still a popular method, used in about one-third of all published articles.

DEFINITION OF CONTENT ANALYSIS

There are many definitions of *content analysis*. Walizer and Wienir (1978) define it as any systematic procedure devised to examine the content of recorded information; Krippendorf (2004) defines it as a research technique for making replicable and valid references from data to their context. Kerlinger's (2000) definition is fairly typical: Content analysis is a method of studying and analyzing communication in a *systematic, objective,* and *quantitative* manner for the purpose of measuring variables.

Kerlinger's definition involves three concepts that require elaboration. First, content analysis is *systematic.* This means that the content to be analyzed is selected according to explicit and consistently applied rules: Sample selection must follow proper procedures, and each item must have an equal chance of being included in the analysis. Moreover, the evaluation process must be systematic: All content under consideration is to be treated in exactly the same manner. There must be uniformity in the coding and analysis procedures and in the length of time coders are exposed to the material. Systematic evaluation simply means that one and only one set of guidelines is used for evaluation throughout the study. Alternating procedures in an analysis is a sure way to confound the results.

Second, content analysis is *objective*; that is, the researcher's personal idiosyncrasies and biases should not enter into the findings. The analysis should yield the same results if another researcher replicates the study. Operational definitions and rules for the classification of variables should be explicit and comprehensive so that other researchers who repeat the process will arrive at the same decisions. Unless a clear set of criteria and procedures is established that fully explains the sampling and categorization methods, the researcher does not meet the requirement of objectivity and the reliability of the results may be called into question. Perfect objectivity, however, is seldom achieved in a content analysis. The specification of the unit of analysis and the precise makeup and definition of relevant categories are areas in which individual researchers must exercise subjective choice. (Reliability, as it applies to content analysis, is discussed at length later in this chapter.)

Third, content analysis is *quantitative*. The goal of content analysis is an accurate representation of a body of messages. Quantification is important in fulfilling that objective because it aids researchers in the quest for precision. The statement "Seventy percent of all prime-time programs contain at least one act of violence" is more precise than "Most shows are violent." Additionally, quantification allows researchers to summarize results and to report them succinctly. If measurements are made over intervals of time, comparisons of the numerical data from one time period to

another can help simplify and standardize the evaluation procedure. Finally, quantification gives researchers additional statistical tools that can aid in interpretation and analysis.

However, quantification should not blind the researcher to other ways of assessing the potential impact or effects of the content. The fact that some item or behavior was the most frequently occurring element in a body of content does not necessarily make that element the most important. For example, a content analysis of the news coverage of the uprisings in North Africa in 2011 might disclose that 70% of the coverage showed nonviolent scenes. Yet the other 30% that contained violence might have been so powerful and so sensational that their impact on the audience was far greater than the nonviolent coverage.

USES OF CONTENT ANALYSIS

Over the past decade, the symbols and messages contained in the mass media have become increasingly popular research topics in both the academic sector and the private sector. Public relations firms use content analysis to monitor the subject matter of company publications, and the *Media Monitor* publishes periodic studies of how the media treat social and political issues.

Although it is difficult to classify and categorize studies as varied and diverse as those using content analysis, the studies are usually conducted for one of six purposes. The following discussion of these six purposes illustrates some ways in which this technique can be applied.

Describing Communication Content

Several recent studies have cataloged the characteristics of a given body of communication content at one or more points in time. These studies demonstrate content analysis used in the traditional, descriptive manner: to identify what exists. For example, Sapolsky, Molitor, and Luque (2003) described trends in the depiction of sex and violence in "slasher" movies. Maier (2010) compared news content that appeared on the web to traditional media coverage. One of the advantages of content analysis is its potential to identify developments over long time periods. Cho (2007) illustrated how TV newscasts portrayed plastic surgery over the course of three decades, and Dudo, Dunwoody, and Scheufele (2011) described news coverage of nanotechnology over a 20-year period.

These descriptive studies also can be used to study societal change. For example, changing public opinion on various controversial issues could be gauged with a longitudinal study (see Chapter 8) of letters to the editor or newspaper editorials. Statements about what values are judged to be important by a society could be inferred from a study of the nonfiction books on the bestseller list at different points in time. Greenberg and Worrell (2007), for example, analyzed changes in the demographic makeup of characters in the broadcast networks' programs that premiered from 1993 to 2004. Harmon and Lee (2010) described changes in how TV newscasts covered strikes from 1968 to 2007.

Testing Hypotheses of Message Characteristics

A number of analyses attempt to relate certain characteristics of the source of a given body of message content to the characteristics of the messages that are produced. As Holsti (1969) points out, this category of content analysis has been used in many studies that test hypotheses of form: "If the source has characteristic *A*, then messages containing elements *x* and *y* will be produced; if the source has characteristic *B*, then messages with elements *w* and *z* will be produced." Smith and Boyson (2002) discovered that rap music videos were more likely to contain violence than any other music genre. Jha (2007) determined that journalists covering a particular social protest in 1999 relied on official sources more than

journalists who covered an antiwar protest in 1967. Finally, Lowry and Naser (2010) found that campaign commercials for winning presidential candidates contained more positive terms whereas commercials for losing candidates contained more self-related words such as "I," "me," and "my."

Comparing Media Content to the "Real World"

Many content analyses are reality checks in which the portrayal of a certain group, phenomenon, trait, or characteristic is assessed against a standard taken from real life. The congruence of the media presentation and the actual situation is then discussed. Probably the earliest study of this type was by Davis (1951), who found that crime coverage in Colorado newspapers bore no relationship to changes in state crime rates. The National Commission on the Causes and Prevention of Violence used content analysis data collected by Gerbner (1969) to compare the world of television violence with real-life violence. Dixon, Azocar, and Casas (2003) compared the portrayal of race and crime on network news programs to crime reports issued by the U.S. Department of Justice, and Jensen, Moriarty, Hurley, and Stryker (2010) contrasted newspaper coverage of cancer with the actual incidence of cancer in the United States.

Assessing the Image of Particular Groups in Society

Ever-growing numbers of content analyses have focused on exploring the media images of certain minority or otherwise notable groups. In many instances, these studies are conducted to assess changes in media policy toward these groups, to make inferences about the media's responsiveness to demands for better coverage, or to document social trends. For example, Poindexter, Smith, and Heider (2003) found that Latinos, Asian Americans, and Native Americans were rarely seen in local television newscasts. Mastro and

Ortiz (2008) noted differences in the way that social groups were portrayed in Spanish-language television, and Fitzgerald (2010) traced how Native Americans were depicted on prime-time TV from 1966 to 2008.

Framing Analysis

Framing analysis has recently enjoyed increasing popularity among mass media researchers. Matthes (2009) identified more than 130 framing studies in communication journals from 1995 to 2005. Of the 59 content analyses published in three leading mass communication journals from 2009 to 2010, nearly 15% used this approach. Most analyses focus on the frames found in news reporting.

Entman (1993) defined framing as selecting some aspects of a perceived reality and making them more salient in a communication text, in such a way as to promote a particular problem definition, causal interpretation, moral evaluation, and/or treatment recommendation for the item described. Frames highlight some bits of information about an item and downplay other aspects. For example, a news report about a change in food stamp eligibility might stress the plight of those who will no longer qualify for the program and downplay the amount of taxpayer money that will be saved by the new regulations.

Framing analysis can be divided into three categories: (1) frame building, (2) frame description and comparison, and (3) framing effects. Frame building refers to what forces shape how news is framed, such as editorial policies, news values, and influence of external forces, such as public relations campaigns. Content analysis is seldom used in frame building research. Content analysis is more common in the second category. Researchers use it to identify and describe how news media frame general and specific issues. In addition, frames can be compared across media to determine whether, for example, print media frame an issue differently from the electronic media.

To illustrate, Kim, Carvalho, and Davis (2010) examined how the news media framed the causes of poverty. They found two main frames: one that stressed personal causes and one that stressed societal causes. In their study of news coverage of the trans fat ban in New York City, Wise and Brewer (2010) found that news media framed the story as a public health issue or a business issue.

The third category, framing effects analysis is discussed in the next section.

Establishing a Starting Point for Studies of Media Effects

The use of content analysis as a starting point for subsequent studies dates back to the 1970s. The best known example is **cultivation analysis**, in which the dominant message and themes in media content are documented by systematic procedures and a separate study of the audience is conducted to see whether these messages are fostering similar attitudes among heavy media users. Gerbner, Gross, Signorielli, Morgan, and Jackson-Beeck (1979) discovered that heavy viewers of television tend to be more fearful of the world around them. In other words, television content—in this case, large doses of crime and violence—may cultivate attitudes more consistent with its messages than with reality. Other work that has used a similar framework includes Busselle and Crandall's (2002) study of TV viewing and perceptions of race differences in socioeconomic success and Mutz and Nir's (2010) analysis that indicated that fictional TV programs can affect public attitudes about policy issues.

Content analysis is also used in studies of agenda setting. An analysis of relevant media content is necessary to determine the importance of news topics. Subsequent audience research looks at the correspondence between the media's agenda and the audience's agenda. For instance, Kim, Scheufele, and Shanahan (2002) discovered that a local newspaper's prominent coverage of certain issues increased the importance of this issue among readers. Sweetser, Golan, and Wanta (2008) found that the content of blogs was strongly related to media content during the 2004 election.

Framing effects analysis is similar to agenda setting research. This approach uses content analysis to define news frames and then conducts audience research to see whether the media frames had an effect on audience perception. To illustrate, Han, Chock, and Shoemaker (2009) found that news frames affected both U.S. and Chinese audiences' perceptions of the 2004 election in Taiwan.

LIMITATIONS OF CONTENT ANALYSIS

Content analysis alone cannot serve as the basis for making statements about the effects of content on an audience. A study of cartoon programs on television might reveal that 80% of these programs contain commercials for sugared cereal, but this finding alone does not allow researchers to claim that children who watch these programs will want to purchase sugared cereals. To make such an assertion, an additional study of the viewers is necessary (as in cultivation analysis). Content analysis cannot serve as the sole basis for claims about media effects.

Also, the findings of a particular content analysis are limited to the framework of the categories and the definitions used in that analysis. Different researchers may use varying definitions and category systems to measure a single concept. In mass media research, this problem is most evident in studies of televised violence. Some researchers rule out comic or slapstick violence in their studies, whereas others consider it an important dimension. Obviously, great care should be exercised in comparing the results of different content analysis studies. Researchers who use different tools of measurement naturally arrive at different conclusions.

Another potential limitation of content analysis is a lack of messages relevant to the research. Many topics or characters receive little

exposure in the mass media. For example, a study of how Native Americans are portrayed in U.S. television commercials would be difficult because such characters are rarely seen (of course, this fact in itself might be a significant finding). A researcher interested in this topic must be prepared to examine a large body of media content to find sufficient quantities for analysis.

Finally, content analysis is frequently time consuming and expensive. The task of examining and categorizing large volumes of content is often laborious and tedious. Plowing through 100 copies of the *New York Times* or 50 issues of *Newsweek* takes time and patience. In addition, if television content is selected for analysis, there must be some means of preserving the programs for detailed examination.

STEPS IN CONTENT ANALYSIS

In general, a content analysis is conducted in several discrete stages. Although the steps are listed here in sequence, they need not be followed in the order given. In fact, the initial stages of analysis can easily be combined. Nonetheless, the following steps may be used as a rough outline:

1. Formulate the research question or hypothesis.
2. Define the universe in question.
3. Select an appropriate sample from the population.
4. Select and define a unit of analysis.
5. Construct the categories of content to be analyzed.
6. Establish a quantification system.
7. Train coders and conduct a pilot study.
8. Code the content according to established definitions.
9. Analyze the collected data.
10. Draw conclusions and search for indications.

Formulating a Research Question

One problem to avoid in content analysis is the syndrome of "counting for the sake of counting." The goal of the analysis must be clearly articulated to avoid aimless exercises in data collection that have little utility for mass media research. For example, after counting the punctuation marks used in the *New York Times* and *Esquire*, one might make a statement such as "*Esquire* used 45% more commas but 23% fewer semicolons than the *New York Times*." The value of such information for mass media theory or policy making is dubious. Content analysis should not be conducted simply because the material exists and can be tabulated.

As with other methods of mass media research, content analysis should be guided by well-formulated research questions or hypotheses. A basic review of the literature is a required step. The sources for hypotheses are the same as for other areas of media research. It is possible to generate a research question based on existing theory, prior research, or practical problems, or as a response to changing social conditions. For example, a research question might ask whether the growing acceptability of motorcycles has produced a change in the way motorcyclists are depicted in TV shows. Or a content analysis might be conducted to determine whether news on a newspaper website differs from the news in the print edition of that same newspaper. Well-defined research questions or hypotheses lead to the development of accurate and sensitive content categories, which in turn helps to produce data that are more valuable.

Defining the Universe

This stage of the content analysis process is not as grandiose as it sounds. To "define the **universe**" is to specify the boundaries of the body of content to be considered, which requires an appropriate operational definition of the relevant population. If researchers are interested in analyzing the content of popular songs, they must define what is meant by a "popular song": All songs listed in *Billboard*'s "Hot 100" chart? The top 50 songs? The top 10? They must also ask what time period will be considered: The past six months? This month only? A researcher who intends to study the image of minority groups on television must first define what the term *television* means. Does it include broadcast and cable networks? Pay television? DVDs? Is it evening programming, or does it also include daytime shows? Will the study examine news content or confine itself to dramatic offerings?

Two dimensions are usually used to determine the appropriate universe for a content analysis—the topic area and the time period. The topic area should be logically consistent with the research question and related to the goals of the study. For example, if a researcher plans a study of news coverage of U.S. involvement in Iraq, should the sample period extend back to the early 1990s? Finally, the time period to be examined should be sufficiently long so that the phenomenon under study has enough time to occur.

By clearly specifying the topic area and the time period, the researcher is meeting a basic requirement of content analysis: a concise statement that spells out the parameters of the investigation. For example:

> This study considers TV commercials broadcast in prime time in the New York City area from September 1, 2012, to August 31, 2013.

or

> This study considers the news content on the front pages of the *Washington Post* and the *New York Times,* excluding Sundays, from January 1 to December 31 of the past year.

A CLOSER LOOK

Content Analysis: Coder Perception versus Audience Perception

One problem with using content analysis as a starting point for studies of audience effects is the possibility of falsely assuming that what trained coders see in a body of content is the same as what audience members perceive. For example, a study of the cultivation effects of TV content on viewers' attitudes toward sexual practices might start with an analysis of the sexual content of specific television programs. Coders might be trained to count how many provocatively dressed characters appear; how many instances of kissing, embracing, caressing, and other forms of sexual behavior occur; and so on. When the coders are finished with this aspect of the study, they could rank-order a list of TV programs with regard to their sexual content. Audience viewings of these shows could then be correlated with audience attitudes toward sexual matters. The trouble is that the researchers do not know whether the audience defines the term *sexual content* in

the same way the coders do. For example, many in the audience might not define all forms of kissing as sexual. Or perhaps programs where sexual activity is only talked about, such as *The View*, are also influential in shaping audience attitudes. Since these shows would probably score low on most of the measures used by coders to gauge sexual content, the influence of these shows might be overlooked.

Manganello et al. (2010) shed some light on this issue. In their study of adolescents' judgment of sexual content on television, they compared the decisions made by trained coders with coding decisions made by untrained adolescents. They found that coders and adolescents generally agreed on manifest content but were less likely to agree on variables that required some judgment, such as whether a character wore a sexy costume.

Selecting a Sample

Once the universe is defined, a sample is selected. Although many of the guidelines and procedures discussed in Chapter 4 are applicable here, the sampling of content involves some special considerations. On one hand, some analyses are concerned with a finite amount of data, and it may be possible to conduct a census of the content. For example, Greenberg and Collette (1997) performed a census of all new major characters added to the broadcast networks' program lineup from 1966 to 1992, a total of 1,757 characters, and Matthes (2009) did a census of all 131 media framing studies in communication journals. On the other

hand, in the more typical situation, the researcher has such a vast amount of content available that a census is not practical. Thus, a sample must be selected.

Most content analysis in mass media involves multistage sampling. This process typically consists of two stages (although it may entail three). The first stage is usually to take a sampling of content sources. For example, a researcher interested in the treatment of the "green" movement by American newspapers would first need to sample from among the 1,400 or so newspapers published each day. The researcher may decide to focus primarily on the way big-city dailies covered the story and opt to analyze only the leading circulation newspapers in the 10 largest American cities. To take another example, a researcher interested in the changing portrayal of elderly people in magazine advertisements would first need to sample from among the thousands of publications available. In this instance, the researcher might select only the top 10, 15, or 25 mass-circulation magazines. Of course, it is also possible to sample randomly if the task of analyzing all the titles is too overwhelming. A further possibility is to use the technique of stratified sampling discussed in Chapter 4. A researcher studying the environmental movement might wish to stratify the sample by circulation size and to sample from within the strata composed of big-city newspapers, medium-city newspapers, and small-city newspapers. The magazine researcher might stratify by type of magazine: news, women's interests, men's interests, and so on. A researcher interested in television content might stratify by network or by program type.

Once the sources have been identified, the second step is to select the dates. In many studies, the time period from which the issues are to be selected is determined by the goal of the project. If the goal is to assess the nature of news coverage of the 2012 election campaign, the sampling period is fairly well defined by the actual duration of the story. If the research question is about changes in the media coverage of a presidential candidate following his nomination, content should be sampled before, at the time of, and after the event. But within this period, which editions of newspapers and magazines and which television programs should be selected for analysis? It would be a tremendous amount of work to analyze each issue of the *Washington Post* and the *New York Times* over an extended period. It is possible to sample from within that time period and obtain a representative group of issues. A simple random sample of the calendar dates involved is one possibility: After a random start, every *n*th issue of a publication is selected for the sample. This method cannot be used without planning, however. For instance, if the goal is 10 edition dates and an interval of 7 is used, the sample might include 10 Saturday editions (a problem called "periodicity"). Because news content is not distributed randomly over the days of the week, such a sample will not be representative.

Another technique for sampling edition dates is stratification by week of the month and by day of the week. A sampling rule that no more than two days from one week can be chosen is one way to ensure a balanced distribution across the month. Another procedure is to construct a **composite week** for each month in the sample. For example, a study might use a sample of one Monday (drawn at random from the four or five possible Mondays in the month), one Tuesday (drawn from the available Tuesdays), and so on, until all weekdays have been included. How many edition dates should be selected? Obviously, this depends on the topic under study. If an investigator is trying to describe the portrayal of Mexican Americans on prime-time television, several dates have to be sampled to ensure a representative analysis. If there is an interest in analyzing the geographic sources of news stories, a smaller number of dates is needed because almost every story is relevant. The number of dates should be a function of the incidence of the phenomenon in question: The lower the incidence, the more dates must be sampled.

There are some rough guidelines for sampling in the media. Stempel (1952) drew separate samples of 6, 12, 18, 24, and 48 issues of a newspaper and compared the average content of each sample size in a single subject category against the total for the entire year. He found that each of the five sample sizes was adequate and that increasing the sample beyond 12 issues did not significantly improve sampling accuracy. Riffe, Aust, and Lacy (1993) demonstrated that a composite week sampling technique was superior to both a random sample and a consecutive day sample when dealing with newspaper content. Similarly, Riffe, Lacy, and Drager (1996) studied the optimum sample sizes for an analysis of weekly newsmagazines, and Lacy, Robinson, and Riffe (1995) did the same for weekly newspapers. They found that a monthly stratified sample of 12 issues was the most efficient sample for both magazines and newspapers. The next most efficient method was a simple random sample of 14 issues.

In television, Gerbner, Gross, Jackson-Beeck, Jeffries-Fox, and Signorielli (1977) demonstrated that, at least for the purpose of measuring violent behavior, a sample of one week of fall programming and various sample dates drawn throughout the year produced comparable results. Riffe, Lacy, Nagovan, and Burkum (1996) examined sample sizes for content analysis of broadcast news and found that two days per month chosen at random proved to be the most efficient method. However, as a general rule, the larger the sample, the better—within reason, of course. If too few dates are selected for analysis, the possibility of an unrepresentative sample is increased. Larger samples, if chosen randomly, usually run less risk of being atypical.

There may be times, however, when purposive sampling is useful. As Stempel (1989) points out, a researcher might learn more about newspaper coverage of South Africa by examining a small sample of carefully selected papers (for example, those that subscribe to the international/national wire services or have correspondents in South Africa) than by studying a random sample of 100 newspapers.

Another problem that can arise during the sampling phase is systematic bias in the content itself. For example, a study of the amount of sports news in a daily paper might yield inflated results if the sampling were done only in April, when three or more professional sports are simultaneously in season. A study of marriage announcements in the Sunday *New York Times* for the month of June from 1932 to 1942 revealed no announcement of a marriage in a synagogue (Hatch & Hatch, 1947). It was later pointed out that the month of June usually falls within a period during which traditional Jewish marriages are prohibited. Researchers familiar with their topics can generally discover and guard against this type of distortion.

Once the sources and the dates have been determined, there may be a third stage of sampling. A researcher might wish to confine his or her attention to the specific content within an edition. For example, an analysis of the front page of a newspaper is valid for a study of general reporting trends but is probably inadequate for a study of social news coverage. Figure 6.1 provides an example of multistage sampling in content analysis.

Sampling online content raises special problems and is discussed below.

Selecting a Unit of Analysis

The next step in the content analysis process is to select the **unit of analysis**, which is the smallest element of a content analysis but also one of the most important. In written content, the unit of analysis might be a single word or symbol, a theme (a single assertion about one subject), or an entire article or story. In television and film analyses, units of analysis can be characters, acts, or entire programs or films. Specific rules and definitions are required for determining these units to ensure closer agreement among coders and fewer judgment calls.

Certain units of analysis are simpler to count than others. It is easier to determine the number of stories on the *CBS Evening News* that deal with international news

---

Figure 6.1   Multistage Sampling in a Hypothetical Analysis Study

Research Question: Have there been changes in the types of products advertised in men's
magazines from 1980 to 2000?

Sampling Stage 1: Selection of Titles

Men's magazines are defined as those magazines whose circulation figures show that 80% or more
of their readers are men. These magazines will be divided into two groups: large and medium
circulation.

Large circulation: reaches more than 1,000,000 men.

Medium circulation: reaches between 500,000 and 999,999 men.

From all the magazines that fall into these two groups, three will be selected at random from each
division, for a total of six titles.

Sampling Stage 2: Selection of Dates

Three issues from each year will be chosen at random from clusters of four months. One magazine
will be selected from the January, February, March, and April issues, and so on. This procedure
will be followed for each magazine, yielding a final sample of 30 issues per magazine, or a total
of 180 issues.

Sampling Stage 3: Selection of Content

Every other display ad will be tabulated, regardless of its size.

---

than the number of acts of violence in a week
of network television because a story is a
more readily distinguishable unit of analysis.
The beginning and ending of a news story are
fairly easy to discern, but suppose that a
researcher trying to catalog violent content
is faced with a long fistfight among three
characters. Is the whole sequence one act of
violence, or is every blow considered an act?
What if a fourth character joins in? Does it
then become a different act?

Operational definitions of the unit of
analysis should be clear-cut and thorough;
the criteria for inclusion should be apparent
and easily observed. These goals cannot be
met without effort and some trial and error.
As a preliminary step, researchers must
form a rough draft of a definition and then
sample representative content to look for
problems. This procedure usually results in
further refinement and modification of the

operational definition. Table 6.1 presents
typical operational definitions of units of
analysis taken from mass media research.

Constructing Content Categories

At the heart of any content analysis is the
category system used to classify media content. The precise makeup of this system, of
course, varies with the topic under study. As
Berelson (1952) points out, "Particular studies have been productive to the extent that
the categories were clearly formulated and
well-adapted to the problem and the content" (p. 147).

There are two ways to go about establishing content categories. **Emergent coding**
establishes categories after a preliminary
examination of the data. The resulting category system is constructed based on common
factors or themes that emerge from the
data themselves. For example, Potter (2002)

Table 6.1 Samples and Operational Definitions of Units of Analysis

Researcher(s)	Topic	Universe	Sample	Unit of Analysis
Haigh and Heresco (2010)	Late-Night Iraq: Monologue Joke Content and Tone 2003–2007	All Iraq-based jokes from the *Tonight Show, Late Show,* and *Late Night*	All jokes in Lexis-Nexis Academic Universe using keywords "Iraq" or "war" from March 2003 to April 2007	Any joke discussing the war
Greer and Ferguson (2011)	Using Twitter for Promotion and Branding	U.S. TV stations with Twitter accounts	First page of 488 TV stations' Twitter accounts	Individual tweets
Schwartz and Andsager (2011)	Images in Gay Male-Targeted Magazines	All issues of *The Advocate* and *Out,* 1967–2008	Random sample of four issues from every third year of issues	Photographic images of men
Aubrey and Frisby (2011)	Sexual Objectification in Music Videos	Popular songs in the pop, R&B, and country genres	Random sample of videos based on Billboard's charts from 2007–2008	Individual artists and overall music video

analyzed the content of FM radio stations' websites and, after examining the frequency of various items, found that they clustered into four major categories: station contact variables, station information variables, news and information, and other.

On the other hand, **a priori coding** establishes the categories before the data are collected, based on some theoretical or conceptual rationale. In their study of media coverage of fundamentalist Christians, Kerr and Moy (2002) developed a 10-category system based on stereotypes that were reported in the American National Election Studies, and then they coded more than 2,000 newspaper articles into the 10 categories.

To be serviceable, all category systems should be mutually exclusive, exhaustive, and reliable. A category system is **mutually exclusive** if a unit of analysis can be placed in one and only one category. If the researcher discovers that certain units fall simultaneously into two categories, then the definitions of those categories must be revised. For example, suppose researchers attempt to describe the ethnic makeup of prime-time television characters using the following category system: (1) African American, (2) Jewish, (3) White, (4) Native American, and (5) other. Obviously, a Jewish person falls into two categories at once, thus violating the exclusivity rule. Or, to take another example, a researcher might start with these categories in an attempt to describe the types of programming on network television: (1) situation comedies, (2) children's shows, (3) movies, (4) documentaries, (5) action/adventure programs, (6) quiz and talk shows, and (7) general drama. This list might look acceptable at first glance, but a program such as *CSI* raises questions. Does it belong in the action/adventure category or in the general drama category? Definitions must be highly specific to ensure accurate categorization.

In addition to exclusivity, content analysis categories must have the property of **exhaustivity**: There must be an existing slot into which every unit of analysis can be placed. If investigators suddenly find a unit of analysis that does not logically fit into a predefined category, they have a problem with their category system. Taken as a whole, the category system should account for every unit of analysis. Achieving exhaustivity is usually not difficult in mass media content analysis. If one or two unusual instances are detected, they can be put into a category labeled "other" or "miscellaneous." (If too many items fall into this category, however, a reexamination of the original category definitions is called for; a study with 10% or more of its content in the "other" category is probably overlooking some relevant content characteristic.) An additional way to ensure exhaustivity is to dichotomize or trichotomize the content: Attempts at problem solving might be defined as aggressive and nonaggressive, or statements might be placed in positive, neutral, and negative categories. The most practical way to determine whether a proposed categorization system is exhaustive is to pretest it on a sample of content. If unanticipated items appear, the original scheme requires changes before the primary analysis can begin.

The categorization system should also be *reliable*; that is, different coders should agree in the great majority of instances about the proper category for each unit of analysis. This agreement is usually quantified in content analysis and is called **intercoder reliability**. Precise category definitions generally increase reliability, whereas sloppily defined categories tend to lower it. Pretesting the category system for reliability is highly recommended before researchers begin to process

the main body of content. Reliability is crucial in content analysis, as discussed in more detail later in this chapter.

Researchers may face the question of how many categories to include in constructing category systems. Common sense, pretesting, and practice with the coding system are valuable guides to aid the researcher in steering between the two extremes of developing a system with too few categories (so that essential differences are obscured) and defining too many categories (so that only a small percentage falls into each, thus limiting generalizations). Generally, many researchers suggest that too many initial categories are preferable to too few, because it is usually easier to combine several categories than it is to subdivide a large one after the units have been coded.

Establishing a Quantification System

Quantification in content analysis can involve all four of the levels of data measurement discussed in Chapter 2, although usually only nominal, interval, and ratio data are used. At the nominal level, researchers simply count the frequency of occurrence of the units in each category. Thus, Signorielli, McLeod, and Healy (1994) analyzed commercials on MTV and found that 6.5% of the male characters were coded as wearing somewhat sexy clothing and none were coded as being dressed in very sexy outfits; among the female characters, however, the corresponding percentages were 24% and 29%. The topics of conversation on daytime television, the themes of newspaper editorials, and the occupations of prime-time television characters can all be quantified by means of nominal measurement.

At the interval level, it is possible to develop scales for coders to use to rate certain attributes of characters or situations. For example, in a study dealing with the images of women in commercials, each character might be rated by coders on several scales like these:

Independent __:__:__:__:__ Dependent

Dominant __:__:__:__:__ Submissive

Scales such as these add depth and texture to a content analysis and are perhaps more interesting than the surface data obtained through nominal measurement. However, rating scales inject subjectivity into the analysis and may jeopardize intercoder reliability unless careful training is undertaken.

At the ratio level, measurements in mass media research are generally applied to space and time. In the print media, column-inch measurements are used to analyze editorials, advertisements, and stories about particular events or phenomena. In television and radio, ratio-level measurements are made concerning time: the number of commercial minutes, the types of programs on the air, the amount of the program day devoted to programs of various types, and so on. Interval and ratio data permit the researcher to use some powerful statistical techniques. For example, Cho and Lacy (2000) used a regression equation (see Chapter 12) to explain variations in coverage of international news that were due to organizational variables.

Training Coders and Conducting a Pilot Study

Placing a unit of analysis into a content category is called **coding**. It is the most time-consuming and least glamorous part of a content analysis. Individuals who do the coding are called coders. The number of coders involved in a content analysis is typically small; a brief examination of a sampling of recent content analyses indicated that typically two to six coders are used.

Careful training of coders is an integral step in any content analysis and usually results in a more reliable analysis. Although the investigator may have a firm grasp of the operational definitions and the category schemes, coders may not share this close knowledge. Consequently, they must become thoroughly familiar with the study's mechanics and peculiarities. To this end, researchers should plan several lengthy training sessions in which sample content is examined and coded. These sessions are used to revise definitions, clarify category boundaries, and revamp coding sheets until the coders are comfortable with the materials and procedure. Detailed instruction sheets should also be provided to coders.

Next, a pilot study is conducted to check intercoder reliability. The pilot study should be conducted with a fresh set of coders who are given some initial training to impart familiarity with the instructions and the methods of the study. Some argue that fresh coders are preferred for this task because intercoder reliability among coders who have worked for long periods of time developing the coding scheme might be artificially high. As Lorr and McNair (1966) suggest, "Interrater agreement for a new set of judges given a reasonable but practical amount of training ... would represent a more realistic index of reliability" (p. 133).

Coding the Content

Standardized sheets are usually used to ease coding. These sheets allow coders to classify the data by placing check marks or slashes in predetermined spaces. Figure 6.2 is an example of a standardized coding sheet, and Figure 6.3 is the coder instruction sheet that accompanies it. If data are to be tabulated by hand, the coding sheets should be constructed to allow for rapid tabulation. Some studies code data on 4-by-6-inch index cards, with information recorded across the top of the card. This method enables researchers to quickly sort the information into categories. Templates are available to speed the measurement of newspaper space. Researchers

Figure 6.2 Standardized Coding Sheet for Studying TV Cartoons

Character Description Code Sheet

Program name _____

A. Character number _____

B. Character name or description _____

C. Role

1-Major		3-Other (individual)
2-Minor		4-Other (group)

D. Species

1-Human	4-Robot	7-Other (specify):
2-Animal	5-Animated object	
3-Monster/Ghost	6-Indeterminate	_____

E. Sex

1-Male	2-Female	3-Indeterminate	4-Mixed (group)

F. Race

1-White	4-Robot	7-Other (specify):
2-African American	5-Native American	
3-Animal	6-Indeterminate	_____

G. Age

1-Child	3-Adult	5-Indeterminate
2-Teenager	4-Mature adult	6-Mixed (group)

who work with television or video games generally record the content and allow coders to stop and start at their own pace while coding data. Additionally, software programs are available that help in coding visual content.

When a computer is used to tabulate data, the data are usually transferred directly to a spreadsheet or data file, or perhaps to mark-sense forms or optical scan sheets (answer sheets scored by computer). These forms save time and reduce data errors. Computers are useful not only in the data-tabulation phase of a content analysis, but also in the actual coding process. Computers perform with unerring accuracy any coding task in which the classification rules are unambiguous. There are many software programs available that can aid in the content analysis of text documents. Some of the more common are TextSmart, VBPro, and ProfilerPlus.

Analyzing the Data

The descriptive statistics discussed in Chapters 10–12, such as percentages, means, modes, and medians, are appropriate for content analysis. If hypothesis tests are

Figure 6.3   Coder Instruction Sheet That Accompanies Form Shown in Figure 6.2

Character Description Code Sheet Instructions

Code all characters that appear on the screen for at least 90 seconds and/or speak more than 15 words (include cartoon narrator when applicable). Complete one sheet for each character to be coded.

A. Character number, code two-digit program number first (listed on page 12 of this instruction book), followed by two-digit character number randomly assigned to each character (starting with 01).

B. Character name: list all formal names, nicknames, or dual identity names (code dual identity behavior as one character's actions). List description of character if name is not identifiable.

C. Role

1. *Major*: major characters share the majority of dialogue during the program, play the largest role in the dramatic action, and appear on the screen for the longest period of time during the program.

2. *Minor*: all codeable characters that are not identified as major characters.

3. *Other (individual)*: one character that does not meet coding requirements but is involved in a behavioral act that is coded.

4. *Other (group)*: two or more characters that are simultaneously involved in a behavioral act but do not meet coding requirements.

D. Species

1. *Human*: any character resembling man, even ghost or apparition if it appears in human form (e.g., the Ghostbusters)

2. *Animal*: any character resembling bird, fish, beast, or insect; may or may not be capable of human speech (e.g., muppets, smurfs, Teddy Ruxpin)

3. *Monster/Ghost*: any supernatural creature (e.g., my pet monster, ghosts)

4. *Robot*: mechanical creature (e.g., transformers)

5. *Animated object*: any inanimate object (e.g., car, telephone) that acts like a sentient being (speaks, thinks, etc.). Do not include objects that "speak" through programmed mechanical means (e.g., recorded voice playback through computer).

6. *Indeterminate*

7. *Other*: if species is mixed within group, code as mixed here and specify which of the species are represented.

E. 1-Male   2-Female   3-Indeterminate: use this category   4-Mixed (group only)
                                 sparingly (if animal has low
                                 masculine voice, code as male)

Note: The remainder of the instructions continue in this format.

planned, then common inferential statistics (whereby results are generalized to the population) are acceptable. The chi-square test is the most commonly used because content analysis data tend to be nominal in form; however, if the data meet the requirements of interval or ratio levels, then a *t*-test, ANOVA, or Pearson's *r* may be appropriate.

Krippendorf (1980) discusses other statistical analyses, such as discriminant analysis, cluster analysis, and contextual analysis.

Interpreting the Results

If an investigator is testing specific hypotheses concerning the relationships between variables, the interpretation will be evident. If the study is descriptive, however, questions may arise about the meaning or importance of the results. Researchers are often faced with a "fully/only" dilemma. Suppose, for example, that a content analysis of children's television programs reveals that 30% of the commercials are for snacks and candy. What is the researcher to conclude? Is this a high amount or a low amount? Should the researcher report, "*Fully* 30% of the commercials fell into this category," or should the same percentage be presented as "*Only* 30% of the commercials fell into this category"? Clearly, the investigator needs some benchmark for comparison; 30% may indeed be a high figure when compared to commercials for other products or for those shown during adult programs.

In a study done by Joseph Dominick, the amount of network news time devoted to the various states was tabulated. It was determined that California and New York receive 19% and 18%, respectively, of non–Washington, D.C., national news coverage. By themselves, these numbers are interesting, but their significance is somewhat unclear. In an attempt to aid interpretation, each state's relative news time was compared to its population, and an "attention index" was created by subtracting the ratio of each state's population to the national population from its percentage of news coverage. This provided a listing of states that were either "over-covered" or "under-covered" (Dominick, 1977). To aid in their interpretation, Whitney, Fritzler, Jones, Mazzarella, and Rakow (1989) created a sophisticated "attention ratio" in their replication of this study.

RELIABILITY

The concept of reliability is crucial to content analysis. If a content analysis is to be objective, its measures and procedures must be reliable. A study is reliable when repeated measurement of the same material results in similar decisions or conclusions. Intercoder reliability refers to levels of agreement among independent coders who code the same content using the same coding instrument. If the results fail to achieve reliability, something is amiss with the coders, the coding instructions, the category definitions, the unit of analysis, or some combination of these. To achieve acceptable levels of reliability, the following steps are recommended:

1. *Define category boundaries with maximum detail.* A group of vague or ambiguously defined categories makes reliability extremely difficult to achieve. Coders should receive examples of units of analysis and a brief explanation of each to fully understand the procedure.

2. *Train the coders.* Before the data are collected, training sessions in using the coding instrument and the category system must be conducted. These sessions help eliminate methodological problems. During the sessions, the group as a whole should code sample material; afterward, they should discuss the results and the purpose of the study. Disagreements should be analyzed as they occur. The result of the training sessions is a "bible" of detailed instructions and coding examples, and each coder should receive a copy.

3. *Conduct a pilot study.* Researchers should select a subsample of the content universe under consideration and let independent coders categorize it. These data are useful for two reasons: Poorly defined categories can be detected, and chronically dissenting coders can be identified. To illustrate these problems, consider Tables 6.2 and 6.3.

A CLOSER LOOK

Reporting Intercoder Reliability

Over the course of a long career that included editing one scholarly journal and serving on the editorial boards of several others, Joseph Dominick has reviewed dozens of content analyses submitted for publication. One common problem that usually got the manuscript returned for further revision was the reporting of intercoder reliability. Many problems showed up again and again: no mention of how much content was involved in the reliability sample, failing to identify what statistic was used, not specifying how many coders performed the check, no indication of how disagreements were handled, and so on. The most vexing problem, however, involved studies that included several variables and where the author made a statement such as "The average reliability coefficient was .82."

If a study has a dozen variables that were placed into categories by coders, then a dozen reliability coefficients should be reported. One overall average coefficient does not make sense because the high reliability of easily coded variables (like counting the number of times a word occurs in a sample of text) could obscure lower reliability estimates of harder-to-code variables (such as themes in a sample of text). Reporting an average coefficient might lead researchers to conclude that the data were more reliable than they actually were.

In Table 6.2, the definitions for categories I and IV appear to be satisfactory. All four coders placed Units 1, 3, 7, and 11 in the first category; in Category IV, item 14 is classified consistently by three of the four coders and items 4 and 9 by all four coders. The confusion apparently lies in the boundaries between categories II and III. Three coders put items 2, 6, and/or 13 in category II, and three placed some or all of these numbers in category III. The definitions of these two categories require reexamination and perhaps revision because of this ambiguity.

Table 6.3 illustrates the problem of the chronic dissenter. Although Coders A and B agree seven of eight times, Coders B and C agree only two of eight times, and Coders A and C agree only once. Obviously, Coder C is going to be a problem. As a rule, the investigator would carefully reexplain to this coder the rules used in categorization and examine the reasons for his or her consistent deviation. If the problem persists, it may be necessary to dismiss the coder from the analysis.

When the initial test of reliability yields satisfactory results, the main body of data is coded. After the coding is complete, it is recommended that a subsample of the data, probably between 10% and 25%, be reanalyzed by independent coders to calculate an overall intercoder reliability coefficient. Lacy and Riffe (1996) note that a reliability check based on a probability sample may contain sampling error. They present a formula for calculating the size of the inter-coder reliability sample that takes this error into account.

Intercoder reliability can be calculated by several methods. Holsti (1969) reports this formula for determining the reliability of nominal data in terms of percentage of agreement:

$$\text{Reliability} = \frac{2M}{N_1 + N_2}$$

where M is the number of coding decisions on which two coders agree and N_1 and N_2 are the total number of coding decisions by the

Table 6.2 Detecting Poorly Defined Categories from Pilot Study Data*

Coders	Categories			
	I	II	III	IV
A	1,3,7,11	2,5,6,8,12,13	10	4,9,14
B	1,3,7,11	5,8,10,12	2,6,13	4,9,14
C	1,3,7,11	2,8,12,13	5,6,10	4,9,14
D	1,3,7,11	5,6	2,8,10,12,13,14	4,9

*Arabic numerals refer to items.

Table 6.3 Identifying a Chronic Dissenter from Pilot Study Data*

Items	Coders		
	A	B	C
1	I	I	II
2	III	III	I
3	II	II	II
4	IV	IV	III
5	I	II	II
6	IV	IV	I
7	I	I	III
8	II	II	I

*Roman numerals refer to categories.

first and second coder, respectively. Thus, if two coders judge a subsample of 50 units and agree on 35 of them, the calculation is

$$\text{Reliability} = \frac{2(35)}{50 + 50} = .70$$

This method is straightforward and easy to apply, but it is criticized because it does not take into account some coder agreement that occurs strictly by chance, an amount that is a function of the number of categories in the analysis. For example, a two-category system has 50% reliability simply by chance, a five-category system generates a 20% agreement by chance, and so on. To take this into account, Scott (1955) developed the pi index, which corrects for the number of categories used and also for the probable frequency of use:

$$\text{Scott's } pi = \frac{\% \text{ observed agreement} - \% \text{ expected agreement}}{1 - \% \text{ expected agreement}}$$

A hypothetical example demonstrates the use of this index. Suppose that two coders are assigning magazine advertisements to the five categories shown here and obtain the following matrix of agreement after each coded 100 ads.

		Coder A					Marginal Totals
	Categories	1	2	3	4	5	
	1	42	2	1	3	0	48
	2	1	12	2	0	0	15
Coder B	3	0	0	10	0	2	12
	4	0	2	1	8	1	12
	5	2	0	1	2	8	13
Marginal Totals		45	16	15	13	11	100

The percentage of observed agreement is found by adding the numbers in the diagonal

$(42 + 12 + 10 + 8 + 8 = 80)$ and dividing by N ($80/100 = .80$). The percentage of agreement expected by chance is a little more complicated. One way to calculate this number is to set up the following table:

Categories	Marginal Totals for Coder A	Marginal Totals for Coder B	Sum of Marginals	Joint Marginal Proportions
1	45	48	93	93/200 = .465
2	16	15	31	31/200 = .155
3	15	12	27	27/200 = .135
4	13	12	25	25/200 = .125
5	11	13	24	24/200 = .120
Totals	100	100	200	1.00

The percentage of expected agreement is found by squaring the proportions in the joint marginals column and summing. Thus:

$$\% \text{ of expected agreement} =$$
$$(.465)^2 + (.155)^2 + (.135)^2 + (.125)^2 + (.120)^2$$

or

$$\% \text{ of expected agreement} =$$
$$.216 + .024 + .018 + .016 + .014 = .288$$

Now we can calculate Scott's *pi*:

$$\text{Scott's } pi = \frac{.80 - .288}{1 - .288} = .719$$

This same technique can be used to calculate reliability when there are more than two coders. In this instance, the statistic is called Cohen's *kappa* (Cohen, 1960; Fleiss, 1971). Estimating reliability with interval data requires care. Using the correlation coefficient, Pearson's *r*, a method that investigates the relationship between two items, requires caution. The Pearson *r* can range from $+1.00$ to -1.00. In estimates of reliability in content analysis, however, if this measure has a high value, it may indicate either that the coders were in agreement or that their ratings were associated in some systematic manner.

For example, suppose an interval scale ranging from 1 to 10 is used to score the degree of favorableness of a news item to some person or topic. (A score of 1 represents very positive; 10 represents very negative.) Assume that two coders are independently scoring the same 10 items.

A CLOSER LOOK

Reliability, *pi,* and *kappa*

Much content analysis research involves two coders placing units of analysis into nominal categories. In such a situation, the generally reported reliability coefficients are Scott's *pi* or *kappa*. Although these are useful measures, researchers should be aware of some of their idiosyncrasies. In the first place, consider the matrix in Example One, where a reliability check used two coders who independently coded 100 items into two nominal categories: yes and no. Note that the coders disagreed 100% of the time, and the corresponding values of *pi* and *kappa*, logically enough, are .00.

Example One: Perfect disagreement (*pi* = .00, *kappa* = .00)

		Coder A	
		Yes	No
Coder B	Yes	0	50
	No	50	0

Now look at Example Two. The coders agreed on 50% of the items, yet the *pi* and *kappa* values are negative, about −.10, an outcome that suggests some agreement is worse than no agreement at all.

(continued)

A CLOSER LOOK

Reliability, *pi,* and *kappa (continued)*

Example Two: 50% agreement (*pi* = −.10 *kappa* = −.09)

		Coder A	
		Yes	No
Coder B	Yes	10	20
	No	30	40

Next, consider Example Three. The two coders agree 96% of the time, and the *pi* and *kappa* coefficients are .92, consistent with the high percentage of agreement.

Example Three: 96% agreement (*pi* = .92, *kappa* = .92)

		Coder A	
		Yes	No
Coder B	Yes	48	2
	No	2	48

Now look at Example Four, where the percentage of perfect agreement is also 96 but *pi* and *kappa* are only about .31, an unacceptable level of reliability.

Example Four: 96% agreement (*pi* = .31, *kappa* = .32)

		Coder A	
		Yes	No
Coder B	Yes	95	1
	No	3	1

What accounts for this counterintuitive difference between Example Three and Example Four? Kilem (2002) suggests that the problem lies in the way *pi* and *kappa* calculate the values expected by chance (the percentage of expected agreement). Kilem argues that "Any agreement between 2 raters, A and B, can be considered as a chance agreement if a rater has performed a random rating (i.e. classified a [unit] without being guided by its characteristics) and both raters have agreed." He goes on to argue that a reasonable value for chance agreement in this situation should not exceed .5. (Readers interested in the math behind his argument should consult Kilem's article.)

In Example Four, the percentage of expected agreement is about .94. This assumes that if Coder A randomly assigned a rating, then coder B should agree 94% of the time. Kilem argues that it is highly unlikely that two coders would agree by chance this often. He offers a formula that would correct for this questionable assumption. (Again, readers should consult Kilem for the calculation details.) Using Kilem's correction on the data in Example Four yields a new coefficient of about .97.

Others argue that the coders must show enough covariation in order to justify a high reliability coefficient (Krippendorf, 2004). In Example 4, Coder A used the "no" code only twice, whereas Coder B used it just four times. In this case, the traditional *pi* and *kappa* calculations severely lower the reliability estimates. One solution is to use a different coding scheme that allows coders more latitude.

In any case, researchers tabulating reliability estimates on content analyses should be aware of the influences on *pi* and *kappa*.

Table 6.4 shows two possible outcomes. In Situation I, the coders agree on every item, and *r* equals 1.00. In Situation II, the coders disagree on every item by three scale positions, yet *r* still equals 1.00. Clearly, the uses of this estimate are not equally reliable in the two situations.

Krippendorf (2004) circumvents this dilemma by presenting what might be termed an "all-purpose reliability measure," *alpha,*

Table 6.4   False Equivalence as a Reliability Measure When *r* Is Used

	Situation I			Situation II	
Items	Coder 1	Coder 2	Items	Coder 1	Coder 2
1	1	1	1	1	4
2	2	2	2	2	5
3	3	3	3	3	6
4	3	3	4	3	6
5	4	4	5	4	7
6	5	5	6	5	8
7	6	6	7	6	9
8	6	6	8	6	9
9	7	7	9	7	10
10	7	7	10	7	10
	$r = 1.00$			$r = 1.00$	

which can be used for nominal, ordinal, interval, and ratio scales and for more than one coder. Though somewhat difficult to calculate, *alpha* is the equivalent of Scott's *pi* at the nominal level with two coders and represents an improvement over *r* in the interval situation.

As may be obvious, calculating a reliability coefficient by hand is tedious. There are software programs that can be helpful. Agree, from SciencePlus, calculates Cohen's *kappa* but as of late 2011 cost about $275. ReCal is a free online utility developed by a doctoral student that calculates Krippendorf's *alpha* and other reliability coefficients, but first-time users will have to contend with a learning curve. For those who are comfortable with macros, *www.afhayes.com/public/kalpha* contains a macro that works with SPSS to calculate Krippendorf's *alpha*. Information on other reliability programs can be found at *http://astro.temple.edu/~lombard/reliability/*.

What is an acceptable level of intercoder reliability? The answer depends on the research context and the type of information coded. In some instances, little coder judgment is needed to place units into categories (for example, counting the number of words per sentence in a newspaper story or tabulating the number of times a network correspondent contributes a story to the evening news), and coding becomes a mechanical or clerical task. In this case, one expects a high degree of reliability, perhaps approaching 100%, since coder disagreements probably result from only carelessness or fatigue. If a certain amount of interpretation is involved, however, reliability estimates are typically lower. In general, the greater the amount of judgmental leeway given to coders, the lower the reliability coefficients.

As a rule of thumb, most published content analyses typically report a minimum reliability coefficient of about 90% or above when using Holsti's formula, and about .75 or above when using *pi* or *kappa*. Neuendorf (2002) offers the following guidelines: Coefficients of .90 or greater are nearly always acceptable, .80 or greater is acceptable in most situations, and .70 may be appropriate in some exploratory studies for some indices.

Note that the previous discussion assumed that at least two independent coders categorized the same content. In some situations, however, *intracoder* reliability also might be assessed. These circumstances occur most frequently when only a few coders are used because extensive training must be given to ensure the detection of subtle message elements. To test intracoder reliability, the same individual codes a set of data twice, at different times, and the reliability statistics are computed using the two sets of results.

Researchers need to pay special attention to reporting intercoder reliability. One recent study (Lombard, Snyder-Duch, & Bracken, 2002) sampled published content analyses in scholarly journals from 1994 to 1998 and found that only 69% contained any report of intercoder reliability, and many contained only a sketchy explanation of how reliability was calculated. Given this lack of rigor in reporting reliability, the same authors recommended that the following information be included in any content analysis report:

- The size of and the method used to create the reliability sample, along with a justification of that method
- The relationship of the reliability sample to the full sample (that is, whether the reliability sample is the same as the full sample, a subset of the full sample, or a separate sample)
- The number of reliability coders (which must be two or more) and whether they include the researcher(s)
- The amount of coding conducted by each reliability and nonreliability coder

- The index or indices selected to calculate reliability, and a justification of this/these selections
- The intercoder reliability level for each variable, for each index selected
- The approximate amount of training (in hours) required to reach the reliability levels reported
- How disagreements in the reliability coding were resolved in the full sample
- Where and how the reader can obtain detailed information regarding the coding instrument, procedures, and instructions (for example, from the authors)

Krippendorf (2004) provides a technical discussion of some of the more popular intercoder reliability statistics.

VALIDITY

In addition to being reliable, a content analysis must yield valid results. As indicated in Chapter 2, *validity* is usually defined as the degree to which an instrument actually measures what it sets out to measure. This raises special concerns in content analysis. In the first place, validity is intimately connected with the procedures used in the analysis. If the sampling design is faulty, if categories overlap, or if reliability is low, the results of the study probably possess little validity. Additionally, the adequacy of the definitions used in a content analysis bears directly on the question of validity. For example, a great deal of content analysis has focused on the depiction of televised violence; different investigators have offered different definitions of what constitutes a violent act. The question of validity emerges when one tries to decide whether each of the various definitions actually encompasses what one might logically refer to as violence. The debate between Gerbner and the television networks vividly illustrates this problem. The definition of violence propounded by Gerbner and his associates in 1977 included accidents, acts of nature, or violence that might occur in a fantasy or a humorous setting. However, network analysts do not consider these phenomena to be acts of violence (Blank, 1977). Both Gerbner and the networks offered arguments in support of their decisions. Which analysis is more valid? The answer depends in part on the plausibility of the rationale that underlies the definitions.

This discussion relates closely to a technique traditionally called *face validity*. This validation technique assumes that an instrument adequately measures what it purports to measure if the categories are rigidly and satisfactorily defined and if the procedures of the analysis have been adequately conducted. Most descriptive content analyses rely on face validity, but other techniques are available.

The use of *concurrent validity* in content analysis is exemplified in a study by Clarke and Blankenburg (1972). These investigators attempted a longitudinal study of violence in TV shows dating back to 1952. Unfortunately, few copies of the early programs were available, and the authors were forced to use program summaries in *TV Guide*. To establish that such summaries would indeed disclose the presence of violence, the authors compared the results of a subsample of current programs coded from these synopses to the results obtained from a direct viewing of the same programs. The results were sufficiently related to convince the authors that their measurement technique was valid. However, this method of checking validity is only as good as the criterion measurement: If the direct-viewing technique is itself invalid, then there is little value in showing that synopsis coding is related to it.

Only a few studies have attempted to document *construct validity*. One instance involves the use of sensationalism in news stories. This construct has been measured by semantic differentials and factor analysis in an attempt to isolate its underlying dimensions, and it is related to relevant message characteristics (Tannenbaum, 1962; Tannenbaum & Lynch, 1960). Another technique that investigators occasionally use is *predictive validity*. For example, certain content attributes from wire stories might allow a researcher to predict which items a newspaper will carry.

In summary, several different methods are used in content analysis to assess validity. The most common is face validity, which is appropriate for some studies. It is recommended, however, that the content analyst also examine other methods to establish the validity of a given study.

EXAMPLES OF CONTENT ANALYSIS

Table 6.5, which summarizes four content analyses, lists the purpose of the analysis, the sample, the unit of analysis, illustrative categories, and the type of statistic used for each study.

CONTENT ANALYSIS AND THE INTERNET

As Stempel and Stewart (2000) put it, the Internet provides both opportunities and challenges for content researchers. On the opportunity side, the Internet opens up huge new areas of content that can be studied. Here is a brief sampling of the possibilities:

- Messages shared by online communities (Ginossar, 2008)
- Facebook pages (Kolek & Saunders, 2008)
- Online food advertising (Moore & Rideout, 2007)
- Online news (Karlsson & Stromback, 2010)

Table 6.5 Summaries of Content Analysis Studies

Researchers	Title of Study	Sample	Unit of Analysis	Representative Categories	Statistic
Mastro and Ortiz (2008)	A content analysis of social groups in prime-time Spanish-language TV	Composite week of fictional prime-time TV from four Spanish-language networks	Main characters	Demographics; physical attributes; speech characteristics	ANOVA
Schaefer and Martinez III (2009)	Trends in network news editing strategies from 1969 through 2005	Network evening newscasts during three days in June, 1969, 1983, 1997, and 2005	Each camera shot	Shot length; type of edit; transition type	ANOVA
Kaye and Sapolsky (2009)	Offensive language in prime-time broadcast and cable programming	Constructed week of prime-time programming of seven broadcast and cable nets	Offensive words	Sexual words; excretory words; cursing	Chi Square
Callister, Stern, Coyne, Robinson, and Bennion (2011)	Evaluation of sexual content in teen-centered films from 1980–2007	30 top grossing films from each of three decades	Scenes	sexual activity; sexual dialog; safe sex practices	ANOVA

- Messages on Twitter (Chew & Eyesenbach, 2010)
- Corporate websites (Yan, 2008)
- Blogs (Cho & Huh, 2007)
- YouTube videos (Duman & Locher, 2008)

Moreover, content can be searched quickly and efficiently by using search engines and electronic archives. If a newspaper, for example, has an online archive of past editions, a search for a research term such as *elections* can be done in a matter of seconds. Finally, the content exists in cyberspace and not on paper or some other medium. Researchers don't have to physically obtain, store, and maintain hard copies of the material.

On the challenge side, sampling can be an issue. Sample frames may not exist for many topics. For example, suppose a researcher wanted to do a content analysis of medical websites. Which sites should be sampled? There is probably no comprehensive list of websites. (A Google search using the exact phrase "*medical websites*" turned up more

Content Analysis of Video Games

Many media researchers have focused on the content of popular video games and have examined such topics as character demographics (Williams, Martin, Consalvo, & Ivory, 2009), female body imagery (Martins, Williams, Harrison, & Ratan, 2009), aggressive behavior (Lachlan, Smith, & Tamborini, 2005), profanity (Ivory, Williams, Martins, & Consalvo, 2009), and racial stereotyping (Burgess, Dill, Stermer, Burgess, & Brown, 2011).

However, coding the content of video games raises special problems. First, how much content should be recorded for analysis? The first five minutes of play? The first 30 minutes? In an informal sampling of recent video game content analyses, recording times varied from 10 minutes to 90 minutes. Second, the actual flow of game play may vary because of choices made by the player or because of varying skill or difficulty levels. Thus, not every person sees the same content. Many researchers address this problem by focusing on the opening levels of the game, but this approach ignores content that appears in more advanced levels. Finally, new editions of video games quickly appear. Since 2003, for example, *Call of Duty* has gone through eight versions.

In order to avoid these problems, some researchers have instead coded game websites (Robinson, Callister, Clark, & Phillips, 2009) or online reviews of the games (Ivory, 2006). Nonetheless, despite the problems, it seems that the most valid way to assess the content of a video game is to code actual game play. Researchers, however, must make sure that they include enough detail about their methods so that readers can fully interpret the results.

than 16,800,000 hits, and many of these were links to other sites for various medical specialties.)

Trying to find an adequate sampling frame for such a study is challenging. A similar situation was faced by Yu, King, and Yoon (2010) in their study of online diet websites in the United States, the United Kingdom, and South Korea. The researchers did a Yahoo search for "weight loss" in each country. Although the search engine returned millions of results, only the first 100 sites for each country were analyzed.

On the other hand, if the topic under study is more limited, generating a sampling frame may be easier. In their study of pro–eating disorder websites, Borzekowski, Schenk, Wilson, and Peebles (2010) searched Google and Yahoo for 15 pro–eating disorder terms and identified 302 unique sites.

From these 302, they eliminated restricted-access sites, medical reference sites, and others that contained little eating disorder content, leaving a manageable 180 websites for analysis.

Another sampling issue is determining how many sample dates are enough when examining online content. In practice, however, it appears that the most popular sample frame is about a week. Hester and Dougall (2007) compared the accuracy of the constructed week sample, the simple random sample, and the consecutive day sample of online news content on the Yahoo! news site. They found that the constructed week sample was the most efficient but that sample sizes needed to be larger than those needed for sampling print newspapers. In their analysis of the *New York Times* website, Wang and Riffe (2010) found that a random sample of six days was enough to represent one year of content. Fernandes, Giurcanu, Bowers, and Neely (2010) used a calendar week in their analysis of Facebook posts, and Himelboim (2010) constructed a Monday–Friday composite week for his study of hyperlinks in news websites. Connolly-Ahern, Ahern, and Bortree (2009) concluded that constructing a week on a quarterly basis was preferable to constructing weeks based on a full year when content-analyzing electronic news source archives.

Electronic archives have disadvantages. Stryker, Wray, Hornik, and Yanovitzky (2006) point out that electronic databases such as LexisNexis are frequently used for content analysis. Their review of nearly 200 content analyses appearing in six communication journals found that more than 40% sampled from databases, but only a third of these reported the search term(s) used and only 6% discussed the validity of using that term. They go on to present an approach that could be used to determine which search term best selects relevant items and rejects extraneous ones.

The choice of a database also raises concerns. Weaver and Bimber (2008) examined the differences among online news archives. They compared searches using LexisNexis with searches using Google News for finding stories in the *New York Times* and in eight large-circulation newspapers. They found wide discrepancies between the two archives in the obtained results. The two agreed more than 80% of the time when the searches focused on the *New York Times* but only 61% of the time when searches focused on the eight large newspapers. Their results suggest that researchers who use online archives in an attempt to find stories on a given topic should be aware of the limitations of these two databases.

Using a software program rather than humans to code data also has its drawbacks. Conway (2006) compared results from computerized coding with those from human coders and found that software programs were better at simple tasks, such as counting words, but humans were better when it came to more nuanced coding tasks.

Another challenge concerns the fluid nature of the Internet. Websites are added and deleted every day, and the content of existing sites is constantly changing. A content analysis done in April might not find the same results as one done in May. Researchers can use programs such as WebShot or Webpage Thumbnail to make copies of the relevant pages so that coders are examining the same material. Finally, in many situations there are challenges in determining the unit of analysis. Is it the home page or the whole website? Some sites have more web pages than other sites. Does this introduce a bias? Are links to other sites included? What about audio and video material? McMillan (2000) discusses these and other problems in doing web content analysis.

SUMMARY

Content analysis is a popular technique in mass media research. Many of the steps followed in laboratory and survey studies are also involved in content analysis; in particular, sampling procedures need to be objective and detailed, and operational definitions are mandatory. Content categories should be reliable, exclusive, and exhaustive.

Coders must be carefully trained to gather accurate data. Interpreting a content analysis, however, requires more caution: No claims about the impact of the content can be drawn from an analysis of the message in the absence of a study that examines the audience. A content analysis should demonstrate acceptable intercoder reliability and validity. The Internet has opened up new opportunities and challenges for content analysis.

A CLOSER LOOK

Abstracts vs. Transcripts

One of the most popular data archives for researchers interested in the content of television news is the Vanderbilt Television News Archive. In addition to collecting videotaped versions of the major networks' newscasts, the Archive also publishes abstracts to help researchers locate specific stories. Many researchers have used these abstracts as proxies for the videotapes and have assumed that the abstracts are an accurate representation of the full stories as recorded on the tapes. This assumption, however, may not be valid in all cases.

Althaus, Edy, and Phalen (2002) conducted an analysis of coverage of the Persian Gulf War that compared the content of the Vanderbilt Archive abstract of a story with the full transcript of the same story. They found that the abstracts are acceptable substitutes in some areas but not in others. For example, researchers are often interested in news sources, people who make statements during the course of a news story. When compared to the full transcripts, the abstracts provided an accurate picture of who speaks during a newscast. The positions of the sources, however, often showed wide differences between abstracts and transcripts. In one instance, a researcher who depended upon the abstracts would have found that a minority (44%) of foreign officials favored a negotiated solution to the conflict. The transcripts, however, revealed that 85% of foreign officials favored such a strategy, a difference of more than 40 points.

In sum, the authors note that the abstracts in the Vanderbilt Archive are written for specific archival purposes that may not meet the needs of content researchers. Although the abstracts might suffice for researchers examining general themes, they may not be adequate for those looking for more specific items.

Key Terms

A priori coding
Coding
Composite week
Cultivation analysis
Emergent coding
Exhaustivity

Intercoder reliability
Mutually exclusive
Scott's *pi*
Unit of analysis
Universe

 Using the Internet

For further information on the topics in this chapter, search the Internet for "content analysis examples," "*intercoder reliability*," "*unit of analysis*," and "*Cohen's kappa.*"

There are several useful Internet sites for a content analysis researcher:

1. A good general introduction to content analysis can be found at *http://writing.colostate.edu/ guides/research/content/pop2a.cfm*

2. The companion website to Neuendorf"s Content Analysis Guidebook, *http://academic.csuohio. edu/kneuendorf/content/index.htm*, contains bibliographies, links to other relevant sites, and examples of coding materials.

3. Information about coding video content can be found at *www.videoanalysis.org/.*

4. For a thorough discussion of intercoder reliability, visit *http://astro.temple.edu/~lombard/ reliability/.*

Questions and Problems for Further Investigation

1. Define a unit of analysis that could be used in each of these content analyses:

   a. Problem solving on television

   b. News emphasis in a daily newspaper and a weekly newspaper

c. Changes in the values expressed by popular songs

d. The role of women in editorial cartoons

e. Content of blogs on the Internet

2. Using the topics in Question 1, define a sample selection procedure appropriate for each.

3. Generate two content analyses that could be used as preliminary tests for an audience study.

4. Conduct a brief content analysis of one of the topics listed next. (Train a second individual in the use of the category system that you develop, and have this person independently code a subsample of the content.)

a. Similarities and differences between local newscasts on two television stations

b. Changes in the subject matter of movies over a selected five-year period

c. The treatment of the elderly on network television

5. Using the topic you selected in Question 4, compute a reliability coefficient for the items that were scored by both coders.

For additional resources, go to *www.wimmer dominick.com* and *www.cengagebrain.com*.

References and Suggested Readings

Althaus, S., Edy, J., & Phalen, P. (2002). Using the Vanderbilt Television News Archives to track broadcast news content. *Journal of Broadcasting & Electronic Media, 46*(3), 473–492.

Aubrey, J., & Frisby, C. (2011). Sexual objectification in music videos: A content analysis comparing gender and genre. *Mass Communication and Society, 14*(4), 475–501.

Berelson, B. (1952). *Content analysis in communication research.* New York, NY: Free Press.

Blank, D. (1977). The Gerbner violence profile. *Journal of Broadcasting, 21,* 273–279.

Borzekowski, D., Schenk, S., Wilson, J., & Peebles, R. (2010). e-Ana and e-Mia: A content analysis of pro-eating disorder websites. *American Journal of Public Health, 100*(8), 1526–1534.

Bramlett-Solomon, S., & Subramanian, G. (1999). Nowhere near picture perfect: Images of the elderly in *Life* and *Ebony* magazines, 1990–1997.

Journalism and Mass Communication Quarterly, 76(3), 565–572.

Brown, S. (1998, April 20). Television violence stays constant. *Broadcasting & Cable,* p. 20.

Burgess, M., Dill, K., Stermer, P., Burgess, S., & Brown, B. (2011). Playing with prejudice: The prevalence and consequence of racial stereotypes in video games. *Media Psychology, 14*(3), 289–311.

Busselle, R., & Crandall, H. (2002). Television viewing and perceptions of traditional Chinese values among Chinese college students. *Journal of Broadcasting & Electronic Media, 46*(2), 265–282.

Callister, M., Stern, L., Coyne, S., Robinson, T., & Bennion, E. (2011). Evaluation of sexual content in teen-centered films from 1980 to 2007. *Mass Communication and Society, 14*(4), 454–474.

Carlyle, K., Slater, M., & Chakroff, J. (2008). Newspaper coverage of intimate partner violence: Skewing representations of risk. *Journal of Communication, 58*(1), 168–186.

Chan-Olmstead, S. M., & Park, J. S. (2000). From on-air to online world: Examining the content and structures of broadcast TV stations' websites. *Journalism & Mass Communication Quarterly, 77*(2), 321–339.

Chang, W. (1975). A typology study of movie critics. *Journalism Quarterly, 52*(4), 721–725.

Chew, C., & Eysenbach, G. (2010). Pandemics in the age of Twitter: Content analysis of tweets during the 2009 H1N1 outbreak. *PLoS One, 5*(11), 1–13.

Cho, S. (2007). TV news coverage of plastic surgery, 1972–2004. *Journalism & Mass Communication Quarterly, 84*(1), 75–89.

Cho, S., & Huh, J. (2007). Corporate blogs as a public relations tool. Conference paper presented to the International Communication Association, San Francisco, CA, May 2007.

Cho, H., & Lacy, S. (2000). International conflict coverage in Japanese local daily newspapers. *Journalism & Mass Communication Quarterly, 77*(4), 830–845.

Clarke, D., & Blankenburg, W. (1972). Trends in violent content in selected mass media. In G. Comstock & E. Rubinstein (Eds.), *Television and social behavior: Media content and control* (188–243). Washington, DC: U.S. Government Printing Office.

Cohen, J. (1960). A coefficient of agreement for nominal scales. *Educational and Psychological Measurement, 20*(1), 37–46.

Connolly-Ahern, C., Ahern, L., & Bortree, D. (2009). The effectiveness of stratified constructed week sampling for content analysis of electronic news source archives. *Journalism & Mass Communication Quarterly, 86*(4), 862–883.

Conway, M. (2006). The subjective precision of computers: A methodological comparison with human coding in content analysis. *Journalism & Mass Communication Quarterly, 83*(1), 186–200.

Cooper, R., Potter, W. J., & Dupagne, M. (1994). A status report on methods used in mass communication research. *Journalism Educator, 48*(4), 54–61.

Coyne, S., & Whitehead, E. (2008). Indirect aggression in animated Disney films. *Journal of Communication, 58*(2), 382–395.

Davis, F. (1951). Crime news in Colorado newspapers. *American Journal of Sociology, 57*, 325–330.

Dixon, T., Azocar, C., & Casas, M. (2003). The portrayal of race and crime on television network news. *Journal of Broadcasting & Electronic Media, 47*(4), 498–523.

Dixon, T., Schell, T., Giles, H., & Drogus, K. (2008). The influence of race in police-civilian interactions. *Journal of Communication, 58*(3), 530–549.

Dominick, J. (1977). Geographic bias in national TV news. *Journal of Communication, 27*, 94–99.

Dovring, K. (1954). Quantitative semantics in 18th century Sweden. *Public Opinion Quarterly, 18*(4), 389–394.

Dudo, A., Dunwoody, S., & Scheufele, D. (2011). The emergence of nana news: Tracking thematic trends and changes in U.S. newspaper coverage of nanotechnology. *Journalism & Mass Communication Quarterly, 88*(1), 55–75.

Duman, S., & Locher, M. (2008). An analysis of the conversation metaphor employed in Clinton's and Obama's YouTube campaign clips. *Multilingua, 27*(3), 193–231.

Evans, W. (2001). Mapping mainstream and fringe medicine on the Internet. *Science Communication, 22*(3), 292–300.

Entman, R. (1993). Framing: Toward clarification of a fractured paradigm. *Journal of Communication, 43*(4), 51–58.

Fernandes, J., Giurcanu, M., Bowers, K., & Neely, J. (2010). The writing on the wall: A content analysis of college students' Facebook groups for the 2008 presidential election. *Mass Communication and Society, 13*(5), 653–675.

Fitzgerald, M. (2010). Evolutionary stages of minorities in the mass media. *Howard Journal of Communications, 21*(4), 367–384.

Fleiss, J. L. (1971). Measuring nominal scale agreement among many raters. *Psychological Bulletin, 76*, 378–382.

Gerbner, G. (1969). The television world of violence. In D. Lange, R. Baker, & S. Ball (Eds.), *Mass media and violence* (311–339). Washington, DC: U.S. Government Printing Office.

Gerbner, G., Gross, L., Jackson-Beeck, M., Jeffries-Fox, S., & Signorielli, N. (1977). One more time: An analysis of the CBS "Final Comments on the Violence Profile." *Journal of Broadcasting, 21*, 297–304.

Gerbner, G., Gross, L., Signorielli, N., Morgan, M., & Jackson-Beeck, M. (1979). The demonstration of power: Violence profile no. 10. *Journal of Communication, 29*(3), 177–196.

Gerbner, G., Holsti, O., Krippendorf, K., Paisley, W., & Stone, P. (1969). *The analysis of communication content.* New York, NY: John Wiley.

Ginossar, T. (2008). Online participation: A content analysis of differences in utilization of two online cancer communities by men, women, patients and family members. *Health Communication, 23*(1), 1–13.

Greenberg, B. (1989). On other perceptions toward message analysis. *American Behavioral Scientist, 33*(2), 183–186.

Greenberg, B. S., & Collette, L. (1997). The changing faces on TV. *Journal of Broadcasting & Electronic Media, 41*(1), 1–13.

Greenberg, B. S., & Worrell, T. (2007). New faces on television: A twelve-season replication. *Howard Journal of Communications, 18*(4), 277–290.

Greer, C., & Ferguson, D. (2011). Using Twitter for promotion and branding: A content analysis of local television Twitter sites. *Journal of Broadcasting & Electronic Media, 55*(2), 198–214.

Haigh, M., & Heresco, A. (2010). Late-night Iraq: Monologue joke content and tone from 2003 to 2007. *Mass Communication and Society, 13*(2), 157–173.

Han, G., Chock, T., & Shoemaker, P. (2009). Issue familiarity and framing effects of online campaign coverage. *Journalism & Mass Communication Quarterly, 86*(4), 739–755.

Harmon, M., & Lee, S. (2010). A longitudinal study of U.S. network TV newscasts and strikes: Political economy on the picket line. *Journalism & Mass Communication Quarterly, 87*(3/4), 501–514.

Hatch, D., & Hatch, M. (1947). Criteria of social status as derived from marriage announcements in the *New York Times. American Sociological Review, 12*, 396–403.

Hennessee, J., & Nicholson, J. (1972, May 28). NOW says: TV commercials insult women. *New York Times Magazine*, 12–14.

Hester, J., & Dougall, E. (2007). The efficiency of constructed week sampling for content analysis of online news. *Journalism & Mass Communication Quarterly, 84*(4), 811–824.

Himelboim, I. (2010). The international network structure of news media: An analysis of hyperlink usage in news websites. *Journal of Broadcasting & Electronic Media, 54*(3), 373–390.

Hinkle, G., & Elliott, W. R. (1989). Science coverage in three newspapers and three supermarket tabloids. *Journalism Quarterly, 66*(2), 353–358.

Holsti, O. (1969). *Content analysis for the social sciences and humanities.* Reading, MA: Addison-Wesley.

Ivory, J. (2006). Still a man's game: Gender representation in online reviews of video games. *Mass Communication and Society, 9*(1), 103–114.

Ivory, J., Williams, D., Martins, N., & Consalvo, M. (2009). Good clean fun? A content analysis of profanity in video games and its prevalence across game systems and ratings. *CyberPsychology & Behavior, 12*(10), 1–4.

Jensen, J., Moriarty, C., Hurley, R., & Stryker, J. (2010). Making sense of cancer news coverage trends: A comparison of three comprehensive content analyses. *Journal of Health Communication, 15*(2), 136–151.

Jha, S. (2007). Exploring Internet influence on the coverage of social protest. *Journalism & Mass Communication Quarterly, 84*(1), 40–57.

Kamhawi, K., & Weaver, D. (2003). Mass communication research trends from 1980 to 1999. *Journalism & Mass Communication Quarterly, 80*(1), 7–27.

Karlsson, M., & Sromback, J. (2010). Freezing the flow of online news. *Journalism Studies, 11*(1), 2–19.

Kaye, B., & Sapolsky, B. (2009). Taboo or not taboo? Offensive language on prime-time broadcast and cable programming. *Journal of Broadcasting & Electronic Media, 53*(1), 22–37.

Kepplinger, H. M. (1989). Content analysis and reception analysis. *American Behavioral Scientist, 33*(2), 175–182.

Kerlinger, F. N. (2000). *Foundations of behavioral research* (4th ed.). New York, NY: Holt, Rinehart & Winston.

Kerr, P., & Moy, P. (2002). Newspaper coverage of fundamentalist Christians, 1980–2000. *Journalism & Mass Communication Quarterly, 79*(1), 54–72.

Kilem, G. (2002). Statistical methods for inter-rater reliability assessment, no. 1. Retrieved from *http://agreestat.com/research_papers/kappa_statistic_is_not_satisfactory.pdf*

Kim, S., Scheufele, D., & Shanahan, J. (2002). Think about it this way: Attribute agenda-setting function of the press and the public's evaluation of a local issue. *Journalism & Mass Communication Quarterly, 79*(1), 7–23.

Kim, S., Carvalho, J., & Davis, A. (2010). Talking about poverty: News framing of who is responsible for causing and fixing the problem. *Journalism & Mass Communication Quarterly, 87*(3/4), 563–581.

Kolek, E., & Saunders, D. (2008). Online disclosure: An empirical examination of undergraduate Facebook profiles. *NASPA Journal, 45*(1), 1–25.

Krippendorf, K. (1980). *Content analysis: An introduction to its methodology.* Beverly Hills, CA: Sage Publications.

Krippendorf, K. (2004). Reliability in content analysis. *Human Communication Research, 30*(3), 411–433.

Lachlan, K., Smith, S., & Tamborini, R. (2005). Models for aggressive behavior: The attributes of violent characters in popular video games. *Communication Studies, 56*(4), 313–329.

Lacy, S., & Riffe, D. (1996). Sampling error and selecting intercoder reliability samples for nominal content categories. *Journalism & Mass Communication Quarterly, 73*(4), 963–973.

Lacy, S., Robinson, K., & Riffe, D. (1995). Sample size in content analysis of weekly newspapers. *Journalism & Mass Communication Quarterly, 72*(2), 336–345.

Lauzen, M. M., & Dozier, D. D. (1999). Making a difference in prime time: Women on screen and behind the screen in the 1994–1995 television season. *Journal of Broadcasting & Electronic Media, 43*(1), 1–19.

Lauzen, M., Dozier, D., & Horan, N. (2008). Constructing gender stereotypes through social roles in prime-time television. *Journal of Broadcasting & Electronic Media, 52*(2), 200–214.

Littleton, C. (1995, September 25). Violence study finds promising signs. *Broadcasting and Cable,* 20.

Lombard, M., Snyder-Duch, J., & Bracken, C. (2002). Content analysis in mass communication. *Human Communication Research, 28*(4), 587–604.

Lorr, M., & McNair, D. (1966). Methods relating to evaluation of therapeutic outcome. In L. Gottschalk & A. Auerbach (Eds.), *Methods of research in psychotherapy* (573–594). Englewood Cliffs, NJ: Prentice Hall.

Lowry, D., & Naser, M. (2010). From Eisenhower to Obama: Lexical characteristics of winning versus losing presidential campaign commercials. *Journalism & Mass Communication Quarterly, 87*(3/4), 530–547.

Martins, N., Williams, D., Harrison, K., & Ratan, R. (2009). A content analysis of female body imagery in video games. *Sex Roles.* Retrieved from *http://dmitriwilliams.com/femalebodies.pdf*

Matthes, J. (2009). What's in a frame? A content analysis of media framing studies in the world's leading communication journals, 1995–2005. *Journalism & Mass Communication Quarterly, 86*(2), 349–367.

Maier, S. (2010). All the news fit to post? Comparing news content on the web to newspapers, television and radio. *Journalism & Mass Communication Quarterly, 87*(3/4), 548–562.

Manganello, J., Henderson, V., Jordan, A., Trentacoste, N., Martin, S., Hennessy, M., & Fishbein, M. (2010). Adolescent judgment of sexual content on television: Implications for future content analysis research. *Journal of Sex Research, 47*(4), 364–373.

Martindale, C., & McKenzie, D. (1995). On the utility of content analysis in author attribution. *Computers and the Humanities, 29*(4), 259–270.

Mastro, D., & Ortiz, M. (2008). A content analysis of social groups in prime-time Spanish-language television. *Journal of Broadcasting & Electronic Media, 52*(1), 101–118.

McMillan, S. J. (2000). The microscope and the moving target: The challenge of applying content analysis to the World Wide Web. *Journalism & Mass Communication Quarterly, 77*(1), 80–98.

Moore, E., & Rideout, V. (2007). *Ready, set, play: A content analysis of online food advertising to children.* Conference paper presented to International Communication Association, San Francisco, CA, May 2007.

Morris, R. (1994). Computerized content analysis in management research. *Journal of Management, 20*(4), 903–931.

Mutz, D., & Nir, L. (2010). Not necessarily the news: Does fictional television influence real-world policy preferences? *Mass Communication and Society, 13*(2), 196–217.

Neuendorf, K. (2002). *The content analysis guidebook.* Thousand Oaks, CA: Sage.

Poindexter, P., Smith, L., & Heider, D. (2003). Race and ethnicity in local television news: Framing, story assignments, and source selections. *Journal of Broadcasting & Electronic Media, 47*(4), 524–536.

Potter, R. (2002). Give the people what they want: A content analysis of FM radio station home pages. *Journal of Broadcasting & Electronic Media, 46*(3), 369–384.

Riffe, D., Aust, C., & Lacy, S. (1993). The effectiveness of random, consecutive day and constructed week sampling in newspaper content analysis. *Journalism Quarterly, 70*(1), 133–139.

Riffe, D., & Freitag, A. (1997). A content analysis of content analyses: Twenty-five years of Journalism Quarterly. *Journalism & Mass Communication Quarterly, 74*(3), 515–524.

Riffe, D., Lacy, S., & Drager, M. W. (1996). Sample size in content analysis of weekly news magazines. *Journalism & Mass Communication Quarterly, 73*(3), 635–644.

Riffe, D., Lacy, S., & Fico, F. G. (2005). *Analyzing media messages.* Mahwah, NJ: Lawrence Erlbaum.

Riffe, D., Lacy, S., Nagovan, J., & Burkum, L. (1996). The effectiveness of simple and stratified random sampling in broadcast news content analysis. *Journalism & Mass Communication Quarterly, 73*(1), 159–168.

Robinson, T., Callister, M., Clark, B., & Phillips, J. (2009). Violence, sexuality, and gender stereotyping: A content analysis of official video game websites. *Web Journal of Mass Communication, 13* (February).

Sapolsky, B., Molitor, F., & Luque, S. (2003). Sex and violence in slasher films: Re-examining the assumptions. *Journalism & Mass Communication Quarterly, 80*(1), 28–38.

Schaefer, R., & Martinez, T. (2009). Trends in network news editing strategies from 1969 through 2005. *Journal of Broadcasting & Electronic Media, 53*(3), 347–364.

Scharrer, E. (2001). From wise to foolish: The portrayal of the sitcom father, 1950s–1990s. *Journal of Broadcasting & Electronic Media, 45*(1), 23–40.

Schwartz, J., & Andsager, J. (2011). Four decades of images in gay male-targeted magazines. *Journalism & Mass Communication Quarterly, 88*(1), 76–98.

Scott, W. (1955). Reliability of content analysis: The case of nominal scale coding. *Public Opinion Quarterly, 17*, 321–325.

Signorielli, N., McLeod, D., & Healy, E. (1994). Gender stereotypes in MTV commercials. *Journal of Broadcasting & Electronic Media, 38*(1), 91–101.

Smith, S., & Boyson, A. (2002). Violence in music videos: Examining the prevalence and content of physical aggression. *Journal of Communication, 52*(1), 61–83.

Stempel, G. H. (1952). Sample size for classifying subject matter in dailies. *Journalism Quarterly, 29*, 333–334.

Stempel, G. H. (1989). Content analysis. In G. H. Stempel & B. H. Westley (Eds.), *Research methods in mass communications* (132–143). Englewood Cliffs, NJ: Prentice Hall.

Stempel, G. H., & Stewart, R. K. (2000). The Internet provides both opportunities and challenges for mass communication researchers. *Journalism & Mass Communication Quarterly, 77*(3), 549–560.

Stryker, J., Wray, R., Hornik, R., & Yanovitzky, I. (2006). Validation of database search terms for content analysis. *Journalism & Mass Communication Quarterly, 83*(2), 381–396.

Sweetser, K., Golan, G., & Wanta, W. (2008). Intermedia agenda setting in television, advertising, and blogs during the 2004 election. *Mass Communication and Society, 11*(2), 197–216.

Tannenbaum, P. (1962). Sensationalism: Some objective message correlates. *Journalism Quarterly, 39,* 317–323.

Tannenbaum, P., & Lynch, M. (1960). Sensationalism: The concept and its measurement. *Journalism Quarterly, 37,* 381–392.

Walizer, M. H., & Wienir, P. L. (1978). *Research methods and analysis: Searching for relationships.* New York, NY: Harper & Row.

Wang, X., & Riffe, D. (2010). An exploration of sample sizes for content analysis of the *New York Times* website. *Web Journal of Mass Communication Research, 20* (May).

Warren, R., Wicks, R., Wicks, J., Fosu, I., & Chung, D. (2008). Food and beverage advertising on U.S. television: A comparison of child-targeted versus general audience commercials. *Journal of Broadcasting & Electronic Media, 52*(2), 231–246.

Weaver, D., & Bimber, B. (2008). Finding news stories: A comparison of searches using LexisNexis and Google News. *Journalism & Mass Communication Quarterly, 85*(3), 515–553.

Whitney, D. C., Fritzler, M., Jones, S., Mazzarella, S., & Rakow, L. (1989). Source and geographic bias in network television news: 1982–1984. *Journal of Broadcasting & Electronic Media, 33*(2), 159–174.

Wilhoit, G., & Sherrill, K. (1968). Wire service visibility of U.S. senators. *Journalism Quarterly, 45,* 42–48.

Williams, D., Martins, N., Consalvo, M., & Ivory, J. (2009). The virtual census: Representation of gender, race and age in video games. *New Media & Society, 11*(5), 815–834.

Wise, D., & Brewer, P. (2010). Competing frames for a public health issue and their effects on public opinion. *Mass Communication and Society, 13*(4), 435–457.

Wu, H., & Bechtel, A. (2002). Website use and news topic and type. *Journalism & Mass Communication Quarterly, 79*(1), 73–86.

Yan, T. (2008). Cultural variance in corporate presentations. *Human Communication, 11*(4), 483–485.

Yu, J., King, K., & Yoon, H. (2010). How much are health websites influenced by culture? Content analysis of online diet programs in the United States, United Kingdom and Korea. *Journal of Promotion Management, 16*(3), 331–359.

Yule, G. (1944). *The statistical study of literary vocabulary.* Cambridge, England: Cambridge University Press.

Zeldes, G., Fico, F., & Lacy, S. (2008). Context and sources in broadcast television coverage of the 2004 Democratic primary. *Mass Communication and Society, 11*(3), 340–357.

CHAPTER 7

SURVEY RESEARCH

CHAPTER OUTLINE

Audience and consumer surveys are commonplace in all areas of life. This becomes immediately evident by searching the Internet for "**audience surveys**" or "**consumer surveys.**" Decision makers in businesses, consumer and activist groups, politics, and the media use survey results as part of their daily routine. Fortunately, the increased use of surveys has created changes in the way many of the studies are conducted and reported. More attention (although not enough) is given to sample selection, questionnaire design, and error rates.

Survey research, including online surveys, requires careful planning and execution, and the research must take into account a wide variety of decisions and problems. The purpose of this chapter is to introduce the basics of survey research.

DESCRIPTIVE AND ANALYTICAL SURVEYS

There are two major types of surveys: descriptive and analytical. A **descriptive survey** attempts to describe or document current conditions or attitudes—that is, to explain what exists at the moment. For example, the Department of Labor regularly conducts surveys on the rate of unemployment in the United States. Professional pollsters survey the electorate to learn its opinions of candidates or issues. Broadcast stations and networks continually survey their audiences to determine programming tastes, changing values, and lifestyle variations that might affect programming. In descriptive surveys, the interest is in discovering the current situation in the area under study.

An **analytical survey** attempts to describe and explain *why* situations exist. In this approach, two or more variables are usually examined to investigate research questions or test research hypotheses. The results allow researchers to examine the interrelationships among variables and to develop explanatory inferences. For example, television station owners survey the market to determine how lifestyles affect viewing habits or to determine whether viewers' lifestyles can be used to predict the success of syndicated programming. On a broader scale, television networks conduct yearly surveys to determine how the public's tastes and desires are changing and how these attitudes relate to viewers' perceptions of the three major commercial networks.

ADVANTAGES AND DISADVANTAGES OF SURVEY RESEARCH

Surveys have several advantages:

1. They can be used to investigate problems in realistic settings. Newspaper reading, television viewing, radio listening, and consumer behavior patterns can be examined where they happen rather than in a laboratory or screening room under artificial conditions.

2. The cost of surveys is reasonable when one considers the amount of information gathered (some online surveys are free). Researchers also can control expenses by selecting from five major types of surveys: mail, telephone, personal interview, group administration, and the Internet.

3. A large amount of data can be collected with relative ease from a variety of people. Surveys allow researchers to examine many variables (demographic and lifestyle information, attitudes, motives, intentions, and so on) and to use a variety of statistics to analyze the data.

4. Surveys are not constrained by geographic boundaries; they can be conducted almost anywhere.

5. Data that are helpful to survey research already exist. Data archives, government documents, census materials, radio and television rating books, and voter registration lists can be used as *primary sources* (main sources of data) or as *secondary sources* (supportive data) of information. With archive data, it is possible to conduct an entire survey study without ever developing a questionnaire or contacting a single respondent.

While survey research has many advantages over other research approaches, it is not a perfect research methodology and there are a few disadvantages:

1. The most important disadvantage is that independent variables cannot be manipulated the way they are in laboratory experiments. Without control over independent variables, the researcher cannot be certain whether the relationships between independent variables and dependent variables are causal or noncausal. That is, a survey may establish that A and B are related, but it is impossible to determine solely from the survey results that A causes B. Causality is difficult to establish because many intervening and extraneous variables are involved. Time series studies can sometimes help correct this problem.

2. Inappropriate wording or placement of questions within a questionnaire can bias results. The questions must be worded and organized unambiguously to collect the desired information. This problem is discussed in detail later in the chapter.

3. The wrong respondents may be included in survey research. For example, in telephone interviews, a respondent may claim to be between 18 and 24 years old but may in fact be over 60 years old; a mail or Internet survey may be completed by a teenager when the target respondent is a parent in the household over the age of 34.

4. Some survey research is becoming difficult to conduct because response rates continue to decline. This is especially true with telephone surveys, where answering machines, call blocking, caller ID, various state and local regulations against calling people at home, and respondents unwilling to participate lower the incidence rates (the percentage of people who agree to participate in the survey). Telemarketers (telephone salespeople) continually affect research in all areas because an increasing number of people refuse to participate in legitimate studies for fear that the interviewer will try to sell them something.

Despite these problems, however, surveys can produce reliable and useful information. They are especially useful for collecting information on audiences and readership.

The remainder of this chapter discusses the various aspects of survey design. While not always mentioned, the discussions relate to all types of surveys—mail, telephone, personal interview, group administration, and the Internet.

CONSTRUCTING QUESTIONS

Although most people think that survey design is simple—just put together a series of questions—the fact is that survey design takes a lot of practice. Part of this practice is to understand five basic rules of questionnaire design:

1. Understand the goals of the project so that only relevant questions are included.

2. Questions should be clear and unambiguous.

3. Questions must accurately communicate what is required from the respondents.

4. Don't assume respondents understand the questions they are asked.

5. Follow Ockham's Razor in question development and order.

The specifics of questionnaire design depend on the choice of data collection technique. Questions written for a **mail survey** must be easy to read and understand because respondents are unable to ask questions. **Telephone surveys** cannot use questions with long lists of response options because the respondent may forget the first few responses by the time the last items are read. Questions written for **group administration** must be concise and easy for the respondents to answer. In a **personal interview**, an interviewer must tread lightly with sensitive and personal questions because his or her physical presence might make the respondent less willing to answer. (These procedures are discussed in later in this chapter.)

A questionnaire's design must always reflect the purpose of the research. A complex research topic such as media use during a political campaign requires more detailed questions than does a survey to determine a favorite radio station or magazine. Nonetheless, there are several general guidelines to follow regarding wording of questions and question order and length for all types of surveys.

Types of Questions

Surveys can include two basic types of questions: open-ended and closed-ended. An **open-ended question** requires respondents to generate their own answers, as in these examples:

What could your favorite radio station change so that you would listen more often?

———————————————————

———————————————————

What type of television program do you prefer to watch most often?

———————————————————

———————————————————

Why do you subscribe to the *Daily Record?*

———————————————————

———————————————————

Open-ended questions allow respondents freedom in answering and an opportunity to provide in-depth responses. Furthermore, they give researchers the option to ask, "Why did you say that?" or "Could you explain your answer in more detail?" The flexibility to follow up on, or probe, certain questions enables the interviewers to gather information about the respondents' feelings and the motives behind their answers.

In addition, open-ended questions allow for answers that researchers did not foresee in designing the questionnaire—answers that may suggest possible relationships with other answers or variables. For example, in response to the question "Which radio stations do you have programmed on the buttons in the vehicle you drive most often?" the manager of a local radio station might expect to receive a list of the local radio stations. However, a subject may give an unexpected response, such as "I have no idea. I thought the stations were programmed by the car dealer." This forces the manager to reconsider his or her perceptions of radio listeners.

Finally, open-ended questions are particularly useful in a pilot test of a study. Researchers may not know what types of responses to expect from subjects, so open-ended questions are used to allow subjects to answer in any way they wish. From the list of responses provided by the subjects, the researcher may select the items most often mentioned and include them in multiple-choice or forced-choice questions. Using open-ended questions in a pilot study usually saves time and resources because all possible responses are more likely to be included on the final measurement instrument, avoiding the need to repeat the analysis.

The major disadvantage associated with open-ended questions is the amount of time needed to collect and analyze the responses. In most cases, open-ended responses require interviewers to record long answers. In addition, because there are so many types of responses, a content analysis of each open-ended question must be completed to produce data that can be tabulated—called coding (see Chapter 6). A content analysis groups common responses into categories, essentially making the question closed-ended. The content analysis results are used to produce a codebook to code the open-ended responses. A **codebook** is a menu or

A CLOSER LOOK

Questionnaire Design

There can be significant differences when designing questionnaires for academic use and those used for the private sector. Academic research usually requires additional explanations, procedures, and anonymity guarantees.

Because of the differences, it is extremely important to contact the appropriate academic

committee that oversees research to ensure that all rules are followed *before* designing any type of academic research project.

If you are in an academic setting, what rules or regulations does your school have in reference to conducting research with humans?

---

list of quantified responses. For example, "I hate television" may be coded as a 5 for analysis.

In the case of **closed-ended questions**, respondents select an answer from a list provided by the researcher. These questions are popular because they provide greater uniformity in responses and the answers are easy to quantify. The major disadvantage is that researchers often fail to include some important responses. Respondents may have an answer different from those that are supplied. One way to solve the problem is to include an "Other" response followed by a blank space to give respondents an opportunity to supply their own answer. The "Other" responses are then handled just like an open-ended question; a content analysis of the responses is completed to develop a codebook. A pilot study or pretest of a questionnaire usually solves most problems with closed-ended questions.

> **Special Note:** Virtually every question in any questionnaire, even the simplest question, should include some form of "Don't Know/No Answer" (DK/NA) response. In many sections of this chapter, we provide samples of questions but to save space do not always include a DK/NA response. Realize, however, that in a real questionnaire, we always include some form of DK/NA response (No opinion, Doesn't apply, etc.).

Problems in Interpreting Open-Ended Questions

Open-ended questions often cause a great deal of frustration because respondents' answers are often bizarre. Sometimes respondents do not understand a question and provide answers that are not relevant to anything. Sometimes interviewers have difficulty understanding respondents, or they may have problems spelling what the respondents say. In these cases, researchers must interpret the answers and determine which code is appropriate.

The following examples are actual comments (called **verbatims**) from telephone surveys and self-administered surveys conducted by the senior author of this text. They show that even the best-planned survey questionnaire can produce a wide range of responses. The survey question asked, "How do you describe the programming on your favorite radio station?"

- The station is OK, but it's geared to Jerry Atrics.
- I only listen because my husband listens to it.
- I don't listen to that station because I live on Chinese time.
- It's great. It has the best floormat in the city.
- The station is good, but sometimes it makes me want to vomit.

Open-Ended Questions

Open-ended questions always include an opportunity for interviewers to ask for additional information. From experience, we have learned that interviewers should ask the respondent "What else?" instead of "Anything more?" or "Is that all?" The "What else?" approach does not give the respondent the same easy opportunity to say, "Nothing."

- My parrot is just learning to talk, and the station teaches him a lot of words.
- It sounds great with my car trunk open.
- There is no way for me to answer that question before I eat dinner.

And then there was a woman who, when asked what her spouse does for a living, wrote "Arrow Space Engeneer." Part of the research process is learning how to decipher respondents' answers.

General Guidelines

Before we examine specific types of questions appropriate in survey research, here are some general dos and don'ts about writing questions:

1. *Make questions clear.* This is logical, but many researchers become so closely associated with a problem that they can no longer put themselves in the respondents' position. What might be perfectly clear to researchers might not be nearly as clear to the respondents. For example, after finding out which radio stations a respondent has been listening to more lately, the researcher might ask, "Why have you been listening more lately to WXXX?" and expect to receive an answer such as "I like the music a lot more." However, the respondent might say, "It's the only station my radio can pick up." The question would be much clearer to a respondent if asked in this form: "Which radio station, or stations, if any, do you enjoy listening to more lately as compared to a few months ago?" The word *enjoy* poses a totally different question that will elicit good information. Questionnaire items must be phrased precisely so that respondents know what is being asked.

Making questions clear also requires avoiding difficult or specialized words, acronyms, and pretentious language. In general, the level of vocabulary commonly found in newspapers or popular magazines is appropriate for a survey. Questions should be phrased in everyday speech, and social science jargon and technical words should be eliminated. For example, "If you didn't have a premium channel, would you consider PPV?" might be better phrased, "If you didn't have a pay channel like Home Box Office or Showtime, would you consider a service where you pay a small amount for individual movies or specials you watch?"

The item "Should the Satellite TV System consider offering an interactive channel for news and weather information" assumes that respondents know what an "interactive channel" actually provides. A better approach is, "An interactive satellite channel is one where viewers can personalize the news and weather information presented on the channel rather than watch information presented by a local or national source. Do you think the Satellite TV System should add this free channel to your satellite service?"

Question clarity can also be affected by double or hidden meanings in the words that are not apparent to researchers. This question, for example, causes such a problem: "How many television shows do you think are a little too violent—most, some, a few, or none?" Some respondents who feel that all TV shows are extremely violent will answer "none" based on the question's wording. These subjects reason that all shows are more than "a little too violent"; therefore, the most appropriate answer to the question is "none." (Deleting the phrase *a little* from the question helps avoid this problem.) In addition, the question inadvertently establishes the idea that at least some shows are violent. The question should read, "How many television shows, if any, do you think are too violent—most, some, a few, or none?" Questions should be written so that they are fair to all respondents.

2. *Keep questions short.* To be precise and unambiguous, researchers sometimes write long and complicated questions. Yet respondents who are in a hurry to complete a questionnaire are unlikely to take the time to figure out the precise intent of the person who drafted the items. Short, concise, and clear questions are best. A good question should not contain more than two short sentences.

3. *Remember the purposes of the research.* It is important to include in a questionnaire only items that relate directly to what is being studied. For example, if the occupation of respondents is not relevant to the purpose of the survey, the questionnaire

should not include a question about it. Beginning researchers often add questions for the sake of developing a longer questionnaire or because the information "will be interesting." Any question that is included only because it would be interesting to find out the answer should be deleted from the questionnaire.

4. *Do not ask double-barreled questions.* A **double-barreled question** is one that asks two or more questions in the same sentence. Whenever the word *and* appears in a question, the sentence structure should be examined to see whether more than one question is being asked. Consider "The ABC network has programs that are funny and sexually explicit. Do you agree or disagree?" Since a program may be funny but not necessarily sexually explicit (or vice versa), a respondent could agree with the second part of the question even though he or she disagrees with the first part. This question should be split into two items.

5. *Avoid biased words or terms.* Consider the following item: "In your free time, would you rather read a book or just watch television?" The word *just* in this example injects a pro-book bias into the question because it implies that there is something less desirable about watching television. Similarly, "Where did you hear the news about the president's new economic program?" is mildly biased against newspapers; the word *hear* suggests that "radio," "television," or "other people" is a more appropriate answer. Items that start with "Do you agree or disagree with so-and-so's proposal to ..." usually bias a question. If the name "Adolf Hitler" is inserted for "so-and-so," the item becomes overwhelmingly negative.

Inserting "the president" creates a potential for both positive bias and negative bias. Any time a specific person or source is mentioned in a question, the possibility of bias arises. If it is necessary to ask questions about a specific person or source, the best way to approach the subject is to ask both positive and negative questions to reduce the possibility of bias.

6. *Avoid leading questions.* A **leading question** suggests a certain response (either literally or by implication) or contains a hidden premise. For example, "Like most Americans, do you read a newspaper every day?" suggests that the respondent should answer in the affirmative or run the risk of being unlike most Americans. The question "Do you still use marijuana?" contains a hidden premise. This type of question is called a **double bind**; regardless of how the respondent answers, an affirmative response to the hidden premise is implied—in this case, that the respondent has used marijuana at some point.

7. *Do not use questions that ask for highly detailed information.* The question "In the past 30 days, how many hours of television have you viewed with your family?" is unrealistic. Few respondents, if any, could answer this question. A more realistic approach is to ask, "How many hours did you spend watching television with your family yesterday?" A researcher interested in a 30-day period should ask respondents to keep a log or diary of family viewing habits.

8. *Avoid potentially embarrassing questions unless they are absolutely necessary.* Most surveys need to collect some form of confidential or personal data, but an overly personal question, such as one that asks about the respondents' income, may cause embarrassment and inhibit respondents from answering honestly. Many people are reluctant to tell their income to strangers conducting a survey. A straightforward "What is your annual income?" often prompts the reply "None of your business." It is better to preface a reading of the

following list with the question, "Which of these categories includes your household's total annual income?"

_____ Under $25,000
_____ $25,000–$29,999
_____ $30,000–$39,999
_____ $40,000–$49,999
_____ $50,000–$59,999
_____ $60,000 or more

The categories are broad enough to allow respondents some privacy but narrow enough for statistical analysis. The income classifications depend on the purpose of the questionnaire and the geographic and demographic distribution of the subjects. However, the average household income in the United States is about $60,000. The $60,000 upper level in the example is too low for many parts of the country. Other potentially sensitive areas are people's sex lives, drug use, religion, and trustworthiness. In all these areas, care should be taken to ensure respondents' confidentiality and anonymity, when possible.

The simplest type of closed-ended question is one that provides a dichotomous response, usually "agree/disagree" or "yes/no." For example:

Local television stations should have longer weather reports in the late evening news.

_____ Agree
_____ Disagree

Although such questions provide little sensitivity to different degrees of conviction, they are the easiest to tabulate of all question forms. Whether they provide enough sensitivity or information about the purpose of the research project are questions the researcher must seriously consider.

The **multiple-choice question** allows respondents to choose an answer from several options. Here is an example:

In general, television commercials include truthful information ...

_____ All of the time

_____ Most of the time

_____ Some of the time

_____ Rarely

_____ Never

Multiple-choice questions should include all possible responses. A question that excludes any significant response usually creates problems. For example:

What is your favorite television network?

_____ ABC

_____ CBS

_____ NBC

Subjects who prefer any other network could not answer this question.

Additionally, multiple-choice responses must be **mutually exclusive**: There should be only one response option per question for each respondent. For instance:

How many years have you been working in the newspaper industry?

_____ Less than 1 year

_____ 1–5 years

_____ 5–10 years

Which blank would a person check who has exactly 5 years of experience? One way to correct this problem is to reword the responses, such as in the following item:

How many years have you been working in the newspaper industry?

_____ Less than 1 year

_____ 1–5 years

_____ More than 5 years

Rating scales are also used widely in mass media research (see Chapter 2). They can be arranged horizontally or vertically:

There are too many commercials on TV during prime time.

_____ Strongly agree   (coded as 5 for analysis)

_____ Agree   (coded as 4)

_____ Neutral   (coded as 3)

_____ Disagree   (coded as 2)

_____ Strongly disagree   (coded as 1)

What is your opinion of the local news on Channel 9?

Fair ____ ____ ____ ____ ____ Unfair
　　(5)　(4)　(3)　(2)　(1)

Semantic differential scales are another form of rating scale frequently used to rate persons, concepts, or objects (see Chapter 2). These scales use bipolar adjectives with seven scale points:

How do you perceive the term *public television*?

Uninteresting	____	____	____	____	____	____	____	Interesting
Good	____	____	____	____	____	____	____	Bad
Dull	____	____	____	____	____	____	____	Exciting
Happy	____	____	____	____	____	____	____	Sad

Next, in situations where there is an interest in the relative perception of several concepts or items, the *rank-ordering* technique is appropriate, such as:

Here is an alphabetical list of several common occupations. Please rank them in terms of their prestige. Put a 1 next to the profession that has the most prestige, a 2 next to the one with the second most, and so on. (The list is alphabetical to avoid presentation bias.)

_____ Banker

_____ Lawyer

_____ Newspaper reporter

_____ Police officer

_____ Politician

_____ Teacher

_____ Television news reporter

Asking respondents to rank more than a dozen objects is not recommended because the process can become tedious and the discriminations exceedingly fine. Furthermore, ranking data imposes limitations on the statistical analysis that can be performed.

The **checklist question** is often used in pilot studies to refine questions for the final project. For example:

What things do you look for in a new television set? (Check as many as apply.)

_____ Automatic fine-tuning

_____ Internet capability

_____ Picture within a picture (the ability to view more than one channel at a time)

_____ Portable

_____ Built-in hard drive for recording

_____ Surround sound

_____ Other

In this case, the most frequently checked answers may be used to develop a multiple-choice question; the unchecked responses are dropped.

Forced-choice questions are frequently used in media studies designed to gather information about lifestyles, and they are always listed in pairs. Forced-choice questionnaires are usually long—sometimes containing dozens of questions—and repeat questions (in a different form) on the same topic. The answers for each topic are analyzed for patterns, and a respondent's interest in that topic is scored. A typical forced-choice questionnaire might contain the following pairs:

Select one statement from each of the following pairs of statements:

_____ Advertising of any kind is a waste of time and money.

_____ I learn a lot from all types of advertising.

_____ The government should regulate television program content.

_____ The government should not regulate television program content.

_____ I listen to the radio every day.

_____ I listen to the radio only when I'm alone.

Respondents generally complain that neither response in a forced-choice question is satisfactory, but they have to select one or the other. From a series of questions on the same topic (violence, lifestyles, career goals), a pattern of behavior or attitude usually develops.

Survey researchers use *fill-in-the-blank* questions infrequently; however, some studies are particularly suited for this type of question. In advertising copy testing, for example, they are often used to test subjects' recall of a commercial. After seeing, hearing, or reading an advertisement, subjects receive

Figure 7.1   "Feeling Thermometer" for Recording a Subject's Degree of Like or Dislike

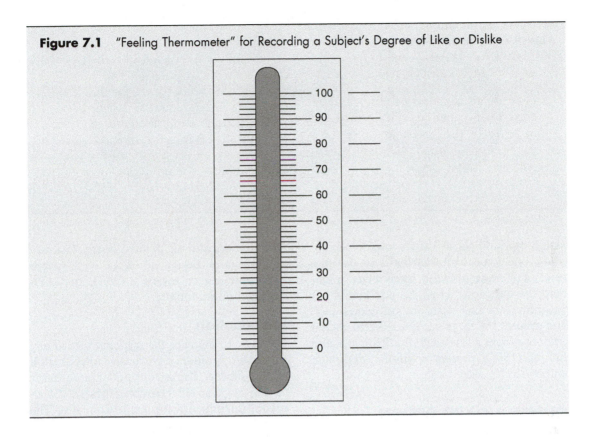

a script of the advertisement in which a number of words have been randomly omitted (often every fifth or seventh word). Subjects are required to fill in the missing words to complete the commercial. Fill-in-the-blank questions also can be used in information tests, such as:

> "The local news anchors on Channel 4 are _____ " or "The headline story on the front page was about _____."

Tables, graphs, and figures are also used in survey research. Some ingenious questioning devices have been developed to help respondents more accurately describe how they think and feel. For example, the University of Michigan Survey Research Center developed the **feeling thermometer,** with which subjects can rate an idea or object.

The thermometer, which is patterned after a normal mercury thermometer, offers an easy way for respondents to rate their degree of like or dislike in terms of "hot" or "cold" (see Figure 7.1). For example:

> How would you rate the coverage your local newspaper provided on the recent school board elections? (Place an X near the number on the thermometer that most accurately reflects your feelings; 100 indicates strong approval, and 0 reflects strong disapproval.)

A search on the Internet for *"feeling thermometer"* shows the diverse uses of the scale.

Some questionnaires designed for children use other methods to collect information. Since young children have difficulty

Figure 7.2   Simple Picture Scale for Use with Young Children

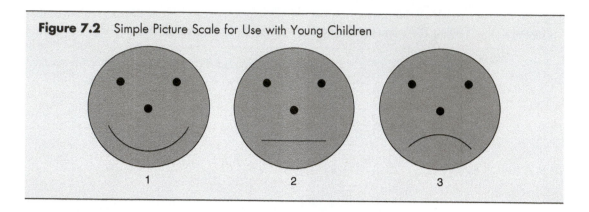

1   2   3

assigning numbers to values and/or perceptions, one logical alternative is to use pictures. For example, the interviewer might read the question "How do you feel about Saturday morning cartoons on television?" and present the faces in Figure 7.2 to elicit a response from a five-year-old. Zillmann and Bryant (1975) present a similar approach with their "Yucky" scale.

QUESTIONNAIRE DESIGN

The approach used in asking questions and, in the case of a self-administered questionnaire, physical appearance can affect the **response rate** (the percentage of respondents who complete the questionnaire among those who are contacted/selected). The time and effort invested in developing a good questionnaire always pay off with more usable data. This section offers some useful suggestions. Many of the suggestions about questionnaire design and layout discussed here are intended for paper or computer questionnaires, not **CATI (computer-aided telephone interviewing)**, which eliminates many problems such as skip patterns and rotation of questions, or **CAPI (computer-assisted personal interviewing)**, where the interview is conducted in person and either the respondent or interviewer enters the information in the computer. However, all researchers

must understand all of the idiosyncrasies of questionnaire design to work with paper questionnaires or review a CATI- or CAPI-designed questionnaire.

Introduction

One way to increase the response rate in any survey is to prepare a persuasive introduction to the survey. Backstrom and Hursh-Cesar (1986) suggest six characteristics of a successful introduction to a questionnaire: The introduction should be short, realistically worded, nonthreatening, serious, neutral, and pleasant but firm.

Although some academic research requires that the purpose of the survey be explained in detail to respondents, this is usually not the case in private-sector research. In private-sector research, there is no need to explain the purpose or value of a survey to respondents or to tell them how long the survey will take to complete. For example, in a telephone survey, telling the respondents "The survey will take only a few minutes" gives them the opportunity to say they do not have time to talk. The introduction should be short so that the respondent can begin writing answers or the interviewer can start asking questions.

Here is an example of an effective introduction for a telephone survey conducted by a field service to show how the interviewer immediately gets into the questionnaire:

Hi, my name is _____ with [INSERT COMPANY NAME]. We're conducting an *opinion* survey about radio in the Chicago area and I'd like to ask you a few questions. We're not trying to sell anything, and this is not a contest or promotion. We're interested only in your opinions. Please tell me which of these age groups you belong to—under 18, 18 to 24, 25 to 34, 35 to 44, 45 to 54, or over 54? [TERMINATE IF UNDER 18 OR OVER 54.]

With some modifications, the same introduction is appropriate for a self-administered questionnaire. The introduction would include the second, third, and fourth sentences along with a final sentence that says, "Please answer the questions as completely and honestly as possible."

The goal of the introduction in telephone surveys is to get into the interview as quickly as possible so that the respondent does not have a chance to say "no" and hang up (referred to as a "terminate"). This may sound overly aggressive, but it works. (Note, however, that many academic research review boards would not approve such an approach and would require that a statement such as "May I continue?" be included before going on with the interview.) The introduction in self-administered questionnaires should be as simple as possible.

Regardless of the survey approach used, a well-constructed introduction usually generates higher response rates than a simple "Please answer the following questions…"

Instructions

All instructions necessary to complete the questionnaire should be clearly stated for respondents or interviewers. These instructions vary depending on the type of survey conducted. Mail surveys and self-administered questionnaires usually require the most specific instructions because respondents are not able to ask questions about the survey. Respondents and interviewers should understand whether the correct response consists of circling or checking an item, placing items in a specific order, or skipping an item.

Procedural instructions for respondents are often highlighted with a different typeface, capital letters, or some graphic device, perhaps arrows or lines. The following is an example from a mail survey:

Do you have a favorite radio station that you listen to most of the time?

_____ Yes _____ No

| If yes, please briefly explain why the radio station is your favorite on the lines below. |

_____

_____

_____

Some questionnaires require respondents to rank a list of items. In this case, the instructions must clearly describe which response represents the highest value:

Please rate the following magazines in order of importance to you. Place a 1 next to the magazine you prefer most, a 2 next to the magazine in second place, and so on up to 5.

_____ *Cycle World Magazine*

_____ *Better Homes and Gardens*

_____ *Consumer Reports*

_____ *Popular Science*

_____ *Time*

Fowler (2002) offers these suggestions for designing a self-administered questionnaire:

- Make the questionnaire self-explanatory.
- Limit the questions to closed-ended items. Checking a box or circling an answer should be the only task required.
- Use only a limited number of question forms.

- Lay out and type the questionnaire in a clear and uncluttered way.
- Limit the amount of instructions. Respondents can be confused easily.

Fowler's second suggestion is too strict. Most respondents are usually able to answer open-ended questions with the same ease (or complication) as closed-ended questions. Whether open-ended or closed-ended, all questions should be pretested to determine whether the directions for answering are clear.

Instructions for interviewers are usually typed in capital letters and enclosed in parentheses, brackets, or boxes. For example, instructions for a telephone survey might look like this:

We'd like to start by asking you some things about television. First, what are your favorite TV shows? [RECORD]

1. _____   2. _____

3. _____   4. _____

> RECORD ALL NAMES OF TV SHOWS. PROBE WITH "ARE THERE ANY MORE?" TO GET AT LEAST THREE SHOWS.

Screener questions, or **filter questions**, are used to eliminate unwanted respondents; that is, to include only respondents who have specific characteristics or who answer questions in a specific manner. These questions often require respondents or interviewers to skip one or more questions. Skips must be clearly specified (recall that a CATI- or CAPI-designed questionnaire automatically skips to the next relevant question). Here is an example:

During a typical week, do you listen to radio stations on the AM dial?

_____ Yes [ASK Q.16]

_____ No [SKIP TO Q.17]

A survey using this question might be designed to question only respondents who

listen to AM radio. The screener question immediately determines whether the subject falls into this group. If the respondent says "no," the interviewer (or respondent, if the survey is self-administered) may skip a certain number of questions or terminate the survey immediately.

When interviewers are used, as is the case in telephone and one-on-one interviews, the questionnaires must have easy-to-follow instructions, including how many responses to take for open-ended questions; simple skip patterns; and enough space to record answers if survey responses are recorded. Telephone questionnaires must include everything an interviewer will say, including introductions, explanations, definitions, transitions, and pronunciations. The last point is particularly important because interviewers should sound as if they know the topic. Don't assume interviewers know how to pronounce names or technical terms. Always use phonetic spellings for potentially troublesome words.

All instructions should be clear and simple. A confusing questionnaire impairs the effectiveness of the interviewer, lowers the number of respondents who complete the test, and increases costs.

Question Order

All surveys flow better when the early questions are simple and easy to answer. Researchers often include one or two "warm-up" questions about the topic under investigation so that respondents become accustomed to answering questions and begin thinking about the survey topic. Preliminary questions can also serve as motivation to create interest in the questionnaire. Demographic data, personal questions, and other sensitive items should be placed at the end of the questionnaire to allow the interviewer to establish a rapport with each respondent or, for a self-administered questionnaire, to relieve any suspicions. Although

A CLOSER LOOK

Questionnaire Design

The best way to start designing a questionnaire is to make a "laundry list" of questions that need to be answered. In this stage, don't worry about how the questions will be asked or what form they will take. This list will also help you design the flow of the questionnaire: what should be asked first, second, third, and so on.

some respondents may still refuse to answer personal items or may hang up the telephone, at least the main body of data is already collected.

Age and gender information are usually included in the first part of a questionnaire, so at least some respondent identification is possible, which may be necessary in determining study quotas.

The questionnaire should be organized in a logical sequence, proceeding from the general to the specific. Questions on similar topics should be grouped together, and the transitions between question sections should be clear and logical.

Poor question order may bias a respondent's answers. For example, suppose that, after several questions about the presence of violence in society, respondents are asked to rank the major problems facing the country today from the following list:

_____ Terrorism

_____ Corrupt government

_____ High prices

_____ Violence on TV

_____ War

Violence on TV might receive a higher ranking than it would if the ranking question had been asked before the series of questions on violence. Or, to take another example, suppose a public relations researcher is attempting to discover the public's attitudes toward a large oil company. If the questionnaire begins with attitudinal questions concerning oil spills and inflated profits and then asks respondents to rate certain oil companies, it is likely that the ratings of all the companies will be lower because of general impressions created by the earlier questions.

There is no easy solution to the problem of question "contamination." Obviously, some questions have to be asked before others. Perhaps the best approach is to be sensitive to the problem and check for it in a pretest. If question order A, B, C may have biasing effects, then another version using the order C, B, A should be tested. Completely neutral positioning is not always possible, however, and when bias may enter because of how responses are ordered, the list of items should be rotated. The command [ROTATE] after a question indicates that the interviewer must change the order of responses for each subject (performed automatically by a CATI- or CAPI-designed questionnaire). In self-administered questionnaires, different question orders can be printed, but make sure that the data are input and analyzed correctly. If several versions of a questionnaire are used, it's easy to get them confused.

Layout

The physical design of the questionnaire is another important factor in survey research. A badly typed, poorly reproduced questionnaire is not likely to attract many responses in a mail survey. Nor does a cramped questionnaire with 40 questions to a page create a positive attitude in respondents. Response categories should be adequately spaced and presented in an unambiguous manner. For example, the following format might lead to problems:

> There are too many commercials on television.
>
> Do you strongly agree ＿＿＿ Agree ＿＿＿
>
> Have no opinion ＿＿＿ Disagree ＿＿＿
>
> Strongly disagree? ＿＿＿

A more effective and less confusing method is to provide a vertical ordering of the response choices:

> There are too many commercials on television.
>
> ＿＿＿ Strongly agree
>
> ＿＿＿ Agree
>
> ＿＿＿ No opinion
>
> ＿＿＿ Disagree
>
> ＿＿＿ Strongly disagree

Some researchers recommend avoiding blanks altogether because respondents and interviewers tend to make a large checkmark or X that covers more than one blank, making interpretation difficult. If blanks are perceived as a problem, boxes to check or numbers to circle are satisfactory. In any case, the response form should be consistent throughout the questionnaire. Changes in format generally create confusion for both respondents and interviewers. Finally, each question must have enough space for answers. This is especially true for open-ended questions. Nothing is more discouraging to respondents and interviewers than to be confronted with a presentation like this:

> What would you change on your favorite radio station? ＿＿＿＿＿＿＿＿
>
> ＿＿＿＿＿＿＿＿＿＿＿＿＿＿＿
>
> Why do you go to the movies? ＿＿＿
>
> ＿＿＿＿＿＿＿＿＿＿＿＿＿＿＿

> What are your favorite television shows?
>
> ＿＿＿＿＿＿＿＿＿＿＿＿＿＿＿
>
> ＿＿＿＿＿＿＿＿＿＿＿＿＿＿＿

If a research budget limits the amount of paper for questionnaires, subjects can be asked to add further comments on the back of the survey.

Questionnaire Length

Questionnaire length is an important concern in any survey because it directly relates to the completion rate. Long questionnaires cause fatigue, respondent dropout (also known as mortality), and low completion rates. Shorter questionnaires guarantee higher completion rates.

Unfortunately, there are no strict guidelines to help in deciding how long a questionnaire should be. The length depends on a variety of factors:

- Amount of money in the research budget
- Purpose of the survey
- Type of problems or questions to be investigated
- Age of respondents involved in the survey
- Type and complexity of questions in the questionnaire
- Location in the country where the study is conducted
- Specific setting of the testing situation
- Time of year and time of day when the study is conducted
- Type of interviewer (professional or amateur)

In most cases, questionnaire length is determined by trial and error. A survey that has more than 10% incompletes or **breakoffs** (the respondent hangs up during a telephone survey or terminates the survey in some way) is probably too long. The length of the survey may not be the only problem, however,

A CLOSER LOOK

Questionnaire Design

One great website is Quaid: Question Understanding Aid from the University of Memphis (*mnemosyne.csl.psyc.memphis.edu/QUAID/ quaidindex.html*). An introduction page on the website states, in part, that "QUAID is a software tool that assists survey methodologists, social scientists, and designers of questionnaires in improving the wording, syntax, and semantics of questions. The tool identifies potential problems that respondents might have in comprehending the meaning of questions on questionnaires." It's free. Try it.

so it is important to take a close look at the questionnaire for other problems.

Our experience during the past 30 years has shown the following time limits as maximum:

Type of Survey	Maximum Time Limit
Self-administered mail	60 min.
Self-administered in a group situation supervised by a researcher	60 min.
One-on-one interview	60 min.
Telephone	20 min.
Internet/online	20 min.
Mall intercept	10 min.

Telephone interviewing can be a difficult approach to use because it takes talent to keep respondents on the telephone answering questions. Professional interviewers can usually hold respondents' attention for about 20 minutes. After 20 minutes, there is a severe drop-off in incidence due to breakoffs.

PRETESTING

Without a doubt, the best way to discover whether a research instrument is adequately designed is to pretest it—that is, conduct a mini-study with a small sample to determine whether the study approach is correct and to help refine the questions. Areas of misunderstanding or confusion can be easily corrected without wasting time or money.

There are several ways to pretest a questionnaire. When an acceptable draft of the questionnaire is completed, a focus group can be used to discuss the questionnaire with potential respondents. However, this is usually too expensive. The best pretest in telephone surveys is for interviewers to call 10 to 20 people and do a run-through. Any problems quickly emerge. Self-administered questionnaires should be pretested with the type of respondent who will participate in the actual study. Once again, any problems should be apparent immediately.

In any type of pretesting situation, it is appropriate to discuss the project with respondents after they complete the questionnaire. They can be asked whether they understood the questions, whether the questions were simple to answer, and so on. Respondents are almost always willing to help researchers.

GATHERING SURVEY DATA

Once a questionnaire is developed and one or more pretests or pilot studies have been conducted, the next step is to gather data from an appropriate group of respondents.

The five basic methods for doing this are mail survey, telephone survey, personal interview, group administration, and Internet survey. Researchers can also use variations and combinations of these five methods, such as mall interviews or CAPI. Each procedure has advantages and disadvantages that must be considered before a choice is made. This section highlights the characteristics of each method.

Mail Surveys

Mail surveys involve sending self-administered questionnaires to a sample of respondents. Stamped reply envelopes are enclosed to encourage respondents to send their completed questionnaires back to the researcher. Mail surveys are popular in some types of businesses, such as consumer panels to gather information about product purchasing behavior, because they can secure a lot of information without spending a lot of time and money. However, novice researchers must understand that mail surveys are usually difficult to conduct because most respondents simply throw the questionnaire in the trash. In research terms, the response rate for mail surveys is low—usually under 40%.

The general stages of a mail survey are discussed next. Although the steps are listed in numerical sequence, many of them are often done in a different order or even simultaneously.

1. *Select a sample.* Sampling is usually accomplished from a prepared frame that contains the names and addresses of potential respondents (see Chapter 4). The most common sampling frame is the **mailing list,** a collection of names and addresses of respondents who belong to a narrowly defined group, which commercial sampling companies prepare.

2. *Construct the questionnaire.* As discussed earlier, mail questionnaires must be concise and specific because no interviewer is present with the respondent to correct misunderstandings, answer questions, or give directions.

3. *Write a cover letter.* A brief note explaining the purpose and importance of the questionnaire usually increases the response rate. The importance of the research study is the key.

4. *Assemble the package.* The questionnaire, cover letter, and return envelope are stuffed into mailing envelopes. Researchers sometimes use bulk mail with first-class return envelopes. Another method is to send questionnaires via first-class mail and use business reply envelopes for responses. This allows researchers to pay postage for only the questionnaires actually returned. Postal options always depend on the research budget.

5. *Mail the surveys.* Bulk-mail regulations require sorting envelopes into ZIP code areas.

6. *Monitor return rates.*

7. *Send follow-up mailings.* The first follow-up should be sent two weeks after the initial mailing, and a second (if necessary) two weeks after the first. The follow-up letter can be sent to the entire sample or to only the subjects who fail to answer.

8. *Tabulate and analyze data.*

Advantages. Mail surveys cover a wide geographic area for a reasonable cost. They are often the only way to gather information from people who live in hard-to-reach areas of the country (or in other countries). Mail surveys also allow for selective sampling using specialized mailing lists. In addition to those mentioned, lists are available that include only people with specific annual incomes, consumers who have bought a car within the past year, subscribers to a particular magazine, or residents of a specific ZIP code. If researchers need to collect information from a highly specialized audience, mail surveys are often better than other approaches.

Another advantage of the mail survey is that it provides anonymity; some respondents are more likely to answer sensitive questions candidly. Questionnaires can be completed at home or in the office, which affords respondents a sense of privacy. People can answer questions at their own pace, and they have an opportunity to look up facts or check past information. Mail surveys also eliminate interviewer bias because there is no personal contact.

Probably the biggest advantage of this method is its low cost. Mail surveys do not require a large staff of trained interviewers. The only costs are for printing, mailing lists, envelopes, and postage. When compared to other data collection procedures, the mail survey has the lowest cost per completed questionnaire.

Disadvantages. First, mail questionnaires must be self-explanatory. No interviewer is present to answer questions or to clear up misunderstandings. Mail surveys are also the slowest form of data collection. Returns start to trickle in a week or so after the initial mailing and continue to arrive for several weeks thereafter. It may be months before some responses are returned. Many researchers set a cutoff date, after which returns are not included in the analysis.

One significant problem with mail surveys is that researchers never know exactly who answers the questions. For example, assistants may complete a survey sent to corporate executives, or a child in the home may complete a survey sent to the "male head of household." Furthermore, replies are often received only from people who are interested in the survey, and this injects bias into the results. Another significant disadvantage of the mail survey is the low return rate. A typical survey (depending on area and type of survey) will achieve a response rate of 5%–40%, and this casts doubt on the reliability of the findings.

Increasing Response Rates

Survey researchers have investigated a number of ways to improve response rates, but there are no surefire guarantees. In a meta-analysis (an analysis in which the findings of several studies are treated as independent observations and combined to calculate an overall or average effect) of numerous studies concerning mail surveys, Fox, Crask, and Kim (1989) found that average response rates can be increased in a variety of ways. In descending order of importance, the following procedures tend to increase mail survey response rates: university sponsorship, stamped return postage as opposed to business reply, written prenotification of the survey sent to the respondent, postcard follow-up, first-class outgoing postage, questionnaire color (green paper as opposed to white), notification of cutoff date, and stamped outgoing postage rather than metered stamping.

Other ways to increase response rates in mail surveys as much as 50% include:

- A drawing that offers a prize of a TV set, Blu-Ray, or MP3 player (academic researchers should check with local institutional review boards for guidelines before using this technique)
- Prepaid telephone calling cards activated when the questionnaire is returned
- Gift cards to local retailers
- Cash (no less than $10)

Telephone Surveys

Telephone surveys and personal interviews use trained interviewers who ask questions and record the responses, usually on a computer. The respondents generally do not see the actual questionnaire. Since telephone and personal interviewing techniques have certain similarities, much of what follows applies to both. Telephone surveys fill a middle ground between mail surveys and personal interviews. They offer more control and higher response rates than most mail surveys, but they are limited in the types of questions that can be asked. Telephone interviews are generally more expensive than mail surveys but less expensive than face-to-face interviews. Because of these factors, telephone surveys are a compromise between the other two techniques, which may account for their popularity in mass media research.

Interviewers are extremely important to both telephone surveys and personal surveys. An interviewer ideally should function as a neutral medium through which the respondents' answers are communicated to the researcher. The interviewer's presence and manner of speaking should not influence respondents' answers in any way. Adequate training and instruction can minimize the bias that the interviewer might inject into the data. For example, if an interviewer shows disdain or shock over an answer, it is unlikely that the respondent will continue to answer questions in an honest manner. Showing agreement with certain responses might prompt similar answers to other questions. Skipping questions, carelessly asking questions, and being impatient with the respondent also cause problems.

As an aid to minimizing interviewer bias, the National Association of Broadcasters (1976, pp. 37–38) published recommendations for interviewers. While the publication is many years old, the recommendations are still relevant:

- Read the questions exactly as worded. Ask them in the exact order listed. Skip questions only when the instructions

on the questionnaire tell you to. There are no exceptions.

- Never suggest an answer, try to explain a question, or imply what kind of reply is wanted. Don't prompt in any way.

- If a question is not understood, say, "Let me read it again" and repeat it slowly and clearly. If it is still not understood, record a "no answer."

- Report answers and comments exactly as given, writing them out fully. If an answer seems vague or incomplete, probe with neutral questions, such as "Will you explain that?" or "How do you mean that?" Sometimes just waiting a bit will convey to the respondent that you want more information.

- Act interested, alert, and appreciative of the respondent's cooperation, but never comment on his or her replies. Never express approval, disapproval, or surprise. Even an "Oh" can cause a respondent to hesitate or refuse to answer further questions. Never talk up or down to a respondent.

- Follow all instructions carefully, whether you agree with them or not.

- Thank each respondent. Leave a good impression for the next interviewer.

- Discuss any communication problems immediately with the researcher in charge.

A general procedure for conducting a telephone survey follows. Again, the steps are presented in numerical order, but it is possible to address many tasks simultaneously.

1. *Select a sample.* Telephone surveys require researchers to specify clearly the geographic area to be covered and to identify the type of respondent to be interviewed in each household contacted. Many surveys are restricted to people over 18, heads of households, and so forth. The sampling procedure used depends on the purpose of the study (see Chapter 4).

2. *Construct the questionnaire.* Telephone surveys require straightforward and uncomplicated response options. For example, ranking a long list of items is especially difficult over the telephone, and this should be avoided. The survey should not exceed 10 minutes for nonprofessional interviewers; interviews up to 20 minutes long require professionals who are trained to keep respondents on the telephone.

3. *Prepare an interviewer instruction manual.* This document should cover the basic mechanics of the survey (telephone numbers to call, when to call, how to record times, and so on). It should also specify which household member to interview and provide general guidelines on how to ask the questions and how to record the responses.

4. *Train the interviewers.* Interviewers need practice going through the questionnaire to become familiar with all the items, response options, and instructions. It is best to train interviewers in a group using interview simulations that allow each person to practice asking questions. It is a good idea to pretest interviewers as well as the questionnaire.

5. *Collect the data.* Data collection is most efficient when conducted from one central location (assuming enough telephone lines are available). Problems that develop are easier to remedy, and important questions raised by one interviewer can easily be communicated to the rest of the group. A central location also makes it easier for researchers to validate the interviewers' work. The completion rate should be monitored daily.

6. *Make necessary callbacks.* Up to three additional callbacks should be made to respondents whose lines were busy or who did not answer during the first session. Callbacks on a different day or evening tend to have a greater chance of reaching someone willing to be interviewed. In most situations, three callbacks produce a contact about 75% of the time.

When the first call produces a busy signal, the rule is to wait one half hour before calling again. If the first call produced a "no answer," wait two to three hours before calling again, assuming it is still a reasonable hour to call. If evening calls produce no answer, call the following day.

7. *Verify the results.* When all questionnaires are complete, 5%–10% of each interviewer's respondents should be called to verify that their answers were accurately recorded. Respondents should be told during the initial survey that they might receive an additional call at a later date. This alerting tends to eliminate any confusion when subjects receive a second call. A typical procedure is to ask the subject's first name in the interview so that it can be used later. The interviewer should ask, "Were you called a few days ago and asked questions about television viewing?" The verification can begin from there—two or three of the original questions are asked again (preferably open-ended and sensitive questions, since interviewers are most likely to omit these).

8. *Tabulate the data.* Along with the normal data analysis, telephone researchers generally compute response rates for the following items: completed interviews, initial refusals, unqualified respondents, busy signals, language barriers, no answers, terminates, breakoffs, and disconnects. The summary of calls is known as a *call disposition sheet.*

Advantages.   The cost of telephone surveys tends to be reasonable. The sampling involves minimal expense, and there are usually no significant transportation costs. Callbacks are simple and economical. The variety of telephone plans from phone companies enable researchers to conduct telephone surveys from any location.

Compared to mail surveys, telephone surveys can include more detailed questions, and, as stated earlier, interviewers can clarify misunderstandings that might arise during the administration of the questionnaire.

The incidences in telephone surveys for mass media research (once a qualified respondent is contacted) are generally high, especially when multiple callbacks are used. This is because most people enjoy answering questions about what they see, hear, or read. In addition, phone surveys are much faster than mail. A large staff of interviewers can collect the data from the designated sample in a short time—400 surveys often can be completed in less than seven days.

Disadvantages.   First, much of what is called survey research by telephone is not research at all but rather an attempt to sell people something. Unfortunately, many companies disguise their sales pitch as a survey. This falsified approach has made many people suspicious about telephone calls to their home and prompts many potential respondents to terminate an interview before it has started.

Additionally, it is impossible to include questions that involve visual demonstrations. A researcher cannot hold up a picture of a product and ask whether the respondent remembers seeing it advertised. Another potentially severe problem is that not everyone in a community is listed in the telephone directory, the sampling frame used most frequently. Not everyone has a telephone, many people have unlisted phone numbers, some numbers are listed incorrectly, and others are too new to be listed. A more recent problem is the growing number of people who no longer have landline telephones in their home and use only their cell phones. Cell phone numbers are not published. These problems would not be serious if the people with no telephones, unlisted numbers, or cell phone only, were just like those listed in the phone book. Unfortunately, researchers generally have no way of checking for such similarities or differences, so it is possible that a sample obtained from a telephone directory may be significantly different from the population. (See Chapter 4 concerning random-digit dialing.)

Finally, telephone surveys require a large number of "dialings" to successfully interview the number of respondents required for a study. To demonstrate this, Table 7.1 shows a summary of the telephone **call disposition sheets** from 50 randomly selected telephone studies conducted by Wimmer Research. The studies included respondents between the ages of 18 and 54 and investigated topics such as radio listening, television viewing, automotive purchases, and other nonmedia topics.

The data in Table 7.1 show what a professional interviewer faces during a typical workday. Of more than 750,000 dialings, only 2.5% were completed interviews. That is, Table 7.1 indicates that for every 100 dialings made, only 2.5 will result in a completed interview. There aren't many other jobs with a success rate this low.

Table 7.1	50-Study Call Disposition Summary	
Call Result	**Number**	**Percentage of Total**
No answer/machine*	443,200	56.3
Initial refusal	99,350	2.6
Busy	74,600	9.5
Did not qualify	34,550	4.4
Call back	30,550	3.9
Disconnect	28,400	3.6
Wrong age	26,000	3.3
Business	9,400	1.2
Computer/modem	6,750	0.9
Over age/sex quota	5,250	0.7
Language barrier	3,750	0.5
Security	3,000	0.4
Breakoff	2,800	0.4
Complete	20,000	2.5
TOTAL CALLS	787,600	

*Probably includes a significant number of caller ID rejections.

Personal Interviews

Personal interviews, also called **one-on-one interviews**, usually involve inviting a respondent to a field service location or a research office, and sometimes interviews are conducted at a person's place of work or home. There are two basic types of interviews: structured and unstructured. In a **structured interview**, standardized questions are asked in a predetermined order; little freedom is given to interviewers. In an **unstructured interview**, broad questions allow interviewers freedom to determine what further questions to ask to obtain the required information. Structured interviews are easy to tabulate and analyze, but they do not achieve the depth or expanse of unstructured interviews. Conversely, the unstructured type elicits more detail but takes a great deal of time to score and analyze.

The steps in constructing a personal interview survey are similar to those for a telephone survey. The following list discusses instances in which the personal interview differs substantially from the telephone method:

1. *Select a sample.* Drawing a sample for a personal interview is essentially the same as selecting a sample in any other research method. In one-on-one interviews, respondents are selected based on a predetermined set of screening requirements. In door-to-door interviews, a multistage sample is used to select first a general area, then a block or a neighborhood, and finally a random household from which a person will be chosen (see Figure 4.2).

2. *Construct the questionnaire.* Personal interviews are flexible: Detailed questions are easy to ask, and the time taken to complete the survey can be greatly extended—many personal interviews take up to one hour. Researchers can also use visual exhibits, lists, and photographs to ask questions, and respondents can be asked to sort photos or materials into categories, or to point to their answers on printed cards. Respondents can have privacy and anonymity by marking ballots, which can then be slipped into envelopes and sealed.

3. *Prepare an interviewer instruction guide.* The detail needed in an instruction guide depends on the type of interview. One-on-one interviewer guides are not very detailed because there is only one location, respondents are prerecruited by a field service, and interviewing times are prearranged. Door-to-door interviewer guides contain information about the household to select, the respondent to select, and an alternative action to take in the event the target respondent is not at home. Interviewer guides often have instructions on how to conduct the interview, how to dress, how to record data, and how to ask questions. (Keep in mind that although door-to-door interviews are mentioned in this chapter, they are rarely used in the United States because of cost and the hesitancy of respondents to participate.)

A CLOSER LOOK

Silence on the Telephone?

Many companies that conduct telephone interviews use a computer system known as a **predictive dialer**. In short, telephone numbers purchased from a sampling company are downloaded into the computer and the computer systematically dials each number in the database. When a voice is detected, the computer "sends" the call to an interviewer, who then begins the interview. When a person at home (or elsewhere) answers the phone and hears a short delay (dead air), the person is receiving a call from a predictive dialer. Many people have learned this and simply hang up if they hear a pause on the other end of the line.

4. *Train the interviewers.* Training is important because the questionnaires in a personal interview are longer and more detailed. Interviewers should receive detailed instructions on establishing a rapport with subjects, on administrative details (for example, time and length of interviews and interviewer salaries), and on asking follow-up questions.

5. *Collect the data.* Personal interviews are both labor and cost intensive. These problems are why most researchers prefer to use other methods. A personal interview project can take several days to several weeks to complete because turnaround is slow. One interviewer can complete only a handful of surveys each day. In addition, costs for salaries and expenses escalate quickly. It is common for research companies to charge as much as $1,000 per respondent in a one-on-one situation.

Interviewers gather data either by writing down answers or by electronically recording the respondents' answers. Both methods are slow, and detailed transcriptions and editing are often necessary.

6. *Make necessary callbacks.* Each callback requires an interviewer to return to a household originally selected or to the location used for the original interview. Additional salary, expenses, and time are required.

7. *Verify the results.* As with telephone surveys, a subsample of each interviewer's completed questionnaires is selected for verification. Respondents can be called on the phone or reinterviewed in person.

8. *Tabulate the data.* Data tabulation procedures for personal interviews are essentially the same as with any other research method. A codebook must be designed, questionnaires coded, and data input into a computer.

Advantages.   Many advantages of the personal interview technique have already been mentioned. It is the most flexible means of obtaining information because the face-to-face situation lends itself easily to questioning in greater depth and detail. Also, the interviewer can observe some information during the interview without adding to the length of the questionnaire. Additionally, the interviewer can develop a rapport with the respondents and may be able to elicit replies to sensitive questions that would remain unanswered in a mail or telephone survey. The identity of the respondent is known or can be controlled in the personal interview survey. Whereas in a mail survey all members of a family might confer on an answer, this can usually be avoided in a face-to-face interview. Finally, once an interview has begun, it is harder for respondents to terminate the interview before all the questions have been asked. In a telephone survey, the respondent can simply hang up the telephone.

Disadvantages.   As mentioned, time and cost are the major drawbacks to the personal interview technique, but another major disadvantage is the potential for interviewer bias. The physical appearance, age, race, gender, dress, nonverbal behavior, and comments of the interviewer may prompt respondents to answer questions untruthfully. Moreover, the organization necessary for recruiting, training, and administering a field staff of interviewers is much greater than that required for other data collection procedures. If a large number of interviewers are needed, it is necessary to hire field supervisors to coordinate their work, which makes the survey even more expensive. Finally, if personal interviews are conducted during the day, most of the respondents will not be employed outside the home. If it is desirable to interview respondents who have jobs outside the home, interviews must be scheduled on the weekends or during the evening.

One alternative now used in personal interviews is a self-administered interview that respondents answer on a personal computer. Respondents are usually invited to the research company or field service to participate in the project by answering questions presented to them on the computer.

A hybrid of personal interviewing is intensive, or in-depth, interviewing, which is discussed in Chapter 5.

Computer-Assisted Personal Interviewing

A recent methodology developed by a small number of research companies is computer-assisted personal interviewing (CAPI), in which laptop computers are used for in-person interview surveys. The respondent or a professional interviewer enters the data directly into the computer, and the results are later uploaded to a master computer for analysis.

Advantages. The main advantage of this approach is that the research questionnaire is taken to the respondent rather than the respondent answering the phone or attending a research location. Complicated questions and visual aids may be used in this approach.

Disadvantages. If CAPI involves respondent data entry, it requires that the respondent be able to use a computer and accurately input his or her responses. In addition, while CAPI may expand the geographic area where respondents are contacted, data collection remains slow because only one questionnaire is completed at a time. Finally, while CAPI may be valuable for certain applications, this use of a computer may actually be a technological step backwards. The goal of research in most cases is speed, and CAPI does not reduce the time required to collect data.

Mall Interviews

Although mall interviews are essentially a form of the personal interviews just discussed, their recent popularity and widespread use warrant individual consideration.

During the late 1980s, **mall intercepts** became one of the most popular research approaches among marketing and consumer researchers. As long ago as 1986, Schleifer found that of all the people who participated in a survey in 1984, 33% were mall intercepts. The popularity of mall intercepts continues even today, a fact that can be verified by a quick search on the Internet for "*mall intercepts.*"

Although mall intercepts use convenience samples so sampling error cannot be determined, the method has become the standard for many researchers. It is rare to enter a shopping mall without seeing an interviewer with a clipboard trying to stop a shopper. The method has become commonplace, but some shoppers resent the intrusion. In fact, shoppers often take paths to avoid the interviewers they can so easily detect.

The procedures involved in conducting mall intercepts are the same as those for personal interviews. The only major difference is that it is necessary to locate the field service that conducts research in the particular mall of interest. Field services pay license fees to mall owners to allow them to conduct research on the premises. Not just any field service can conduct research in any mall.

One recent trend in mall intercept research is the use of a personal computer for data collection. As with one-on-one interviews conducted in a field service, the respondents simply answer questions posed to them on the computer monitor.

Advantages. Mall intercepts are a quick and inexpensive way to collect data.

Disadvantages. Most of the disadvantages of mall intercepts have been discussed in other sections of this book. The three major problems are that convenience sampling restricts the generalizability of the results (not all people in a given area shop at the same mall), the interviews must be short (no more than about 10 minutes), and there is no control over data collection (researchers are at the mercy of the field service to conduct a proper interview).

Group Administration

Group administration combines some of the features of mail surveys and personal interviews. In the group-administered survey, a group of respondents is gathered together (prerecruited by a field service) and given individual copies of a questionnaire or asked to participate in a group interview (a large focus group). The session can take place in a natural setting, but it is usually held at a field service location or a hotel ballroom. For example, respondents may be recruited to complete questionnaires about radio or television stations, students in a classroom may complete questionnaires about their newspaper reading habits, or an audience may be asked to answer questions after viewing a sneak preview of a new film.

The interviewer in charge of the session may or may not read questions to respondents. Reading questions aloud may help respondents who have reading problems, but this is not always necessary. (It is possible to screen respondents for reading or language skills.) The best approach is for several interviewers to be present in the room so that individual problems can be resolved without disturbing the other respondents.

Some group-administered sessions include audio and video materials for respondents to analyze. The session allows respondents to proceed at their own pace, and in most cases interviewers allow respondents to ask questions, although this is not a requirement.

Advantages. The group administration technique has certain advantages. For example, a group-administered questionnaire can be longer than the typical questionnaire used in a mail survey. Because the respondents are usually assembled for the sole purpose of completing the questionnaire, the response rates are usually quite high. The opportunity for researchers to answer questions and handle problems that might arise generally means that fewer items are left blank or answered incorrectly.

Disadvantages. On the negative side, if a group-administered survey leads to the perception that some authority sanctions the study, respondents may become suspicious or uneasy. For example, if a group of teachers is brought together to fill out a questionnaire, some might think that the survey has the approval of the local school administration and that the results will be made available to their superiors. Also, the group environment makes interaction possible among the respondents; this can make the situation more difficult for the researcher to control. In addition, not all surveys can use samples that can be tested together in a group. Surveys often require responses from a wide variety of people, and mixing respondents together may bias the results.

Finally, group administration is very expensive. Costs usually include recruiting fees, co-op payments, hotel rental, refreshments, audiovisual equipment, and salaries for interviewers. Many companies no longer use group administration because of the high costs involved.

Internet Surveys

Nothing has changed the world of research more than the Internet. While the validity and reliability of some methods may be questioned, the fact is that virtually any type of research can now be conducted on, or via, the Internet. In this section, however, we will focus on survey research and the Internet.

During the late 1990s, researchers capitalized on the popularity of the Internet. Collecting research data via the Internet is now commonplace. The process is simple: A respondent is contacted via telephone, letter, or email and asked to participate in a research project. Respondents who agree are either sent a questionnaire via email or given a link to access the questionnaire online. In most situations, respondents are given a password to access the website. When finished, respondents either click on a "submit" button or email the questionnaire back to the research company or business conducting the study.

Online research, which often consists only of data collection, has become amazingly easy to conduct with websites such as Survey Monkey, Zoomerang, PollDaddy, and many more. In many cases, small research studies can be conducted free, and these websites have become extremely popular with students and professional researchers alike. The survey websites allow virtually anyone to conduct his or her own research.

Advantages.   Online research offers a huge list of advantages, including—but not limited to—low costs, no geographic limitations, no specific time constraints because respondents can complete the survey or measurement instrument at their convenience, flexibility in the approach used to collect data, and the ability to expose respondents to almost any type of audio or visual materials.

Disadvantages.   The primary disadvantage of online research is that there is not yet a way to ensure that the person recruited for the study is actually the person who completes the questionnaire. For example, an adult may be recruited for a study, but the adult may ask a child in the house to answer the questions. Internet research, like any electronic gathering procedure, has no control over data-gathering procedures. This lack of control may have a profound negative effect on the results gathered and the decisions made. However, we address this situation in the next section.

A SPECIAL NOTE ON USING THE INTERNET FOR DATA COLLECTION

Some researchers include a variety of questions (screener questions) to try to identify the person who participates in a research study. However, despite these efforts, when it comes to online research, no "Big Brother" mechanism exists to help researchers know with 100% certainty the identity of the respondents who complete an online research project. If appropriate controls are used, most of the respondents will probably belong to the target sample, but it is likely that the sample will include a number of bogus respondents. While the warnings about this problem are widespread, the reality is that both experienced and novice researchers in every field continue to use the Internet to conduct research. Online sampling problems are well known, but we predict that in the future the majority of all data in all research areas will be collected via the Internet.

With the maxim "Use online research regardless of warnings" in mind, we would like to offer a suggestion that will reduce the amount of error in online data collection. Do not presume that our suggestion is a **carte blanche** endorsement of using the Internet for data collection. It is not. Instead, we offer this suggestion because we feel that regardless of how many warnings are presented, the warnings will fall on deaf ears and many (if not most) people who conduct online research continue to do so with little concern for the validity and reliability of the data. With that as a foundation, we offer this advice.

During our decades of mass media research in both the academic and private sectors, we have witnessed a countless number of characteristics and idiosyncrasies of research, many of which are discussed in this book. In relation to respondent behavior, we have found that the responses and respondents in *virtually all types of research* tend to fall into a typical normal distribution pattern; that is, most respondents' answers cluster around the middle of the curve (the mean), with smaller groups of respondents "tailing off" to the right or left of the mean—the outliers, as we have mentioned in other chapters. However, we have also found in almost every study, a few respondents are *extreme outliers*—respondents who differ *dramatically* from the sample (standard deviation $\geq \pm 2.0$), even with samples that are supposedly homogeneous. The phenomenon of omnipresent outliers and extreme outliers in all types of online research is the foundation for our suggestion in dealing with the fact that there is no way to know, with 100% certainty, the identity of the respondents who participated in an online research project.

In virtually all of the research studies we have conducted during the past 35+ years, we have made attempts to identify extreme outliers. In some cases, these respondents can be identified simply by looking at the data, such as when respondents' answers constitute a *response set* (the same or similar answers). However, to ensure accuracy, we always identify extreme outliers using one of two simple procedures: one is for questionnaires that include ratings and other numerical-answer questions; the second is for questionnaires that include only open-ended questions.

In questionnaires with ratings and other numerical-answer questions, we identify extreme outliers by first calculating the means and standard deviations of all respondents' answers for every rating or numerical-answer question in the study. Next, we convert the means and standard deviations to *z*-scores (see Chapter 10) to make identification easier. We look for respondents with *z*-scores that differ substantially from the remaining sample (usually $z \geq \pm 2.0$), but

there is no set guideline because each research study is unique. If an extreme outlier appears in the analysis, we review the person's entire questionnaire or instrument to determine whether the person should remain in the sample. If enough evidence in the questionnaire indicates that the person differs markedly from the sample and does not qualify for the study, the respondent is discarded and replaced with someone else. In some situations, telephone calls to extreme outliers are helpful in proving that the respondents do not belong in the sample.

In questionnaires with only open-ended questions, we always include a "Code 98" in the codebook used to code the respondents' answers. The 98 code stands for "Unique answer," and if coders find a respondent with an answer that differs substantially from the other respondents in the study, the respondent receives two codes—one for the answer and one for the unique answer. When the data tables are run, respondents with 98 codes are scrutinized to determine whether they belong in the sample. If detailed scrutiny determines that the respondent should not be included in the study, the person is replaced with a qualified respondent.

These same procedures can be used to obtain an indication of the correctness of respondents included in an online study. Therefore, we suggest that researchers compute *z*-scores on the means and standard deviations for all ratings and numerical-answer questions, or that they use unique answer codes in open-ended surveys. The procedures do not offer a 100% guarantee that all invalid respondents will be located. However, the procedures, which we have tested repeatedly for more than 35 years, have proven to be extremely successful in identifying respondents who do not belong in a study. The procedures have become known in many mass media research circles as the *Wimmer Outlier Analysis*.

Finally, the procedures do not violate the tenet of "letting the data fall where they may." On the contrary, the procedures are objective methods to determine whether the data are valid and reliable.

One example may help. In a recent online survey conducted by a radio station in New Mexico, respondents were asked several questions about their use of text messages. The sample was supposed to include adults 35–54. One question asked the respondents how many text messages they sent during a typical week, which produced an average of 7.5 per week. However, z-scores computed on the standard deviations and 98 codes for all questions identified five respondents who sent more than 200 text messages per week. After further investigation, as well as follow-up telephone calls to verify the respondents, the researchers discovered that all five respondents were teenagers, and their questionnaires were deleted.

ACHIEVING A REASONABLE RESPONSE RATE

Regardless of which type of survey is conducted, it is virtually impossible to obtain a 100% response rate. Researchers have more control with some types of surveys (personal interview) and less with others (mail survey). However, in all situations, not all respondents will be available for interviews and not all will cooperate. Consequently, the researcher must try to achieve the highest response rate possible under the circumstances.

What constitutes an acceptable response rate? Obviously, the higher the response rate, the better: As more respondents are sampled, response bias is less likely. But is there a minimum rate that should be achieved? Not everyone agrees on an answer to this question, and it is difficult to develop a standard because of the variety of research studies conducted, methods of recruiting used,

research topics, and times of year and places that studies are conducted. However, this textbook's authors' experience suggests these response rate ranges:

- Mail surveys: 1%–5%
- Telephone surveys: 5%–80%
- Internet surveys: 5%–80%
- Mall intercept: 5%
- Personal (face-to-face) interviews: 40% (depends on recruiting method)

Regardless of the response rate, the researcher is responsible for examining any possible biases in response patterns. Were females more likely to respond than males? Older people more likely to respond than younger ones? A significant lack of response from a particular group might weaken the significance of any inferences from the data to the population under study. To be on the safe side, the researcher should attempt to gather information from other sources about the people who did not respond; by comparing such additional data with those from respondents, the researcher may be able to determine whether underrepresentation introduced any bias into the results.

Using common sense will help increase the response rate. In telephone surveys, respondents should be called when they are likely to be at home and receptive to interviewing. Do not call when people are likely to be eating or sleeping. In a one-on-one situation, the interviewer should be appropriately attired. In addition, the researcher should spend time tracking down some of the nonrespondents and asking them why they refused to be interviewed or why they did not fill out the questionnaire. Responses such as "The interviewer was insensitive and pushy," "The questionnaire was delivered with postage due," and "The survey sounded like a ploy to sell something" can be illuminating.

Along with common sense, certain elements of the research design can have a significant impact on response rates. Yu and Cooper (1983), in their survey of 93 published studies, made these discoveries that continue to be important today:

- Monetary incentives increased the response rate, with larger incentives being the most effective.

- Preliminary notification, personalization of the questionnaire, a follow-up letter, and assertive "foot-in-the-door" personal interview techniques all significantly increased the response rate.

- A cover letter, the assurance of anonymity, and a statement of a deadline did not significantly increase the response rate (the authors did not investigate a cover letter that stressed the importance of the research).

- Stressing the social utility of the study and appealing to the respondent to help out the researcher did not affect response rates.

GENERAL PROBLEMS IN SURVEY RESEARCH

Although surveys are valuable tools in mass media research, several obstacles are frequently encountered. Experience in survey research confirms the following points:

1. Subjects or respondents are often unable to recall information about themselves or their activities. This inability may be caused by memory failure, nervousness related to being involved in a research study, confusion about the questions asked, or some other intervening factor. Questions that are glaringly simple to researchers may cause significant problems for respondents.

For example, as mentioned earlier, radio station managers often want to ask respondents which radio stations they have set on their vehicle's radio pushbuttons. The managers are surprised to discover the number of people who not only do not know which stations are programmed on their radio buttons but also do not know how many buttons are on their radio.

2. Due to respondents' feelings of inadequacy or lack of knowledge about a particular topic, they often provide "prestigious" answers rather than admit to not knowing something. This is called **prestige bias.** For example, as mentioned earlier in this book, some respondents claim to watch public TV and listen to public radio when in fact they do not.

3. Subjects may purposely deceive researchers by giving incorrect answers to questions. Almost nothing can be done about respondents who lie. A large sample may discount this type of response. However, there is no acceptable and valid method to determine whether respondents' answers are truthful; the answers must be accepted as they are given, although one way to discover deception is to ask the same question in different ways a few times throughout the survey. (Note: It may be possible to identify respondents who lie by computing z-scores, as discussed earlier in this chapter.)

4. Respondents often give elaborate answers to simple questions because they try to figure out the purpose of a study and what the researcher is doing. People are naturally curious, but they become even more curious when they are the focus of a scientific research project. In addition, some respondents use a research study as a soapbox for their opinions. These people want to have all of their opinions known and use the research study to attempt to deliver the messages.

5. Surveys are often complicated by the inability of respondents to explain their true feelings, perceptions, and beliefs—not because they do not have any but because they cannot put them into words. The question "Why do you like to watch soap operas?" may be particularly difficult for some people. They may watch soap operas

every day but respond by saying only, "Because I like them." From a research perspective, this answer does not provide much information and probing respondents for further information may help, but not in every case.

Conducting survey research is an exciting activity. It is fun to find out why people think in certain ways or what they do in certain situations. But researchers must continually remain aware of obstacles that may hinder data collection, and they must deal with these problems. In many areas around the world, many citizens now refuse to take part in any type of research project. Researchers must convince respondents and subjects that their help is important in making decisions and solving problems.

The face of survey research is continually changing. One-on-one and door-to-door interviews are now difficult to conduct. The emphasis is now on research via the Internet, and it will be interesting to see how the Internet continues to change the research survey process.

SUMMARY

Survey research is an important and useful method of data collection. The survey is also one of the most widely used methods of media research, primarily because of its flexibility. Surveys, however, involve a number of steps. Researchers must decide whether to use a descriptive or analytical approach; define the purpose of the study; review the available literature in the area; select the survey approach, questionnaire design, and sample; analyze and interpret the data; and, finally, decide whether to publish or disseminate the results. These steps are not necessarily taken in that order, but all must be considered in conducting a survey.

To ensure that all the steps in the survey process are in harmony, researchers should conduct one or more pilot studies to detect any errors in the approach. Pilot studies save time, money, and frustration because an error that could void an entire analysis sometimes surfaces at this stage.

Questionnaire design is also a major step in any survey. This chapter included examples to show how a question or an interviewing approach may elicit a specific response. The goal in questionnaire design is to avoid bias in answers. Question wording, length, style, and order may affect a respondent's answers. Extreme care must be taken when developing questions to ensure that they are neutral. To achieve a reasonable response rate, researchers should consider including an incentive, notifying survey subjects beforehand, and personalizing the questionnaire. Also, researchers should mention the response rate when they report the results of the survey.

Finally, researchers must select the most appropriate survey approach from among five basic types: mail and telephone surveys, personal interviews, and group-administered, and online surveys. Each approach has advantages and disadvantages that must be weighed. The type of survey used depends on the purpose of the study, the amount of time available to the researcher, and the funds available for the study. It is clear that many researchers now depend less on the face-to-face survey and more on computer-assisted telephone interviewing and Internet data collection.

Key Terms

Analytical surveys	Door-to-door survey
Breakoffs	Double-barreled
Call disposition sheet	question
CAPI	Double-bind question
CATI	Feeling thermometer
Checklist question	Filter question
Closed-ended	Forced-choice
question	question
Codebook	Group administration
Descriptive surveys	Internet survey

Leading question
Mail survey
Mailing list
Mall intercept
Multiple-choice
   question
Mutually exclusive
One-on-one interview
Open-ended question
Personal interview
Pop-up survey

Prestige bias
Response rate
Screener question
Structured interview
Telephone survey
Unstructured
   interview
Verbatims
Wimmer Outlier
   Analysis

 Using the Internet

Search the Internet for more information on these topics:

- *"survey research," "surveys," "questionnaire design,"* and *"Internet research"*
- *"mail surveys" advantages disadvantages*
- *"questionnaire instructions"*
- *research survey advantages*
- *"constructing questions"*
- *"questionnaire design"*
- *problems with questionnaire design*

Questions and Problems for Further Investigation

1. Practical research example.

   a. Design a questionnaire with 5–10 questions on a topic related to the mass media.

   b. Post your survey on one of the free online survey websites, such as Survey Monkey.

   c. Collect 20–25 responses from respondents. Don't worry about a target sample or a small sample. The purpose of this exercise is to get you familiar with the online research process, data collection, and data analysis.

   d. Analyze your data and write a short report of your study. Be sure to include a section discussing any problems you encountered and what would need to be changed if someone else replicated your study.

2. Locate one or more survey studies in journals on mass media research. Answer the following questions in relation to the article(s):

   a. What was the purpose of the survey?

   b. How were the data collected?

   c. What type of information was produced?

   d. Did the data answer a particular research question or hypothesis?

   e. Were any problems evident with the survey and its approach?

3. Design a survey to collect data on a topic of your choice. Be sure to address these points:

   a. What is the purpose of the survey? What is its goal?

   b. What research questions or hypotheses are tested?

   c. Are any operational definitions required?

   d. Develop at least 10 questions relevant to the problem.

   e. Describe the approach to be used to collect data.

   f. Design a cover letter or an interview schedule for the study.

   g. Conduct a pretest to test the questionnaire.

For additional resources go to *www.wimmer dominick.com* and *www.cengagebrain.com*.

References and Suggested Readings

Babbie, E. R. (1990). *Survey research methods* (2nd ed.). Belmont, CA: Wadsworth.

Beville, H., Jr. (1988). *Audience ratings* (Rev. ed.). Hillsdale, NJ: Lawrence Erlbaum.

Brighton, M. (1981). Data capture in the 1980s. Communicare. *Journal of Communication Science, 2*(1), 12–19.

Chaffee, S. H., & Choe, S. Y. (1980). Time of decision and media use during the Ford–Carter campaign. *Public Opinion Quarterly, 44,* 53–70.

Dillman, D. (1978). *Mail and telephone surveys.* New York, NY: John Wiley.

Erdos, P. L. (1974). Data collection methods: Mail surveys. In R. Ferber (Ed.), *Handbook of marketing research* (90–104). New York, NY: McGraw-Hill.

Fletcher, J. E., & Wimmer, R. D. (1981). *Focus group interviews in radio research*. Washington, DC: National Association of Broadcasters.

Fowler, F. (2002). *Survey research methods* (3rd ed.). Newbury Park, CA: Sage Publications.

Fox, R. J., Crask, M. R., & Kim, J. (1989). Mail survey response rate. *Public Opinion Quarterly, 52*(4), 467–491.

Groves, R., & Mathiowetz, N. (1984). Computer assisted telephone interviewing: Effects on interviewers and respondents. *Public Opinion Quarterly, 48*(1), 356–369.

Hornik, J., & Ellis, S. (1989). Strategies to secure compliance for a mall intercept interview. *Public Opinion Quarterly, 52*(4), 539–551.

Hsia, H. J. (1988). *Mass communication research methods: A step-by-step approach*. Hillsdale, NJ: Lawrence Erlbaum.

Kerlinger, F. N., & Lee, H. B. (2000). *Foundations of behavioral research* (4th ed.). New York, NY: Holt, Rinehart & Winston.

Lavrakas, P. J. (1993). *Telephone survey methods: Sampling, selection, and supervision* (2nd ed.). Newbury Park, CA: Sage Publications.

Marketing News. (1983). Inflation adjusted spending is on rise for consumer research. *Marketing News, 17*(1), 13.

Miller, D. C. (1991). *Handbook of research design and social measurement* (5th ed.). New York, NY: Longman.

National Association of Broadcasters. (1976). *A broadcast research primer*. Washington, DC: Author.

Oppenheim, A. N. (1992). *Questionnaire design and attitude measurement*. New York, NY: Pinter.

Poindexter, P. M. (1979). Daily newspaper nonreaders: Why they don't read. *Journalism Quarterly, 56*, 764–770.

Rea, L. M., Parker, R. A., & Shrader, A. (1997). *Designing and conducting survey research: A comprehensive guide*. New York, NY: Jossey-Bass.

Rosenberg, M. (1968). *The logic of survey analysis*. New York, NY: Basic Books.

Schleifer, S. (1986). Trends in attitudes toward and participation in survey research. *Public Opinion Quarterly, 50*(1), 17–26.

Sewell, W., & Shaw, M. (1968). Increasing returns in mail surveys. *American Sociological Review, 33*, 193.

Sharp, L., & Frankel, J. (1983). Respondent burden: A test of some common assumptions. *Public Opinion Quarterly, 47*(1), 36–53.

Singer, E., & Presser, S. (Eds.) (1989). *Survey research methods: A reader*. Chicago, IL: University of Chicago Press.

Wakshlag, J. J., & Greenberg, B. S. (1979). Programming strategies and the popularity of television programs for children. *Journal of Communication, 6*, 58–68.

Walizer, M. H., & Wienir, P. L. (1978). *Research methods and analysis: Searching for relationships*. New York, NY: Harper & Row.

Weisberg, H. F., & Bowen, B. D. (1996). *An introduction to survey research and data analysis* (3rd ed.). Glenview, IL: Scott, Foresman.

Williams, F., Rice, R. E., & Rogers, E. M. (1988). *Research methods and the new media*. New York, NY: Free Press.

Wimmer, R. D. (1976). *A multivariate analysis of the uses and effects of the mass media in the 1968 presidential campaign*. Unpublished doctoral dissertation, Bowling Green University, Ohio.

Wimmer, R. D. (1995). *Comparison of CATI and non-CATI interviewing*. Unpublished company paper. Denver, CO: The Eagle Group.

Winkler, R. L., & Hays, W. L. (1975). *Statistics: Probability, inference and decision* (2nd ed.). New York, NY: Holt, Rinehart & Winston.

Yu, J., & Cooper, H. (1983). A quantitative review of research design effects on response rates to questionnaires. *Journal of Marketing Research, 20*(1), 36–44.

Zillmann, D., & Bryant, J. (1975). Viewers' moral sanctions of retribution in the appreciation of dramatic presentations. *Journal of Experimental Social Psychology, 11*, 572–582.

# CHAPTER 8

LONGITUDINAL RESEARCH

CHAPTER OUTLINE

Most of the research discussed to this point has been cross-sectional. In **cross-sectional** research, data are collected from a representative sample at only one point in time. Longitudinal research, in contrast, involves the collection of data at different points in time. Although longitudinal investigations are relatively rare in mass media research, several longitudinal studies have been among the most influential and provocative in the field.

Of the 14 studies Lowery and DeFleur (1995) consider to be milestones in the evolution of mass media research, four involve the longitudinal approach: Lazarsfeld, Berelson, and Gaudet's *The People's Choice* (1944), which introduced the two-step flow model; Katz and Lazarsfeld's *Personal Influence* (1955), which examined the role of opinion leaders; the *Surgeon General's Report on Television and Social Behavior*, particularly as used in the study by Lefkowitz, Eron, Walder, and Huesmann (1972), which found evidence that viewing violence on television caused subsequent aggressive behavior; and the 10-year update of the Lefkowitz et al. report (Pearl, Bouthilet, & Lazar, 1982), which cited the longitudinal studies that affirmed the link between TV violence and aggression. Other longitudinal studies also figure prominently in the field, including the elaborate **panel study** done for NBC by Milavsky, Kessler, Stipp, and Rubens (1982); the cross-national comparisons cited in Huesmann and Eron (1986); and the studies of mass media in elections as summarized by Peterson (1980). Thus, although it is not widely used, the longitudinal method can produce theoretically and socially important results.

DEVELOPMENT

Longitudinal studies have a long history in the behavioral sciences. In psychology in particular, they have been used to trace the development of children and the clinical progress of patients. In medicine, longitudinal studies have been used widely to study the impact of disease and treatment methods. Sociologists studying the 1924 election campaign did the pioneering work in political science. Somewhat later, Newcomb (1943) conducted repeated interviews of Bennington College students from 1935 to 1939 to examine the impact of a liberal college environment on respondents who came from conservative families.

In the mass media area, the first major longitudinal study was done by Lazarsfeld, Berelson, and Gaudet (1944) during the 1940 presidential election. Lazarsfeld pioneered the use of the panel technique in which the same individuals are interviewed several times. Lazarsfeld also developed the 16-fold table, one of the earliest statistical techniques to attempt to derive causation from longitudinal survey data. Another form of longitudinal research, **trend studies** (in which different people are asked the same question at different points in time) began showing up in mass media research in the 1960s. One of the most publicized trend studies was the continuing survey of media credibility done by the Roper organization. Trend studies by Gallup and Harris, among others, also gained prominence during this time.

More recently, the notion of **cohort analysis**, a method of research developed by demographers, has become popular. Cohort analysis involves the study of specific populations, usually all those born during a given period, as they change over time. Other significant developments in longitudinal research have taken place as more sophisticated techniques for analyzing longitudinal data were developed. More technical information about advanced computational strategies for longitudinal data is contained in Magnusson, Bergman, Rudinger, and Torestad (1991) and in Toon (2000).

Cross-lagged correlations are computed when information about two variables is gathered from the same sample at two different times. The correlations between variables at the same point in time are compared with the correlations at different points in time. Three other forms of analysis using advanced statistical techniques have had relevance in longitudinal studies: path analysis, log-linear models, and structural equations. *Path analysis* is used to chart directions in panel data. *Log-linear models* are used with categorical panel data and involve the analysis of multivariate contingency tables. *LISREL* (*LInear Structural RELations*), a model developed by Joreskog (1973), is another statistical technique that has broad application in longitudinal analysis.

TYPES OF LONGITUDINAL STUDIES

The three main types of longitudinal studies are trend study, cohort analysis, and panel study. Each is discussed in this section.

Trend Studies

The trend study is probably the most common type of longitudinal study in mass media research. Recall that a trend study samples different groups of people at different times from the same population. Trend studies are common around presidential election time. In the 2008 presidential election, approximately 15 polling organizations conducted national trend studies at regular intervals during the campaign.

Trend studies are useful, but they have limitations. Suppose that a sample of adults is selected three months before an election and 57% report that they intend to vote for Candidate A and 43% for Candidate B. A month later, a different sample drawn from the same population shows a change: 55% report that they are going to vote for A and 45% for B. This is a simple example of a trend study. Trend studies provide information about net changes at an aggregate level. In the example, we know that in the period under consideration, Candidate A lost 2% of his support. We do not know how many people changed from B to A or from A to B, nor do we know how many stayed with their original choice. We know only that the net result was a two-point loss for A. To determine both the gross change and the net change, a panel study is necessary.

Advantages. Trend studies are valuable in describing long-term changes in a population. They can establish a pattern over time to detect shifts and changes in some event. Broadcast researchers, for example, compile trend studies that chart fluctuations in viewing levels for the major networks. Another advantage of trend studies is that they can be based on a comparison of survey data originally constructed for other purposes. Of course, in using such data, the researcher needs to recognize any differences in question wording, context, sampling, or analysis techniques from one survey to the next. Hyman (1987) provides extensive guidance on the secondary analysis of survey data. The growing movement to preserve data archives and the ability of the Internet to make retrieval and sharing much easier will help this technique gain in popularity. A few of the databases that have been used in recent mass media research studies include the "life style study" conducted periodically for the DDB advertising agency, surveys done for the Brigham Young University's Center for the Study of Elections and Democracy, and the Annenberg National Health Communication Surveys. *The Gale Directory of Online, Portable, and Internet Databases* lists resources that might be useful for mass media researchers. Also, see the using the Internet section at the end of this chapter.

As noted in Chapter 1, secondary analysis saves time, money, and personnel; it also makes it possible for researchers to understand long-term change. In fact, mass media researchers might want to consider what socially significant data concerning media behaviors should be collected and archived at regular intervals. Economists have developed regular trend indicators to gauge the health of the economy, but mass communication scholars have developed almost no analogous social indicators of the media or audiences.

Disadvantages.   Trend analysis is only as good as the underlying data. If data are unreliable, false trends will show up in the results. Moreover, to be most valuable, trend analysis must be based on consistent measures. Changes in the way indexes are constructed or the way questions are asked produce results that are not comparable over time. In addition, there is a problem when comparing the results of two different samples. See "A Closer Look: Using Different Samples" in this section.

Examples of Trend Studies.   Both university and commercial research firms have asked some of the same questions for many national and statewide trend studies. For example, in the United States, a question about satisfaction with the president's performance has been asked hundreds of times, dating back to the administration of Harry Truman. *Public Opinion Quarterly* has a regular section entitled "the polls" that allows researchers to construct trend data on selected topics. In recent issues the following trend data have appeared: (1) a 2-year sampling of public opinion about the economic health of the real estate market, (2) a 12-year sampling of attitudes toward immigration, and (3) a 32-year compilation of public attitudes about energy policy.

Of specific interest in the field of mass media research are the trend data on changing patterns of media credibility, compiled for more than three decades by the Roper organization (summarized in Mayer, 1993), and the Violence Index constructed by Gerbner and his associates (Gerbner, Gross, Signorielli, Morgan, & Jackson-Beeck, 1979). The Pew Center has collected data on Internet usage from 2000 to 2009 and the Pew Center's Project for Excellence in Journalism has trend data for the audiences for the various news media.

Recent examples of academic trend studies include Barnes and Mattson's (2009) study of social media use in fast-growing corporations over a three-year period and Korhonen and Lahikainen's (2008) analysis of children's television-induced fears using survey data from 1993 and 2003. In the professional arena, the diary surveys conducted by the Arbitron Company and A. C. Nielsen in smaller television and radio markets are examples of trend studies.

Cohort Analysis

To the Romans, a cohort was one of the 10 divisions of a military legion. For research purposes, a *cohort* is any group of individuals who are linked in some way or who have experienced the same significant life event within a given period. Usually the "significant life event" is birth, in which case the group is termed a *birth cohort*. However, there are many other kinds of cohorts, including marriage (all those married between 2000 and 2010), divorce (all those divorced between 1990 and 2010), education (the class of 2012), and others such as all those who attended college during the Vietnam era.

Any study in which some characteristic of one or more cohorts is measured at two or more points in time is a cohort analysis. Cohort analysis attempts to identify a *cohort effect*: Are changes in the dependent variable due to aging, or are they present because the sample members belong to the same cohort? To illustrate, suppose that 50% of college seniors report that they regularly read news magazines, whereas only 10% of college freshmen in the same survey give this answer. How might the difference be explained? One

Using Different Samples

Most longitudinal studies, particularly trend studies, use different samples at each testing or measurement period. One well-known example of this method is Arbitron, the company that collects radio listening data for about 300 radio markets in the United States. Since its inception in 1949, Arbitron has conducted surveys to collect radio-listening data and has published the information in quarterly reports known as books, although hardcopy books are no longer printed because the information is now available online.

Arbitron, however, has been criticized for decades for the reliability of the data it produces, namely that the data "bounce around" from one book to another. In one ratings period, a radio station may rank number one in the market, and even without making any programming changes, the radio station may fall to a much lower ranking in the next ratings period. Why does this happen? Although there are many possible reasons, the two most important are (1) listenership to the radio station did actually decline or (2) the drop in audience figures is a result of the use of different samples from one ratings period to the next. In most situations, the second reason is the culprit for the change, and that's what happens in many trend studies. (A. C. Nielsen does not have this problem with TV ratings data because it uses a panel study.)

Although every effort may be made to ensure that the samples are as similar as can be, the fact is that the samples are not the same—the samples may be completely different. This has to be true because the same people are not used in the different testing or measurement periods—each sample has its own unique characteristics and its own unique sampling error. Because of these differences, it is not valid to compare one testing or measurement period to another. Statements by radio managers such as "We're up from the last book" are erroneous because comparisons from one measurement situation cannot be made to another situation without accounting for the differences in samples (to be discussed shortly).

Even though comparisons of different sample trend studies cannot be made, the fact is that such comparisons are made all the time, not just in the mass media, but in advertising and public relations to determine the success of campaigns, political polling to predict the winner of an election or the opinions about a political issue, and virtually all consumer research that tests the potential success of a product or service. Even though the data are collected from different samples, the two data sets are treated as though they came from the same sample. Quite frankly, this falls into the category of "bad science."

The only way to compare data from two or more samples in a trend study is to convert the data into z-scores, which, as mentioned elsewhere in this book, allow for an "apples-to-apples" comparison. Any data comparisons made in multisample trend studies without converting the data to z-scores are not valid.

Note: During 2008, Arbitron began to use a panel design with the introduction of its new electronic Portable People Meter methodology, which was designed to help to eliminate the problem of not being able to compare one ratings period to another, but there are still many complaints about Arbitron's sampling even in mid-2012. (See Chapter 14.)

explanation is that freshmen change their reading habits as they progress through college. Another is that this year's freshman class is composed of people with reading habits different from those who were enrolled three years earlier.

There are two ways to distinguish between these explanations. One way involves questioning the same students during their freshman year and again during their senior year and comparing their second set of responses to those of a group of current freshmen. (This is the familiar panel design, which is discussed in detail later.) Or a researcher can take two samples of the student population, at Time 1 and Time 2.

Each survey has different participants—the same people are not questioned again, as in a panel study—but each sample represents the same group of people at different points in their college career. Although we have no direct information about which individuals changed their habits over time, we do have information on how the cohort of people who entered college at Time 1 changed by the time they became seniors. If 15% of the freshmen at Time 1 read news magazines and if 40% of the seniors at Time 2 read them, we can deduce that students change their reading habits as they progress through college.

Typically, a cohort analysis involves data from more than one cohort, and a standard table for presenting the data from multiple cohorts was proposed by Glenn (1977). Table 8.1 is such a table. It displays news magazine readership for a number of birth cohorts. Note that the column variable (read down) is age, and the row variable (read across) is the year of data collection. Because the interval between any two periods of measurement (that is, surveys)

corresponds to the age class intervals, cohorts can be followed over time. When the intervals are not equal, the progress of cohorts cannot be followed with precision.

This type of table allows a researcher to make three types of comparisons. First, reading down a single column is analogous to a cross-sectional study and presents comparisons among different age cohorts at one point in time (*intercohort differences*). Second, reading across the rows shows trends at each age level that occur when cohorts replace one another. Third, reading diagonally toward the right reveals changes in a single cohort from one time to another (an *intracohort study*). Thus, Table 8.1 suggests that news magazine reading increases with age (reading down each column). In each successive time period, the percentage of younger readers has diminished (reading across the rows), and the increase in reading percentage as each cohort ages is about the same (reading diagonally to the right).

The variations in the percentages in the table can be categorized into three kinds of effects. (For the moment, we assume that there is no variation due to sampling error or to changing composition in each cohort as it ages.) First, influences produced by the sheer fact of maturation, or growing older, are called **age effects**. Second, influences associated with members in a certain birth cohort are called **cohort effects**. Finally, influences associated with each particular time period are called **period effects**.

To recognize these various influences at work, examine the hypothetical data in Tables 8.2, 8.3, and 8.4. Again, we assume that the dependent variable is the percentage of the sample that regularly reads a news magazine. Table 8.2 demonstrates a "pure" age effect. Note that the rows are identical and the columns show the same pattern of variation. Apparently, it does not matter when a person was born or in which period he or she lived. As the individual becomes

Table 8.1   Percentage of Adults Who Regularly Read News Magazines

| | Year | | |
Age	2000	2004	2008
18–21	15	12	10
22–25	34	32	28
26–29	48	44	35

Table 8.2 Cohort Table Showing Pure Age Effect

	Year		
Age	1992	1996	2000
18–21	15	15	15
22–25	20	20	20
26–29	25	25	25
Average	20	20	20

Table 8.3 Cohort Table Showing Pure Period Effect

	Year		
Age	1992	1996	2000
18–21	15	20	25
22–25	15	20	25
26–29	15	20	25
Average	15	20	25

Table 8.4 Cohort Table Showing Pure Cohort Effect

	Year		
Age	1992	1996	2000
18–21	15	10	5
22–25	20	15	10
26–29	25	20	15
Average	20	15	10

older, news magazine readership increases. For ease of illustration, Table 8.2 shows a linear effect, but this is not necessarily the only effect possible. For example, readership might increase from the first age interval to the next but not from the second to the third.

Table 8.3 shows a "pure" period effect. There is no variation by age at any period; the columns are identical, and the variations from one period to the next are identical. Furthermore, the change in each cohort (read diagonally to the right) is the same as the average change in the total population. The data in this table suggest that year of birth and maturation have little to do with news magazine reading. In this hypothetical case, the time period seems to be most important. Knowing when the survey was done enables the researcher to predict the variation in news magazine reading.

Table 8.4 shows a "pure" cohort effect. Here the cohort diagonals are constant and the variation from younger to older respondents is in the opposite direction from the variation from earlier to later survey periods. In this table, the key variable seems to be date of birth. Among those who were born between 1971 and 1974, news magazine readership was 15% regardless of their age or when they were surveyed.

Of course, these pure patterns rarely occur in actual data. Nonetheless, an examination of Tables 8.2, 8.3, and 8.4 can help develop sensitivity to the patterns one can detect in analyzing cohort data. In addition, the tables illustrate the logic behind the analysis.

An example using actual data might also be helpful. Table 8.5 contains excerpts from a cohort analysis done by Peiser (2000b) that examined the cohort effect on newspaper readership. Although these data comprise only part of the cohort data analyzed by Peiser, they do represent his general findings.

As Table 8.5 indicates, there is an apparent age effect (read down the columns). With minor exception, older people are more likely

Table 8.5 Cohort Analysis of Daily Newspaper Reading (percentage reading paper every day)*

Age	Year		
	1972	1982	1991
18–22	47	28	20
28–32	66	55	39
38–42	78	51	60

*Data excerpted from Peiser (2000b). Readers are urged to consult the article for the full cohort table and Peiser's interpretation.

to be newspaper readers. In addition, reading across the rows suggests that younger people are reading less than older people. Finally, a possible cohort effect can be detected by looking at the diagonals.

Advantages.   Cohort analysis is an appealing and useful technique because it is highly flexible. It provides insight into the effects of maturation and social, cultural, and political change. In addition, it can be used with either original data or secondary data. In many instances, a cohort analysis can be less expensive than experiments or surveys.

Disadvantages.   The major disadvantage of cohort analysis is that the specific effects of age, cohort, and period are difficult to untangle through purely statistical analysis of a standard cohort table. In survey data, much of the variation in percentages among cells is due to sampling variability. Testing cohort differences for significance is difficult and requires advanced statistical techniques (see Anderson & Fetner, 2008, for an example). Moreover, as a cohort grows older, many of its members die. If the remaining cohort members differ in regard to the variable under study, the variation in the cohort table may simply reflect this change. Finally, as Glenn (1977) points out, no matter how a cohort table is examined, three of the

basic effects—age, cohort, and period—are confounded. Age and cohort effects are confounded in the columns; age and period effects in the diagonals; and cohort and period effects in each row. Even the patterns of variations in the "pure" cohort Tables 8.2, 8.3, and 8.4 could be explained by a combination of influences.

Several authors have developed techniques to try to sort out these effects. Three of the most useful are Palmore's (1978) triad method, the constrained multiple regression model (Rentz, Reynolds, & Stout, 1983), and the goodness-of-fit technique (Feinberg & Mason, 1980). If the researcher is willing to make certain assumptions, these methods can provide some tentative evidence about the probable influences of age, period, and cohort. Moreover, in many cases there is only one likely or plausible explanation for the variation. Nonetheless, a researcher should exercise caution in attributing causation to any variable in a cohort analysis. Theory and evidence from outside sources should be used in any interpretation. For example, in his study of the influences of television watching and newspaper reading on cohort differences in verbal ability, Glenn (1994) assumed that there were no period effects on changes in adult vocabulary during the duration of his study. As a result, he was able to demonstrate a cohort effect suggesting that decreases in verbal ability were associated with a decline in newspaper reading and an increase in TV viewing.

A second disadvantage of the technique is sample mortality. If a long period is involved or if the specific sample group is difficult to reach, the researcher may have some empty cells in the cohort table or some that contain too few members for meaningful analysis.

Examples of Cohort Analysis.   Cohort analysis is useful in the study of public opinion. Jennings (1996) analyzed cohort data on political knowledge gathered from a sample of twelfth graders and their parents and found both period and cohort effects. Peiser (2000b) looked at cohort trends in media use, and Schuman and Corning (2006) looked at cohort differences in recalling the Vietnam war.

PANEL STUDIES

Panel studies measure the same sample of respondents at different points in time. Unlike trend studies, panel studies can reveal information about both net change and gross change in the dependent variable. For example, a study of voting intentions might reveal that between Time 1 and Time 2, 20% of the panel switched from Candidate A to Candidate B and 20% switched from Candidate B to Candidate A. Where a trend study would show a net change of zero because the gross changes simply canceled each other out, the panel study would show a high degree of volatility in voting intention.

Similar to trend and cohort studies, panel studies can make use of mail questionnaires, telephone interviews, personal interviews, or the Internet via web panels. Television networks, advertising agencies, and marketing research firms use panel studies to track changes in consumer behavior. Panel studies can reveal shifting attitudes and patterns of behavior that might go unnoticed with other research approaches; thus, trends, new ideas, fads, and buying habits are among the variables investigated. For a panel study on the effectiveness of political commercials, for example, all members of the panel would be interviewed periodically during a campaign to determine whether and when each respondent makes a voting decision.

Depending on the purpose of the study, researchers can use either a continuous panel, consisting of members who report specific attitudes or behavior patterns on a regular basis, or an interval panel, whose members agree to complete a certain number of measurement instruments (usually questionnaires) only when the information is needed. Panel studies produce data suitable for sophisticated statistical analysis and enable researchers to predict cause-and-effect relationships.

Advantages. Panel data are particularly useful in answering questions about the dynamics of change. For example, under what conditions do voters change political party affiliation? What are the respective roles of mass media and friends in changing political attitudes? In addition, repeated contacts with the respondents may help reduce their suspicions, so that later interviews yield more information than the initial encounters. Of course, the other side to this benefit is the sensitization effect, discussed in the disadvantages section. Finally, panel studies help solve the problems normally encountered when defining a theory based on a one-shot case study. Since the research progresses over time, the researcher can allow for the influences of competing stimuli on the subject.

Disadvantages. On the negative side, panel members are often difficult to recruit because of an unwillingness to fill out questionnaires

A CLOSER LOOK

Panel Studies

Panel studies are rarely used in research because of their enormous expense. An "easy" national study with 1,000 respondents over five years may cost at least $100,000 per year.

One of the most significant problems in this type of research is getting respondents to commit to more than one interview.

or submit to interviews several times. The number of initial refusals in a panel study fluctuates, depending on the amount of time required, the prestige of the organization directing the study, and the presence or absence of some type of compensation.

Once the sample has been secured, the problem of mortality emerges—panel members drop out for one reason or another. Because the strength of panel studies is that they interview the same people at different times, this advantage diminishes as the sample size decreases. Because mortality is such a problem, many panel studies start with a large initial sample so that the number who eventually participate in the entire study will be adequate. For example, in their panel study of local media use, Hoffman and Eveland (2010) had 3,388 respondents in the first wave of their four-wave study. Two years later, about 971 of the original panel completed the final survey. Pearson, Ball, and Crawford (2011) started with 3,264 respondents in their analysis of TV viewing and eating behaviors and ended

with 1,729 who completed surveys in both waves of their two-year study.

Sullivan, Rumptz, Campbell, Eby, and Davidson (1996) present several helpful techniques that have minimized sample mortality:

- Offer a stipend or payment to panel members. (However, Wimmer [2001] found that even a cash incentive may not increase a respondent's willingness to participate in a panel study.)

- Establish the credibility and value of the research project.

- Gather detailed information about panel member's friends, coworkers, and family who might know the whereabouts of the panel member.

- Contact the panel member between data collection waves.

- Give panel members a card with a phone number to call if they change addresses.

Another serious problem is that respondents often become sensitized to measurement

---

A CLOSER LOOK

Panel Studies: Minimizing Attrition

One of the most common causes of attrition (mortality) in panel research is the inability to locate the original respondents for a follow-up study. The longer the time lag between the waves of data collection, the more severe this problem becomes. A variety of tracking strategies are available, however, for persistent researchers who wish to overcome this problem. Call, Otto, and Spenner (1982) offer the following suggestions for finding those missing respondents:

- Use the U.S. Postal Service to find forwarding addresses.
- Check with the phone company for new phone numbers.
- Question family and relatives for current location.

- Ask neighbors for current information.
- Interview former classmates.
- Enlist the aid of a high school class reunion committee.
- Check with former employers.
- Examine records of college alumni associations.
- Inquire at churches in the area.
- Examine driver's license registration records.
- Use military locator services.
- Hire a professional tracking company (such as Equifax or Tracers Company of America).

To this list we add: Use one of the Internet websites that specializes in finding people.

instruments after repeated interviewing, thus making the sample atypical. For example, panelists who know in advance that they will be interviewed about public-TV watching might alter their viewing patterns to include more PBS programs (or fewer). Menard (1991) suggests that a revolving panel design might overcome the sensitization problem. In this design, after the first measurement period, new members replace some of the original members of the panel. (This is the procedure A. C. Nielsen uses with its metered national television sample.) For example, a researcher concerned that increased PBS viewing is the result of sensitization could interview 100 viewers during Week 1 and then replace 25 of the original sample with new panel members in Week 2. The viewing data from those who had been interviewed twice could then be compared with the data from those who participated in a single interview. (Researchers who use replacement should not replace more than 25% of the original sample in replications of the first measurement.)

Finally, respondent error is always a problem in situations that depend on self-administered measurement instruments. For example, panelists asked to keep a diary over a certain period may not fill it out until immediately before it is due. And, of course, panel studies require much more time than other types of studies and can be quite expensive.

Examples of Panel Studies. Perhaps the most famous example of the panel technique in mass media research is the collection of national television audience data by the A. C. Nielsen company. Nielsen's current sample consists of approximately 21,000 households located across the united states (soon to be increased to 37,000). These homes are equipped with *people meters*—devices that record when the television set is turned on, which channel is tuned in, and who is watching. (see Chapter 14 for more

information about people meters.) Nielsen//NetRating also maintains a large panel to track Internet usage. Other panels are maintained by such commercial research organizations as Market Facts, Inc.; National Family Opinion, Inc.; and the Home Testing Institute.

A well-publicized panel study was carried out with the support of the National Broadcasting Company (Milavsky et al., 1982). The overall purpose of this study was to isolate any possible causal influence on aggression among young people from viewing violence on television. Three panel studies were conducted, with the most ambitious involving boys between the ages of 7 and 12. In brief, the methodology in the study involved collecting data on aggression, TV viewing, and a host of sociological variables from children in Minneapolis, Minnesota, and Fort Worth, Texas, on six occasions. About 1,200 boys participated in the study. The time lags between each wave of data collection were deliberately varied so that the effects of TV viewing could be analyzed over different durations. Thus, there was a five-month lag between Waves 1 and 2, a four-month lag between Waves 2 and 3, and a three-month lag between Waves 3 and 4. The lag between Waves 1 and 6 constituted the longest elapsed time (three years). As is the case in all panel studies, the NBC study suffered from attrition. The particular design, however, magnified the effects of attrition. When respondents left the sixth grade, they frequently left the panel. Consequently, only a small number of children (58 of the 1,200 who participated) were available for observing and analyzing the long-term effects of viewing violence on TV.

The participant losses reported by the NBC team illustrate the impact of year-to-year attrition on a sample of this age group. About 7% of the sample was lost in the first year, approximately 37% in the first two years, and 63% over all three years.

The study also illustrates how a panel design influences the statistical analysis. The most powerful statistical test would have incorporated data from all six waves and simultaneously examined all the possible causal relationships. This was impossible, however, because due to the initial study design and subsequent attrition, the sample size fell below minimum standards. Instead, the investigators worked with each of the 15 possible wave pairs in the sample. The main statistical tests used the analytical technique of partial regression coefficients to remove the impact of earlier aggression levels. In effect, the researchers sought to determine whether TV viewing at an earlier time added to the predictability of aggression at a later time, once the aggression levels present before the test began had been statistically discounted. After looking at all the resulting coefficients for all the possible wave pairs, the investigators concluded that there was no consistent statistically significant relationship between watching violent TV programs and later acts of aggression. Nonetheless, they did find a large number of small but consistently positive coefficients that suggested the possibility of a weak relationship that might not have been detected by conventional statistical methods. Upon further analysis, however, the researchers concluded that these associations were due to chance. This study has value for anyone interested in longitudinal research. Many of the problems encountered in panel studies and the compromises involved in doing a three-year study are discussed in detail.

The panel technique continues to be popular for studying the impact of TV violence. Singer, Singer, Desmond, Hirsch, and Nicol (1988) used this technique to examine the effects of family communication patterns, parental mediation, and TV viewing on children's perceptions of the world and their aggressive behavior. Ninety-one first and second graders were interviewed during the first phase of the study. One year later, 66 of the original sample were reinterviewed. Concerned about the effects of attrition, the researchers compared their final sample with the original on a wide range of demographic variables and found that attrition did not cause any significant differences between the two groups. Singer and colleagues found that family communication patterns during the first phase were strong predictors of children's cognitive scores but were only weakly related to emotional and behavioral variables. The influence of TV viewing on aggression was greatest among heavy viewers who were least exposed to parental mediation.

Cho et al. (2003) used a two-wave panel design to investigate media use and public reaction to the September 11, 2001, terrorist attacks. Four months separated the two waves of the survey, with an attrition rate of 48%. Bickham et al. (2003) used panel data from the Child Development Supplement of the Panel Study of Income Dynamics to examine predictors of children's electronic media use. The Child Development Supplement is a longitudinal database maintained by the University of Michigan that uses a national sample. Attrition rates from various waves of data collection are about 10%. More recently, Moriarty and Harrison (2008) conducted a panel study to investigate the effects of television watching on eating disorders. Collecting data in two waves that were one year apart, they found that television viewing was related to eating disorders among girls but not among boys. In their study of media exposure during a political campaign, Overby and Barth (2009) used three-wave panel data collected by Brigham Young University's Center for the Study of Elections and Democracy. They found that media exposure affected citizens' political attitudes but that different media exerted different effects.

SPECIAL PANEL DESIGNS

Panel data can be expensive to obtain, but analysis cannot begin until at least two waves of data are available. For many panel studies, this may take years. Researchers who have limited time and resources might consider one of the following alternatives.

Schulsinger, Mednick, and Knop (1981) outlined a research design called a **retrospective panel**. In this method, the respondent is asked to recall facts or attitudes about education, occupations, events, situations, and so on, from the past. These recalled factors are then compared with a later measure of the same variable, thus producing an instant longitudinal design. Belson (1978) used a variation of this design in his study of the effects of exposure to violent TV shows on the aggressive behavior of teenage boys when he asked his respondents to recall when they first started watching violent TV programs.

There are several problems with this technique. Many people have faulty memories; some deliberately misrepresent the past; and others try to give a socially desirable response. Only a few research studies have examined the extent to which retrospective panel data might be misleading. Powers, Goudy, and Keith (1978) reanalyzed data from a 1964 study of adult men. In 1974, all the original respondents who could be located were reinterviewed and asked about their answers to the 1964 survey. In most instances, the recall responses presented respondents in a more favorable light than did their original answers. Interestingly, using the 1974 recall data produced almost the same pattern of correlations as using the 1964 data, suggesting that recall data might be used, albeit with caution, in correlational studies. In 1974, Norlen (1977) reinterviewed about 4,700 people originally questioned in 1968. Of those reinterviewed, 464 had originally reported that they had written

a letter to the editor of a newspaper or magazine, but in 1974 about a third of this group denied ever having written to a newspaper or magazine. Auriat (1993) found that respondents were more likely to recall correctly the month of a major life event (in this case, a family move) than they were the year the event occurred. In addition, women were slightly better than men were at remembering exact dates. Clearly, the savings in time and money accrued by using retrospective data must be weighed against possible losses in accuracy.

A **follow-back panel** selects a cross-sectional sample in the present and uses archival data from an earlier point in time to create the longitudinal dimension of the study. The advantages of such a technique are clear: Changes that occurred over a great many years can be analyzed in a short time period. This design is also useful in studying dwindling populations because the researcher can assemble a sample from baseline investigations conducted earlier, probably at great expense. The disadvantages are also obvious. The follow-back panel depends on archival data, and archives do not contain many variables that interest mass media researchers. In addition, the resulting sample in a follow-back design may not represent all possible entities. For example, a follow-back study of the managerial practices of small radio stations will not represent stations that went out of business and no longer exist.

A **catch-up panel** involves selecting a cross-sectional study done in the past and locating all possible units of analysis for observation in the present. The catch-up design is particularly attractive if the researcher has a rich source of baseline data in the archive. Of course, this is usually not the case because most data sources lack enough identifying information to allow the investigator to track down the respondents. When the appropriate data exist, however, the catch-up study can be highly useful.

A CLOSER LOOK

Cell Phones, Brain Tumors, and Retrospective Panels

Does heavy usage of a cell phone increase a person's risk of brain cancer? This has been a controversial question since cell phone use became popular. As might be expected, numerous studies have looked at this question but their results have not been consistent. A 2010 study found a weak association between very heavy cell phone use and a deadly form of brain cancer. This study, and others that found a link, prompted the International Agency for Research on Cancer to list radiation from cell phones as a "possible carcinogen," along with other items including coffee, gasoline engine exhaust, and leather dust. On the other hand, several studies have found no evidence of a link, including a 2011 study of 350,000 people in Denmark, the largest study ever conducted on the topic.

There are many possible reasons for the lack of consistency, including differences in the radiation given off by various phone models, where the calls took place, and whether the calls were made with hands-free devices. Of more relevance to this chapter is the way some researchers gathered data on the history of cell phone use. Because the relationship between cancer and cell phone usage is an important health concern, timely information on the issue is desirable. But any cancer caused by cell phone radiation may take a decade or more to develop. Consequently, to provide more immediate information, many studies used a retrospective panel design where respondents were asked to report their cell phone usage in the past, sometimes many years in the past. It is possible that many people have faulty memories and overestimate their past cell phone use. One study compared actual usage records with recalled use and found that overestimates were common and that some overestimated their usage by a factor of three.

The 2011 study in Denmark mentioned above used a different strategy. Denmark assigns each resident a unique ID number at birth, and over time that number is used for medical purposes, such as being admitted to a hospital for cancer treatment, and for commercial transactions, such as subscribing to a cell phone service. The 350,000 people in the study were first divided into cell phone subscribers and nonsubscribers, and these two groups were then analyzed for incidence of cancer and other diseases over time. The data showed no overall association between usage and incidences of brain cancer.

Although retrospective panels can be useful, actual historical data, if available, are usually more accurate.

Huesmann, Moise-Titus, Podolski, and Eron (2003) collected data concerning TV watching and aggressive behavior from a sample of 6- to 10-year-olds growing up in the 1970s and 1980s and reinterviewed them 15 years later. They found that early exposure to TV violence was linked to increased aggression during the respondents' young adult years. Beam, Weaver, and Brownlee (2009) reinterviewed journalists five years after they had participated in the 2002 American Journalist survey. They found that journalists had become more ethically cautious during the five-year span of the study.

Another problem associated with the catch-up panel involves the comparability of measures. If the earlier study was not constructed to be part of a longitudinal design, the original measurement instruments have to be modified. For example, a study of 10-year-olds might

Figure 8.1 Comparison of Retrospective, Follow-back, and Catch-up panels

Retrospective panel

Step 1: Select current sample.
Step 2: Interview sample about past recollections concerning topic of interest.
Step 3: Collect current data on topic of interest.
Step 4: Compare data.

Follow-back panel

Step 1: Select current sample.
Step 2: Collect current data on topic of interest.
Step 3: Locate archival data on sample regarding topic of interest.
Step 4: Compare data.

Catch-up panel

Step 1: Locate archival data on topic of interest.
Step 2: Select current sample by locating as many respondents as possible for whom data exist in the archive.
Step 3: Collect current data on topic of interest.
Step 4: Compare data.

have used teacher ratings to measure aggressiveness; however, such a measure is not appropriate with 20-year-olds.

Finally, the researcher in the catch-up situation is confined to the variables measured in the original study. In the intervening time, new variables might have been identified as important, but if those variables were not measured during the original survey, they are unavailable to the researcher. Figure 8.1 shows the similarities and differences among retrospective, follow-back, and catch-up panel designs.

ANALYZING CAUSATION IN PANEL DATA

The panel design provides an opportunity for the researcher to make statements about the causal ordering among different variables. Three conditions are necessary for determining cause and effect. The first is time order. Causation is present if and only if the cause precedes the effect. Second, causation can occur only if some tendency for change in A results in change in B. In other words, there is an association between the two variables. Third, before effects are attributed to causes, all other alternative causes must be ruled out. Cross-sectional surveys, for which the data are collected at a single point in time, can meet only two of these three criteria. A cross-sectional survey allows the researcher to say that Variables A and B are associated. A skillfully constructed questionnaire and statistical controls such as partial correlation can help the researcher rule out alternative explanations. Nonetheless, only if the time order between A and B is evident can statements of cause be inferred. For example, a person's education is typically acquired before his or her occupational status. Thus, the statement that education is a cause of occupational status (all other things being equal) can be inferred. If there is no distinguishable temporal sequence in the data (as is the case with viewing violence on TV and aggressive behavior), causal statements are conjectural. In a panel study, the variables are measured across time, which makes causal inferences more defensible.

However, there are two important points: On one hand, the interval between measurement periods must be long enough to allow the cause to produce an effect. For example, if it takes a full year for exposure to TV violence to have an effect on viewers' aggressive behavior, then a panel study with only six months between measurement periods will not discover any effect. On the other hand, if a cause produces an effect that does not remain stable over the long run, an overly long interval between measurement waves will fail to discover an effect. Continuing the example, let us suppose that exposure to TV violence produces an effect that appears three months after exposure but quickly disappears. A panel survey with six months between waves will totally miss observing this effect. The hard part, of course, is determining the proper time intervals. Most researchers rely on past research and appropriate theories for some guidelines.

Many statistical techniques are available for determining a causal sequence in panel data. A detailed listing and explanation of the computations involved are beyond the scope of this book. Nonetheless, some of the following references will be helpful to readers who desire more detailed information. Menard (1991) discusses common methods for analyzing panel data measured at the interval level. Similarly, Toon (2000) gives computational methods for analyzing panel data, including the increasingly popular log-linear technique. Asher (1983) provides a detailed discussion of path analysis. Trumbo (1995) describes statistical methods for analyzing panel data, including time series analysis and Granger verification, and illustrates their use in a longitudinal study of agenda setting. Those readers looking for a general description should consult Frees (2004).

Finally, the most mathematically sophisticated technique—linear structural relations, or LISREL—is discussed in Joreskog (1973), Long (1976), Hayduk (1996), and Diamantopoulos and Siguaw (2000). Because it appears that the LISREL method has much to recommend it (it was used in the NBC panel study discussed previously), researchers who intend to do panel studies should be familiar with its assumptions and techniques.

COMBINING QUALITATIVE AND QUANTITATIVE DATA IN LONGITUDINAL RESEARCH

Although the discussion up until now has examined longitudinal research from the traditional quantitative survey perspective, it is possible to combine quantitative and qualitative data in a study that extends over time. One possible technique involves selecting a smaller sample of people at each measurement interval for more intensive study. These people might participate in focus groups or in-depth interviews.

Using both qualitative and quantitative techniques provides certain advantages. First, the qualitative data can aid in the interpretation of the quantitative data and provide insights that might have been missed. For example, qualitative data used in conjunction with a panel survey looking at media exposure and vote choice might reveal why certain changes occurred among sample respondents. Additionally, qualitative data might suggest new hypotheses that could be examined in subsequent waves of data collection. To continue with the last example, focus group data could suggest that exposure to negative advertising might play a key role in determining vote choice. This relationship could be examined quantitatively the next time the panel survey is conducted. However, using both approaches requires more effort on the part of the researcher and increases the time spent in analyzing and interpreting the data.

McMillan (2001) combined qualitative and quantitative data in her longitudinal study of health-related websites. Data from an email survey found that sites with more financial backing were more likely to survive and that the technological sophistication of the site had no relation to its long-term viability. Qualitative data revealed that site managers considered promotion and marketing as keys to their survival. Shaw, Scheufele, and Catalono (2005) combined surveys with intensive interviews in their study of instant messaging in a large organization. Their quantitative findings revealed that instant messaging had a positive effect on productivity while their interviews made apparent that one of the reasons for increased productivity was that workers who used instant messaging spent less time on the phone and voice mail.

LONGITUDINAL RESEARCH ON THE INTERNET

The Internet has made it possible to collect longitudinal data online. An Internet survey panel consists of individuals who have been prerecruited to participate in a number of surveys over time. There are obvious advantages to this arrangement. A large number of individuals can be recruited to serve as potential panel members. This makes it easier for researchers to target and collect data from low-incidence groups (for example, those with iPad magazine apps or 3DTV owners). Data collection over the Internet is rapid, and researchers can access previously collected demographic information from their respondents.

Internet panels also have disadvantages. As with other online data-gathering techniques, Internet panels may not be representative of the entire population. Not everyone is skilled at completing online surveys. Further, Internet panels may suffer from a "churn" problem, a situation in which respondents sign up for the panel and then get bored or

lose interest and drop out. As a result, the potential mortality rates for longitudinal samples become a concern. Third, it is possible that web panel members become "professional respondents" whose answers are influenced by their participation in panel studies (Dennis, 2001). For example, a panel member who fills out several online questionnaires over a period of months about his or her online shopping habits might be encouraged to do even more online shopping. Finally, there is often no way to verify the person who actually completed the research project.

Longitudinal studies of Internet content can reveal long-term trends. Xigen and Lin (2007) investigated the content of banner ads on selected websites in 2000, 2003, and 2007. They found that utilitarian appeals dominated in all three sample periods.

Many private research companies offer Internet panel research to their clients. Esearch.com, for example, has a pool of more than 200,000 respondents.

LONGITUDINAL DESIGN IN EXPERIMENTS

Although the preceding discussion was concerned with survey research, experimental research has a longitudinal dimension that should not be overlooked. Many research designs are based on a single exposure to a message, with the dependent variable measured almost immediately afterward.

This procedure might be appropriate in many circumstances, but a longitudinal treatment design may be necessary to measure subtle, cumulative media effects. Furthermore, delayed assessment is essential to determine the duration of the impact of certain media effects. (For example, how long does it take a persuasive effect to disappear?)

Bryant, Carveth, and Brown (1981) illustrated the importance of the longitudinal design to the experimental approach. In investigating TV viewing and anxiety, they divided their subjects into groups and assigned to each a menu of TV shows they could watch. Over a six-week period, one group was assigned a light viewing schedule and a second was directed to watch a large number of shows that depicted a clear triumph of justice. A third group was assigned to view several shows in which justice did not triumph. One of the dependent variables was also measured over time. The investigators obtained voluntary viewing data by having students fill out diaries for another three weeks. The results of this study indicated that the cumulative exposure to TV shows in which justice does not prevail seems to make some viewers more anxious, thus offering some support to Gerbner's cultivation hypothesis.

Roessler and Brosius (2001), in their study of the cultivation phenomenon, exposed their experimental subjects to screenings of TV talk shows for five consecutive days and measured the impact of this exposure a week later. Their data showed that a limited cultivation effect did occur. Grabe, Kamhawi, and Yegiyan (2009) examined educational differences in remembering news content across newspapers, TV, and websites. They measured recall immediately after their experiment and again two days later. Clearly, the longitudinal design can be of great value in experimental research.

SUMMARY

Longitudinal research involves the collection of data at different points in time. The three types of longitudinal study are trend, cohort, and panel. A trend study asks the same questions of different groups of people at different points in time. A cohort study measures some characteristic of a sample whose members share some significant life event (usually the same age range) at two or more points in time. In a panel study, the same respondents are measured at least twice. One advantage of the panel design is that it allows the researcher to make statements about the causal ordering of the study variables, and several different statistical methods are available for this task.

Key Terms

Age effect	Follow-back panel
Catch-up panel	Longitudinal study
Cohort analysis	Panel study
Cohort effect	Period effect
Cross-lagged correlation	Retrospective panel
Cross-sectional research	Trend studies

 Using the Internet

For more information on the methods discussed in this chapter, search the Internet for *"longitudinal analysis," "panel studies," "cohort studies,"* and *"trend studies."*

There are many archives that are valuable resources for media researchers interested in longitudinal data. Here are a few examples:

1. National Opinion Research Center—General Social Survey. Among other things, this database contains data on newspaper readership, radio listening, and TV viewing from 1972 to the late 2000s. *www3.norc.org/GSS+Website/*

2. The Odum Institute for Research in the Social Sciences. This database at the University of North Carolina requires a subscription for access to all of its contents, but some data are open to all. It contains a searchable database of public opinion poll data from 1970 to the present. *www.irss.unc.edu/odum/jsp/home.jsp*

3. The Gallup Organization. The website for this well-known polling organization contains data covering the period 1985–2005 on mass media use, media credibility, bias, and sources of most news. *www.gallup.com*

4. The Roper Center. This website requires a membership fee (but many universities are

members) to access data on public opinion polls that date back to the 1930s. *www. ropercenter.uconn.edu/*

5. The Pew Center. The Pew Center specializes in studies that look at the public's attitudes toward the news media. A data archive contains polling results from 1997 to the present. *www.people-press.org/*

Questions and Problems for Further Investigation

1. Search recent issues of scholarly journals for examples of longitudinal studies. Which of the three designs discussed in this chapter are used? Try to find additional longitudinal studies done by commercial research firms. Which design is used most often?

2. What mass media variables are best studied using the cohort method?

3. What are some possible measures of media or audience characteristics that might be regularly made and stored in a data archive for secondary trend analysis?

4. How might a panel study make use of laboratory techniques?

5. Find information about Arbitron's new sampling methods with the Portable People Meter data collection methodology. What are the advantages and disadvantages of this technique?

For additional resources, go to *www.wimmer dominick.com* and *www.cengagebrain.com*.

References and Suggested Readings

Andersen, R., & Fetner, T. (2008). Cohort differences in tolerance of homosexuality. *Public Opinion Quarterly, 72*(2), 311–330.

Asher, H. (1983). *Causal modeling* (2nd ed.). Beverly Hills, CA: Sage Publications.

Auriat, N. (1993). A comparison of event dating accuracy between the wife, the husband, and the couple, and the Belgian population register. *Public Opinion Quarterly, 57*(2), 165–190.

Barnes, N., & Mattson, E. (2009). Social media in the 2009 Inc. 500: New tools and new trends. *Journal of New Communications Research, 4*(2), 70–79.

Beam, R., Weaver, D., & Brownlee, B. (2009). Changes in professionalism of U.S. journalists in the turbulent twenty-first century. *Journalism & Mass Communication Quarterly, 86*(2), 277–298.

Belson, W. (1978). *Television violence and the adolescent boy.* Hampshire, England: Saxon House.

Bickham, D., Vandewater, E., Huston, A., Lee, J., Caplovitz, A., & Wright, J. (2003). Predictors of children's electronic media use. *Media Psychology, 5*(2), 107–138.

Bryant, J., Carveth, R., & Brown, D. (1981). Television viewing and anxiety. *Journal of Communication, 31*(1), 106–119.

Call, V., Otto, L., & Spenner, K. (1982). *Tracking respondents.* Lexington, MA: Lexington Books.

Cho, J., Boyle, M., Keum, H., Shevy, M., McLeod, D., Shah, D., & Pan, Z. (2003). Media, terrorism, and emotionality. *Journal of Broadcasting & Electronic Media, 47*(3), 309–327.

Dennis, J. M. (2001). Are Internet panels creating professional respondents? *Marketing Research, 13*(2), 34–38.

Diamantopoulos, A., & Siguaw, J. (2000). *Introducing Lisrel: A guide for the uninitiated.* London: Sage.

Fienberg, S. E., & Mason, W. M. (1980). Identification and estimation of age-period-cohort models in the analysis of archival data. In K. F. Schuessler (Ed.), *Sociological methodology* (pp. 1–67). San Francisco, CA: Jossey-Bass.

Frees, E. (2004). *Longitudinal and panel data: Analysis and applications in the social sciences.* New York, NY: Cambridge University Press.

Gerbner, G., Gross, L., Signorielli, N., Morgan, M., & Jackson-Beeck, M. (1979). The demonstration of power: Violence profile no. 10. *Journal of Communication, 29*(3), 177–196.

Glenn, N. (1977). *Cohort analysis.* Beverly Hills, CA: Sage Publications.

Glenn, N. (1994). Television watching, newspaper reading and cohort differences in verbal ability. *Sociology of Education, 67*(2), 216–230.

Grabe, E., Kamhawi, R., & Yegiyan, N. (2009). Informing citizens: How people with different levels of education process television, newspaper and web news. *Journal of Broadcasting & Electronic Media, 53*(1), 90–111.

Hayduk, L. A. (1996). *LISREL: Issues, debates, strategies.* Baltimore, MD: Johns Hopkins University Press.

Hoffman, L., & Eveland, W. (2010). Assessing causality in the relationship between community attachment and local media use. *Mass Communication & Society, 13*(2), 174–195.

Huesmann, L., Moise-Titus, J., Podolski, C., & Eron, L. (2003). Longitudinal relations between children's exposure to TV violence and violent behavior in young adulthood: 1977–1992. *Developmental Psychology*, 39(2), 210–222.

Huesmann, L. R. (1986). Psychological processes promoting the relation between exposure to media violence and aggressive behavior by the viewer. *Journal of Social Issues*, 42(3), 125–139.

Huesmann, L. R., & Eron, L. D. (1986). *Television and the aggressive child*. Hillsdale, NJ: Lawrence Erlbaum.

Hyman, H. H. (1987). *Secondary analysis of sample*. Middletown, NY: Wesleyan University Press.

Jennings, M. K. (1996). Political knowledge over time and across generations. *Public Opinion Quarterly*, 60(2), 228–252.

Johnsson-Smaragdi, U., & Jonsson, A. (2006). Book reading in leisure time: Long-term changes in young peoples' book reading habits. *Scandinavian Journal of Educational Research*, 50(5), 519–541.

Joreskog, K. (1973). A general method for estimating a linear structural equation system. In A. Goldberger & O. Duncan (Eds.), *Structural equations models in the social sciences* (pp. 85–101). New York, NY: Seminar Press.

Katz, E., & Lazarsfeld, P. F. (1955). *Personal influence*. New York, NY: Free Press.

Korhonen, P., & Lahikainen, A. (2008). Recent trends in young children's television-induced fears in Finland. *Journal of Children & Media*, 2(2), 147–162.

Lazarsfeld, P., Berelson, B., & Gaudet, H. (1944). *The people's choice*. New York, NY: Columbia University Press.

Lefkowitz, M., Eron, L., Walder, L., & Huesmann, L. (1972). Television violence and child aggression. In E. Rubinstein, G. Comstock, & J. Murray (Eds.), *Television and adolescent aggressiveness* (pp. 35–135). Washington, D.C.: U.S. Government Printing Office.

Lindstrom, P. B. (1997). The Internet: Nielsen's longitudinal research on behavior changes in use of this counterintuitive medium. *Journal of Media Economics*, 10(2), 35–40.

Long, J. (1976). Estimation and hypothesis testing in linear models containing measurement error. *Sociological Methods and Research*, 5, 157–206.

Lowery, S., & DeFleur, M. (1995). *Milestones in mass communication research* (3rd ed.). White Plains, NY: Longman.

Magnusson, D., Bergman, L., Rudinger, G., & Torestad, B. (1991). *Problems and methods in longitudinal research*. Cambridge: Cambridge University Press.

Markus, G. (1979). *Analyzing panel data*. Beverly Hills, CA: Sage Publications.

Mayer, W. (1993). Trends in media usage. *Public Opinion Quarterly*, 57(4), 593–610.

McMillan, S. J. (2001). Survival of the fittest online: A longitudinal study of health-related websites. *Journal of Computer Mediated Communication*, 6(3). *www.ascusc.org/jcmc/vol6/issue3/mcmillan.html*

Menard, S. (1991). *Longitudinal research*. Newbury Park, CA: Sage Publications.

Milavsky, J., Kessler, R. C., Stipp, H. H., & Rubens, W. S. (1982). *Television and aggression*. New York, NY: Academic Press.

Moriarty, C., & Harrison, K. (2008). Television exposure and disordered eating among children: A longitudinal panel study. *Journal of Communication*, 58(2), 361–381.

Newcomb, T. (1943). *Personality and social change*. New York, NY: Dryden.

Norlen, V. (1977). Response errors in the answers to retrospective questions. *Statistik Tidskrift*, 4, 331–341.

Overby, L., & Barth, J. (2009). The media, the medium, and malaise: Assessing the effects of campaign media exposure with panel data. *Mass Communication & Society*, 12(3), 271–290.

Palmore, E. (1978). When can age, period and cohort effects be separated? *Social Forces*, 57, 282–295.

Pearl, D., Bouthilet, L., & Lazar, J. (1982). *Television and behavior: Ten years of scientific progress and implications for the eighties*. Washington, DC: U.S. Government Printing Office.

Pearson, N., Ball, K., & Crawford, D. (2011). Mediators of longitudinal associations between television viewing and eating behaviors in adolescents. *International Journal of Behavioral Nutrition and Physical Activity*, 8(23), 1–9.

Peiser, W. (2000a). Cohort replacement and the downward trend in newspaper readership. *Newspaper Research Journal*, 42(3), 380–389.

Peiser, W. (2000b). Cohort trend in media use in the United States. *Mass Communication & Society*, 3(2/3), 185–203.

Peterson, T. (1980). *The mass media election*. New York, NY: Praeger.

Porter, W. J. (1992). How do adolescents' perceptions of television reality change over time? *Journalism Quarterly*, 69(2), 392–405.

Powers, E., Goudy, W., & Keith, P. (1978). Congruence between panel and recall data in longitudinal research. *Public Opinion Quarterly*, 42(3), 380–389.

Rentz, J., Reynolds, F., & Stout, R. (1983). Analyzing changing consumption patterns with cohort analysis', *Journal of Marketing Research*, 20(1), 12–20.

Roessler, P., & Brosius, H. B. (2001). Do talk shows cultivate adolescents' views of the world? A prolonged-exposure experiment. *Journal of Communication, 51*(1), 143–163.

Schulsinger, F., Mednick, S., & Knop, J. (1981). *Longitudinal research*. Boston, MA: Nijhoff Publishing.

Schuman, H., & Corning, A. (2006). Comparing Iraq to Vietnam: Recognition, recall and the nature of cohort effects. *Public Opinion Quarterly, 70*(1), 78–88.

Shaw, B., Scheufele, D., & Catalano, S. (2005). *The role of presence awareness in organizational communication*. Conference paper presented to the International Communication Association, New York, NY, May 2005.

Singer, J. L., Singer, D. G., Desmond, R., Hirsch, B., & Nicol, A. (1988). Family mediation and children's cognition, aggression and comprehension of television. *Journal of Applied Developmental Psychology, 9*(3), 329–347.

Sullivan, C. M., Rumptz, M. H., Campbell, R., Eby, K. K., & Davidson, W. S. (1996). Retaining participants in longitudinal community research. *Journal of Applied Behavioral Science, 32*(3), 262–276.

Toon, T. W. (2000). *A primer in longitudinal data analysis*. London: Sage Publications.

Trumbo, C. (1995). Longitudinal modeling of public issues. *Journalism and Mass Communication Monographs, 152*, 1–53.

Wimmer, R. D. (2001). *An analysis of panel study participation methods: Replication of 1995 results*. Denver, CO: Wimmer Research.

Xigen, L., & Lin, Z. (2007). Cultural values in Internet advertising. *Southwestern Mass Communication Journal, 23*(1), 57–73.

CHAPTER 9

EXPERIMENTAL RESEARCH

CHAPTER OUTLINE

Although the experimental method is the oldest approach in mass media research and continues to provide a wealth of information for researchers and critics of the media, experimental research is used relatively infrequently in mass media research. Nevertheless, its popularity has risen somewhat in recent years. A study of the most frequently used data-gathering methods in major academic journals (Kamhawi & Weaver, 2003) found that the experiment accounted for only 11% of the research techniques published from 1980 to 1984 but rose to 21% of the techniques published from 1995 to 1999. By comparison, the survey method accounted for 37% of the data-gathering methods in 1980–1984 but declined to 24% in the 1995–1999 period. An informal content analysis of three mass communication journals for 2009–2010 found slightly different results. Surveys were used in about 35% of the studies, while experiments were used in 16%.

We examine only the more basic techniques in this chapter, with discussions of the controlled **laboratory experiment**, quasi-experimental designs, and field experiments. For more information about advanced experimental procedures, you should consult Christensen (2004) and Montgomery (2008).

ADVANTAGES AND DISADVANTAGES OF LABORATORY EXPERIMENTS

There are several reasons to use the experimental method:

1. *Evidence of causality.* Experiments help establish cause and effect. Although some researchers argue whether we can ever really *prove* a cause-and-effect link between two variables, the experiment is undoubtedly the best social science research method for establishing causality. The researcher controls the time order of the presentation of two variables and thus makes sure that the cause actually precedes the effect. In addition, the experimental method allows the researcher to control other possible causes of the variable under investigation.

2. *Control.* As suggested earlier, control is an advantage of the experimental method. Researchers have control over the environment, the variables, and the subjects. Laboratory research allows researchers to isolate a testing situation from the competing influences of normal activity. Researchers are free to structure the experimental environment in almost any way. Lighting and temperature levels, proximity of subjects to measuring instruments, soundproofing, and nearly every other aspect of the experimental situation can be arranged and altered. However, environmental control has its drawbacks, and the artificially created environment of the laboratory is one of the main disadvantages of the technique.

Laboratory studies also allow researchers to control the numbers and types of independent and dependent variables selected and the way these variables are manipulated. Variable control strengthens internal validity and helps eliminate confounding influences. For example, Gilbert and Schleuder (1990), were able to control almost every detail of their laboratory analysis of the effects of color and complexity in still photographs.

The experimental approach also allows researchers to control subjects, including control over the selection process, assignment to the control or the experimental group, and exposure to experimental treatment. Limits can be placed on the number of subjects who participate in a study, and specific types of subjects can be selected for exposure in varying degrees to the independent variable. For example, researchers may select subjects according to which medium they use for news information and vary each subject's exposure to commercials of different types to determine which is the most effective.

3. *Cost.* In relative terms, the cost of an experiment can be low when compared to

other research methods. For example, an advertising researcher can examine the impact of two different ad designs using an experimental design with as few as 40–50 subjects. A comparable test done in the field would be far more costly.

4. *Replication.* Finally, the experimental method permits replication. Typically, the conditions of the study are clearly spelled out in the description of an experiment, which makes it easier for others to replicate. In fact, classic experiments are often repeated, sometimes under slightly different conditions, to ensure that the original results were not unique in some way.

The experimental technique, however, is not perfect. It has three major disadvantages.

1. *Artificiality.* Perhaps the biggest problem with using this technique is the artificial nature of the experimental environment. The behavior under investigation must be placed in circumstances that afford proper control. Unfortunately, much behavior of interest to mass media researchers is altered when studied out of its natural environment. Critics claim that the sterile and unnatural conditions created in the laboratory produce results that have little direct application to real-world settings, where subjects are continually exposed to competing stimuli. Miller (2002) notes that critics of the laboratory method often resort to ambiguous and disjunctive arguments about the artificiality of the procedure; he suggests that contrasting the "real" world with the "unreal" world may, in fact, be merely a problem in semantics. He claims the main point is that both the laboratory method and the field method investigate communication behavior, and if viewed in this way, it is meaningless to speak of behavior as "real" or "unreal": All behavior is real.

Miller also notes that it is unsatisfactory and unscientific to dodge the problem of artificiality in laboratory procedures by including a disclaimer in a study indicating that the findings are applicable only to a particular audience, to the environmental conditions of the analysis, and to the period during which the study was conducted. Since external validity is a major goal of scientific research, a disclaimer of this nature is counterproductive. If researchers are not willing to expand their interests beyond the scope of a single analysis, such studies have only heuristic value; they make little or no contribution to the advancement of knowledge in mass media.

Many researchers have conducted field experiments in an attempt to overcome the artificiality of the laboratory. Although field experiments take place in natural surroundings, they are likely to face problems with control.

2. *Researcher (experimenter) bias.* Experiments can be influenced by experimenter bias (see Chapter 1). Rosenthal and Jacobson (1966) discovered that researchers who were told what findings to expect had results more in line with the research hypothesis than researchers who were not told what to expect. To counteract this problem, researchers can use the **double-blind technique,** in which neither subjects nor researchers know whether a given subject belongs to the control group or to the experimental group.

3. *Limited scope.* Finally, some research questions simply do not lend themselves to the experimental approach. Many of the more interesting research topics in mass media are concerned with the collective behavior of perhaps millions of people. Experiments on this scale are much too massive to conduct. Consider, for example, the **cultivation effect** (discussed in more detail on this book's website), which involves the long-term impact of television on society. Any experimental design that would "test" the cultivation effect would be too time-consuming, expensive, and ethically questionable to take place. Although it is possible to conduct some smaller-scale experiments on this topic with small groups of subjects, it is unclear how these experiments relate to the larger-scale phenomenon.

CONDUCTING EXPERIMENTAL RESEARCH

The experimental method involves both manipulation and observation. In the simplest form of an experiment, researchers manipulate the independent variable and then observe the responses of subjects on the dependent variable. Although every experiment is different, most researchers agree that the following eight steps should be followed when conducting an experiment:

1. *Select the setting.* Many experiments are best conducted in a laboratory or in another environment under the direct control of the researcher. Others are best conducted in more natural surroundings where the researcher has little, if any, control over the experimental situation. This latter type of experiment is discussed in more detail later in this chapter.

2. *Select the experimental design.* The appropriate design depends on the nature of the hypothesis or the research question, types of variables to be manipulated or measured, availability of subjects, and amount of resources available.

3. *Operationalize the variables.* In the experimental approach, independent variables are usually operationalized in terms of the manipulation done to create them. Dependent variables are operationalized by constructing scales or rules for categorizing observations of behavior.

4. *Decide how to manipulate the independent variable.* To manipulate the independent variable (or variables), a set of specific instructions, events, or stimuli is developed for presentation to the experimental subjects. There are two types of manipulations: straightforward and staged.

In a **straightforward manipulation**, written materials, verbal instructions, or other stimuli are presented to the subjects. For example, Baran, Mok, Land, and Kang (1989) used a straightforward manipulation

of their independent variable—product positioning. One group of subjects was presented with a "generic" shopping list that contained items such as ice cream, frozen dinners, mustard, and coffee. Another group saw the "practical" list with items such as *Borden's* ice cream, *Swanson's* frozen dinners, *French's* mustard, and *Maxwell House* coffee. A third group was presented with the "upscale" list consisting of *Häagen-Dazs* ice cream, *Lean Cuisine* frozen dinners, *Grey Poupon* mustard, *General Foods International* coffee, and similar items. Each group was then asked to make judgments about the character of the person to whom the list belonged. As predicted by the researchers, the shopping lists had an impact on the way subjects evaluated the general goodness and responsibility of the lists' authors. Cho, Shah, Nah, and Brossard (2009) used a straightforward manipulation in their study of production variables in a televised debate. One experimental group saw the traditional single-screen coverage that showed each candidate speaking, while another group saw the same debate segment on a split screen where both candidates were in view at all times. Viewers who saw the split-screen version perceived the debate as being higher in incivility than did the single-screen group.

In a **staged manipulation**, researchers construct events and circumstances that enable them to manipulate the independent variable. Staged manipulations can be relatively simple or rather elaborate. They frequently involve the use of a confederate, a person who pretends to be a subject but who is actually part of the manipulation. For example, staged manipulations and confederates have been used in experiments that examine the impact of media portrayals of antisocial behavior. In their study of rock music videos, Hansen and Hansen (1990) showed half of their sample three music videos that depicted antisocial behavior; the other half of the sample viewed three rock videos depicting a more "neutral" type of behavior. The subjects then watched a videotaped job interview of a person applying for a position with the campus TV station's rock video program. One version of this tape showed the applicant (who was actually a confederate of the researchers) making an obscene gesture while the interviewer's back was turned. Subjects who had previously viewed the rock videos depicting "neutral" behaviors evaluated the applicant's behavior more negatively than did the subjects who saw the videos depicting antisocial behaviors.

Hoyt (1977) investigated the effects of television coverage on courtroom behavior. In a staged manipulation of three groups of subjects, he separately questioned the groups about a film they had just viewed. One group answered questions in the presence of a TV camera at the front of the room; a second group answered questions with the camera concealed behind a full-length mirror; and a third group answered questions without being filmed. Hoyt found no differences in subjects' verbal behaviors across the three conditions. McGarva, Ramsey, and Shear (2006) used an imaginative staged manipulation in their study of cell phone use and driver aggression. A confederate driving an old car slowed and stopped at a red light. The researchers instructed the confederate to remain at the light for 15 seconds after it had turned to green unless the car behind the confederate's vehicle honked the horn. Half the time the confederate looked straight ahead and half the time he held a cell phone to his ear and engaged in a mock-animated conversation. A second member of the research team sat in the passenger seat and surreptitiously videotaped the reactions of the driver in the following car. The study revealed that female drivers were more visibly angered when delayed at a stop light due to a cell phone user, but that male drivers were quicker to blow their horns when frustrated by a cell phone user than a non–cell phone user.

No matter what manipulation technique is used, a general principle for the researcher to follow is to construct or choose a manipulation that is as strong as possible to maximize potential differences between the experimental groups. For example, if a researcher is trying to assess the effects of different degrees of newspaper credibility on audience perceptions of the accuracy of a story, one condition might attribute the story to the *New York Times* and another might attribute it to the *National Enquirer* or the *Star*. A strong manipulation maximizes the chances that the independent variable has an effect.

5. *Select and assign subjects to experimental conditions.* Recall from Chapter 1 that to ensure external validity, experimental subjects should be selected randomly from the population under investigation. The various random sampling techniques discussed in Chapter 4 are appropriate for selecting subjects for experimental studies.

6. *Conduct a pilot study.* A pilot study with a small number of subjects will reveal problems and allow the researcher to make a **manipulation check**—a test to determine whether the manipulation of the independent variable actually has the intended effect. For example, suppose a researcher wants to assess the effect of viewers' involvement in a TV show on how well they remember the ads in the show. The researcher constructs TV shows labeled "high involvement" (a cliff-hanger with lots of suspense), "medium involvement" (a family drama), and "low involvement" (a Senate committee hearing recorded from C-SPAN). To check whether these programs actually differ in involvement, the researcher must measure the degree to which subjects were involved with the programs under each of the conditions. Such a check might include a self-report, an observational report (such as counting the number of times a subject looked away from the screen), or even a physiological measure. If the check shows

that the manipulation was not effective, the researcher can change the manipulation before the main experiment is conducted. (It is also a good idea to include a manipulation check in the main experiment.)

7. *Administer the experiment.* After the problems are corrected and the manipulation is checked, the main phase of data collection begins. Experimental manipulations can be carried out on either individuals or groups. The dependent variable is measured, and the subjects are **debriefed**. During debriefing, the researcher explains the purpose and the implications of the research.

If the manipulation required deception, the researcher must explain why and how the deception was used. (See Chapter 3 for more about deception and other ethical problems of research.)

8. *Analyze and interpret the results.* The subjects' scores on the dependent variable(s) are tabulated, and the data are analyzed. Many statistics discussed in Chapters 10 and 12 are used to analyze the results of experiments. Finally, the researcher must decide what the results indicate—the most difficult task in many experiments.

A CLOSER LOOK

Physiological Measurements in Experiments

Although physiological measurements are often used in psychology, they are relatively rare in mass media research. At their simplest level, physiological measurements quantify changes in the body's nervous system as a person processes certain information. Some dependent variables that seem especially appropriate for physiological measures include attention, arousal, interest, and habituation.

What follows is a brief description of three of the more common physiological measurements:

- Galvanic skin response (GSR) measures the variations in the electrical conductance of human skin caused by tiny changes in perspiration level. Two electrodes are attached to a person's fingers, and a small current is sent across the surface of the skin from one electrode to the other. Changes in GSR can help researchers gauge how a subject responds to a message.
- Blood pressure is the level of force exerted against the walls of the arteries when the heart is contracting (called systolic blood pressure) and when the heart is resting

(called diastolic blood pressure). Blood pressure is measured using the familiar arm cuff and is expressed as two numbers with the systolic figure first followed by the diastolic (such as 120/80). Some researchers combine these two measures to create an index called *mean arterial pressure*. Blood pressure can be used to measure excitement, arousal, and involvement.

- Pupillometry involves measuring changes in the size of the pupils of the eyes that are due to changes in the body's sympathetic nervous system. These changes are recorded by a special camera that is focused on the eye. Advertising researchers have used pupillometry to measure attention and attraction.

One advantage of physiological measures is that they are hard to fake. There is no possibility for a social desirability bias or other distortions of a subject's self-report. On the other hand, they require special equipment and extra effort to calculate. Nonetheless, they should not be overlooked as potential measures when designing an experiment.

CONTROL OF CONFOUNDING VARIABLES

As discussed in previous chapters, researchers must ensure the internal validity of their research by controlling for the effects of **confounding variables** (*extraneous variables*) that might contaminate their findings. These variables can be controlled through the environment, experimental manipulations, experimental design, or assignment of subjects. This section concentrates on techniques used to ensure that the groups in an experiment are comparable before the experimental treatment is administered. Group comparability is an important consideration because it helps to rule out possible alternative explanations based on the natural differences among people.

Perhaps an example will illustrate this point. Suppose a researcher wants to determine whether different versions of a TV commercial's musical soundtrack have different impacts on what is remembered from that ad. The researcher uses a media research class as the sample and assigns an ad with a rap soundtrack to the students in the first three rows. Students in the last three rows view the same ad but hear a heavy metal soundtrack. Both groups are then given a recall test, and the results show that the group that heard the rap soundtrack remembered more information from the ad. How confident should the researcher be of this conclusion? Not too confident: it is entirely possible that the people who sat in the first three rows of the class are different from those who sat in the back. The "fronters" might have chosen the front seats because they are more intelligent, more attentive, and more alert than the "backers," who might have sat in the rear of the room so that they could sleep, talk, or otherwise amuse themselves. Consequently, the superior performance of the "fronters" might be due to these factors rather than to the effectiveness of the soundtrack. How can researchers ensure that their groups are equivalent? There are three main techniques: randomizing, matching, and including the confounding variable in the design.

Randomization

A powerful technique for eliminating the influence of extraneous variables is **randomization**: randomly assigning subjects to various treatment groups. Random assignment means that each subject has an equal chance of being assigned to each treatment group. This method works because the variables to be controlled are distributed in approximately the same way in all groups. In the preceding example, suppose that the researcher had randomly assigned students to one group or the other instead of assigning them according to where they sat. It is highly probable that the average level of intelligence in the two groups would have been the same, as would have been their levels of attentiveness and alertness, thus ruling out those variables as alternative explanations. In addition, randomization would equalize some other confounding factors that the researcher might have overlooked. Random

---

A CLOSER LOOK

Confounding Variables

Whenever you conduct a research study and are ready to interpret the results, go through every step of the research to determine what could have produced the results. Don't immediately accept that your data are correct.

assignment would avoid the presence of a disproportionate number of men or women in one or the other group, which skews the results. The same might be said for geographic background: Randomization would provide for proportionate numbers of urban versus rural residents in each group.

There are several ways randomization can be achieved. If there are only two groups in the experiment, the researcher might simply flip a coin. If heads comes up, the subject goes to Group 1; if tails, Group 2. Experimental designs with more than two groups might use a table of random numbers to assign subjects. In a four-group design, a two-digit random number might be assigned to each subject. Those assigned 00–24 are placed in Group 1, 25–49 in Group 2, 50–74 in Group 3, and 75–99 in Group 4.

Randomization is not perfect. The smaller the sample size in the experiment, the greater the risk that randomization will produce nonequivalent groups. This is another reason that researchers must use an adequate sample size in an experiment.

Matching

Another way to control for the impact of confounding variables is to match subjects on characteristics that may relate to the dependent variable. There are two primary methods of **matching**. The first, *matching by constancy*, makes a variable uniform for all of the experimental groups. For example, let's say a researcher is interested in assessing the impact of playing two types of video games on aggressiveness in children. Past research strongly suggests that gender is related to the levels and types of aggressive acts performed. To match the sample by constancy and control for gender effects, the researcher may decide to perform the experiment using only boys or only girls in the sample.

The second type of matching involves *matching by pairing*. In this method, subjects are paired on a similar value of a relevant variable before being assigned to different groups. Using the video game example, suppose the researcher suspects that a subject's prior level of aggressive tendencies has an impact on how that subject is affected by violent video games. The researcher would administer a test of aggressiveness to all subjects and calculate their scores. For simplicity's sake, let's say that there are only three possible scores on this test: low, medium, and high. The researcher would find two people who scored high on this test, pair them up, and then assign one at random to one treatment group and the other to the second. A similar procedure would be followed for those scoring low and medium. When finished, the researcher would be confident that equal numbers of high-, medium-, and low-aggression subjects were placed in each treatment group. This process, of course, is not necessarily restricted to pairs. If an experiment had three groups, subjects could be matched as triplets and then randomly assigned to groups.

In addition to gaining control over confounding variables, matching subjects increases the sensitivity of the experimental design. Because the treatment groups become more homogeneous, smaller differences that might have been obscured by individual variations can be detected.

On the other hand, this method does have some disadvantages. Matching by constancy limits the generalizability of the study and restricts the size of the population available for sampling. Both forms of matching also require at least some prior knowledge about the subjects and may require the extra effort of a pretest.

Including the Confounding Variable in the Design

Another way to control the impact of confounding variables in an experiment and to increase the sensitivity of the experiment is to incorporate the confounding variable(s) into the design. For instance, let's return to the video game example. Instead of controlling for the effects of gender by restricting the study to only boys or to only girls, the researcher might include gender as an independent variable. After the sample is divided by gender, each male or female would be randomly assigned to a condition. The resulting design would have four groups: males who play video game A, males who play video game B, females who play video game A, and females who play video game B. (Note that this is an example of the factorial design described later in this chapter.) An added benefit of this design is that it can provide information about the interaction—the combined effects of the confounding variable and independent variable of interest. Again, there are disadvantages to this method. Including another factor in the design increases the number of subjects needed for the experiment and also increases the time and energy necessary to complete it.

EXPERIMENTAL DESIGN

When used in the context of experimental research, the word *design* can have two different meanings. On one hand, it can refer to the statistical procedures used to analyze the data, and it is common to hear about an analysis of variance design or a repeated-measures *t*-test design. On the other hand, *design* can refer to the total experimental plan or structure of the research. Used in this sense, it means selecting and planning the entire experimental approach to a research problem. This chapter uses the latter meaning. The appropriate statistical techniques for the various experimental designs in this chapter are discussed in Part Three.

An **experimental design** does not have to be a complicated series of statements, diagrams, and figures; it may be as simple as

Pretest > Experimental treatment > Posttest

A CLOSER LOOK

Importance of Pretesting

The following scenario illustrates the importance of pretesting in an experiment. A researcher was planning to conduct a study with high school students. After completing the laborious process of securing approval from the appropriate authorities, the researcher scheduled a date and showed up bright and early to collect the data. About 70 students were assembled in the auditorium, and the school's principal had given the researcher 45 minutes to collect the data. No problem, thought the researcher. The subjects merely had to listen to a few musical selections and fill out rating scales. The researcher passed out the sheets containing the rating scales and told students to get their pencils or pens ready. At this point the students looked perplexed, and many protested that they did not have pencils or pens with them. Unlike the college students that the researcher was used to, high school students do not routinely carry pens or pencils.

With the allotted time quickly running out, the researcher ran to the principal's office and asked to borrow pencils. Luckily, there were several boxes in the supply cabinet. The researcher hurried back into the auditorium and started to pass out the pencils when he suddenly discovered that they were not sharpened. A frenzied search of the auditorium revealed exactly one pencil sharpener that probably dated from the 1930s. Needless to say, the experiment had to be rescheduled. Since that experience, the researcher has never failed to run a pretest before doing an experiment and to always bring along enough pencils!

Although other factors—such as variable and sample selection, control, and construction of a measurement instrument—enter into this design, the diagram does provide a legitimate starting point for research.

To facilitate the discussion of experimental design, the following notations are used to represent specific parts of a design (Campbell & Stanley, 1963):

- R represents a random sample or random assignment.

- X represents a treatment or manipulation of the independent variables so that the effects of these variables on the dependent variables can be measured.

- O refers to a process of observation or measurement; it is usually followed by a numerical subscript indicating the number of the observation (O_1 = Observation 1).

A left-to-right listing of symbols, such as R O_1 X O_2, indicates the order of the experiment. In this case, subjects are randomly selected or assigned to groups (R) and then observed or measured (O_1). Next, some type of treatment or manipulation of the independent variable is performed (X), followed by a second observation or measurement (O_2).

Each line in experimental notation refers to the experience of a single group. Consider the following design:

$$R \quad O_1 \quad X \quad O_2$$
$$R \quad O_1 \qquad O_2$$

This design indicates that the operations in the experiment are conducted simultaneously on two different groups. Notice that the second group, the control group, does not receive the experimental treatment.

Basic Experimental Designs

Each experimental design makes assumptions about the type of data the researcher wants to collect because different data require different research methods. Several questions need to be answered by the researcher before any type of design is constructed:

1. What is the purpose of the study?
2. What is to be measured or tested?
3. How many factors (independent variables) are involved?
4. How many levels of the factors (degrees of the independent variables) are involved?
5. What type of data is desired?
6. What is the easiest and most efficient way to collect the data?
7. What type of statistical analysis is appropriate for the data?
8. How much will the study cost?
9. How can costs be trimmed?
10. What facilities are available for conducting the study?
11. What types of studies have been conducted in the area?
12. What benefits will be received from the results of the study?

The answer to each question has a bearing on the sequence of steps a study should follow. For example, if a limited budget is available for the study, a complicated four-group research design cannot be conducted. Or if previous studies have shown the "posttest-only" design to be useful, another design may be unjustified.

Not all experimental designs are covered in this section; only the most widely used are considered. The sources listed at the end of the chapter provide more information about these and other designs.

Pretest–Posttest Control Group. The pretest–posttest control group design is a fundamental and widely used procedure in all research areas. The design controls many of the rival hypotheses generated by artifacts;

the effects of maturation, testing, history, and other sources are controlled because each group faces the same circumstances in the study. As shown in Figure 9.1, subjects are randomly selected or assigned, and each group is given a pretest. However, only the first group receives the experimental treatment. The difference between O_1 and O_2 for Group 1 is compared to the difference between O_1 and O_2 for Group 2. If a significant statistical difference is found, it is assumed that the experimental treatment was the primary cause.

Posttest-Only Control Group. When researchers are hesitant to use a pretest because of the possibility of subject sensitization to the posttest, the design in Figure 9.1 can be altered to describe a **posttest-only control group** (see Figure 9.2). Neither group has a pretest, but Group 1 is exposed to the treatment variable, followed by a posttest. The two groups are compared to determine whether statistical significance is present.

The posttest-only control group design is also widely used to control rival explanations. Both groups are equally affected by maturation, history, and so on. Also, both normally call for a *t*-test, a test to compare the significance between two groups, to determine whether a significant statistical difference is present (see Chapter 12).

Solomon Four-Group Design. The **Solomon four-group design** combines the first two designs and is useful if pretesting is considered to be a negative factor (see Figure 9.3). Each alternative for pretesting and posttesting is accounted for in the design, which makes it attractive to researchers.

For example, consider the hypothetical data presented in Figure 9.4. The numbers represent college students' scores on a test of current events knowledge. The X represents a program of regular newspaper reading. If the newspaper reading had an effect, O_2 should be significantly different from O_1 and also significantly different from O_4. In addition, O_2 should be significantly different from O_6 and also from O_3. If we assume that

Figure 9.3   Solomon Four-Group Design

R	O_1	X	O_2
R	O_3		O_4
R		X	O_5
R			O_6

Figure 9.1   Pretest–Posttest Control Group Design

R	O_1	X	O_2
R	O_1		O_2

Figure 9.2   Posttest-Only Control Group Design

R		X	O_1
R			O_2

Figure 9.4   Hypothetical Data for Solomon Four-Group Design

Group				
1	R	20 (O_1)	X	40 (O_2)
2	R	20 (O_3)		20 (O_4)
3	R		X	40 (O_5)
4	R			20 (O_6)

the 20-point difference shown in Figure 9.4 is significant, it appears that the independent variable in our example is indeed having an effect on current events knowledge. Note that other informative comparisons are also possible in this design. To assess the possible effects of pretesting, O_4 can be compared with O_6. Comparing O_1 and O_3 allows the researcher to check on the efficacy of randomization, and any possible pretest manipulation interaction can be detected by comparing O_2 and O_5.

The biggest drawback of the Solomon four-group design is a practical one—the design requires four separate groups, which means more subjects, more time, and more money. Further, some results produced from this design can be difficult to interpret. For example, what does it mean if O_2 is significantly greater than O_4 even though O_5 is significantly less than O_6?

Factorial Studies

Research studies involving the simultaneous analysis of two or more independent variables are called **factorial designs**, and each independent variable is called a **factor**. The approach saves time, money, and resources and allows researchers to investigate the interaction between the variables. That is, in many instances it is possible that two or more variables are *interdependent* (dependent on each other) in the effects they produce on the dependent variable, a relationship that could not be detected if two simple randomized designs were used. The factorial design is popular in mass communication research. Of all the experiments reported in three mass communication journals from 2009 to 2010, about two-thirds used a factorial design.

The term *two-factor design* indicates that two independent variables are manipulated, a *three-factor design* includes three independent variables, and so on. (A *one-factor design* is a simple random design because only one independent variable is involved.) A factorial design for a study must have at least two factors or independent variables.

Factors may also have two or more levels. Therefore, the 2 × 2 factorial design has two independent variables, each with two levels. A 3 × 3 factorial design has three levels for each of the two independent variables. A 2 × 3 × 3 factorial design has three independent variables: The first has two levels, and the second and third have three levels each.

To demonstrate the concept of levels, imagine that a TV station program director (PD) wants to study the success of a promotional campaign for a new movie-of-the-week series. The PD plans to advertise the new series on radio and in newspapers. Subjects selected randomly are placed into one of the cells of the 2 × 2 factorial design in Figure 9.5. This allows for the testing of two levels of two independent variables—exposure to radio and exposure to newspapers.

Figure 9.5 2 × 2 Factorial Design

	Radio	No radio
Newspapers	I	II
No newspapers	III	IV

Four groups are involved in the study: Group I is exposed to both newspaper material and radio material, Group II is exposed to only newspaper, Group III is exposed to only radio, and Group IV serves as a control group and receives no exposure to either radio or newspaper. After the groups have undergone the experimental treatment, the PD can administer a short questionnaire to determine which medium, or combination of media, worked most effectively.

A 2 × 3 factorial design, which adds a third level to the second independent variable, is illustrated in Figure 9.6. This design demonstrates how the PD might investigate the relative effectiveness of full-color versus black-and-white newspaper advertisements while also measuring the impact of the exposure to radio material.

Assume the PD wants to include promotional advertisements on television as well as use radio and newspaper. The third factor produces a 2 × 2 × 2 factorial design. This three-factor design in Figure 9.7 shows the eight possibilities of a 2 × 2 × 2 factorial study. Note that the subjects in Group I are exposed to newspaper, radio, and television announcements, whereas those in Group VIII are not exposed to any of the announcements.

The testing procedure in the three-factor design is similar to that of previous methods. Subjects in all eight cells are given some type of measurement instrument, and differences between the groups are tested for statistical significance. For example, Williams (2011) used a 2 × 2 factorial design in his study of video game violence. Factor One was the content of the game (violent or nonviolent)

Figure 9.6   2 × 3 Factorial Design

	Radio	No radio
Full-color newspaper ad	I	II
Black-and-white newspaper ad	III	IV
No newspaper	V	VI

Figure 9.7   2 × 2 × 2 Factorial Design

	Radio		No radio	
	TV	No TV	TV	No TV
Newspaper	I	II	III	IV
No newspaper	V	VI	VII	VIII

and Factor Two was the physical resemblance of the player's avatar to the player (similar or nonsimilar). The results showed that playing a violent video game with an avatar that resembles the player resulted in greater levels of hostility than playing a violent game with a dissimilar avatar.

Other Experimental Designs

Research designs are as unique and varied as the questions and hypotheses they help to study. Designs of different types yield different types of information. If information about the effects of multiple manipulations is desired, a **repeated-measures design** (several measurements of the same subject) is appropriate. In this design, instead of assigning different people to different manipulations, the researcher exposes the same subjects to multiple manipulations. The effects of the various manipulations appear as variations within the same person's performance rather than as differences *between* groups of people. Figure 9.8 shows a simple example of the repeated-measures design that assumes order effects do not matter.

One obvious advantage of the repeated-measures design is that fewer subjects are necessary because each subject participates in all conditions. Furthermore, because each subject acts as his or her own control, the design is quite sensitive to detecting treatment differences. On the other hand,

repeated-measures designs are subject to *carryover effects*: The effects of one manipulation may still be present when the next manipulation is presented. Another possible disadvantage is that the subjects experience all of the various experimental conditions, and they may figure out the purpose behind the experiment. As a result, they may behave differently than they would have if they were unaware of the study's goals.

Unfortunately, there is no way to totally eliminate carryover effects, but the researcher can at least balance them out by varying the order in which the treatments are presented. For example, if there are three treatment conditions—A, B, and C—the first subject might receive them in ABC order, the order for subject number two might be ACB, for subject three CBA, and so forth until all of the six possible combinations are used. Of course, the larger the number of treatments, the larger the number of combinations that have to be considered. For an experiment with five treatment levels, there are 120 possible combinations. One possible solution to this dilemma is to use a Latin square design.

If the researcher thinks that the order of presentation of the independent variables in a repeated-measures design will be a problem, a **Latin square design** is appropriate. Figure 9.9 shows an example of a Latin square design for a repeated-measures experiment with four subjects. Notice that each subject is exposed

Figure 9.8	Repeated-Measures Design with Five Subjects and Three Treatments		
Subject	Treatment 1	Treatment 2	Treatment 3
1	X_1O_1	X_2O_2	X_3O_3
2	X_1O_1	X_2O_2	X_3O_3
3	X_1O_1	X_2O_2	X_3O_3
4	X_1O_1	X_2O_2	X_3O_3
5	X_1O_1	X_2O_2	X_3O_3

A CLOSER LOOK

Repeated-Measures Designs

In many research studies, it doesn't matter if the respondents or subjects "figure out" the purpose of the research. In most cases, there is nothing to figure out. For example, a commonly used repeated-measures design in radio research is the auditorium music test, where respondents rate several hundred song segments (hooks). There is nothing hidden in the research, and the respondents' rating of one song has no effect on the ratings of other songs. In other words, the respondents don't learn anything from one song to the next.

Figure 9.9   Latin Square Design

Subjects	Experimental conditions			
A	1	2	3	4
B	2	3	4	1
C	3	4	1	2
D	4	1	2	3

to all conditions, and that each of the four conditions appears only once per row and once per column. The Latin square arrangement also can be used when repeated measures are made on independent groups rather than on individual subjects.

Let's take a straightforward example of a repeated-measures design. Suppose a researcher is interested in the effects of screen size on the arousal caused by scenes of violence. The researcher recruits a dozen subjects and decides to measure arousal by means of a physiological measurement, galvanic skin response (GSR—See A Closer Look on page 250). The first subject watches a violent scene on a small portable DVD screen while her GSR is monitored. The subject's GSR is then measured while watching the scene on a 22-inch screen and again on a 50-inch screen. The next subject follows the same protocol but watches on the biggest screen first, the smallest screen next, and then finally the middle-sized screen. The same routine is followed with the rest of the subjects with the order of screen size varied to guard against carryover effects. After the data are collected, they can be analyzed using a type of analysis of variance procedure (see Chapter 12).

The repeated-measures approach can also be used in factorial designs. In the previous example, the same experimental procedure could be done with repeated measures on a group of 12 males and a group of 12 females. The resulting analysis could test for differences due to screen size, gender, and the interaction between the two. An example of a repeated-measures, $2 \times 2 \times 3$ factorial design can be found in Bolls and Muehling (2007).

Quasi-Experimental Designs

Sometimes a researcher does not have the luxury of randomly assigning subjects to experimental conditions. Suppose, for example, a researcher knows that a local radio station is about to be sold and is interested in determining the effects of this change of ownership on employee morale. The researcher measures the morale of a sample of employees at the station before and after the sale. At the same time, the researcher collects data on morale from a sample of employees at a comparable station in the same community. This test design is similar to the pretest–posttest control group design discussed on page 255, but it does not involve the random assignment of subjects to experimental groups. Using Campbell and Stanley's (1963) terminology, we call it a **quasi-experiment**. Quasi-experiments are a valuable source of information, but there are design faults that must be considered in the interpretation of the data.

This chapter discusses only two types of quasi-experimental designs: the **pretest–posttest nonequivalent control group** design and the **interrupted time series** design. For more information, consult Campbell and Stanley (1963) and Cook and Campbell (1979).

Pretest–Posttest Nonequivalent Control Group Design. This approach, illustrated in Figure 9.10, is used by the hypothetical researcher studying employee morale at radio stations. One group is exposed to the experimental manipulation and is compared to a similar group that is not exposed. The pre- and posttest differences are compared to determine whether the experimental condition had an effect.

In the radio station example, assume the pretest of employee morale showed that the workers at both radio stations had the same morale level before the sale. The posttest, however, showed that the morale of the employees at the sold station decreased

significantly after the sale, but the morale level at the other (control) station remained constant. This result indicates that the station sale had an impact on morale, but this may not be true. The two groups might have been different on other variables at the time of the pretest. For example, suppose the two groups of employees were of different ages. It is possible that the effect of the station sale on older employees produced the difference. The quasi-experimental design does not rule out this alternative selection-treatment interaction explanation.

Interrupted Time Series Design. In this arrangement, illustrated in Figure 9.11, a series of periodic measurements is made of a group. The series of measurements is interrupted by the experimental treatment, and then measurements are continued.

This design can rule out threats to internal validity. If there is a significant difference between O_5 and O_6, maturation can be ruled out by examining the scores for all the intervals before the manipulation. If maturation did occur, it would probably produce differences between O_1 and O_2, O_2 and O_3, and so on. If the only difference is between O_5 and O_6, then maturation is not a plausible explanation. The same logic can be applied to rule out the sensitizing effects of testing. The biggest threat to the internal validity in this design is history. It is possible that any apparent changes occurring after the experimental manipulation will be due to some other event that occurred at the same time as the experimental treatment. Donohew, Lorch, and Palmgreen (1998) describe an example of an interrupted time series design. Monthly samples of 100 teenagers were

---

Figure 9.10 Pretest–Posttest Nonequivalent Control Group Design

O_1	X	O_2
O_3		O_4

Note: The line dividing the two groups indicates that no random assignment occurred.

Figure 9.11 Interrupted Time Series Design

O_1	O_2	O_3	O_4	O_5	X	O_6	O_7	O_8	O_9	O_{10}

interviewed about their exposure to anti-marijuana public service announcements and their attitudes toward marijuana use in two matched cities over a 32-month period. A four-month public service announcement campaign featuring the anti-marijuana public service announcements took place in both cities at different times. Comparison of the month-to-month data revealed changes in attitudes and behaviors.

FIELD EXPERIMENTS

Experiments conducted in a laboratory can be disadvantageous for many research studies because of certain problems they present: They are performed in controlled conditions that are unlike natural settings, they are generally considered to lack external validity, and they usually necessitate subject awareness of the testing situation. Because of these shortcomings, many researchers prefer to use field experiments (Haskins, 1968).

The exact difference between laboratory experiments and field experiments has been a subject of debate for years, especially with regard to the "realism" of the situations involved. Many researchers consider field and laboratory experiments to be on opposite ends of the realism continuum. However, the main difference between the two approaches is the setting. As Westley (1989) points out:

> The laboratory experiment is carried out on the researcher's own turf; the subjects come into the laboratory. In the field experiment, the researcher goes to the subject's turf. In general, the physical controls available in the laboratory are greater than those found in the field. For that reason, statistical controls are often substituted for physical controls in the field. (p. 129)

The presence or absence of rules and procedures to control the conditions and the subjects' awareness or unawareness of being subjects can also distinguish the two approaches. If the researcher maintains tight control over the subjects' behavior and the subjects are placed in an environment they perceive to be radically different from their everyday life, the situation is probably better described as a laboratory experiment. On the other hand, if the subjects function primarily in their everyday social roles with little investigator interference or environmental restructuring, the case is probably closer to a field experiment. Basically, the difference between laboratory experiments and field experiments is one of degree.

Advantages of Field Experiments

The major advantage of field experiments is their external validity: Because study conditions closely resemble natural settings, subjects usually provide a truer picture of their normal behavior and are not influenced by the experimental situation. For example, consider a laboratory study designed to test the effectiveness of two versions of a television commercial. One group views Version A, and the other group views Version B. Both groups are then given a questionnaire to measure their willingness to purchase the advertised product. After the study is conducted, the results may indicate that Version B is more effective in selling the product. Although this may actually be the case, the validity of the experiment is questionable because the subjects knew they were being studied. (See the discussion of demand characteristics in Chapter 1.) Another problem is that answering a questionnaire cannot be equated to buying a product. Furthermore, viewing commercials in a laboratory setting is different from the normal viewing situation, in which competing stimuli (other media, crying children, ringing telephones, and so on) are often present.

In a field experiment, these commercials might be tested by showing Version A in one market and Version B in a similar, but different, market. Actual sales of the product in both markets might then be monitored to determine which commercial was the more successful in persuading viewers to buy the product. As can be seen, the results of the field experiment have more relevance to reality, but the degree of control involved is markedly less than in the laboratory experiment.

Some field studies have the advantage of being nonreactive. **Reactivity** is the influence that a subject's awareness of being measured or observed has on his or her behavior. Laboratory subjects are almost always aware of being measured. Although this is also true of some field experiments, many can be conducted without the subjects' knowledge of their participation. (See, for example, McGarva, Ramsey, and Shear, 2006.)

Field experiments are useful for studying complex social processes and situations. In their classic study of the effects of the arrival of television in an English community, Himmelweit, Oppenheim, and Vince (1958) recognized the advantages of the field experiment. Because television has an impact on several lifestyle variables, the researchers used a range of analysis techniques, including diaries, personal interviews, direct observation, questionnaires, and teachers' ratings of students, to document this impact. Such a broad topic area does not easily lend itself to laboratory research.

Field experiments can be inexpensive. Most studies require no special equipment or facilities; however, expenses increase rapidly with the size and scope of the study (Babbie, 2010). Finally, the field experiment may be the only research option to use. For example, suppose a researcher is interested in examining patterns of communication at a television station before and after a change in management—a problem difficult, if not impossible, to simulate in a laboratory. The only practical option is to conduct the study in the field—that is, at the station.

Disadvantages of Field Experiments

The disadvantages of the field experiment are mostly practical ones. However, some research is impossible to conduct because of ethical considerations. The difficult question of the effects of television violence on young viewers provides a good example of this problem. Probably the most informative study that could be performed in this area would be a field experiment in which one group of children is required to watch violent television programs and another similar group to watch only nonviolent programs. The subjects could be carefully observed over a number of years to check for any significant difference in the number of aggressive acts committed by the members of each group. However, the ethics involved in controlling the television viewing behavior of children and in possibly encouraging aggressive acts are extremely questionable. Therefore, scientists have resorted to laboratory and survey techniques to study this problem.

On a more practical level, field experiments often encounter external hindrances that cannot be anticipated. For example, a researcher may spend weeks planning a study to manipulate the media use of students in a summer camp, only to have camp counselors or a group of parents cancel the project because they do not want the children to be used as guinea pigs. Also, it takes time for researchers to establish contacts, secure cooperation, and gain necessary permissions before beginning a field experiment. In many cases this phase of the process may take weeks or months to complete.

Finally, and perhaps most importantly, researchers cannot control all the intervening variables in a field experiment. The presence of extraneous variables affects the precision of the experiment and the confidence of the researchers in its outcome.

Types of Field Experiments

There are two basic categories of field experiments: those in which the researcher manipulates the independent variable(s) and those in which independent variable manipulation occurs naturally as a result of other circumstances. To illustrate the first type, suppose that a researcher is interested in investigating the effects of not being able to read a newspaper. A possible approach would be to select two comparable samples and not allow one of the samples to read any newspapers for a period of time; the second sample (the control group) would continue to read the newspaper as usual. A comparison could then be made to determine whether abstinence from newspapers has any effect in other areas of life, such as interpersonal communication. In this example, reading the newspaper is the independent variable that has been manipulated.

The second type of field experiment involves passive manipulation of independent variables. Suppose a community with no broadband connection to the Internet is scheduled for installation in the future. In an attempt to gauge the effects of broadband service on television viewing and other media use, a researcher might begin studying a large sample of television set owners in the community long before the broadband service is available. A few months after it is introduced, the researcher could return to the original sample, sort out the households that subscribed to broadband and those that did not, and then determine the effects of the service. In this case, there is no control over the independent variable (broadband service); the researcher is merely taking advantage of existing conditions.

Note that in some field experiments, the researcher is not able to assign subjects randomly to treatment groups. As a result, many field experiments are classified as quasi-experiments. As Cook and Campbell (1979)

point out, the extent to which causal statements can be made from the results of these studies depends on the ability to rule out alternative explanations. Consequently, researchers who use field experiments must pay close attention to threats to internal validity.

Examples of Field Experiments

Tan (1977) was interested in what people would do during a week without television. He recruited a sample of 51 adults and paid them each $4 a day not to watch television for an entire week. Before depriving these subjects of television, Tan requested that they watch television normally for a one-week period and keep a detailed diary of all their activities. At the start of the experimental week, Tan's assistants visited the subjects' homes and taped up the electrical plugs on their television sets to lessen temptation. Again, the subjects were requested to record their activities for the week. To maintain some control over the experiment, the assistants visited the subjects' homes periodically during the week to ensure that the television was not being viewed.

One week later, the diaries completed during the week of deprivation were collected, and the data were compared to the week of normal television viewing. Tan discovered that when deprived of television, subjects turned more to radio and newspapers for entertainment and information. They also tended to engage in more social activities with their friends and family.

This study illustrates some of the strengths and weaknesses of field experiments. In the first place, they are probably the only viable technique available to investigate this particular topic. A survey (see Chapter 7) does not permit the researcher to control whether the subjects watch television, and it would be impossible in the United States to select a representative sample composed of people who do not own a television set. Nor would it be feasible to bring people into the laboratory for an entire week of television deprivation.

On the other hand, the ability of the field researcher to control independent variables is not conclusively demonstrated here: Tan had no way to be sure that his sample subjects actually avoided television for the entire week. Subjects could have watched at friends' homes or at local bars, or even at home by untaping the plugs. Moreover, Tan mentioned that several individuals who fell into the initial sample refused to go without television for only $4 per day. As a result, the nonprobability sample did not accurately reflect the general makeup of the community.

Smith and Hand (1987) took advantage of a natural occurrence in their field experiment on the effects of viewing pornography. One XXX-rated film was shown every year at the small college that served as the site of the research. About one-third of all the male students on campus typically attended this film at its annual showing. One week before the film was shown, the investigators surveyed 230 female students of the college about their contact with aggression. The same measurement was taken on the Monday following the film and then again a week later. The researchers then analyzed the amount of violence experienced by females whose male companions had seen the film as compared to females whose male companions had not seen the film. The results showed no differences in the amount of violence experienced by the two groups of females.

This study represents one of the few times that the effects of exposure to pornographic films have been studied experimentally outside of the laboratory. Nonetheless, the study suffers from some common limitations of field experiments. First, the researchers were unable to make random assignments of sample subjects. Consequently, this study is more accurately described as a quasi-experiment. The males who went to the film may have been different from those who stayed away.

Second, the researchers had no control over the content of the film that was shown. The actual film may have been too mild to elicit much aggression. Third, the researchers could not control how many females or which particular females had contact with males who attended the movie. They were able to find only 38 of 230 whose companions saw the film. These 38 might not be typical of the rest of the population.

Williams and her colleagues (1986) conducted an elaborate field experiment on the impact of television on a community. In 1973, she was able to identify a Canadian town that, because of its peculiar geographic location, was unable to receive television. This particular town, however, was scheduled to acquire television service within a year. Given this lead time, the researchers could match the town with two others that were similar in population, area, income, transportation systems, education, and other variables. Residents of the three towns completed questionnaires that measured a large number of variables, including aggressive behavior, personality traits, reading ability, creativity, sex-role perceptions, intelligence, and vocabulary. Two years later, the research team went back to the three communities, and residents completed a posttest with questions that measured the same variables as before. The design of this field experiment is illustrated in Figure 9.12. Note that it is a variation of the quasi-experimental pretest–posttest nonequivalent control group design discussed earlier.

This field experiment provided a wealth of data. Among other things, the researchers found that the arrival of TV apparently slowed down the acquisition of reading skills, lowered attendance at outside social events,

Figure 9.12   Design of Canadian Field Experiment

Town	Time one	Time two
A	No TV reception	One TV channel
B	One TV channel	Two TV channels
C	Four TV channels	Four TV channels

fostered more stereotypical attitudes toward sex roles, and increased children's verbal and physical aggression.

Two rather ambitious field experiments were conducted by Milgram and Shotland (1973) with the cooperation of the CBS television network. The researchers arranged to have three versions of the then-popular television series *Medical Center* constructed. One version depicted antisocial behavior that was punished by a jail sentence; another portrayed antisocial behavior that went unpunished; and a third contained prosocial (favorable) behavior. The antisocial behavior consisted of scenes of a distraught young man smashing a plastic charity collection box and pocketing the money.

In the first experiment, the researchers used two methods to recruit subjects: Ads placed in New York City newspapers promised a free transistor radio to anyone willing to view a one-hour television show, and business reply cards containing the same message were passed out to pedestrians near several subway stops. Subjects were asked to report to a special television theater to view the program. Upon arrival, each person was randomly assigned to one of four groups, and each group was shown a different program (the three programs described earlier plus a different nonviolent show used as a control). After viewing the program (with no commercial interruptions) and completing a short questionnaire about it, the subjects were instructed to go to an office in a downtown building to receive their free radios.

The downtown office, monitored by hidden cameras, was part of the experiment. The office contained a plastic charity collection box with about $5 in it, and a notice informed the subjects that no more transistor radios were available. Their behavior on reading the notice was the dependent variable: How many would emulate the antisocial act seen in the program and take the money from the charity box? Milgram and Shotland found no differences in antisocial behavior among the groups of viewers; no one broke into the charity box.

The second study tried to gauge the immediate effects of televised antisocial acts on viewers. Subjects were recruited from the streets of New York City's Times Square area and ushered into a room with a color television set and a plastic charity collection box containing $4.45. Subjects viewed one of the *Medical Center* episodes described earlier. A hidden camera monitored the subjects' behavior, even though they were told that they would not be observed. Although this time some subjects broke into the box, once again no differences emerged between the groups.

These two studies demonstrate several positive and negative aspects of field experiments. In the first place, Milgram and Shotland had to secure the cooperation of CBS to conduct their expensive experiments. Second, volunteer subjects were used, and it is reasonable to assume that the sample was unrepresentative of the general population. Third, in the first experiment the researchers did not control for the amount of time that passed between viewing the program and arriving at the testing center. Some participants arrived 24 hours after watching *Medical Center*, whereas others came several days later. Clearly, the subjects' experiences during this interval may have influenced their responses. Finally, Milgram and Shotland reported that the second experiment had to be terminated early because some of the subjects started resorting to behavior that the researchers could not control. On the positive side, the first experiment clearly shows the potential of the field experiment to simulate natural conditions and to provide a nonreactive setting. Upon leaving the theater after seeing the program, subjects had no reason to believe that they would be participating in another phase of the research. Consequently, their behavior at the supposed gift center was probably genuine and not a reaction to the experimental situation.

The Milgram and Shotland studies also raise the important question of ethics in field experiments. Subjects were observed without their knowledge and apparently were never told about the real purpose of the study, or even that they were involved in a research study. Does the use of a hidden camera constitute an invasion of privacy? Does the experimental situation constitute entrapment? How about the subjects who stole the money from the charity box? Did they commit a crime? Field experiments can sometimes pose difficult ethical considerations, and these points *must be dealt with before the experiment is conducted*, not afterward, when harm may already have been inflicted on the subjects.

Two field experiments concerned the impact of media on politics. Donsbach, Brosius, and Mattenklott (1993) compared the perceptions of people who attended a political event in person with those of people who saw different versions of the same event on television. They concluded that participants in the event and those who saw the television coverage did not differ significantly in their perceptions of the event and the people involved. However, those who watched the TV versions were more likely to hold polarized opinions than those who had seen the event in person. Cappella and Jamieson (1994) conducted a field experiment that evaluated the effects of *adwatches*—analyses by some TV networks of misleading political

ads during the 1992 presidential election. The researchers recruited subjects from 12 cities across the country and paid respondents $10 per day for participating in the study—165 individuals provided useful data. Six groups of respondents were given videotapes that contained several news items and different versions of an adwatch report. The number of exposures per group was also manipulated. One group received a tape that contained only the news reports. All respondents were instructed to view the tapes at home. After exposure, each participant was asked questions about the tapes, including information about the particular adwatch he or she had viewed. Results showed that exposure to the adwatches had an impact on the perceived fairness and importance of the ad.

This study is another illustration of the complexity that can be involved in a field experiment. The experimental tapes were constructed with the cooperation of CNN, each research location had to have a research coordinator on site, participants had to be paid for their efforts, and so forth. In addition, it points out some of the difficulties in control and generalization. Respondents were volunteers; they might not be a representative sample of the total population. The researchers could not control exposure to other sources of political information. Some sensitization to the study's purpose might have occurred. Field experiments can go a long way toward providing more external validity, but substantial efforts can be involved in carrying out the study.

CONDUCTING EXPERIMENTS ONLINE

The Internet has created new possibilities in experimental research. So far, however, few mass communication researchers have taken advantage of this new approach. Psychologists have been more willing to explore the potential of online experiments. As of 2011, there were more than 100 psychological experiments online, including such projects as the psychological outcomes of playing video games and the impact of personality on decision making. (For examples of current online experiments, see the Web Experiment List: *www.wexlist.net/*.)

As more mass media researchers learn about the potential of Internet experiments, it is expected that the online experiment will be used more frequently in mass media research. This section will take a brief look at the advantages and disadvantages of online experiments, examine how to recruit subjects, and conclude with a look at the validity of Internet experiments.

Advantages and Disadvantages

Reips (2000) offers a succinct listing of the main advantages of Internet experiments:

- They offer access to a large and demographically diverse sample, including individuals who would not normally be part of a traditional laboratory experiment—for example, the elderly.

- Internet experiments make possible a potentially large sample size that improves statistical power.

- A subject can participate in an Internet experiment 24 hours a day, 7 days a week.

- The experimenter need not be present.

- Internet experiments may be less expensive because they don't require lab space, special equipment, or supervisory personnel.

- Online experiments provide more convenience for participants because the experiment goes to the subjects rather than the other way around. Subjects do not have to find certain buildings and wander down hallways looking for the right room.

- Internet experiments present no possibility of experimenter bias.

On the downside:

- There is a lack of experimental control over the circumstances in which the subject participates in the study.

- Some subjects may participate in the experiment more than once; that is, they may "cheat." (This is becoming less of a problem with various computer identification software.)

- Participants are self-selected, creating an unqualified volunteer sample, as mentioned in Chapter 4. Only those who are motivated and interested in the topic will participate.

- Questions from subjects regarding the instructions or methods are not possible. In the traditional lab experiment, an experimenter would be present to handle such queries.

- The potential for technical problems is greater for Internet experiments (for example, the website doesn't load properly, monitors are set for the wrong display mode, and so on).

- Because it's easy to terminate an online experiment, the dropout rate may be greater.

Recruiting Participants

Finding subjects for traditional experiments conducted at colleges and universities is typically not a problem. They are usually recruited from classes and offered some kind of incentive (for example, extra credit) for participation. In some psychology departments, participation in experiments might be part of a course requirement. However, Internet experiments offer challenges to the researcher when it comes to recruiting subjects.

Bailey, Foote, and Throckmorton (2000) discuss several ways that a researcher could recruit subjects. If a suitable email list of the target audience exists, an email message could be sent to some or all members of the list, inviting their participation. The researcher could also post a recruiting message on relevant news group sites. Another method might be placing a banner ad on relevant websites, assuming, of course, that the sites cooperate. Reips (2002) suggests using online panels, newsgroups, search engines, banners, and email lists. Yet another possibility is to recruit subjects offline. For example, in their study of reactions to news photos, Kim and Kelly (2010) recruited participants by posting messages to Internet bulletin boards and sending email messages to several social organizations listed by Google groups.

Another alternative involves indexing an experiment under various search engines. The researcher can add certain keyword "meta-tags" to make it more likely that the search engine will display the site in response to a search. In this circumstance, the recruit finds information about the experiment when searching for a related term. Finally, the researcher could place a link to the experiment on such sites as Psychological Research on the Net or the Web Experimental Psychology Lab.

Dealing with Dropouts

As mentioned earlier, it is easier for subjects in an online experiment to leave a study than it is for subjects in a lab environment. Reip (2002) offers two suggestions to minimize

---

A CLOSER LOOK

Practical Experiments on the Web: eBay

Millions of people have used the auction site eBay to buy and sell various items. An online experiment conducted by Gregg and Walczak (2008) illustrated how researchers can use eBay to study consumer behavior in real life.

The researchers hypothesized that web design can influence the success of an online auction. They created two different websites. One was labeled a "high-quality" site and included a picture of the product, a seller name with a professional image (Collegiate-Sales), a detailed product description, customer service policies and an aesthetically pleasing layout. On the other hand, the "low–quality" site had an identical picture of the item but a nonprofessional seller name (NotaPro2003), no product information, no customer service policies, and a plain design. The experimenters had judges evaluate the quality of the two websites, and raters agreed that the high-quality site was more desirable.

The researchers auctioned a number of electronic items (DVDs, jump drives, used zip drives), with each item appearing on both the high-quality and the low-quality pages. The starting price, starting date, and duration of the auctions were the same for both versions. The experiment took a year to complete.

The results showed that the quality of the website influenced a number of variables. The high-quality sites received their first bid more than a day earlier than the low-quality sites and wound up with more bidders and more bids. Items on the high-quality sites sold for an average of 17% more than the identical items on the low-quality sites. The authors note that in addition to the findings about high- and low-quality sites, the experiment "demonstrates the ability to use eBay as an experimental laboratory for testing hypotheses about purchasing behavior online."

dropouts. The *high hurdle* approach entails informing subjects upfront about possible adverse factors, including a long participation time, slow-loading web pages, and the possibility that subject identities might be traced. Presumably, subjects who continue on to the actual experiment are motivated enough to finish.

Research has indicated that most dropouts occur during the beginning of an online study. Consequently, in the *warm-up* technique, the experiment begins several web pages into the process. The first pages may contain practice trials, checks that the subjects are following instructions, or even pilot studies for subsequent experiments. In this situation, most dropout occurs before the actual experiment begins.

Validity of Online Experiments

Recall from Chapter 1 that there are two types of validity: internal and external. Internal validity permits researchers to rule out plausible but incorrect explanations of results. External validity pertains to how well the results of a study can be generalized across populations, settings, and time. Online experiments raise new challenges and possibilities in both areas.

One of the threats against internal validity mentioned in Chapter 1 is history—events that occur during a study might have an impact on its results. A traditional lab experiment might be completed in a few hours or days. An online experiment, however, may be posted for several weeks or even months, thus increasing the odds that history might play a role in the results. Experimental mortality, or dropout, is another threat. Subjects may drop out of the experiment before it is over. As mentioned, it is easier to drop out of an online experiment than in the traditional interpersonal lab setting, thus introducing another confounding factor to internal validity. On the other hand, the experimenter bias mentioned in Chapter 1 can be a factor in traditional experiments. This factor is absent in the online setting.

As for external validity, Internet experiments raise many of the same issues as online surveys (discussed in Chapter 7). One of the oldest criticisms leveled at much of the experimental research in the social sciences has been the limited nature of its external validity. As early as 1942, McNemar noted, "The existing science of human behavior is largely the science of the behavior of sophomores" (p. 333). Internet experiments have access to a more diverse pool of subjects (Reips, 2000). Further, now that more and more people are online, the Internet population is becoming more similar to the population as a whole. Mueller, Jacobsen, and Schwarzer (2000) argue that Internet samples are more representative of the "real world" than other common forms of data gathering. Fraley (2007) notes that much of current social psychological research conducted at universities is done with young, middle-class, and increasingly female samples. He argues that conducting an experiment on the Internet yields samples with a broader age range across several socioeconomic levels and usually has more male participants. In addition there are possible safeguards against multiple responses from a single subject (for example, limiting the number of responses from a single Internet protocol [IP] address).

Schmidt (1997) recommends that Internet researchers gather data about the demographics of their subjects to make judgments about the populations to which the results might be generalized. Moreover, several studies indicate that the results of web experiments are consistent with those obtained from traditional lab experiments (see, for example, Krantz and Dalal, 2000). In sum, greater external validity might be one of the biggest advantages of Internet experiments.

Reips (2002) argues that online experiments have ecological validity. Because the subjects in web experiments are generally in familiar, real-life surroundings, as opposed to a lab, the effects cannot be attributed to being in an unfamiliar setting.

In summary, a researcher needs to weigh the advantages and disadvantages of online experiments. If a researcher desires to study a population segment other than college students, the Internet experiment seems appropriate. Similarly, if tight control of the experimental setting is not a crucial element of the study, then an online experiment is a good alternative.

Turning to specific examples, Cho (2003) conducted an Internet experiment that looked at the impact of product involvement on clicking on a banner ad at a website. The researcher posted recruiting messages for the study on 165 listservs that dealt with advertising and marketing topics. Those who responded to the recruiting message were randomly assigned to one of the experimental groups. Cho was able to amass a sample of 751 participants, a sample size much greater than that of a typical traditional experiment. He found that those with high product involvement were significantly more likely to click on a banner than those with low involvement. Williams (2006) performed an experiment dealing with cultivation in the context of the online multiplayer game Asheron's Call. He recruited participants from message boards on game websites and randomly assigned them to a treatment and a control group. Those in the treatment group received a free copy of the game and were asked to record their game play for a month. At the end of a month, players in both groups were asked questions concerning the probability of being a victim of various crimes. The cultivation effect was found for situations that existed in the game world but not for other real-world crimes.

SUMMARY

Mass media researchers have a number of research designs from which to choose when analyzing a given topic. The laboratory experiment has been a staple in mass media research for several decades. Though criticized by many researchers as being artificial, the method offers a number of advantages that make it particularly useful to some researchers. Of specific importance is the researcher's ability to control the experimental situation and to manipulate experimental treatments.

This chapter also described the process of experimental design—the researcher's blueprint for conducting an experiment. The experimental design provides the steps the researcher will follow to accept or reject a hypothesis or research question. Some experimental designs are simple and take little time to perform; others involve many different groups and numerous treatments.

Quasi-experimental designs are used when random selection and random assignment of subjects are not possible. Field experiments take place in natural settings, which aids the generalizability of the results but introduces problems of control. The Internet represents a promising new area for experimental researchers.

Key Terms

Confounding
  variables
Cultivation effect
Debriefed
Double-blind
  technique
Experimental design
Factor
Factorial designs
Interrupted time
  series
Laboratory
  experiment

Latin square design
Manipulation check
Matching
Posttest-only control
  group
Pretest–posttest
  control group
Quasi-experiment
Randomization
Reactivity
Repeated-measures
  design

Solomon four-group design

Staged manipulation

Straightforward manipulation

 ## Using the Internet

1. To learn more about the topics mentioned in this chapter, search the Internet for *"experimental design," "Latin square design," "field experiments," "repeated-measures design"* and *"Internet experiments."*

2. See *http://allpsych.com/psychology101/experiment.html* for a good introduction to experimental methods.

3. The web page *www.experiment-resources.com/conducting-an-experiment.html* provides a user-friendly step-by-step guide on how to conduct an experiment.

Questions and Problems for Further Investigation

1. Develop four research questions or hypotheses for any mass media area. Which of the designs described in this chapter is best suited to investigate the problems?

2. What are the advantages and disadvantages of each of the following four experimental designs?

   a. $X \quad O_1$
      $\quad\quad O_2$

   b. $R \quad X \quad O_1$

   c. $R \quad O_1 \quad X \quad O_2$
      $R \quad X \quad O_3$

   d. $R \quad O_1 \quad X \quad O_2$

3. Which research questions are best answered by field experiments?

4. Which research questions are best answered by online experiments?

For additional resources, go to *www.wimmerdominick.com* and *www.cengagebrain.com.*

References and Suggested Readings

Babbie, E. R. (2010). *The practice of social research* (11th ed.). Belmont, CA: Wadsworth.

Bailey, R., Foote, W., & Throckmorton, B. (2000). Human sexual behavior: A comparison of college and Internet surveys. In M. Birnbaum (Ed.), *Psychological experiments on the Internet.* New York, NY: Academic Press.

Baran, S. B., Mok, J. J., Land, M., & Kang, T. Y. (1989). You are what you buy. *Journal of Communication, 39*(2), 46–55.

Bolls, P., & Muehling, D. (2007). The effects of dual-task processing in consumers' response to high-imagery and low-imagery radio advertisements. *Journal of Advertising, 36*(4), 35–48.

Bruning, J. L., & Kintz, B. L. (1997). *Computational handbook of statistics* (4th ed.). Chicago, IL: Scott, Foresman.

Campbell, D. T., & Stanley, J. C. (1963). *Experimental and quasi-experimental designs and research.* Skokie, IL: Rand McNally.

Cappella, J., & Jamieson, K. (1994). Broadcast adwatch effects. *Communication Research, 21*(3), 342–365.

Cho, C. (2003). The effectiveness of banner advertising. *Journalism & Mass Communication Quarterly, 80*(3), 623–645.

Cho, J., Shah, D., Nah, S., & Brossard, D. (2009). Split screens and spin rooms: Debate modality, post-debate coverage, and new video malaise. *Journal of Broadcasting & Electronic Media, 53*(2), 242–261.

Christensen, L. B. (2004). *Experimental methodology.* Boston, MA: Allyn & Bacon.

Cook, T. D., & Campbell, D. T. (1979). *Quasiexperimentation: Designs and analysis for field studies.* Skokie, IL: Rand McNally.

Donohew, L., Lorch, E. P., & Palmgreen, P. (1998). Applications of a theoretic model of information exposure to health interventions. *Human Communication Research, 24*(3), 454–468.

Donsbach, W., Brosius, H., & Mattenklott, A. (1993). How unique is the perspective of television? A field experiment. *Political Communication, 10*(1), 37–53.

Fraley, R. (2007). Using the Internet for personality research. In R. Robins, R. Fraley, & R. Krueger (Eds.), *Handbook of research methods in personality psychology* (pp. 130–148). New York, NY: Guilford.

Gilbert, K., & Schleuder, J. (1990). Effects of color and complexity in still photographs on mental effort and memory. *Journalism Quarterly, 67*(4), 749–756.

Gregg, D., & Walczak, S. (2008). Dressing your online business for success: An experiment comparing two eBay businesses. *MIS Quarterly, 32*(3), 653–670.

Hansen, C., & Hansen, R. (1990, December). Rock music videos and antisocial behavior. *Basic and Applied Social Psychology, 11,* 357–369.

Haskins, J. B. (1968). *How to evaluate mass communication.* New York, NY: Advertising Research Foundation.

Haskins, J. B. (1981). A precise notational system for planning and analysis. *Evaluation Review, 5*(1), 33–50.

Himmelweit, H., Oppenheim, A. N., & Vince, P. (1958). *Television and the child.* London: Oxford University Press.

Hoyt, J. L. (1977). Courtroom coverage: The effects of being televised. *Journal of Broadcasting, 21*(41), 487–496.

Kamhawi, R., & Weaver, D. (2003). Mass communication research trends from 1980 to 1999. *Journalism & Mass Communication Quarterly, 80*(1), 7–27.

Keppel, G., & Wickens, T. (2004). *Design and analysis: A researcher's handbook* (3rd ed.). Englewood Cliffs, NJ: Prentice Hall.

Kim, Y., & Kelly, J. (2010). Public reactions toward an ethical dilemma faced by photojournalists. *Journalism & Mass Communication Quarterly, 87*(1), 23–40.

Krantz, J., & Dalal, R. (2000). Validity of web-based psychological research. In M. Birnbaum (Ed.), *Psychological experiments on the Internet* (pp. 35–60). New York, NY: Academic Press.

McBurney, D. H. (1990). *Experimental psychology.* Belmont, CA: Wadsworth.

McGarva, A., Ramsey, M., & Shear, S. (2006). Effect of cell-phone use on driver aggression. *The Journal of Social Psychology, 146*(2), 133–146.

McNemar, Q. (1942). Opinion-attitude methodology. *Psychological Bulletin, 43,* 289–324.

Milgram, S., & Shotland, R. (1973). *Television and antisocial behavior.* New York, NY: Academic Press.

Miller, D. C. (2002). *Handbook of research design and social measurement* (5th ed.). White Plains, NY: Longman.

Montgomery, D. C. (2008). *Design and analysis of experiments.* New York, NY: John Wiley.

Mueller, J., Jacobsen, D., & Schwarzer, R. (2000). What are computing experiments good for? In M. Birnbaum (Ed.), *Psychological experiments on the Internet* (pp. 196–214). New York, NY: Academic Press.

Nunnally, J. C. (1994). *Psychometric theory* (3rd ed.). New York, NY: McGraw-Hill.

Reips, U. (2000). The web experiment method: Advantages, disadvantages, solutions. In M. Birnbaum (Ed.), *Psychological experiments on the Internet* (pp. 89–120). New York, NY: Academic Press.

Reips, U. (2002). Standards for Internet-based experimenting. *Experimental Psychology, 49*(4), 243–256.

Roscoe, J. T. (1975). *Fundamental research statistics for the behavioral sciences.* New York, NY: Holt, Rinehart & Winston.

Rosenberg, M. J. (1965). When dissonance fails: On eliminating evaluation apprehension from attitude measurement. *Journal of Personality and Social Psychology, 1,* 28–42.

Rosenthal, R. (1976). *Experimenter effects in behavioral research* (2nd ed.). New York, NY: Irvington.

Rosenthal, R., & Jacobson, L. (1966). Teacher's expectancies: Determinants of pupils' IQ gains. *Psychological Reports, 19,* 115–118.

Rosenthal, R., & Rosnow, R. L. (1969). *Artifact in behavioral research.* New York, NY: Academic Press.

Schmidt, W. (1997). World wide web survey research. *Behavior Research Methods, Instruments and Computers, 29,* 270–273

Smith, M. D., & Hand, C. (1987). The pornography/aggression linkage: Results from a field study. *Deviant Behavior, 8*(4), 389–400.

Tan, A. S. (1977). Why TV is missed: A functional analysis. *Journal of Broadcasting, 21,* 371–380.

Walizer, M. H., & Wienir, P. L. (1978). *Research methods and analysis: Searching for relationships.* New York, NY: Harper & Row.

Westley, B. H. (1989). The controlled experiment. In G. H. Stempel & B. H. Westley (Eds.), *Research methods in mass communication* (pp. 200–220). Englewood Cliffs, NJ: Prentice Hall.

Williams, D. (2006). Virtual cultivation: Online worlds, offline perceptions. *Journal of Communication, 56*(1), 69–87.

Williams, K. (2011). The effects of homophily, identification, and violent video games on players. *Mass Communication and Society, 14*(1), 3–24.

Williams, T. B. (1986). *The impact of television.* New York, NY: Academic Press.

# CHAPTER 10

INTRODUCTION TO STATISTICS

CHAPTER OUTLINE

Statistics are *mathematical methods to collect, organize, summarize, and analyze data.* Statistics cannot perform miracles. Statistics alone will not "correct" a misdirected, poorly phrased, or ambiguous research question or hypothesis, or a study that uses sloppy measurement and design and contains numerous errors. Statistics provide valid and reliable results only when the data collection and research methods follow established scientific procedures.

The science of statistics and the ease with which they can be used have changed dramatically since the development of computers. Only a few decades ago, researchers spent weeks or months performing hand-calculated statistical procedures—calculations that now take only seconds or minutes on a handheld calculator or personal computer. In addition, there are now dozens of excellent computer software programs and spreadsheets to calculate nearly any type of statistical test, all of which have simplified all types of statistical analysis.

Much of the groundwork for statistics was established in 1835 by Lambert Adolphe Quetelet ('kay-tuh-lay), a Belgian mathematician and astronomer, with his paper entitled *On Man and the Development of His Faculties.* In addition to other techniques, Quetelet developed the ideas behind the normal distribution and formed the basics of probability theory from preliminary work by French mathematician and physicist Pierre-Simon Laplace (la-'plas) and others. Quetelet's background is similar to that of others who were instrumental in the development of statistics. Almost all were Renaissance men involved in such disciplines as astronomy, mathematics, physics, and philosophy.

This chapter introduces descriptive statistics and some of the methods used in mass media research. We encourage you to consult other sources for more information.

DESCRIPTIVE STATISTICS

Descriptive statistics condense data sets to allow for easier interpretation. If a random sample of 100 people were asked how long they listened to the radio yesterday and all 100 answers were recorded on a sheet of paper, it would be difficult to draw conclusions by simply looking at that list. Analysis of this information is much easier if the data are organized in some meaningful way—the function of descriptive statistics. These statistical methods allow researchers to take random data and organize them into some type of order.

During a research study, investigators typically collect data consisting of measurements or observations of the people or items in a sample. These data usually have little meaning or usefulness until they are displayed or summarized using one of the techniques of descriptive statistics. Mass media researchers use two primary methods to make their data more manageable: data distributions and summary statistics.

Data Distributions

A **data distribution** is simply a collection of numbers. Table 10.1 shows a hypothetical distribution of 20 respondents' answers to the question, "How many hours did you spend in the past two days listening to the radio and watching TV?" While the distribution may appear adequate, it is difficult to draw any conclusions or to generalize from this collection of unordered scores.

As a preliminary step toward making these numbers more manageable, the data may be arranged in a **frequency distribution**—a table of the scores ordered according to magnitude and frequency of occurrence. Table 10.2 presents the data from the hypothetical radio/TV survey in a frequency distribution.

Now the data begin to show a pattern. Note that the typical frequency distribution

Table 10.1 Distribution of Responses to "How many hours did you spend in the past two days listening to the radio and watching TV?"

Respondent	Hours	Respondent	Hours
A	12	K	14
B	9	L	16
C	18	M	23
D	8	N	25
E	19	O	11
F	21	P	14
G	15	Q	12
H	8	R	19
I	11	S	21
J	6	T	11

Table 10.2 Frequency Distribution of Responses to "How many hours did you spend in the last two days listening to the radio and watching TV?"

Hours	Frequency ($N = 20$)
6	1
8	2
9	1
11	3
12	2
14	2
15	1
16	1
18	1
19	2
21	2
23	1
25	1

Table 10.3 Frequency Distribution of Radio and TV Listening and Viewing Hours Grouped in Intervals

Hours	Frequency
0–10	4
11–15	8
16–20	4
21–25	4

table includes two columns. The column on the left contains all the values of the variable under study; the column on the right shows the number of occurrences of each value. The sum of the frequency column is the number (N) of persons or items in the distribution.

A frequency distribution can also be constructed using grouped intervals, each of which contain several score levels. Table 10.3 shows the data from the hypothetical survey with the scores grouped together in intervals. This table is a more compact frequency distribution than Table 10.2, but the scores have lost their individual identity.

Other columns can be included in frequency distribution tables, such as proportions or percentages. To obtain the percentage of a response, divide the frequency of the individual responses by N, the total number of responses in the distribution. Percentages allow comparisons to be made between different frequency distributions that are based on different values of N.

Table 10.4 Frequency Distribution with Columns for Percentage, Cumulative Frequency, and Cumulative Frequency as a Percentage of N

Hours	Frequency	Percentage	cf	cf Percentage of N
6	1	5	1	5
8	2	10	3	15
9	1	5	4	20
11	3	15	7	35
12	2	10	9	45
14	2	10	11	55
15	1	5	12	60
16	1	5	13	65
18	1	5	14	70
19	2	10	16	80
21	2	10	18	90
23	1	5	19	95
25	1	5	20	100
	N = 20	100%		

Some frequency distributions include the **cumulative frequency** (*cf*), constructed by adding the number of scores in one interval to the number of scores in the intervals above it. Table 10.4 displays the frequency distribution from Table 10.2 with the addition of a percentage column, a cumulative frequency column, and a column showing cumulative frequency as a percentage of *N*.

Sometimes it is best to present data in graph form. The graphs shown in this section contain the same information as frequency distributions. Graphs usually consist of two perpendicular lines, the *x-axis,* or **abscissa** (horizontal), and the *y-axis,* or **ordinate** (vertical), and statisticians have developed

certain standards regarding graphic format. One common standard is to list the scores along the *x*-axis and the frequency or relative frequency along the *y*-axis. Thus, the height of a line or bar indicates the frequency of a score. One common form of graph is the **histogram,** or **bar chart,** where vertical bars represent frequencies. Figure 10.1 is a histogram constructed from the data in Table 10.1. Note that the scores on the *x*-axis are actually the scores (hours) listed from the lowest value to the highest; the *y*-axis shows the frequency of scores.

If a line is drawn from the midpoint of each interval at its peak along the *y*-axis to

Figure 10.1   Histogram of Radio Listening/TV Viewing

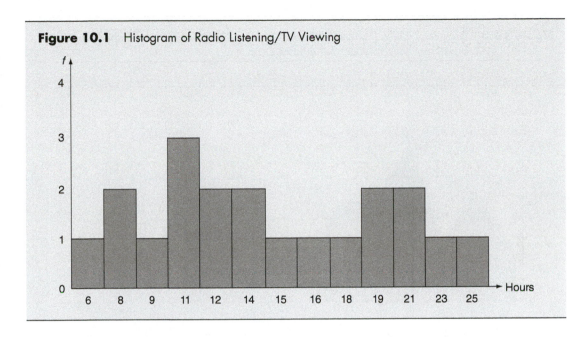

Figure 10.2   Frequency Polygon of Radio Listening/TV Viewing Hours Superimposed on a Histogram of the Same Data

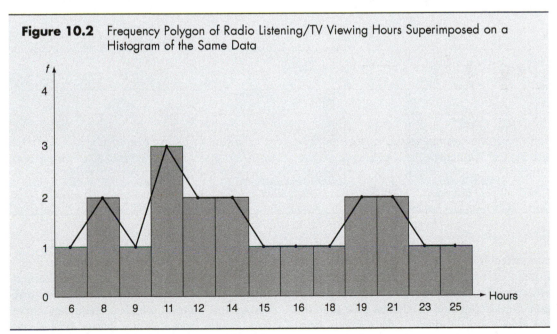

each adjacent midpoint/peak, the resulting graph is called a **frequency polygon**. Figure 10.2 shows a frequency polygon superimposed on the histogram from Figure 10.1.

As can be seen, the two figures display the same information.

A **frequency curve** is similar to a frequency polygon except that the points are

Figure 10.3   Frequency Curve (Shaded) of Radio Listening/TV Viewing Hours Superimposed on a Frequency Polygon of the Same Data

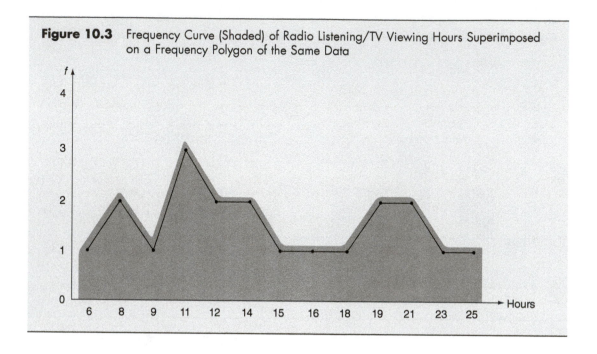

Figure 10.4   Skewness and the Normal Curve

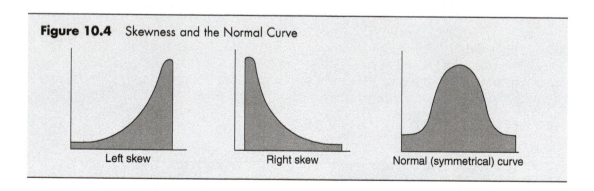

Left skew   Right skew   Normal (symmetrical) curve

connected by a continuous, unbroken curve instead of by lines. The curve assumes that any irregularities shown in a frequency polygon are simply due to chance and that the variable being studied is distributed continuously over the population. Figure 10.3 superimposes a frequency curve onto the frequency polygon shown in Figure 10.2.

Frequency curves are described in relation to the **normal curve**, a symmetrical bell-shaped curve whose properties are discussed more fully later in this chapter. Figure 10.4 illustrates the normal curve and shows the ways in which a frequency curve can deviate from it. These patterns of deviation are called skewness.

Skewness refers to the concentration of scores around a particular point on the x-axis. If this concentration lies toward the low end of the scale, with the tail of the curve

A CLOSER LOOK

Skewness

Although the word *skewness* is still a valid statistical term, the fact is that it is not used much in research. Instead, variations of the word *lean* are used. That is, researchers may say that the data lean one way or another, such as "The data lean to the younger demographic groups." (In other words, there are more younger respondents or subjects in the data distribution.)

trailing off to the right, the curve is called a *right skew*. Conversely, if the tail of the curve trails off to the left, it is a *left skew*. If the halves of the curve are identical, it is *symmetrical,* or normal.

A normal distribution of data is not skewed in either direction. If data produce a curve that deviates substantially from the normal curve, then the data may have to be transformed in some way (discussed later in this chapter) to achieve a more normal distribution.

Summary Statistics

The data in Table 10.1 can be condensed still further through the use of **summary statistics** that help make data more manageable by measuring two basic tendencies of distributions: central tendency and dispersion, or variability.

Central Tendency.   **Central tendency** statistics answer the question: What is a typical score? The statistics provide information about the grouping of the numbers in a distribution by giving a single number that characterizes the entire distribution. Exactly what constitutes a "typical" score depends on the level of measurement and how the data will be used.

For every distribution, three characteristic numbers can be identified. One is the **mode** (Mo), or the score or scores that occur most frequently. A calculation is usually not necessary to determine the mode; it is most often found by inspecting the distribution. For the data in Table 10.1, the mode is 11.

Table 10.5 The Mode as a Potentially Misleading Statistic

Score	F
70	2
35–69	0
34	1
33	1
32	1
31	1
30	1
29	1
28	1
27	1
26	1

Though easy to determine, the mode has some serious drawbacks as a descriptive statistic. The mode focuses attention on only one score, which can hide important facts about the data when considered alone. This is illustrated by the data in Table 10.5. The mode is 70, but the most striking feature about the numbers is the way they cluster around 30. Another serious drawback is that a distribution of scores can have more than one mode. When this happens, the mode does not provide an effective way of analyzing data.

A second summary statistic is the **median** (Mdn), which is the midpoint of a distribution—half of the scores lie above it and half lie below it. If the distribution has an odd number of scores, the median is the middle score; if there is an even number, the median is a hypothetical score halfway between the two middle scores. To determine the median, the scores are ordered from smallest to largest and the midpoint is identified by inspection. (The median is 14 in the sample data in Table 10.1.)

Consider another example for the median with nine scores:

0   2   2   5   ⑥   17   18   19   67

The median score is 6 because there are four scores above this number and four below it.

Now consider these 10 scores:

0 2 2 5 6   17 18 19 67 75
$$\uparrow$$
11.5

In this example, no score neatly bisects this distribution. To determine the median, the two middle scores must be added and divided by 2:

$$Mdn = \frac{6 + 17}{2} = 11.5$$

When several scores in the distribution are the same, computing the median becomes more complicated. See *Comprehending Behavioral Statistics* by Hurlburt (1998, p. 52) for a detailed description of how to compute the median when there are duplications of middle scores.

The third type of central tendency statistic is the **mean**. The mean represents the average of a set of scores and is probably the most familiar summary statistic. Mathematically speaking, we define the mean as *the sum of all scores, divided by N, the total number of scores.* Because the mean is used widely in both descriptive statistics and inferential statistics, it is described here in detail.

As a first step, some basic statistical notation is required:

X = any score in a series of scores
$\overline{X}$ = the mean (read "X bar"; M is also commonly used to denote the mean)
Σ = summation (symbol is Greek capital letter sigma)
N = the total number of scores in a distribution

Using these symbols, we can write the formula for the calculation of the mean as

$$\overline{X} = \frac{\Sigma X}{N}$$

This equation indicates that the mean is the sum of all scores (ΣX) divided by the total number of scores (N). From the data in Table 10.1, the mean is

$$\overline{X} = \frac{293}{20} = 14.65$$

If the data are contained in a frequency distribution, a slightly different formula is used to calculate the mean:

$$\overline{X} = \frac{\Sigma fx}{N}$$

In this case, x represents the midpoint of any given interval, and f is the frequency of that interval. Table 10.6 uses this formula to calculate the mean of the frequency distribution in Table 10.2.

Unlike the mode and the median, the mean takes all the values in the distribution into account, which makes it especially sensitive to **outliers** and **extreme outliers**. Outliers pull the mean toward their direction. For example, suppose Table 10.1 contained another response, from Respondent U, who reported 100 hours of radio and television use. The new mean would then be approximately 18.71, an increase of about 28% due to the addition of only one large number.

Table 10.6 Calculation of Mean from Frequency Distribution

Hours	Frequency	fx
6	1	6
8	2	16
9	1	9
11	3	33
12	2	24
14	2	28
15	1	15
16	1	16
18	1	18
19	2	38
21	2	42
23	1	23
25	1	25
	$N = 20$	$\Sigma fx = 293$

$$\overline{X} = \frac{293}{20} = 14.65$$

One way to look at the mean is that it could be assigned to each individual or element if the total were evenly distributed among all members of the sample. It is also the only measure of central tendency that can be defined algebraically. As we show later, this allows the mean to be used in a variety of situations. It also suggests that the data used to calculate the mean should be at the interval or ratio level (see Chapter 2).

Two factors must be considered in decisions about which of the three measures of central tendency to report for a given data set. First, the level of measurement used may determine the choice: If the data are at the nominal level, only the mode is

meaningful; with ordinal data, either the mode or the median may be used. All three measures are appropriate for interval and ratio data, however, and it may be desirable to report more than one.

Second, the purpose of the statistic is important. If the ultimate goal is to describe a set of data, the measure that is most typical of the distribution should be used. To illustrate, suppose the scores on a statistics exam are 100, 100, 100, 100, 0, and 0. To say that the mean grade is 67 does not accurately portray the distribution; the mode provides a more characteristic description.

Dispersion. A second type of descriptive statistic is used to measure **dispersion,** or variance. Measures of central tendency determine the typical score of a distribution; dispersion measures describe the way the scores are spread out about this central point. Dispersion measures can be particularly valuable in comparisons of different distributions. For example, suppose the average grades for two classes in research methods are the same, but one class has several excellent students and many poor students, and the other class has students who are all about average. A measure of dispersion must be used to reflect this difference. In many cases, a data set can be described adequately by simply reporting a measure of central tendency (usually the mean) and an index of dispersion.

The three measures of dispersion, or variation, are range, variance, and standard deviation. (Some statisticians include a fourth measure—sum of squares.) The simplest measure, **range** (R), is the difference between the highest and lowest scores in a distribution of scores. The formula used to calculate the range is

$$R = X_{hi} - X_{lo}$$

where X_{hi} is the highest score and X_{lo} is the lowest score. The range is sometimes reported simply as, for example, "the range among scores is 40."

Because the range uses only two scores out of the entire distribution, it is not particularly descriptive of the data set. In addition, the range often increases with the sample size because larger samples tend to include more extreme values (outliers). For these reasons, the range is seldom used in mass media research as the sole measure of dispersion.

A second measure, **variance**, is a mathematical index of the degree to which scores deviate (differ) from, or are at variance with, the mean. A small variance indicates that most of the scores in the distribution lie fairly close to the mean—the scores are very much the same; a large variance represents widely scattered scores. Therefore, variance is directly proportional to the degree of dispersion or difference among the group of scores.

To compute the variance of a distribution, the mean is first subtracted from each score; these *deviation scores* are then squared, and the squares are summed and divided by $N - 1$. Strictly speaking, this formula is used to find the variance of a sample of scores, where the sample variance is used to estimate the population variance. If a researcher is working with a population of scores, the denominator becomes N rather than $N - 1$. The formula for variance (usually symbolized as S^2, although many textbooks use a different notation) is:

$$S^2 = \frac{\Sigma(X - \overline{X})^2}{N - 1}$$

In many texts, the expression $(X - \overline{X})^2$ is symbolized by x^2. The numerator in this formula, $\Sigma(X - \overline{X})^2$, is called the *sum of squares*. Although this quantity is usually not reported as a descriptive statistic, the sum of squares is used to calculate several other statistics. An example using this variance formula is shown in Table 10.7.

Table 10.7 Calculation of Variance: $X =$ Score

X	$\overline{X}$	$(X - \overline{X})$	$(X - \overline{X})^2$
6	14.65	−8.65	74.8
8	14.65	−6.65	44.2
8	14.65	−6.65	44.2
9	14.65	−5.65	31.9
11	14.65	−3.65	13.3
11	14.65	−3.65	13.3
11	14.65	−3.65	13.3
12	14.65	−2.65	7.0
12	14.65	−2.65	7.0
14	14.65	−0.65	0.4
14	14.65	−0.65	0.4
15	14.65	0.35	0.1
16	14.65	1.35	1.8
18	14.65	3.35	10.2
19	14.65	4.35	18.9
19	14.65	4.35	18.9
21	14.65	6.35	40.3
21	14.65	6.35	40.3
23	14.65	8.35	69.7
25	14.65	10.35	107.1

$$S^2 = \frac{\Sigma(X - \overline{X})^2}{N - 1} = \frac{558}{19} = 29.4$$

This equation may not be the most convenient for calculating variance, especially if N is large. A simpler, equivalent formula is

$$S^2 = \frac{\Sigma X^2}{N} - \overline{X}^2$$

The expression ΣX^2 indicates to square each score and sum the squared scores. [Note that this is not the same as $\Sigma(X)^2$, which indicates to sum all the scores and then square the sum.]

Variance is a commonly used and highly valuable measure of dispersion. In fact, it is at the heart of one powerful technique, *analysis of variance* (see Chapter 12), which is widely used in inferential statistics. However, variance does have one minor inconvenience: It is expressed in terms of squared deviations from the mean rather than in terms of the original measurements. To obtain a measure of dispersion that is calibrated in the same units as the original data, it is necessary to take the *square root of the variance*. This quantity, called the **standard deviation**, is the third type of dispersion measure. The standard deviation is more meaningful than the variance because it is expressed in the same units as the measurement used to compute it.

To illustrate, assume that a research project involves a question on household income that produces a variance of $90,000—interpreted as 90,000 "squared dollars." Because the concept of "squared dollars" makes no sense, a researcher would choose to report the standard deviation: 300 "regular dollars" ($\sqrt{90,000} = 300$). Usually symbolized as S (or SD), standard deviation is computed using either of these formulas:

$$S = \sqrt{\frac{\Sigma(X - \overline{X})^2}{N - 1}}$$

$$S = \sqrt{\frac{\Sigma X^2}{N - 1} - \overline{X}^2}$$

Note that these two equations correspond to the two variance formulas given earlier. Standard deviation represents a specific distance a score is from the mean of a distribution. (Another way to consider standard deviation is to think of it as each element's "average difference" from the mean of the data set.)

The standard deviation is especially helpful in describing the results of standardized tests. For example, most modern intelligence tests have a mean of 100 and a standard deviation of 15. A person with a score of 115 is 1 standard deviation above the mean; a person with a score of 85 is 1 standard deviation below the mean.

The notions of variance and standard deviation are easier to understand if they are visualized. Figure 10.5 shows two sets of frequency curves. Which curve in each set has the larger S^2 and S?

By computing the mean and standard deviation of a set of scores or measurements, researchers can compute **standard scores** (*z-scores*) for any distribution of data. *z*-scores allow researchers to compare scores or measurements obtained from totally different methods; they allow for comparisons of "apples and oranges." This is possible because all *z*-score computations are based on the same metric; they all have a mean of 0 and a standard deviation of 1.

z-scores are useful and are easy to compute and interpret. They are probably one of the most widely used statistics in private-sector mass media research (see the "Readings" section on the authors' textbook website: *www.wimmerdominick.com*). The formula for computing *z*-scores is simply the score (X) minus the mean ($\overline{X}$), divided by the standard deviation (S):

$$z = \frac{X - \overline{X}}{S}$$

Interpretation is easy because each score represents how many standard deviation units a score, rating, or entity is above or below the mean of the data set.

The computation of *z*-scores and the ability to compare different measurements or methods can be demonstrated with a brief example. Suppose that two roommates are in different sections of a mass media research course. On a particular day, the two sections

Figure 10.5   Variance as Seen in Frequency Curves

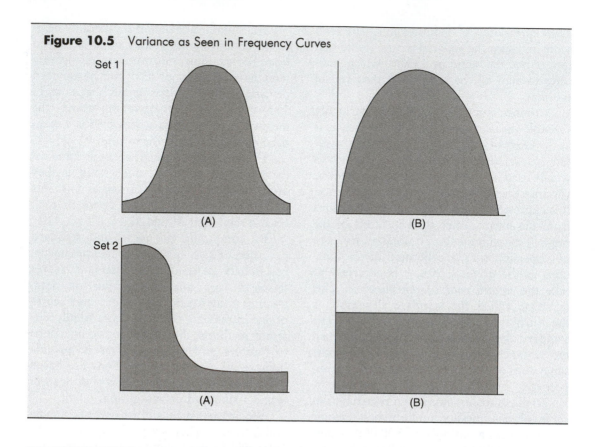

Set 1

(A)   (B)

Set 2

(A)   (B)

A CLOSER LOOK

z-Scores

Search the Internet for several examples of how *z*-scores are used in research: *z-scores research, z-scores prediction, z-score calculator,* and *z-scores research uses.* In addition,

see the "W-X-Z" questions in Roger Wimmer's "The Research Doctor Archive" for several questions and answers about *z*-scores (*www.wimmerdominick.com*).

are given different exams, and both students score 73. However, the first roommate receives a letter grade of C, whereas the second roommate gets an A. How can this be? To understand how the professors arrived at the different grades, it is necessary to look at each section's *z*-scores.

Table 10.8 shows the hypothetical data for the two research sections. Each section

contains 20 students. The scores in the first roommate's section range from a low of 68 to a high of 84 (range = 16), whereas the scores in the second roommate's section range from a low of 38 to a high of 73 (range = 35). The differences in scores could be due to a variety of things, including the difficulty of the tests, the ability of students in each section, and the teaching approach used by the professors.

Table 10.8   z-Score Hypothetical Data

	First Roommate's Section				Second Roommate's Section		
	Scores	(Computation)	z-Score	Scores	(Computation)	z-Score	
	84	$(84 - 74.6)/4.9 =$	1.9	73	$(73 - 43.9)/7.5 =$	3.9	A grade
B grade	81	$(81 - 74.6)/4.9 =$	1.3	50	$(50 - 43.9)/7.5 =$	0.8	
	81	$(81 - 74.6)/4.9 =$	1.3	50	$(50 - 43.9)/7.5 =$	0.8	
	79	$(79 - 74.6)/4.9 =$	0.9	47	$(47 - 43.9)/7.5 =$	0.4	
	79	$(79 - 74.6)/4.9 =$	0.9	46	$(46 - 43.9)/7.5 =$	0.3	
	79	$(79 - 74.6)/4.9 =$	0.9	45	$(45 - 43.9)/7.5 =$	0.2	
	78	$(78 - 74.6)/4.9 =$	0.7	43	$(43 - 43.9)/7.5 =$	−0.1	
	77	$(77 - 74.6)/4.9 =$	0.5	43	$(43 - 43.9)/7.5 =$	−0.1	
	77	$(77 - 74.6)/4.9 =$	0.5	42	$(42 - 43.9)/7.5 =$	−0.2	
C grade	75	$(75 - 74.6)/4.9 =$	0.1	41	$(41 - 43.9)/7.5 =$	−0.4	
	73	$(73 - 74.6)/4.9 =$	−0.3	41	$(41 - 43.9)/7.5 =$	−0.4	C grade
	71	$(71 - 74.6)/4.9 =$	−0.7	41	$(41 - 43.9)/7.5 =$	−0.4	
	71	$(71 - 74.6)/4.9 =$	−0.7	40	$(40 - 43.9)/7.5 =$	−0.5	
	71	$(71 - 74.6)/4.9 =$	−0.7	40	$(40 - 43.9)/7.5 =$	−0.5	
	70	$(70 - 74.6)/4.9 =$	−0.9	40	$(40 - 43.9)/7.5 =$	−0.5	
	70	$(70 - 74.6)/4.9 =$	−0.9	40	$(40 - 43.9)/7.5 =$	−0.5	
	70	$(70 - 74.6)/4.9 =$	−0.9	40	$(40 - 43.9)/7.5 =$	−0.5	
				39	$(39 - 43.9)/7.5 =$	−0.6	
	69	$(69 - 74.6)/4.9 =$	−1.1	38	$(38 - 43.9)/7.5 =$	−0.8	
D grade	68	$(68 - 74.6)/4.9 =$	−1.3	38	$(38 - 43.9)/7.5 =$	−0.8	
	68	$(68 - 74.6)/4.9 =$	−1.3				

Mean 74.6

S 4.9

Mean 43.9

S 7.5

The mean score in the first roommate's section is 74.6, with a standard deviation of 4.9 (43.9 and 7.5, respectively, in the other roommate's section). If we assume that the professors strictly followed the normal curve (discussed later in the chapter), it is easy to see why two scores of 73 can result in different grades. The first roommate's performance is about average in comparison to the other students in the section; the second roommate is clearly above the performance of the other students.

The distribution of scores in Table 10.8 is not normal (discussed later). In reality, the professors might transform (change to a different metric) the scores to produce a more normal distribution, or they might set grade cutoffs at other scores to spread the grades out. When any collection of raw scores is transformed into z-scores, the resulting distribution possesses certain characteristics. Any score below the mean becomes a *negative* z-score, and any score above the mean is *positive*. The mean of a distribution of z-scores is always 0, which is also the z-score assigned to a person whose raw score equals the mean. As mentioned, the variance and the standard deviation of a z-score distribution are always both 1.00. z-scores are expressed in units of the standard deviation; thus a z-score of 3.00 means that the score is 3 standard deviation units above the mean.

z-scores are used frequently in all types of research because they allow researchers to directly compare the performances of different subjects on tests using different measurements (assuming the distributions have similar shapes). Assume for a moment that the apple harvest in a certain year was 24 bushels per acre, compared to an average annual yield of 22 bushels per acre, with a standard deviation of 10. During the same year, the orange crop yielded 18 bushels per acre, compared to an average of 16 bushels, with a standard deviation of 8. Was it a better year for apples or for oranges? The

standard score formula reveals a z-score of .20 for apples $[(24 - 22)/10]$ and .25 for oranges $[(18 - 16)/8]$. Relatively speaking, oranges had a better year.

	Apples	Oranges
Average bushel yield	22	16
Standard deviation	10	8
Current bushel yield	24	18
z-score	.20	.25

The Normal Curve

An important tool in statistical analysis is the normal curve, which was introduced briefly in Chapter 4. z-scores enable comparisons to be made between dissimilar measurements and, when used in connection with the normal curve, also allow statements to be made regarding the frequency of occurrence of certain variables. Figure 10.6 shows an example of the typical normal curve. The curve is symmetrical and achieves its maximum height at the mean, which is also its median and its mode. Also note that the curve in Figure 10.6 is calibrated in standard score units. When the curve is expressed in this way, it is called a **standard normal curve** and has all the properties of a z-score distribution.

Statisticians have studied the normal curve closely to describe its properties, most of which are discussed in articles available on the Internet. The most important of these properties is that a fixed proportion of the area below the curve lies between the mean and any unit of standard deviation. The area under a certain segment of the curve represents the frequency of the scores that fall therein. From Figure 10.7, which portrays the areas under the normal curve between several key standard deviation units, it can be determined that roughly 68% of the total area (the scores) lies within -1 and $+1$ standard deviations from the mean; about 95% lies within -2 and $+2$ standard deviations; and so forth.

Figure 10.6   The Normal Curve

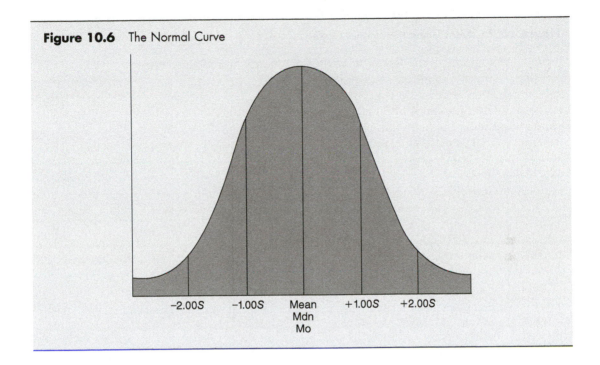

-2.00S   -1.00S   Mean   +1.00S   +2.00S
                        Mdn
                        Mo

This knowledge, together with the presence of a normal distribution, allows researchers to make useful predictive statements. For example, suppose that TV viewing is normally distributed with a mean of 2 hours per day and a standard deviation of 0.5. What proportion of the population watches between 2 and 2.5 hours of TV? First, we convert the raw scores to z-scores:

$$\frac{2-2}{0.5} = 0 \quad \text{and} \quad \frac{2.5-2}{0.5} = 1.00$$

In other words, the z-score for 2 hours of TV watching is 0; the z-score for 2.5 hours of TV watching is 1.00.

Figure 10.7 shows that approximately 34% of the area below the curve is contained between the mean and 1 standard deviation. Thus, about 34% of the population watches between 2 and 2.5 hours of television daily.

The same data can be used to find the proportion of the population that watches more than 3 hours of TV per day. Again,

the first step is to translate the raw figures into z-scores. In this case, 3 hours corresponds to a z-score of 2.00. A glance at Figure 10.7 shows that approximately 98% of the area under the curve falls below a score of 2.00 (50% in the left half of the curve plus about 48% from the mean to the 2.00 mark). Thus, only 2% of the population views more than 3 hours of TV daily.

Table 3 in Appendix 1 lists all the areas under the normal curve between the mean of the curve and some specified distance. To use this table, we match the row and the column represented by some standard score. For example, let's assume that the z-score of a normally distributed variable is 1.79. In Table 3, first find the row labeled 1.7 and then find the column labeled .09. At the intersection of the 1.7 row and the .09 column is the number .4633. The area between the mean of the curve (the midpoint) and a z-score of 1.79 is .4633, or roughly 46%. To take another example, what is the distance

Figure 10.7   Areas Under the Normal Curve

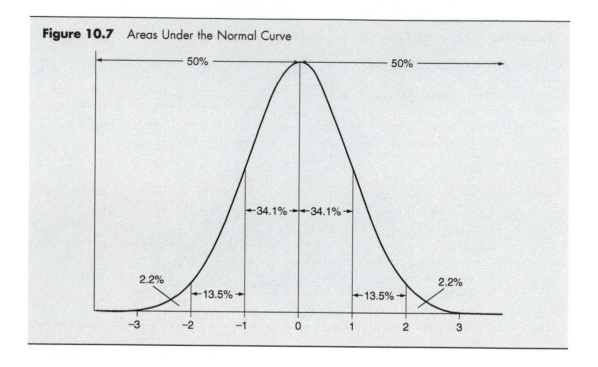

from the midpoint of the curve to the *z*-score of −1.32? According to Table 3, 40.66% of the curve lies between these two values. (In the left column, find 1.3; then go over to the column labeled .02.) Note that the area is always positive even though the *z*-score was expressed as a negative value.

To make this exercise more meaningful, let's go back to our example of the two roommates (see Table 10.8). Assume that the scores were normally distributed in the class that had a mean of 74.6 and a standard deviation of 4.9. The instructor decided to assign the letter grade C to the middle 50% of the class. What numerical scores would receive this grade? To begin, remember that "the middle 50% of the grades" actually means "25% above the mean and 25% below the mean." Which standard deviation unit corresponds to this distance? To answer this question, it is necessary to reverse the process just performed.

Specifically, the first thing that we must do is examine the body of Table 3 in Appendix 1 for the corresponding *z* value of .2500. Unfortunately, it does not appear. However, there are two percentages bracketing it: .2486 (*z* = .67) and .2517 (*z* = .68). Because .2486 is a little closer to .2500, let's use it as our area. Examining the row and column intersection at .2486, we find that it corresponds to 0.67 standard deviation units. We can now quickly calculate the test scores that receive Cs. First, we find the upper limit of the C range by taking the mean (74.6) and adding it to 0.67 × 4.9, or 3.28. This yields 77.88, which represents the quarter of the area above the mean. To find the lower limit of the range, we take the mean (74.6) and subtract from it 0.67 × 4.9, or 74.6 − 3.28. This gives us 71.32. After rounding, we find that all students who scored between 71 and 78 would receive the C grade.

A CLOSER LOOK

Statistical Computations

Virtually all of the statistical methods discussed in this book can be computed using a spreadsheet program, such as Microsoft's Excel. While many of the statistics are included in the software, many statistical procedures can be computed in Excel by using the steps provided in *Computational Handbook of Statistics* by Bruning and Kintz.

The normal curve is important because many of the variables encountered by mass media researchers are distributed in a normal manner, or normally enough that minor departures can be overlooked. Furthermore, the normal curve is an example of a probability distribution that is important in inferential statistics. Finally, many of the more advanced statistics discussed in later chapters assume normal distribution of the variable(s) under consideration.

Characteristic	Sample Statistic	Population Parameter
Average	$\overline{X}$ (or M)	μ (mu)
Variance	S^2	σ^2 (sigma squared)
Standard deviation	S (or SD)	σ (sigma)

SAMPLE DISTRIBUTION

A **sample distribution** is the distribution of some characteristic measured on the individuals or other units of analysis that were part of a sample. If a random sample of 1,500 college students is asked how many movies they attended in the last month, the resulting distribution of the variable "number of movies attended" is a sample distribution, with a mean (X) and variance (S^2). It is theoretically possible (though not practical) to ask the same question of every college student in the United States. This would create a **population distribution** with a mean (μ) and a variance (σ^2). *A statistic is a measure based on a sample, whereas a parameter is a measure taken from a population.* Ordinarily, the precise shape of the population distribution and the values of μ and σ^2 are unknown and are estimated from the sample. This estimate is called a **sampling distribution.**

In any sample drawn from a specified population, the mean of the sample, $\overline{X}$, probably differs somewhat from the population mean, μ. For example, suppose that the average number of movies seen by each college student in the United States during the past month was exactly 3.8. It is unlikely that a random sample of 10 students from this population would produce a mean of exactly 3.8. The amount that the sample mean differs from μ is called the *sampling error*. If more random samples of 10 were selected from this population, the values calculated for $\overline{X}$ that are close to the population mean would become more numerous than the values of $\overline{X}$ that are greatly different from μ. If this process were repeated an infinite number of times and each mean were placed on a frequency curve, the curve would form a sampling distribution.

Once the sampling distribution has been identified, statements about the *probability of occurrence* of certain values are possible. There are many ways to define the concept of probability. Stated simply, the probability that an event will occur is equal to the relative frequency of occurrence of that event in the population under consideration (Roscoe, 1975). To illustrate, suppose a large urn contains 1,000 marbles, of which 700 are red and 300 white. The probability of drawing a red marble at random is 700/1,000, or 70%. It is also possible to calculate probability when the relative frequency of occurrence of an event is determined theoretically. For example, what is the probability of randomly guessing the answer to a true/false question? One out of two, or 50%. What is the probability of guessing the right answer on a four-item multiple-choice question? One out of four, or 25%. Probabilities can range from 0 (no chance) to 1 (a sure thing). The sum of all the probable events in a population must equal 1.00, which is also the sum of the probabilities that an event will and will not occur. For instance, when a coin is tossed, the probability that it will land face up ("heads") is .50, and the probability that it will not land face up ("tails") is .50 (.50 + .50 = 1.00).

There are two important rules of probability. The "addition rule" states that the probability that any one of a set of mutually exclusive events will occur is the sum of the probabilities of the separate events. (Two events are mutually exclusive if the occurrence of one precludes the other. In the marble example, the color of the marble is either red or white; it cannot be both.) To illustrate the addition rule, consider a population in which 20% of the people read no magazines per month, 40% read only one, 20% read two, 10% read three, and 10% read four. What is the probability of selecting at random a person who reads at least two magazines per month? The answer is .40 (.20 + .10 + .10), the sum of the probabilities of the separate events.

The "multiplication rule" states that the probability of a combination of independent events occurring is the product of the separate probabilities of the events. (Two events are

independent when the occurrence of one has no effect on the other. For example, getting "tails" on the flip of a coin has no impact on the next flip.) To illustrate the multiplication rule, calculate the probability that an unprepared student will guess the correct answers to the first four questions on a true/false test. The answer is the product of the probabilities of each event: .5 (chance of guessing right on Question 1) × .5 (chance of guessing right on Question 2) × .5 (chance of guessing right on Question 3) × .5 (chance of guessing right on Question 4) = .0625.

Probability is important in inferential statistics because sampling distributions are a type of probability distribution. When the concept of probability is understood, a formal definition of "sampling distribution" is possible. A sampling distribution *is a probability distribution of all possible values of a statistic that would occur if all possible samples of a fixed size from a given population were taken.* For each outcome, the sampling distribution determines the probability of occurrence. For example, assume that a population consists of six college students. Their film viewing for the last month was as follows:

Student	Number of Films Seen
A	1
B	2
C	3
D	3
E	4
F	5

$$\mu = \frac{1+2+3+3+4+5}{6} = 3.00$$

Suppose a study is conducted using a sample of two ($N = 2$) from this population. As is evident, there is a limit to the number of combinations that can be generated, assuming that sampling is done without replacement (putting elements back into the population after they have already been selected). Table 10.9 shows the possible outcomes. The mean of this sampling distribution is equal to μ, the mean of the population. The likelihood of drawing a sample whose mean is 2.0 or 1.5 or any other value is found simply by reading the figure in the far right column.

Table 10.9 is an example of a sampling distribution determined by empirical means. Many sampling distributions, however, are not derived by mathematical calculations but are determined theoretically. For example, sampling distributions often take the form of a normal curve. When this is the case, the researcher can make use of everything that is known about the properties of the normal curve. Consider a hypothetical example using dichotomous data—data with only two possible values. (This type of data is chosen because it makes the mathematics less complicated. The same logic applies to continuous data, but the computations are elaborate.) A TV ratings firm is attempting to estimate from the results of a sample the total number of people in the population who saw a given program. One sample of 100 people might produce an estimate of 40%, a second an estimate of 42%, and a third an estimate of 39%. If, after a large number of samples have been taken, the results are expressed as a sampling distribution, probability theory predicts that it would have the shape of the normal curve with a mean equal to μ. This distribution is shown in Figure 10.8. It is interesting that if a person draws samples of size N repeatedly from a given population, the sampling distribution of the means of these samples, assuming N is large enough, will almost always be normal. This holds even if the population itself is not normally distributed. Furthermore, the mean of the sampling distribution will equal the population mean— the parameter.

In earlier discussions of the normal curve, the horizontal divisions along the base of the curve were expressed in terms of standard deviation units. With sampling distributions, this unit is called the **standard error of the**

Table 10.9 Generating a Sampling Distribution Population = (1,2,3,3,4,5) N = 2

$\overline{X}$	Number of possible sample combinations producing this $\overline{X}$	Probability of occurrence
1.5	2 (1,2) (2,1)	2/30 or .07
2.0	4 (1,3) (1,3) (3,1) (3,1)	4/30 or .13
2.5	6 (1,4) (2,3) (2,3) (3,2) (3,2) (4,1)	6/30 or .20
3.0	6 (1,5) (2,4) (3,3) (3,3) (4,2) (5,1)	6/30 or .20
3.5	6 (2,5) (3,4) (3,4) (4,3) (4,3) (5,2)	6/30 or .20
4.0	4 (3,5) (3,5) (5,3) (5,3)	4/30 or .13
4.5	2 (4,5) (5,4)	2/30 or .07
		1.00

Total number of possible sample combinations = 30

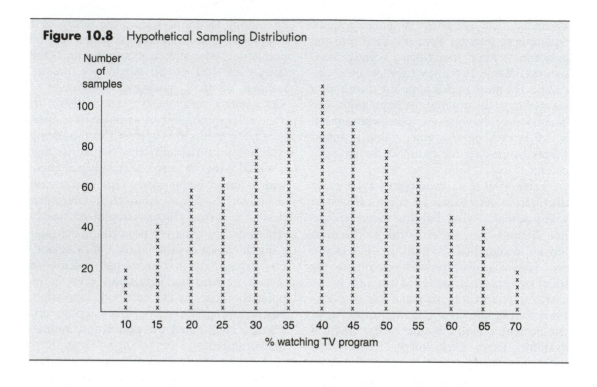

Figure 10.8   Hypothetical Sampling Distribution

mean (*SE*) and serves as the criterion for determining the probable accuracy of an estimate. As is the case with the normal curve, roughly 68% of the sample falls within ±1 standard error of the population mean, and about 95% falls within ±2 standard errors.

In most actual research studies, a sampling distribution is not generated by taking large numbers of samples and computing the probable outcome of each, and the standard error is not computed by taking the standard deviation of a sampling distribution of means. Instead, a researcher takes only one sample and uses it to estimate the population mean and the standard error. The process of inference from only one sample works in the following way: The sample mean is used as the best estimate of the population mean, and the standard error is calculated from the sample data. Suppose that in the foregoing TV viewing example, 40 of a sample of 100 people

were watching a particular program. This number, in this case symbolized as *p* because the data are dichotomous, is 40% (dichotomous data require this unique formula). The formula for standard error in a dichotomous situation is

$$SE = \sqrt{\frac{pq}{N}}$$

where *p* is the proportion viewing, $q = 1 - p$, and *N* is the number in the sample. In the example, the standard error at the 95% **confidence level** (corresponding *z*-score is 1.96) is

$$\sqrt{\frac{(.4)(.6)}{100}} \times 1.96 = \sqrt{\frac{.24}{100}} \times 1.96$$
$$= 0.96 \text{ or } 9.6\%$$

Standard error is used in conjunction with the **confidence interval** (*CI*) set by the researcher. Recall from Chapter 4 that a confidence interval establishes an interval in which researchers state, with a certain degree of probability, that the statistical result found will fall. In the previous example, this means that at the 68% confidence interval, 68% of all possible samples taken will fall within the interval of plus and minus one standard error, or 35.2 (40 − 4.8) and 44.8 (40 + 4.8), and at the 95% confidence level, 95% of all samples will fall between plus and minus 1.96 (*SE*) or 30.4 (40 − 9.6) and 49.6 (40 + 9.6). The most commonly used confidence level is .95, which is expressed by this formula:

$$.95CI = p \pm 1.96SE$$

where p is the proportion obtained in the sample, SE is the standard error, and 1.96 is the specific value to use for enclosing exactly 95% of the scores in a normal distribution.

As an example, consider that a television ratings firm sampled 400 people and found that 20% of the sample was watching a certain program. What is the .95 confidence interval estimate for the population mean? The standard error is equal to the square root of [(.20)(.80)]/400, or .02. Inserting this value into the formula previously presented yields a .95 confidence interval of .20 ± (1.96)(.02), or .16 − .24. In other words, there is a .95 chance that the population average lies between 16% and 24%. There is also a 5% chance of error that μ lies outside this interval. If this 5% chance is too great a risk, it is possible to compute a .99 confidence interval estimate by substituting 2.58 for 1.96 in the formula. (In the normal curve, 99% of all scores fall within ±2.58 standard errors of the mean.) For a discussion of confidence intervals using continuous data, consult Hays (1973).

The concept of sampling distribution is important to statistical inference. Confidence intervals represent only one way in which sampling distributions are used in inferential statistics. They are also important in hypothesis testing, where the probability of a specified sample result is determined under assumed population conditions.

DATA TRANSFORMATION

Most statistical procedures are based on the assumption that the data are normally distributed. Although many statistical procedures are "robust," or conservative, in their requirement of normally distributed data, in some instances the results of studies using data that show a high degree of skewness may be invalid. The data used for any study should be checked for normality, a procedure easily accomplished with most statistical software.

Most non-normal distributions are created by outliers. When such anomalies arise, researchers can attempt to transform the data to achieve normality. Basically, transformation involves performing some type of mathematical adjustment to each score to try to bring the outliers closer to the group mean. This may take the form of multiplying or dividing each score by a certain number, or even taking the square root or log of the scores.

It makes no difference which procedure is used (although some methods are more powerful than others), as long as the same procedure is applied to all the data. This is known as a **monotonic transformation** (see Table 10.10).

Transformation is a simple process and can be computed either in statistical software packages or on spreadsheets. Table 10.10 demonstrates how two transformations (square root and $\log_{10}$ of the original scores) "pull in" the outliers. The data remain the same as long as the same transformation is used for all scores. In other words, any statistical test conducted on the original scores

Table 10.10 Example of Monotonic Transformation

	Original score	Square root	Log$_{10}$
	98	9.9	1.99
	84	9.2	1.92
	82	9.1	1.91
	78	8.8	1.89
	75	8.7	1.88
	68	8.2	1.83
	61	7.8	1.79
	50	7.1	1.70
	48	6.9	1.68
	11	3.3	1.04
Mean	65.5	7.9	1.8
SD	24.6	1.9	0.3
High score	98	9.9	1.99
Low score	11	3.3	1.04

will have the same result if the square root or log$_{10}$ scores are used.

SUMMARY

This chapter introduced some of the more common descriptive and inferential statistics used by mass media researchers. Little attempt has been made to explain the mathematical derivations of the formulas and principles presented; rather, the emphasis here (as throughout the book) has been on understanding the reasoning behind these statistics and their applications. Unless researchers understand the logic underlying such concepts as mean, standard deviation, and standard error, the statistics themselves are of little value.

Key Terms

Abscissa
Bar chart
Central tendency
Confidence interval
Confidence level
Cumulative frequency
Data transformation
Descriptive statistics
Dispersion
Distribution
Extreme outlier
Frequency curve
Frequency distribution
Frequency polygon
Histogram
Mean
Median
Mode
Monotonic transformation
Normal curve
Ordinate
Outlier
Population distribution
Range
Sample distribution
Sampling distribution
Sigma
Skewness
Standard deviation
Standard error of the mean
Standard normal curve
Standard scores
Summary statistics
Variance
z-score

 Using the Internet

1. There are many excellent statistical software packages available—search the Internet for "*statistical methods,*" "*statistical tests,*" and "*statistics software packages.*" However, one of the most popular software packages is SPSS. A step-by-step explanation of SPSS is beyond the scope of this text. However, an excellent summary, *Learner's Guide to SPSS 11.0,* is available on Earl Babbie's website, located here: *http://www.wadsworth.com/ sociology_d/templates/student_resources/ 0534519040_babbie/primers/SPSS_11.0_ complete/index.html.*

2. Go to *http://nilesonline.com/stats* for a discussion of statistics used by journalists.

3. *z*-scores are used in several areas such as the stock market and banking. Search the Internet for "*z*-scores" for examples of how the statistic is used in nonmedia areas.

Questions and Problems for Further Investigation

1. Find the mean, variance, and standard deviation for these two sets of data (answers appear at the end of the exercises):

   Group 1:   5, 5, 5, 6, 7, 5, 4, 8, 4, 5, 8, 8, 7, 6, 3, 3, 2, 5, 4, 7

   Group 2:   19, 21, 22, 27, 16, 15, 18, 24, 26, 24, 22, 27, 16, 15, 18, 21, 20

2. From a regular deck of playing cards, what is the probability of randomly drawing an ace? An ace or a nine? A spade or a face card?

3. Assume that scores on the Mass Media History Test are normally distributed in the population with a μ of 50 and a population standard deviation of 5. What are the probabilities of these events?

   a. Someone picked at random has a score between 50 and 55.

   b. Someone picked at random scores 2 standard deviations above the mean.

   c. Someone picked at random has a score of 58 or higher.

4. Assume that a population of scores is 2, 4, 5, 5, 7, and 9. Generate the sampling distribution of the mean if $N = 2$ (sampling without replacement).

5. Confidence intervals and probability are discussed in a variety of places on the Internet and elsewhere. From the information you can find, how are the two concepts related?

   Answers to Question 1:

   Group 1: $\overline{X} = 5.35$, $S^2 = 3.08$, $S = 1.76$

   Group 2: $\overline{X} = 20.6$, $S^2 = 16.2$, $S = 4.0$

For additional resources, go to *www.wimmer dominick.com* and *www.cengagebrain.com*.

References and Suggested Readings

Blalock, H. M. (1972). *Social statistics*. New York, NY: McGraw-Hill.

Bruning, J. L., & Kintz, B. L. (1997). *Computational handbook of statistics* (4th ed.). New York, NY: Longman.

Champion, D. J. (1981). *Basic statistics for social research* (2nd ed.). New York, NY: Macmillan.

Hays, W. L. (1973). *Statistics for the social sciences*. New York, NY: Holt, Rinehart & Winston.

Hurlburt, R. T. (1998). *Comprehending behavioral statistics* (2nd ed.). Pacific Grove, CA: Brooks/Cole.

Jaccard, J., & Becker, M. A. (1996). *Statistics for the behavioral sciences* (3rd ed.). Belmont, CA: Wadsworth.

Lehmann, E. L. (2005). *Testing statistical hypotheses* (3rd ed.). New York, NY: Springer.

Maleske, R. T. (1995). *Foundations for gathering and interpreting behavioral data: An introduction to statistics*. Pacific Grove, CA: Brooks/Cole.

Mason, R. D., Lind, D. A., & Marchal, W. G. (1998). *Statistics: An introduction*. Belmont, CA: Duxbury.

Moore, D. S. (1998). *Introduction to the practice of statistics*. New York, NY: W. H. Freeman.

Nunnally, J. (1994). *Psychometric theory* (3rd ed.). New York, NY: McGraw-Hill.

Rasmussen, S. (1992). *An introduction to statistics with data analysis*. Pacific Grove, CA: Brooks/Cole.

Roscoe, J. T. (1975). *Fundamental research statistics for the behavioral sciences*. New York, NY: Holt, Rinehart & Winston.

Rummel, R. J. (1970). *Factor analysis*. Chicago, IL: Northwestern University Press.

Siegel, S. (1988). *Nonparametric statistics for the behavioral sciences*. New York, NY: McGraw-Hill.

Toothaker, L. E. (1996). *Introductory statistics for the behavioral sciences* (2nd ed.). Pacific Grove, CA: Brooks/Cole.

Williams, F., & Monge, P. R. (2001). *Reasoning with statistics: How to read quantitative research* (5th ed.). New York, NY: Harcourt.

CHAPTER 11

HYPOTHESIS TESTING

CHAPTER OUTLINE

Scientists rarely begin a research study without a problem or a question to test. That would be similar to holding a cross-country race without telling the runners where to start. Both events need an initial step: The cross-country race needs a starting line, and the research study needs a research question or hypothesis to test. This chapter describes the procedures for developing research questions and the steps involved in testing them.

RESEARCH QUESTIONS AND HYPOTHESES

Mass media researchers use a variety of approaches to answer questions. Some research is informal and seeks to solve relatively simple problems; some research is based on theory and requires formally worded questions. However, all researchers must start with some tentative generalization regarding a relationship between two or more variables. These generalizations may take two forms: *research questions* and *statistical hypotheses*. The two are identical except for the aspect of prediction—hypotheses predict an outcome; research questions do not.

Research Questions

Research questions are used frequently in problem- or policy-oriented studies where the researcher is not interested in testing the statistical significance of the findings. For example, researchers analyzing television program preferences or newspaper circulation may be concerned only with discovering general *indications*, not with gathering data for statistical testing. However, research questions can be tested for statistical significance. They are not merely weak hypotheses; they are valuable tools for many types of research.

Research questions are frequently used in areas that have been studied only marginally or not at all. Studies of this type are classified as **exploratory research** because researchers have no clear idea what they may find—they have no prior information to use for predictions. Legendary statistician John Tukey (1915–2000) suggested that exploratory research is intended to search for data *indications* rather than to attempt to find causality (Tukey, 1962, 1986). The goal is to gather *preliminary* data, to be able to refine research questions, and possibly to develop hypotheses—an approach often used by graduate students for theses and dissertations.

Research questions may be stated as simple questions about the relationship between two or more variables or about the components of a phenomenon. Tukey (1986) suggested that exploratory research responds to the question: What appears to be going on? For example, researchers might ask, "What are the characteristics of environmental reporters?" (Detjen, Fico, Li, & Kim, 2000) or "Do wire services differ in how they cover AIDS-HIV in different world regions?" (Bardhan, 2001). Walsh-Childers, Chance, and Swain (1999) posed several research questions about the way daily newspapers cover health care: (1) To what extent are health issues covered in daily newspapers relative to other topics? (2) How often does coverage include information about organization, delivery, and financing of health services? (3) Do major national and regional newspapers cover health issues differently than other newspapers?

Research Hypotheses

In many situations, researchers develop studies based on existing theory and are able to make predictions about the outcome of their work. Tukey (1986) said that **hypotheses** ask, "Do we have firm evidence that such-and-such is happening (has happened)?"

To facilitate the discussion of research testing, the remainder of this chapter uses only the word *hypothesis*. However, recall that research questions and hypotheses are

Benefits of Hypotheses
- Provide direction for a study
- Eliminate trial-and-error research
- Help rule out intervening and confounding variables
- Allow for quantification of variables

Criteria for Good Hypotheses
- Compatible with current knowledge
- Logically consistent
- Succinct
- Testable

identical except for the absence of the element of prediction in the former.

Purposes of Hypotheses

Hypotheses offer researchers a variety of benefits. First, they *provide direction for a study*. As indicated in the opening of the chapter, research that begins without hypotheses offers no starting point; there is no blueprint of the sequence of steps to follow. Hypothesis development is usually the conclusion of a rigorous literature review and emerges as a natural step in the research process. Without hypotheses, research lacks focus and clarity.

A second benefit of hypotheses is that they *eliminate trial-and-error research*—that is, the chaotic investigation of a topic in the hope of finding something significant. Hypothesis development requires researchers to isolate a specific area for study. Trial-and-error research is time consuming and wasteful. The development of hypotheses eliminates this waste.

Hypotheses also help *rule out intervening* and *confounding variables*. Because hypotheses focus research to precise testable statements, other variables, whether relevant or not, are excluded. For instance, researchers interested in determining how the media are

used to provide consumer information must develop a specific hypothesis stating which media are included, which products are being tested for which specific demographic groups, and so on. Through this process of narrowing, extraneous and intervening variables are eliminated or controlled. This does not mean that hypotheses eliminate all error in research; nothing can do that. Error in some form is present in every study.

Finally, hypotheses allow for quantification of variables. As stated in Chapter 2, any concept or phenomenon can be quantified if it is given an adequate operational definition. All terms used in hypotheses must have an operational definition. For example, to test the hypothesis "There is a significant difference between the recall of television commercials for subjects exposed to low-frequency broadcasts and that for subjects exposed to high-frequency broadcasts," researchers need operational definitions of *recall, low frequency*, and *high frequency*. Terms that cannot be quantified cannot be included in a hypothesis.

In addition, some concepts have a variety of definitions, such as *violence*. The complaint of many researchers is not that violence cannot be quantified, but rather that it can be operationally defined in more than

A CLOSER LOOK

Syllogism

A syllogism is a sequence of three propositions such that the first two propositions imply the third proposition, the conclusion. There are three major types of syllogism. The most common is the "hypothetical syllogism," which is demonstrated by the Stevie Wonder example that is included in the "Criteria for Useful Hypotheses" section. The hypothetical syllogism uses the first premise as a conditional hypothesis: If P then Q, if Q then R, (therefore) if P then R.

one way. Therefore, before comparisons are made among the results of studies of media violence, it is necessary to consider the definition of violence used in each study. Contradictory results may be due to the definitions used, not to the presence or absence of violence.

Criteria for Useful Hypotheses

A useful hypothesis must have at least four essential characteristics: It should be compatible with current knowledge in the area, it should be logically consistent, it should be stated concisely, and it should be testable.

That hypotheses must be in harmony with current knowledge is obvious. If available literature strongly suggests one point of view, researchers who develop hypotheses that oppose this knowledge without basis only slow the development of the area. For example, it has been demonstrated in several research studies that an increasing number of people are obtaining their news from the Internet, and has recently passed newspapers as a primary news source. It would be wasteful for a researcher to develop a hypothesis suggesting that this is not true. There is simply too much evidence to the contrary. (This is not to say that existing knowledge cannot be challenged; significant advances in science are made sometimes by doubting conventional wisdom, but researchers who do challenge existing knowledge should have a compelling reason to do so.)

The criterion of logical consistency means that if a hypothesis suggests that A = B and B = C, then A must also equal C. That is, if reading the *New York Times* implies a knowledge of current events, and a knowledge of current events means greater participation in social activities, then readers of the *New York Times* should exhibit greater participation in social activities. (Logical consistency relates to Aristotle's notion of *syllogism*, which produces such pop culture "logical consistencies" as: God is Love/Love is blind/[therefore] Stevie Wonder is God.)

It should come as no surprise that hypotheses must be stated as succinctly as possible. A hypothesis such as "Intellectual and psychomotor creativity possessed by an individual positively coincides with the level of intelligence of the individual as indicated by standardized evaluative procedures measuring intelligence" is not exactly concise. Stated simply, the same hypothesis could read, "Psychomotor ability and IQ are positively related."

Most researchers agree that developing an untestable hypothesis is unproductive, but there is a fine line between what is and what is not testable. We agree that untestable hypotheses will probably create a great deal of frustration, and the information collected and tested will probably add nothing to the development of knowledge. However, the situation here is similar to some teachers who say (and really mean) on the first day of class, "Don't ever be afraid to ask me a question because you think it is stupid. The only stupid question is the one that is not asked." We consider hypothesis development a similar situation. It is much better to form an untestable hypothesis than to form none at all. The developmental process itself is a valuable experience, and researchers will no doubt soon find their error. The untestable ("stupid") hypothesis may eventually become a respectable research project. Our suggestion is to try not to develop untestable hypotheses but to accept the fact when it happens, correct it, and move on. Beginning researchers should not try to solve the problems of the world. Take small steps.

What are some unrealistic and untestable hypotheses? Read the following list of hypotheses (some relate to areas other than mass media) and determine what is wrong with each one. Feldman (2006) was used in preparing some of these statements.

1. Watching too many soap operas on television creates antisocial behavior.

2. Clocks run clockwise because most people are right-handed.

3. High school students with no exposure to television earn higher grades than those who watch television.

4. Students who give teachers gifts tend to earn higher grades.

5. People who read newspapers wash their hands more frequently than those who do not read newspapers.

6. Movies rated XXX are 10 times worse than movies rated XX and 20 times worse than movies rated X.

7. College students who cut classes have more deceased relatives than students who attend classes.

8. Einstein's theory of relativity would not have been developed if he would have had access to television.

9. Sales of Ford automobiles in America would be higher if Lexus did not exist.

10. World opinion of the United States would be different if Barack Obama had never been the president.

The Null Hypothesis

The **null hypothesis** (also called the "hypothesis of no difference") asserts that the statistical differences or relationships discovered in an analysis are due to *chance* or *random error*. The null hypothesis (H_0) is the logical alternative to the research hypothesis (H_1). For example, the hypothesis "The level of attention paid to radio commercials is positively related to the amount of recall of the commercial" has its logical alternative (null hypothesis): "The level of attention paid to radio commercials is *not* related to the amount of recall of the commercial."

In practice, researchers rarely state the null hypothesis. Since every research hypothesis does have its logical alternative, stating the null form is redundant (Williams & Monge, 2001). However, the null hypothesis is always present and plays an important role in the rationale underlying hypothesis testing.

TESTING HYPOTHESES FOR STATISTICAL SIGNIFICANCE

In hypothesis testing, or significance testing, the researcher either rejects or accepts the null hypothesis. That is, if H_0 is accepted (supported), it is assumed that H_1 is rejected; and if H_0 is rejected, H_1 must be accepted.

To determine the statistical significance of a research study, the researcher must set a **probability** level, or **significance level**, against which the null hypothesis is tested. If the results of the study indicate a probability lower than this level, the researcher can reject the null hypothesis. If the research outcome has a high probability, the researcher must support (or, more precisely, fail to reject) the null hypothesis. In reality, since the null hypothesis is not generally stated, acceptance and rejection apply to the research hypothesis, not to the null hypothesis. The probability level is expressed by a lowercase letter p (indicating probability), followed by a "less than" or "less than or equal to" sign and then a value. For example, "$p \leq .01$" means that the null hypothesis is being tested at the .01 (1%) level of significance and that the results will be considered statistically significant if the probability is equal to or lower than this level. The level of significance also indicates the potential for error. For example, a .05 level of significance indicates that the researcher has a 5% chance of making a wrong decision about rejecting the null hypothesis (or accepting the research hypothesis). Establishing a level of significance depends on the amount of error researchers are willing to accept (in addition to other factors peculiar to the particular research study). The question of error is discussed in detail later in this chapter.

It is common practice in mass media research studies to set the probability level at .01 or .05, which means that either 1 or 5 times out of 100 significant results of the study occur because of random error or chance. There is no logical reason for using these figures; the practice has been followed for many years because Sir Ronald A. Fisher, who developed the concept of significance testing, formulated tables based on the areas under the normal curve defined by .01 and .05. In many research areas, however, researchers set the significance level according to the purpose of the study rather than by general convention. Some studies use .10 or .20, depending on the goals of the research, whereas many studies in the medical fields use levels of .0001 (1 in 10,000 chance that significant results of the study

occur because of random error or chance). In exploratory research especially, levels that are more liberal are generally used; these are made more restrictive as further information is gathered.

In a theoretical sampling distribution (a graphed display of sampling results), the proportion of the area in which the null hypothesis is rejected is called the **region of rejection**. This area is defined by the level of significance chosen by the researcher. If the .05 level of significance is used, then 5% of the sampling distribution becomes the critical region. Conversely, the null hypothesis is retained in the region between the two rejection values (or levels).

As Figure 11.1 shows, the regions of rejection are located in the tails, or outer edges, of the sampling distribution. The terms *one-tail testing* and *two-tail testing* refer to the type of prediction made in a research study. A **one-tail test** predicts that the results will fall in only one direction—either positive or negative. This approach is more stringent than the **two-tail test**, which does not predict a direction. Two-tail tests are generally used when little information is available about the research area. One-tail tests are used when researchers have knowledge of the area and are able to more accurately predict the outcome of the study.

For example, consider a study of the math competency of a group of subjects who receive a special learning treatment, possibly a series of television programs on mathematics. The hypothesis is that the group, after viewing the programs, will have scores on a standardized math test significantly different from those of the remainder of the population that has not seen the programs. The level of significance is set at .05, indicating that for the null hypothesis to be rejected, the mean test score of the sample must fall outside the boundaries in the normal distribution that are specified by the statement "$p \leq .05$." These boundaries, or values, are determined by a simple

Figure 11.1   Regions of Rejection for $p \leq .05$ (Two-Tail)

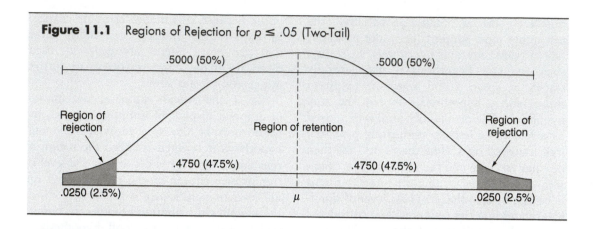

.5000 (50%)   .5000 (50%)

Region of rejection   Region of retention   Region of rejection

.4750 (47.5%)   .4750 (47.5%)

.0250 (2.5%) μ .0250 (2.5%)

computation. First, the critical values of the boundaries are found by consulting the normal distribution table (see Appendix 1, Table 3).

In Figure 11.1, the area from the middle of the distribution, or μ (mu, the hypothesized mean, denoted by the vertical broken line), to the end of the tails is 50%. At the .05 level, with a two-tail test, there is a 2.5% (.0250) area of rejection in each tail. Consequently, the area from the middle of the distribution to the region of rejection is equal to 47.5% (50% – 2.5% = 47.5%).

It follows that the corresponding z values that define the region of rejection are those that cut off 47.5% (.4750) of the area from μ to each end of the tail. To find this z value, use Table 3 of Appendix 1 (Areas Under the Normal Curve). This table provides a list of the proportions of various areas under the curve as measured from the midpoint of the curve out toward the tails. The far left column displays the first two digits of the z value. The row across the top of the table contains the third digit. For example, find the 1.0 row in the left column. Next, find the entry under the .08 column in this row. The table entry is .3599, meaning that 35.99% of the curve is found between the midpoint and a z value of 1.08. Of course, another 35.99% lies in the other direction, from the midpoint to a

z value of –1.08. In our current example, it is necessary to work backward. We know the areas under the curve that we want to define (.4750 to the left and right of μ), and we need to find the z values. An examination of the body of Table 3 shows that .4750 corresponds to a z value of ±1.96.

These values are then used to determine the region of rejection:

$$-1.96(\alpha_m) + \mu = \text{lower boundary}$$
$$+1.96(\alpha_m) + \mu = \text{upper boundary}$$

where α_m is the standard deviation of the distribution and μ is the population mean.

Assume that the population mean for math competency is 100 and the standard deviation is 15. Thus, the sample must achieve a mean math competency score lower than 70.60 or higher than 129.40 for the research study to be considered significant:

$$-1.96(15) + 100 = 70.60$$
$$+1.96(15) + 100 = 129.40$$

If a research study produces a result between 70.60 and 129.40, then the null hypothesis cannot be rejected; the instructional television programs had no significant effect on math levels. When we use the normal distribution to demonstrate these boundaries, the area of rejection is illustrated in Figure 11.2.

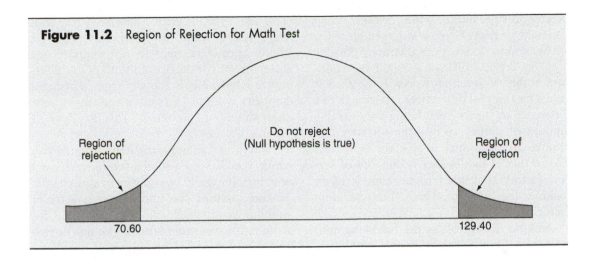

Figure 11.2   Region of Rejection for Math Test

Region of rejection

Do not reject
(Null hypothesis is true)

Region of rejection

70.60   129.40

The Importance of Significance

The concept of significance testing causes problems for many people, primarily because too many researchers overemphasize the importance of **statistical significance**. When researchers find that the results of a study are nonsignificant, it is common to downplay the results—to deemphasize the finding that the results were not statistically significant. But there is really no need to use this approach.

There is no difference in value between a study that finds statistically significant results and a study that does not. Both studies provide valuable information. Discovering that some variables are not significant is just as important as determining which variables are significant. A nonsignificant study can save time for other researchers working in the same area by ruling out worthless variables. Both significant and nonsignificant research studies are important in collecting information about a theory or concept.

Also, there is nothing wrong with the idea of proposing a null hypothesis as the research hypothesis. For example, a researcher could formulate this hypothesis: "There is no significant difference in comprehension of program content between a group

of adults (ages 18–49) with normal hearing that views a television program with closed-captioned phrases and a similar group that views the same program without captions." A scientific research study does not always have to test for significant relationships; it can also test for nonsignificance.

However, sloppy research techniques and faulty measurement procedures can add to error in a study and contribute to the failure to reject a hypothesis of no difference as well as jeopardize the entire study. This is a danger in using a null hypothesis as a substantive hypothesis.

Finally, it is important to remember that a statistically significant result is not necessarily a meaningful result. A significant statistical test simply tells the researcher that an observed result is probably not the result of chance or error. It is up to the researcher to determine whether that result has any social significance. For example, suppose a company is interested in buying a new software program that claims to improve keyboard skills. A researcher conducts an experiment where one group uses the software and the other does not. The keyboard skills of the two groups are then measured. Suppose the group using the software typed an average of 65 words per minute while the other group had a 63 average. Given a large sample and a small variance in scores, it is entirely possible that this 2-point difference might be significant at the .05 level. However, is the 2-point gain a meaningful difference? Is it enough of a difference to justify spending a considerable amount of money to buy the software and require all personnel to use the program? The statistical significance is only one of several factors that need to be considered in making the decision; it is not the only factor.

Salkind (2007) offers the following considerations when evaluating the importance of statistical significance:

- Significance is not very meaningful unless the study has a sound conceptual base that lends meaning to the results.

- Significance cannot be interpreted independently of the context in which it occurs.

- Significance should not be the end-all of all research. If a study is designed correctly, failing to reject the null hypothesis might be an important finding.

Error

As with all steps in the research process, testing for statistical significance involves error. Two types of error particularly relevant to hypothesis testing are called **Type I error** and **Type II error**. Type I error is the rejection of a null hypothesis that should be accepted, and Type II error is the acceptance of a null hypothesis that should be rejected. Whenever we conduct research, there is a chance that we'll get data that support our alternative hypothesis simply by luck or random accident, not because our alternative hypothesis is actually true. When this happens, we incorrectly reject a null hypothesis that actually should be retained (accepted).

This is Type I error. Similarly, random error could work the other way, and we could have data that do not support our alternative hypothesis even though our alternative hypothesis is actually true. When this happens, we fail to reject a null hypothesis that should be rejected. This is Type II error.

Maybe an analogy will help. Assume you think you have a problem with your car's steering and you take your car to a mechanic. Further, assume you know there is actually nothing wrong with your car's steering. Ultimately, the mechanic can tell you one of two things: (1) there is a problem with the steering or (2) there is no problem with the steering. If the mechanic says, "No problem," that is great because it is the correct decision. However, the mechanic might misread some test results and say, "There is a problem." This is an error. In this situation, we will have falsely rejected a true null hypothesis ("There is nothing wrong with the steering.") and committed a Type I error.

Now, suppose there really *is* something wrong with the steering. If the mechanic says, "You have a problem," that is great. That is a correct decision. But the mechanic may be having a bad day, or overlook some test results, and say, "There's no problem." This is an error. We have failed to reject a false null hypothesis. We have committed a Type II error. These error types are represented in Figure 11.3.

The probability of making a Type I error, often called *alpha error*, is equal to the established level of significance and is therefore under the direct control of the researcher. That is, to reduce the probability of Type I error, the researcher can simply set the level of significance closer to zero.

Type II error, often called *beta error*, is a bit more difficult to conceptualize. The researcher does not have direct control over Type II error; instead, Type II error is controlled, though indirectly, by the design of

Figure 11.3   Type I and Type II Errors

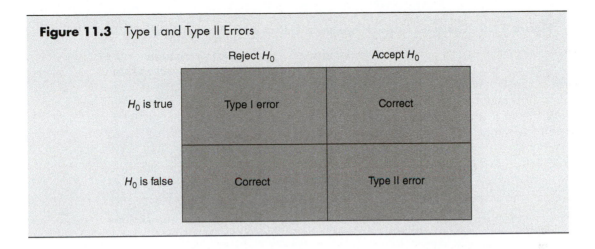

	Reject H_0	Accept H_0
H_0 is true	Type I error	Correct
H_0 is false	Correct	Type II error

Figure 11.4   Inverse Relationship Between Type I and Type II Errors

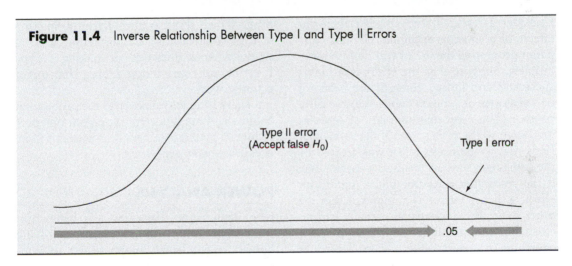

Type II error
(Accept false H_0)

Type I error

.05

the research. In addition, the level of Type II error is inversely proportional to the level of Type I error: As Type I error decreases, Type II error increases, and vice versa. The potential magnitude of Type II error depends in part on the probability level and in part on which of the possible alternative hypotheses actually is true. Figure 11.4 shows the inverse relationship between the two types of error.

As mentioned earlier, most research studies do not state the null hypothesis because it is assumed. However, there is a way to depict Type I and Type II errors without considering the null hypothesis, and this approach may help to demonstrate the relationship between Type I and Type II errors. As Figure 11.5 demonstrates, the research hypothesis is used to describe Type I and Type II errors instead of the null hypothesis. To use the table, start at the desired row on the left side and then read the column entry that completes the hypothesis to be tested. For example, "Significant difference found where none exists = Type I error" or "No significant difference found where one exists = Type II error."

Let's illustrate Type I and Type II errors one more time with a hypothetical example.

Figure 11.5   Use of the Research Hypothesis to Distinguish Between Type I and Type II Errors

	Where one exists	Where none exists
Significant difference found	Correct	Type I error
No significant difference found	Type II error	Correct

Consider a research study to determine the effects of a short-term public relations campaign promoting the use of seat belts in automobiles. Suppose that the effort was highly successful and indeed changed the behavior of a majority of subjects exposed to the campaign. (This information is, of course, unknown to the researcher.) If the researcher finds that a significant effect was created by the campaign, the conclusion is a correct one; if the researcher does not find a significant effect, a Type II error is committed. On the other hand, if the campaign actually had no effect but the researcher concludes that the campaign was successful, a Type I error is committed.

Balancing Type I and Type II Error

Although researchers would like to be right all the time, it is just not possible. There is always the possibility of making an error in rejecting or failing to reject a null hypothesis. Under these circumstances, researchers must evaluate the various consequences of making a Type I or a Type II error. There are different consequences for different decisions. Setting a significance level at .0001 will virtually eliminate Type I error but will dramatically increase the odds of Type II error. Suppose a researcher is testing the efficacy of a new

drug. Which result is more harmful: making a Type I error and claiming that a drug works when it does not, or making a Type II error and overlooking a drug that might actually work?

There is no easy answer to the problem of balancing these two error types, but one procedure to help researchers deal with this issue is called *power analysis*.

POWER ANALYSIS

One significant decision all behavioral researchers face with any study involving human respondents/subjects relates to sample size—How many respondents are needed to test or evaluate the question(s) under analysis? This is extremely important because a study that uses too few respondents may not be able to uncover significant differences among respondents or other significant findings. Psychologist Jacob Cohen (1923–1998) first addressed the question of sample size in 1960 and subsequently developed what is known as **statistical power analysis**, or simply **power analysis**. In brief, power analysis provides an estimate of the minimum number of respondents needed to provide the best chance to discover if something does or does not exist.

The concept of power is directly related to Type I and Type II errors. Cohen (1988) said that power indicates the probability that a statistical test of a null hypothesis will conclude that the phenomenon under study actually exists. There are a variety of power analysis computations for different statistical methods, and in every situation, a researcher wants to use a sample size and a statistical test that can detect if a phenomenon does exist.

To illustrate, let's go back to the steering problem and the mechanic example mentioned earlier. First, what are the consequences of a Type I and a Type II error in this situation? If your car's steering is *really* broken but your mechanic fails to identify it (Type II error), you might have an accident. On the other hand, if your steering is actually working properly and the mechanic mistakenly says it is broken (Type I error), the consequences are bad (you will pay for unnecessary repairs) but not as bad as having an accident. Obviously, if you really have a problem with your steering, you want a mechanic who will be able to discover it. Similarly, if there is a difference between two variables in a research project, you want a statistical method that is powerful enough to detect it.

Statistical power is a function of three parameters: probability level, sample size, and effects size. As we know, the probability level is under the direct control of the researcher and the level predetermines the probability of committing a Type I error. Sample size refers to the number of subjects used in an experiment. The most difficult concept is **effects size**. Basically, the effects size is the degree to which the null hypothesis is rejected; this can be stated either in general terms (such as any nonzero value) or in exact terms (such as .40). That is, when a null hypothesis is false, it is false to some degree; researchers can say the null hypothesis is false and leave it at that, or they can specify

exactly how false it is. The larger the effects size, the greater the degree to which the phenomenon under study is present (Cohen, 1988).

Researchers seldom know the exact value of the effects size, and in these cases, they can use one of three alternatives:

1. Estimate the effects size based on knowledge in the area of investigation or indications from previous studies in the area, or simply state the size as "small," "medium," or "large." (Cohen describes these values in greater detail.)

2. Assume an effects size of "medium."

3. Select a series of effects sizes and conduct several experiments.

The formula for the power of a statistical test is 1 − the probability of Type II error. When the probability level, sample size, and effects size are known, researchers can consult power tables to determine the level of power in their study. Power tables consist of sets of curves that represent different sample sizes, levels of significance (.05 etc.), and types of tests (one- or two-tail). For example, in a two-tail test with a probability of .05 and a sample size of 10, the probability of rejecting the null hypothesis (that is, assuming that it is false) is .37 and the probability of accepting or retaining the hypothesis is .63. Power tables show that by increasing the sample size to 20, the probability of rejecting the null hypothesis jumps to .62 and the probability of retaining the hypothesis drops to .38. Many researchers suggest that a desirable power value is .80 when working at the .05 level of significance. Researchers can find out what sample size will yield a power of .80 by consulting online power calculators or power curves.

Determining power is important for two reasons. First and most important, if a low power level prevents researchers from arriving at statistical significance, a Type II error may result. However, if the power of the statistical test is increased, the results may become significant. Second, the high power level may help interpret the research results. If an experiment just barely reaches the significance level but has high power, researchers can place more faith in the results. Without power figures, researchers must be more hesitant in their interpretations.

Statistical power should be considered in all research studies. Although power is only an approximation, computation of the value helps control Type II error. In addition, as power increases, there is no direct effect on Type I error; power acts independently of Type I error.

Finally, there are several power analysis calculators on the Internet, such as the SPSS version located at *www.spss.com/sample-power/index.htm.* For other calculators, search the Internet for *"power analysis calculator."*

EPA Statistical Primer

Interesting and relevant information can often be found in the most unlikely places. One such case is information about power analysis from the Environmental Protection Agency (EPA) website. One part of the EPA website is called the Statistical Primer, which includes a section on power analysis.

The following information is from the EPA's website (*www.epa.gov/bioiweb1/statprimer/power.html*), and the description provides a different perspective in explaining power analysis.

Statistical power is a function of the amount of change (or effect size) that you are trying to detect, the level of uncertainty you are willing to accept, the sample size, the variance of the indicator, and the statistical model you are using for testing.

$$\text{Power} = ES \times \alpha \times \sqrt{n/\sigma}$$

In words, this equation says, "Statistical power is proportional to the effect size multiplied by the alpha-level of the test, multiplied by the square root of the sample size, and divided by the standard deviation (square root of the variance)."

Effect size: The larger the difference you are trying to detect, the greater chance you will have of detecting it. This relationship is summarized in the preceding equation such that large values for the effect size also increase the power of the test.

Alpha (Type I error): If you are willing to get a false positive more often, you will be more likely to detect a change. In the preceding equation, a larger alpha translates into a greater statistical power. For power analysis, the alpha level is often relaxed from the traditional .05 to 0.10.

N: A larger sample size will increase the probability of detecting a change. Power increases with N.

Variance: The estimate of variance used in power calculations typically refers to measurement error associated with repeat sampling. Statistical power and variance are inversely related; when the variance goes up, the power goes down.

Keep in mind that the results of the power analysis depend on the statistical test being used. For example, a different number of samples will likely be needed to detect a 10% change for a regression model than for an analysis of variance (ANOVA) model.

SUMMARY

Hypothesis development in scientific research is important because the process refines and focuses the research by excluding extraneous variables and permitting variables to be quantified. Rarely will researchers conduct a project without developing some type of research question or hypothesis.

Research without this focus usually proves to be a waste of time (although some people may argue that many inventions, theories, and new pieces of information have been found without the focus provided by a research question or hypothesis).

An applicable hypothesis must be compatible with current related knowledge, and it must be logically consistent. It should also be stated as simply as possible and, generally speaking, it should be testable. Hypotheses must be tested for statistical significance. This testing involves error, particularly Type I and Type II error. Error must be considered in all research. An understanding of error, such as Type I and Type II does not make research foolproof, but it makes the process somewhat easier because researchers must pay closer attention to the elements involved in the project.

Often, too much emphasis is placed on significance testing. It is possible that a nonsignificant test will add information to an available body of knowledge simply by finding what "does not work" or "should not be investigated." However, some nonsignificant research projects may be more valuable if the statistical power is analyzed.

Key Terms

Effects size
Exploratory research
Hypothesis
Null hypothesis
One-tail and
   two-tail tests
Power analysis

Probability level
Region of rejection
Research question
Statistical power
Statistical significance
Type I and
   Type II error

 Using the Internet

The following are some examples of Internet searches you can run to find additional information about the topics discussed in this chapter.

- "hypothesis testing"
- "research questions" examples

- "hypothesis testing" methods
- "hypothesis testing" examples
- "null hypothesis"
- Type I and Type II errors
- "sample size calculator" and "sample size calculators"
- "sample size" research
- "power analysis" statistical
- "sample size" power
- "power analysis calculator" (there are several on the Internet)

Questions and Problems for Further Investigation

1. Develop three research questions and three hypotheses in any mass media area that could be investigated or tested.

2. What is your opinion about using levels of significance .10 or greater in exploratory research?

3. Conduct a brief review of published research in mass media. How many articles or publications report the results of a power analysis calculation?

4. Explain the relationship between Type I error and Type II error.

5. Under what circumstances might a mass media researcher use a probability level of .001?

6. If a researcher's significance level is set at $p \leq$ .02 and the results of the experiment indicate that the null hypothesis cannot be rejected, what is the probability of a Type I error?

For additional resources, go to *www.wimmer dominick.com* and *www.cengagebrain.com*.

References and Suggested Readings

Bardhan, N. (2001). Transnational AIDS-HIV news narratives. *Mass Communication & Society*, 4(3), 283–309.

Cohen, J. (1960). A coefficient of agreement for nominal scales. *Educational and Psychological Measurement*, 20, 37–46.

Cohen, J. (1962). The statistical power of abnormal-social psychological research: A review. *Journal of Abnormal and Social Psychology, 65*(3), 145–150.

Cohen, J. (1969). *Statistical power analysis for the behavioral sciences*. Hillsdale, NJ: Lawrence Erlbaum Associates.

Cohen, J. (1988). *Statistical power analysis for the behavioral sciences* (2nd ed.). Hillsdale, NJ: Lawrence Erlbaum Associates.

Cohen, J. (1992). A power primer. *Psychological Bulletin, 112*(1), 155–159. PDF reprint: *www. education.wisc.edu/elpa/academics/syllabi/2006/ 06Spring/825Borman/Cohen1992.pdf*

Detjen, J., Fico, F., Li, X., & Kim, Y. (2000). Changing work environment of environmental reporters. *Newspaper Research Journal, 21*(1), 2–12.

Feldman, D. (2006). *Why do clocks run clockwise?* New York, NY: Harper & Row.

Roscoe, J. T. (2004). *Fundamental research statistics for the behavioral sciences* (2nd ed.). New York, NY: Holt, Rinehart & Winston.

Salkind, N. (2007). *Statistics for people who think they hate statistics*. Thousand Oaks, CA: Sage.

Smith, B. (2010). *Making sense of statistics in research*. *http://nichcy.org/research/basics/makingsense*

StatSoft Electronic Statistics Textbook. *Power analysis. www.statsoft.com/textbook/power-analysis/*

Tukey, J. W. (1962). The future of data analysis. *Annals of Mathematical Statistics, 33*, 1–67.

Tukey, J. W. (1986). *The collected works of John W. Tukey* (Vols. III–IV). Belmont, CA: Wadsworth and Brooks/Cole.

Walsh-Childers, K., Chance, J., & Swain, K. (1999). Daily newspaper coverage of the organization, delivery and financing of health care. *Newspaper Research Journal, 20*(2), 2–22.

Williams, F., & Monge, P. (2001). *Reasoning with statistics: How to read quantitative statistics* (5th ed.). New York, NY: Harcourt, Rinehart & Winston.

Note: Several eBooks on the topic of statistics and testing statistical hypotheses are now available. Search the Internet to see the variety available.

# CHAPTER 12

BASIC STATISTICAL PROCEDURES

CHAPTER OUTLINE

Before we begin the discussion of statistics, we would like to address one question we hear repeatedly: "Why do I need to learn about statistics? It's boring." Well, boring as they may be, statistics are necessary when you follow the scientific method of research. To have valid and reliable results, any question—regardless of what it relates to—must be analyzed using some type of statistical method. If not, the results of the analysis will be based on the methods of intuition, tenacity, or authority, and we already know that results from these methods usually cannot be verified. We apologize if you're bored with statistics, but learning about them is a necessary evil. Statistics are how we advance our knowledge of everything, including our understanding of the mass media.

Researchers often wish to do more than merely describe a sample. In many cases researchers want to use their results to make inferences about the population from which the sample has been taken. Tukey (1986), in his typically nonpresumptuous manner, identifies four purposes of statistics:

1. To aid in summarization
2. To aid in "getting at what is going on"
3. To aid in extracting "information" from the data
4. To aid in communication

With these four purposes as a foundation, this chapter describes some of the basic inferential statistical methods used in mass media research and suggests ways in which these methods may help answer questions.

HISTORY OF SMALL-SAMPLE STATISTICS

Using a sample selected from the population or universe to investigate a problem or question has been common for many centuries. Documented use of sampling in scientific research is found as long ago as 1627, when Sir Francis Bacon published an account of tests he had conducted to measure wheat seed growth in various forms of fertilizer. In 1763, Arthur Young began a series of experiments to discover the most profitable method of farming, and in 1849 James Johnston published a book called *Experimental Agriculture*, in which he provided advice on scientific research (Cochran, 1976).

One influential investigator of the early twentieth century was William S. Gossett, who in 1908 attempted to quantify experimental results in a paper entitled *The Probable Error of the Mean*. Under the pen name Student, Gossett published the results of small-sample investigations he had conducted while working in a Dublin brewery. The *t*-distribution statistics Gossett developed were not widely accepted at the time; in fact, it took more than 15 years before other researchers took an interest in his work. However, the *t*-test, as will be seen, is now one of the most widely used statistical procedures in all areas of research.

British mathematician Sir Ronald Aylmer (R. A.) Fisher (1890–1962) provided a stepping stone from early work in statistics and sampling procedures to modern statistical inference techniques. Fisher introduced the idea of "likelihood"; that is, what is the *likelihood* that an event will occur. This idea provided the basis for developing statistical approaches to answer such questions. Fisher also developed the concept of probability and established the use of the .01 and .05 levels of probability testing (see Chapter 10). Until Fisher, statistical methods were not perceived as practical in areas other than agriculture, for which they were originally developed.

DEGREES OF FREEDOM

Before discussing basic statistical methods, it is important to understand a statistical term known as the **degrees of freedom** (*df*).

A CLOSER LOOK

Statistical Calculations

There are at least four basic ways to calculate the statistics mentioned in this chapter:

1. Do them by hand.
2. Use statistical calculators found online.
3. Use a spreadsheet such as Excel.
4. Use a statistical program such as SPSS.

Although we recognize that most students will not calculate statistics by hand, we think it is useful for students to see the basic logic behind the statistics. Therefore, we have provided formulas and simple examples to follow. Understanding how the numbers are used by the statistic will make it easier for students to make sense of the results of online statistical calculators and statistical packages, spreadsheets, and SPSS.

The concept involves subtracting a number, usually 1 or 2, from a sample (N or n), a group (K), a row (R), a column (C), or other subset designation, such as: N − 1, N − 2, K − 1, R − 1, and so on. For purposes of discussion, we will use N − 1 to represent all letter variations and number variations of degrees of freedom.

Sample size, or subset size (hereafter referred to only as sample size), is a fundamental component of virtually all statistical formulas—it is added to something, multiplied by something, or divided by something to arrive at a result. The understanding of the crucial importance of sample size led to the development of degrees of freedom.

Because degrees of freedom are relevant to virtually all statistical methods, it is important to understand what the concept actually means. However, the problem is that most definitions of degrees of freedom are confusing. For example, in most definitions, degrees of freedom is defined something like, "The number of elements free to vary," and is usually followed by an example, such as: "Assume we have five ratings on a 1–10 scale from five different respondents, and the sum of the five ratings is 32. If we know that one person's rating is 2, the four remaining ratings are free to vary (5 − 1 = 4 degrees of freedom) to account for the remaining 30 points." This means that since we know one of the five ratings is 2, the four remaining scores can be any score from 1 to 10, such as 6, 9, 8, 7 or 3, 9, 9, 9 or 6, 5, 9, 10—four ratings, or four degrees of freedom, are free to vary from 1 to 10.

While the use of the words *free to vary* in defining degrees of freedom may sound intriguing and has been used in the definition for nearly 100 years, the definition elicits this question: "So what? What effect does 'free to vary and N − 1' have on the data or the interpretation of the data?" This is an excellent question, and we will try to clarify the mystery. But first, we need a little history of the development of degrees of freedom.

Most statistics historians would probably agree that the concept of degrees of freedom was first developed by British mathematician Karl Pearson (1857–1936) around 1900 but was refined—or, more appropriately, corrected—by R. A. Fisher in an article published in 1922. Pearson and Fisher shared a hatred of being wrong (and also reportedly shared a hatred for each other), and in their quest for correctness, they realized that something was needed in statistical calculations to compensate for possible errors made in data collection, analysis, and interpretation. The fear of making an error is actually the foundation for the development of degrees of freedom.

In their work, Pearson and Fisher concentrated on creating statistics to use in analyzing data from a sample selected from a population so that the results could be generalized to the population. They knew early on the importance of sample size in statistics, and they also knew, as we have discussed, that no matter how many controls are established in a research study, there will always be some error involved in projecting the results from the sample to the population.

With the reality of ever-present error, Pearson developed, and Fisher refined, a method to account for the problem that was directly associated with sample size. However, as indicated, the main problem with the term *degrees of freedom* is similar to the problem with other statistics terms—the term itself is confusing. For example, students often have difficulty understanding the concept "standard deviation," but when we tell them the term basically means "average difference from the mean," the usual comment is something like, "Now I understand. Why didn't they say that in the first place?" *Degrees of freedom* falls into the same category—it is an ambiguous term. It is possible that if a different term were used, there wouldn't be as much confusion with the concept.

Recall that the philosophy behind degrees of freedom is very simple—fear of being wrong. Because most research studies analyze data from a sample where the results are projected to the population, there is a need to make a slight adjustment to the sample to compensate for errors made in data collection, analysis, and/or interpretation. This is because population parameters (the "real" data) are rarely, if ever, known to researchers. When calculating statistics for a sample, there is a need to have results that are somewhat conservative (corrected, adjusted) to compensate for any errors that may be present. A brief example should help.

Assume we have a sample of 10 respondents selected from a population. (The small sample is only for demonstrating the concept of degrees of freedom and would never be used in a legitimate research study.) The sample is asked to rate a new TV show on a 1–10 scale, where the higher the number, the more the respondent likes the show. The following table summarizes the computation of the standard deviation for the hypothetical sample. As a reminder, the formula for standard deviation is

$$S = \sqrt{\frac{\Sigma(X - \overline{X})^2}{N - 1}}$$

Table 12.1 shows that the mean rating for the 10 respondents is 5.8. The second column shows the deviation scores $(X - \overline{X})$, and the third column shows the squared deviation scores, which are used to produce the sum of squares used in the numerator of the standard deviation formula. Line A at the bottom of Table 12.1 shows the standard deviation for the 10 respondents using N in the denominator (referred to as *biased*) of the standard deviation formula—2.56. Line B shows the standard deviation with $N - 1$ in the denominator (referred to as *unbiased*) of the formula—2.70.

The difference of .14 (2.70 − 2.56) in the two standard deviations, while small, demonstrates that using $N - 1$ (degrees of freedom) in the denominator produces a slightly larger standard deviation than N alone. The larger standard deviation (with $N - 1$), which is a slightly more conservative estimate, compensates for the fact that the biased standard deviation formula (N in the denominator) may be too restrictive when the results are generalized to the population. This situation is true for every nonparametric and parametric statistic (discussed next) using $N - 1$ (or other variation) in its formula—the resulting computation will always be slightly larger (more conservative) because the sample size is reduced by at least 1, although the difference between the two calculations (N or $N - x$) gets smaller as sample size increases.

Table 12.1 Degrees of Freedom Example			
Respondent	Rating	x	x^2
1	4.0	−1.8	3.2
2	5.0	−0.8	0.6
3	3.0	−2.8	7.8
4	8.0	2.2	4.8
5	3.0	−2.8	7.8
6	9.0	3.2	10.2
7	9.0	3.2	10.2
8	7.0	1.2	1.4
9	2.0	−3.8	14.4
10	8.0	2.2	4.8
Mean	5.8		
Sum of squares			65.6
A. Standard deviation computed with N			2.56
B. Standard deviation computed with $N − 1$			2.70

As mentioned, the confusion surrounding degrees of freedom might be reduced if the concept had another name or definition. From our previous discussion, we can say that, in essence, the "key" to degrees of freedom is not that data are free to vary but rather that the concept relates to an adjustment made to data to provide a slightly more conservative estimate of the data to compensate for the possibility of errors in data collection, analysis, or interpretation. Therefore, our formally stated definition for *degrees of freedom* is:

An intentional and predetermined reduction in sample size to provide a conservative data adjustment to compensate for research error.

NONPARAMETRIC STATISTICS

Statistical methods are commonly divided into two broad categories: **parametric** and **nonparametric**. Historically, researchers have recognized three primary differences between parametric and nonparametric statistics:

1. Nonparametric statistics are appropriate with only nominal and ordinal data. Parametric statistics are appropriate for interval and ratio data.

2. Nonparametric results cannot be generalized to the population. Generalization is possible only with parametric statistics.

3. Nonparametric statistics make no assumption about normally distributed data, whereas parametric statistics assume normality. Nonparametric statistics are said to be "distribution-free."

For the most part, the distinctions in items 1 and 2 have vanished. We agree with most researchers who argue that both parametric statistics and nonparametric statistics can be used successfully with all types of data, and that both are appropriate for generalizing results to the population.

The following sections introduce some of the basic statistical procedures encountered by and used by mass media research. As we have stated before, this text is not a statistics text. For more information about any of these basic procedures, consult a statistics book or search for the specific methodology on the Internet.

Chi-Square Goodness of Fit

Mass media researchers often compare the observed frequencies of a phenomenon with the frequencies that might be expected or hypothesized. For example, assume a researcher wants to determine whether the sales of television sets by four manufacturers in the current year are the same as the sales during the previous year. A logical hypothesis might be: "Television set sales of four major manufacturers are significantly different this year from those of the previous year."

Suppose the previous year's television set sales were distributed as follows:

Manufacturer	Percentage of Sales
RCA	22
Sony	36
Sharp	19
Mitsubishi	23

From these previous year's sales, the researcher can calculate the expected frequencies (using a sample of 1,000) for each manufacturer's sales by multiplying the percentage of each company's sales by 1,000. These are the expected frequencies:

Manufacturer	Expected Frequency
RCA	220
Sony	360
Sharp	190
Mitsubishi	230

Next, the researcher surveys a random sample of 1,000 households known to have purchased one of the four manufacturers' television sets during the current year. The data from this survey provide the following information:

Manufacturer	Expected Frequency	Observed Frequency
RCA	220	180
Sony	360	330
Sharp	190	220
Mitsubishi	230	270

The researcher now must interpret these data to determine whether the change in frequency is actually significant. This can be done by reducing the data to a chi-square statistic and performing a test known as the chi-square "goodness of fit" test.

A **chi-square** (X^2) is simply a value that shows the relationship between expected frequencies and observed frequencies. It is computed by this formula:

$$X^2 = \Sigma \frac{(O_i - E_i)^2}{E_i}$$

where O_i is the observed frequencies and E_i is the expected frequencies. This means that the difference between each expected and observed frequency must be squared and then divided by the expected frequency. The sum of the quotients is the **chi-square** for those frequencies. For the frequency distribution just shown, chi-square is calculated as follows:

$$X^2 = \frac{(O_1 - E_1)^2}{E_1} + \frac{(O_2 - E_2)^2}{E_2}$$
$$+ \frac{(O_3 - E_3)^2}{E_3} + \frac{(O_4 - E_4)^2}{E_4}$$
$$= \frac{(180 - 220)^2}{220} + \frac{(330 - 360)^2}{360}$$
$$+ \frac{(220 - 190)^2}{190} + \frac{(270 - 230)^2}{230}$$
$$= \frac{(-40)^2}{220} + \frac{(-30)^2}{360} + \frac{(30)^2}{190} + \frac{(40)^2}{230}$$
$$= \frac{(1600)}{220} + \frac{(900)}{360} + \frac{(900)}{190} + \frac{(1600)}{230}$$
$$= 7.27 + 2.50 + 4.73 + 6.95$$
$$= 21.45$$

Once the chi-square value is known, the goodness-of-fit test determines whether this value represents a significant difference in frequencies. The test requires two values:

the probability level and the **degrees of freedom**.

In the goodness-of-fit test, degrees of freedom are expressed in terms of $K - 1$ where K is the number of categories. In the television sales study, $K = 4 - 1 = 3$. Next, a chi-square significance table is consulted (see Appendix 1, Table 4). These tables are arranged by probability level and degrees of freedom. A portion of the chi-square table relevant to the hypothetical study is reproduced here to show how the table is used:

		Probability		
df	.10	.05	.01	.001
1	2.706	3.841	6.635	10.827
2	4.605	5.991	9.210	13.815
3	6.251	7.815	11.345	16.266
4	7.779	9.488	13.277	18.467

If the calculated chi-square value equals or exceeds the value found in the table, the differences in the observed frequencies are considered to be statistically significant at the predetermined alpha level; if the calculated value is smaller, the results are nonsignificant.

In the television sales example, suppose the researcher finds a chi-square value of 21.45, with degrees of freedom of 3, and has established a probability level of .05. The chi-square table shows a value of 7.815 at this level when $df = 3$. Because 21.45 is greater than 7.815, the difference is significant, and the hypothesis is accepted (supported): Television set sales of the four manufacturers are significantly different in the current year from sales in the previous year.

The chi-square goodness-of-fit test can be used in a variety of ways to measure changes. Researchers might use them, for example, to study audience perceptions of advertising messages over time, to plan changes in television programming, and to analyze the results of public relations campaigns.

There are limitations to the use of the goodness-of-fit test. Because it is a nonparametric statistical procedure, the variables must be measured at the nominal or ordinal level. The categories must be mutually exclusive, and each observation in each category must be independent from all others. Additionally, because the chi-square distribution is sharply skewed (see Chapter 10) for small samples, Type II errors (see Chapter 11) may occur: Small samples may not produce significant results in cases that could have yielded significant results if a larger sample had been used. To avoid this problem, most researchers suggest that each category contain at least five observations. Other researchers suggest that 20% of the cells should have an expected frequency of at least 5, and none should have expected frequencies of 0.

As an alternative to the chi-square goodness-of-fit test, some researchers prefer the Kolmogorov–Smirnov test, which is considered more powerful than the chi-square approach. In addition, a minimum number of expected frequencies in each cell, as in the chi-square, is not required.

Contingency Table Analysis

Another nonparametric procedure used in mass media research is the **contingency table** analysis, frequently called **cross-tabulation**, or simply **crosstabs**. Crosstab analysis is an extension of the goodness-of-fit test. The primary difference is that two or more variables can be tested simultaneously. Consider a study to determine the relationship between gender and use of the media to obtain information on new products. Suppose a researcher selects a random sample of 210 adults and obtains the information displayed in Figure 12.1.

The next step is to calculate the expected frequencies for each cell. This procedure is

Figure 12.1 Description of Random Sample of Media Users in Study of Sources of New Product

Media Most Used for New Product Information

	Radio	Newspapers	Television	
Male	3	26	71	100
Female	18	31	61	110
	21	57	132	

Sex (row label)

similar to that used in the goodness-of-fit test, but it involves a slightly more detailed formula:

$$E_{ij} = \frac{R_i C_j}{N}$$

where E_{ij} is the expected frequency for the cell in row i, column j; R_i is the sum of frequencies in row i; C_j is the sum of frequencies in column j; and N is the sum of frequencies for all cells. Using this formula, the researcher in the hypothetical example can calculate the expected frequencies:

$$\text{Male/radio} = \frac{100 \times 21}{210} = \frac{2,100}{210} = 10$$

$$\text{Female/radio} = \frac{110 \times 21}{210} = \frac{2,310}{210} = 11$$

and so forth. Each expected frequency is placed in a small square in the upper right corner of the appropriate cell, as illustrated in Figure 12.2.

After the expected frequencies have been calculated, the investigator must compute the chi-square using this formula:

$$X^2 = \Sigma \frac{(O_{ij} - E_{ij})^2}{E_{ij}}$$

With the same example:

$$X^2 = \frac{(3 - 10)^2}{10} + \frac{(26 - 27)^2}{27}$$

$$+ \frac{(71 - 63)^2}{63} + \frac{(18 - 11)^2}{11}$$

$$+ \frac{(31 - 30)^2}{30} + \frac{(61 - 69)^2}{69}$$

$$= \frac{49}{10} + \frac{1}{27} + \frac{64}{63} + \frac{49}{11} + \frac{1}{30} + \frac{64}{69}$$

$$= 4.90 + 0.04 + 1.01 + 4.45 + 0.03$$

$$+0.92$$

$$= 11.35$$

To determine statistical significance, it is necessary to consult the chi-square table. In a crosstab analysis, the degrees of freedom are expressed as $(R - 1)(C - 1)$, where R is the number of rows and C is the number of columns. If $p \leq .05$, the chi-square value listed in Table 4 of Appendix 1 is 5.991, which is lower than the calculated value of 11.35. Therefore, there is a significant relationship between gender and the media used to acquire new product information. The test indicates that the two variables are somehow related, but it does not tell exactly how. To find this out, we need to go back and examine the original crosstab data in Figure 12.1. According to

Figure 12.2 Random Sample of Media Users Showing Expected Frequencies

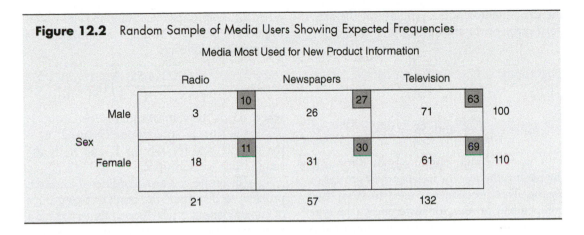

Media Most Used for New Product Information

	Radio	Newspapers	Television	
Male	3 [10]	26 [27]	71 [63]	100
Female	18 [11]	31 [30]	61 [69]	110
	21	57	132	

(Sex on left axis)

the distribution, it is easy to see that radio use is higher among females than males.

For a 2 × 2 crosstab (where $df = 1$), computational effort is saved when the corresponding cells are represented by the letters A, B, C, and D, such as:

A	B
C	D

The following formula can then be used to compute chi-square:

$$X^2 \frac{N(AD - BC)^2}{(A + B)(C + D)(A + C)(B + D)}$$

Crosstab analysis is used frequently in mass media research and can be conducted on almost any computer statistics package.

PARAMETRIC STATISTICS

The sections that follow discuss the parametric statistical methods usually used with interval and ratio data. Recall that these methods assume that data are normally distributed. The most basic parametric statistic is the t-test, a procedure widely used in all areas of mass media research.

The *t*-Test

Many research studies test two groups of subjects: One group receives some type of treatment, and the other serves as the control group. After the treatment has been administered, both groups are tested, and the results are compared to determine whether a statistically significant difference exists between the groups. In other words, did the treatment have an effect on the results of the test? In cases such as this, the mean score for each group is compared with a t-test. The Internet provides a variety of t-test calculators, or see Bruning and Kintz (1997) for a step-by-step t-test algorithm.

The **t-test** is the most elementary method for comparing two groups' mean scores. Several t-test alternatives are available to use with different types of research studies. Variations of the t-test include testing independent groups, related groups, and cases in which the population mean is either known or unknown.

The t-test assumes that the variables in the populations from which the samples are drawn are normally distributed (see Chapter 10). The test also assumes that the data have *homogeneity of variance*—that is, that they deviate equally from the mean.

The basic formula for the t-test is relatively simple. The numerator of the formula is the difference between the sample mean and the hypothesized population mean, and the denominator is the estimate of the standard error of the mean (S_m):

$$t = \frac{\overline{X} - \mu}{S_m}$$

where

$$S_m = \sqrt{\frac{SS}{n-1}} \quad \text{and} \quad SS = \Sigma(X - \overline{X})^2$$

One of the more commonly used forms of the *t*-test is the test for independent groups or means. This procedure is used to study two independent groups for differences (the type of study described at the beginning of this section). The formula for the independent *t*-test is

$$t = \frac{\overline{X}_1 - \overline{X}_2}{S_{\overline{x}_1 - \overline{x}_2}}$$

where $\overline{X}_1$ is the mean for Group 1, $\overline{X}_2$ is the mean for Group 2, and $S_{\overline{x}_1 - \overline{x}_2}$ is the standard

error for the groups. The standard error is an important part of the *t*-test formula and is computed as follows:

$$S_{\overline{x}_1 - \overline{x}_2} = \sqrt{\left(\frac{SS_1 + SS_2}{n_1 + n_2 - 2}\right)\left(\frac{1}{n_1} + \frac{1}{n_2}\right)}$$

where SS_1 is the sum of squares for Group 1, SS_2 is the sum of squares for Group 2, n_1 is the sample size for Group 1, and n_2 is the sample size for Group 2.

To illustrate a *t*-test, consider a research problem to determine the recall of two groups of subjects about a television commercial for a new household cleaner. One group consists of 10 males, and the other consists of 10 females. Each group views the commercial once and then completes a 15-item questionnaire. The hypothesis predicts a significant difference between the recall scores of males and females.

With the data from Table 12.2, using the *t*-test formula, the researcher computes the

Table 12.2   Data on Recall Scores for Men and Women

Female Recall Scores			Male Recall Scores		
X	x	x^2(SS)	X	x^2	x^2(SS)
4	−4	16	2	−4	16
4	−4	16	3	−3	9
5	−3	9	4	−2	4
7	−1	1	4	−2	4
7	−1	1	4	−2	4
8	0	0	6	0	0
9	1	1	6	0	0
9	1	1	8	2	4
12	4	16	10	4	16
15	7	49	13	7	49
80		110	60		106
$\overline{X} = 8$			$\overline{X} = 6$		

Table 12.3 Portion of the *t*-Distribution Table for the Two-Tail Test

	Probability			
n	.10	.05	.01	.001
1	6.314	12.706	63.657	636.619
2	2.920	4.303	9.925	31.598
*				
*				
*				
17	1.740	2.110	2.898	3.965
18	1.734	2.101	2.878	3.992
19	1.729	2.093	2.861	3.883
*				
*				
*				

standard error for the groups using the previous formula:

$$S_{\bar{x}_1 - \bar{x}_2} = \sqrt{\left(\frac{110 + 106}{10 + 10 - 2}\right)\left(\frac{1}{10} + \frac{1}{10}\right)}$$

$$= 1.55$$

The researcher then substitutes this standard error value into the *t*-test formula:

$$t = \frac{8 - 6}{1.55}$$

$$= 1.29$$

To determine whether the *t* value of 1.29 is statistically significant, a *t*-distribution table is consulted. The *t*-distribution is a family of curves closely resembling the normal curve. The portion of the *t*-distribution table relevant to the sample problem is reproduced in Table 12.3. Again, to interpret the table, two values are required: degrees of freedom and level of probability. (For a complete *t*-distribution table, see Appendix 1, Table 2.)

For purposes of the *t*-test, degrees of freedom are equal to $(n_1 + n_2) - 2$, where n_1 and n_2 are the sizes of the respective groups. In the example of advertising recall, $df = 18$ $(10 + 10 - 2)$. If the problem is tested at the .05 level of significance, a *t* value equal to or greater than 2.101 is required for the results to be considered statistically significant. However, because the sample problem is a two-tail test (the hypothesis predicts only a difference between the two groups, not that one particular group will have the higher mean score), the required values are actually $t \leq -2.101$ or $t \geq +2.101$. The conclusion of the hypothetical problem is that there is no significant difference between the recall scores of the female group and the recall scores of the male group because the calculated t does not equal or exceed the table values.

There are many examples of the t-test in mass media research that demonstrate the versatility of the method. One classic example is Garramone's (1985) study of political advertising that explored the roles of the commercial sponsor (the source of the message) and the rebuttal commercial (a message that charges as false the claims of another commercial). Among six separate hypotheses that were tested, Garramone predicted:

H_1: Viewers of a negative political commercial will perceive an independent sponsor as more trustworthy than a candidate sponsor.

H_2: Viewers of an independent commercial opposing a candidate will demonstrate
   a. More negative perceptions of the target's image.
   b. Lesser likelihood of voting for the target than viewers of a candidate commercial.

H_3: Viewers of an independent commercial opposing a candidate will demonstrate
   a. More positive perceptions of the target's opponent.
   b. Greater likelihood of voting for the target's opponent than viewers of a candidate commercial.

Among other findings, Garramone concluded that

The first hypothesis ... was not supported. [However,] hypotheses 2 and 3 ... were supported. Viewers of an independent commercial opposing a candidate demonstrated a more negative perception of the target's image, $t(110) = 2.41$, $p \leq .01$, and a lesser likelihood of voting for the target, $t(110) = 1.83$, $p \leq .05$, than did viewers of a

candidate commercial. Also as predicted, viewers of an independent commercial demonstrated a more positive perception of the target's opponent, $t(110) = 1.89$, $p \leq .05$, and a greater likelihood of voting for the target's opponent, $t(110) = 2.45$, $p \leq .01$, than did viewers of a candidate commercial.

Analysis of Variance

The t-test allows researchers to investigate the effects of one independent variable on two samples of people, such as the effect of room temperature on subjects' performance on a research exam. One group may take the test in a room at 70°F, while another group takes the same test in a room at 100°F. The mean test scores for each group are used to calculate t. In many situations, however, researchers want to investigate several levels of an independent variable (rooms set at 70°, 80°, 90°, and 100°F), or possibly several independent variables (heat and light), and possibly several different groups (freshmen, sophomores, etc.). A t-test is inappropriate in these cases because the procedure is valid for only a single comparison. What may be required is an **analysis of variance** (ANOVA).

ANOVA is essentially an extension of the t-test. The advantage of ANOVA is that it can be used to simultaneously investigate several independent variables (also called *factors*). An ANOVA is named according to the number of factors involved in the study: A one-way ANOVA investigates one independent variable, a two-way ANOVA investigates two independent variables, and so on. An additional naming convention is used to describe an ANOVA that involves different levels of an independent variable. A 2 × 2 ANOVA studies two independent variables, each with two levels. For example, using the room temperature study just described, an ANOVA research project may include two levels of room temperature (70° and 100°F) and two levels of room lighting (dim and bright). This provides four different effects possibilities on test scores: 70°/dim lighting; 70°/bright lighting; 100°/dim lighting; and 100°/bright lighting.

ANOVA allows the researcher in this example to look at four unique situations at the same time. ANOVA is a versatile statistic that is widely used in mass media research. However, the name of the statistic is somewhat misleading because the most common form of ANOVA tests for significant differences between two or more group means and says little about the analysis of variance differences. Additionally, ANOVA breaks down the total variability in a set of data into its different **sources of variation**; that is, it "explains" the sources of variance in a set of scores on one or more independent variables. An ANOVA identifies or explains two types of variance: systematic and error. **Systematic variance** in data is attributable to a *known* factor that predictably increases or decreases all the scores it influences. One such factor commonly identified in mass media research is gender: Often, an increase or decrease in a given score can be predicted simply by determining whether a subject is male or female. **Error variance** in data is created by an *unknown* factor that most likely has not been examined or controlled in the study. A primary goal of all research is to eliminate or control as much error variance as possible, a task that is generally easier to do in a laboratory setting.

The ANOVA model assumes that (1) each sample is normally distributed, (2) variances in each group are equal, (3) subjects are randomly selected from the population, and (4) scores are statistically independent—they have no concomitant (related) relationship with any other variable or score. The ANOVA procedure begins with the selection of two or more random samples. The samples may be from the same or different populations. Each group is subjected to different

experimental treatments, followed by some type of test or measurement. The scores from the measurements are then used to calculate a ratio of variance, known as the **F ratio** (F).

To understand this calculation, it is necessary to examine in detail the procedure known as **sum of squares**. In the sum of squares procedure, raw scores or deviation scores are squared and summed to eliminate dealing with negative numbers. The squaring process does not change the meaning of the data as long as the same procedure is used on all the data (known as a *monotonic transformation*); it simply converts the data into a more easily interpreted set of scores.

In ANOVA, sums of squares are computed *between groups* (of subjects), *within groups* (of subjects), and in *total* (the sum of the between and within figures). The sums of squares between groups and within groups are divided by their respective degrees of freedom (as will be illustrated) to obtain a *mean square*: mean squares between (MS_b) and mean squares within (MS_w). The F ratio is then calculated using this formula:

$$F = \frac{MS_b}{MS_w}$$

where MS_b $df = K - 1$; MS_w $df = N - K$; K is the number of groups, and N is the total sample. The F ratio derived from the formula is then compared to the value in the F-distribution table (Tables 5 and 6 in Appendix 1) that corresponds to the appropriate degrees of freedom and the desired probability level. If the calculated value equals or exceeds the tabled value, the ANOVA is considered to be statistically significant. The F table is similar to the t table and the chi-square table except that two different degrees of freedom are used, one for the numerator of the F ratio and one for the denominator.

The ANOVA statistic can be illustrated with an example from advertising. Suppose that three groups of five subjects each are selected randomly to determine the credibility of a newspaper advertisement for a new laundry detergent. The groups are exposed to versions of the advertisement that reflect varying degrees of design complexity: easy, medium, and difficult. The subjects are then asked to rate the advertisement on a 1–10 scale, with 10 indicating believable and 1 indicating not believable. The null hypothesis is advanced: "There is no significant difference in credibility among the three versions of the ad."

To test this hypothesis, it is first necessary to calculate the three sums of squares: total, within, and between. The formulas for sums of squares (*SS*) are

$$\text{Total}_{ss} = \Sigma X^2 - \frac{(\Sigma X)^2}{N}$$

where N represents total sample size,

$$\text{Within}_{ss} = \Sigma X^2 - \frac{\Sigma(\Sigma X)^2}{n_k}$$

where n_k represents the sample size of each group, and

$$\text{Between}_{ss} = T_{ss} - W_{ss}$$

The scores for the three groups furnish the data shown next:

Group A (easy)		Group B (medium)		Group C (difficult)	
X	X^2	X	X^2	X	X^2
1	1	4	16	6	36
2	4	5	25	7	49
4	16	6	36	7	49
4	16	6	36	8	64
5	25	8	64	10	100
16	62	29	177	38	298

$$\Sigma X = (16 + 29 + 38) = 83$$
$$\Sigma X^2 = (62 + 177 + 298) = 537$$

By inserting the data into the formulas, the researchers are able to calculate the sums of squares as follows:

$$T_{ss} = \Sigma X^2 - \frac{(\Sigma X)^2}{N} = 537 - \frac{(83)^2}{15}$$

$$= 537 - 459.2 = 77.8$$

$$W_{ss} = \Sigma X^2 - \frac{\Sigma(\Sigma X)^2}{n_k}$$

$$= 537 - \frac{16^2}{5} - \frac{29^2}{5} - \frac{38^2}{5}$$

$$= 537 - 51.2 - 168.2 - 288.8 = 28.8$$

$$B_{ss} = T_{ss} - W_{ss} = 77.8 - 28.8 = 49$$

With this information, we can calculate the mean squares between and within groups (*SS/df*) which can then be divided (MS_b/MS_w) to obtain the value of the *F* ratio. These results are displayed in Figure 12.3.

If we assume a significance level of .05, the *F*-distribution data (Table 5, Appendix 1) for degrees of freedom of 2 and 12 indicate that the *F* ratio must be 3.89 or greater to show statistical significance. Because the calculated value of 10.2 is greater than 3.89, there is a significant difference in credibility among the three types of advertisements, and the researchers must reject the null hypothesis.

Two-Way ANOVA

Researchers often examine more than one independent variable in a study. In the preceding example, we may have wanted to investigate simultaneously a second independent variable, product knowledge. If so, then we could have used a two-way ANOVA. In a **two-way ANOVA**, as with the one-way ANOVA, the data are gathered and organized in table form. But the two-way table has both rows and columns, where each row and column represents an independent

Figure 12.3 Values for One-Way ANOVA

Sources of variation	df	Sums of squares	Mean square	F
Between groups	2 $(K-1)$	49	24.50	10.19
Within groups	12 $(n-K)$	28.8	2.4	xxxx
Total	14 $(n-1)$	77.8	xxxx	

Figure 12.4 Two-Way ANOVA

	Group A (Easy)	Group B (Medium)	Group C (Hard)
No product knowledge	$X_{111}, X_{112} \cdots \cdots$	$X_{121}, X_{122} \cdots \cdots$	$X_{131}, X_{132} \cdots \cdots$
Product knowledge	$X_{211}, X_{212} \cdots \cdots$	$X_{221}, X_{222} \cdots \cdots$	$X_{231}, X_{232} \cdots \cdots$

X represents a dependent measurement score.

The subscripts identify the subject who received that score.

For example:

X_{111} — Group A

— No product knowledge

— Subject number 1

variable. The dependent variable score, represented by the letter X for each subject, is entered into each cell of the table. This procedure is demonstrated in Figure 12.4. The two-way ANOVA can save time and resources because studies for each independent variable are being conducted simultaneously. In addition, we are able to calculate two types of independent variable effects on the dependent variable: main effects and interactions. (A one-way ANOVA tests for only main effects.) A **main effect** is simply the influence of an independent variable on the dependent variable. **Interaction** refers to the concomitant influence of two or more independent variables on the single dependent variable. For example, it may be found that a subject's educational background has no effect on media used for entertainment, but education and socioeconomic status may interact to create a significant effect.

The main effects plus interaction in a two-way ANOVA create a summary table slightly different from that shown for the one-way ANOVA, as illustrated by comparing Figures 12.3 and 12.4. Instead of computing only one F ratio as in one-way ANOVA, a two-way ANOVA involves four F ratios, and each is tested for statistical significance on the F-distribution table (Between columns, Between rows, Interaction, Within cells). "Between columns" (a main effect) represents the test of the independent variable levels located in the columns of a two-way ANOVA. (From the preceding example, this would be a test for the differences between groups easy, medium, and hard.) "Between rows" is another main effects test; it represents the significance between levels of the independent variable identified in the rows of the two-way ANOVA (product knowledge and no product knowledge). The "Interaction" section is the test for interaction between both independent variables in the study, and "Within cells" tests for significant differences between each cell in the study to determine how each individual group performed in the analysis. F ratios are not computed for the "Total," which accounts for the X's in the mean square and F columns.

Basic Correlation Statistics

Assume that a researcher hypothesizes an association between the number of pictures on the cover of a magazine and the total number of copies sold at newsstands. If the observations reveal that more magazines are sold when more pictures are used, there may be a relationship between the two variables. Numerical expressions of the degree to which two variables change in relation to each other are called *measures of association*, or **correlation**. When making two different measurements of the same entity or person, researchers commonly designate one measure as the X *variable* and the other as the Y *variable*. For example, in a study of whether a relationship exists between the size of a subject's family and the frequency with which that person reads a newspaper, the measure of family size could be the X variable and the measure of newspaper reading the Y variable. Note that each subject in the group under study must be measured for both variables.

Figure 12.5 shows hypothetical data collected from a study of eight subjects. The Y variable is the number of times per week the newspaper is read; the X variable is the number of persons in the household. The two scores for each subject are plotted on a **scattergram**, a graphic technique for portraying a relationship between two or more variables. As indicated, family size and newspaper reading increase together. This is an example of a *positive relationship*.

An *inverse* (or *negative*) *relationship* exists when one variable increases while the other correspondingly decreases. Sometimes the relationship between two variables is positive up to a point and then becomes inverse (or vice versa). When this happens, the relationship is said to be *curvilinear*. When there is no tendency for a high score on one variable to be associated with a high or low score on another variable, the two are said to be *uncorrelated*. Figure 12.6 illustrates these relationships.

Many statistics are available to measure the degree of relationship between two variables, but the most commonly used is the *Pearson product-moment correlation*, symbolized as r. It varies between -1.00 and $+1.00$. A correlation coefficient of $+1.00$ indicates a perfect positive correlation: X and Y are completely covariant (they vary together). A Pearson r of -1.00 indicates a

Figure 12.5   Scattergram of Family Size and Newspaper Reading Scores

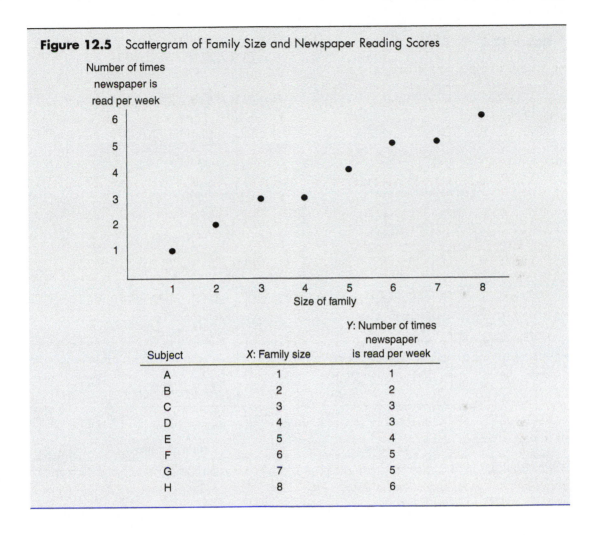

Subject	X: Family size	Y: Number of times newspaper is read per week
A	1	1
B	2	2
C	3	3
D	4	3
E	5	4
F	6	5
G	7	5
H	8	6

perfect relationship in the negative direction. The lowest value the Pearson r can have is 0.00, which represents absolutely no relationship between two variables. Thus, the **Pearson r** contains two pieces of information: (1) an estimate of the strength of the relationship, as indicated by the number, and (2) a statement about the direction of the relationship, as shown by the $+$ or $-$ sign. Keep in mind that the strength of the relationship depends solely on the number, and it must be interpreted in terms of absolute value. A correlation of $-.83$ is a stronger relationship than one of $+.23$.

The formula for calculating r looks sinister, but it actually includes only one new expression:

$$r = \frac{N\Sigma XY - \Sigma X \Sigma Y}{\sqrt{[N\Sigma X^2 - (\Sigma X)^2][N\Sigma Y^2 - (\Sigma Y)^2]}}$$

where X and Y stand for the original scores, N is the number of pairs of scores, and Σ again is the summation symbol. The only new term is ΣXY, which stands for the sum of the products of each X and Y. To find this quantity, simply multiply each X variable by its corresponding Y variable and then add

Figure 12.6   Scattergram of Possible Relationships

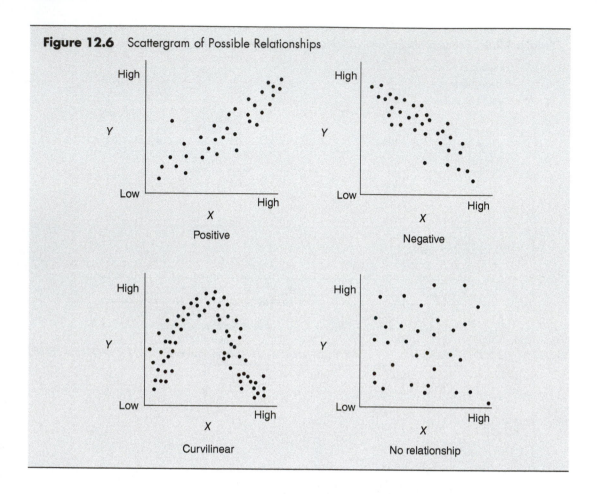

the results. Table 12.4 demonstrates a computation of *r*.

A correlation coefficient is a pure number; it is not expressed in feet, inches, or pounds, nor is it a proportion or percentage. The Pearson *r* is independent of the size and units of measurement of the original data. (In fact, the original scores do not have to be expressed in the same units.) Because of its abstract nature, *r* must be interpreted with care. In particular, it is not as easy as it sounds to determine whether a correlation is large or small. Some writers have suggested various adjectives to describe certain ranges of *r*. For example, an *r* between .40 and .70 might be called a "moderate" or

"substantial" relationship, whereas an *r* of .71 to .90 might be termed "very high."

These labels are helpful, but they may lead to confusion. The best advice is to consider the nature of the study. For example, an *r* of .70 between frequency of viewing television violence and frequency of arrest for violent crimes would be more than substantial; it would be phenomenal. Conversely, a correlation of .70 between two coders' timings of the lengths of news stories on the evening news is low enough to call the reliability of the study into question. Additionally, correlation does not in itself imply causation. Newspaper reading and income might be strongly related, but this does not mean

Table 12.4 Calculation of *r*

Subject	X	X²	Y	Y²	XY
A	1	1	1	1	1
B	2	4	2	4	4
C	3	9	3	9	9
D	4	16	3	9	12
E	4	16	4	16	16
F	5	25	5	25	25
G	6	36	5	25	30
H	8	64	6	36	48
N = 8	$\Sigma X = 33$	$\Sigma X^2 = 171$	$\Sigma Y = 29$	$\Sigma Y^2 = 125$	$\Sigma XY = 145$

$$(\Sigma X)^2 = 1,089$$
$$(\Sigma Y)^2 = 841$$

$$r = \frac{(8)(145) - (33)(29)}{\sqrt{[(8)(171) - 1,089][(8)(125) - 841]}}$$

$$= \frac{203}{(279)(159)} = \frac{203}{(16.7)(12.6)}$$

$$= \frac{203}{210.62} = .964$$

r formula:

$$\frac{N\Sigma XY - \Sigma X \Sigma Y}{\sqrt{[N\Sigma X^2 - (\Sigma X)^2][N\Sigma Y^2 - (\Sigma Y)^2]}}$$

that earning a high salary causes people to read the newspaper. Correlation is just one factor in determining causality.

Furthermore, a large *r* does not necessarily mean that the two sets of correlated scores are equal. What it does mean is that there is a high likelihood of being correct when predicting the value of one variable by examining another variable that correlates with it. For example, there may be a correlation of .90 between the amount of time people spend reading newspapers and the amount of time

they spend watching television news. That is, the amount of time reading newspapers correlates with the amount of time watching television news. The correlation figure says nothing about the *amount* of time spent with each medium. It suggests only that there is a strong likelihood that people who spend time reading newspapers also spend time watching TV news.

Perhaps the best way to interpret *r* is in terms of the **coefficient of determination**, or the proportion of the total variation of one measure that can be determined by the other. This is calculated by squaring the Pearson r to arrive at a ratio of the two variances: The denominator of this ratio is the total variance of one of the variables, and the numerator is the part of the total variance that can be attributed to the other variable. For example, if $r = .40$ then $r^2 = .16$. One variable explains 16% of the variation in the other. Or, to put it another way, 16% of the information necessary to make a perfect prediction from one variable to another is known. Obviously, if $r = 1.00$, then $r^2 = 100\%$; one variable allows perfect predictability of the other. The quantity $1 - r^2$ is usually called the **coefficient of nondetermination** because it represents that proportion of the variance left unaccounted for or unexplained.

Suppose that a correlation of .30 is found between children's aggression and the amount of television violence the children watch. This means that 9% of the total variance in aggression is accounted for by television violence. The other 91% of the variation is unexplained (it is not accounted for by the television variable). Note that the coefficient of determination is not measured on an equal interval scale: .80 is twice as large as .40, but this does not mean that an r of .80 represents twice as strong a relationship between two variables as an r of .40. In fact, the r of .40 explains 16% of the variance, while the r of .80 explains 64%—four times as much.

The Pearson r can be computed between any two sets of scores. For the statistic to be a valid description of the relationship, however, three assumptions must be made: (1) the data represent interval or ratio measurements; (2) the relationship between X and Y is linear, not curvilinear; and (3) the distributions of the X and Y variables are symmetrical and comparable. (Pearson's r can also be used as an inferential statistic. When this is the case, it is necessary to assume that X and Y come from normally distributed populations with similar variances.) If these assumptions cannot be made, the researcher must use another kind of correlation coefficient, such as Spearman's *rho* or Kendall's *W*. For a thorough discussion of these and other correlation coefficients, consult Nunnally (1994).

Partial Correlation

Partial correlation is a method researchers use when they believe that a confounding or spurious variable may affect the relationship between the independent variables and the dependent variable: If such an influence is perceived, they can "partial out" or control the confounding variable. For example, consider a study of the relationship between exposure to television commercials and purchasing the advertised products. The researchers select two commercials for a liquid laundry detergent (a "straight sell" version with no special video or audio effects, and a "hard sell" version that includes special effects). The commercials are shown to two groups of subjects: people who use only powdered detergent and people who use only liquid detergent. The study design is shown in Figure 12.7.

If the results show a very low correlation, indicating that any prediction made based on these two variables would be very tenuous, the researchers should investigate the presence of a confounding variable. An examination might reveal, for example, that the technicians had problems adjusting the color definition of the recording equipment; instead of its natural blue color, the detergent appeared dingy brown on the television screen. The study could be repeated to control (statistically eliminate) this variable by filming new commercials with the color controls properly adjusted. The design for the new study is shown in Figure 12.8.

The partial correlation statistical procedure would enable the researchers to

Figure 12.7 Basic Product Purchase Study Design

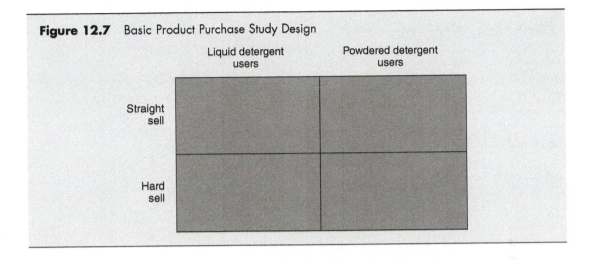

Figure 12.8 Product Purchase Study Design Incorporating Partial Correlation Analysis

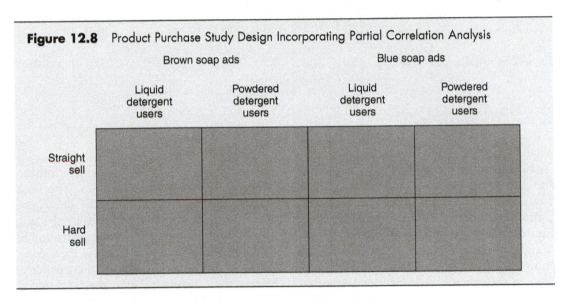

determine the influence of the controlled variable. With the new statistical method, the correlation might increase from the original study.

Simple Linear Regression

Simple correlation involves measuring the relationship between two variables. The statistic is used to determine the degree to which one variable changes with a given change in another variable. Thus, **linear regression** is a way of using the association between two variables as a method of prediction. Let's take the simplest case to illustrate the logic behind this technique.

Suppose two variables are perfectly related ($r = 1.00$). Knowledge of a person's score on one variable allows the researcher to determine the score on the other. Figure 12.9 is a scattergram that portrays this situation.

Figure 12.9 Perfect Linear Correlation

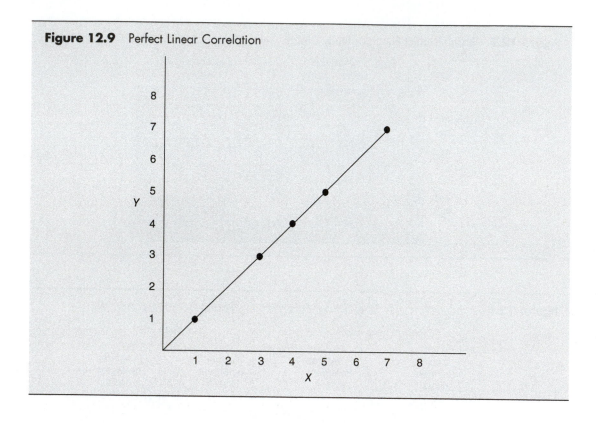

Note that all the points lie on a straight line, the *regression line*. Unfortunately, relationships are never this simple, and scattergrams more often resemble the one shown in Figure 12.10(a). Obviously, no single straight line can be drawn through all the points in the scattergram. It is possible, however, to mathematically construct a line that best fits all the observations in the figure. This line comes closest to all the dots even though it might not pass through any of them. Mathematicians have worked out a technique to calculate such a line. In 1794, German mathematician Karl Gauss developed the "least squares" method to relocate Ceres, the first recorded asteroid.

The least squares technique produces a line that is the best summary description of the relationship between two variables. For example, Figure 12.10(a) shows the data points that represent the relationship between eight *x* and *y* variables. The least squares technique determines the line equation for the data points such that the line passes through, or near, the greatest number of points. The computed line is then compared to the true, or perfect, line to determine the accuracy of the computed (predicted) line. The closer the computed line is to the true line, the more accurate the prediction.

The solid line in Figure 12.10(b) represents the best fitting line that passes through, or closest to, the greatest number of data points. The broken line connects the actual data points. It is clear that the broken line does not fall on the true line. The data points are some distance away from the true line (showing that the prediction is not perfect).

Figure 12.10   (a) Scattergram of X and Y; (b) Scattergram with Regression Line

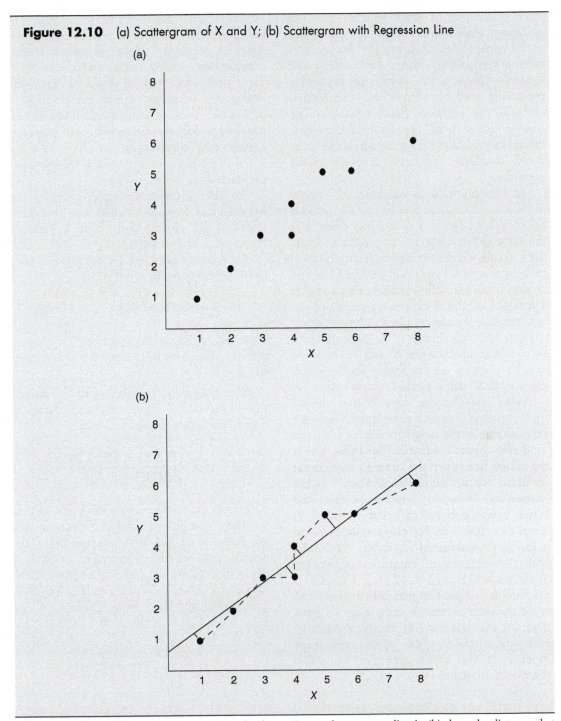

Note: The solid perpendicular lines connecting the data points to the computer line in (b) show the distances that must be determined and squared.

The method of least squares involves measuring the distances from the data points to the perfect line, *squaring* the distances to eliminate negative values, and adding the squared distances. A computer does this repeatedly until the sum of the squared distance is the smallest (least squares). The smaller the sum of the squared distances, the greater the accuracy with which the computed formula predicts the dependent variable.

At this point, it is necessary to review some basic analytical geometry. The general equation for a line is $Y = a + bX$, where Y is the variable we are trying to predict and X is the variable we are predicting from. Furthermore, a represents the point at which the line crosses the y-axis (the vertical axis), and b is a measure of the slope (or steepness) of the line. In other words, b indicates how much Y changes for each change in X. Depending on the relationship between X and Y, the slope can be positive or negative. To illustrate, Figure 12.9 shows that every time X increases one unit, so does Y. In addition, the a value is 0 because the line crosses the vertical axis at the origin.

Strictly speaking, the equation for a regression line is not the same as the general equation for a line, because the Y in the regression equation represents not the actual variable Y but rather a predicted Y. Therefore, the Y in the regression equation is usually symbolized $\hat{Y}$ (called "Y hat"), and the regression equation is written $\hat{Y} = a + bX$.

Now let us put this general equation into more concrete terms. Assume that we have data on the relationship between years of education and number of minutes spent looking at the newspaper per day. The regression equation is

Minutes reading newspaper =
2 + 3(education)

What can we assume from this? In the first place, the a value tells us that a person with no formal education spends 2 minutes per day looking at the newspaper. The b value indicates that time spent with the newspaper increases 3 minutes with each additional year of education. What is the prediction for someone with 10 years of education? Substituting, we have $\hat{Y} = 2 + 3(10) = 32$ minutes spent with the newspaper each day.

To take another example, consider the hypothetical regression equation predicting hours of TV viewed daily from a person's IQ score: $\hat{Y} = 5 - .01(IQ)$

How many hours of TV are viewed daily by someone with an IQ of 100?

$$\hat{Y} = 5 - .01(100) = 5 - 1 = 4 \text{ hours}$$

Thus, according to this equation, TV viewing per day decreases 0.01 hour for every point of IQ.

The arithmetic calculation of the regression equation is straightforward. First, to find b, the slope of the line, use

$$b = \frac{N\Sigma XY - (\Sigma X)(\Sigma Y)}{N\Sigma X^2 - (\Sigma X)^2}$$

Note that the numerator is the same as that for the r coefficient, and the denominator corresponds to the first expression in the denominator of the r formula. Thus, b is easily calculated once the quantities necessary for r have been determined. To illustrate, using the data from Table 12.4, we have

$$b = \frac{8(145) - (33)(29)}{8(171) - 1089}$$
$$= \frac{203}{279}$$
$$= 0.73$$

The value of the $\hat{Y}$ intercept (a) is found by the following:

$$a = \overline{Y} - b\overline{X}$$

Again, using the data in Table 12.4 and the calculation of b, we get

$$\begin{aligned} a &= 3.63 - (0.73)(4.125) \\ &= 3.63 - 3.01 \\ &= 0.62 \end{aligned}$$

The completed regression equation is $\hat{Y} = 0.62 + 0.73X$.

Of course, as the name suggests, simple linear regression assumes that the relationship between X and Y is linear (the data increase or decrease in the same way). If an examination of the scattergram suggests a curvilinear relationship, other regression techniques are necessary. The notion of regression can be extended to the use of multiple predictor variables to predict the value of a single criterion variable.

Multiple Regression

Multiple regression, an extension of linear regression, is another parametric technique used to analyze the relationship between two or more independent variables and a single dependent (criterion) variable. Though similar in some ways to an analysis of variance, multiple regression serves basically to *predict* the dependent variable using information derived from an analysis of the independent variables.

In any research problem, the dependent variable is affected by a variety of independent variables. The primary goal of multiple regression is to develop a formula that accounts for, or explains, as much variance in the dependent variable as possible. It is widely used by researchers to predict success in college, sales levels, and so on. These dependent variables are predicted by **weighted linear combinations** of independent variables. A simple model of multiple regression is shown in Figure 12.11.

Linear combinations of variables play an important role in higher-level statistics.

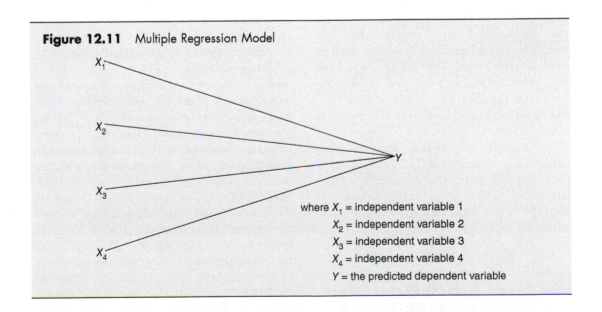

Figure 12.11   Multiple Regression Model

where X_1 = independent variable 1
X_2 = independent variable 2
X_3 = independent variable 3
X_4 = independent variable 4
Y = the predicted dependent variable

To understand the concept of a weighted linear combination, consider two methods of classroom grading. One instructor determines each student's final grade by his or her performance on five exams: The scores on these exams are summed and averaged to obtain each final grade. A student receives the following scores for the five exams: B (3.0), D+ (1.5), B (3.0), B+ (3.5), and A (4.0); thus the final grade is a B (15/5 = 3.0). This grade is the dependent variable determined by the linear combination of five exam scores (the independent variables). No test is considered more important than another; hence, the linear combination is not said to be weighted (except in the sense that all the scores are "weighted" equally).

The second instructor also determines the final grades by students' performances on five exams; however, the first exam counts 30%, the last exam 40%, and the remaining three exams 10% each in the determination. A student with the same five scores as in the previous example thus receives a final grade of 3.3. Again, the scores represent a linear combination, but it is a weighted linear combination: The first and last exams contribute more to the final grade than do the other tests. The second grading system is used in multiple regression. The independent variables are weighted and summed to predict a dependent variable. The weight of each variable in a linear combination is referred to as its *coefficient*.

A multiple regression formula may involve any number of independent variables, depending on the complexity of the dependent variable. A simple formula of this type might look like this (hypothetical values are used):

$$\hat{Y} = 0.89X_1 = 2.5X_2 - 3$$

where $\hat{Y}$ is the predicted score or variable, X_1 is Independent Variable 1, and X_2 is

Independent Variable 2. The number 3 in the formula, a constant subtracted from each subject's scores, is derived as part of the multiple regression formula. All formulas produced by multiple regression analyses represent a line in space; that is, the dependent variable is interpreted as a linear combination, or line, of independent variables. The slope of this line is determined by the *regression coefficients* assigned to the variables. The goal of the researcher is to derive a formula for a line that coincides as closely as possible with the true line (a mathematically determined line that represents a perfect prediction) of the dependent variable: The closer the computed line comes to the true line, the more accurate the prediction.

Another important value that must be calculated in a multiple regression analysis is the *coefficient of correlation* (R), which represents the product-moment correlation between the predicted $\hat{Y}$ score and the weighted linear combination of the X scores. The square of this coefficient (R^2) indicates the proportion of variance in the dependent variable that is accounted for by the predictor variables. The higher the R^2 (that is, the closer the figure is to 1.00), the more accurate the prediction is considered to be.

Drew and Reeves (1980) conducted a multiple regression analysis to determine what factors affect the way children learn from television news stories. They defined the dependent variable, "learning," in terms of performance on a 10-point questionnaire regarding a news program the children watched in an experimental setting. The selection of independent variables was based on the results of previous studies; they decided to measure (1) whether the children liked the program, (2) whether the children liked the particular news story, (3) the credibility of the program, and (4) the informational content of the particular story. The results, shown in Table 12.5, indicate that all the

Table 12.5 Drew and Reeves's Multiple Regression Analysis

Predictor Variables	Beta Weights
Like program	.15**
Credibility	.10*
Informational content	.39***
Like story	.25***
Multiple R	.546
R^2	.298

*$p < .05$
**$p < .01$
***$p < .001$

independent variables were statistically significant in their relation to learning. As the **beta weights** show, "informational content" seems to be the best predictor of learning, and "credibility" accounts for the least amount of variance. The multiple R of .546 could be considered highly significant; however, because it means that only 30% $(.5462)^2$ of the variance in the dependent variable is accounted for by the four predictor variables, this value may not substantially explain the variance.

SUMMARY

Mass media research has made great strides in both the number of research studies completed and the types of statistical methods used. This chapter introduced some of the more widely used basic statistical procedures involving one dependent variable and one or more independent variables. The information is intended to help beginning researchers read and analyze published research.

The emphasis in this chapter was on using statistical methods rather than on the statistics themselves. The basic formula for each statistic was briefly outlined so that beginning researchers can understand how the data are derived; the goal, however, has been to convey a knowledge of how and when to use each procedure. It is important that researchers be able to determine not only what the problem or research question is but also which statistical method most accurately fits the requirements of a particular research study.

Key Terms

Analysis of variance
ANOVA
Beta weight
Chi-square goodness
   of fits
Coefficient of
   determination
Coefficient of
   nondetermination
Contingency table
Correlation
Crosstab
Cross-tabulation
Degrees of freedom
Error variance
F ratio
Interaction

Linear regression
Main effect
Multiple regression
Nonparametric
   statistics
Parametric statistics
Partial correlation
Pearson r
Scattergram
Sources of variation
Sum of squares
Systematic variance
t-test
Two-way ANOVA
Weighted linear
   combination

 Using the Internet

1. There are several good (free) online statistical packages and statistics calculators available online. Search for "*statistical package*" *online* and "*statistical packages*" *online* for packages and "*statistics calculators*" for calculators.

2. The Internet is a valuable source for a great deal of information about statistics. For example, search for "analysis of variance," "linear regression," "Sir Ronald Fisher," "multiple regression," "multicollinearity," and "multiple dependence."

Questions and Problems for Further Investigation

1. Design a mass media study for which a chi-square analysis is appropriate. Consult the Internet for help, using *"mass media questions"* as a starting point.

2. In the chi-square example of television set sales, assume that the observed sales frequencies are 210 (RCA), 350 (Sony), 200 (Sharp), and 240 (Mitsubishi). What is the chi-square value? Is it significant?

3. What are the advantages of using an ANOVA rather than conducting several separate *t*-tests of the same phenomena?

4. How could multiple regression be used to predict a subject's television viewing, radio listening, and newspaper reading behavior?

5. We state that a Pearson *r* can be computed between any two sets of scores. Does that mean that all Pearson correlations will be logical? Why can some correlations be called pseudoscience or bad science?

6. Calculate *r* for the following sets of scores:

   X: 1 1 3 2 2 4 5 7

   Y: 8 6 5 4 3 5 2 3

   Answer = −.65. If you use Excel and enter the data in columns A and B, rows 1 through 8, use this formula to calculate the answer: =CORREL(A1:A8, B1:B8).

7. Input the pairs of data from question 6 in a different order and recalculate the correlation. What happens to the correlation?

8. Add 10 to every score in Question 6 and recalculate the correlation. What happens to the correlation?

For additional resources, go to *www.wimmer dominick.com* and *www.cengagebrain.com*.

References and Suggested Readings

Bruning, J. L., & Kintz, B. L. (1997). *Computational handbook of statistics* (4th ed.) New York, NY: Longman.

Cochran, W. G. (1976). Early development of techniques in comparative experimentation. In D. B. Owen (Ed.), *On the history of statistics and probability*. New York, NY: Marcel Dekker.

Cohen, J., & Cohen, P. (1975). *Applied multiple regression/correlation analysis for the behavioral sciences*. Hillsdale, NJ: Lawrence Erlbaum.

Drew, D., & Reeves, B. (1980). Learning from a television news story. *Communication Research, 7*, 121–135.

Fisher, R. A. (1922). On the mathematical foundations of theoretical statistics. *Philosophical Transactions of the Royal Society, (A) 222*, 309–368.

Garramone, G. (1985). Effects of negative political advertising: The roles of sponsor and rebuttal. *Journal of Broadcasting & Electronic Media, 29*, 147–159.

Kerlinger, F. N., & Pedhazur, E. J. (1997). *Multiple regression in behavioral research* (3rd ed.). New York, NY: Holt, Rinehart & Winston.

Nie, N. H., Hull, C. H., Jenkins, J. G., Steinbrenner, K., & Bent, D. H. (1975). *Statistical package for the social sciences*. New York, NY: McGraw-Hill.

Nunnally, J. C. (1994). *Psychometric theory* (4th ed.). New York, NY: McGraw-Hill.

Reeves, B., & Miller, M. (1977). A multidimensional measure of children's identification with television characters. *Journal of Broadcasting, 22*, 71–86.

Thorndike, R. M. (1978). *Correlational procedures for research*. New York, NY: Gardner Press.

Tukey, J. W. (1986). *The collected works of John W. Tukey* (Vols. *III–IV*). Belmont, CA: Wadsworth.

CHAPTER 13

NEWSPAPER AND MAGAZINE RESEARCH

CHAPTER OUTLINE

In earlier editions of this book, this chapter was titled "Research in the Print Media." That title is inappropriate now because the print media are no longer simply print media—they are both print and online media. In fact, the online part of many operations has become more important than the traditional print version. The *Christian Science Monitor*, published for more than 100 years, ended its print edition in 2009 and shifted to the Internet, as did the *Seattle Post-Intelligencer*. The *Detroit News* and the *Detroit Free Press* cut back their home delivery to three days a week and urged subscribers to visit their websites on the other days. Several magazines have dropped or suspended their print versions and exist only online.

The reason for this shift is primarily economic. Newspaper advertising revenue has declined significantly as websites such as Craigslist and Monster.com have siphoned off classified ad business. The recession that started at the beginning of the 21st century caused advertisers to cut back their budgets. Many people, particularly younger people, are getting their news and entertainment from online sites and reading the newspaper less and less. As a result, much of today's research in the publishing business entails finding ways to stay in business. In addition, a good deal of current research is proprietary as newspaper and magazine publishers examine such topics as paywalls (barring users from accessing web page content without a paid subscription), the impact of mobile media (smartphones, e-readers, and tablet computers) on newspaper and magazine reading, and the best app (application) designs for online readers. To date, little academic research on these topics has appeared in scholarly journals.

Methodologies used to study the print and online media are similar to those used in most areas of research; academic and commercial research organizations often use content analysis, experiments, focus groups, and surveys, among other procedures, to study newspapers and magazines. Now more than ever, print media research tends to be narrowly focused and oriented toward practical application. This chapter provides a brief overview of the most common types of studies in newspaper and magazine research, both print and online, with a special emphasis on the research most likely to be conducted by advertiser-supported publications.

This chapter does not address basic market studies and advertising exposure studies. A basic market study provides a demographic or psychographic portrait of the potential readers of a newspaper or magazine; this market research technique is more fully described by Aaker, Kumar, and Day (2009). Advertising exposure studies (also called *reader traffic studies*) are conducted to determine which ads are noticed or read by a publication's audience; for more information on these studies, see Chapter 15.

BACKGROUND

Much of early print media research was qualitative. The first volume of *Journalism Quarterly,* founded in 1928, contained articles on press law, history, international comparisons, and ethics. However, quantitative research soon began to make its appearance in this academic journal. An article published in March 1930 surveyed the research interests of those currently working in the newspaper and magazine fields and found the most prevalent type of study to be the survey of reader interest in newspaper content. The June 1930 issue contained an article by Ralph Nafziger, "A Reader Interest Survey of Madison, Wisconsin," which served as the prototype for hundreds of future research studies. The 1930s also saw the publication of many studies designed to assess the results of print media advertising. This led to studies in applied research, and several publications began to sponsor their own readership surveys. However, most of the results of these studies were considered proprietary.

As the techniques of quantitative research became more widely known and adopted, newspaper and magazine research became more empirical. Wilbur Schramm (1957) first recognized this trend in an article in *Public Opinion Quarterly* that reviewed 20 years of research as reported in *Journalism Quarterly.* Schramm found that only 10% of the 101 articles published between 1937 and 1941 concerned quantitative analyses; between 1952 and 1956, nearly half of the 143 articles published were quantitative, a fivefold increase in only 15 years. The reasons for this trend, according to Schramm, were the growing availability of basic data, the development of more sophisticated research tools, and the increase in institutional support for research.

By 1960, newspapers and magazines were competing with television and radio for audience attention and advertiser investment. This situation greatly spurred the growth of private-sector research. The Bureau of Advertising of the American Newspaper Publishers Association (subsequently called the Newspaper Advertising Bureau) began conducting studies on all aspects of the press and its audience. In the 1970s, it founded the News Research Center, which reported the results of research to editors. The Magazine Publishers Association also began to sponsor survey research at this time. The continuing interest of academics in print media research led to the 1979 creation of the *Newspaper Research Journal,* a publication devoted entirely to research that has practical implications for newspaper management.

In 1976, the Newspaper Readership Project was instituted to study the problems of declining circulation and sagging readership. As a major part of the 6-year, $5 million study, a news research center was set up at Syracuse University to abstract and synthesize the results of more than 300 private and published studies of newspaper reading habits. The Newspaper Advertising Bureau produced dozens of research reports and conducted extensive focus group studies. In addition, regional workshops were held across the country to explain to editors the uses and limitations of research. By the time the Readership Project ended, most editors had accepted research as a necessary tool of the trade. Bogart (1991) presents a thorough history of the Readership Project.

In 1977 the Newspaper Research Council (NRC), a subgroup of the Newspaper Advertising Bureau, was incorporated with 75 members. This group was involved with the American Society of Newspaper Editors in a circulation retention study and with the International Newspaper Marketing Association on how to convert Sunday-only readers to daily readers. In 1992 the Newspaper Advertising Bureau merged with the American Newspaper Publishers Association to create the Newspaper Association of America (NAA). The NAA continued the efforts of the NRC in the research area by sponsoring a number of studies that looked at such topics as attracting younger readers and how to use advertising to encourage newspaper reading. The most recent effort of the NAA, launched in 1999, was a five-year readership initiative study that examines the relationship of newspaper content to its readers. The Readership Institute at the Media Management Center at Northwestern University supervised this initiative. In 2000, the Readership Institute launched the Impact Study, which gathered information from 37,000 readers and 100 newspapers in an attempt to increase readership. Results from this study were reported at the 2004 Newspaper Advertising Association/American Society of Newspaper Editors convention.

The Pew Research Center's Project for Excellence in Journalism has published annual reports on the state of the news media since 2004. These reports contain useful descriptive statistics about the audience for newspapers and news magazines. The 2011 report, for example, contains a ranking of the top 15 newspaper e-editions.

The declining fortunes of the print media have prompted new research efforts as traditional newspapers and magazines try to assess the competition from the Internet, examine how online versions relate to their traditional paper counterparts, and look for new ways to improve their financial situation.

TYPES OF RESEARCH

Newspaper and magazine researchers conduct four basic types of studies: readership, circulation, management, and website usability. Most of their research focuses on readership; studies of circulation and management rank next. Usability research is a new but growing area.

Readership Research

Many readership studies were done in the United States in the years immediately preceding and following World War II. The George Gallup organization was a pioneer in developing the methodology of these studies—namely, a personal interview in which respondents were shown a copy of a newspaper and asked to identify the articles they had read. The American Newspaper Publishers Association (ANPA) undertook a comprehensive study of newspaper readership. The ANPA's *Continuing Studies of Newspapers* involved more than 50,000 interviews with readers of 130 daily newspapers between 1939 and 1950 (Swanson, 1955).

Readership research became important to management during the 1960s and 1970s, as circulation rates in metropolitan areas began to level off or decline. Concerned with holding the interest of their readers, editors and publishers began to depend on surveys for the detailed audience information they needed to shape the content of a publication.

The uncertain economy at the end of the first decade of the new century and the increasing competition from online media have made readership research even more important today. This is most evident in the Readership Institute's Impact Study, mentioned previously, and in the growing number of studies that examine the impact of new media (websites, smartphones, and tablet computers) on newspaper and magazine consumption.

As mentioned in Chapter 1, mass media research progresses through identifiable phases. Phase 1 consists of studies that examine the media itself, including how it is similar to or different from what already exists, whereas Phase 2 looks at users and uses of the new medium. Most readership studies of how the new media relate to print newspapers and magazines fall into these first two phases.

Research into newspaper readership in traditional or new media is composed primarily of four types of studies: reader profiles, item-selection studies, uses and gratifications studies, and journalist–reader comparisons.

Reader Profiles

There are two types of reader profiles. The traditional **reader profile** provides a demographic summary of the readers of a particular online or print publication. For example, in 2011, *People.com* reported that its readership was 70% female, median age 38, with 26% having a household income in excess of $100,000. The typical *New York Times* reader is male, 49 years old, has a college degree, and has a median household income of about $100,000. These data can be used to focus the content of the publication, prepare advertising promotions, and increase subscriptions.

Because there may be significant differences in the nature and extent of print and online newspaper and magazine reading among individuals who have the same demographic characteristics, researchers have turned to psychographic and **lifestyle segmentation studies** to construct reader profiles. Both procedures go beyond the traditional demographic portrait and describe readers in terms of what they think or how they live. **Psychographic studies** usually ask readers to indicate their level of agreement or disagreement with a large number of attitudinal statements. Subsequently, patterns of response are analyzed to see how they correlate or cluster together. People who show high levels of agreement with questions that cluster together can be described with labels that summarize the substance of the questions. On one hand, people who tend to agree with statements such as "I like to think I'm a swinger," "I'm a night person," and "Sex outside marriage can be a healthy thing" might be called "progressives." On the other hand, people who agree with items such as "Women's lib has gone too far," "Young people have too much freedom," and "The good old days were better" might be labeled "traditionalists."

Lifestyle segmentation research takes a similar approach. Respondents are asked a battery of questions concerning their activities, hobbies, interests, and attitudes. Again, the results are analyzed to see which items cluster together. Groups of individuals who share the same attitudes and activities are identified and labeled. To illustrate, Davis (2001) describes newspaper industry research that segmented readers based on how people manipulated time. The research identified three groups of readers: routinized,

relaxed, and harried. The strategy for improving readership could then be tailored to each specific segment.

Both psychographic and lifestyle segmentation studies are designed to provide management with additional insights about editorial aims, target audiences, and circulation goals. In addition, they give advertisers a multidimensional portrait of the publications' readers. Two of the most popular scales designed to measure these variables are the List of Values (LOV) and the Values and Life Styles test (VALS II). Descriptions and comparisons of these scales are found in Novak and MacEvoy (1990).

The second type of reader profile study we examine has become increasingly important. A recent survey noted that more people get news from online sources than from the print version of the newspaper. About 34% of respondents reported that they got news "yesterday" from online sources compared to 31% who named the newspaper (Pew Research Center, 2010a).

As readers shift from the print newspaper to online and mobile versions, publishers are interested in knowing about those who read on the web and on mobile media compared to those who read the traditional paper. Bartlett (2001) conducted a survey that indicated that those with greater experience and Internet access, typically younger individuals, rely more on the Internet and less on the newspaper for their news. Kayani and Yelsma

A CLOSER LOOK

Readership Research: What Isn't Investigated

While many national advertisers use insert advertising (the various forms of advertising inserted into a magazine or newspaper, usually in the Sunday edition of the newspaper), the companies do not conduct research on the effectiveness of these inserts. The advertisers do not know what types of messages these inserts communicate. They merely insert them and hope for the best.

(2000) reported similar findings. Their survey revealed that newspaper reading declined as Internet usage went up.

The Pew Research Center's news consumption survey found that the percentage of people who read only a print newspaper dropped from 34% in 2006 to 25% in 2008. During the same period, the percentage that read only the online version of a newspaper increased from 5% to 9%. The same survey contained data from a cohort study (see Chapter 8) indicating that for those born in or after 1977, the proportion who read only a print version was equal to the proportion who read only the online version, providing further evidence that young readers are continuing to migrate to the Internet. The Pew Center's data also contained more bad news for the print edition. The older age cohort was also reading the newspaper less and less (Pew Research Center, 2009). Additional survey data also indicated that online news readers tended to be younger, better educated, and more affluent than the rest of the population (Pew Research Center, 2006).

Olmstead, Mitchell, and Rosenstiel (2011) suggest that there are two types of readers for online news. Casual users visit news sites just a few times a month and stay only a few minutes per visit. About 85% of visitors to *USA.com*, for example, accessed the site just two or three times a month. On the other hand, power users return to a news site more than 10 times per month and spend more than an hour a month on the site. The researchers recommend that newspaper websites develop separate strategies to attract both groups.

About 30 million iPads have been sold as of late 2011. Many newspapers have created their own apps for this new device, hoping that it will become a significant revenue stream. How much of an impact will the iPad have on traditional newspapers? Two surveys provide some preliminary information.

A 2011 Pew Research Center report on the use of tablet computers (mainly the iPad) for accessing news found that more than half of the researchers' sample used a tablet computer to consume news. A majority of respondents also reported that they prefer getting news on their tablets over traditional computers, print newspapers, and television. The Pew survey also found that the revenue potential for newspapers from tablet computes might be limited since just 14% of respondents had paid to access news on their tablets (Pew Research Center, 2011).

A 2011 survey by the Reynolds Journalism Institute at the University of Missouri found that the number one use of the iPad was catching up with the news using apps that aggregate information from several sources. Reading newspapers within their apps ranked second. The two most regularly used news apps were both newspaper apps: the *New York Times* and *USA Today*. When it came to what was read, iPad users ranked general news as the content they accessed most frequently, followed by technology news, weather, business, and sports.

Only 6% of the sample had purchased a subscription to an app-based newspaper, but about half of the sample reported that they were somewhat or very likely to purchase such a subscription in the next 6 months. On the other hand, about 5% had canceled their print newspaper subscription after purchasing an iPad, and another 24% reported that they were somewhat or very likely to cancel their print subscription in the next 6 months (Fidler, 2011).

Magazines, of course, are faced with the same dilemma: audiences abandoning the print edition for the online version. Naturally, publishers are interested in the characteristics of their digital readership. One survey of digital magazine readers found that they tended to be older than the average newspaper online user and slightly more likely to be males. The average digital reader spent about 30 minutes reading the online version (Texterity, 2008). A study conducted by MRI and Nielsen/NetRatings disclosed that 83% of visitors to the websites of 23 large-circulation magazines read those publications only online (Leggatt, 2007).

Magazine publishers are also hoping that tablet computers (again, mainly the iPad) will increase their readership. Big magazine companies, including Conde Nast and Hearst, now offer magazine subscriptions over the iPad. Fidler (2011) found that two-thirds of the respondents in the Reynolds Journalism Institute iPad survey purchased at least one magazine to read within the magazine's app, and 11% purchased five or more. The survey noted that one in five tablet users reported reading magazines of some kind at least weekly. In addition, nearly 40% of tablet users read previous issues of the magazine on their devices (Pew Research Center, 2011). Finally, many magazines conduct proprietary research to compare their online and print readership.

Item-Selection Studies

A second type of newspaper readership study, the **item-selection study**, is used to determine who reads specific parts of the print or online version. The readership of a particular item in the print version is usually measured by means of **aided recall**, whereby the interviewer shows a copy of the paper to the respondent to find out which stories the respondent remembers. In one variation on this technique, the interviewer preselects items for which readership data are to be gathered and asks subjects about those items only. Because of the expense involved in conducting personal interviews, most researchers now use phone interviews to collect readership data. Calls are made on the same day the issue of the paper is published. The interviewer asks the respondent to bring a copy of the paper to the phone, and

together they go over each page, with the respondent identifying the items he or she has read. Although this method saves money, it excludes from study those readers who do not happen to have a copy of the paper handy. An alternative technique asks users to go to a website that contains a replica edition of the paper, and respondents indicate which articles they read.

The unit of analysis in an item-selection study is a specific news article (such as a front-page story dealing with a fire) or a specific content category (such as crime news, sports, and obituaries). The readership of items or categories is then related to certain audience demographics or psychographic characteristics. For example, Gersh (1990) reported that teenage readers have reading habits different from adults. The most popular sections of the newspaper among teens were comics, sports, and entertainment; finance, food, and home sections were the least popular. Stone and Boudreau (1995) compared data from a 1985 survey of newspaper reader preferences with data gathered in 1994. They found that content preferences changed remarkably little during the time period. An industry study of item readership (Astor, 2000) found that local news was the number one category of news preferred by readers. Fashion news ranked last.

A 2004 survey of readership of special sections of the newspaper found that the business/finance section ranked first, followed by classified ads and the comics ("Who's Reading What?" 2004). More recently, the Newspaper Association of America (2011) reported that the most popular parts of the newspaper were main news, followed by local news, sports, entertainment, and international news.

Measuring the readership for a specific item on a newspaper or magazine website or app is a little more complicated. One problem has to do with the time frame. In traditional print media, item readership is usually based on the reading of one day's copy of a newspaper or a weekly or monthly issue of a magazine. However, on the Internet, items may stay posted for varying lengths of time. As a result, item readership could be based on daily, weekly, or even monthly reading. Many newspapers and magazines pay attention to hits (the number of times a story is requested from a website) or the number of page views over a specified time to judge the popularity of an item.

Another technique tracks the popularity of certain website arrangements and story presentations. One method involves the use of an **eye camera**—a device that can track how a person's gaze travels over an image. For example, research at the Digital Effects Story Lab at the University of Minnesota found that online readers were more apt to click on a headline that led to a full story rather than on a headline plus a brief blurb. Eye camera studies revealed that readers read around an ad that was embedded in the middle of a news story. Researchers also found that readers preferred dynamic story forms (ones that contained motion and let readers click on options for more information) to static, text-only stories. (See *www.diselproject.org/*.)

Qualitative techniques have also been used. The Media Management Center at Northwestern University conducted a study using intensive interviews with 27 heavy online users (Lynch, 2008). The study revealed that reading news items online is a different process from reading a print edition. Online readers reported several different types of reading: scanning, searching for a specific item, and reading to pass the time. In addition, those who described themselves as light users were often overwhelmed by the sheer number of items on a news website and tuned out most of the information. The study also revealed that national news and local news items were most preferred.

Reader–Nonreader Studies

The third type of newspaper readership research is called the **reader–nonreader study**. This type of study can be conducted via personal, telephone, online, or mail interviews with minor modifications. This type of research is becoming more important because newspapers are trying to identify nonprint readers and attract them to their online editions. It is difficult, however, to establish an operational definition for the term *nonreader*. In some studies, a nonreader is determined by a "no" answer to the question "Do you generally read a newspaper?" Others have used the more specific question "Have you read a newspaper yesterday or today?" (The rationale is that respondents are more likely to admit they have not read a paper today or yesterday than that they never read one.) A third form of this question uses multiple-response categories. Respondents are asked "How often do you read a daily paper?" and they are given five choices of response: "very often," "often," "sometimes," "seldom," and "never." Nonreaders are defined as those who check the "never" response or, in some studies, "seldom" or "never." Obviously, the form of the question has an impact on how many people are classified as nonreaders. The largest percentage of nonreaders generally occurs when researchers ask, "Have you read a newspaper today or yesterday?" (Penrose, Weaver, Cole, & Shaw, 1974); the smallest number is obtained by requiring a "never" response to the multiple-response question (Sobal & Jackson-Beeck, 1981).

Once the nonreaders are identified, researchers typically attempt to describe them by means of traditional demographic variables. A study by Stone (1994) found that education was a better predictor of newspaper readership than race among a sample of 18-34-year-olds. Davis (2001) reported that as today's young people grow older, they are more likely to become non-readers. More recently, several studies have shown that young people are far more likely to skip reading the print newspaper. For example, a 2008 survey done by Internet ratings company comScore found that those in the 18–24 age group were about 40% more likely than average to not read a newspaper at all during a typical week. The same survey also noted that even though they may not read a traditional newspaper, nonreaders are still interested in news but they prefer to receive their news online. Nonreaders, for example, were frequent visitors to the websites of the *New York Times*, the *Los Angeles Times*, and the *Chicago Tribune*. This finding suggests that print news sites are not merely an extension of the traditional paper but have a separate online audience ("Younger, Heavy Online-News Consumers Don't Read Newspapers," 2008).

Broader studies in this area have included variables that are beyond the control of the newspaper. In a longitudinal study, Chaffee and Choe (1981) found that changes in marital status, residence, and employment had an impact on newspaper readership. Cobb-Walgren (1990) focused on why teenagers do not read the newspaper. She found that both teenagers' home environment and their image of the newspaper were important in determining why they do not read newspapers. Nonreader teens perceived that reading the paper took too much time and effort, and they were more likely to have parents who also did not read newspapers. In a study of readers of a campus newspaper, Collins (2003) found that students who lived off campus and who did not belong to student groups were more likely to be nonreaders.

Ellonen, Tarkiainen, and Kuivalainen (2010) examined website usage and the readership of print magazines. They found that those people who visited a magazine's website were more likely to be nonreaders of the print magazine.

Uses and Gratifications Studies

A uses and gratifications study is used to study media content. For newspapers, it can determine the motives that lead to newspaper reading and the personal and psychological rewards that result from it. The methodology of the uses and gratifications study is straightforward: Respondents are given a list of possible uses and gratifications and are asked whether any of these are the motives behind their reading. The technique can be applied to both print and online versions. For example, a reader might be presented with this question:

Here is a list of some things people have said about why they read the newspaper. How much do you agree or disagree with each statement?

1. I read the newspaper because it is entertaining.
2. I read the newspaper because I want to kill time.
3. I read the newspaper to keep up to date with what's going on around me.
4. I read the newspaper to relax and to relieve tension.
5. I read the newspaper so that I can find out what other people are saying about things that are important to me.

The responses are then summed, and an average score for each motivation item is calculated.

A Readership Institute (2001) survey attempted to generate a list of common motivations for reading a newspaper. The survey found 26 different "motivators" that were related to increased newspaper readership. Some of the motivators included "makes me smarter," "touches and inspires me," and "makes me more interesting."

Recent uses and gratifications studies in this area compare the gratifications of a print newspaper with those of an online version. Papacharissi and Rubin (2000) found five main motivations for using the Internet to read an online version of the newspaper: interpersonal utility, passing time, convenience, information seeking, and entertainment. Lee (2001) surveyed college students and compared their motives for reading an online paper with their motives for reading a print paper. He found that motives were generally similar but that convenience and entertainment were more important factors for online newspaper readers. Salwen, Garrison, and Driscoll (2005) compared offline and online news gratifications and found that the motivations were similar for both versions but that online versions were more convenient to read. These findings do not bode well for the print version of the newspaper: It appears that all gratifications associated with the print version are also provided by the online version, and the online version is easier to use.

Kaye (2010) developed a uses and gratifications scale for news blog reading. Her research discovered nine categories of motivations, including political debate, antitraditional media sentiment, opinion seeking, and expression/affiliation.

Journalist–Reader Comparisons

In the final area of newspaper readership research, **journalist–reader comparisons**, a group of journalists is questioned about a certain topic, and their answers are compared to those of their readers to see whether there is any correspondence between the two groups. Bogart (1989) presented two examples of such research. In one study, a group of several hundred editors was asked to rate 23 attributes of a high-quality newspaper. The editors ranked "high ratio of staff-written copy to wire service copy" first, "high amount of non-advertising content" second, and "high ratio of news interpretations … to spot news reports" third. When a

sample of readers ranked the same list, the editors' three top attributes were ranked seventh, eleventh, and twelfth, respectively. The readers rated "presence of an action line column" first, "high ratio of sports and feature news to total news" second, and "presence of a news summary" and "high number of letters to the editor per issue" in a tie for third. In short, there was little similarity among the two groups in their perceptions of the attributes of a high-quality newspaper.

Gladney (1996) explored whether editors and readers agreed on what makes a good newspaper. A survey revealed that both groups agreed on the importance of many journalistic standards, but readers didn't value professional staffing goals and enterprise reporting as highly as the editors did. Bernt, Fee, Gifford, and Stempel (2000) compared editors' estimates of readers' interest in certain news topics with actual estimates taken from a survey. The results demonstrated that editors overestimated readers' interest in crime, religion, stock market, and local business news. Beaudoin and Thorson (2002) found that journalists viewed media reporting more positively than did the general population.

The same approach can be used concerning online news. Curtin, Dougall, and Mersey (2007) compared the topic preferences of news producers and the users of Yahoo!'s news website. They found that breaking news was valued more by news producers, whereas consumers put more emphasis on human interest, entertainment, and stories about the odd or unusual.

A 2010 Pew Center study compared news topics covered by traditional media and mentioned on Twitter, YouTube, and in blogs. The researchers found that stories and issues that were popular in social media differed substantially from those covered most by the mainstream press. Bloggers were more likely to write about political issues, whereas Twitter stressed technological news, and

YouTube videos emphasized more foreign stories than the mainstream press (Pew Research Center, 2010b).

Specialized Magazine Readership Research

Magazine readership surveys are fundamentally similar to those conducted for newspapers but tend to differ in the particulars. Some magazine research is done by personal interview; respondents are shown a copy of the magazine under study and asked to rate each article on a four-point scale ("read all," "read most," "read some," or "didn't read"). The mail survey technique, also frequently used, involves sending a second copy of the magazine to a subscriber shortly after the regular copy has been mailed, with instructions on how to mark the survey copy. For example, the respondents might be instructed to mark with a check the articles they scanned, to draw an X through articles read in their entirety, and to underline titles of articles that were only partly read. Laitin (1997) presents a basic outline of the methods used to survey magazine subscribers.

Most consumer magazines use audience data compiled by Experian Simmons (formerly Simmons Market Research Bureau) and GfK MRI (formerly Mediamark Research Inc.). Both companies select a large random sample of households and identify readers by showing household members cards displaying a magazine's title. Once a magazine's readers are identified, detailed data are collected in follow-up interviews. Because many magazines are passed from person to person, GfK MRI also measures audience accumulation by tracking daily magazine reading behavior in a typical week using a special sample of 10,000 respondents. Variables include time spent reading, place of reading, and whether this was the first time the issue was read.

Both companies face a troublesome problem caused by the proliferation of magazines targeted for a narrow readership. It is difficult to draw a sample that includes enough readers of specialized publications to generate statistically reliable results. As of 2011, GfK MRI was interviewing about 26,000 people.

Many magazines maintain *reader panels* of 25 to 30 people who are selected to participate for a predetermined period. All feature articles that appear in each issue of the magazine are sent to these panel members, who rate each article on a number of scales, including interest, ease of reading, and usefulness. Over time, a set of guidelines for evaluating the success of an article is drawn up, and future articles can be measured against that standard. The primary advantage of this form of panel survey is that it can provide information about audience reactions at a modest cost. Other publications might use surveys that are included with the magazine itself.

The most recent trend is to use online reader panels. The sample size of the online panel is much larger than that of a traditional panel, and much more information can be gathered. The downside of the online panel is that it is probably not a representative sample of all readers. Nonetheless, online panels are cheap and quick, and many magazines use them (Lindsay, 2002). *Rolling Stone*, for example, launched a 10,000-member panel in 2001. *YM* maintained an online panel of several hundred teenage females to evaluate the magazine's content and to spot new trends.

The Magazine Publishers of America commissioned the Media Management Center to conduct a comprehensive study of the magazine readership experience. As part of this project, the Center employed the uses and gratifications approach to isolate 39 dimensions of the readership experience (*Magazine Reader Experience Study*, 2004). Some of the uses that emerged were "to get value for time and money," "to make me smarter," and "it's part of my routine."

Readership: Measuring Daily or Weekly

Since newspaper readership research began, it has been geared to measure the amount of readership garnered by daily newspapers. One of the most common questions used to measure readership has been "Did you read a newspaper today or yesterday?" This question, however, is not adequate to measure weekly newspaper reading. Surveys done on Mondays, Tuesdays, Wednesdays, Saturdays, and Sundays would probably not accurately assess the reading of a weekly that appears on Thursday.

Thurlow and Milo (1993) suggest that more research should be devoted to the readership of weeklies. Their study of college students revealed that about half of them reported reading every issue of their campus weekly and a local paper weekly. In contrast, 56% of the students reported that they never read the local paper daily, and only about 3% were classified as everyday readers. The authors note that it is important to track these students to see whether they continue to prefer the weekly over the daily or whether they join the ranks of nonreaders.

Circulation Research

Before the Internet complicated things, circulation referred to the number of people who received a newspaper or magazine via subscription or who bought a paper or magazine at a newsstand or vending machine. Today, however, with newspapers and magazines available on multiple platforms (computer, tablet, smartphone, e-reader) circulation is a less useful measurement. A copy of a newspaper or magazine may be read by more than one person and may be read in print or on an electronic device. Consequently, publishers prefer to measure **reach,** or the total audience that reads a newspaper or magazine in print or digitally.

Measuring reach across platforms is a challenging task and there are several different techniques. Scarborough Research, for example, defines reach as the percentage of adults in the market who have read the printed newspaper over 5 weekdays or on Sunday, or who visited the newspaper's website(s), or did both during the past 7 days. The Audit Bureau of Circulations (ABC) reports online audiences for both 7 days and 30 days. In addition, as of 2011, the

ABC now reports a publication's total average circulation, a number that includes both print and digital editions.

Measuring the traffic to a publication's website presents additional problems. The typical unit of measurement is "unique users," the total number of different people who have accessed a website at least once in a month. The problem with this metric is that a person who visited a newspaper website 20 times in a month is counted the same as a person who visited the site only once. In addition, a person who accessed the site via both a computer and a smartphone would be counted as two unique visitors.

Other measures are also available. Internet research company comScore reports average daily visitors, average visits per visitor, total pages viewed, and average minutes per visit. For example, in October 2011 newspaper websites averaged more than 24 million daily visitors who averaged about 10 visits a month and spent about 4 minutes on the site per visit. As advertisers learn more about what measures are most useful for their needs, it is likely that industry standards will take better shape.

Affinity, a market research company, provides information about the reach of particular magazines. Working with Experian Simmons, Affinity publishes the American Magazine Study (AMS). Based on a sample of 60,000 readers, Affinity's website states that the AMS measures "total audience estimates for magazine brands, including traditional printed magazines as well as a magazine's digital audience across a variety of platforms—magazine websites, social networks, electronic subscriptions and magazine apps designed for iPads, e-readers and other mobile devices." For example, the Spring 2011 AMS reported that *Vogue*'s print version reached about 9 million adults while its digital edition reached another 2 million.

Much of current **circulation research** that focuses on print newspapers examines how to maintain a circulation base that is attractive to advertisers and is also profitable for the publication. Several metropolitan papers have conducted cost/benefit analyses to determine whether circulation in areas distant from the city center is worth keeping. Some, including the *Atlanta Journal Constitution*, have ceased delivery to outlying counties in an effort to cut expenses. Lindsay (2009), for example, outlines "customer profitability analysis," a technique that describes how newspapers can distinguish profitable subscribers and preprint advertisers from less profitable ones, with the goal of maximizing profits.

A second area of traditional newspaper circulation research looks at the effects of content variables on circulation. Lacy and Fico (1991) demonstrated that measures of the content quality of a newspaper were positively related to circulation figures. Ha and Litman (1997) conducted a longitudinal analysis of the impact of magazine advertising clutter on the circulation of 10 magazines. They found that increased clutter had a negative impact on the circulation of entertainment magazines but not of news magazines. Lastly, Cho, Thorson, and Lacy (2004) documented that staff increases and more local news helped improve circulation at selected papers.

A third area looks at economic influences on circulation. Lewis (1995) found that increases in price were related to declines in circulation. Marchetti (1996) detailed several economic factors that were related to declining circulation, including increased advertising cost, cutbacks in newsstand distribution, and a concentration on core market areas. Finally, Bakker (2007) found that competition from free daily newspapers had minimal impact on the circulation of paid newspapers. Currently, newspapers and magazines are exploring how digital paid subscription models (such as those available through Apple) will impact their reach.

A fourth type of traditional circulation research uses the individual reader as the unit of analysis to measure the effects of certain aspects of delivery on reader behavior. For example, McCombs, Mullins, and Weaver (1974) studied why people cancel their subscriptions to newspapers. They found that the primary reasons had less to do with content than with circulation problems, such as irregular delivery and delivery in unreadable condition. Seamon (2000) looked at several newspaper delivery variables and concluded that the age of the carrier was not a factor in missed or late delivery.

Magazine publishers often conduct this type of circulation research by drawing samples of subscribers in different states and checking on the delivery dates of their publication and its physical condition when received. Other publications contact subscribers who do not renew to determine what can be done to prevent cancellation (Sullivan, 1993). Calvacca (2003) reports the results of a survey sponsored by the Audit Bureau of Circulations that asked consumers about their magazine purchases at newsstands. The survey revealed that single-copy purchasers would become regular subscribers if the subscription price were perceived as a bargain and that direct-mail campaigns were still effective at building circulation.

Some circulation research uncovers facts that management would probably never be aware of. For example, at the *Wichita Eagle*, management was puzzled about circulation losses. A survey found that many subscribers were canceling because the plastic delivery bags used by the paper on rainy days were not heavy enough, and many readers were fed up with soggy papers. In short, this type of circulation research investigates the effect on readership or subscription rates of variables that are unrelated to a publication's content.

In closing, research about online circulation is an evolving area. One avenue of research looks at geographic differences among online readers. This is a significant topic because if most of an online publication's audience are logging onto the publication's website from long distances, it may make the website less attractive for local advertisers. Sylvie and Chyi (2007) used comScore data to determine that all newspapers attract a substantial number of readers from outside of the print newspaper's market. Out-of-market readers comprised about half of all visitors.

Other avenues of emerging research involve the effect of paywalls on subscriptions; audiences' preferences for apps or browsers to access newspapers and magazines; and the

A CLOSER LOOK

New Media, New Research Topics

As more newspapers and magazines funnel their resources into their digital versions, new research topics become important. Below is a sample of some recent research done by private-sector firms concerning the new media landscape that confronts the traditional print media:

- Localytics, a research firm that specializes in app usage, reported that iPad users' sessions on news sites were 2.5 times longer than the average iPad visit.
- Digital research company L2 Think Tank surveyed Americans born between 1977 and 2002 and found that 65% accessed newspaper content through their computers, compared to 19% who read a print version. Another 14% read the news on their phone or e-reader.
- Market Research firm Outsell Inc. surveyed online news users and found that 44% scanned the headlines on Google News and didn't access any newspaper sites.

- A study by industry publication *Adweek* disclosed that 43% of people ignored Internet banner ads, but only 6% ignored print newspaper ads.
- A Pew Center study found that only 19% of its sample were willing to pay for online news. When asked whether people had to pay for online news, 54% preferred a full subscription plan as opposed to paying for individual stories.
- Research consultant Chris Snider found that the top three newspapers with the most Facebook fans were the *New York Times,* the *Wall Street Journal,* and the *Washington Post.*

(Note that when the first edition of this book was published, the above research projects would have been impossible to do because the technologies did not yet exist. New technologies inevitably generate new research topics.)

impact of tablet computers, e-readers, and smartphones on print subscriptions.

Newspaper Management Research

The declining fortunes of the print newspaper industry have refocused this area of research. For example, before the current economic downturn, job satisfaction among newspaper employees was the topic of several studies. Now, with some newspapers cutting back on staff and some going out of business, job satisfaction is less of an issue. Most journalists are probably happy to have a job.

Several researchers have looked at the impact of downsizing. Besley and Roberts (2010) discovered that cuts in the number of employees at a newspaper resulted in less coverage of public meetings. Reinardy (2010) surveyed editors at 23 newspapers and found that reduced numbers of employees in the newsroom resulted in complaints about work overload and that many veteran journalists were uncomfortable with an increasing emphasis on reporting for the web.

The effect of various management structures at newspapers and magazines is still a significant research area and will probably remain important as newspapers and magazines downsize and streamline. Neuzil, Hansen, and Ward (1999) analyzed the impact of participatory management and topic teams on employees' feelings of empowerment. They found little evidence that such an approach was beneficial. A study conducted by the Readership Institute (2001) looked at the management culture of 90 newspapers across the United States. Their results suggested that the culture at more than 70 of the papers could be classified as "defensive," whereas only 17 evidenced what was called a "constructive" atmosphere. Adams (2008) concluded that most weekly newspapers did not follow any type of management strategy when developing an online edition.

Another area of management research looks at the impact of concentration of ownership in the newspaper industry. For example, Akhavan-Majid, Rife, and Gopinah (1991) studied editorial positions taken by Gannett-owned papers. They found that the Gannett papers were more likely than other newspapers to endorse similar editorial positions. Coulson (1994) sampled 773 journalists at independent and group-owned papers about the quality of their publications. Reporters at independently owned papers were more likely to rate their paper's commitment to quality local coverage as excellent. Coulson and Hansen (1995) examined the news content of the *Louisville Courier-Journal* after its purchase by the Gannett organization. Results indicated that the total amount of news space increased but that the average length of stories and the amount of hard news coverage decreased. Lacy and Blanchard (2003) found that public ownership of a newspaper was associated with a smaller newsroom staff and higher profits. Martin (2003) found that clustered ownership of newspapers was associated with increased operating efficiency, and Beam (2008) discovered that the content of publicly owned papers did not differ significantly from the content of privately owned papers.

Readability Research

Simply defined, **readability** is the sum total of all the elements and their interactions that affect the success of a piece of printed material. Success is measured by the extent to which readers understand the piece, are able to read it at an optimal speed, and find it interesting (Dale & Chall, 1948).

Several formulas have been developed to determine objectively the readability of text. One of the best known is the **Flesch** (1948) **reading ease formula**, which requires the researcher to select systematically 100 words from the text, determine the total number of syllables in those words (*wl*), determine the average number of words per sentence (*sl*), and perform the following calculation:

$$\text{Reading ease} = 206.835 - 0.846wl - 1.015sl$$

The score is compared to a chart that provides a description of style (such as "very easy") or a school grade level for the potential audience. An alternate version of the Flesch formula is the **Flesch–Kincaid Readability Test,** which uses a score of 0–100. This number is translated to a corresponding school reading level. For example, the Flesch–Kincaid grade level for this chapter is calculated as twelfth grade.

Another measure of readability is the **Fog Index,** developed by Gunning (1952). To compute the Fog Index, researchers must systematically select samples of 100 words each, determine the mean sentence length by dividing the number of words by the number of sentences, count the number of words with three or more syllables, add the mean sentence length to the number of words with three or more syllables, and multiply this sum by 0.4. Like the Flesch index, the Gunning formula suggests the educational level required for understanding a text. The chief advantages of the Fog Index are that the syllable count and the overall calculations are simpler to perform. (Check the Internet for online calculation programs to compute the Fog Index.)

Taylor (1953) developed yet another method for measuring readability, called the **Cloze procedure.** This technique departs from the formulas described in that it does not require an actual count of words or syllables. Instead, the researcher chooses a passage of about 250–300 words, deletes every fifth word from a random starting point, and replaces it with a blank. The researcher then gives the passage to subjects and asks them to fill the blanks with what they think are the correct words; the researcher then counts the

number of times the blanks are replaced with the correct words. The number of correct words or the percentage of correct replacement constitutes the readability score for that passage. The following paragraph is a sample of what a passage might look like after it has been prepared for the Cloze procedure:

> The main stronghold of the far left _____ to be large _____ centers of north Italy. _____ is significant, however, that _____ largest relative increase in _____ leftist vote occurred in _____ areas where most of _____ landless peasants live—in _____ and south Italy and Sicily and Sardinia. The _____ had concentrated much of its efforts on winning the _____ of those peasants.

Nestvold (1972) found that Cloze procedure scores were highly correlated with readers' own evaluations of content difficulty. The Cloze procedure was also found to be a better predictor of evaluations than several other common readability tests.

Although they are not used extensively in newspaper and magazine research, readability studies can provide valuable information. Smith (1984) found differences in readability among categories of newspaper content, with features and entertainment more readable than national-international or state and local news. Smith also noted that three popular readability formulas did not assign the same level of reading difficulty to his sample of stories. Porter and Stephens (1989) found that a sample of Utah managing editors consistently underestimated the Flesch readability scores of five different stories from five different papers. They also found that the common claim that reporters write front-page stories at an eighth-grade level was a myth. The hard news stories they analyzed were written at an average twelfth-grade level. McAdams (1992/1993) computed a Fog Index for 14 news stories that were then given to a sample of readers. Results suggest that a high Fog Index did not adversely affect readers who found a story to have high overall quality. Lastly, Bodle (1996) compared the readability levels of a sample of student newspapers with a sample of private-sector papers and found that the private-sector dailies had a higher score than the student papers.

Several online calculators measure the readability of websites. See, for example, *www.read-able.com* and *http://juicystudio.com/services/readability.php*. The Flesch-Kincaid level for the companion website for this book, *wimmerdominick.com,* is about the eighth grade.

Qualitative Methods and the Print Media

Private-sector researchers often use qualitative techniques to uncover factors related to print media readership that might have been overlooked by quantitative methods. For example, Lyon (1998) reported the results of focus group interviews that revealed some reasons people did not read the newspaper: having to recycle, perceived bias, and reliance on TV news. Mason (2000) did field observations and interviews in a donut shop. She found that some people did not read a newspaper because they didn't have the change necessary to buy a paper from a vending machine. Saba (2004) reported findings from a series of focus groups among teens that looked at their attitudes toward newspaper reading. The results suggested that teens wanted concise news and didn't like news that was "dumbed down." The focus groups also revealed that newspapers have an image problem among teens. When the groups were asked to respond to photos of teens reading newspapers, the participants snickered and some said the kids in the pictures were acting "nerdy."

The Readership Institute also relied on qualitative methods in their study of newspaper and magazine readership experiences. Intensive interviews that lasted more than an hour were conducted with both newspaper and magazine readers. Researchers took the results of these interviews and used them to develop items for a quantitative survey.

WEBSITE USABILITY RESEARCH

As of 2011, more than 1,200 newspapers were publishing both traditional print and online versions. The total number of magazines online is harder to pin down. In 2010 the Magazine Publishers of America Association listed more than 13,000 online magazines. As online readership continues to increase and becomes more important to the publication's bottom line, new lines of research develop. One such area that has become popular in recent years is website **usability research.** On a general level, usability research is a method by which users of a product or service are asked to perform certain tasks in an effort to measure the product or service's ease of use, its task time, and the user's perception of the experience. With regard to newspapers and magazines, usability research deals with the usefulness and convenience of a publication's website or app.

Stewart (2008) provides a description of a small-scale usability study done by a local newspaper. The paper posted an online questionnaire about its site and invited 16 readers to its office to participate in a testing session. Some readers tested the old site while others did back-to-back comparisons of the old site and a new site. In a typical study, readers might be asked to find an email address for a reporter, post a comment, read certain stories, search for a topic, or navigate through certain menus. Researchers observe the behaviors of those using the site, keep track of how much time they take in completing the assigned tasks, and encourage the readers to voice comments. Usability research can uncover problems in navigating around the site, detect confusing designs, and identify distracting or annoying placement of advertising.

Lynch (2009) reports the results of a qualitative usability study using intensive interviews with 15 individuals who were heavy Internet users. An analysis of the interviews suggested that the most usable and convenient websites shared a number of features: They communicated clearly what they had to offer, helped users find where to look for information, made it easy to tell what was new, and did not overload the user with information.

Usability research is also a common technique in research about online magazines. Faydeyev (2009) summarizes several mistakes made by magazines and other online sites that make their sites less usable. They include, among others, tiny clickable areas, content that is difficult to scan, no way to get in touch with content creators, and no way to search the site. Budiu and Nielsen (2011) analyzed changes in the usability of the *USA Today* app. They found that tiny icons and tiny search boxes hurt usability. Krug (2005) has a detailed discussion on usability and website design. (Krug's First Law of Usability is "Don't Make Me Think.")

SUMMARY

Magazine and newspaper research began in the 1920s and for much of its early existence was qualitative in nature. Typical research studies dealt with law, history, and international press comparisons. During the 1930s and 1940s, readership surveys and studies of the effectiveness of print media advertising were frequently done by private firms. By the 1950s, quantitative research techniques became common in print media research. The continuing competition between television and radio for advertisers and audiences during the past three decades has spurred the growth of private-sector research.

Research done by newspapers and magazines encompasses readership studies, circulation studies, management studies, readability studies, and online usability studies. Readership research is the most extensive area; it serves to determine who reads a publication, what items are read, and what gratifications the readers get from their choices. Circulation studies examine the various aspects of the delivery and pricing systems. Management studies look at management structure and the impact of consolidation of ownership on newspaper and magazine content and quality.

Readability studies investigate the textual elements that affect comprehension of a message. A more recent research area examines the usability of newspaper and magazine websites.

Key Terms

Aided recall	Magazine readership
Circulation research	survey
Cloze procedure	Psychographic studies
Eye camera	Reach
Flesch formula	Readability study
Fog Index	Reader profile
Item-selection study	Reader–nonreader
Journalist–reader	study
comparison	Tracking study
Lifestyle segmentation	Usability research
studies	Uses and gratifications

 Using the Internet

For more information on the topics mentioned in this chapter, search the Internet for "*tracking study*," "*eye camera*," "*readership studies*," and "*usability research*." Many websites contain useful information for anyone interested in newspaper and magazine research. The sites mentioned here represent only a small sampling.

1. *www.empowermemagazine.com/index.php/ category/readers-panel/* You can join Empower Me! magazine's online reader panel at this site. Note the kind of information the magazine wants to know about its readers.

2. *http://readership.org* This site of the Readership Institute of the Media Management Center at Northwestern University contains links to reports of surveys, content analyses, and management studies pertaining to newspapers.

3. *www.magazine.org* The Magazine Publishers of America maintains this site that contains links to magazine readership and advertising data.

4. *www.naa.org* The Newspaper Association of America's home page contains links to several research studies concerning both print and online newspapers.

Questions and Problems for Further Investigation

1. Assume you are the editor of an afternoon newspaper faced with a declining circulation. What types of research projects could you conduct to help increase your readership?

2. Now suppose you have decided to publish a new magazine about women's sports. What types of research would you conduct before starting publication? Why?

3. Conduct a uses and gratifications pilot study of 15–20 people to determine why they do or do not read the local daily newspaper.

4. Examine the websites of several online newspapers. Conduct an informal usability study of each.

5. Assume your newspaper is developing an app for mobile devices. What information about your potential audience would you want to know?

For additional resources, go to *www.wimmer dominick.com* and *www.cengagebrain.com.*

References and Suggested Readings

Aaker, D., Kumar, V., & Day, G. (2009). *Marketing research*. New York, NY: Wiley.

Adams, J. (2008). Innovation management and U.S. weekly newspaper websites. *International Journal on Media Management, 10*(1), 64–73.

Akhavan-Majid, A. M., Rife, A., & Gopinah, S. (1991). Chain ownership and editorial independence. *Journalism Quarterly, 68*(1/2), 59–66.

Ambroz, J. (2004). From the reader's modem to the advertiser's ear. *Folio, 33*(1), 10–11.

Astor, D. (2000). Relative readership of syndicated stuff. *Editor & Publisher, 133*(33), 21.

Bakker, P. (2007). The impact of free daily newspapers on the circulation of paid newspapers. Conference paper presented to the International Communication Association.

Bartlett, M. (2001, June 22). Study predicts black skies ahead for newspapers. Retrieved August 18, 2001, from *www.newsbytes.com*

Beam, R. (2008). Content in publicly, privately owned newspapers more alike than different. *Newspaper Research Journal, 29*(4), 74–80.

Beaudoin, C., & Thorson, E. (2002). Journalists, public differ on perception of media coverage. *Newspaper Research Journal, 23*(4), 52–62.

Besley, J., & Roberts, M. (2010). Cuts in newspaper staffs change meeting coverage. *Newspaper Research Journal, 31*(3), 22–35.

Bernt, J. P., Fee, F. E., Gifford, J., & Stempel, G. (2000). How well can editors predict reader interest in news? *Newspaper Research Journal, 21*(2), 2–11.

Bleyer, W. (1924). Research problems and newspaper analysis. *Journalism Bulletin, 1*(1), 17–22.

Bodle, J. V. (1996). Assessing news quality: A comparison between community and student daily newspapers. *Journalism & Mass Communication Quarterly, 73*(3), 672–686.

Bogart, L. (1989). *Press and public*. Hillsdale, NJ: Lawrence Erlbaum.

Bogart, L. (1991). *Preserving the press*. New York, NY: Columbia University Press.

Budiu, R., & Nielsen, J. (2011). *Usability of iPad apps and websites*. Fremont, CA: Nielsen Norman Group.

Calvacca, L. (2003). The sweet buy and buy. *Folio, 32*(11), 19.

Chaffee, S., & Choe, S. (1981). Newspaper reading in longitudinal perspective. *Journalism Quarterly, 58*(2), 201–211.

Ciotta, R. (1996). Baby, you should drive this CAR. *American Journalism Review, 18*(2), 34–39.

Click, J. W., & Stempel, G. (1982). *Reader response to front pages with modular format and color* (ANPA News Research Report No. 35). Reston, VA: ANPA News Research Center.

Cobb-Walgren, C. J. (1990). Why teenagers do not read all about it. *Journalism Quarterly, 67*(2), 340–347.

Collins, S. (2003). Level of on-campus activities predicts student paper readership. *Newspaper Research Journal, 24*(4), 102–106.

Coulson, D. (1994). Impact of ownership on newspaper quality. *Journalism Quarterly, 71*(2), 403–410.

Coulson, D., & Hansen, A. (1995). The *Louisville Courier-Journal*'s news content after purchase by Gannett. *Journalism & Mass Communication Quarterly, 72*(1), 205–215.

Curtin, P., Dougall, E., & Mersey, R. (2007). Study compares Yahoo! news story preferences. *Newspaper Research Journal, 28*(4), 22–36.

Dale, E., & Chall, J. S. (1948). A formula for predicting readability. *Education Research Journal, 27*(1), 11–20.

Davis, N. (2001). Measures for measures. *Presstime, 23*(4), 38–44.

Ellonen, H., Tarkiainen, A., & Kuivalainen, O. (2010). The effect of magazine website usage on print magazine loyalty. *The International Journal on Media Management, 12*(1), 21–37.

Faydeyev, D. (2009). 9 common usability mistakes in web design. Smashing Magazine. Retrieved March 15, 2009, from *www.smashingmagazine.com/2009/02/18/9-common-usability-blunders*

Fidler, R. (2011). RJI-DPA spring 2011 iPad survey results. Reynolds Journalism Institute. Retrieved November 12, 2011, from *www.rjionline.org/news/rji-dpa-spring-2011-ipad-survey-results*

Fisher, C. (1993, July 26). Newspaper readers get choosier. *Advertising Age, 64*(28) p. 22.

Fitzgerald, M. (2000). Reading edge report. *Editor & Publisher, 133*(41), 22–27.

Flesch, R. (1948). A new readability yardstick. *Journal of Applied Psychology, 32*(2), 221–233.

Gersh, D. (1990, April 7). Reaching the teenage reader. *Editor & Publisher, 123*(15) p. 18.

Gladney, G. A. (1996). How editors and readers rank and rate the importance of eighteen traditional standards of newspaper excellence. *Journalism & Mass Communication Quarterly, 73*(2), 319–331.

Gunning, R. (1952). *The technique of clear writing.* New York, NY: McGraw-Hill.

Ha, L., & Litman, B. R. (1997). Does advertising clutter have diminishing and negative returns? *Journal of Advertising, 26*(1), 31–42.

Harper, C. (1996). Online newspapers: Going somewhere or going nowhere? *Newspaper Research Journal, 17*(3/4), 2–13.

Janofsky, M. (1993, July 22). A survey shows Tina Brown's *New Yorker* is attracting more and wealthier readers. *New York Times*, p. D21.

Kayani, J. M., & Yelsma, P. (2000). Displacement effects on online media in the socio-technical contexts of households. *Journal of Broadcasting & Electronic Media, 44*(2), 215–229.

Kaye, B. (2010). Going to the blogs. *Atlantic Journal of Communication, 18*(1), 194–210.

Krug, S. (2005). *Don't make me think.* Berkeley, CA: New Riders Press.

Lacy, S., & Blanchard, A. (2003). The impact of public ownership, profits and competition on number of newspaper employees and starting salaries at mid-sized daily newspapers. *Journalism & Mass Communication Quarterly, 80*(4), 949–968.

Lacy, S., & Fico, F. (1991). The link between content quality and circulation. *Newspaper Research Journal, 12*(2), 46–56.

Laitin, J. A. (1997, June 1). Subscriber surveys that sing. *Folio, 26*(8), 88–89.

Lee, D. W. (2001). *A comparative study: Use of online vs. print media newspapers and gratifications.* Unpublished master's thesis. Department of Telecommunication, University of Georgia, Athens, Georgia.

Lewis, R. (1995). Relation between newspaper subscription price and circulation. *Journal of Media Economics, 8*(1), 25–41.

Lindsay, G. (2002). Lights, camera, research. *Folio, 31*(7), 22–25.

Lindsay, M. (2009). *Customer profitability analysis.* Conference paper presented to the Newspaper Association of America, San Diego, CA., April, 2009.

Lynch, S. (2008). *What it takes to be a web favorite.* Evanston, IL: Northwestern University Media Management Center.

Lynch, S. (2009). *How to become "easy to use" online.* Evanston, IL: Northwestern University Media Management Center.

Lyon, C. (1998). Women grade the newspaper. *Presstime, 20*(12), 65.

Magazine reader experience study. (2004). Evanston, IL: Northwestern University.

Martin, H. (2003). Clustered newspapers operate more efficiently. *Newspaper Research Journal, 24*(4), 6–22.

Mason, K. (2000). Price vs. sales. *Presstime, 22*(11), 37–40.

Marchetti, M. (1996). The scoop on circulation. *Sales & Marketing Management, 148*(3), 61–62.

McAdams, K. (1992/1993). Readability reconsidered. *Newspaper Research Journal, 13/14*(4/1), 50–59.

McCombs, M., Mullins, L. E., & Weaver, D. (1974). *Why people subscribe and cancel: A stop-start survey of three daily newspapers* (ANPA News Research Bulletin No. 3). Reston, VA: ANPA News Research Center.

Nafziger, R. (1930). A reader interest survey of Madison, Wisconsin. *Journalism Quarterly, 7*(2), 128–141.

Nestvold, K. (1972). Cloze procedure correlation with perceived readability. *Journalism Quarterly, 49*(3), 592–594.

Neuzil, M., Hansen, K., & Ward, J. (1999). Twin Cities journalists' assessment of topic teams. *Newspaper Research Journal, 20*(1), 2–16.

Newspaper Association of America. (2011). Daily newspaper section readership. Retrieved November 16, 2011, from *http://www.naa.org/Trends-and-Numbers/Readership/~/media/NAACorp/Public% 20Files/TrendsAndNumbers/Readership/Daily_ Sections_2011.ashx*

Novak, T. P., & MacEvoy, B. (1990, June). On comparing alternative schemes: LOV and VALS. *Journal of Consumer Research, 17*(1), 105–109.

Olmstead, K., Mitchell, A., & Rosenstiel, T. (2011). *Navigating news online: Where people go, how they get there and what lures them away.* Washington, DC: Pew Research Center's Project for Excellence in Journalism.

Papacharissi, Z., & Rubin, A. R. (2000). Predictors of Internet use. *Journal of Broadcasting & Electronic Media, 44*(2), 175–196.

Penrose, J., Weaver, D., Cole, R., & Shaw, D. (1974). The newspaper non-reader ten years later. *Journalism Quarterly, 51*(4), 631–639.

Perse, E., & Courtright, A. (1993). Normative images of communication media. *Human Communication Research, 19*(4), 485–503.

Pew Research Center for People and the Press, (2006). *Online papers modestly boost newspaper readership.* Washington, D.C.: Pew Research Center.

Pew Research Center for People and the Press (2009). *Newspapers face a challenging calculus.* Washington, DC: Pew Research Center.

Pew Research Center for People and the Press (2010a). *Americans spending more time following the news.* Washington, DC: Pew Research Center.

Pew Research Center for People and the Press (2010b). *New media. Old media.* Washington, DC: Pew Research Center.

Pew Research Center for People and the Press (2011). *The tablet revolution.* Washington, DC: Pew Research Center.

Porter, W. C., & Stephens, F. (1989). Estimating readability: A study of Utah editors' abilities. *Newspaper Research Journal, 10*(2), 87–96.

Readership Institute. (2001). *Impact study.* Evanston, IL: Northwestern University Media Management Center.

Reinardy, S. (2010). Need for speed onto Internet clashes with journalistic values. *Newspaper Research Journal, 31*(1), 69–84.

Saba, J. (2004). Study says papers not reaching teens. *Editor & Publisher, 137*(5), 18.

Schramm, W. (1957). Twenty years of journalism research. *Public Opinion Quarterly, 21*(1), 91–108.

Seamon, M. (2000). How demographic variables affect newspaper delivery. *Newspaper Research Journal, 21*(1), 91–101.

Smith, R. (1984). How consistently do readability tests measure the difficulty of newswriting? *Newspaper Research Journal, 5*(4), 1–8.

Stewart, S. (2008). News sites large and small can measure usability. *Online Journalism Review.* Retrieved March 15, 2009, from *www.ojr.org/ojr/stories/ 08117/stewar/*

Stone, G. (1994). Race yields to education as predictor of newspaper use. *Newspaper Research Journal, 15*(1), 115–126.

Stone, G., & Boudreau, T. (1995). 1985, 1994: Comparison of reader content preferences. *Newspaper Research Journal, 16*(4), 13–28.

Sullivan, C. (1993, November 1). Expire research is no dead end. *Folio, 22*(11), pp. 39–40.

Swanson, C. (1955). What they read in 130 daily newspapers. *Journalism Quarterly, 32*(3), 411–421.

Sylvie, G. (1996). Departmental influences on interdepartmental cooperation in daily newspapers. *Journalism & Mass Communication Quarterly, 73*(1), 230–241.

Sylvie, G., & Chyi, H. (2007). One product two markets: How geography differentiates online newspaper audiences. *Journalism & Mass Communication Quarterly, 84*(3), 562–581.

Taylor, W. (1953). Cloze procedure: A new tool for measuring readability. *Journalism Quarterly, 30*(4), 415–433.

Thurlow, G., & Milo, K. (1993). Newspaper readership. *Newspaper Research Journal, 14*(3/4), 34–43.

Wanta, W., Hu, Y. W., & Wu, Y. C. (1995). Getting more people to read more newspapers. *Newspaper Research Journal, 16*(1), 103–115.

Who's reading what? (2004). *Editor & Publisher, 137*(8), 49.

Younger, heavy online-news consumers don't read newspapers. (2008). Retrieved November 17, 2011, from *www.marketingcharts.com/print/ younger-heavy-online-news-consumers-dont-read-newspapers-3841*

CHAPTER 14

RESEARCH IN THE ELECTRONIC MEDIA

CHAPTER OUTLINE

Research in the electronic media has been a staple management tool for successful managers for several decades because managers need to know what their target audience wants. As Phil LoCascio (2012), a major market program director from New Jersey (USA), says:

> Research is the only way to find out about target listeners and what they want from a station. Research helps us determine when we must adjust our business to meet new demands. This is important because changes in broadcasting can happen in a matter of minutes. Competition has increased dramatically with the advent of the Internet. We are now competing with stations from around the world in addition to local competition. How do we best serve your audience? We have to ask them.
>
> The ratings winners in broadcasting use quality research and accurately analyze the data. Some stations conduct research yet lose in the ratings because they either have used inferior research or have come to the wrong conclusions. In broadcasting, there is no replacement for quality research information.

There are many types of researchers in the electronic media who provide the quality information that is needed. For example, there are professional research companies; in-house research departments in most radio, television, cable, TV network, and satellite operations; and many research departments or divisions in colleges and universities. Electronic media research is a multimillion-dollar business that continually changes because of advancements in technology and improved research methods. This chapter introduces some of the more widely used research procedures in this area.

BACKGROUND

Broadcast research has developed rapidly in sophistication and volume since its beginnings in the 1920s. In the early years of broadcasting, broadcasters were experimenters and hobbyists who were interested mainly in making sure that their signal was being sent and received. The popularity of radio was unknown, and there was no reason to be concerned with audience size at that time.

The situation changed quickly during the 1930s as radio became a popular mass medium. When radio began to attract large audiences, concern emerged over how radio would be financed. After much discussion, advertising emerged as the choice over government financing or taxes on sales of equipment. The acceptance by radio listeners of advertising on radio was the first step in the development of electronic media research.

Advertisers, not broadcasters, were the initiators of broadcast research. When commercials began airing on radio stations, advertisers naturally wondered how many listeners were exposed to their messages and how effective the messages were. It became the responsibility of broadcasters to provide empirical information about the size and characteristics of their audience. This situation still exists—advertisers continually want information about the people who hear and see their commercial announcements.

In addition to information about audience size, advertisers became interested in *why* people behave the way they do. This led to the development of the research area known as **psychographics**. However, because psychographics data are rather vague, they were not adequate predictors of audience behavior, and advertisers wanted more information. Research procedures were then designed to study lifestyle patterns and how they affect media use and buying behavior. Such information is valuable in designing advertising campaigns: If advertisers understand the lifestyle patterns of the people who purchase their products, they can design commercials to match those lifestyles.

Electronic media research studies today fall into two broad categories: ratings and nonratings research. The remainder of this chapter discusses these two areas.

RATINGS RESEARCH

When radio became popular and advertisers began to grasp its potential for attracting customers, they were faced with the problem of documenting audience size. The print media were able to provide circulation figures, but broadcasters had no equivalent "hard" information, just unsubstantiated estimates. The early attempts at audience measurement failed to provide adequate data. Mail and telephone calls to the radio station from listeners were the first sources of data, but it is now a well-known fact that mail and telephone calls from a handful of listeners or viewers do not represent the general audience. A myth that someone started long ago, which many people still believe today, is that one letter or one telephone call to a radio station represents 10 listeners. Advertisers and broadcasters quickly realized that more information was urgently needed.

Since 1930, when a group called the Cooperative Analysis of Broadcasting conducted one of the first audience surveys for radio, several companies have attempted to provide syndicated audience information. Two companies have survived and provide the bulk of syndicated ratings information for radio, television, and cable: Nielsen Media Research for television and Arbitron for radio. The United States is divided into about 366 metropolitan markets or areas. Nielsen conducts TV ratings in 210 of the markets; Arbitron conducts radio ratings in 284. In many markets, both companies provide ratings data throughout the year, known as *continuous measurement*, not just during certain times of the year as in the past.

Nielsen

Nielsen Media Research is located in Northbrook, Illinois, and is a subsidiary of the Nielsen Company (see *www.nielsen.com*). The original company (A. C. Nielsen) was founded in 1945 and is now owned by Nielsen Holdings N.V., a group of investors (N.V. is an abbreviation for two Dutch words that have an equivalent English meaning of "Limited Liability Corporation"). Nielsen is one of the world's largest market research companies.

Nielsen Media Research is involved in television ratings in several countries throughout the world and includes ratings and research for "national broadcast and cable networks, regional networks, syndicators, television stations, local cable TV systems, satellite distributors, advertising agencies and advertisers, program producers, station representatives and buying services" *(www.nielsenmedia.com)*.

Nielsen Media Research uses two types of data collection methods: diaries and electronic meters. The information is divided into two broad categories: *national* and *local*. This brief summary of Nielsen is from the company's website:

Meters & Diaries

Electronic metering technology is the heart of the Nielsen Media Research ratings process. We use two types of meters: Set Meters capture what channel is being viewed, while People Meters add information about who is watching. Diaries continue to be a valuable instrument in our measurement toolbox and are used to collect viewing information from sample homes in almost every television market in the United States. Each year we process approximately 2 million paper diaries from households across the country for the months of November, February, May and July—also known as the "sweeps" rating periods. This local viewing information provides a basis for program scheduling and advertising decisions for local television stations, cable systems, and advertisers. In some of the larger markets, diaries provide viewer information for up to three additional "sweeps" months (October, January and March).

Over the course of a sweeps month, diaries are mailed to a new panel of homes each week. At the end of the month, all of the viewing data from the individual weeks is aggregated.

People Meter Samples

Our national sample, composed of a cross-section of representative homes throughout the United States, is measured by People Meters, a technology that has been in place since 1987. These meters give us information about not only what is being viewed on the set, but also exactly which members of the household are watching.

The People Meter is a "box"—about the size of a paperback book—that's hooked up to each television set and is accompanied by a remote control unit. Each family member in a sample household is assigned a personal viewing button, which is matched to that person's age and sex. Whenever the TV is turned on, a light flashes on the meter, reminding viewers to press their assigned button and to indicate that they're watching television. Additional buttons on the People Meter enable guests who are also watching to participate in the sample by entering their age, sex and viewing status into the system.

In addition to our national measurement, Nielsen also measures some of the nation's largest local markets (such as New York, Los Angeles and Chicago) with Local People Meter Technology.

Set Meter Samples

Large to mid-sized local markets (such as Seattle, San Antonio and Memphis) are measured by a different type of meter—one that gives information about set-tuning only. In these markets, demographic information is provided by a separate sample of people who fill out seven-day paper diaries (or eight-day diaries in homes with DVRs).

Diary Samples

Smaller markets ... are measured by paper diaries only. These seven-day diaries (or eight-day diaries in homes with DVRs) are mailed to homes to keep a tally of what is watched on each television set and by whom.

Nielsen produces a variety of audience measurement reports, such as the *National Television Index* (NTI) for national measurements and the *National Station Index* (NSI) for local measurements. These publications and other information from Nielsen are discussed on the company's website, particularly in the sections titled "Measurement" and "News & Insights."

The metered data are used for NTI and NSI reports and for **overnights**, which are preliminary ratings data gathered to give network and station executives, program producers, advertising agencies, and others an indication of the performance of the previous night's programs. Because the sample sizes involved in overnights are small, the actual ratings for the programs do not appear until several days later, when an additional sample is added to increase statistical reliability.

In addition, Nielsen is also involved in Internet research with two products. First, Nielsen produces Nielsen Online, a variety of measurement services for the Internet, including audience measurement, Internet marketing, and online advertising (see *www.nielsen-online.com*.) Second, Nielsen's Net Ratings is a panel study to investigate Internet users' surfing along with consumer surveys designed to provide business and websites with consumer information.

Finally, Nielsen also produces a variety of research products for the mass media, such as SoundScan for radio station monitoring. See Nielsen's website for a complete description of the company's research products.

Arbitron

Arbitron (*www.arbitron.com*) was founded in 1949 as the American Research Bureau (ARB). The company name was changed to The Arbitron Company in 1972, then to The Arbitron Ratings Company in 1982, and back to The Arbitron Company in 1989. It is now **Arbitron, Inc.** Arbitron's headquarters are in New York City and Columbia, Maryland. For more information about the history of broadcast ratings, see Beville (1988).

Information from Arbitron's website says:

Arbitron Inc. (NYSE: ARB) is an international media and marketing research firm serving the media—radio, television, cable and out-of-home; the mobile industry as well as advertising agencies and advertisers around the world. Arbitron's businesses include: measuring network and local market radio audiences across the United States; surveying the retail, media and product patterns of U.S. consumers; providing mobile audience measurement and analytics in the United States, Europe, Asia and Australia, and developing application software used for analyzing media audience and marketing information data.

The Company has developed the Portable People Meter™ (PPM™) and the PPM 360™, new technologies for media and marketing research.

Arbitron's headquarters and its world-renowned research and engineering organizations are located in Columbia, Maryland.

Until 1995, Arbitron provided ratings for local television, but it now focuses only on radio by collecting information via diaries and the **Portable People Meter (PPM)**, discussed later in this chapter.

Although Arbitron continually measures most of the larger markets in the United States, the most important ratings period, historically called "books" because of their printed format, are produced in the winter, spring, summer, and fall, which are identified in Arbitron materials as WI, SP, SU, and FA. Arbitron also produces network radio ratings with its service called RADAR (Radio's All-Dimension Audience Research), with a complete explanation located at *www.arbitron.com/national_radio/radar_accountability.htm*.

We urge you to visit the Arbitron's website for extensive information about Arbitron products, services, and methodologies. We especially suggest that you print the publication titled *Arbitron Radio Market Report Reference Guide*, more commonly known as *The Purple Book*, which is located at *www.arbitron.com/downloads/purplebook.pdf*. This reference guide provides an excellent summary of Arbitron's methods and procedures.

Finally, Arbitron also conducts what the company calls Cross-Platform Services, which is described on the website (*www.arbitron.com/crossplatform/home.htm*) as follows:

Media are evolving, expanding beyond consumers' living rooms into the workplace, retail locations, restaurants, bars and more. Media have integrated into consumers' daily lives, nearly every hour of every day.

Television programs and events are no longer only fodder for the water cooler, they're consumed more than once, and on multiple platforms. Videos reach across the Internet as friends share links through mobile phones, social sites, email and instant messenger.

Now, more than ever, media companies, advertisers and agencies need research that evolves with their audiences to meet the changing needs of today's advertising marketplace. It's time to unchain media research and let it follow today's mobile consumer.

Focusing on the Consumer

Arbitron Cross-Platform Services focus on the consumer, whether he or she is in-home or away from home. With Arbitron's patented Portable People Meter™ system, the person—not the device—is measured, so that media are able to give advertisers a complete picture of their audience and a comprehensive measure of advertising impressions.

Demonstrate the Power of Your Audience

By capturing an individual's exposure to media, Arbitron provides media with a deeper understanding of their networks' and stations' reach. With this enhanced knowledge, media are able to give advertisers the insight they need to make effective media buying decisions.

Research from Arbitron makes it possible for media companies to drive increased value from their many platforms and enables advertisers to connect advertising exposure to business outcomes.

Ratings Controversy. Broadcast ratings create controversy in many areas. TV viewers complain that "good" shows are canceled; radio listeners complain that their favorite station changed its format; producers, actors, and other artists complain that "numbers" are no judge of artistic quality (they are not intended to be); radio and television station owners and operators complain that the results are not reliable; and advertisers balk at the lack of good information. Although there may be merit to some of

these complaints, one basic fact remains: Regardless of the amount of criticism about radio, television, and cable ratings, the basic procedures as they currently exist will remain the primary decision-making tool in programming and advertising.

Because ratings will continue to be used to make programming and nonprogramming decisions, it is important to understand two important facts: (1) Ratings are only approximations or estimates of audience size—the data do not measure either the quality of programs or opinions about the programs, and (2) not all ratings are equally dependable because each company uses it own methodology.

Because broadcast ratings are only estimates, they are not error free. The data must be interpreted in light of several limitations, which are always included in all Arbitron and Nielsen publications, such as this disclaimer from Arbitron's PPM website:

> PPM ratings are based on audience estimates and are the opinion of Arbitron and should not be relied on for precise accuracy or precise representativeness of a demographic or radio market.

Keep this in mind: Interpreting radio and television ratings as though they are facts (that is, 100% error-free) is a misuse of the data.

Ratings Methodology

The research methodologies used by Arbitron and Nielsen are complex, and each company publishes several documents describing its methods and procedures that should be consulted for specific information. As mentioned, the data for ratings surveys are currently gathered by two methods: diaries and electronic meters/recorders. Each method has advantages and disadvantages.

Broadcast ratings provide a classic example of the need to sample the population. With about 114.7 million households in the

United States in 2012, it would be impossible for any ratings company to conduct a census of media use. The companies naturally resort to sampling to produce data that are generalized to the population. For example, Nielsen's national samples are selected using national census data and involve multistage area probability sampling that ensures that the sample reflects actual population distributions. That is, if Los Angeles accounts for 10% of the television households in the United States, Los Angeles households should comprise 10% of the sample. Nielsen uses four stages in sampling: selection of counties in the country, selection of block groups within the counties, selection of certain blocks within the groups, and selection of individual households within the blocks. Nielsen claims that about 20% of the households in the NTI-metered sample of approximately 21,000 households are replaced each year.

To obtain samples for producing broadcast audience estimates, Arbitron and Nielsen use recruitment by telephone, which includes calls to listed and unlisted telephone numbers, as well as cell phone–only households. Although all ratings companies begin sample selection from telephone directories, each firm uses a statistical procedure to ensure that unlisted telephone numbers are included. This approach eliminates the bias that would be created if only people or households listed in telephone directories were asked to participate in broadcast audience estimates. Nielsen calls its procedure a Total Telephone Frame; Arbitron uses the term *Expanded Sample Frame*, as well as address-based sampling and sampling to reach cell phone–only households.

Target sample sizes for local audience measurements vary from market to market. Each ratings service uses a formula to establish a minimum sample size required for a specific level of statistical efficiency, but there is no guarantee that this number of subjects will actually be produced. Although many people may agree to participate in an audience survey, there is no way to force them all to complete the diaries they are given or to use electronic meters accurately. Additionally, completed diaries are often rejected because they are illegible or obviously inaccurate. The companies are often lucky to get a 50% response rate in their local market measurements.

Finally, because participation by minority groups in audience surveys is generally lower than for the remainder of the population, the companies make an extra effort to collect

A CLOSER LOOK

Ratings Diaries and Reports

In the previous editions of this textbook, we included sample pages from Arbitron and Nielsen diaries as well as pages from each company's ratings books. The problem with reproducing sample pages of these pages is that they become out of date very quickly. The Internet has changed our approach. Instead of including examples of diaries here, we will direct you to each company's website to see the most current examples. The Internet has also changed our typical procedure of including sample pages from each company's ratings books. Hard copies of ratings books are no longer published. All of the information for broadcasters and advertisers is available only online. However, we offer an alternative in the Reading a Ratings Book section of this chapter. Don't overlook these sources of additional information.

data from these groups by contacting households by telephone or in person to assist them in completing the diary. These methods are used in high-density Hispanic (HDHA) and high-density African American (HDBA) areas; otherwise, return rates could be too low to provide any type of audience estimates. When the return (*intab* or *in-tab*) is low, statistical weighting or sample balancing is used to compensate for the shortfall. This topic is discussed later.

Data Collection. Perhaps the best-known method of gathering ratings data from a sample is by means of electronic ratings-gathering instruments, such as Arbitron's Portable People Meter (PPM) and the Nielsen People Meter, as mentioned earlier in the chapter. The People Meter was introduced as the *audimeter* in 1936 to record radio use on a moving roll of paper. (A. C. Nielsen purchased the audimeter from Robert Elder and Louis Woodruff, professors at the Massachusetts Institute of Technology.) In 1973, the audimeter changed to a new technology and the device was called the *storage instantaneous audimeter* (SIA). Finally, during the 1987–1988 television season, Nielsen offered service with the new People Meter. The meter records viewing data, and the central computer in Dunedin, Florida, calls each NTI household each day to retrieve the stored data. These data are used to compute the National Television Index. The data collection is automatic and does not require participation by anyone in the NTI households.

Arbitron's PPM was introduced in the mid-1990s to improve the validity and reliability of radio ratings. When the PPM was first introduced, Arbitron described the new procedure this way:

> The Arbitron Portable People Meter (PPM) system replaces the Arbitron personal Diary with a small, portable, personal electronic meter that automatically records

exposures to encoded stations. Participating broadcasters encode their stations by installing Arbitron encoding equipment, which embeds a unique inaudible code into their audio signals. Whenever a PPM detects this signal—which is acoustically masked from listeners, but receivable by the Meter—the Meter records the code, along with the date and time of the exposure. A station receives credit for a quarter-hour of listening if the Meter records five or more minutes of exposure to the station's encoded signal within that quarter-hour. [The five minutes need not be contiguous.]

Further information about PPM was included on Arbitron's website in early 2012:

> After years of research, field tests and industry review, Arbitron's revolutionary radio audience measurement system—the Portable People Meter (PPM™)—is now being rolled out as a commercial radio ratings service.
>
> The PPM service will replace Arbitron's current diary-based ratings with passive, electronic measurement. Current plans call for the PPM to be deployed in the Top 48 radio markets by 2010.
>
> At the same time, Arbitron is exploring—and will be testing in the field—different approaches to using electronic measurement in markets ranked 51+.

Invitation to Encode

The PPM system automatically reports audience exposure to inaudible codes embedded in a broadcast signal.

In the Top 50 markets, Arbitron will provide PPM encoders free of charge and report PPM audience estimates for all FCC-licensed AM and FM radio stations—including noncommercial stations—that wish to participate. The PPM data, however, will only be provided to those who subscribe to the PPM service.

Members of the public are selected as respondents in each new PPM market at random, based on landline and cell phone–only sample frames. These respondents, called "panelists," are asked to wear or carry the Meter each day from the time they rise until the time they retire at bedtime. Each individual six years of age or older in a participating household receives his or her own Meter and individual docking station. The panelists dock their Meters when they retire. The docking station transmits the data to a collector located in the panelist's home, which transmits the recorded exposure data to Arbitron. While docked, the Meter's battery is also recharged and its internal clock reset. In addition, to help identify at-home listening, the collector emits a low-power Radio Frequency (RF) signal that can be detected by a Meter when listening takes place at home.

The PPM measures all types of radio listening, including listening to radio stations on the Internet. However, for the PPM to recognize a radio station, the station's signal must be encoded. Arbitron states that "A radio station (FM/AM/HD Radio/Internet) whose broadcasts include unique inaudible codes that can be heard by the meters carried by PPM panelists. Only encoded stations can be measured in the PPM service. A station is not required to subscribe to the PPM data in order to encode."

For a detailed description of Arbitron's PPM, please consult the information located on the company's website: *www.arbitron. com/downloads/guide_to_using_ppm_data. pdf*. (If the link is no longer valid, conduct a search for "*Arbitron PPM guide.*")

In March 2012, Arbitron announced that it was introducing a new PPM, called the PPM 360. The new meter is mobile-enabled, which means the company can retrieve panel data without being connected to a phone line, as is necessary for the first PPM. The PPM 360 is scheduled to be in service in late 2012.

The second major form of data collection—diaries—requires subjects to record the channels they tuned to or the stations they listened to and to indicate when they watched or listened (time periods, or **dayparts**), such as "prime time" (8:00 P.M.–11:00 P.M. EST). Arbitron continues to use diaries for radio ratings information in most radio markets; Nielsen uses diaries for the households in its NAC (National Audience Composition) sample to supplement the information gathered from the metered households because the audimeter cannot record the number of people who are watching each television set.

The telephone is the third major technique used to collect, but it is not currently used by any accredited ratings research company. However, Arbitron and Nielsen do use the telephone for initial sample recruiting and to conduct a variety of special studies, allowing clients to request almost any type of survey research project. One of the most frequent types of custom work is the **telephone coincidental**. This procedure measures the size of the medium's audience at a given time; the survey coincides with actual viewing or listening. The method involves selecting a sample of households at random and calling these homes during the viewing or listening period of interest. Respondents are simply asked what they are watching or listening to at that moment. This method avoids having respondents trying to recall information from the previous day. Coincidentals are inexpensive (generally a few thousand dollars) and are frequently used by station management to receive immediate feedback about the success of special programming. In most cases, coincidentals are used for advertising sales purposes.

In summary, each audience data collection method has its critics: Electronic meters are criticized because they do not provide specific audience information and may cause respondent fatigue; diaries, because participants may fail to record viewing or listening as it happens and may rely on recall to complete the diary at the end of the week. In addition, many critics contend that diaries are used to "vote" for or against specific shows and that actual viewing is not recorded. Arbitron's PPM is criticized for potentially reducing the size of some radio station's audience because the device is not universally accepted by all types of respondents. And, finally, critics of data collection by telephone (although the method is not currently used by any national company) say that it favors responses by younger people, who are more willing to talk on the telephone, and misses many qualified respondents because of cell phone–only households. Data collection by telephone is becoming increasingly more difficult because of caller ID, call blocking, and a low response rate.

One thing is certain: While the debate about the accuracy of the various audience ratings methods will continue, research companies, including Arbitron and Nielsen, will continue their pursuit of more valid and reliable data collection procedures.

Interpreting the Ratings

Interpreting broadcast ratings and understanding the terminology used can best be explained with an example. While this example uses television, the procedures are the same for radio ratings. Let's assume that Nielsen has collected TV viewing information (see Table 14.1) for a specific daypart on "traditional" network television. (Only three networks are shown to simplify the discussion. In reality, the list would include dozens of TV stations, cable channels, and networks.)

Recall that Nielsen's NTI sample includes about 21,000 households in the United States, and the data collected from them are generalized to the total population of about 114.7 million television households. The first number to compute is the rating for each network.

Table 14.1   Hypothetical TV Viewing Data

Network	Households
ABC	4,620
CBS	4,200
NBC	3,780
Not watching	8,400
Total	21,000

Rating.   An audience **rating** is the percentage of people or households in a population with a television or radio tuned to a specific station, channel, or network. Thus, the rating is expressed as the station or network's audience divided by the total number of television households or people in the target population:

$$\text{Rating} = \frac{\text{People or Housholds}}{\text{Population}}$$

This formula is typical in mass media research. The numerator in the formula is People or Households Viewing TV or People Listening to Radio. For example, using the hypothetical data in Table 14.1, ABC's rating is computed as:

$$\text{Rating} = \frac{4,620}{21,000} = 0.22 \text{ or } 22\% \text{ or } 22$$

This indicates that approximately 22% of the sample of 21,000 households was tuned to ABC at the time of the survey. Notice that even though ratings and shares are percentages, when the data are reported, the decimal point and % symbol are usually eliminated.

The combined ratings of all the networks or stations during a specific time period (daypart) provide an estimate of the total number of *Homes Using Television* (HUT). Because radio ratings deal with people rather than households, the term *Persons Using Radio* (PUR) is used. The HUT or PUR can be found either by adding together the households or persons using radio or television or by computing the total rating and multiplying it by the sample (or population, when generalized). The total rating in the sample data in Table 14.1 is .60, which is computed as follows:

$$\text{ABC} = \frac{4,620}{21,000} = .22 \text{ or } 22\%$$

$$\text{CBS} = \frac{4,200}{21,000} = .20 \text{ or } 20\%$$

$$\text{NBC} = \frac{3,780}{21,000} = .18 \text{ or } 18\%$$

HUT = 12,600 Total Rating = .60 or 60%

In other words, about 60% of all households (HH) with television were tuned to one of the three networks at the time of the survey. As mentioned, the HUT can also be computed by multiplying the total rating by the sample size: 0.60 × 21,000 = 12,600. The same formula is used to project to the population. The population HUT is computed as 0.60 × 114.7 million = 68,820,000.

TV stations, networks, and advertisers naturally wish to know the estimated number of households in the HUT tuned to specific channels. Ratings data from the sample of 21,000 households are used to provide a *rough* estimate of the households tuned to each network (or station), as shown in Table 14.2.

Share.   An audience **share** is the percentage of the HUT or PUR that is tuned to a specific station, channel, or network. It is determined by dividing the number of households or persons tuned to a station or network by the number of households or persons using their sets:

$$\text{Share} = \frac{\text{Persons or Households}}{\text{HUT or PUR}}$$

From Table 14.1, the sample HUT is 12,600 (4,620 + 4,200 + 3,780), or 60% of 21,000. The audience share for ABC would be:

$$\text{ABC Share} = \frac{4,620}{12,600} = .367 \text{ or } 36.7\%$$

Table 14.2 Household Estimates Using Ratings and Shares

Network	Rating		Population		Rough Population HH Estimate
ABC	22.0	×	114,700,000	=	25,234,000
CBS	20.0	×	114,700,000	=	22,940,000
NBC	18.0	×	114,700,000	=	20,646,000
Total	60.0				68,820,000
Network	**Share**		**HUT**		**Exact Population HH Estimate**
ABC	36.7	×	68,820,000	=	25,256,940
CBS	33.3	×	68,820,000	=	22,710,600
NBC	30.0	×	68,820,000	=	20,646,000
Total	100				68,613,540

That is, of the households in the sample whose television sets were on at the time of the survey, 36.7% were tuned to ABC. (People may not have been watching the set but may have recorded that they did in a diary, or the People Meter recorded the information.) The shares for CBS and NBC are computed in the same manner: CBS Share = 4,200/12,600, or 33.3%; NBC Share = 3,780/12,600, or 30.0%.

Shares are also used to provide an *exact* estimate of households in the target population, computed by multiplying the share by the HUT or PUR. The rough and exact household estimates for each network are shown in Table 14.2.

Estimating the number of households tuned to specific channels and networks provides a broad indication of audience size. However, broadcasters, advertisers, and other people who use TV ratings are also interested in estimates of the number of people tuned to a channel or network. Most references in books and on the Internet say

that to estimate the number of people tuned to a channel or network, Nielsen multiplies the number of estimated households by the average household size (average number of people per household) in the United States— 3, 4, or 5. Actually, both items are incorrect. Nielsen does not multiply the number of households by a constant number such as 3, 4, 5, or any other number. In addition, references using 3, 4, or 5 as the average number of people per household in the United States in 2012 are wrong. In 2012, the average is 2.6 people per household in the United States, although the number varies by region of the country.

If Nielsen does not multiply household estimates by the average number of people per household (constant) to estimate the number of viewers, how does the company produce the estimates? To explain the procedure, we will use actual Nielsen data for the week of February 27, 2012, shown in Table 14.3—the top 10 programs for the week. Nielsen releases this information to

Table 14.3　Nielsen Top 10 Primetime Broadcast Network TV Programs for the Week of February 27, 2012

Rank	Program	Network	Rating	Households Estimate (000)	Viewers Estimate (000)	Viewers Per HH
1	NCIS	CBS	11.3	12,961	18,200	1.40
2	American Idol-Thursday	FOX	10.8	12,388	18,452	1.49
3	American Idol-Wednesday	FOX	10.1	11,585	17,228	1.49
4	NCIS: Los Angeles	CBS	9.9	11,355	15,853	1.40
5	American Idol-Tuesday	FOX	9.4	10,782	16,110	1.49
6	Voice	NBC	8.7	9,979	14,894	1.49
7	FOX NASCAR Daytona 500	FOX	8.0	9,176	13,669	1.49
8	Criminal Minds	CBS	7.8	8,947	12,539	1.40
9	FOX Daytona 500 Red Flag	FOX	7.5	8,603	12,471	1.45
10	Two and a Half Men	CBS	7.5	8,603	11,921	1.39

the public because the data show only total household estimates and total viewers over 1-year old (referred to as the 2+ [2 plus] audience). Broadcasters do not sell, and advertisers do not buy, advertising based on Household and 2+ ratings and shares because the data are for the total audience, and there is no interest in this group. The interest is in specific demographic targets, known as "demographics," "demos," "demo cells," or simply "cells," such as Females 25–34. Every TV program is designed for a specific demo (cell), and that is how advertising time is bought and sold— an advertiser purchases time on a program because the program attracts a specific audience the advertiser wants to reach. (See the special note on demos at the end of this chapter.)

Now refer to Table 14.3. The actual Nielsen data include everything but the column titled Viewers Per HH (VPHH). The authors calculated the data for this column. (Nielsen rarely includes the VPHH number in public information because there is no specific use for the number.) Looking at the VPHH column, the two often-stated "facts" about how Nielsen computes the number of viewers are immediately proved to be wrong—Nielsen does not use a constant for the average number of people per household, and the number is not 3, 4, or 5. So what is the source of the numbers in the Viewers per HH column?

To demonstrate that VPHH is not a constant number, we computed the numbers in a simple way—we "backed into" the VPHH numbers. That is, we divided the number of estimated viewers by the number of estimated households. For example, the VPHH for *NCIS* is 1.40 (18,200/12,961 = 1.40).

Table 14.3 demonstrates that the VPHH is not a constant, and none are 2.6, the 2012 average people per household in the United States. The reason each VPHH is different is that each program attracts a different audience. While some programs may be popular among a wide audience, others appeal to a smaller group of people. For example, the *American Idol* programs and the two **NASCAR** programs have the largest VPHH numbers at 1.49, because the programs are designed for a broad audience—males and females of all ages. On the other hand, *Two and a Half Men* has the lowest VPHH, 1.39, because a narrower group of viewers is attracted to the show.

In summary, Viewers Per HH is not computed with a constant number. It is a weighted number calculated by Nielsen prior to a ratings period, and that number is multiplied by the Households estimate to produce the "Viewers Estimate (000)" shown in Table 14.3 (the data released to the public). The weighted number is calculated by using several items including, but not limited to, the program's target demographic, what time the program is aired, and historical viewing data from previous ratings periods. (Incidentally, notice that the episode of *NCIS* was in first place with a rating of only 11.3. This is more than 50% lower than the rating that the number one ranked TV program received just a few years ago. The large number of choices on television has fragmented the television audience.)

One final point about audience ratings and shares is that whereas television uses both ratings and shares for decision making and advertising sales, radio uses only shares because the ratings are too small and offer little information.

Cost Per Thousand. Stations, networks, and advertisers need to be able to assess the efficiency of advertising on radio and television so that they can determine which advertising buy is the most cost effective. One common way to express advertising efficiency is in **cost per thousand (CPM)**, or what it costs an advertiser to reach 1,000 households or persons. The CPM provides no information about the effectiveness of a commercial message, only the dollar estimate of its reach. It is computed according to the following formula:

$$CPM = \frac{\text{Cost of advertisement}}{\text{Audience size (in thousands)}}$$

Using the hypothetical television rough estimate data from Table 14.2, assume that a single 30-second commercial (spot) on ABC costs $275,000. The CPM for the commercial is computed as:

$$ABC\ CPM = \frac{\$275,000}{25,234(000)} = \$10.90$$

That is, it costs an advertiser $10.90 to reach each 1,000 households on ABC for a specific program at a specific time period. If we assume that the advertising costs were the same for CBS and NBC, the corresponding CPMs are: CBS = $11.99 and NBC = $13.32.

The CPM is used regularly when advertisers buy commercial time. Advertisers and stations or networks usually negotiate advertising contracts using CPM figures; the advertiser might agree to pay $11.50 per thousand households. In some cases, no negotiation is involved—a station or network may simply offer a program to advertisers at a specified CPM, or an advertiser may offer to pay only a specific CPM.

The CPM is seldom the only criterion used in purchasing commercial time. Other information, such as audience demographics and the type of program on which the advertisement will be aired, is considered before a contract is signed. An advertiser may be willing to pay a higher CPM to a network or station that is reaching an audience that is more desirable for its product. Cost per thousand should be used as the sole purchasing criterion *only* when all else is equal: demographics, programming, advertising strategy, and so on.

Related Ratings Concepts

Ratings, shares, and other figures are computed for a variety of survey areas and are split into several demographic categories. The current online delivery of ratings information allows stations and networks to produce custom information such as ratings in specific ZIP codes or other target area. Although ratings and shares are important in audience research, a number of other computations can be performed with the data.

A **metro survey area** (**MSA**) corresponds to the Consolidated Metropolitan Statistical Areas (CMSA) for the country as defined by the U.S. Office of Management and Budget. The MSA generally includes the town, the county, or some other designated area closest to the station's transmitter. The **designated market area** (**DMA**), another area for which ratings data are gathered, defines each television or radio market in exclusive terms. (At one time Arbitron used the term *Area of Dominant Influence*, or ADI, to describe the DMA but has since changed to Nielsen's designation.) Each county in the United States belongs to one and only one DMA, and rankings are determined by the number of television households in the DMA. Radio ratings use the DMAs established from television households; they are not computed separately.

The **total survey area** (**TSA**) includes the DMA and MSA as well as some other areas the market's stations reach (known as adjacent DMAs). Broadcasters are most interested in TSA data because they represent the largest number of households or people. In reality, however, advertising agencies look at DMA figures when purchasing commercial time for television stations and MSA figures when purchasing radio time. The TSA is used infrequently in the sale or purchase of advertising time; it serves primarily to determine the reach of the station, or the total number of people or households that

A CLOSER LOOK

The Stability of Radio Ratings

Everyone involved in radio has encountered situations in which a radio station's shares "bounce around" from one ratings period ("book") to another. This is a common complaint about Arbitron and one that all broadcasters must understand. Although a radio station's shares may change because of changes in actual listening, a primary reason for the change is that different samples are used for each rating's period. By virtue of using different samples of listeners, there are different sampling error percentages. Even if no programming changes were made, radio broadcasters must expect changes in their radio station's shares. Nielsen does not encounter this problem often because the company uses respondent panels for ratings information, which are more stable and reliable. Arbitron is attempting to correct this problem by using panels for its PPM methodology.

---

listened to or watched a station or a channel. Nielsen's term *NSI area* is equivalent to Arbitron's *TSA*.

Ratings reports contain information about the TSA/NSI, DMA, and MSA. Each area is important to stations and advertisers for various reasons, depending on the type of product or service being advertised and the goals of the advertising campaign. For instance, a new business that places a large number of spots on several local stations may be interested in reaching as many people in the area as possible. In this case, the advertising agency or individual client may ask for TSA/NSI numbers only, disregarding the DMA and Metro data.

The **cume** (cumulative audience) or **reach** is an estimate of the number of different people who listened to or viewed at least five minutes within a given daypart (the five minutes do not have to be consecutive). The cume is also referred to as the *unduplicated audience*. For example, a person who watches a soap opera at least five minutes each day Monday through Friday would be counted only once in a cume rating, whereas the person's viewing would be "duplicated" five times in determining average quarter-hours, which is discussed next.

The **average quarter-hour** (**AQH**) is an estimated average of the number of persons or households tuned to a specific station for at least 5 minutes during a 15-minute time segment (the 5 minutes do not have to be consecutive). Unlike the cume, where a person is counted only once during a Monday–Friday program, the listener or viewer would be counted five times for the time period.

Cume represents the number of different people in the audience; AQH represents the average number of people in the audience.

Cume and AQH estimates are provided for the TSA/NSI, DMA, and MSA in all ratings books. Stations are obviously interested in obtaining high AQH figures in all demographic areas because these figures indicate how long an audience is tuned in and thus how loyal the audience is to the station. The AQH data are used to determine the average radio listener's **Time Spent Listening** (**TSL**) or **Average Weekly Time Exposed** (**AWTE**) in Arbitron's PPM markets, and **Time Spent Viewing** (**TSV**) for television during a given day, time period, or daypart. All stations try to increase the time their audience spends with the station because increased listening or viewing time means that the audience is not continually switching to other stations or turning off the radio or TV.

The **gross rating points (GRPs)** are a total of a station's ratings during two or more dayparts and estimate the size of the gross audience. Advertising purchases are often made via GRPs. For example, a radio advertiser who purchases 10 commercials on a station may wish to know the gross audience that will be reached. Using hypothetical data, the GRP calculation is shown in Table 14.4. The gross rating point indicates that about 32.4% of the listening audience will be exposed to the 10 commercials.

A useful figure for radio stations is the **audience turnover,** or the number of times the audience changes during a given daypart. A high turnover is not always a negative factor in advertising sales; some stations have naturally high turnover (such as Top 40 stations, whose audiences comprise mostly younger people, who tend to change stations frequently). A high turnover simply means that an advertiser needs to run more spots to reach the station's audience. Usually such stations compensate by charging less for commercial spots than stations with low turnovers.

Turnover is computed by dividing a station's cume audience by its average persons total. (Both these figures are reported in ratings books.) Consider three stations in the Monday–Friday, 3:00 P.M.–6:00 P.M. daypart, as shown in Table 14.5. In this market, an advertiser on Station C would need to run more commercials to reach all listeners than one who advertises on Station A or Station B. However, although Station C has a smaller audience, it may have the demographic audience most suitable for the advertiser's product.

Table 14.4   Calculation of GRP for Five Dayparts

Daypart	Number of Spots		Station Rating		GRP
M–F, 6 A.M.–9 A.M.	2	×	3.1	=	6.2
M–F, 12 P.M.–3 P.M.	2	×	2.9	=	5.8
M–F, 1 P.M.–6 P.M.	2	×	3.6	=	7.2
Sat, 6 A.M.–9 A.M.	2	×	2.5	=	5.0
Sun, 3 P.M.–6 P.M.	2	×	4.1	=	8.2
	10				32.4

Table 14.5   Computation of Turnover for Three Stations

Station	Cume Audience		Average Persons		Turnover
A	2,900	÷	850	=	3.4
B	1,750	÷	850	=	2.1
C	960	÷	190	=	5.1

Reading a Ratings Book

As mentioned earlier, Arbitron and Nielsen no longer publish hard copies of ratings books; all reports are available only online. Both Arbitron and Nielsen provide their clients with access to virtually all ratings information, which allows the clients to produce an unlimited number of reports for programs, dayparts, and demographic cells. (Note: Arbitron allows free access to Topline [information for the Total 6+ audience] on its website. At the Arbitron homepage, click on "Radio Ratings" at the right of the screen and enter the appropriate name and email address. Any market's Topline information can be viewed.)

When most people view Arbitron and Nielsen ratings data for the first time, many are shocked by the thousands of numbers included on the pages. However, although radio and TV ratings are organized differently, they are easy to read once the layout is understood. Remember that even though most numbers in ratings books are percentages, all decimal points and percent signs are deleted. In addition, all numbers are rounded.

Let's take a look at an example of Arbitron's PPM data, which is available on the company's website. Table 14.6 shows only a small portion of the data available from the Denver-Boulder, Colorado, PPM survey reported in February 2012. The data show the shares for the top 100 radio stations for the 6+ audience (*Total Audience*) for Mon–Sun, 6 AM–Mid (*Total Day*).

However, before discussing the PPM data, we need to specify a set of rules to follow when reading any broadcast information. To accurately read any ratings information, you must know the following:

1. name of the market where the survey was conducted

2. geography (Metro, DMA, TSA, county, or a unique special area)

3. demographic (age and sex)

4. source (households or persons)

5. daypart (time period, daypart, program, Total Day, or Total Week)

6. type of data (rating, share, cume, AQH)

7. when the survey was conducted (and other surveys for trend purposes)

When these items are known, it's time to read the information, so let's see what the Arbitron 6+ Total Week audience shares indicate in the Denver-Boulder market for January 2012 and the two previous surveys. Note: The center column is labeled "HOL 11," which is the "Holiday Ratings" period from December 8, 2011, to January 4, 2012, and this is why there are 13 PPM reports each year—one for each month and one for the special Holiday season because many radio stations in the United States have special programming during this time.

First, referring to the 12-Jan column, KOA-AM, a News/Talk radio station, leads the market with a 5.9 share, which is the same at its 11-Jan share. KOA-AM's HOL 11 share is slightly lower at 5.6, but considering sampling error, the radio station was consistent during the three periods reported. However, it's easy to see how holiday programming can affect a radio station's performance by looking at KOSI-FM, which received a 6.2 share for 11-Dec, then jumped significantly to 9.3 for HOL 11, and then back to 4.8 for 12-Jan. The ability to look at smaller time periods is one major advantage of PPM ratings. In fact, it is possible for a radio station to produce minute-by-minute shares for any time period or program.

Table 14.6 is a good example of how difficult it is sometimes to analyze a radio station's performance. Is an increase or decrease in a radio station's share due to performance alone, or could the season (time of year) have an effect? It appears that KOSI-FM

Table 14.6 Arbitron PPM Ratings Data

Arbitron PPM Data:
Denver-Boulder, Colorado.
AQH Share for Persons 6+, Mon–Sun, 6 A.M.–Mid
(only top 10 stations shown). Ranked on most current survey: Jan. 2012

Ranking	Outlet	Format	11-Dec	HOL 11	12-Jan
1	KOA-AM	News Talk Information	5.9	5.6	5.9
2	KQMT-FM	Classic Rock	4.6	4.3	5.1
3	KLDV-FM	Contemporary Christian	3.6	4.0	4.9
4	KOSI-FM	Adult Contemporary	6.2	9.3	4.8
5	KBCO-FM	Album Adult Alternative	4.2	4.2	4.6
6	KXPK-FM	Mexican Regional	4.7	5.1	4.5
7t	KALC-FM	Modern Adult Contemporary	4.2	4.2	4.3
7t	KTCL-FM	Alternative	4.2	4.2	4.3
7t	KYGO-FM	Country	3.9	4.1	4.3
10t	KQKS-FM	Rhythmic Contemporary Hits	4.9	4.2	4.2
10t	KXKL-FM	Adult Hits	3.8	3.5	4.2

benefitted greatly from its Holiday programming, because the station's share dropped to a 4.8 in 12-Jan, which is significantly lower than its 11-Dec share of 6.2. The radio station's management must analyze why many listeners left the radio station (11-Dec to 12-Jan) and why so many of the HOL 11 listeners didn't stay with the radio station after the holiday season ended.

Comparisons from one Arbitron ratings period to another are valid in PPM markets because a panel sample is used; such comparisons are not valid in diary markets because different samples are used for each ratings period (book). Recall from our discussion of statistics that it isn't valid to compare one Arbitron or Nielsen diary ratings period to another unless the ratings, shares, or other data are converted to *z*-scores.

Table 14.6 also indicates several other things including, but not limited to:

1. The number one station in 12-Jan in the Denver-Boulder market is an AM News/Talk radio station. This is rare since music stations are usually number one in most radio markets. Even though there are other AM radio stations in the Denver-Boulder market, KOA-AM is the only AM station that appears in the Top 10.

2. Excluding KOSI-FM, the other radio stations in the Top 10 did not benefit from holiday programming and all stayed fairly consistent from 11-Dec to 12-Jan.

3. The format names shown are those that are used in the radio industry

and are not usually used by "average" radio listeners.

4. There are a variety of types of music stations in the top 10 in Denver-Boulder; the market cannot be classified by one type of music, such as "Rock" or "Oldies."

5. No one in the radio industry would use the information shown in Table 14.6 for advertising sales or programming decisions because it includes only information for the 6+ audience. Like TV programs, all radio stations have a target audience, such as Females 25–34 or Males 35–49. There isn't one radio station in the United States that has a 6+ target, and that's why the 6+ data are the only numbers Arbitron releases to the public. Specific target information is available only to Arbitron subscribers. The 6+ audience in the radio industry is known as a "Family Reunion," not a target, and the information is essentially useless for everyone in the radio industry except for "bragging rights" in discussions about the radio station.

6. Excluding KOSI-FM's performance during HOL 11, it is clear from the numbers that the Denver-Boulder radio market is very competitive.

For additional information about Arbitron's PPM data, go to *www.arbitron.com/portable_people_meters/home.htm.*

To view older versions of ratings information from Arbitron and Nielsen, go to the text's website, *www.wimmerdominick.com,* and then to the "Additional Materials" box and click on "Supplemental Information."

Decline in Ratings and Shares

The definition of success varies from one area to another. In broadcasting, the number of viewers or listeners determines success—the networks or stations with the highest numbers (ratings and/or shares) are considered successful—the winners. But how many people are these successful radio and television stations reaching? How big is the audience?

Until a few years ago, successful TV stations garnered ratings of 20–30% and shares of 30–40% for most prime-time programs and nightly network news; successful radio stations had shares of 10–20% in most daytime dayparts. This is no longer the case.

In television, it is now common to see the leading show with a 6.0 rating and 14 share. In radio, a successful station garners a 3.0–5.0 share of the audience. The huge radio and TV audiences are gone; they have disappeared because (1) there are many choices for listeners and viewers and (2) there is a lack of concern by many broadcasters to find out what the audience wants to hear or see.

Have the lower numbers created a new atmosphere for broadcasters? What do broadcasters do about the lower numbers? To be honest, most broadcasters "take it easy" when they reach the number one position in their market (or the nation)—they perceive that they have given the audience what it wants. Is that true? Let's look at the situation from a different perspective. In radio, for example, a program director and the morning show team may be ecstatic if they win the 6:00 A.M.–10:00 A.M. daypart with a 4.0 share in the target demographic. Ecstatic! Bonuses are handed out, parties are held, and everyone is happy ("We killed 'em."). But wait a minute—the 4.0 share means that 96% of the target demographic is *not listening to their radio station!* Is the radio station giving the audience what it wants to hear? Sure it is—to 4% of them. This is the reality of today's broadcasting.

Adjusting for Unrepresentative Samples

Because ratings are computed using samples from the population, a certain amount of error is always associated with the data.

This error, designated by the notation $SE(p)$, is known as **standard error**. Standard error must always be considered before ratings are interpreted, to determine whether a certain gender/age group has been undersampled or oversampled.

There are several approaches to calculating standard error. One standard formula is

$$SE(p) = \sqrt{\frac{p(100 - p)}{n}} \times 1.96$$

where p is the sample percentage or rating, n is sample size, SE is the standard error, and 1.96 is the corresponding z-score for the 95% confidence interval. For example, suppose a random sample of 1,200 households produces a rating of 20. The standard error can be expressed as follows:

$$SE(P) = \sqrt{\frac{20(100 - 20)}{1,200}} \times 1.96$$

$$= \sqrt{\frac{20(80)}{1200}} \times 1.96$$

$$= \sqrt{1.33} \times 1.96$$

$$= \pm 2.26$$

The 20 rating has a standard error of ± 2.26 points, which means that at the 95% confidence level, the rating ranges from 17.74 to 22.26. Standard error formulas are available to both Arbitron and Nielsen clients.

Weighting is another procedure used by ratings companies to adjust for samples that are not representative of the population. In some situations, a particular gender/age group cannot be adequately sampled, and a correction must be made.

Assume that population estimates for a DMA indicate that it includes 41,500 men ages 18–34 and that this group accounts for 8.3% of the population over the age of 12. The researchers distribute diaries to a sample of the DMA population, of which 950 are returned and usable (in-tab diaries). They would expect about 79 of these to be from

men ages 18–34 (8.3% of 950). However, they find that only 63 of the diaries are from this demographic group—16 short of the anticipated number ($0.066 = 63/950$). The data must be weighted to adjust for this deficiency. The weighting formula is:

$$\text{Weight}_{\text{MSA men, 18–24}} = \frac{0.083}{0.066}$$

$$= 1.25$$

This number (1.25) must be multiplied by the number of persons in the group that each would normally represent. That is, instead of each diary representing 525 men ($41,500 \div 79$), each diary would represent 656 men (1525×1.252). The ideal is to have no weighting at all, which indicates that the group was adequately represented in the sample. On occasion, a group may be oversampled, in which case the weighting value is a negative number, such as -1.25.

Both Arbitron and Nielsen provide detailed explanations of error rates, weighting, and other methodological considerations. Each company includes pages of information on how to interpret the data considering different sample sizes and weighting. In reality, however, the vast majority of people who interpret and use broadcast and cable ratings consider the printed numbers as gospel. If they are considered at all, error rates, sample sizes, and other artifacts related to audience ratings are considered only when an owner or manager's station performs poorly in the ratings.

NONRATINGS RESEARCH

Although audience ratings are the most visible research data used in broadcasting, broadcasters, production companies, advertisers, and broadcast consultants use numerous other research methodologies. Ratings provide estimates of audience size and composition. Nonratings research provides information about what the audience likes and dislikes, analyses of different types of programming, demographic and lifestyle information about the audience, and more. These data provide decision makers with information they can use to eliminate some of the guesswork involved in giving the audience what it wants. Nonratings research is important to broadcasters in all markets, and one characteristic of all successful broadcast or cable operations is that the management uses research in all types of decision making.

What is the importance of nonratings research to a newcomer to the broadcast field? Renowned American broadcaster Frank Bell (2012) says:

> Imagine yourself as a pilot, attempting to safely guide your plane through a bank of thunderstorms, and all of your navigation instruments are out of commission. As heavy turbulence bounces your craft up and down, passengers, each with a different perspective, shout suggestions: "Pull up, watch out for the mountains ahead!" "Don't fly into those clouds; they're full of lightning!" "Hey, there's another plane off to the right!" That's what it is like to program a radio or TV station today without the benefit of ongoing local market research.
>
> If you don't know the strengths and weaknesses of your own station and your primary competitors, if you don't have a handle on your market's tastes, if you're unsure what would happen if a new competitor signed on tomorrow, then you are truly "flying blind." Better keep your parachute packed!
>
> Local market research provides something unattainable from inside a radio or TV station: the unvarnished perspective of those wonderful people who actually tune in every week and keep us in business. As a wise man said many years ago, "The only reality that counts is that of the audience."

The following section describes some nonratings research methods conducted in the electronic media to provide information to decision makers so that they don't "fly blind," as Frank Bell says.

Program Testing

Research is an accepted step in the development and production of programs and commercials. It is common to test these products in each state of development: initial idea or plan, rough cut, and postproduction. A variety of research approaches can be used in each stage, depending on the purpose of the study, the amount of time allowed for testing, and the types of decisions that will be made with the results. The researcher must determine what information the decision makers will need to know and must design an analysis to provide that information.

Since programs and commercials are expensive to produce, success-minded producers and directors are interested in gathering preliminary reactions to a planned project. It would be ludicrous to spend thousands or millions of dollars on a project that has no audience appeal, although it has been done many times.

Although the major TV networks, large advertising agencies, and production companies conduct most program testing, many local TV stations are involved in programming research. Stations test promotional campaigns, prime-time access scheduling, the acceptability of commercials, and various programming strategies.

One way to collect preliminary data is to have respondents read a short statement that summarizes a program or commercial and ask them for their opinions about the idea, their willingness to watch the program, or their intent to buy the product based on the description. The results may provide an indication of the potential success of a program or commercial.

However, program or commercial descriptions often cannot adequately describe the characters and their relationships to other characters in the program or commercial. This can be done only through the program dialogue and the characters' on-screen performance. For example, the ABC-TV program *Lost* might not sound appealing as it is described on the program's website:

> After Oceanic Air flight 815 tore apart in mid-air and crashed on a Pacific island, its survivors were forced to find inner strength they never knew they had in order to survive. But they discovered that the island holds many secrets, including a mysterious smoke monster, polar bears, a strange French woman and another group of island residents known as "The Others." The survivors have also found signs of those who came to the island before them, including a 19th century sailing ship called *The Black Rock*, the remains of an ancient statue, as well as bunkers belonging to the Dharma Initiative—a group of scientific researchers who inhabited the island in the recent past.

To many people, this statement might describe the type of show generally referred to as a "bomb." However, the indescribable on-screen relationships between the characters and the intricate story lines have made *Lost* one of the most popular television shows in the past several years. If producers relied only on program descriptions in testing situations, many successful shows would never reach the air.

If an idea tests well in the preliminary stages (or if the producer or advertiser wishes to go ahead with the project regardless of what the research indicates), a model or simulation is produced. These media "hardware" items are referred to as *rough cuts, storyboards, photomatics, animatics,* or *executions.* The **rough cut** is a simplistic production that usually uses amateur actors, little or no editing, and makeshift sets. The other models are photographs, pictures, or drawings of major scenes designed to give the basic idea of a program or commercial to anyone who looks at them.

Testing rough cuts is not expensive, which is important if the tests show a lack of acceptance or understanding of the product. The tests provide information about the script, characterizations, character relationships, settings, cinematic approach, and overall appeal. Rough cut tests seldom identify the reasons why a program or commercial tests poorly, but they provide an overall indication that something is wrong and provide information for more specific tests.

When the final product is available, postproduction research can be conducted. Finished products are tested in experimental theaters, in shopping centers (where mobile vans are used to show commercials or programs), at respondents' homes in cities where cable systems provide test channels, or (in the case of radio commercials) via telephone. Results from postproduction research often indicate that, for example, the ending of a program is unacceptable and must be re-edited or reshot. Many problems that were not foreseen during production may be encountered in postproduction research, and the data usually provide producers with an initial audience reaction to the finished, or partially finished, product.

The major TV networks use their own approaches to testing new programs. One approach is to test pilot programs on cable TV outlets throughout the country, where respondents are prerecruited to watch the program. Another approach is to test pilot programs in large focus group settings. Regardless of the type of pretesting, the networks continually test the programs using a variety of qualitative and quantitative approaches such as focus groups and telephone interviews.

There are many ways to test commercials or programs. Some researchers test commercials and consumer products by showing different versions of commercials on cable systems. Prototype (test) commercials can be "cut into" a program (they replace a regularly scheduled commercial with a test spot) in target households. The other households on the cable system view the regular spot. Shortly after airing the test commercial to the target households, follow-up research is conducted to determine the success of the commercial or the response to a new consumer product.

Commercials can also be tested in focus groups, via shopping center intercepts, in auditorium-type situations, and on the Internet. Leading companies and advertising agencies rarely show their commercials on television until they are tested in a variety of situations. The companies and their agencies do not want to communicate the wrong message to the audience.

Music Research

Music is the product of a music radio station, and failing to analyze the product invites ratings disaster. To provide the radio station's listeners with music they like to hear and to avoid the songs that they do not like or are tired of hearing (*burned out*), radio programmers use three primary research procedures: auditorium music testing (AMT), callout research, and online music tests (OMT).

The **Auditorium test (AMT)** is designed to evaluate *recurrents* (popular songs of the past few years) and *oldies* (songs older than 10 years), but this method is being used less often during the past few years because of the high costs involved in conducting the test. **Callout research, conducted via telephone,** is used to test music currently on the air (*currents*), and even recurrents and oldies. However, as with auditorium testing, increases in costs have forced radio station management to either eliminate music research or elect to use the third method of music testing, the Internet. The online music

test (OMT) has respondents listen to and rate songs on their home computers. All types of music can be tested, including new music, since an entire song can be included.

The three types of music tests serve the same purpose: to provide a program director or music director with information about the songs the audience likes, dislikes, is tired of hearing, or is unfamiliar with. This information allows the program director to make decisions based on audience reaction rather than gut feelings or guessing.

The three music testing methods involve playing **hooks** (short segments) of several songs for a sample of listeners. A hook is a 5- to 10-second (usually 8-second) representative sample of the song—enough for respondents to identify the song if it is already familiar to them and to rate the song on some type of evaluation scale. Our experience indicates that respondents who are familiar with a song can identify it in three seconds or less.

Research companies and program directors have a variety of scales for listeners to use in evaluating the music they hear. For example, respondents can be asked to rate a hook on a 5-, 7-, or 10-point scale, where 1 represents "hate" and 5, 7, or 10 usually represents something like, "like a lot" or "favorite." Or the scales can be used without labels, and respondents are instructed to rate the songs on the scale, where the higher the number, the more the song is liked. There are also options for "unfamiliar" and "tired of hearing." (A respondent who is unfamiliar with a song does not rate the song.) Which scale is best? Research conducted over several years by the senior author of this book indicates that either a 7-point or 10-point scale provides the most reliable results.

Sometimes researchers ask respondents to rate whether each song "fits" the music they hear on their favorite radio station. This additional question helps program directors determine which of the tested songs might be inappropriate for their station. In addition, some research companies ask listeners whether they would like radio stations in the area to play a particular song more, less, or the same amount as they currently do. This is an inefficient and inaccurate way to determine the frequency with which a song should be played. The reason is that there is no common definition of *more*, *less*, or *same*, and listeners are poor judges of how often a station currently plays the songs in its playlist.

The bottom line in all music testing is that program directors should use the data as a guide for selecting their radio station's music, not as a music selection "bible."

Auditorium Testing. In this method, between 75 and 200 people are invited to a large room or hall, often a hotel ballroom. Subjects always match specific screening requirements determined by the radio station or the research company, such as listeners between the ages of 25 and 40 who listen to soft rock stations in the client's market. Respondents are usually recruited by a field service that specializes in recruiting people for focus groups or other similar research projects. Respondents are generally paid $50 or more for their cooperation. The auditorium setting—usually a comfortable location away from distractions at home—allows researchers to test several hundred hooks in one 90- to 120-minute session. Usually 200–600 hooks are tested, although some companies routinely test up to 800 hooks in a single session. However, after 600 songs subject fatigue becomes evident by explicit physical behavior (looking around the room, fidgeting, talking to neighbors), and statistical reliability decreases. It is easy to demonstrate that scores for songs after 600 are not reliable (Wimmer, 2001), specifically in reference to unstable respondent standard deviations for the songs.

While auditorium music testing is a relatively simple project, there are many things

to consider to ensure that the test is successful. Among numerous procedures and steps, some basic procedures to follow when conducting an auditorium music test include the following:

1. All respondents should be rescreened before they are allowed to enter the room and should present a photo ID to verify that they are the respondents who were recruited. In addition, any person who is younger or older than the desired age group should not be allowed to participate (people often lie about their age in order to participate).

2. The key to a successful test is a good introduction that explains the purpose of the test and how important the respondents' answers are to hearing good music on the radio. It is important to stress that there are no right or wrong answers in the test and that the goal is to collect a variety of opinions.

3. The moderator must be in total control over the situation to ensure that respondents do not talk among themselves or try to influence other respondents' answers.

4. Adequate breaks must be taken during the session. Respondents shouldn't listen to more than 200 hooks without a break.

5. The moderator must make sure that all respondents understand the scoring system. After the test begins, the moderator should check to see that each person is rating the songs correctly.

6. The moderator should not allow the respondents to sing along with the songs, which distracts the other respondents.

7. The moderator must always expect the unexpected, including such things

as electrical outages, sick respondents, unruly respondents, equipment failures, or problems with the hotel arrangements.

In the late 1990s, a few radio research companies developed alternative approaches to the firmly established (reliable and valid) AMT methodology. One method is callout, where song hooks are tested over the telephone, and the other is online music testing (OMT) where hooks are tested via the Internet. Both methods face the same problem of relinquishing control over the testing situation, and there is no way to know who is actually rating the songs. While the authors' experience shows that telephone and Internet music testing should not be used because there is no publicly available research evidence to support that it is reliable and valid, we know that many program directors and general managers use them anyway.

Callout Research.   The purpose of callout research is the same as that of auditorium testing; only the procedure for collecting the data is changed. Instead of inviting people to a large hall or ballroom, researchers call randomly selected or prerecruited subjects on the telephone. Subjects are given the same rating instructions as in the auditorium test; they listen to the hook and provide a verbal response to the researcher making the telephone call. Callout research is usually used to test only newer music releases.

While callout methodology is adequate because only a few songs are tested, the limitation on the songs tested is also the methodology's major fault. Well-designed callout research involves testing a maximum of 20 songs because subject fatigue sets in quickly over the telephone. Other problems include the distractions that are often present in the home, the poor quality of sound

transmission created by the telephone equipment, and the fact that there is no way to determine exactly who is answering the questions.

Even with such limitations, many radio stations throughout the country use callout research. Because callout research is inexpensive compared with the auditorium method, the research can be conducted frequently to track the performance of songs in a particular market. Auditorium research, which can cost between $20,000 and $40,000 to test approximately 600–800 songs, is generally conducted only once or twice per year.

Online music testing.   Online music testing is a convenient and simple way to test music, and the costs are extremely low, especially if the respondents are not paid to participate. Hundreds of songs, even new music where the entire song is played, can be tested because respondents can complete the test on their own time, and virtually any type of rating scale can be used. The results can be tabulated quickly or even in real time as each respondent completes the test.

The OMT offers several advantages over the two other music testing methods, but there is one significant problem: There is no way to verify who is actually completing the online test. The respondent may be the person who was recruited, or he or she may be the respondent's friend, relative, or someone else. Researchers may include various types of security questions to verify the identity of the respondent, but it's possible for the respondent to answer those questions and then turn over the rating of songs to someone else, even a child in the household. However, even with this major flaw, OMTs are used regularly in the radio industry because of their low cost in cases where cost is more important than the validity or reliability of the information.

Corrective Measure for Sampling in Music Testing and All Research

Regardless of how often legitimate researchers warn of the potential inaccuracy of using callout or OMT research, the fact remains that many radio broadcast will continue to use both research methodologies. Why? A typical answer is, "It's cheap and it's better than nothing." However, at least in the case of OMT research, "nothing" is probably better than "something." With that in mind, we repeat the importance of running the Wimmer Outlier Analysis discussed in Chapter 7. The procedure is an excellent approach to use for **respondent verification**.

All research uses respondents who vary in a number of ways, but in almost every type of research respondents are recruited via a set of screener questions and so are similar in one or more ways; they therefore tend to be similar in their responses. The similarity of responses is the key to the method of respondent verification.

Regardless of how many safeguards a researcher includes in a research study, it is possible that one or more respondents included in the sample should not have been included. That's just the way it is. This is true for all types of behavioral research, not just music testing, and the respondent verification procedure the authors have developed is intended to eliminate inappropriate respondents, although no method is guaranteed 100%.

The Wimmer Outlier Analysis involves calculating standard deviations for every respondent in a study that uses rating scales of some form. For example, in music testing the mean and corresponding standard deviation is computed for each respondent's rating for all songs included in the test. The standard deviations are then converted to z-scores to determine if there are any outliers in the sample. In most situations, the respondents' standard deviation scores will hover near the average standard deviation for the entire sample. However, if a respondent has a standard deviation z-score that is significantly different from the rest of the sample, usually a z-score $\geq \pm 2.0$, or even ± 1.5, that person's answers should be reviewed. If it appears that the person does not belong in the sample, such as rating all songs as a "1" or "2," then the person should be eliminated from the study.

All research for which rating scales are employed should use respondent verification, but this is especially true for all music testing methodologies.

Programming Research and Consulting

Several companies conduct mass media research. Although each company specializes in specific areas of broadcasting and uses different procedures, they all have a common goal: to provide management with data to use in decision making. These companies offer custom research in almost any area of broadcasting—from testing call letters and slogans to air talent, commercials, music, importance of programming elements, and the overall sound of a station.

Broadcast consultants can be equally versatile. The leading consultants have experience in broadcasting and offer their services to radio and television stations. Although some of their recommendations are based on research, many are based on past experience. A good consultant can literally "make or break" a broadcast station, and the task of a consultant is probably best described by E. Karl (2012), a former leading international radio consultant who was asked to describe what a consultant does for a radio station. He said:

> A consultant works with research data to help a station's management team design its overall strategy. A consultant puts research findings into a strategic action

plan that will make sure the target audience's most important programming elements are on the air, and that the station is positioned correctly in listeners' minds. A consultant also helps market and advertise the station to attract listeners to try the station. The consultant does everything from designing music rotations, creating "clock hours" on the station, and selecting air talent … to developing television commercials, executing direct marketing campaigns to ask listeners to listen, designing website content, and working with the station staff to make sure the "promise" of the station's position stays on track.

Performer Q

Producers and directors in broadcasting naturally want to have an indication of the popularity of various performers and entertainers. A basic question in the planning stage of any program is this: What performer or group of performers should be used to give the show the greatest appeal? Not unreasonably, producers prefer to use the most popular and likable performers in the industry rather than taking a chance on an unknown entertainer.

Marketing Evaluations, Inc., of Manhasset, New York, meets the demand for information about performers, entertainers, and personalities (*www.qscores.com*). The company conducts nationwide telephone surveys using panels of about 1,250 households and interviewing about 5,400 people 6 years of age and older. The surveys are divided into seven types of "Q" scores, such as the Performer Q, TVQ, and Cartoon Q. The Performer Q portion of the analysis provides Familiarity and Appeal scores for more than 1,000 different personalities. The Target Audience Rankings provide a rank-order list of all personalities for several different target audiences, such as women aged 18–49. The target rank tells producers and directors which personalities appeal to specific demographic groups.

Focus Groups

The focus group, discussed in Chapter 5 and on *www.wimmerdominick.com*, is a common research procedure in electronic media research, probably because of its versatility. Focus groups are used to develop questionnaires for further research and to provide preliminary information on a variety of topics, such as format and programming changes, personalities, station images, and lifestyle characteristics of the audience. Data in the last category are particularly useful when the focus group consists of a specific demographic segment.

Miscellaneous Research

The electronic media are unique, and each requires a different type of research. Here are examples of research conducted by and for stations:

1. *Market studies.* A market study investigates the opinions and perceptions of the entire market, usually within a specific age range, such as 25–44. There are no requirements for respondents to meet in terms of station listening or viewing, and the sample matches the population distribution and makeup of the market.

2. *Format studies.* A format study for a radio station involves a sample of respondents who listen to or prefer a certain type of music. These respondents are asked a series of questions to determine which stations provide the best service in a variety of areas, such as music, news, traffic reports, and community activities.

3. *Format search studies.* The title of the study explains its purpose—to find an available radio format in a given market. An experienced

researcher can accurately predict a potential format hole with a specifically designed three-module questionnaire.

4. *Program element importance.* A program element importance study identifies the specific elements on radio or television that are most important to a specific audience. Station managers use this information to ensure that they are providing what the audience wants.

5. *Station image.* It is important for a station's management to know how the public perceives the station and its services. Public misperception of management's purpose can decrease audience size and, consequently, advertising revenue. For example, suppose a radio station has been CHR (Contemporary Hits Radio) for 10 years and switches to a Country format. It is important that the audience and advertisers be aware of this change and have a chance to voice their opinions. This can be accomplished through a station image study, where respondents are asked questions such as "What type of music does WAAA-FM play?" "What types of people do you think listen to WAAA-FM?" and "Did you know that WAAA-FM now plays country music?" If research reveals that only a few people are aware of the change in format, management can develop a new promotional strategy. Or the station might find that the current promotional efforts have been successful and should not be changed. Station image studies are conducted periodically by most large radio stations to gather current information on how the audience perceives each station

in the market. If station managers are to provide the services that listeners and viewers want, they must understand audience trends and social changes.

6. *Personality (talent) studies.* Radio and television managers of successful stations frequently test the on-air personalities. Announcers (DJs or jocks), news anchors, and all other personalities are tested for their overall appeal and fit with other station personalities. Personality studies are often conducted for stations to find new talent from other markets or even to test personalities who are on other stations in the market with the intent of hiring them in the future.

7. *Advertiser (account) analysis.* To increase the value of their service to advertisers, many stations conduct studies with local business executives. Some typical questions are "When did your business open?" "How many people own this business?" "How much do you invest in advertising per year?" "When are advertising purchase decisions made?" and "What do you expect from your advertising?" Information obtained from client questionnaires is used to help write more effective advertising copy, to develop better advertising proposals, and to allow the sales staff to know more about each client. Generally, the questionnaires are administered before a business becomes an advertiser on the station, but they can also be conducted with advertisers who have done business with the station for several years.

8. *Account executive research.* Radio and television station managers throughout the country conduct

Watching or Tuned In?

In this chapter, you may have noticed that in discussions of television viewing, we use a variation of the word *tune* (*tuned in, tuned to*, etc.) instead of variations of the word *watch*. We did this for a reason, and that reason relates to concepts known as *monochronic* and *polychronic behavior*. A person who is monochronic tends to do one thing at a time; the person who is polychronic does more than one thing at a time, more commonly known as *multitasking*. These terms relate to the use of the media.

In the past 35+ years, the senior author of this text has conducted dozens of studies to find out what people 18–54 years old do while they watch TV and listen to the radio. All of the studies have produced virtually the same results. In reference to TV viewing, every study has shown that about 75% of adults 18–54 do something else while watching TV—75% are polychronic TV viewers, and 25% are monochronic TV viewers ("I just sit and watch TV and that's all I do"). The list of activities in which polychronic viewers engage is extensive, but some commons activities include such things as eating; reading; talking to family or friends in person or on the telephone; playing with children; working on projects, hobbies, or work-related items; and many more.

In addition, polychronic viewers are always asked to estimate the amount of time they do not look at the TV screen during a typical 30- or 60-minute program. The average estimate is about 30%. In other words, about 75% of adult TV viewers say that they do not look at the TV screen about 30% of the time they are "watching" TV (about 18 minutes during a typical one-hour program). What this means is that about 30% of all visual information on the TV screen is not seen by about 75% of the adult audience. These viewers, the vast majority, are merely tuned to a TV program and should not be classified as watching TV.

While the lack of actually watching the TV screen is significant in many areas, it is of ultimate importance to advertisers. But many advertisers seem not to understand the reality of television viewing because they (or their advertising agencies) produce commercials that have no audio information other than some type of background music; the only information about the product or service is visual in nature—it is information missed by as much as 75% of the audience. The purpose of advertising is to communicate a message to consumers. Many of the commercials on television communicate absolutely nothing. You can verify this on your own. When watching TV, turn your eyes away from the screen and determine how much you learn about the product or service being advertised. All TV commercials should include both audio and visual information about the advertised product or service. A visual-only approach is a waste of time and money. Advertisers who use (or agree to use) such an approach would receive more value for their advertising investment if they donated the money (commercial production costs and airtime) to a worthy charity.

Polychronic behavior also affects radio listening. Once again, the senior author of this text has repeatedly found that, in virtually all radio formats with all age groups, adults 18–54 misunderstand, or do not hear at all, about 35% of all nonmusic material they are exposed to on the radio. Radio broadcasters are constantly amazed that their listeners do not know about a program change, a contest, a news item, or something at the radio station. Radio broadcasters think their audience hears everything that is on their radio station, when quite the opposite is true.

See Chapter 15 for more information about monochronic and polychronic behavior.

surveys of advertising agency personnel, usually buyers, to determine how their sales executives are perceived. It is vitally important to know how the buyers perceive the salespeople. The results of the surveys indicate which salespeople are performing well and which may need additional help. These surveys often disclose that problems between a sales executive and a buyer are due to personality differences, and the station can easily correct the problem by assigning another salesperson to the business or advertising agency.

9. *Sales research*. In an effort to increase sales, many stations conduct research for local clients. For example, a station may conduct a "bank image" study of all banks in the area to determine how residents perceive each bank and the service it provides. The results from such a study are then used in an advertising proposal for the banks in the area. For example, if it is discovered that First National Bank's 24-hour automatic teller service is not well understood by local residents, the station might develop an advertising proposal to concentrate on this point.

10. *Diversification analyses*. The goals of any business are to expand and to achieve higher profits. In an effort to reach these goals, most large stations, partnerships, and companies engage in a variety of studies to determine where investments should be made. Should other stations be purchased? What other types of activities should the business invest in? Such studies are used for forecasting and represent a major portion of the research undertaken by larger stations and companies. The changes in broadcast ownership rules made by the FCC have significantly increased the amount of acquisition research conducted by individuals, group owners, and other large companies in the broadcasting industry.

11. *Qualitative research*. Managers of successful broadcasting and cable operations leave nothing to chance, which means that they test every aspect of their station or network. Research is conducted to test billboard advertising, logo designs, bumper stickers, bus advertising, direct mail campaigns, programming interests, and more.

12. *TV programming research*. This is a broad category that includes testing local news programs, promotional materials used by the station (known as *topicals*), entertainment programming, and everything else that appears on the station.

SUMMARY

This chapter introduced some of the more common methodologies used in broadcast research. Ratings are the most visible form of research used in broadcasting as well as the most influential in the decision-making process. However, nonratings approaches such as focus groups, music research, image studies, and program testing are all used frequently to collect data. The importance of research is fueled by an ever-increasing desire by management to learn more about broadcast audiences and their uses of the media.

Audience fragmentation is now an accepted phenomenon of the electronic media, and the competition for viewers and listeners has created a need for research data.

Broadcast owners and managers realize that they can no longer rely on gut feelings when making programming, sales, and marketing decisions. The discussions in this chapter have been designed to emphasize the importance of research in all areas of broadcasting.

Key Terms

A.C. Nielsen	Nonratings research
Arbitron, Inc	Overnights
Audience turnover	People Meter
Auditorium music test	Polychronic behavior
Average quarter-hour	Portable People Meter
Callout research	Psychographics
Cost per thousand (CPM)	PUR
Cume	Rating
Daypart	Reach
Designated market area	Rough cut
Gross rating points	Share
Hook	Standard error
HUT	Sweeps
Metro survey area	Telephone coincidental
Monochronic behavior	Time spent listening
	Total survey area

 Using the Internet

Search the Internet for:

1. *Broadcast ratings controversies* and *"broadcast ratings" methodology*

2. *Radio history; television history; cable television history*

3. Radio and TV market ranks—*Nielsen TV markets, Arbitron radio markets*

4. Market diary information: *www.arbitron.com/diary/home.htm*

5. Arbitron's PPM: *www.arbitron.com/portable_people_meters/home.htm*

6. Nielsen's history of the People Meter: *www.nielsenmedia.com/lpm/history/History.html*

Questions and Problems for Further Investigation

1. Assume that a local television market has three stations: Channel 2, Channel 7, and Channel 9. There are 200,000 television households in the market. A ratings company samples 1,200 households at random and finds that 25% of the sample is tuned to Channel 2; 15% is tuned to Channel 7; and 10% is tuned to Channel 9.

   a. Calculate each station's share of the audience.

   b. Project the total number of households in the population that tune to each channel.

   c. Calculate the CPM for a $1,000, 30-second spot on Channel 2.

   d. Calculate the standard error involved in Channel 2's rating.

2. What are the major data-gathering problems associated with each of the following instruments?

   a. Diaries

   b. Telephone interviews

   c. Personal People Meters

   d. People Meters

3. Find out what you can find about A. C. Nielsen's idea for "sticker diaries" in radio audience measurement.

4. Search the Internet for websites for radio and TV stations in your market. Can you detect any type of research the station may have used in designing its site? Pay attention to content areas and links to other websites.

5. Perform your own music callout research. Edit several songs to 5–10 seconds in length and ask people to rate them on a 7-point scale. Compute means and standard deviations for the results. What can you conclude?

6. In early 2009, Arbitron announced that it would begin including cell-phone households in its sampling. Determine the progress of the new methodology by visiting this Arbitron website: *www.arbitron.com/home/cell_phone_markets.htm*.

For additional resources, go to *www.wimmerdominick.com* and *www.cengagebrain.com*.

References and Suggested Readings

Arbitron, Inc. (2012). *Arbitron radio market report reference guide*. Arbitron, Inc. Retrieved from *www.arbitron.com/downloads/purplebook.pdf*

Arbitron, Inc. (2012). *PPM encoding handbook for radio*. Arbitron, Inc. Retrived from *www.arbitron.com/downloads/ppm_encoding_handbook.pdf*

Bell, F. (2012). Personal correspondence to Roger Wimmer.

Beville, H. M. (1988). *Audience ratings: Radio, television, cable* (Rev. ed.). Hillsdale, NJ: Lawrence Erlbaum.

Hawkins, W. J. (1990, February). TV views viewers. *Popular Science, 236*, pp. 74–75.

Karl, E. (2012). Personal correspondence to Roger Wimmer.

LoCascio, P. (2012). Personal correspondence to Roger Wimmer.

Webster, J., & Lichty, L. (2006). *Ratings analysis*. Hillsdale, NJ: Lawrence Erlbaum.

Wimmer, R. D. (2000). Research in advertising. In C. Chakrapani (Ed.), *Marketing research: State-of-the-art perspectives*, pp. 454–478. New York, NY: American Marketing Association.

Wimmer, R. D. (2001). *An analysis of the reliability of auditorium music tests*. Denver, CO: Wimmer Research. (Proprietary data.)

Special Note about Demographics, Demos, Demo Cells, Cells

In all mass media, but particularly radio and television, the adult audience is divided into age groups: 18–24, 25–34, 35–44, 45–54, 55–64, and 65+ (children are defined as 2–11; teens are 12–17). Age groups are used extensively in programming to define a target audience, and in sales, where advertising is sold and purchased according to specific age cells. However, in reality, programming decisions and advertising sales do not focus on listeners and viewers who are over 55 years old—virtually all targets are somewhere between 18 and 54. Because programming and sales almost always exclude the 55+ audience, the age cells in the industry are referred to as 18–24, 25–34, 35–44, 45–54, and 55 to Dead. While the 55 to Dead category may sound crass, derogatory, or disparaging, the term is commonly used in many areas of broadcasting. For example, a radio station general manager may say something like, "We need to do a research study because the last few Arbitrons show that most of our audience is 55 to Dead. We need to find out why."

We wanted to prepare you for this term/phrase in the event you have never heard it. Again, the term is not intended to be demeaning. It is just a commonly used term to describe people who are beyond the usual upper limit (54 years old) of targets in programming and advertising.

There has been a gradual acceptance of the 55+ age group in programming and advertising for two reasons: (1) the large number of people who are 55+ and (2) the relative affluence of this group.

CHAPTER 15

RESEARCH IN ADVERTISING

CHAPTER OUTLINE

For many years, research was not widely used in advertising and decisions were made on an intuitive basis. However, with increased competition, mass markets, and mounting costs, more and more advertisers have come to rely on research as a basic management tool.

Much of the research in advertising is **applied research,** which attempts to solve a specific problem and is not concerned with theorizing or generalizing to other situations. Advertising researchers want to answer questions such as whether a certain product should be packaged in blue or red or whether *Cosmopolitan* is a better advertising buy than *Vogue.* Advertising research does not involve any special techniques; the methods discussed earlier—laboratory, survey, field research, focus groups, and content analysis—are in common use. They have been adapted, however, to provide specific types of information that meet the needs of this industry.

This chapter discusses the more common areas of advertising research and the types of studies they entail. In describing these research studies, we aim to convey the facts the reader must know to understand the methods and to use them intelligently.

A significant portion of the research in these areas involves market studies conducted by commercial research firms; these studies form the basis for much of the more specific research that follows in either the academic sector or the private sector. The importance of market research notwithstanding, this chapter does not have sufficient space to address this topic. Readers who want additional information about market research techniques should consult

A CLOSER LOOK

Statistics Used by Advertising Researchers

A recent study (Yoo, Joo, Choi, & Reid, 2012) examined the use of statistical techniques in published articles in four major advertising journals from 1980 to 2010. Articles were grouped into 5-year intervals, and the statistics used in each article were classified as basic (descriptive statistics, analysis of variance, Chi Square, *t*-test, correlation); intermediate (regression, analysis of covariance, partial correlation); or advanced (factor analysis, path analysis, canonical correlation, and several others).

Some of the major findings:

- Over the years, the percentage of articles using statistical analysis ranged from about 52% to 83%. Overall, about 69% of the published articles used statistical analysis.
- The percentage of articles using basic statistics decreased from 1980 to 2010, while those using intermediate and advanced statistics increased.

- Overall, basic statistics were used in 56% of the articles, intermediate in 23%, and advanced in 21%.
- Content analyses were most likely to use basic statistics. Surveys and experiments were more likely to use intermediate and advanced techniques.

One of the authors' conclusions has special relevance for those planning an academic career in advertising research: "To get ahead and enjoy career success, future scholar/educators must have a substantial foundation not only in basic and intermediate statistics, but also in advanced techniques. Such knowledge is needed to (1) read and comprehend the published research literature and (2) to ensure success in publishing their research in the major advertising journals." Those planning on a career in private-sector research would also benefit from a solid foundation in intermediate and advanced techniques.

McQuarrie (2011) and McDaniel and Gates (2011).

The three functional research areas in advertising are copy research, media research, and campaign assessment research. Each is discussed in this chapter, and the syndicated research available in each case is described when appropriate. Next, because qualitative research is popular with advertisers, the chapter includes a discussion of three specific qualitative approaches used to investigate advertising's impact. Finally, advertisers are shifting a significant portion of their budgets to the Internet. Measuring the traditional concepts in advertising research on the Internet presents difficult challenges for both practitioners and investigators. This chapter closes with an examination of some of the techniques that researchers use to study online advertising audiences, strategies, and consequences.

COPY TESTING

Copy testing refers to research that helps develop effective advertisements and then determines which of several advertisements is the most effective. Copy testing is done for ads in all media—print, audio, video, and digital. It takes place at every stage of the advertising process. Before a campaign starts, copy pretesting indicates what to stress and what to avoid. After the content of the ad is established, tests are performed to determine the most effective way to structure the ideas. For example, in studying the illustration copy of a proposed magazine spread, a researcher might show an illustration of the product photographed from different angles to three or more groups of subjects. The headline can be evaluated by having subjects rate the typefaces used in several versions of the ad, and copy can be tested for readability and recall. In all cases, the aim is to determine whether the variable tested significantly affects the liking or the recall of the ad.

In TV, a rough cut of an entire commercial might be produced. The rough cut is a film or video version of the ad in which amateur actors are used, locations are simplified, and the editing and narration lack the smoothness of broadcast (final cut) commercials. In this way, variations in the ad can be tested without incurring great expense.

The final phase of copy testing, which occurs after the finished commercials have appeared, serves to determine whether the campaign is having the desired effects. Any negative or unintended effects can be corrected before serious damage is done to a company's sales or reputation. This type of copy testing requires precisely defined goals. For example, some campaigns are designed to draw customers away from competitors; others are conducted to retain a company's present customers. Still others are intended to enhance the image of a firm and may not be concerned with consumers' purchase preferences. As we discuss later, this type of copy testing blends in with campaign assessment research.

There are several different ways to categorize copy testing methods. Perhaps the most useful, summarized by Leckenby and Wedding (1982), suggests that there are appropriate copy testing methods for each of the three dimensions of impact in the persuasion process. Although the model suggests a linear process starting with the cognitive dimension (knowing) and continuing through the affective dimension (feeling) to the conative dimension (doing), it is not necessary for the steps to occur in this order—see Table 15.1. In any event, the model serves as a convenient guide for discussing copy research methods.

The Cognitive Dimension

In the cognitive dimension, the key dependent variables are attention, awareness, exposure, recognition, comprehension, and recall. Studies that measure attention to

Table 15.1   Typology of Copy Testing Effects

Dimension of Impact	Typical Dependent Variables
Cognitive	Attention
	Exposure
	Awareness
	Recognition
	Comprehension
	Recall
	Engagement
Affective	Attitude change
	Liking/disliking
	Involvement
Conative	Intention to buy
	Purchase behavior

advertising can use various methods. One strategy involves a consumer jury, where a group of 50–100 consumers looks at test ads and indicates which ad, if any, was best at catching their attention. A physiological measurement technique, known as an eye-tracking study (see Chapter 13), is also used to determine which parts of an ad are noticed. A camera records the movement of the eye as it scans printed and graphic material. Analyzing the path the eye follows allows researchers to determine which parts of the ad attracted initial attention.

A tachistoscope (or T-scope) is one way to measure recognition of an ad. The T-scope is actually a slide projector with adjustable levels of illumination and with projection speeds that can be adjusted down to a tiny fraction of a second. Ads are tested to determine how long it takes a consumer to recognize the product, the headline, or the brand name.

Ad comprehension is an important factor in advertising research. One study found that all 60 commercials used in a test were misunderstood by viewers (Jacoby & Hofer, 1982). To guard against results such as these, advertising researchers typically test new ads with focus groups (see Chapter 5) to make sure their message is getting across as intended. The T-scope is also used to see how long it takes subjects to comprehend the theme of an ad—an important consideration for outdoor advertising, where drivers may have only a second or two of exposure.

Awareness, exposure, and recall are determined by several related methods. The print media use one measurement technique that taps these variables: Subjects look at a copy of a newspaper or magazine and report which advertisements they remember seeing or reading. The results are used to tabulate a "reader traffic score" for each ad.

This method is open to criticism because some respondents confuse the advertisements or the publications in which they saw the ads, and some try to please the interviewer by reporting that they saw more than they actually did (prestige bias). To control this problem, researchers often make use of **aided recall** techniques. For instance, they might also show the respondent a list of advertisers, some whose advertisements actually appeared in the publication and some whose did not. For obvious reasons, this type of **recall study** is not entirely suitable for testing radio and television commercials; a more commonly used method in such cases is the telephone or online survey. Two variations of this approach are sometimes used. In aided recall, the interviewer mentions a general class of products and asks whether the respondent remembers an ad for a specific brand. A typical question might be "Have you seen or heard any ads for soft drinks lately?" In the **unaided recall** technique, researchers ask a general question such as "Have you seen any ads that interested you lately?" Obviously, it is harder for the consumer to respond to the second type of question. Only truly memorable ads score high on this form of measurement. Some researchers suggest that the most sensitive way to measure recall is to ask consumers whether they remember any recent advertising for each particular brand whose advertising is of interest.

Several private sector research firms provide posttesting services. Gallup & Robinson offer the InTeleTest method, which measures the percentage of respondents who remember seeing a commercial and the percentage of those who can remember specific points. Additionally, they provide a score that indicates the degree of favorable attitude toward the product, based on positive statements made by the subjects during the interview.

Gallup & Robinson also conduct pretests and posttests of magazine advertisements. Their Magazine Impact Research Service (MIRS) measures the recall of advertisements that appear in general-interest magazines. Copies of a particular issue containing the advertisement under study are mailed to approximately 150 readers. (In the case of a pretest, the MIRS binds the proposed advertisement into each magazine.) The day after delivery of the magazines, respondents are telephoned and asked which advertisements they noticed in the magazine and what details they can remember about them. These results are reported to the advertiser.

One of the best-known professional research firms is Gfk MRI, which conducts posttest recall research. The company's Issue Specific Readership Study uses online interviews to report how many people saw a particular ad in a specific issue of a magazine. Data are reported by age, gender, and household income level.

Starch Advertising Research (also a part of Gfk MRI) has provided advertising readership information for more than 80 years. Respondents look through an issue of a magazine and indicate their readership of individual ads. Readers are classified into four categories:

1. Nonreader (did not recall seeing the advertisement)

2. Noted reader (remembered seeing the advertisement)

3. Associated reader (not only saw the advertisement but also read some part of it that clearly indicated the brand name)

4. Read most reader (read more than half the written material in the advertisement)

The Starch organization reports the findings of its recall studies in a novel manner. Advertisers are given a copy of the magazine in which readership scores printed on yellow stickers have been attached to each advertisement.

The newest measure in advertising and media research is called **engagement**, a multidimensional measure that attempts to determine how involved a consumer is with an advertisement or media content. The method combines cognitive measures with some of the affective and conative measures discussed in the next sections. Engagement can be measured in several ways. Researchers may ask about recall of the ad, whether the consumer liked the ad, and whether the consumer talked about the content of the ad with others. There is evidence to suggest that engagement measures are positively correlated with intent to purchase a product (Kilger & Romer, 2007).

Peacock, Purvis, and Hazlett (2011) examined 16 advertising campaigns that used both radio and television ads. They found that engagement was positively related to brand recall but that TV ads generated a slightly higher negative emotional reaction.

A CLOSER LOOK

Cautions about Advertising Research

The perception that many people have who are *outside* the advertising community is that all businesses and their advertising agencies use the latest and most effective forms of advertising—that print and electronic advertising is on the "cutting edge" of knowledge of advertising (persuasion). With all due respect to advertising agencies and others involved in the development of advertising, this is not true. An example will help with this misperception.

When it comes to television viewing, it is common knowledge that about 75% of all TV viewers do not watch the TV screen all the time. Instead of constantly watching the TV screen, these people *listen* to TV while they participate in other activities such as reading, eating, playing with children, and so on. As mentioned in Chapter 14, the people who simultaneously participate in two or more activities, such as TV viewing and reading, belong to a category known as **polychronic behavior**. In current terms, these people are multitasking. The people who do not participate simultaneously in two or more activities belong to a category known as **monochronic behavior**. People exhibiting monochronic behavior watch TV and do nothing else.

Because the majority of TV viewers are polychronic, it is scientifically logical that commercials should include both visual *and* audio information. Audio information does not mean music. It means spoken words. TV commercials that include only visual information, including commercials that have words that must be read, are a complete waste for as much as 75% of the audience. In other words, a polychronic viewer obtains no information from a visual-only commercial. This is demonstrated easily in tests of TV commercials in which respondents are asked to rate commercials by looking away from the TV screen. When visual-only commercials are tested and the respondents are asked to rate the commercial or explain what information they obtained from it, the answer to both questions is always, "I don't know."

Therefore, it is clear from the countless number of visual-only commercials on American television that advertising experts do not incorporate "cutting-edge" research into the development of commercials. Instead, advertising agencies create commercials for other reasons—to win awards, to be considered "artistic," or to mimic other advertising agencies. There is no concern about the success of the ad in relation to its ability to communicate a message to the audience. A significant amount of advertising money in the United States is wasted on messages that have no purpose or meaning. This is primarily the fault of advertising agency employees who don't know much, if anything, about advertising (communication/persuasion), and of clients who unfortunately don't know enough to question the advertisements presented to them by their agencies. For more information about this topic, see Wimmer (2000).

Mersey, Malthouse, and Calder (2010) found two types of engagement for online media: personal engagement and social-interactive engagement. Both types of engagement were related to online ad readership.

The Affective Dimension

The affective dimension usually involves research into whether consumers' attitudes toward a particular product have changed because of exposure to an ad or a campaign. The techniques used to study the affective dimension include projective tests, theater testing, physiological measures, semantic differential scales, and rating scales. Projective tests provide an alternative to the straightforward "Do you like this ad?" approach. Instead, respondents are asked to draw a picture or complete a story that involves the ad or the product mentioned in the ad. Analysis of these responses provides additional insight and depth into consumers' feelings. We discuss projective tests later in this chapter.

Theater tests involve bringing an audience to a special facility where they are shown a TV program that is embedded with test commercials. Respondents are given electronic response indicators (ERIs—similar to handheld calculators) that allow them to instantaneously rate each commercial they see. There are a variety of ERI devices, but all have buttons, a dial, or a sliding device so that respondents can rate the commercials (or other content) on a scale, such as "very negative" to "very positive." The respondents record their perceptions while watching the commercial or other content. The miniaturization of handheld rating devices allows tests to be conducted in focus room facilities or in specially equipped vans parked outside shopping malls. These tests have been criticized because they require respondents to make too many responses and analyze content that may be too minute to be put into practical use, and they do not allow respondents to change their answers because the answers are recorded instantaneously in a computer. (Sometimes a researcher's desire to use technology to impress clients overshadows the validity and reliability of a research approach. That is, the use of technology in research can create a "leap backward" in data collection and analysis).

Four physiological tests (see Chapter 9) are used in this area of advertising research. In the pupilometer test, a tiny camera focused on the subject's eye measures the amount of pupil dilation that occurs while the person is looking at an ad. Changes in pupil diameter are recorded because findings from psychophysiology suggest that people tend to respond to appealing stimuli with dilation (enlargement) of their pupils. Conversely, when unappealing, disagreeable stimuli are shown, the pupil narrows. The second test measures galvanic skin response, or GSR, where changes in the electrical conductance of the surface of the skin are measured. A change in GSR while the subject is looking at an ad is taken to signify emotional involvement or arousal. The third technique, brain wave analysis, monitors brain activity during exposure to a television commercial in order to measure the level of interest and involvement by a viewer (Percy & Rossiter, 1997). As advances in neuroscience continue, it is likely that studies of the brain will become more important in advertising research. This area has been given its own name, **neuromarketing** (Marci, 2008). In 2011 the Advertising Research Foundation issued a report that recommended standards for neuromarketing (Stipp, Weber, & Varan, 2011).

Hazlett (1999) describes a method whereby facial electromyography (fEMG—a technique that measures the electrical activity of facial muscles) was used to track consumers' responses to TV commercials. The results suggested that fEMG was a better measure of emotion than relying on viewers' self-reports. The research company Gallup & Robinson offers a service called Continuous Emotional Response Analysis (CERA) that uses fEMG to track consumers' emotional arousal while watching an ad. The big advantage of fEMG is that it can differentiate negative arousal from positive arousal because different facial muscles are involved in each response.

Semantic differential scales and rating scales (see Chapter 2) are used most often to measure attitude change. For these measurements to be most useful, it is necessary to (1) obtain a picture of consumers' attitudes before exposure to the ad, (2) expose consumers to the ad or ads under examination, and (3) remeasure their attitude after exposure. To diminish the difficulties associated with achieving all three goals in testing television ads, many researchers prefer a **forced-exposure** method. In this technique, respondents are invited to a theater for a special screening of a TV program. Before viewing the program, they are asked to fill out questionnaires concerning their attitudes toward several different products, one of which is of interest to the researchers. Next, the respondents watch the TV show, which contains one or more commercials for the product under investigation in addition to ads for other products. When the show is over, the respondents complete another questionnaire concerning product attitudes. Change in evaluation is the essential variable of interest. The same basic method can be used in testing attitudes toward print ads except that the testing is done individually, often at the respondent's home. Typically, a consumer is interviewed about product attitudes, a copy of a magazine that includes the test ad (or ads) is left at the house, and the respondent is asked to read or look through the publication before the next interview. A short time later, the interviewer calls the respondent and asks whether the magazine has been read. If it has, product attitudes are once again measured.

The importance of the affective dimension was emphasized by Walker and Dubitsky (1994), who noted that the degree of liking expressed by consumers toward a commercial was significantly related to awareness, recall, and greater persuasive impact. Indeed, several advertising researchers have suggested that liking an ad is one of the most important factors in determining its impact (Haley, 1994).

Multidimensional measures of emotion are useful. Micu and Plummer (2010) evaluated three measures of affect: physiological (GSR, heart rate, and fEMG), symbolic (a picture-sorting technique), and self-reports (verbal and ERI). They recommended that all measures be used in combination because less intense emotions are tapped by physiological measurements while self-report measures capture conscious emotional reactions. Symbolic measures provide a mental map of the brand.

The Conative Dimension

The conative dimension deals with actual consumer behavior; in many instances, it is the most important of all dependent variables. The two main categories of behavior usually measured are buying predisposition and actual purchasing behavior. In the first category, the usual design gathers precampaign predisposition data and reinterviews the subjects after the advertising has been in place. Subjects are typically asked a question such as "If you were going shopping tomorrow to buy breakfast cereal, which brand would you buy?" This might be followed by "Would you consider buying any other brands?" and "Are there any cereals you would definitely not buy?" (The last question is included to determine whether the advertising campaign had any negative effects.) Additionally, some researchers (Haskins, 1976) suggest using a buying intention scale, which instructs respondents to check the one position on the scale that best fits their intention. Such a scale might look like this:

_____ I'll definitely buy this cereal as soon as I can.

_____ I'll probably buy this cereal sometime.

_____ I might buy this cereal, but I don't know when.

_____ I'll probably never buy this cereal.

_____ I wouldn't eat this cereal even if somebody gave it to me.

The scale allows advertisers to see how consumers' buying preferences change during and after the campaign.

Perhaps the most reliable methods of post-testing are those that measure actual sales, direct response, and other easily quantifiable behavior. For newspaper or magazines, direct response might be measured by inserting a coupon that readers can mail in for a free sample or redeem online. Different forms of an ad might be run in different publications and websites to determine which elicits the most inquiries. Another alternative suitable for use in both print media advertising and electronic media advertising is to include a toll-free telephone number or an Internet address that consumers can contact for more information or to order the product.

Three studies illustrate how researchers can examine behavioral response. Bates and Buckley (2000) examined the influence of exposure to TV commercials that urged people to return their 2000 census forms on the actual rate of returned forms. They found that exposure to advertising was related to knowing more about the census but that there was no relationship between exposure to the ads and actually returning a form. Burton, Lichtenstein, and Netemeyer (1999) discovered that exposure to an advertising sales flyer for retail supermarkets resulted in more than a 100% increase in the number of advertised products that were purchased. More recently, Bronnenberg, Dube, and Mela (2010) studied whether DVR usage (specifically fast-forwarding through commercials) hurt the sales of advertised products. They monitored DVR behavior and household purchases over a one- and two-year period. Interestingly, they could find no statistical support for the assertion that DVRs affect the purchasing of advertised products.

Some research companies measure direct response by means of a laboratory store. Usually used in conjunction with theater testing, this technique involves giving people chits with which they can buy products in a special store, which in most cases is a special trailer or field service conference room furnished to look like a store. Subjects are then shown a program containing some test commercials, given more chits, and allowed to shop again. Changes in pre- and post-exposure choices are recorded. Symphony IRI (formerly Information Resources Inc.) has taken this concept online. It offers a virtual shopping experience where consumers can pick up, rotate, and buy products just as they would in a real store.

Actual sales data can be obtained in many ways. Consumers may be asked directly, "Which brand of breakfast cereal did you most recently purchase?" However, the findings from this survey would be subject to error due to faulty recall, courtesy bias, and so forth. For this reason, more direct methods are usually preferred. If enough time and money are available, direct observation of people's selections in the cereal aisles at a sample of supermarkets can be a useful source of data. Store audits that list the total number of boxes sold at predetermined times are another possibility. Last, and possibly most expensive, is the household audit technique, in which an interviewer visits the homes of a sample of consumers and actually inspects their kitchen cupboards to see which brands of cereals are there. In addition to the audit, a traditional questionnaire is used to gather further information about the respondents' feelings toward the commercials.

MEDIA RESEARCH

Two important terms in media research are **reach** and frequency. Reach is the total number of households or persons that are supposedly exposed to a message in a particular medium at least once over a certain time period. Reach can be thought of as the cumulative audience, and it is usually expressed as a percentage of the total universe of households that have been exposed to a message.

For example, if 25 of a possible 100 households are exposed to a message, then the reach is 25%. **Frequency** refers to the number of exposures to the same message that each household or person receives. Of course, not every household or person in the sample will receive exactly the same number of messages. Consequently, advertisers prefer to use the average frequency of exposure, expressed by this formula:

$$\frac{\text{Total exposures for all households/persons}}{\text{Reach}} = \text{Average frquency}$$

Thus, if the total number of exposures for a sample of households is 400 and the reach is 25, the average frequency is 16. In other words, the average household was exposed 16 times. Notice that if the reach were 80%, the frequency would be 5. As reach increases, average frequency drops. (Maximizing reach and frequency is directly related to the amount of money invested in an advertising campaign.)

A concept closely related to reach and frequency is **gross rating points** (GRPs), introduced in Chapter 14. GRPs are useful when it comes to deciding between two media alternatives. For example, suppose Program A has a reach of 30% and an average frequency of 2.5, whereas Program B has a reach of 45% and a frequency of 1.25. Which program offers a better reach–frequency relationship? First, determine the GRPs of each program using the following formula:

$$\text{GRPs} = \text{Reach} \times \text{Average frequency}$$

For A:

$$\text{GRPs} = 30 \times 2.5 = 75.00$$

For B:

$$\text{GRPs} = 45 \times 1.25 = 56.25$$

In this example, Program A scores better in the reach–frequency combination, and this would probably be a factor in deciding which one is the better buy.

Media research falls into three general categories: studies of the size and composition of an audience of a particular medium or media (reach studies), studies of the relative efficiency of advertising exposures provided by various combinations of media (reach and frequency studies), and studies of the advertising activities of competitors.

Audience Size and Composition

Analyses of audiences are probably the most commonly used advertising studies in print and electronic media research. Because advertisers spend large amounts of money in the print and electronic media, they have an understandable interest in the audiences for those messages. In most cases, audience information is gathered using techniques that are compromises between the practical and the ideal.

As noted in Chapter 13, the audience size of a newspaper or magazine is commonly measured in terms of the number of copies distributed per issue. This number, which is called the publication's **circulation**, includes both copies delivered to subscribers and those bought at newsstands or from other sellers. Because a publication's advertising rate is determined directly by its circulation, the print media have developed a standardized method of measuring circulation and have instituted an organization, the Audit Bureau of Circulations (ABC), to verify that a publication actually distributes the number of copies per issue that it claims. (The specific procedures used by the ABC are discussed later in this chapter.)

Circulation figures are used to compute the cost per thousand (CPM) of various publications. For example, suppose Newspaper X charges $1,800 for an advertisement and has an ABC-verified circulation of 180,000, whereas Newspaper Y has a circulation of 300,000 and charges $2,700 for a space of

Table 15.2 Determining Advertising Efficiency from Ad Cost and Circulation Data

	Newspaper X	Newspaper Y
Ad cost	$1,800	$2,700
Circulation	180,000	300,000
Cost per thousand circulated copies	$\dfrac{\$1,800}{180} = \$10.00$	$\dfrac{\$2,700}{300} = \$9.00$

the same size. Assuming the newspapers are the same in all respects except for advertising costs, Table 15.2 shows that Newspaper Y is a slightly more efficient advertising vehicle because of a lower CPM.

Note that this method considers only the number of circulated copies of a newspaper or magazine. This information is useful, but it does not necessarily indicate the total number of readers of the publication. To estimate the total audience, the circulation figure must be multiplied by the average number of readers of each copy of an issue. This information is obtained by performing audience surveys.

A preliminary step in conducting such surveys is to operationally define the concept *magazine reader* or *newspaper reader*. There are many possible definitions, but the one most commonly used is fairly liberal: A *reader* is a person who has read or at least looked through an issue in a certain time frame.

Three techniques are used to measure readership. The most rigorous is the unaided recall method, in which respondents are asked whether they have read any newspapers or magazines in the past month (or other time period). If the answer is "yes," subjects are asked to specify the magazines or newspapers they read. When a publication is named, the interviewer attempts to verify reading by asking questions about the contents of that publication. The reliability of the unaided recall method is open to question

(as has been discussed) because of the difficulty respondents often have in recalling specific content.

A second technique is aided recall, where the interviewer names several publications and asks whether the respondent has read any of them lately. Each time the respondent claims to have read a publication, the interviewer asks whether he or she remembers seeing the most recent copy. The interviewer may jog a respondent's memory by describing the front page or the cover. Finally, the respondent is asked to recall anything that was seen or read in that particular issue. In a variation on this process, **masked recall**, respondents are shown the front page or the cover of a publication with the name blacked out and are asked whether they remember reading that particular issue. Those who respond in the affirmative are asked to recall any items they have seen or read.

The third technique, called the **recognition** method, involves showing respondents the logo or cover of a publication. For each publication respondents have seen or read, the interviewer produces a copy and the respondents leaf through it to identify the articles or stories they recognize. Respondents who definitely remember reading the publication are counted in its audience. To check the accuracy of the respondent's memory, dummy articles may be inserted into the interviewer's copy of the publication;

Table 15.3   Determining Ad Efficiency from an Extended Database

	Newspaper X	Newspaper Y
Ad cost	$1,800	$2,700
Circulation	180,000	300,000
CPM	$10.00	$9.00
Number of people who read the issue	630,000 (3.5 readers per copy)	540,000 (1.8 readers per copy)
Revised CPM	$2.86	$5.00

respondents who claim to have read the dummy items thus may be eliminated from the sample or given less weight in the analysis. Many advertising researchers consider the recognition technique to be the most accurate predictor of readership scores.

When the total audience for each magazine or newspaper is tabulated, the advertiser can determine which publication is the most efficient buy. For example, returning to the example of Table 15.2, let's suppose that Newspaper X and Newspaper Y have the audience figures listed in Table 15.3. Based on these figures, Newspaper X, because it has more readers, would be considered the more efficient choice.

Another variable to consider in determining the advertising efficiency (or **media efficiency**) of a newspaper or magazine is the number of times a person reads each issue. For example, imagine two newspapers or magazines that have the same number of readers per issue. Publication A consists primarily of pictures and contains little text; people tend to read it once and not look at it again. Publication B, on the other hand, contains several lengthy and interesting articles; people pick it up several times. Publication B would seem to be a more efficient advertising vehicle because it provides several possible exposures to an advertisement for the same cost as Publication A.

Unfortunately, a practical and reliable method for measuring the number of exposures per issue has not yet been developed.

Perhaps the most important gauge of advertising efficiency is the composition of the audience. It matters little if 100,000 people see an advertisement for farm equipment if only a few of them, or none, are in the market for such products. To evaluate the number of potential customers in the audience, an advertiser must first conduct research to determine the demographic characteristics of people who purchase a particular product. For example, potential customers for beer might be described typically as males 18–49; those for fast-food restaurants might be households in which the primary wage earner is 18–35 with at least two children under 12. The demographic characteristics of typical consumers are then compared with the characteristics of a publication's audience for the product. The cost of reaching this audience is also expressed in CPM units, as shown in Table 15.4. The numbers indicate that Newspaper X is slightly more efficient as a vehicle for reaching potential beer customers and much more efficient in reaching fast-food restaurant patrons.

Because of the ephemeral nature of radio and television broadcasts, determining audience size and composition in the electronic

Table 15.4   Calculation of Ad Efficiency Incorporating Demographic Survey Results

	Newspaper X	Newspaper Y
Ad cost	$1,800	$2,700
Circulation	180,000	300,000
CPM	$10.00	$9.00
Number of people who read average issue	630,000	540,000
Number of potential beer drinkers	150,000	220,000
Number of potential fast-food customers	300,000	200,000
CPM (beer drinkers)	$12.00	$12.27
CPM (fast-food customers)	$6.00	$13.50

A CLOSER LOOK

Target Audience Language

Each mass medium has several target audiences, usually one broad target and many others for specific elements, such as a TV program, radio show, or newspaper insert. In programming, editorial, and advertising sales discussions, the audience target is generally shortened to the words "target" or "demo," so it is common to hear a question such as "What's the demo for this program?"

media poses special problems for advertising researchers. One problem in particular involves the use of the CPM measure for media planning. The various measures of program audience discussed in Chapter 14 may or may not reflect the number of people who actually watch a TV program. Industry experts suggest that engagement measures (discussed previously in this chapter) are more useful for advertisers (Marich, 2008).

Frequency of Exposure in Media Schedules

In some situations, advertisers with a small advertising or promotion budget are limited to using only one medium. However, advertisers with a good budget often use several media simultaneously, which is known as *synergistic advertising* or *synergistic marketing*. The task is to determine which media combination will provide the greatest reach and frequency for the product or service. A substantial amount of media research has been devoted to this question, much of it concentrated on the development of mathematical models of advertising media and their audiences. The mathematical derivations of these models are beyond the scope of this book. However, the following paragraphs describe in simplified form the concepts underlying two models: stepwise analysis and decision calculus. Readers who wish to pursue these topics in more rigorous detail should consult Rust (1986) and the Internet (see "Using the Internet" at the end of this chapter for suggestions to find more information about synergistic advertising/marketing).

Stepwise analysis is called an iterative model because the same series of instructions to the computer is repeated over and over with slight modifications until a predetermined best or optimal solution is reached. The Young & Rubicam agency pioneered development in this area with its stepwise "high-assay" model. Stepwise analysis constructs a media schedule in increments, initially choosing a particular vehicle based on the lowest cost per potential customer reached. After this selection has been made, all the remaining media vehicles are reevaluated to determine whether the optimal advertising exposure rate has been achieved. If not, the second most efficient vehicle is chosen, and the process is repeated until the optimal exposure rate is reached. This method is called the high-assay model because it is analogous to gold mining. The easiest-to-get gold is mined first, followed by less accessible ore. In like manner, the consumers who are the easiest to reach are targeted first, followed by consumers who are harder to find and more costly to reach.

Decision calculus models make use of an **objective function,** a mathematical statement that provides a quantitative value for a given media combination (also known as a schedule). This value represents the schedule's effectiveness in providing advertising exposure. The advertising researcher determines which schedule offers the maximum exposure for a given product by calculating the objective functions of various media schedules.

Calculations of objective functions are based on values generated by studies of audience size and composition for each vehicle or medium. In addition, a schedule's objective function value takes into account such variables as the probability that the advertisement will be forgotten, the total cost of the media schedule compared with the advertiser's budget, and the "media option source effect"—that is, the relative impact of exposure in a particular advertising vehicle. (For example, an advertisement for men's clothes is likely to have more impact in *Gentlemen's Quarterly* than in *True Detective*.)

In the last 20 years or so, many new mathematical models for predicting the optimum combination of reach, frequency, and cost have been developed. The more recent formulations take into account both traditional and digital advertising channels. Cheong, Leckenby, and Eaton (2011) compared nine multivariate media exposure models and concluded that a newly developed measure, the Multivariate Beta Binomial Distribution, performed the best.

Media Research by Private Firms

As mentioned earlier, the Audit Bureau of Circulations (ABC) supplies advertisers with data on the circulation figures of newspapers and magazines. As of 2012, ABC measured the circulation of about 75% of all print media vehicles in the United States and Canada. ABC requires publishers to submit a detailed report of their circulation every six months; it verifies these reports by sending field workers to conduct an audit at each publication. The auditors typically examine records of the publications' press runs, newsprint bills, or other invoices for paper, as well as transcripts of circulation records and related files.

In 2010 the ABC announced a new formula for calculating circulation. Newspapers that publish "branded" editions, such as a Spanish-language version, can now include them in their total average circulation figures. In addition, the new ABC rules let newspapers count a subscriber more than once if he or she pays or registers to access content via a print subscription, website, mobile media, or e-reader. Finally, the ABC also provides an estimate of the total audience for a newspaper that includes both print and online readers.

As mentioned in Chapter 13, Gfk MRI provides comprehensive feedback about magazine readership. Gfk MRI uses the measurement technique called the *recent reading method*. The company selects a large random sample of readers and shows them the logos of about 70 magazines to determine which ones they have recently read or looked through. At the same time, data are gathered about the ownership, purchase, and use of a variety of products and services. This information is tabulated by Gfk MRI and released in a series of detailed online reports on the demographic makeup and purchasing behavior of each magazine's audience. Using these data, advertisers can determine the cost of reaching potential buyers of their products or services.

Two companies—Arbitron and Nielsen—supply broadcast audience data for advertisers. Arbitron measures radio listening in about 270 markets across the United States, and Nielsen provides audience estimates for network TV and local television markets. (Chapter 14 has more information on the methods used by these two companies and others.)

Competitors' Activities

Advertisers like to know the media choices of their competitors, which can help them avoid making mistakes of less successful competitors and imitate the strategies of more successful competitors. In addition, advertisers seeking to promote a new product who know that the leading competitors are using the same media mix might feel that their approach is valid, though this is not always true.

An advertiser can collect data on competitors' activities either by setting up a special research team or by subscribing to the services of a syndicated research company. Because the job of monitoring the media activity of a large number of firms advertising in several media is so difficult, most advertisers rely on a syndicated service. The companies gather data by direct observation—that is, by tabulating the advertisements that appear in a given medium. In addition to information about the frequency of advertisements, cost figures are helpful. The estimates are obtained from the published rate cards used by the media.

Advertisers also find it helpful to know what competitors are saying, and many advertising agencies conduct systematic content analyses of the messages in a sample of the competitors' advertisements to obtain the information. The results often provide insight into the persuasive themes, strategies, and goals of competitors' advertising and are the reason so many commercials look and sound alike—successful approaches are often mimicked.

Kantar Media provides comprehensive information about advertisers' activities and expenditures. Kantar reports advertising expenditures in newspapers and magazines and on television, radio, and the web.

CAMPAIGN ASSESSMENT RESEARCH

Campaign assessment research builds on copy and media research, but its research strategies are generally different from those used in the other areas. In general, there are two kinds of assessment research. The pretest/posttest method takes measurements before and after the campaign, and **tracking studies** assess the impact of the campaign by measuring effects at several times during the progress of the campaign.

The major advantage of a tracking study is that it provides important feedback to the advertiser while the campaign is still in progress. This feedback might lead to changes in the creative strategy or the media strategy. No matter what type of assessment research is chosen, one problem is deciding on the dependent variable.

The objective of the campaign should be spelled out before the campaign is executed so that assessment research is most useful. For example, if the objective of the campaign is to increase brand awareness, this measure should be the dependent variable rather than recall of ad content or actual sales increases. Schultz and Barnes (1994) list several campaign objectives that might be examined, including liking for the brand, ad recall, brand preference, and purchasing behavior.

Pretest/posttest studies typically use personal interviews to collect data. At times, the same people are interviewed before the campaign starts and again after its close (a panel study), or two groups are chosen and asked the same questions (a trend study; see Chapter 8). In any case, measures before and after the campaign are examined to gauge the effects of advertising. Winters (1983) reports several pretest/posttest studies done for a major oil company. In one study a pretest showed that about 80% of the sample agreed that a particular oil company made too much profit. Five months later, a posttest revealed that the percentage had dropped slightly among those who had seen an oil company newspaper ad but had remained the same among those who had not seen the ad. Additionally, the study disclosed that people who saw both print ads and TV ads showed less attitude change than those who saw only the TV ads, suggesting that the print ad might have had a dampening effect.

Hall (2007) discusses a study done by the United Kingdom's Institute of Practitioners in Advertising that is a variation of the pretest/posttest design. In a study of the effectiveness of campaign appeals, the Institute analyzed 880 case studies of ads that had won the group's award for effectiveness. This quasi-experimental design is similar to the posttest-only situation mentioned in Chapter 9. The study concluded that campaigns based on emotional appeal were more effective in the long run.

Tracking studies also rely on personal or telephone interviews for data collection. Thomas (1997) notes that tracking studies can be continuous (a certain number of interviews are conducted every day or every week for a certain time period) or pulsed (the interviews are conducted in waves, perhaps every three or six months). Continuous tracking is more expensive, but it smooths out the effects of short-term factors, such as bad weather or bad publicity. Pulsed tracking can be timed to coincide with specific schedules of ads, thus offering a more precise before–after comparison.

For example, Block and Brezen (1990) analyzed a tracking study of 223 households over 88 weeks concerning their spaghetti sauce purchases. They discovered that brand loyalty was the most important variable in predicting buying behavior. Jones (1995) reported the results of an elaborate tracking study of the advertising and purchasing behavior of 2,000 homes and 142 brands over an entire year. The study found evidence of pronounced short-term effects of advertising, but long-term effects were more difficult to isolate.

Tracking studies are useful, but they do have drawbacks. Perhaps the biggest problem is cost. Tracking studies typically require large samples; in fact, a sample of less than 1,500 cases per year is unusual. If a detailed analysis of subgroups is needed, the sample must be much larger. Furthermore, if the product is available nationwide, test markets across the country might be necessary to present a complete picture of the results. Finally, the use of sophisticated research methods, such as single-source data, makes the research even more expensive. For those who can afford it, the tracking study provides continuous measurement of the effects of a campaign and an opportunity to fine-tune the copy and the media schedule.

QUALITATIVE TECHNIQUES IN ADVERTISING RESEARCH

In addition to the qualitative methods discussed in Chapter 5, advertising researchers have developed unique ways to investigate consumer attitudes and behavior.

Projective Techniques

One approach involves projective techniques. Most readers are probably familiar with the Rorschach ink-blot test, one of the most famous **projective techniques**. The idea behind the inkblot test and other projective techniques is that some people will not divulge their true feelings and attitudes about a product or company because they feel uncomfortable about sharing their personal opinions with researchers. In addition, there may be others who may not even be aware of their motivations for buying a product. Projective techniques address these problems by allowing respondents to project their feelings onto others or into other situations. Researchers who use these methods argue that they provide a person with an unthreatening situation that might reveal the respondent's unconscious or deep-seated beliefs (Donoghue, 2000).

Consumers are typically presented with an unstructured task or other stimuli and asked to respond. The actual responses represent one source of data for analysis, but a more valuable source of information might be the discussion that follows the projective testing session in which respondents are asked to explain why they answered the way they did. These remarks can be recorded and content-analyzed for underlying themes and frequently mentioned topics.

Some specific types of projective techniques include association, immersion, and role playing. The association approach is the familiar "What is the first word that pops into your mind?" technique that has been used in psychotherapy and other areas. An advertising researcher presents a list of words to respondents and instructs them to respond with the first word they think of. In addition to examining the actual response, researchers may also analyze how long it took a consumer to respond and patterns of response that emerge throughout the list. For example, a researcher investigating the image of a certain brand of laundry detergent might present respondents with words such as *clean, fresh,* and *gentle,* as well as the names of some of the leading competitors.

The role-playing method presents the respondent with a series of drawings or photographs that seem to tell a story and asks him or her to assume the role of a person shown in the photos and complete the story. For example, a researcher might show respondents a series of drawings or photographs of a shopper and a salesperson in a car showroom. One series of pictures takes place in a Ford car showroom while another is set in some other venue. In each situation, the researcher asks respondents to take the role of the person shopping for the car and explain how the story ends. A variation of this technique can be used in focus groups where a couple members of the group are assigned roles to play and the rest of the group becomes the audience.

The completion technique involves presenting words, phrases, or questions to respondents, who are then asked to complete them. For example, one item might be "When I think of coffee, I think of _____." Or "If my favorite brand of coffee were a movie star, it would be _____." Similarly, "If my brand were a person, it would look like _____." A variation of this technique makes the respondents use their imagination. The researcher might say, "Imagine a hand picking up a Miller Lite beer. What does the hand look like? What does the owner of the hand look like? Where does the owner live?" "Now imagine a hand picking up Michelob Lite, what does that hand look like?" and so on. WPP Group, a leading ad agency, uses a method called Added Value in which consumers are asked to imagine themselves using a product and then write a story about it (Halliday, 2007).

Another version of this technique presents consumers with cartoon characters with empty "bubbles" by their heads (much like those used in comic books) and asks consumers to fill in the bubble with what the cartoon character is thinking or saying. For example, one set of cartoons might show a person in the coffee aisle at the supermarket, and the respondents might be asked to fill in what the person is thinking about while shopping for coffee.

Advantages and Disadvantages. Probably the biggest disadvantage of projective techniques is the difficulty in data analysis. The questions can be complicated, and the answers are usually phrased indirectly, making it difficult to draw concrete conclusions about a specific brand or product. It is also difficult to sort out the truly meaningful responses—those that might shape purchasing decisions—from the large number of responses that are obtained.

A second disadvantage is one common to qualitative data. How valid are the responses? Are the actions of a consumer in a role-playing situation the same actions that would be found in a real-life situation? How valid are the words consumers add to the bubbles above cartoon characters' heads? Soley (2010) presents evidence that at least one projective technique is as valid and reliable as quantitative methods.

A final disadvantage is that with projective techniques, it takes a relatively long amount of time to collect and analyze the data. On the plus side, projective techniques provide a substantial amount of rich and detailed data. They can also provide in-depth detail about closely held attitudes or perceptions that might not be uncovered via surveys or other quantitative methods.

Additionally, projective techniques work well with younger children and others who lack the verbal or reading skills needed to respond to questionnaire items. Finally, they can provide starting points for quantitative methods.

Respondent Diaries

The *diary method* is used extensively in calculating the ratings of radio and television programs (see Chapter 14), but it can also be used as a qualitative data-gathering tool. The diary method is basically an extension of the observational method discussed in Chapter 5. It allows a researcher to gather information from situations that cannot be easily observed, such as in a respondent's home or while an informant is on the road.

A common arrangement is to provide informants with small diaries that can be carried in a pocket or purse and to instruct them to keep track of a certain behavior and of their feelings, attitudes, and emotions while performing that behavior. For example, a group of informants might be given diaries to record which beverages they drink when they are eating at restaurants. The informants might also record their impressions of the various beverages they consume and how their choice of beverage enhanced or detracted from their dining experience. For instance, a diary might show that some people refrain from ordering wine at a restaurant because they are intimidated by a huge wine list. Diaries might also be product-specific. A group of consumers might be instructed to record their purchases of a specific product over time and write down the price, where they bought it, whether they saw any advertising that influenced their purchase, and whether they were satisfied with the product.

Diaries can be structured or free-form. A structured diary might set limits on the lengths of responses and ask the informant to group entries under such broad headings as "Events," "Activities," and "Feelings." A free-form diary permits respondents to choose what information is pertinent and how much information to include. A compromise involves using the free-form arrangement but limiting respondents to a prescribed length.

A variation of this technique consists of having respondents keep a photographic diary in connection with a product class or a certain brand. Ishmael and Thomas (2006) present an example of this method using skin care products. Respondents were asked to take digital pictures of their health and beauty products in their normal storage space and were asked to write stories about what was in the picture and to keep a diary of their related purchases. The researchers then conducted intensive interviews with the respondents about the content of their pictures.

Advantages and Disadvantages. Diary entries are described in the consumers' natural language. The data may allow a researcher to better understand the respondents' perspectives concerning a specific product or service. In short, they let the researcher see the world through the eyes of the consumer. Diaries can be kept by a panel of respondents to provide a record of reactions and feelings over time. For example, diary entries may reveal patterns of shopping behavior that might otherwise be overlooked.

On the downside, because diaries require a lot of respondent time and energy, many people are unwilling to participate in such a study. There is also a high mortality rate because many respondents who initially agree to accept a diary decide later that it is too much work and stop filling it out.

Finally, the diary method works best with people who can express themselves in writing. Those who are less literate or who have difficulty with writing skills may not provide the most useful data.

Directed Observation

This is a variation on the participant observation method discussed in Chapter 5. There may be times when advertising researchers want to find out specific information about various behaviors of the target market. In this situation, the researcher observes one or two narrowly focused activities. Two types of directed observation are accompanied shopping and pantry checks.

As the name suggests, *accompanied shopping* consists of the researcher sharing the shopping experience with informants. For example, suppose a manufacturer of tablet computers wants to know what factors are important in purchasing such a device. An advertising researcher could go shopping with one or more consumers who were in the market for such a device and note such items as the following:

- Where the consumers chose to look for such a device
- How long they spent in a particular store
- Whether they needed to ask questions of a salesperson
- Whether they paid attention to the packaging
- Whether they read the information on the package
- Whether they spent time with a demo model

Morrison, Haley, Sheehan, and Taylor (2002) call accompanied shopping "an interview on the move." In many cases the interviewer might question consumers during the shopping experience to find out which features

A CLOSER LOOK

Advertising and Mobile Eye Tracking

Although it varies by product and location, research suggests that up to three-quarters of buying decisions take place at the point of purchase. As noted in the text, advertising researchers have used accompanied shopping to examine many in-store purchasing decisions. Recently, researchers in Australia have come up with a new technique to investigate what goes on when a consumer goes shopping.

The technique is called "magic glasses" and builds on the idea behind the eye camera, discussed in Chapter 13. The consumer wears glasses that contain two tiny video cameras. One looks outward and records the shopper's field of vision. The second looks at the shopper's eye and records exactly where it focuses in the field of vision. Video from the two cameras is combined to determine exactly what each shopper looks at and for how long.

Initial results from supermarket tests have been revealing. Some shoppers bought some products without a second glance while others spent minutes deciding which special to buy. Advertising on supermarket floors tended to be ignored, and many consumers spent a significant amount of time checking out other shoppers.

To be most helpful, the results from the magic glasses are combined with in-depth interviews to find out what the consumer was thinking when they were looking at a particular product. In short, the technique offers a unique perspective on the shopping experience.

they were looking for, how much price was a factor, and their general impression of the various makes and models. This technique allows researchers and clients to find out how consumers make sense of the shopping experience and perhaps uncover some attitudes that might otherwise be missed.

Pantry checks are often done with a panel of consumers and are used to chart changes in buying behavior over time. One of the advantages of a pantry check is that it goes beyond measuring brand image or brand attitudes and allows advertisers to gauge actual purchasing behavior. At regular intervals a researcher is permitted to examine a consumer's pantry (or other storage space of interest, such as a medicine cabinet or make-up drawer) to keep track of what products were recently purchased, which products were used, which products were discarded, and so on. In addition, consumers are asked why they bought certain brands, what they thought of them, and whether they would buy them again. Pantry checks

are often used in measuring the long-term success of an ad campaign.

Advantages and Disadvantages. One advantage of directed observation is that it goes beyond gauging such abstract concepts as brand image or brand personality. It takes place in a real-world environment and investigates actual purchasing behavior, the activity of interest to most advertisers. Moreover, it gives researchers a window into the often overlooked everyday, practical considerations that go into product purchases. On the downside, directed observation requires that researchers first obtain permissions from those who are being studied. Not all people jump at the chance to let a stranger peer into their pantry or follow them around the mall. It may take some time before the researchers are permitted access to these activities. Additionally, as is the case with all observational research, the act of observation might change the behavior under study. Some people might shop differently when they have somebody looking over their shoulders and taking notes.

ADVERTISING RESEARCH AND THE INTERNET

The Internet poses special problems for audience measurement. Reliable data on who is looking at web pages and banners are important because without such data advertisers are reluctant to spend money on Internet advertising. As in other media, advertisers want to know who is visiting a website, how often they visit, and whether the CPM is reasonable. However, obtaining such data is difficult.

Measuring the Internet Audience

The first attempts to monitor web page traffic consisted of software programs that measured the number of "hits," or the number of times someone visits the page. These numbers were unreliable because the programs measured hits in different ways, depending on the server. Moreover, there were self-running programs available that repeatedly visited websites to artificially inflate the number of hits. Advertisers preferred to have an independent organization count the numbers (Green, 1998), and it wasn't long before Internet ratings companies came into existence.

As of 2012, the two most visible organizations that measure Internet audiences are comScore Media Metrix and Nielsen//NetRatings. Both companies use a media panel of consumers to collect their data. Media Metrix provides its panel members with software that monitors online and offline activity and also collects demographic and behavioral data. Media Metrix measures Internet activity at home and work. Similarly, Nielsen//NetRatings collects data from panel members in the United States and across the world. The U.S. panel sample consists of at-home and at-work users. Like Media Metrix, Nielsen provides its panel members with software that tracks their online activity.

Both firms face a difficult problem in gathering accurate web data. Much web surfing is done at work, and many businesses have been reluctant to allow ratings companies to install tracking software on office computers because they fear the software might also be used to access confidential information. As a result, all research firms may underreport office use.

In addition to Media Metrix and Nielsen, other organizations offer audits and verifications of traffic on a particular website. For example, the Audit Bureau of Circulations provides an ABC Interactive audit that ensures that the data reported by the website's log is accurate and supports any claim of viewership made by the website owner.

An additional problem arises with regard to exactly what is being measured. An advertiser would be interested in the total number of times a page has been viewed, how many different people visited, and how long each visitor spent at the site. Consequently, web audience measurement uses a variety of concepts (see "A Closer Look: Terms Used in Measuring the Internet Audience").

Panel study results offer some data about the demographics of website visitors. For example, visitors to the *Wall Street Journal*'s *wsj.com* are 64% male, 39% are over the age of 50, and 36% have a household income over $100,000. Website psychographics are typically measured by online surveys completed by a random sample of visitors to a particular site. For example, a psychographic survey of the business social network LinkedIn found that some were people looking for jobs, others were looking to network, and still others joined only because they didn't want to be left out (Bulik, 2008).

Measuring the Effectiveness of Internet Advertising

The Internet offers a unique advantage over traditional media—the potential for directly measuring results. Advertisers have always

A CLOSER LOOK

Terms Used in Measuring the Internet Audience

A number of variables can be measured concerning visitors to a website. Here are just a few:

- Hits—the number of times a file (a page or elements within a page such as a video file) is requested from an Internet site.
- Page views—the number of times a particular page is accessed during the measurement period. Page views can include duplicate visits.
- Unique audience—includes anyone who went to a site during the reporting period. Anyone who went more than once during the reporting period is not counted again.

Unique visitors are determined by cookies placed on the visitor's computer, IP address, or member name, if registration is required to visit the site.

- Active reach—the percentage of active "web users" who went to a specific site during the reporting period. Active web users include anyone who went online or used an Internet application at least once during the reporting period.
- Time per person—the average time spent per person at a site during the reporting period (usually one month).

---

had problems linking exposure to a given advertisement and a sale. However, things are different with the Internet. In addition to simply viewing a banner ad on a website, consumers can click on that ad and be given more specific information about a product and even buy it online. Not surprisingly, in addition to wanting to know how many times websites are visited, advertisers want information about what viewers do when they are there.

The first type of measurement that was used to determine this information was a behavioral one, the "click-through," which measured the number of times a visitor clicked on a banner ad at the site. In addition, advertisers could track how many sales resulted from click-throughs. For many years, this was the industry standard and everybody seemed pleased. In the mid-1990s, click-through rates for some banner ads were around 30%. But the novelty of banner ads soon wore off, and as more and more banners cluttered website pages, there was a dramatic decline in click-through rates. A 2001 study revealed that the click-through

rate had plummeted to only 0.3% (Green & Elgin, 2001).

Given these dismal numbers, it is not surprising that researchers looked for ways to improve the effectiveness of banner ads. In one instance, it was found that reducing the number of banner ads on a web page significantly increased the click-through rate of those that remained (Klaassen, 2009). Robinson, Wysocka, and Hand (2007) used click-through data to determine that larger banner ads with longer messages tended to be the most effective.

Additional research examined the relative efficacy of different kinds of display ads including the *skyscraper ad* (tall and skinny ads at the right and left side of a website), *pop-up* and *pop-under ads* (ads that appear when a web page is opened and have to be closed to view the content underneath), *square* and *rectangular ads* that appear within the text portion of the website, and *floating ads* that appear to hover over the content of a web page. One study found that consumers were most annoyed by pop-up and floating ads (Burns & Lutz, 2006).

Danaher and Mullarkey (2003) noted that the longer a person is exposed to a web page, the more likely they are to remember an ad. They also found that consumer motivation for visiting the site had an impact on recall of ads. Those who were looking for a specific piece of information were less likely to remember an ad than those who were simply surfing the Internet.

Researching New Advertising Channels

As new channels for reaching consumers continue to emerge, advertising researchers look for ways to measure their impact. Much of the recent research about new advertising channels can be divided into four categories: (1) viral, (2) search engine, (3) social media, and (4) mobile.

Viral advertising consists of marketing techniques that use preexisting social networks to produce increases in brand awareness or sales. One content analysis of 360 viral ads revealed that advertisers predominantly constructed their message strategies on ego-oriented appeals that were based on such themes as humor and sexuality (Golan & Zaidner, 2008). Using data from the Harris Research Company, Allsop, Bassett, and Hoskins (2007) found that some individuals in social networks were more important than others and that the context and specific situation of the viral campaign were important factors in determining effectiveness. After analyzing 102 viral TV ads, Southgate (2011) found that traditional advertising pretest measures, such as enjoyment, involvement, and branding, helped predict what ads might go viral. In addition, the distinctiveness of the video and the presence of a celebrity also played a major role.

Keyword search ads let advertisers target specific web visitors by associating ads with pre-identified words of phrases. Thus, if a person searched for "shoelaces," several sponsored links for companies selling shoelaces

might appear to the side of the search results along with a short message. Naturally, advertisers are interested in what factors lead people to click on the sponsored links. In an experiment, Yoo (2011) found that the subjects' involvement with the product and the positive or negative framing of the sponsored link's message had an effect on clicking the link. Yuan (2006) surveyed college students and discovered that, compared with pop-up ads, sponsored links were perceived as more informative, entertaining, and trustworthy and less annoying. Chan, Yuan, Koehler, and Kumar (2011) examined how many clicks on paid ad links were incremental (that is, whether the presence of paid links increased the number of clicks over the number that would have occurred if the paid links were not there). They found that more than 89% of the clicks were incremental in the sense that the visits to the advertiser's site would not have occurred without the paid link.

Turning to social media, as of 2012 Facebook had about 800 million members, more than 200 million people had Twitter accounts, and millions watched YouTube videos. Advertisers are interested in how best to reach these huge audiences. Taylor, Lewin, and Strutton (2011) looked at users' attitudes toward advertising on social media sites. They found that users were more likely to have a favorable attitude toward advertising on social media when the ads were entertaining or had informational or social value. Chatterjee (2011) discovered that certain members of social networks were "influencers" whose opinions on products were more likely to be passed along by others than recommendations by product marketers.

Many amateurs create serious or humorous ads for products and post them on YouTube. Several researchers have examined the impact of these user-generated messages. For example, Paek, Hove, Jeong, and Kim (2011) concluded that advertising produced by a person perceived as a peer by the consumer was more effective in creating positive attitudes towards the ad than was an ad that was professionally done. Vanden Bergh, Lee, Quilliam, and Hove (2011) examined parodies of real ads created by amateurs that were posted in social media. They found that users of social media had positive attitudes toward such parodies as long as they were humorous and truthful. In addition, members were more likely to transmit them to other members. Interestingly, they found that ad parodies had no impact on consumer attitudes toward the brand being parodied.

Finally, mobile advertising, particularly to cell phones, is attracting significant research attention. A 2011 survey sponsored by Google revealed that more than 8 out of 10 mobile phone users notice mobile ads and that half of those who notice them take some kind of action, such as visiting a website or making a purchase (Ipsos OTX, 2011).

Peters, Amato, and Hollenbeck (2007) employed the uses and gratifications approach to investigate how consumers perceived cell phone advertising. Respondents thought that mobile advertising kept them "in the know" and helped build relationships with companies. Respondents also said that they would discontinue the service if companies sent unsolicited messages. Park, Shenoy, and Salvendi (2008) analyzed 53 case studies of mobile advertising and concluded that ad characteristics, audience variables, and the environment influenced its effectiveness. Kolsaker and Drakatos (2009) demonstrated that consumers who have a strong sense of emotional attachment to their phones were more receptive to mobile advertising.

Advances in technology will continue to present challenges for advertising research. For example, in early 2009 advertising agency WPP and Google announced a $4.6 million, 3-year research program to determine how online ads influence consumer choices.

SUMMARY

The three main areas of advertising research are copy testing, media research, and campaign assessment research. Copy testing consists of studies that examine the advertisement or the commercial itself. The three main dimensions of impact examined by copy testing are cognitive (knowing), affective (feeling), and conative (doing). Media research helps determine which advertising vehicles are the most efficient and what type of media schedule will have the greatest impact. Campaign assessment studies examine the overall response of consumers to a complete campaign. The two main types of campaign assessment research are the pretest/posttest and the tracking study. Many private firms specialize in supplying copy, media, and assessment data to advertisers. Qualitative research techniques, such as projective tests, diaries, and directed observation, are becoming popular with advertising researchers.

Online advertising is increasingly the subject of research. Key topics are measuring the online audience, assessing the effectiveness of online ads, and examining the advertising potential of new channels. Other significant areas of new research include advertising on social media and on smart phones.

Key Terms

Aided recall	Objective function
Applied research	Polychronic behavior
Circulation	Projective techniques
Copy testing	Reach
Engagement research	Recall study
Forced exposure	Recognition
Frequency	Synergistic
Gross rating points	advertising
Masked recall	Synergistic marketing
Media efficiency	Tracking study
Monochronic	Unaided recall
behavior	
Neuromarketing	

Using the Internet

For additional information on some of the concepts discussed in this chapter, search the Internet for *"copy testing," "engagement research," "advertising campaigns,"* and *"mobile advertising."*

The following are some of the more useful sites for information about advertising research:

1. *www.thearf.org* This is the site of the Advertising Research Foundation, an organization founded in 1936 whose members consist of advertisers, advertising agencies, research firms, media companies, and colleges. The site contains links to various advertising reports, the organization's newsletter, and award-winning ad campaigns.

2. *www.esomar.org* ESOMAR is the World Association of Research Professionals. The site contains a directory of companies across the globe that provide advertising research, links to codes of good conduct in advertising and marketing research, and recent news about advertising research.

3. *www.ipsos-asi.com* Ipsos-ASI bills itself as "The Advertising Research Specialists." Its site contains a description of the types of reports and other products that are available from a big research company. One link describes its ad-tracking service.

4. *www.aef.com* This site is the home of the Advertising Educational Foundation. Once registered on the site, visitors can read the online version of *Advertising & Society Review,* which often contains articles about research.

5. For more information about using several media simultaneously, conduct a search for *advertising several media simultaneously.*

Questions and Problems for Further Investigation

1. Suppose you develop a new diet soft drink and are ready to market it. Develop a research study for identifying the elements and topics that should be stressed in your advertising.

2. A full-page advertisement costs $16,000 in Magazine A and $26,000 in Magazine B. Magazine A has a circulation of 100,000 and 2.5 readers per copy, whereas Magazine B has a circulation of 150,000 and 1.8 readers per copy. In terms of CPM readers, which magazine is the most efficient advertising vehicle?

3. Select a sample of newspaper and magazine advertisements for two competing products. Conduct a content analysis of the themes or major selling points in each advertisement. What similarities and differences are there?

4. Survey a number of people about their attitudes toward advertising on their mobile phones.

For additional resources, go to *www.wimmer dominick.com* and *www.cengagebrain.com.*

References and Suggested Readings

Allsop, D., Bassett, B., & Haskins, J. (2007). Word-of-mouth research. *Journal of Advertising Research, 47*(4), 398–411.

Bates, N., & Buckley, S. K. (2000). Exposure to paid advertising and returning a census form. *Journal of Advertising Research, 40*(1/2), 65–73.

Block, M. P., & Brezen, T. S. (1990). Using database analysis to segment general media audiences. *Journal of Media Planning, 5*(4), 1–12.

Bronnenberg, B., Dube, J., & Mela, C. (2010). Do digital video recorders influence sales? *Journal of Marketing Research, 47*(6), 998–1010.

Bulik, B. (2008). Finally find out who LinkedIn users are. *Advertising Age, 79*(42), 12.

Burns, K., & Lutz, R. (2006). The function of format: Consumer responses to six online advertising formats. *Journal of Advertising, 35*(1), 53–64.

Burton, S., Lichtenstein, D. R., & Netemeyer, R. G. (1999). Exposure to sales flyers and increased purchases in retail supermarkets. *Journal of Advertising Research, 39*(5), 7–14.

Chan, D., Yuan, Y., Koehler, J., & Kumar, D. (2011). Incremental clicks: The impact of search advertising. *Journal of Advertising Research, 51*(4), 643–647.

Chatterjee, P. (2011). Drivers of new product recommending and referral behavior on social networks. *International Journal of Advertising, 30*(1), 77–101.

Cheong, Y., Leckenby, J., & Eakin, T. (2011). Evaluating the multivariate beta binomial distribution for estimating magazine and Internet exposure frequency distributions. *Journal of Advertising,* 40(1), 7–23.

Danaher, P., & Mullarkey, G. (2003). Factors affecting online advertising recall. *Journal of Advertising Research,* 42(3), 252–263.

Donoghue, S. (2000). Projective techniques in consumer research. *Journal of Family Ecology and Consumer Sciences,* 28, 47–53.

Golan, G., & Zaidner, L. (2008). Creative strategies in viral advertising. *Journal of Computer-Mediated Communication,* 13(4), 959–973.

Green, H. (1998, April 27). The new web ratings game. *Business Week,* pp. 73–78.

Green, H., & Elgin, B. (2001, Jan. 22). Do e-ads have a future? *Business Week,* pp. EB46–51.

Green, P. E., Tull, D. S., & Albaum, G. (1988). *Research for marketing decisions.* Englewood Cliffs, NJ: Prentice Hall.

Haley, R. (1994). A rejoinder to conclusions from the ARF's copy research validity project. *Journal of Advertising Research,* 34(3), 33–34.

Hall, E. (2007). Effective ads work on the heart, not the head. *Advertising Age,* 78(28), 30.

Halliday, J. (2007). WPP shop tries to rewrite research. *Advertising Age,* 78(47), 8.

Haskins, J. (1976). *An introduction to advertising research.* Knoxville, TN: Communication Research Center.

Hazlett, R. L. (1999). Emotional response to television commercials. *Journal of Advertising Research,* 39(2), 7–23.

Ipsos OTX. Smartphone user study shows mobile movement underway. Retrieved December 21, 2011, from *http://googlemobileads.blogspot.com/ 2011/04/smartphone-user-study-shows-mobile.html*

Ishmael, G., & Thomas, J. (2006). Worth a thousand words. *Journal of Advertising Research,* 46(3), 274–279.

Jacoby, J., & Hofer, W. D. (1982). Viewers' miscomprehension of televised communication. *Journal of Marketing,* 46(4), 12–27.

Jones, J. (1995). Single-source research begins to fulfill its promise. *Journal of Advertising Research,* 35(3), 9–11.

Kilger, M., & Romer, C. (2007). Do measures of media engagement correlate with product purchase likelihood? *Journal of Advertising Research,* 47(3), 313–326.

Klaassen, A. (2009). SmartMoney finds fewer ads can boost click-throughs. *Advertising Age,* 80(8), 6.

Kolsaker, A., & Drakatos, N. (2009). Mobile advertising: The influence of emotional attachment to mobile devices on consumer receptiveness. *Journal of Marketing Communications,* 15(4), 267–280.

Leckenby, J., & Wedding, N. (1982). *Advertising management.* Columbus, OH: Grid Publishing.

Loughney, M., Eichholz, M., & Hagger, M. (2008). Exploring the effectiveness of advertising on the ABC.com full-episode player. *Journal of Advertising Research,* 48(3), 320–329.

Marci, C. (2008). Minding the gap: The evolving relationship between affective neuroscience and advertising research. *International Journal of Advertising,* 27(3), 477–479.

Marich, R. (2008). Measuring engagement. *Broadcasting & Cable,* 138(17), 12–13.

McDaniel, C., & Gates, R. (2011). *Marketing research.* Hackensack, NJ: Wiley.

McQuarrie, E. F. (2011). *The market research toolbox.* Thousand Oaks, CA: Sage Publications.

Mersey, R., Malthouse, E., & Calder, B. (2010). Engagement with online media. *Journal of Media Business Studies,* 7(2), 39–56.

Micu, A., & Plummer, J. (2010). Measurable emotions: How television ads really work. *Journal of Advertising Research,* 50(2), 137–153.

Morrison, M., Haley, E., Sheehan, K., & Taylor, R. (2002). *Using qualitative research in advertising.* Thousand Oaks, CA: Sage.

Paek, H., Hove, T., Jeong, H., & Kim, M. (2011). Peer or expert? *International Journal of Advertising,* 30(1), 161–168.

Park, T., Shenoy, R., & Salvendi, G. (2008). Effective advertising on mobile phones. *Behavior Information and Technology,* 27(5), 355–373.

Peacock, J., Purvis, S., & Hazlett, R. (2011). Which broadcast medium better drives engagement? *Journal of Advertising Research,* 51(4), 578–585.

Percy, L., & Rossiter, J. R. (1997). A theory-based approach to pretesting advertising. In W. D. Wells (Ed.), *Measuring advertising effectiveness* (pp. 267–282). Mahwah, NJ: Lawrence Erlbaum.

Peters, C., Amato, C., & Hollenbeck, C. (2007). An exploratory investigation of consumers' perceptions of wireless advertising. *Journal of Advertising,* 36(4), 125–145.

Robinson, H., Wysocka, A., & Hand, C. (2007). Internet advertising effectiveness. *International Journal of Advertising,* 26(4), 527–542.

Rossi, P., & Freeman, H. (1982). *Evaluation: A systematic approach.* Beverly Hills, CA: Sage Publications.

Rust, R. T. (1986). *Advertising media models.* Lexington, MA: D. C. Heath.

Ryan, M., & Martinson, D. C. (1990). Social science research, professionalism and PR practitioners. *Journalism Quarterly,* 67(2), 377–390.

Schultz, D., & Barnes, B. (1994). *Strategic advertising campaigns.* Lincolnwood, IL: Business Books.

Soley, L. (2010). Projective techniques in U.S. marketing and management research. *Qualitative Market Research*, *13*(4), 334–353.

Southgate, D. (2011). Creative determinants of viral video viewing. *International Journal of Advertising*, *29*(3), 349–368.

Stipp, H., Weber, R., & Varan, D. (2011). *Developing best practices in neuromarketing research*. New York, NY: Advertising Research Foundation.

Taylor, D., Lewin, J., & Strutton, D. (2011). Friends, fans and followers: Do ads work on social networks? *Journal of Advertising Research*, *51*(1), 258–275.

Thomas, J. W. (1997). Tracking can determine if your advertising works. *Business First—Louisville*, *13*(42), 38–41.

Vanden Bergh, B., Lee, M., Quilliam, E., & Hove, T. (2011). The multidimensional nature and brand impact of user-generated ad parodies in social media. *International Journal of Advertising*, *30*(1), 103–131.

Walker, D., & Dubitsky, T. (1994). Why liking matters. *Journal of Advertising Research*, *34*(3), 9–18.

Wimmer, R. D. (2000). Research in advertising. In C. Chakrapani (Ed.), *Marketing research: State-of-the-art perspective*, 454–478. New York, NY: American Marketing Association.

Winski, J. M. (1992, January 20). Who we are, how we live, what we think. *Advertising Age*, *63*(4), pp. 16–20.

Winters, L. (1983). Comparing pretesting and posttesting of corporate advertising. *Journal of Advertising Research*, *23*(1), 33–38.

Yoo, C. (2011). Interplay of message framing, keyword insertion and levels of product involvement in click-through of keyword search ads. *International Journal of Advertising*, *30*(3), 399–424.

Yoo, K., Joo, E., Choi, H., & Reid, L. (2012). Use of statistical techniques in major advertising and public relations journals, 1980–2010. Paper presented to the 2012 conference of the American Academy of Advertising. Myrtle Beach, SC, May 15–18, 2012.

Yuan, X. (2006). Assessing college students' attitudes toward two forms of Internet advertising: Pop-up ads and search engine sponsored links. Paper presented to the International Communication Association. Dresden, Germany, June 19–23, 2006.

# CHAPTER 16

RESEARCH IN PUBLIC RELATIONS

CHAPTER OUTLINE

Much like advertising, public relations has become more research-oriented. As a leading text pointed out:

> Research is a vital function in the process of public relations. It provides the initial information necessary to plan public relations action and to evaluate its effectiveness. Management demands hard facts, not intuition or guesswork. (Baskin, Aronoff, & Lattimore, 1997, p. 107)

In addition, at a 2010 meeting of the European Summit on Measurement in Barcelona, Spain, delegates adopted a statement of principles to guide measurement and evaluation of public relations (Barcelona Declaration, 2010). In abbreviated form, the seven principles endorsed by the group are:

1. Goal setting and measurement are fundamental to public relations.

2. Media measurement requires both quantity and quality.

3. Advertising Value Equivalents are not useful measures of public relations effectiveness.

4. Social media can and should be measured.

5. Measuring outcomes is preferred to measuring media results.

6. Where possible, business results should be measured.

7. Sound measurement is built on transparency and replicability.

As is evident, the Barcelona declaration suggests that public relations practitioners are adopting a more research-oriented approach to the profession.

Traditional research techniques, both qualitative and quantitative, are widely used in the field, but recent evidence suggests that quantitative methods are becoming more popular. Pompper (2006) conducted a census of all research published in two scholarly public

relations journals from 1975 to 2005. She found that approximately 58% of the studies used qualitative research, 37% used quantitative research, and the remainder used mixed methods. The most popular qualitative method was intensive interviewing; the most used quantitative method was the survey, followed by content analysis. Using a different sample of journals and a different time frame (1989–2007), Pasadeos, Lamme, Gower, and Tian (2011) found that 65% of the studies used quantitative techniques while 35% were qualitative. The most used quantitative technique was the survey (56%), followed by content analyses and experiments. Historical studies ranked first in the qualitative area, followed by case studies. Yoo, Joo, Choi, and Reid (2012) examined 326 articles appearing in the *Journal of Public Relations Research* and *Public Relations Review* from 1980 through 2010 and found that 47% contained statistical analysis.

TYPES OF PUBLIC RELATIONS RESEARCH

Pavlik (1987) defined three major types of public relations research: applied, basic, and introspective. **Applied research** examines specific practical issues; in many instances, it is conducted to solve a specific problem. A branch of applied research, **strategic research**, is used to develop public relations campaigns and programs. According to Broom and Dozier (1990), strategic research is "deciding where you want to be in the future … and how to get there (Page. 23)." A second branch, **evaluation research**, is conducted to assess the effectiveness of a public relations program and is discussed in more detail later in this chapter. A content analysis by Jelen (2008) found that about 80% of all published public relations research in the last two decades was applied research and 20% was basic research.

Basic research in public relations creates knowledge that cuts across public relations situations. It is most interested in examining the underlying processes and in constructing theories that explain the public relations process. For example, Aldoury and Toth (2002) presented the beginnings of a theory that could explain the gender discrepancies in the field, and Sisco (2012) examined the applicability of situational crisis communication theory.

The third major type of public relations research is **introspective research,** which examines the field of public relations. Sallot, Lyon, Acosta-Alzuru, and Jones (2003) categorized more than 700 abstracts and articles published in public relations academic journal and found that nearly 40% fell into the introspective category. Some examples: Wrigley (2002) examined how women felt about the perceived "glass ceiling" in the profession. Edwards (2008) surveyed public relations professionals to determine their cultural capital—that is, the knowledge, experience, and/or connections people have that make it possible for them to be successful. Meng, Berger, Gower, and Heyman (2012) analyzed the responses of senior-level public relations executives in order to determine what qualities of leadership were most important in the field.

RESEARCH IN THE PUBLIC RELATIONS PROCESS

Perhaps a more helpful way to organize public relations research is to examine the various ways research is used in the public relations process. A leading public relations textbook (Broom, 2012) presents a four-step model of the public relations process:

1. Defining public relations problems
2. Planning public relations programs
3. Implementing public relations programs through actions and communications

4. Evaluating the program

This chapter uses this model to organize the various forms of public relations research.

Defining Public Relations Problems

The first phase in the process consists of gathering information that helps define and anticipate possible public relations problems. Several techniques are useful at this stage: environmental monitoring (also called boundary scanning), public relations audits, communications audits, and social audits.

Environmental Monitoring Programs. Researchers use environmental monitoring programs to observe trends in public opinion and social events that may have a significant impact on an organization. Environmental monitoring can use both content analysis and surveys.

Public relations practitioners often monitor the traditional mass media for mentions of their clients. The results include a tabulation of total mentions by source and frequently report whether the mentions were positive, negative, or neutral. The growth of blogs and social media has added additional complexity to this task. In addition to the traditional media, organizations are also interested in what the general public is saying about them. Accordingly, practitioners have developed a new technique to monitor blogs and social media such as Facebook and Twitter. Message analytics is a group of detailed descriptive content analysis statistics that examine online message volume, tone, and engagement. At their basic level, message analytics track mentions across social media, blogs, and online news sources. In addition, sophisticated computer programs can also determine the tone of the content and track that sentiment over time. These programs are about 80% accurate and indicate whether

Figure 16.1 Sample Message Analytics Report

Time period Jan. 1, 2012–Dec. 31, 2012

Variable	Totals
# of Blog Mentions	378
Positive Mentions	78
Negative Mentions	100
Neutral Mentions	200
# of Comments	240
# of Times Focus of Discussion	16
# of Twitter Mentions	109
Average Length of Facebook Thread	8
# of Facebook "Likes"	690

the mentions are positive or negative. By looking at the trends over time, an organization can compare the tone of its comments with that of its competitors. A qualitative analysis can also reveal underlying themes and context of the messages. Figure 16.1 shows the results of a hypothetical message analytics report.

Online databases have made monitoring studies more efficient. Moreover, several commercial firms provide Internet monitoring services. CyberAlert, for example, tracks publicity about a company or product on thousands of news and information sites, discussion groups, and other areas of the web. The site *Pollingreport.com* contains a large database of public opinion polls on topics ranging from politics to the economy.

Grunig (2006) argued that environmental monitoring should be integrated into a company's strategic management function. Generally, two phases are involved. The early warning phase, an attempt to identify emerging issues, often takes the form of a systematic content analysis of publications likely to signal new developments. For example, one corporation may conduct a content analysis of scholarly journals in the fields of economics, politics, and science; another company may sponsor a continuing analysis of trade and general newspapers; yet another organization might monitor website message analytics. Gregory (2001) presents a typology of monitoring that divides the environment into four sectors: political, economic, social, and lifestyles. Gronstedt (1997) describes the SWOT technique of analyzing a company's *strengths* and *weaknesses* in meeting the *opportunities* and *threats* in the external environment.

An alternative method is to perform panel studies of community leaders or other influential and knowledgeable citizens. These people are surveyed regularly about the ideas they perceive to be important, and the interviews are analyzed to identify new topics of interest. Whether these techniques are used may depend on several factors. Okura, Dozier, Sha, and Hofstetter (2009) found that the use of formal environmental scanning methods was dependent on environmental conditions and also on the internal characteristics of the organization.

Brody and Stone (1989) list other forms of monitoring. One technique is to have the monitors look for a **trigger event,** which is an event or activity that might focus public concern on a topic or issue. For example, the Exxon *Valdez* oil spill in Alaska and the BP oil spill in the Gulf of Mexico brought visibility to environmental concerns. However, there is no scientific way to determine what is or what may become a trigger event. Monitors are left to trust their instincts and judgment.

The technique of precursor analysis is similar to trigger events analysis. **Precursor analysis** assumes that leaders establish trends that ultimately trickle down to the rest of society. For example, Japanese businesses tend to lead in innovative management techniques, many of which have caught on in the United States. At home, California tends to be a leader in insurance concerns and Florida in health issues. Monitors are instructed to pay particular attention to developments in these states.

The second phase of environmental monitoring consists of tracking public opinion on major issues. Typically, this involves either a longitudinal panel study, in which the same respondents are interviewed several times during a specified interval, or a cross-sectional opinion poll, in which a random sample is surveyed only once. AT&T, General Electric, General Motors, and the Dow Chemical Company have conducted elaborate tracking studies. The Insurance Research Council conducts a program called the Public Attitude Monitoring Series. This continuing nationwide study examines enduring consumer attitudes that affect the insurance industry. A 2011 survey asked consumers whether local governments should charge accident response fees to individuals involved in traffic accidents. The Partnership for a Drug-Free America conducts a tracking study using annual surveys of about 7,000 teens.

An **omnibus survey** is a regularly scheduled personal interview, with questions provided by various clients. Survey questions might ask about a variety of topics, ranging from political opinions to basic market research information. For example, the Opinion Research Corporation sponsors CARAVAN, a national omnibus consumer survey of public opinion. Public relations professionals who specialize in political campaigns make extensive use of public opinion surveys. Some of the polling techniques used include:

- *Baseline polling*—an analysis of the current trends in public opinion in a given state or community that could be helpful for a candidate.

- *Threshold polling*—surveys that attempt to assess public approval of changes in services, taxation, fees, and so on. Such a poll can be used to establish positions on various issues.

- *Tracking polls*—polls that take place after a baseline poll and that are used to look at trends over time.

Public Relations Audits. The public relations audit, as the name suggests, is a comprehensive study of the public relations position of an organization. Such studies are used to measure a company's standing both internally (employee perceptions) and externally (opinions of customers, stockholders, community leaders, and so on). In short, as summarized by Simon (1986), the public relations audit is a "research tool used specifically to describe, measure, and assess an organization's public relations activities and to provide guidelines for future public relations programming" (p. 150). An audit is useful because the research may unearth basic issues that the organization might not be aware of. For example, it might reveal that something as simple as a company's product terminology is confusing reporters and customers.

The first step in a public relations audit is to list the segments of both internal and external groups that are most important to the organization. This phase has also been called *identifying the key stakeholders in the organization.* These might include customers, employees, investors, regulators, and the public. This stakeholder analysis is usually conducted via personal interviews with key management in each department and by a content analysis of the company's external communications. The second step is to determine how the organization is viewed by each of these audiences. This involves conducting a corporate image study—that is, a survey of audience members. The questions are designed to measure familiarity with the organization (Can the respondents recognize the company logo? Identify a product it manufactures? Remember the president's name?) as well as attitudes and perceptions toward it.

Ratings scales are often used. For example, respondents might be asked to rank their perceptions of the ideal electric company on a seven-point scale for a series of adjective pairs, as shown in Figure 16.2. Later the respondents would rate a specific electric company on the same scale. The average score for each item would be tabulated and the means placed on a figure to form a composite profile. Thus, in Figure 16.3, the ideal electric company's profile is represented by the O's and the actual electric company's standing by the X's. By comparing the two, public relations researchers can readily identify the areas in which a company falls short of the ideal. Corporate image studies can be conducted before the beginning of a public relations campaign and again at the conclusion of the campaign to evaluate its effectiveness. A search of the Internet will reveal that many marketing companies offer public relations auditing services.

In sum, a public relations audit evaluates how well the current public relations process meets an organization's objectives. It is a valuable tool for unearthing problems that may exist in a public relations program.

Communication Audits. The communication audit resembles a public relations audit but has narrower goals; it concerns the internal and external means of communication used by an organization rather than the company's entire public relations program. The audit may be general, examining all of the company's communication efforts, or specific (e.g., looking at only the company's online communication).

Kopec (n.d.) presents a step-by-step guide for conducting both an internal and external

---

Figure 16.2 A Semantic Differential Scale for Eliciting Perceptions of Electric Companies

The Ideal Electric Company

good	___ : ___ : ___ : ___ : ___ : ___ : ___	bad
unconcerned	___ : ___ : ___ : ___ : ___ : ___ : ___	concerned
responsive	___ : ___ : ___ : ___ : ___ : ___ : ___	unresponsive
cold	___ : ___ : ___ : ___ : ___ : ___ : ___	warm
big	___ : ___ : ___ : ___ : ___ : ___ : ___	small

Figure 16.3 Profiles of Ideal ("Os") and Actual ("Xs") Electric Companies Resulting from Ratings Study

Comparison of Ideal and Actual Electric Company

good	_O_ : ___ : _X_ : ___ : ___ : ___ : ___	bad
unconcerned	___ : ___ : ___ : ___ : ___ : _X_ : _O_	concerned
responsive	_O_ : _X_ : ___ : ___ : ___ : ___ : ___	unresponsive
cold	___ : ___ : ___ : ___ : ___ : _X_ : _O_	warm
big	_X_ : _O_ : ___ : ___ : ___ : ___ : ___	small

communications audit. For the internal audit, he suggests the following steps:

1. Interview top management to pinpoint communication problems.

2. Content-analyze a sample of all the organization's relevant publications and other communication vehicles.

3. Conduct focus groups and intensive interviews with employees that examine their attitudes toward company communications. Use this information to develop a survey questionnaire.

4. Conduct the survey.

5. Analyze and report results to employees.

An external communications audit follows the same procedure, but the focus groups, interviews, and survey are done among audience members, shareholders, and other external groups.

Vahouny (2009) presents a list of items that might be included in a communications audit:

- A review of communication plans and policies

- A review of communication structure and staffing

- Analysis of communication vehicles

- Interviews with senior managers, communication staff, and other key constituents

- News media analysis

- Audience surveys

- An assessment of strengths and weaknesses

Two research techniques generally used in conducting such an audit are readership surveys and readability studies. Readership surveys are designed to measure how many people read certain publications (such as employee newsletters or annual reports) and remember the messages they contain. The results are used to improve the content, appearance, and method of distribution of the publications. Sparks (1997), for example, measured the attitudes of employees and retirees of a large public utility toward its newsletter. She found several areas where readers thought the publication might improve. The Mayo Clinic surveyed more than 7,000 readers of its *Embody Health* newsletter and discovered that 68% of its audience read all of the articles in an issue and 72% shared the newsletter with family and friends (Mayo Clinic, n.d.).

Readability studies help a company gauge the ease with which its employee publications and press releases can be read. Gagliano (2010) offers a do-it-yourself newsletter readability test using the Flesch–Kincaid tool in Microsoft Word (see Chapter 13).

Social Audits. A social audit is a small-scale environmental monitoring program designed to measure an organization's social performance—that is, how well it is living up to its public responsibilities. The audit provides feedback on company-sponsored social action programs such as minority hiring, environmental cleanup, and employee safety.

Social audits are the newest form of public relations research and the most challenging. Researchers are currently studying such questions as which activities to audit, how to collect data, and how to measure the effects of the programs. Nevertheless, several large companies, including General Motors and Celanese, have already conducted lengthy social audits. When the Unilever Company acquired Ben & Jerry's ice cream in 2000, Unilever agreed to conduct a social audit so that the company would continue to carry out the original social missions of Ben & Jerry's. The *Guardian*, a leading British newspaper, conducted a social audit to determine whether its performance matched its core principles of independence, liberalism, and a commitment to exposing

A CLOSER LOOK

The Importance of Readability in Public Communication

When a foodborne illness occurs, such as the 2011 cantaloupe listeria outbreak, the U.S. Food and Drug Administration (FDA) and the U.S. Department of Agriculture (USDA) typically provide information about alerts and recalls on their websites. This procedure assumes that individuals are able to understand and follow the instructions posted on the website. But are the messages on the website written in such a way that everybody can understand them? This was the question asked by public relations researchers Julie Novak and Paula Biskup (Novak & Biskup, 2011).

The researchers examined 88 press releases and warnings posted on the FDA and USDA websites from January to June in 2008. The messages were then analyzed using common readability measures including the Flesch

Reading Ease Scale, the Gunning Fog Index, and the SMOG index (see Chapter 13). These measures provide an estimate of the grade level of readability for the potential audience.

Across all three scales, the warnings and releases issued by both agencies required upper levels of readability literacy, averaging about a 12th-grade level, a relatively high score. In fact, as the authors conclude, "[The messages] are written at a higher grade level than nearly half of the U.S. population.... The public, therefore, would have a difficult time understanding and acting upon the written crisis communication."

This study highlights the importance of tailoring a message to its audience. Warnings and other communications during times of crisis must first be understood before the audience can apply the recommendation.

injustice. The newspaper employed a reader survey and independent consultants to judge how well it was fulfilling its mission (Jaehnig & Onyebadi, 2011).

Planning Public Relations Programs

After gathering the information from the various methods of environmental scanning, the next step in the process is to interpret the information to identify specific problems and opportunities that can be addressed by a systematic public relations program. For example, the results of the public relations audit can be used to identify the needs of each of the key stakeholder groups and construct behavioral objectives that can be achieved with each group. A behavioral objective concerning customers might be to take occasional users of the product and

turn them into loyal users. Among investors, the goal might be to increase stock purchases by small investors.

For example, environmental monitoring by the U.S. Army turned up the fact that recruitment numbers were down and young people were voicing negative attitudes about the military. The army asked a public relations agency to plan a program to increase recruitment. As a first step, the agency needed to find out which specific public relations problems the Army faced. Surveys and focus group research revealed that young people valued such qualities as independence and individualism, things they thought were lacking in a military career. In fact, the Army was viewed as authoritarian and repressive. The image of the Army among 17- to 20-year-olds was one of screaming generals, pushups, and no respect.

Analyzing Annual Reports

The top management of most publicly owned companies is interested in how their company's annual report is received. It is not unusual for a company to spend $50,000 or more to analyze reactions to its annual report.

Using this knowledge, the agency designed a new marketing and public relations program. The 2001 program dropped the old "Be All You Can Be" slogan and replaced it with a new tag line—"An Army of One"—that emphasized individuality. The agency pilot-tested a number of variations and executions of this theme. Approaches that did not reflect their target group were scrapped. Eventually, an acceptable program was launched. Measurable goals included increasing recruitment, increasing the number of hits on *GoArmy.com*, and increasing the number of calls to the Army's 800 number ("How Research Helps," 2001).

The program succeeded in raising recruitment levels in 2002 and 2003, but it was criticized by another group of stakeholders—veteran Army officers. They noted that the slogan ran counter to the Army's emphasis on teamwork. In 2006, the Army changed direction once again as it introduced its "Army Strong" campaign, aimed not only at new recruits but also at their families. Further, the Army introduced *America's Army*, a computer game that can be played for free over the Internet, as another recruitment device. As social media became more important, the Army included them in its campaign. The Army started *Army Strong Stories*, the official soldier blog, and integrated the site with Facebook and Twitter as well as creating an Army Strong Stories iPhone app. The campaign exceeded expectations: The initiatives generated more than 1 million visits in 2010, a 250% increase over 2009 ("Weber Shandwick wins best use of social media," 2011).

Additionally, the qualitative techniques discussed in Chapter 5 can be used in the planning phase. For example, State Farm Insurance conducted a campaign in which the company tried to identify the 10 most hazardous intersections in the United States. In an attempt to find a name for the campaign that would resonate with consumers, the company conducted a number of focus groups to try to identify which word would embody the essence of the campaign. Several adjectives were discussed, including *deadly*, *crash-prone*, and *hazardous*, but most focus group participants thought that *dangerous* was the most appropriate. As a result, State Farm labeled its campaign "The Ten Most Dangerous Intersections." In addition, researchers also conducted intensive interviews with local officials in those communities with the dangerous intersections to see how they would react to being named in the "Ten Most Dangerous" list. The results of the interviews suggested that most public officials would welcome the publicity because they felt it might help them fix the problem and that State Farm would experience no significant public relations problems as a result of the campaign (Russell, 2000).

The planning phase also involves research that attempts to determine the most effective media for delivering the program. At its most basic level, this research entails finding the reach, frequency, and demographic characteristics of the audiences for the various mass and specialized communication media.

A second type of media research is the **media audit**. A media audit is a survey of reporters, editors, and other media personnel that asks about their preferences for stories and how they perceive the public relations agency's clients. Most media audit surveys contact about 50–75 media professionals ("Media Audits," 2000). For example, the public relations division at a leading telecommunications market research company conducted a media audit with reporters at 16 trade publications. The survey revealed that the reporters had little knowledge about the firm or understanding about what it did. Other questions asked what kinds of information the reporters would most like to receive from companies. Responses revealed that case studies were the preferred format. As a result, the company changed its public relations approach and was able to place stories in trade and national publications such as *USA Today* ("Score Big Hits," 2001).

Adams (2002) reported the results of a media audit of Florida journalists that revealed, among other things, that "localism" was not an important consideration in evaluating news releases. Journalists ranked news value and an interesting story as the two factors that were most significant in successfully getting a news release covered. The survey also revealed that the chief complaint of the journalists was that public relations practitioners were not familiar with the publications they were contacting. Ledingham and Bruning (2007) provide another example of a media audit. More recently, media audits have included influential bloggers and individuals with large Facebook or Twitter audiences (Bruell, 2011).

Implementing Public Relations Programs

The most common type of research during the implementation phase consists of monitoring the efforts of the public relations program.

Three of the most frequently used monitoring techniques are **gatekeeping research**, **output analysis**, and **outcome analysis**.

Gatekeeping Research. A gatekeeping study analyzes the characteristics of press releases and video news releases that allow them to "pass through the gate" and appear in a mass medium. Both content and style variables are typically examined. For example, Walters, Walters, and Starr (1994) examined the differences between the grammar and syntax of original news releases and published versions. They found that editors typically shorten the releases and make them easier to read before publication. Hong (2007) noted that the newsworthiness of a press release is a strong predictor of whether the release is used but is not related to the prominence given to the story.

Gaschen (2001) surveyed TV stations about their use of VNRs (video news releases) and found that those stations that used VNRs generally used some of the visuals that accompanied the story but seldom ran the entire package. Harmon and White (2003) analyzed the use of 14 VNRs that were aired more than 4000 times across the United States. They found that most were used in early evening newscasts, and VNRs about children or health got the greatest exposure. A study by Jensen, Coe, and Tewksbury (2006) found that labeling the VNR as a product of an outside organization did not affect judgments of the credibility of the story, the reporter, or the news industry. Connolly-Ahern, Grantham, and Cabrera-Baukus (2010) compared credibility ratings of a VNR attributed to a government agency to the same VNR minus the attribution. They found that credibility was not affected by attribution but was affected by partisanship.

Output Analysis. Lindenmann (1997) defines output as the *short-term or immediate results of a particular public relations* *program or activity*. Output analysis measures how well the organization presents itself to others and the amount of exposure or attention that the organization receives. Several techniques can be used in output analysis. One way is to measure the total number of stories or articles that appear in selected mass media. In addition, it is possible to gauge the tone of the article. A public relations campaign that results in a large number of stories that are negative about the organization is less useful than a campaign that results in positive coverage. Over the past few years, it has become important to monitor mentions in blogs and social media.

Lindenmann (2003) lists several types of specific output analysis. For example, traditional content analysis is used to determine the type of story that appeared in the media (news, feature, editorial, blog mention, and so on); the source of the story (press release, press conference, special event); degree of exposure (column inches in print media, number of minutes of air time in the electronic media, number of views on YouTube, website hits, Facebook "likes," etc.); and topic variables such as what company officials were quoted, what issues were covered, how much coverage was given to competitors, and so on. Additionally, content analysis is used to look at more subtle qualities. Public relations researchers can judge the tone of the article—whether it is positive, neutral, or negative; balanced or unbalanced; or favorable or unfavorable. As Lindenmann points out, this type of analysis must be based on clearly defined criteria for assessing positives and negatives.

Nonmedia activities can also be studied with output analysis, such as attendance at special events and trade shows. In addition, attendees can be analyzed according to the types of people who show up and their level of influence within the field. Researchers can also tabulate the number of promotional materials distributed and the number of interviews or speaking engagements generated by the event.

Another facet of output analysis is measuring the total number of impressions attributed to a public relations campaign. This measurement is determined by calculating the reach and frequency of the various media in which campaign-related stories appeared to determine the number of people who might have been exposed to the message (see Chapters 14 and 15). The reach of a print publication is usually based on its total audited circulation. For example, if an article related to a public relations campaign appeared in the *San Francisco Chronicle*, which has an audited circulation of about 200,000, that article would generate 200,000 impressions or opportunities to see the story. If two stories appeared, they would create 400,000 impressions. In addition, researchers can determine how many of those impressions actually reached an organization's target group by examining detailed media audience data as compiled by firms such as MRI and Nielsen (see Chapter 14).

The problem with using impressions is that the researcher has to make several assumptions. For instance, it is assumed that all readers included in the circulation reports actually read the articles associated with the campaign and that everyone who visits the company website has also read the item. In reference to that connection, Brody (2003) points out the following: Suppose a news release is published in a newspaper that reaches 60% of the households in a market, is noticed by 50% of readers, and read by 25%; the actual exposure rate is only 7.5% (.60 × .50 × .25). In sum, the impressions method does not measure *actual exposure* to the message, but it does estimate the potential audience that might be reached.

Yet another method is to calculate **advertising equivalency**. This is done by counting the number of column inches in newspapers and magazines and the number of seconds of broadcast and cable coverage for a client and converting them into the equivalent advertising costs. For example, assume a local TV station charges $1,000 for a 30-second spot. A public relations firm manages to place a 90-second VNR on the station's local newscast. The advertising equivalency would be $3,000. The problem with this method is that the public relations firm cannot control the content of the news story or television item. The 90-second spot on the local TV newscast might have been edited so that all references and visuals related to the client were removed. Consequently, as mentioned in the opening of this chapter, the Barcelona Principles suggest that advertising equivalencies are not useful measures for effectiveness.

Evaluation Research. Evaluation research refers to the process of judging the effectiveness of program planning, implementation, and impact. Lattimore, Baskin, Heiman, and Toth (2011) suggest that evaluation should be involved in virtually every phase of a program.

Specifically, they propose the following specific phases:

1. *Implementation checking.* This phase investigates whether the intended target audience is actually being reached by the message.

2. *In-progress monitoring.* Shortly after the campaign starts, researchers check to see whether the program is having its intended effects. If there are unanticipated results or if results seem to be falling short of objectives, the program might still be modified.

3. *Outcome evaluation.* When the campaign is finished, the program's results are assessed. These findings are used to suggest changes for the future.

Broom and Dozier (1990) compare evaluation research to a field experiment (discussed in Chapter 5). The public relations campaign is similar to an experimental treatment, and the target public is similar to the subjects in the experiment. If possible, public relations researchers should try to construct control groups to isolate campaign effects from other spurious factors. The public relations researcher takes before-and-after measures and determines if any significant differences exist that can be attributed to the campaign. However, Broom and Dozier point out that public relations campaigns occur in dynamic settings, and as with most field experiments, it is difficult to control extraneous variables. As a result, it may not be scientifically possible to *prove* the program caused the results. However, from a management standpoint, systematic evaluation research may still represent the best available evidence of program effectiveness.

Perhaps the most important of the three phases mentioned above is outcome research. Michaelson and Stacks (2011) call for a standard terminology for outcome research. They suggest that outcome research should focus on several variables: awareness, knowledge, relevance, action, and advocacy. Possible measures of awareness include self-administered or interviewer-administered unaided or aided recall questions. Knowledge is measured by a series of questions that ask about facts included in the public relations campaign. Michaelson and Stacks recommend measuring relevance using a series of Likert scales that rate statements such as "Based on what I know of it, this product is very good," "This product is something that is like me," and "Based on what I know of it, this product is an excellent choice for me." Measures of action include items that ask whether a person is likely to buy an item or use a service. Finally, the authors propose measuring advocacy with a Likert scale that rates statements such as

"I will recommend this (product/service) to friends and relatives" and "People like me can benefit from this (product/service)."

Public relations researchers should be aware of some common mistakes that can affect evaluation research. Baskin, Aronoff, and Lattimore (1997) caution against the following:

1. Confusing volume with results. This is a case of confusing output research with outcome research. A huge pile of press clippings may document effort, but the pile does not document that the clippings had an effect.

2. Substituting estimation for measurement. Public relations practitioners should not substitute intuition or approximations for objective measurement—guesswork has no place in evaluation research (or any research).

3. Using unrepresentative samples. Analyzing only volunteer or convenience samples may lead to errors.

4. Confounding knowledge and attitudes. It is possible that the public might have gained more knowledge as the result of a public relations campaign, but this increased knowledge does not necessarily mean that attitudes have been positively influenced.

5. Confusing attitudes with behavior. Similar to item 4, it is incorrect to assume that favorable attitudes will result in favorable behavior.

Benchmarking is another method used to assess impact. A benchmark is a standard of comparison used by a company to track its public relations progress; research is conducted before the campaign to establish the standards of comparison. Other ways to establish a benchmark might include examining existing data to find industry averages and looking at past performance numbers.

Gronstedt (1997) describes a continuing benchmarking study done by a top European design firm. The company annually surveys its employees with questions such as "My job makes good use of my abilities" and "There are sufficient opportunities for me to improve my skills in my current job." Employee responses are then compared to a benchmark average calculated from a large-scale survey given to other employees in more than 40 countries.

The Institute for Public Relations' website contains many articles about evaluation research: *www.instituteforpr.org/topic/measurement-and-evaluation/*.

Qualitative Methods in Public Relations

The qualitative technique has seen growing popularity in public relations research. Daymon and Holloway (2002) suggest that one reason behind this trend is that public relations practitioners have shifted their focus from one-way communication and control to dialogue and collaboration so that now organizations must hear, appreciate, understand, and identify with those with whom they are talking—tasks that are best addressed by qualitative methods.

Not surprisingly, the qualitative methods increasingly used by public relations practitioners are generally the same techniques mentioned in Chapter 5. For example, Reber, Cropp, and Cameron (2003) conducted a case study of the public relations implications of Norfolk Southern's hostile takeover bid of Conrail, and Bardhan (2003) conducted intensive interviews in her study of the cultural context of public relations in India. Bush (2009) used the snowball sampling technique to recruit intensive interviewing participants in his study of student public relations agencies.

Two specific qualitative methods, however, are becoming more popular in public relations research: critical incident technique and discourse analysis.

Critical Incidents

The **critical incident technique** is a combination of in-depth interviewing and the case study approach. Its chief value is that it allows the researcher to gather in-depth information about a defined significant incident from the perspective of those who were involved in it. A critical incident is defined as an incident in which the purpose or intent of the act is clear to the observer and the consequences are definite. Further, the event must have a clearly demarcated beginning and ending, and a researcher must be able to obtain a detailed account of the incident.

In general terms, a critical incident analysis includes the following characteristics:

- It focuses on a particular event or phenomenon.
- It uses informants' detailed narrative descriptions of their experiences with the phenomenon.
- It employs content analysis to analyze these descriptions.
- It derives interpretive themes based on the results of the content analysis.

One common method is to ask about both positive and negative incidents. Johnson (2002), for example, used the critical incident technique to examine the public relations implications of the experiences of guests at a large Las Vegas hotel/casino. Guests were asked to identify two incidents during their stay—one satisfying and one dissatisfying. They were then asked a series of questions about the incidents. The researchers next asked employees to also identify one satisfying and one dissatisfying incident and respond to the interviewer's questions from the point of view of the customer. The responses were categorized into major themes and analyzed. The results highlighted those areas that management could emphasize to improve their public relations with consumers. More details about critical incident analysis can be found in Schwester (2012).

Advantages and Disadvantages.   The major advantage of the technique is that it focuses on real-world incidents as seen through the eyes of those who are directly involved. Further, a number of different critical incidents can be examined and compared, a process that can lead to greater theoretical understanding of public relations operations and a better formulation of public relations practices. One limitation of the critical incidents technique is that it depends on the memory of the informants for its data. Some people may remember more details than others, and some may have their memories distorted by selective perceptions. Researchers using this technique need to consider the reliability of the information that they gather. A second limitation is linked to the sometimes sensitive nature of critical incidents, particularly those that involve negative events. For example, employees might be reluctant to divulge information that might reflect badly on superiors or the organization for which they work. Researchers should follow established ethical practices concerning the confidentiality of information gained during a critical incident analysis (see Chapter 3).

Discourse Analysis

Discourse analysis is a more recently developed qualitative technique that has been used to study public relations communication. To put it simply, discourse analysis examines the organization of language at a level of analysis beyond the clause or the sentence. It focuses on larger linguistic units, such as whole conversations or written messages. Discourse analysis is also concerned with the way language is used in social contexts and how people make sense of one another's messages. As summarized by van Dijk (1997), discourse analysis examines who uses language, how, why, and when.

Daymon and Holloway (2002) suggest that researchers who use discourse analysis analyze three specific aspects of language:

1. The form and content of the language used
2. The ways people use language to communicate ideas and beliefs
3. Institutional and organizational factors that might shape the way the language is used

Data collection in discourse analysis involves gathering examples of texts and messages that are relevant to the problem being investigated. These may consist of existing documents, such as speeches by company executives, press releases, internal memos, and advertisements. In addition, the researcher can generate new data by conducting interviews with key informants.

There is no concrete set of procedures for conducting a discourse analysis. Data analysis usually consists of focusing on large segments of language to identify key words, themes, imagery, and patterns in the text. In addition, the researcher might conduct a rhetorical analysis that looks at how various arguments are constructed and arranged within a given body of language. Finally, the investigator should pay special attention to the context of the language, examining such factors as who is speaking, the circumstances surrounding the message, and the intended audience.

Levin and Behrens (2003), for example, presented a discourse analysis of Nike's internal and external communications. They analyzed such linguistic structures as semantic association, opposites, degradation, genre manipulation, pronoun selection, obfuscation, slanting, speech acts, restricted style, and metaphor. They found that during the height of Nike's popularity, both company literature and media reports contained a preponderance of positive imagery. However, this changed when the company was accused of unfair labor practices. The media abandoned their positive portrayal and used the same linguistic devices to create a more negative image. In another example, Holtzhausen and Voto (2002) conducted a discourse analysis of interviews conducted with public relations professionals and found that many were endorsing postmodern values. Brooks and Waymer (2009) used discourse analysis to examine Crystallex International Corporation's mining operations in South America. They looked at press release archives, news and advertising archives of Venezuelan newspapers, and the archives of specialized media in the mining area. They found that the

A CLOSER LOOK

Inquiry Studies

Lindenmann (2006) suggests another type of qualitative study for public relations practitioners: an inquiry study. An inquiry study is a systematic review and analysis of the range and types of unsolicited inquiries that an organization receives from the key audience groups with which it communicates. Such a study could be done by traditional content analysis or by telephone or online interviewing.

For example, it might benefit an organization to interview those people who contacted it requesting background, information, samples, or promotional materials. Of course, such a group of people is a self-selected, unscientific sample, but interviewing these people would provide information about the very target audience that the organization is trying to reach.

company's public relations efforts improved once it started emphasizing corporate responsibility. Finally, Walsh and McAllister-Spooner (2011) analyzed the public relations campaign to repair the image of Michael Phelps after a photo of him smoking marijuana appeared in a British tabloid. They found that the campaign used such themes as mortification, atonement, and bolstering to create a successful outcome.

Advantages and Disadvantages. Discourse analysis can be used to study different situations and subjects. It allows public relations researchers to uncover deeply held attitudes and perceptions that are important in an organization's image and communication practices that might not be uncovered by any other method. On the other hand, discourse analysis can take large amounts of time and effort. A second disadvantage is that this technique focuses solely on language. Although language may be an important component of public relations practice, it rarely tells the whole story. Consequently, discourse analysis should be supplemented by other qualitative techniques such as observation or focus group interviewing.

PUBLIC RELATIONS RESEARCH: THE INTERNET AND SOCIAL MEDIA

Much of the current research in public relations is focused on the Internet and social media. Specifically, research falls into four specific areas: (1) practitioners' attitudes toward the Internet and social media, (2) the role of social media in public relations, (3) characteristics of websites used for public relations, and (4) usability studies.

The first category of research is another branch of introspective research mentioned at the beginning of the chapter. Several surveys have tried to describe how public relations professionals feel about using the various features of the Internet. For example,

Wright and Hinson (2009) surveyed practitioners and found that 73% agreed that blogs had changed the way their organizations communicated, 71% felt that blogs served as a watchdog for traditional media, and 25% reported that their companies had commissioned research looking at blog content. Eyrich, Padman, and Sweetser (2008) surveyed professionals about their adoption of 18 social media tools and their perceptions of how social media are changing public relations. More recently, Sweetser and Kelleher (2011) found that internal motivation was an important factor in predicting the social media use of public relations practitioners.

An emerging area of research describes how social media operate in the full range of public relations activities. For example, Waters, Burnett, Lamm, and Lucas (2009) analyzed 275 nonprofit organizations' profiles on Facebook and discovered that most of the organizations did not make use of all the social networking advantages of the service. Rybalko and Seltzer (2010) examined how Fortune 500 companies used Twitter to communicate with stakeholders. They looked at 930 individual "tweets" and found that companies that encouraged the exchange of opinions and ideas were more likely to keep visitors engaged with the companies' online presence. Using a qualitative approach, Vorvoreanu (2009) found that college students had unfavorable attitudes about a company's public relations efforts on Facebook. Finally, taking a different perspective, Lariscy, Avery, Sweetser, and Howes (2009) examined how business journalists used social media for story ideas. They found that journalists embraced the concept of social media but made little use of them.

Other researchers have studied the use of social media in "damage control." Over the past decade, many organizations and individuals have found themselves in crisis situations that have damaged their reputations and have looked to public relations professionals to repair their image using social media as well as traditional media channels. Liu, Austin, and Jine (2011) discovered that audience members were more likely to accept defensive, supportive, and evasive crisis responses via traditional media rather than social media. Shultz, Utz, and Goritz (2011) found that message strategy was less important than the medium that carried the message. Crisis communication using Twitter led to less negative crisis reactions than blogs or newspaper articles. Kim and Liu (2012) conducted a content analysis of messages generated by 13 corporate and government organizations in response to the 2009 swine flu epidemic. They found that both government and corporate organizations used social media more often than traditional media in responding to the crisis.

Numerous studies have analyzed the characteristics of public relations websites. Ingenhoff and Koelling (2009) analyzed nonprofit organizations' websites and found that technical and design aspects were emphasized more than interactive features. Hickeson and Thompson (2007) analyzed wiki health websites (collaborative websites that can be edited by anyone with access to them) and discovered that wikis were more likely to use dialogic public relations techniques than non-wiki sites. Finally, Gomez and Chalmeta (2011) examined corporate responsibility in U.S. corporate websites and found that presentational features were more developed than interactive features.

The last area of research uses methods similar to the usability research discussed in Chapter 13. Vorvoreanu (2008) describes this method as Website Experience Analysis. This method requires research participants to use a website and answer a series of questions about their experience. Because first impressions are important, the researcher may interrupt participants' website experience after about 10 seconds, or at the moment of the first click away from the home page, and ask them to answer questions about the first impression phase. One disadvantage of this technique is that it looks at website usage in an artificial environment.

SUMMARY

Research in public relations takes place at all phases of the public relations process. Research such as environmental monitoring, public relations audits, communication audits, and social audits are used to define problems.

During the planning stage, quantitative and qualitative techniques are used to test various public relations strategies, and media audits are done to identify the most effective media for a campaign. Gatekeeping research and output analysis are done during the program implementation phase. Evaluation research is done both during and after a campaign to assess whether the stated goals were achieved. Qualitative methods are becoming more common in public relations research. Examining the relationship between public relations, the Internet and social media is also becoming a major research area.

Key Terms

Advertising equivalency	Introspective research
Applied research	Media audit
Basic research	Omnibus survey
Benchmarking	Output analysis
Communication audit	Outcome analysis
Critical incident analysis	Precursor analysis
Discourse analysis	Public relations audit
Environmental monitoring	Social audit
Evaluation research	Strategic research
Gatekeeping research	Trigger event

 Using the Internet

For more information on the concepts discussed in this chapter, search the Internet for "*environmental scanning*," "*public relations audit*," "*omnibus survey*," and "*Barcelona Principles*."

There are several websites that contain useful information about public relations research:

1. *www.pollingreport.com* Calling itself "an independent, non-partisan resource on trends in American public opinion," this site contains a great deal of data about public opinion.

2. *www.prsa.org/awards/silveranvil/* The Silver Anvil award is to public relations campaigns what the Emmy is to TV programs. The site has an archive of past winning campaigns. Visitors can learn how research played a role in the way the campaigns were planned, executed, and evaluated.

3. *www.prsa.org* This is the home of the Public Relations Society of America. The site contains a professional resource center that is helpful for researchers.

4. *www.instituteforpr.org* The Institute for Public Relations is an independent foundation whose main concerns are research and education. Several articles directly related to public relations research are available on this site.

Questions and Problems for Further Investigation

1. Assume you are the public relations director for a large auto company. How would you go about conducting an environmental monitoring study?

2. How would you assess the effectiveness of a public relations campaign designed to encourage people to conserve water?

3. What is the difference between an output measure and an outcome measure?

4. What factors might account for the relatively large numbers of introspective studies done in the public relations field?

5. What are the advantages and disadvantages of using messages on social media for public relations research?

For additional resources, go to *www.wimmer dominick.com* and *www.cengagebrain.com*.

References and Suggested Readings

Adams, W. (2002). South Florida media audit challenges assumptions, reveals journalist complaints. *Public Relations Quarterly, 47*(1), 40–45.

Aldoury, L., & Toth, E. (2002). Gendered discrepancies in a gendered profession. *Journal of Public Relations Research, 14*(2), 103–126.

Barcelona declaration of measurement principles (2010). Gainesville, FL: Institute for Public Relations.

Bardhan, N. (2003). Rupturing public relations meta-narratives: The example of India. *Journal of Public Relations Research, 15*(3), 225–248.

Brody, E. W. (2003). For public relations success, track results not messages. *Public Relations Quarterly, 48*(4), 37–38.

Brody, E. W., & Stone, G. C. (1989). *Public relations research.* New York, NY: Praeger.

Brooks, K., & Waymer, D. (2009). Public relations and strategic issues management challenges in Venezuela. *Public Relations Review, 35*(1), 31–39.

Broom, G. (2012). *Cutlip and Centers effective public relations.* New York, NY: Pearson.

Broom, G. M., & Dozier, D. M. (1990). *Using research in public relations.* Englewood Cliffs, NJ: Prentice Hall.

Bruell, A. (2011). PR's new best friend: Social-media-savvy journos. *Advertising Age, 82*(33), 63.

Bush, L. (2009). Student public relations agencies: A qualitative study of the pedagogical benefits, risks, and a framework for success. *Journalism & Mass Communication Educator, 64*(1), 27–38.

Connolly-Ahern, C., Grantham, S., & Cabrera-Baukus, M. (2010). The effect of attribution of VNRs and risk on news viewers' assessments of credibility. *Journal of Public Relations Research, 22*(1), 49–64.

Daymon, C., & Holloway, I. (2002). *Qualitative research methods in public relations and marketing communication.* New York, NY: Routledge.

Edwards, L. (2008). PR practitioners' cultural capital. *Public Relations Review, 24*(4), 367–373.

Eyrich, N., Padman, M., & Sweetser, K. (2008). PR practitioners' use of social media tools and communication technology. *Public Relations Review, 34*(4), 412–414.

Gagliano, K. (2010). Test your e-newsletter's readability. Retrieved Jan. 20, 2012 from *www.amplifymarketinggroup.com/blog/email-content/test-your-e-newsletters-readability.*

Gaschen, D. (June, 2001). What TV stations really think about VNRs. *Public relations tactics, 8*(6), 10.

Gomez, L., & Chalmeta, R. (2011). Corporate responsibility in U.S. corporate websites: A pilot study. *Public Relations Review, 37*(1), 93–95.

Gregory, A. (2001). Public relations and management. In A. Theaker (Ed.), *The public relations handbook* (pp. 35–51). London: Routledge.

Gronstedt, A. (1997). The role of research in public relations strategy and planning. In C. Caywood (Ed.), *The handbook of strategic public relations & integrated communications.* (pp. 34–57) New York, NY: McGraw Hill.

Grunig, J. (2008). Conceptualizing quantitative research in public relations. In B. van Ruler, A. Vercic, and D. Vercic (Eds.), *Public relations metrics.* (pp. 88–119) New York, NY: Routledge.

Grunig, J. (2006). Furnishing the edifice. *Journal of Public Relations Research, 18*(2), 151–177.

Harmon, M., & White, C. (2003). How television news programs use video news releases. *Public Relations Review, 27*(2), 213–223.

Hickerson, C., & Thomas, S. (2007). Dialog through wikis. Conference paper presented to the National Communication Association. Chicago, November 15-18, 2007.

Holtzhausen, D., & Voto, R. (2002). Resistance from the margins: The postmodern public relations practitioner as organizational activist. *Journal of Public Relations Research, 14*(1), 57–82.

Hong, S. (2007). Gatekeeping of news releases. Conference paper presented to the International Communication Association. San Francisco, May 24–28, 2007.

How research helps the Army be all it can be. (2001). *Ragan's PR Intelligence, 4*(1), 1.

Ingelfoff, D., & Koelling, M. (2009). The potential of websites as a relationship building tool for charitable fundraising NPOs. *Public Relations Research, 35*(1), 66–73.

Jaehnig, W., & Onyebadi, U. (2011). Social audits as media watchdogging. *Journal of Mass Media Ethics, 26*(1), 2–20.

Jelen, A. (2008). The nature of scholarly endeavors in public relations. In B. van Ruler, A. Vercic, and D. Vercic (Eds.), *Public relations metrics.* (pp.36–59) New York, NY: Routledge.

Jensen, J., Coe, K., & Tewksbury, D. (2006). The impact of video source labeling on the perceived credibility of news. Conference paper presented to the International Communication Association. Dresden, Germany, June 19–23, 2006.

Johnson, L. (2002). Using the critical incident technique to assess gaming customer satisfaction. *Gaming Research and Review Journal, 6*(2), 1–13.

Kim, S., & Liu, B. (2012). Are all crises opportunities? A comparison of how corporate and government organizations responded to the 2009 flu pandemic. *Journal of Public Relations Research, 24*(1), 69–85.

Kopec, J. (n.d.). Tips and techniques: The communications audit. Retrieved June 14, 2004, from *www.prsa.org/resources/resources/commaudit.asp*

Lariscy, R., Avery, E., Sweetser, K., & Howes, P. (2009). An examination of the role of online social media in journalists' source mix. *Public Relations Review, 35*(3), 314–316.

Lattimore, D., Baskin, O., Heiman, S., & Toth, E. (2011). *Public relations: The profession and the practice.* New York, NY: McGraw-Hill.

Ledingham, J., & Bruning, S. (2007). The media audit. *Journal of Promotion Management, 13*(3/4), 189–203.

Levin, L., & Behrens, S. (2003). From swoosh to swoon: Linguistic analysis of Nike's changing image. *Business Communication Quarterly, 66*(3), 52–65.

Lindenmann, W. (1997). *Public relations research for planning and evaluation.* Gainesville, FL: The Institute for Public Relations.

Lindenmann, W. (2003). *Guidelines and standards for measuring and evaluating PR effectiveness.* Gainesville, FL: The Institute for Public Relations.

Liu, B., Austin, L., & Jin, Y. (2011). How publics respond to crisis communication strategies: The interplay of information form and source. *Public Relations Review, 37*(4), 345–353.

Mayo Clinic (n.d.). A summary of key findings and implications of a Mayo Clinic *EmbodyHealth Newsletter.* Retrieved January 20, 2012, from *www.mayoclinichealthsolutions.com/products/EmbodyHealth-Newsletter-Readership-Survey-Results.cfm*

Media audits are a growing trend. (2000, June 5). *Media Relations Report,* p. 1.

Meng, J., Berger, B., Gower, K., & Heyman, W. (2012). A test of excellent leadership in public relations. *Journal of Public Relations Research, 24*(1), 18–36.

Michaelson, D., & Stacks, D. (2011). Standardization in public relations measurement and evaluation. *Public Relations Journal, 5*(2), 1–22.

Novak, J., & Biskup, P. (2011). Food warnings and recalls: Remembering readability in crisis communication. *Public Relations Journal, 5*(2), 1–11.

Okura, M., Dozier, D., Sha, B., & Hofstetter, C. (2009). Use of scanning methods in decision making. *Journal of Public Relations Research, 21*(1), 51–81.

Pasadeao, Y., Lamme, M., Gower, K., & Tian, S. (2011). A methodological evaluation of public relations research. *Public Relations Review*, 37(2), 163–165.

Pavlik, J. V. (1987). *Public relations: What the research tells us.* Beverly Hills, CA: Sage Publications.

Pompper, D. (2006). 30 years of public relations scholarship. Conference paper presented to the International Communication Association. Dresden, Germany, June 19–23, 2006.

Reber, B., Cropp, F., & Cameron, G. (2003). Impossible odds: Contributions of legal counsel and public relations practitioners in hostile takeover bid for Contrail, Inc. by Norfolk Southern Corporation. *Journal of Public Relations Research*, 15(1), 1–25.

Russell, F. (2000). Dangerous intersections. *Marketing News*, 34(5), 18–19.

Rybalko, S., & Seltzer, T. (2010). Dialogic communication in 140 characters or less: How Fortune 500 companies engage stakeholders using Twitter. *Public Relations Review*, 36(4), 336–341.

Sallott, L., Lyon, L., Acosta-Alzuru, C., & Jones, K. (2003). From aardvark to zebra: A new millennium analysis of theory development in public relations academic journals. *Journal of Public Relations Research*, 15(1), 27–90.

Schwester, R. (Ed.). (2012). *Handbook of critical incident analysis.* Armonk, NY: M. E. Sharpe.

Score big hits with audits. (2001). *Ragan's PR Intelligence*, 4(1), 2.

Shultz, F., Utz, S., & Goritz, A. (2011). Is the medium the message? Perceptions of and reactions to crisis communication via Twitter, blogs and traditional media. *Public Relations Review*, 37(1), 20–27.

Simon, R. (1986). *Public relations: Concepts and practices.* Columbus, OH: Grid Publishing.

Sisco, H. (2012). Nonprofit in crisis: An examination of the applicability of situational crisis communication theory. *Journal of Public Relations Research*, 24(1), 1–17.

Sparks, S. D. (1997). Employee newsletter readability for a large public utility. *Public Relations Quarterly*, 42(3), 37–40.

Sweetser, K., & Kelleher, T. (2011). A survey of social media use, motivation and leadership among public relations practitioners. *Public Relations Review*, 37(4), 425–428.

Vahouny, K. (2009). Get started on your communication audit. *Communication World*, 26(4), 35–37.

van Dijk, T. (1997). *Discourse studies.* London: Sage.

Vorvoreanu, M. (2008). Website experience analysis. *Journal of Website Promotion*, 3(3/4), 222–249.

Vorvoreanu, M. (2009). Perceptions of corporations on Facebook: An analysis of Facebook social norms. *Journal of New Communications Research*, 4(1), 67–86.

Walsh, J., & McAllister-Spooner, S. (2011). Analysis of the image repair discourse in the Michael Phelps controversy. *Public Relations Review*, 37(2), 157–162.

Walters, T., Walters, L., & Starr, D. (1994). After the highwayman: Syntax and successful placement of press releases in newspapers. *Public Relations Review*, 20(4), 345–356.

Waters, R., Burnett, E., Lamm, A., & Lucas J. (2009). Engaging stakeholders through social networking: How nonprofit organizations are using Facebook. *Public Relations Review*, 35(2), 102–106.

Weber Shandwick Wins Best Use of Social Media and PR Innovation of the Year at 2011 PRWeek Awards, (2011). Retrieved January 25, 2012, from *www.webershandwick.com/Default.aspx/AboutUs/Press Releases/2011/WeberShandwickWinsBestUseof SocialMediaandPRInnovationoftheYearat2011PR WeekAwards.*

Wright, D., & Hinson, M. (2009). *An analysis of increasing impact of social and other new media.* Gainesville, FL: Institute for Public Relations.

Yoo, K., Joo, E., Choi, H., & Reid. L. (2012). Use of statistical techniques in major advertising and public relations journals, 1980-2010. Paper presented at the 2012 Conference of the American Academy of Advertising. Myrtle Beach, SC, May 15–18, 2012.

TABLES

APPENDIX OUTLINE

Table 1　Random Numbers

```
0 8 9 5 6 4 4 8 9 4 0 7 5 9 7 0 4 5 3 1 2 7 8 6 6
8 2 4 4 8 8 0 2 6 5 5 0 3 5 9 1 3 8 6 8 8 3 1 8 5
3 1 2 3 7 6 4 1 1 4 3 5 2 7 4 9 3 2 7 5 5 4 7 6 2
2 3 8 1 8 6 6 1 0 8 4 1 0 5 0 4 8 5 3 7 8 7 6 5 7
0 0 4 3 6 5 5 2 3 5 2 4 3 3 9 3 2 5 2 0 8 4 6 2 1
1 2 8 9 7 5 8 9 7 8 6 7 4 0 4 0 4 9 7 8 5 0 2 9 8
9 8 4 6 9 9 0 8 0 2 3 2 8 0 5 4 5 0 6 7 6 2 3 9 8
0 7 3 6 9 5 1 6 3 8 0 5 9 0 0 2 0 9 3 6 8 8 2 4 3
2 2 3 9 5 7 9 4 0 6 7 3 6 9 6 4 1 7 3 6 5 1 8 2 6
4 9 5 6 9 3 1 4 7 8 1 5 6 7 2 2 4 6 3 6 5 4 2 1 2
4 0 6 6 8 5 4 3 7 8 3 2 6 8 1 2 2 7 0 6 5 3 5 8 4
6 3 3 2 0 3 9 7 0 2 3 6 9 5 3 4 1 6 1 8 3 9 4 3 3
0 6 1 8 4 2 1 8 6 7 5 4 1 9 0 3 2 4 1 5 7 7 4 0 8
2 2 4 2 9 6 8 5 8 2 6 1 0 7 6 1 7 9 2 0 9 2 8 7 8
8 3 2 3 0 7 4 3 5 8 9 0 8 0 5 8 8 7 1 3 6 0 1 3 9
2 3 1 8 2 3 1 0 9 0 0 8 9 1 2 0 3 7 0 2 0 1 8 1 7
0 8 7 3 4 4 5 1 8 7 4 5 1 9 9 0 3 2 2 3 1 2 6 4 6
5 8 5 6 7 6 1 0 1 6 7 0 2 1 9 1 6 3 2 0 1 1 5 5 9
6 1 1 0 5 1 3 6 7 7 7 8 2 4 5 9 3 0 7 6 7 9 1 1 6
5 3 6 1 2 7 2 6 2 7 3 3 6 8 2 6 5 5 8 4 2 4 2 1 8
8 7 3 9 5 1 1 8 4 1 8 5 6 6 0 6 9 2 2 6 8 2 5 8 5
2 9 1 9 9 5 6 1 8 6 6 4 0 5 0 0 8 8 2 5 9 2 0 1 2
8 1 0 2 1 7 2 0 2 7 6 8 4 8 0 2 6 2 8 0 8 3 6 0 7
9 7 1 5 5 7 4 6 1 5 6 5 9 9 2 2 7 1 2 7 0 0 5 0 9
6 3 7 9 8 8 7 4 9 5 0 3 3 0 3 7 0 7 5 8 1 2 8 3 1
9 4 2 2 1 3 2 0 5 6 0 6 0 9 0 9 3 1 7 8 1 2 3 1 1
5 2 8 5 1 0 2 4 6 0 8 3 4 2 9 0 2 4 0 5 2 7 8 8 8
7 9 7 1 3 7 2 4 6 3 8 4 0 2 5 5 4 6 1 6 5 4 6 3 0
0 1 5 0 6 5 1 1 8 0 9 4 1 1 2 6 1 4 2 0 8 6 3 1 0
5 8 1 7 4 7 5 6 2 1 9 3 7 4 0 4 6 4 6 9 6 7 5 0 6
2 5 0 7 5 1 6 0 4 0 4 1 9 4 9 8 3 6 3 8 0 0 1 7 9
8 8 3 7 8 1 4 6 3 8 0 5 6 4 4 3 5 0 6 9 5 5 0 6 0
4 3 1 8 7 3 4 1 7 1 6 1 5 2 7 9 4 0 2 9 9 9 6 8 7 6
9 1 4 7 7 4 3 7 4 2 5 5 0 2 1 1 1 4 0 6 4 7 5 9 6
8 6 0 8 2 9 3 4 3 4 7 6 9 6 1 8 2 3 3 8 3 4 6 8 3
3 3 0 6 2 3 8 7 4 3 8 3 1 1 5 9 7 4 4 4 9 7 6 0 9
1 8 2 0 2 9 8 8 0 1 6 8 0 7 5 6 0 8 3 9 2 1 1 2 0
4 7 4 1 1 8 5 9 6 9 7 7 8 0 8 0 8 5 7 2 6 9 4 6 7
7 2 8 1 1 0 4 0 5 0 0 8 2 5 7 4 9 4 0 6 9 7 1 8 0
8 4 0 0 8 1 8 7 1 5 0 1 3 7 3 1 1 4 1 9 7 1 7 8 5
1 5 0 5 3 1 9 7 5 0 3 7 6 3 4 7 2 2 0 5 0 0 7 5 1
6 8 5 1 2 4 1 0 4 6 2 5 9 9 3 2 5 6 0 1 2 0 6 7 7
7 6 5 5 4 6 1 9 1 1 7 9 9 9 6 6 7 1 3 7 7 4 8 8 2
7 8 2 4 2 1 6 4 3 9 7 2 6 6 5 7 0 1 2 8 9 7 1 4 5
9 0 3 3 8 1 3 5 1 4 2 8 7 7 0 3 5 8 0 8 4 2 6 6 4
5 5 4 8 6 5 6 8 0 3 2 0 4 8 4 5 6 6 5 4 7 1 3 1 2
0 6 4 9 7 7 9 8 0 6 4 0 9 2 4 7 8 2 5 1 7 2 3 5 2
6 0 6 7 8 0 8 7 6 8 5 0 1 3 4 3 0 4 7 0 5 2 4 1 3
1 6 3 6 4 9 6 5 3 5 5 3 0 3 3 8 3 7 9 1 1 5 8 2 2
2 1 5 9 7 1 2 6 4 4 5 0 2 1 4 5 1 1 7 0 4 0 1 3 0
```

Table 1   Random Numbers *(continued)*

```
5 0 3 9 1 8 3 8 9 5 5 6 7 3 0 6 7 9 7 1 4 9 2 3 3
3 5 8 1 8 1 6 3 4 7 0 6 7 7 8 9 6 2 0 8 5 0 4 3 7
7 0 6 4 0 6 9 0 5 9 3 3 7 7 1 1 4 4 3 8 0 6 2 1 8
1 0 4 9 2 7 8 1 6 4 4 9 3 2 9 6 7 3 2 4 2 6 4 9 6
7 7 7 0 3 2 5 7 9 3 0 5 6 6 5 8 7 6 2 8 5 2 5 3 8
3 1 4 2 0 1 2 3 5 8 0 4 9 9 9 5 6 4 8 6 4 3 5 0 8
8 7 9 8 4 6 4 1 7 0 8 6 0 0 6 1 7 0 9 0 2 9 8 4 2
5 0 6 9 7 6 4 6 4 9 6 6 0 5 3 2 7 9 2 4 4 4 0 6 5
0 9 7 6 2 3 7 3 6 5 7 7 4 8 5 9 4 9 6 6 0 9 5 6 3
1 1 2 9 9 4 6 0 0 6 3 7 1 3 1 9 1 2 6 6 0 8 7 5 2
9 5 5 5 1 9 7 5 9 0 3 2 1 5 6 1 1 1 2 8 3 5 9 5 5
5 6 2 2 6 5 2 0 4 0 5 8 1 8 6 1 2 3 9 0 3 4 3 0 3
3 0 8 5 5 8 7 5 1 7 1 0 7 0 2 7 4 9 9 5 4 9 3 4 6
1 9 4 1 2 5 8 1 2 4 4 9 7 5 9 7 5 8 8 6 2 2 2 4 0
1 6 0 1 7 5 6 9 4 1 7 3 2 2 6 5 1 4 5 9 8 9 9 2 4
9 4 3 4 6 5 3 2 3 0 8 5 6 6 1 1 0 6 6 9 9 6 0 1 1
3 8 5 2 2 5 3 1 3 4 8 8 2 8 7 5 4 6 4 6 4 0 3 3 4
6 5 9 8 7 5 1 5 0 1 3 1 3 5 7 1 1 7 6 6 6 6 8 4 5
9 9 7 6 9 8 8 7 0 6 1 5 7 9 7 1 5 9 7 9 2 6 7 1 1
3 2 8 0 3 7 7 6 8 3 1 2 6 3 0 8 1 4 8 6 1 2 6 6 8
8 9 9 2 9 7 7 4 2 3 3 5 9 2 3 5 8 6 7 3 0 6 4 9 9
5 2 2 0 3 2 8 7 3 4 1 2 6 8 9 6 8 9 4 1 7 6 8 2 9
9 3 7 1 9 8 3 6 0 2 8 6 3 5 3 0 1 6 1 3 3 8 3 4 8
0 6 7 9 9 0 3 7 7 2 6 0 7 7 1 1 8 1 2 9 9 7 8 0 6
6 5 3 1 0 4 2 4 5 1 4 9 5 3 9 0 2 2 4 5 9 9 9 0 0
4 1 8 9 1 7 4 3 6 4 4 6 6 6 0 7 6 3 2 5 8 2 0 6 8
4 5 4 7 1 1 4 5 0 4 7 9 4 0 6 1 2 1 9 4 9 9 0 2 3
2 5 4 3 3 6 3 1 4 0 9 3 7 9 1 1 8 8 1 8 0 3 1 9 5
4 3 6 4 0 1 7 8 2 0 4 9 5 9 7 9 0 3 3 7 2 9 9 4 0
2 3 8 5 4 4 3 3 0 6 1 0 7 3 5 3 1 3 2 0 6 0 9 1 7
1 6 4 8 7 9 9 9 1 3 1 0 8 6 7 5 6 9 0 3 1 ·6 8 2 0
4 8 1 6 3 4 5 0 2 7 5 7 0 8 3 2 4 8 5 3 2 9 6 8 1
4 2 1 9 4 6 2 3 0 1 1 6 1 0 7 2 2 3 4 8 7 9 1 4 6
4 0 7 6 5 4 2 9 5 3 3 9 0 6 3 0 2 5 4 9 5 3 6 0 8
8 4 9 3 0 8 2 8 4 0 4 5 6 9 0 6 8 1 1 4 6 7 4 8 1
1 7 6 3 8 1 4 6 2 2 9 4 5 0 3 5 7 0 0 2 4 1 7 1 2
5 6 4 6 9 0 1 5 1 5 5 0 3 1 4 5 1 2 7 0 2 4 9 9 6
0 3 6 0 7 1 4 8 0 3 5 4 8 8 0 4 0 6 7 3 3 1 1 7 4
6 7 2 9 0 4 2 9 2 6 4 6 4 6 4 6 9 4 6 2 3 9 4 8 8
0 3 1 4 5 9 5 0 8 2 6 5 0 8 5 8 0 7 5 0 9 5 3 1 5
7 3 0 9 3 6 1 9 3 1 3 9 8 3 9 7 7 6 6 5 3 0 2 6 8
8 6 7 9 6 6 8 3 4 0 5 9 5 1 7 8 0 1 0 8 9 7 1 4 6
4 9 5 8 6 8 0 4 4 4 5 6 7 4 8 1 7 1 4 9 2 9 5 1 9
6 0 3 9 9 5 8 4 4 1 5 4 0 0 1 2 1 8 2 9 5 4 8 7 2
4 1 0 5 3 6 3 5 0 6 4 0 0 1 2 1 8 2 9 5 4 8 7 2 5
5 2 7 9 6 5 7 4 5 1 3 3 8 8 4 4 0 4 1 8 9 1 1 6 5
3 4 6 1 2 1 8 7 4 7 6 3 3 5 0 0 7 9 1 6 4 0 7 4 6
8 2 2 0 8 8 8 7 3 8 3 1 5 8 4 9 5 1 9 1 7 9 7 9 9
4 8 7 0 7 8 9 4 3 0 9 2 3 5 4 7 2 1 4 6 6 8 6 3 2
9 0 4 3 8 0 1 5 7 6 7 1 6 3 0 5 7 3 7 1 0 9 5 6 6
```

Table 1   Random Numbers *(continued)*

```
8 2 8 9 7 9 6 9 7 9 0 8 2 9 8 1 5 6 9 3 2 9 2 3 3
9 4 6 9 2 6 8 4 4 7 8 3 5 1 0 1 3 9 9 2 9 0 4 0 8
5 6 7 4 2 7 4 1 2 7 3 1 5 8 3 1 0 7 3 8 7 5 2 5 1
8 0 9 9 8 3 2 9 7 5 5 8 0 5 2 1 3 4 2 3 8 6 8 3 6
6 7 0 3 7 9 8 8 2 0 9 1 0 6 0 7 2 4 5 1 3 3 5 1 0
8 1 3 0 0 8 3 4 8 8 3 4 8 9 9 2 0 4 3 9 6 7 6 5 7
1 7 6 2 5 8 6 2 6 6 8 0 8 3 9 8 8 7 4 2 1 3 3 3 2
9 9 7 1 7 5 9 1 3 2 4 6 0 5 9 0 7 3 8 2 3 5 4 7 1
0 4 6 4 0 1 7 9 9 3 6 8 1 5 3 7 1 1 9 5 1 0 1 4 8
9 7 8 2 1 2 9 7 2 0 6 4 2 5 2 7 0 8 1 1 9 7 7 7 0
2 4 6 4 6 3 6 7 5 2 0 0 5 4 7 3 3 4 1 0 7 4 4 0 9
8 5 4 5 4 7 7 4 0 0 5 0 6 4 2 8 8 0 8 0 9 9 0 5 8
5 8 6 7 6 6 4 7 0 1 4 9 9 5 7 2 1 4 1 1 9 7 7 3 5
1 3 8 1 4 7 0 7 4 8 8 4 4 0 1 2 5 1 4 8 1 7 7 3 2
4 1 5 9 7 9 5 6 6 7 4 5 6 1 8 8 8 2 8 9 0 0 9 2 5
9 5 4 7 0 6 8 1 2 1 4 0 4 5 8 3 1 6 0 1 9 7 5 6 0
3 7 2 7 4 1 4 8 3 6 4 1 6 1 9 0 4 1 3 2 6 8 9 2 5
9 7 1 8 1 0 8 3 6 0 1 7 5 0 6 3 2 7 9 2 5 6 2 9 9
9 9 9 9 1 9 4 2 6 9 5 8 5 6 8 3 9 8 6 9 9 6 8 2 5
9 3 0 1 8 1 5 8 8 1 1 4 4 6 6 4 1 0 9 6 6 7 5 5 8
7 9 4 6 8 9 0 6 6 9 5 4 3 1 9 5 1 9 5 6 2 8 2 7 4
3 5 5 4 5 2 5 2 2 1 4 8 2 0 9 1 8 4 3 5 0 3 2 6 5
6 7 2 1 9 0 5 4 3 3 9 8 9 0 1 2 6 6 1 3 0 4 5 4 1
4 0 5 3 9 2 6 3 2 2 0 4 2 0 9 1 0 0 8 8 8 0 2 8 1
2 1 5 7 3 7 3 6 2 8 9 3 2 8 7 9 6 7 9 5 1 9 5 5 4
8 2 9 1 7 6 5 0 5 7 4 2 4 7 5 1 4 2 8 4 0 2 0 4 5
0 4 9 2 5 9 9 8 7 4 7 3 2 2 1 7 7 1 9 5 1 4 4 9 4
3 8 6 7 5 6 1 5 3 0 9 0 8 4 0 4 6 7 2 2 6 8 4 3 5
7 1 8 8 3 6 3 7 4 3 6 3 3 0 1 3 4 9 7 3 8 9 2 3 6
2 3 0 4 7 4 6 9 9 9 8 7 4 4 2 8 1 4 4 4 0 0 6 0 8
8 6 4 4 0 7 1 2 9 6 3 1 3 4 9 1 6 2 9 3 7 6 1 1 0
0 5 5 4 6 7 7 9 6 9 0 2 5 5 3 5 8 5 1 2 9 6 9 3 9
5 7 4 3 2 8 8 4 4 2 0 8 9 6 3 0 5 1 1 2 7 3 7 8 0
8 3 2 7 1 2 7 0 2 9 1 1 7 1 5 4 8 1 9 1 2 5 0 5 3
3 1 2 1 0 7 7 3 0 4 7 1 3 8 9 3 8 7 2 7 5 1 4 8 9
0 7 9 7 0 6 4 5 3 0 5 8 2 7 3 7 3 0 6 2 4 3 3 9 1
9 0 3 4 4 3 1 8 2 1 0 4 5 9 7 2 9 0 5 5 4 7 1 5 9
1 5 7 9 2 9 5 2 8 9 1 8 6 4 2 3 4 0 6 1 4 1 7 9 9
7 3 8 2 7 8 4 7 5 9 3 4 2 9 9 4 8 3 1 1 6 5 1 5 6
2 4 0 4 4 0 4 5 0 7 6 4 9 2 0 5 3 9 2 8 1 1 8 0 2
2 9 9 9 6 6 6 8 0 6 9 4 0 8 4 2 4 0 4 6 0 2 1 2 2 4
5 8 2 2 2 1 7 7 2 5 9 4 2 1 7 2 1 7 7 9 3 3 5 9 8
7 3 7 4 3 6 3 0 9 9 1 6 3 9 2 3 0 2 6 8 9 8 9 0 7
8 8 9 7 6 2 9 9 0 1 2 0 0 1 0 2 4 7 8 9 6 6 9 7 8
1 4 0 9 6 1 0 9 8 7 0 5 8 0 6 5 8 0 5 0 1 9 3 0 1
1 6 4 2 4 7 6 7 7 3 5 9 3 2 2 9 2 7 8 6 3 7 7 8 1
1 2 9 8 1 2 5 7 7 9 6 8 4 4 0 6 3 3 1 1 6 7 2 5 8
5 7 7 5 3 5 5 5 6 7 9 4 3 1 5 7 2 7 6 9 7 6 1 0 3
2 4 7 9 1 7 2 8 3 4 4 1 1 1 3 0 6 9 1 4 8 8 7 5 6
0 2 5 9 4 0 8 2 5 6 0 4 7 1 6 3 6 5 5 5 6 1 1 6 7 6
```

Table 1 Random Numbers *(continued)*

```
8 9 0 8 8 8 7 4 1 9 9 9 5 5 1 8 2 1 3 7 5 7 8 7 1
1 1 0 4 2 7 2 3 9 9 5 7 5 0 9 5 3 9 6 8 6 7 4 9 0
0 0 6 6 6 3 1 5 6 3 8 9 7 2 9 0 9 8 4 9 4 2 5 0 0
2 8 5 9 9 3 5 2 5 2 1 1 7 4 0 7 9 0 1 4 9 1 9 8 9
7 5 8 0 7 9 4 5 7 9 3 2 0 7 6 3 2 6 3 6 0 9 7 8 5
2 8 1 2 4 9 9 2 0 1 9 7 9 7 2 0 8 1 4 9 2 8 6 5 9
1 6 5 9 5 2 6 8 5 8 1 8 0 6 1 2 2 7 1 0 8 6 1 9 9
3 8 0 2 2 2 0 4 5 5 5 4 5 6 9 9 1 4 2 6 7 3 9 3 5
7 0 7 8 2 1 9 6 3 1 1 8 1 1 7 8 1 6 0 3 9 6 7 1 0
9 5 9 2 6 6 6 7 4 1 9 5 1 9 8 4 2 7 9 3 8 5 5 0 8
9 9 3 7 7 0 5 3 1 2 2 4 7 0 2 2 4 0 2 1 4 5 2 6 9
2 8 6 7 5 0 2 8 7 0 4 2 5 4 1 5 3 3 7 0 7 8 8 0 8
5 8 4 6 5 0 3 6 4 5 2 4 7 9 6 7 7 3 1 5 9 7 7 4 2
2 7 9 4 0 0 1 7 0 7 2 0 0 5 1 8 6 4 9 7 9 7 0 4 8
3 2 0 4 1 5 9 2 4 0 8 3 9 0 6 9 8 3 7 7 2 6 0 6 8
9 4 4 2 4 3 1 3 1 3 0 2 2 8 2 7 5 6 8 5 3 2 9 9 9
1 4 7 7 0 3 1 3 3 5 9 6 5 1 6 4 0 6 9 7 3 9 2 1 6
2 7 4 6 7 2 6 2 7 2 5 1 3 8 7 7 8 2 1 9 2 5 0 9 0
5 3 2 1 6 4 9 4 4 6 2 5 3 3 3 5 2 5 4 9 5 7 4 4 6
6 0 9 6 4 0 0 9 3 2 7 7 6 6 7 9 7 8 1 8 0 4 1 8 1
6 8 6 5 0 5 3 4 2 3 3 7 5 7 7 9 7 4 7 0 5 6 5 1 3
7 2 1 3 4 1 7 8 1 8 4 4 1 6 6 6 2 5 6 6 2 0 4 1 9
7 5 9 1 3 2 7 1 2 6 3 1 3 3 1 2 9 0 9 8 9 8 6 9 8
8 7 7 6 8 8 8 1 6 8 6 1 8 8 6 1 7 5 6 8 6 4 3 6 9
0 4 6 4 6 1 9 6 1 4 5 9 1 1 3 6 1 4 5 7 0 8 2 5 4
9 6 8 6 1 6 3 0 3 7 0 4 9 8 8 7 7 6 8 1 7 1 5 0 8
7 6 9 7 0 9 8 7 1 2 0 9 0 3 8 5 3 9 3 7 4 1 1 5 7
3 2 7 0 9 2 7 5 8 0 4 7 8 1 4 2 4 0 0 9 6 5 9 2 5
4 2 6 8 9 1 9 0 4 2 1 3 4 3 2 0 6 7 4 7 1 3 9 7 9
6 8 6 5 1 4 1 3 0 6 7 0 9 5 2 8 7 0 9 3 8 5 1 3 5
6 3 5 7 2 0 2 8 6 3 3 8 5 3 1 0 4 6 6 3 1 7 9 9 7
7 3 7 7 3 4 5 2 3 6 2 3 6 5 5 3 9 2 1 7 0 6 4 2 0
6 0 1 2 5 0 2 9 4 9 8 3 5 9 5 7 4 5 2 8 4 7 6 6 4
2 6 6 8 6 5 0 7 7 5 5 4 9 1 2 0 3 4 8 9 6 4 9 8 9
3 6 8 7 2 9 9 2 7 5 6 0 9 0 6 5 8 8 2 8 3 4 7 4 0
4 2 5 5 7 2 6 5 9 4 3 8 7 5 6 5 3 6 3 4 3 8 5 4 7
3 2 3 1 1 5 6 5 8 3 9 6 2 2 0 2 9 0 9 3 1 1 3 1 4
0 2 3 6 6 9 4 4 6 6 0 9 9 7 4 0 1 3 2 5 6 9 4 5 1
6 5 6 9 4 1 6 8 8 6 7 0 0 6 0 8 8 3 9 7 8 4 1 7 6
7 3 1 3 9 1 2 0 7 1 5 2 1 2 0 7 0 1 7 8 6 4 6 6 3
3 5 2 5 5 9 9 0 1 5 3 2 1 7 0 1 9 3 6 3 3 4 5 0 9
2 7 6 2 3 9 6 7 5 3 6 1 5 0 2 0 3 2 9 1 6 2 1 4 6
7 8 9 1 3 0 3 0 0 2 8 5 5 4 3 8 9 6 8 2 2 1 8 8 1
1 1 0 8 2 7 9 9 8 5 5 1 9 0 7 1 2 5 7 6 8 5 8 2 8
9 6 3 9 6 2 1 1 1 0 3 2 1 7 5 0 6 9 0 6 2 0 9 5 1
1 0 3 2 4 6 1 9 9 8 8 6 5 7 6 9 8 9 1 2 4 9 1 3 5
2 3 7 1 5 7 2 5 8 1 1 7 6 6 4 9 1 3 0 3 5 2 6 3 3
2 3 6 4 7 5 3 4 7 7 7 6 4 3 5 9 6 3 8 7 8 0 1 3 2
9 3 6 1 5 4 4 5 3 3 5 4 1 5 2 3 4 6 4 5 3 7 6 9 2
0 4 0 4 6 7 0 2 9 4 3 5 9 9 7 4 9 0 6 8 7 5 9 3 6
```

Table 1 Random Numbers *(continued)*

```
9 3 6 4 8 6 5 9 2 6 4 5 1 6 9 9 0 8 6 7 4 5 7 2 8
1 1 5 8 8 6 9 0 3 3 6 8 4 1 8 1 3 9 0 8 3 4 5 6 5
7 2 8 1 8 8 3 7 4 4 3 5 0 2 1 3 1 9 9 1 1 1 7 0 0
1 8 4 9 4 8 6 2 6 5 1 7 6 9 5 8 8 2 8 4 0 6 2 7 8
2 7 3 0 6 1 3 6 4 1 9 2 4 5 4 4 9 5 4 7 1 4 2 0 0
2 1 0 3 9 9 3 2 8 0 0 3 4 6 2 9 2 5 5 9 6 5 0 7 8
5 1 2 1 7 3 1 5 7 1 5 8 7 7 5 7 9 8 0 8 5 3 2 5 8
2 5 3 5 4 8 4 5 2 5 7 7 2 8 7 1 8 2 3 9 3 1 5 9 9
0 6 1 5 3 1 9 8 0 4 3 2 0 1 4 5 4 2 9 8 2 9 1 5 5
4 7 0 9 2 7 5 8 6 1 5 4 0 9 9 7 3 9 6 5 5 4 0 1 4
4 6 1 4 8 5 7 1 9 7 0 9 4 2 8 0 1 3 6 4 0 4 9 7 2
8 5 2 7 5 0 5 6 6 3 3 3 1 8 1 6 7 3 2 4 9 6 6 8 9
1 9 5 1 2 4 1 4 7 2 9 8 7 7 4 9 5 1 2 8 6 7 0 0 7
1 1 7 5 2 6 4 7 5 9 2 9 2 7 0 9 3 3 1 6 2 1 0 8 2
6 0 4 0 7 7 9 9 5 0 3 8 6 9 8 9 1 2 5 2 6 3 3 6 5
4 2 8 8 4 2 2 6 5 9 7 6 4 5 2 4 4 4 7 2 3 3 8 0 1
6 3 1 3 5 0 4 8 3 4 1 7 2 9 0 6 3 3 5 0 4 0 4 5 1
4 9 9 6 2 8 3 1 8 4 8 1 1 0 9 4 6 4 2 1 5 9 4 8 6
5 5 8 5 7 3 5 3 1 0 8 9 8 0 1 0 6 2 1 6 9 7 3 5 1
0 8 3 6 4 9 7 5 6 2 8 7 3 8 9 0 0 2 2 0 0 4 9 9 0 9
5 6 2 1 3 3 7 4 0 7 1 9 3 3 8 7 6 5 8 9 0 8 3 7 1 4
6 7 6 6 5 2 7 1 5 0 1 5 8 3 1 5 3 5 5 2 2 4 2 5 4
1 0 2 9 2 0 9 5 4 1 6 9 6 8 4 0 2 6 5 3 2 2 1 3 9
9 7 3 0 4 1 8 8 6 5 9 3 9 1 2 2 0 7 2 3 8 9 9 7 8
3 6 6 7 1 6 5 6 6 9 6 7 8 6 2 1 4 1 1 0 8 8 5 4 0
2 4 3 9 7 6 0 0 6 2 8 4 3 4 4 1 1 5 9 3 7 9 4 8 3
0 4 7 0 4 1 0 7 2 9 6 4 5 2 7 2 9 8 3 4 5 6 8 8 2
6 0 5 9 1 1 1 4 4 6 9 7 8 8 6 3 6 7 6 0 5 1 0 5 5
1 1 5 1 6 6 0 5 1 5 6 0 7 5 2 7 3 7 2 4 8 6 2 5 4
3 4 2 3 2 5 9 4 7 1 7 8 4 1 3 8 8 5 3 7 6 8 8 6 4
8 3 3 6 5 8 0 5 9 6 6 1 3 4 5 4 2 8 3 9 5 0 8 9 1
9 2 1 2 4 7 6 5 9 3 6 0 5 0 7 5 3 7 9 3 8 5 1 7 6
2 6 6 8 4 7 5 4 7 0 8 4 2 6 8 3 1 4 5 9 8 7 5 0 6
6 6 4 6 5 8 8 5 9 8 5 9 4 6 5 2 4 0 7 1 4 1 8 7 0
1 1 6 5 4 5 4 0 4 1 7 2 1 5 7 5 8 5 7 4 4 8 2 6 2
3 0 8 3 7 1 3 1 9 0 7 7 5 2 2 7 6 3 9 9 9 0 3 8 6
8 0 2 6 1 8 5 9 3 1 7 9 4 7 5 5 4 9 6 4 6 1 6 0 1
4 5 2 7 5 1 0 6 4 2 1 6 2 4 9 1 8 3 1 8 8 2 7 4 1
0 5 6 1 3 8 3 9 8 3 6 9 4 9 1 5 2 5 6 5 8 4 5 1 9
7 4 1 5 0 4 4 3 4 8 7 4 8 7 4 5 1 3 9 2 4 1 2 2 5
7 4 5 7 0 9 8 3 4 9 7 8 1 3 2 2 8 3 7 3 8 5 2 6 1
5 8 8 2 4 5 4 9 9 5 6 5 5 0 1 7 6 3 6 1 6 6 5 6 8 9
1 4 9 9 2 0 5 4 1 2 6 4 3 8 4 3 4 3 2 4 4 4 2 9 5 6
2 3 5 4 3 3 6 9 2 8 2 1 1 5 5 0 7 1 4 5 0 5 6 3 0
9 6 1 5 9 9 1 2 9 2 5 3 9 9 4 1 6 2 3 4 0 8 8 6 9
0 7 2 9 3 7 5 5 5 0 5 7 3 3 6 8 6 2 7 2 1 5 0 0 3
6 2 8 1 5 1 1 4 8 2 9 5 5 6 5 2 0 6 7 3 3 9 2 2 2
2 7 8 8 9 0 4 1 4 6 9 7 5 4 9 2 4 4 0 6 9 5 4 4 4
4 3 3 9 1 2 1 3 6 3 4 3 4 8 8 6 9 3 2 3 3 4 7 1 2
8 8 0 5 2 2 8 0 8 5 3 0 3 7 4 9 6 0 1 8 5 3 8 6 4
```

Table 2 Distribution of *t*

	Level of Significance for One-Tailed Test					
	.10	.05	.025	.01	.005	.0005
df	Level of Significance for Two-Tailed test					
	.20	.10	.05	.02	.01	.001
1	3.078	6.314	12.706	31.821	63.657	636.619
2	1.886	2.920	4.303	6.965	9.925	31.598
3	1.638	2.353	3.182	4.541	5.841	12.941
4	1.533	2.132	2.776	3.747	4.604	8.610
5	1.476	2.015	2.571	3.365	4.032	6.859
6	1.440	1.943	2.447	3.143	3.707	5.959
7	1.415	1.895	2.365	2.998	3.499	5.405
8	1.397	1.860	2.306	2.896	3.355	5.041
9	1.383	1.833	2.262	2.821	3.250	4.781
10	1.372	1.812	2.228	2.764	3.169	4.587
11	1.363	1.796	2.201	2.718	3.106	4.437
12	1.356	1.782	2.179	2.681	3.055	4.318
13	1.350	1.771	2.160	2.650	3.012	4.221
14	1.345	1.761	2.145	2.624	2.977	4.140
15	1.341	1.753	2.131	2.602	2.947	4.073
16	1.337	1.746	2.120	2.583	2.921	4.015
17	1.333	1.740	2.110	2.567	2.898	3.965
18	1.330	1.734	2.101	2.552	2.878	3.992
19	1.328	1.729	2.093	2.539	2.861	3.883
20	1.325	1.725	2.086	2.528	2.845	3.850
21	1.323	1.721	2.080	2.518	2.831	3.819
22	1.321	1.717	2.074	2.508	2.819	3.792
23	1.319	1.714	2.069	2.500	2.807	3.767
24	1.318	1.711	2.064	2.492	2.797	3.745
25	1.316	1.708	2.060	2.485	2.787	3.725
26	1.315	1.706	2.056	2.479	2.779	3.707
27	1.314	1.703	2.052	2.473	2.771	3.690
28	1.313	1.701	2.048	2.467	2.763	3.674
29	1.311	1.699	2.045	2.462	2.756	3.659
30	1.310	1.697	2.042	2.457	2.750	3.646
40	1.303	1.684	2.021	2.423	2.704	3.551
60	1.296	1.671	2.000	2.390	2.660	3.460
120	1.289	1.658	1.980	2.358	2.617	3.373
∞	1.282	1.645	1.960	2.326	2.576	3.291

Source: From R. A. Fisher and F. Yates, *Statistical Tables for Biological, Agricultural and Medical Research*, 6e © Pearson Education, Ltd. Used by permission.

Table 3 Areas Under the Normal Curve. Proportion of Area Under the Normal Curve Between the Mean and a *z* Distance from the Mean.

$\frac{x}{O}$ or z	.00	.01	.02	.03	.04	.05	.06	.07	.08	.09
.0	.0000	.0040	.0080	.0120	.0160	.0199	.0239	.0279	.0319	.0359
.1	.0398	.0438	.0478	.0517	.0557	.0596	.0636	.0675	.0714	.0753
.2	.0793	.0832	.0871	.0910	.0948	.0987	.1026	.1064	.1103	.1141
.3	.1179	.1217	.1255	.1293	.1331	.1368	.1406	.1443	.1480	.1517
.4	.1554	.1591	.1628	.1664	.1700	.1736	.1772	.1808	.1844	.1879
.5	.1915	.1950	.1985	.2019	.2054	.2088	.2123	.2157	.2190	.2224
.6	.2257	.2291	.2324	.2357	.2389	.2422	.2454	.2486	.2517	.2549
.7	.2580	.2611	.2642	.2673	.2704	.2734	.2764	.2794	.2823	.2852
.8	.2881	.2910	.2939	.2967	.2995	.3023	.3051	.3078	.3106	.3133
.9	.3159	.3186	.3212	.3238	.3264	.3289	.3315	.3340	.3365	.3389
1.0	.3413	.3438	.3461	.3485	.3508	.3531	.3554	.3577	.3599	.3621
1.1	.3643	.3665	.3686	.3708	.3729	.3749	.3770	.3790	.3810	.3830
1.2	.3849	.3869	.3888	.3907	.3925	.3944	.3962	.3980	.3997	.4015
1.3	.4032	.4049	.4066	.4082	.4099	.4115	.4131	.4147	.4162	.4177
1.4	.4192	.4207	.4222	.4236	.4251	.4265	.4279	.4292	.4306	.4319
1.5	.4332	.4345	.4357	.4370	.4382	.4394	.4406	.4418	.4429	.4441
1.6	.4452	.4463	.4474	.4484	.4495	.4505	.4515	.4525	.4535	.4545
1.7	.4554	.4564	.4573	.4582	.4591	.4599	.4608	.4616	.4625	.4633
1.8	.4641	.4649	.4656	.4664	.4671	.4678	.4686	.4693	.4699	.4706
1.9	.4713	.4719	.4726	.4732	.4738	.4744	.4750	.4756	.4761	.4767
2.0	.4772	.4778	.4783	.4788	.4793	.4798	.4803	.4808	.4812	.4817
2.1	.4821	.4826	.4830	.4834	.4838	.4842	.4846	.4850	.4854	.4857
2.2	.4861	.4864	.4868	.4871	.4875	.4878	.4881	.4884	.4887	.4890
2.3	.4893	.4896	.4898	.4901	.4904	.4906	.4909	.4911	.4913	.4916
2.4	.4918	.4920	.4922	.4925	.4927	.4929	.4931	.4932	.4934	.4936

Table 3   Areas Under the Normal Curve. Proportion of Area Under the Normal Curve Between the Mean and a *z* Distance from the Mean. *(continued)*

$\frac{x}{\sigma}$ or z	.00	.01	.02	.03	.04	.05	.06	.07	.08	.09
2.5	.4938	.4940	.4941	.4943	.4945	.4946	.4948	.4949	.4951	.4952
2.6	.4953	.4955	.4956	.4957	.4959	.4960	.4961	.4962	.4963	.4964
2.7	.4965	.4966	.4967	.4968	.4969	.4970	.4971	.4972	.4973	.4974
2.8	.4974	.4975	.4976	.4977	.4977	.4978	.4979	.4979	.4980	.4981
2.9	.4981	.4982	.4982	.4983	.4984	.4984	.4985	.4985	.4986	.4986
3.0	.4987	.4987	.4987	.4988	.4988	.4989	.4989	.4989	.4990	.4990
3.1	.4990	.4991	.4991	.4991	.4992	.4992	.4992	.4992	.4993	.4993
3.2	.4993	.4993	.4994	.4994	.4994	.4994	.4994	.4995	.4995	.4995
3.3	.4995	.4995	.4995	.4996	.4996	.4996	.4996	.4996	.4996	.4997
3.4	.4997	.4997	.4997	.4997	.4997	.4997	.4997	.4997	.4997	.4998
3.5	.4998									
4.0	.49997									
4.5	.499997									
5.0	.4999997									

Table prepared by Roger D. Wimmer using Microsoft *Excel* function NORMSDIST.

Table 4 Distribution of Chi-Square

df	Probability					
	.20	.10	.05	.02	.01	.001
1	1.642	2.706	3.841	5.412	6.635	10.827
2	3.219	4.605	5.991	7.824	9.210	13.815
3	4.642	6.251	7.815	9.837	11.345	16.266
4	5.989	7.779	9.488	11.668	13.277	18.467
5	7.289	9.236	11.070	13.388	15.086	20.515
6	8.558	10.645	12.592	15.033	16.812	22.457
7	9.803	12.017	14.067	16.622	18.475	24.322
8	11.030	13.362	15.507	18.168	20.090	26.125
9	12.242	14.684	16.919	19.679	21.666	27.877
10	13.442	15.987	18.307	21.161	23.209	29.588
11	14.631	17.275	19.675	22.618	24.725	31.264
12	15.812	18.549	21.026	24.054	26.217	32.909
13	16.985	19.812	22.362	25.472	27.688	34.528
14	18.151	21.064	23.685	26.873	29.141	36.123
15	19.311	22.307	24.996	28.259	30.578	37.697
16	20.465	23.542	26.296	29.633	32.000	39.252
17	21.615	24.769	27.587	30.995	33.409	40.790
18	22.760	25.989	28.869	32.346	34.805	42.312
19	23.900	27.204	30.144	33.687	36.191	43.820
20	25.038	28.412	31.410	35.020	37.566	45.315
21	26.171	29.615	32.671	36.343	38.932	46.797
22	27.301	30.813	33.924	37.659	40.289	48.268
23	28.429	32.007	35.172	38.968	41.638	49.728
24	29.553	33.196	36.415	40.270	42.980	51.179
25	30.675	34.382	37.652	41.566	44.314	52.620

Table 4   Distribution of Chi-Square *(continued)*

	Probability					
df	.20	.10	.05	.02	.01	.001
26	31.795	35.563	38.885	42.856	45.642	54.052
27	32.912	36.741	40.113	44.140	46.963	55.476
28	34.027	37.916	41.337	45.419	48.278	56.893
29	35.139	39.087	42.557	46.693	49.588	58.302
30	36.250	40.256	43.773	47.962	50.892	59.703
32	38.466	42.585	46.194	50.487	53.486	62.487
34	40.676	44.903	48.602	52.995	56.061	65.247
36	42.879	47.212	50.999	55.489	58.619	67.985
38	45.076	49.513	53.384	57.969	61.162	70.703
40	47.269	51.805	55.759	60.436	63.691	73.402
42	49.456	54.090	58.124	62.892	66.206	76.084
44	51.639	56.369	60.481	65.337	68.710	78.750
46	53.818	58.641	62.830	67.771	71.201	81.400
48	55.993	60.907	65.171	70.197	73.683	84.037
50	58.164	63.167	67.505	72.613	76.154	86.661
52	60.332	65.422	69.832	75.021	78.616	89.272
54	62.496	67.673	72.153	77.422	81.069	91.872
56	64.658	69.919	74.468	79.815	83.513	94.461
58	66.816	72.160	76.778	82.201	85.950	97.039
60	68.972	74.397	79.082	84.580	88.379	99.607
62	71.125	76.630	81.381	86.953	90.802	102.166
64	73.276	78.860	83.675	89.320	93.217	104.716
66	75.424	81.085	85.965	91.681	95.626	107.258
68	77.571	83.308	88.250	94.037	98.028	109.791
70	79.715	85.527	90.531	96.388	100.425	112.317

Source: From R. A. Fisher and F. Yates, *Statistical Tables for Biological, Agricultural and Medical Research*, 6e © Pearson Education, Ltd. Used by permission.

Table 5 Distribution of F: .05 Level

df_2 \ df_1	1	2	3	4	5	6	7	8	9	10	12	15	20	24	30	40	60	120	∞
1	161.4	199.5	215.7	224.6	230.2	234.0	236.8	238.9	240.5	241.9	243.9	245.9	248.0	249.1	250.1	251.1	252.2	253.3	254.3
2	18.51	19.00	19.16	19.25	19.30	19.33	19.35	19.37	19.38	19.40	19.41	19.43	19.45	19.45	19.46	19.47	19.48	19.49	19.50
3	10.13	9.55	9.28	9.12	9.01	8.94	8.89	8.85	8.81	8.79	8.74	8.70	8.66	8.64	8.62	8.59	8.57	8.55	8.53
4	7.71	6.94	6.59	6.39	6.26	6.16	6.09	6.04	6.00	5.96	5.91	5.86	5.80	5.77	5.75	5.72	5.69	5.66	5.63
5	6.61	5.79	5.41	5.19	5.05	4.95	4.88	4.82	4.77	4.74	4.68	4.62	4.56	4.53	4.50	4.46	4.43	4.40	4.36
6	5.99	5.14	4.76	4.53	4.39	4.28	4.21	4.15	4.10	4.06	4.00	3.94	3.87	3.84	3.81	3.77	3.74	3.70	3.67
7	5.59	4.74	4.35	4.12	3.97	3.87	3.79	3.73	3.68	3.64	3.57	3.51	3.44	3.41	3.38	3.34	3.30	3.27	3.23
8	5.32	4.46	4.07	3.84	3.69	3.58	3.50	3.44	3.39	3.35	3.28	3.22	3.15	3.12	3.08	3.04	3.01	2.97	2.93
9	5.12	4.26	3.86	3.63	3.48	3.37	3.29	3.23	3.18	3.14	3.07	3.01	2.94	2.90	2.86	2.83	2.79	2.75	2.71
10	4.96	4.10	3.71	3.48	3.33	3.22	3.14	3.07	3.02	2.98	2.91	2.85	2.77	2.74	2.70	2.66	2.62	2.58	2.54
11	4.84	3.98	3.59	3.36	3.20	3.09	3.01	2.95	2.90	2.85	2.79	2.72	2.65	2.61	2.57	2.53	2.49	2.45	2.40
12	4.75	3.89	3.49	3.26	3.11	3.00	2.91	2.85	2.80	2.75	2.69	2.62	2.54	2.51	2.47	2.43	2.38	2.34	2.30
13	4.67	3.81	3.41	3.18	3.03	2.92	2.83	2.77	2.71	2.67	2.60	2.53	2.46	2.42	2.38	2.34	2.30	2.25	2.21
14	4.60	3.74	3.34	3.11	2.96	2.85	2.76	2.70	2.65	2.60	2.53	2.46	2.39	2.35	2.31	2.27	2.22	2.18	2.13

15	4.54	3.68	3.29	3.06	2.90	2.79	2.71	2.64	2.59	2.54	2.48	2.40	2.33	2.29	2.25	2.20	2.16	2.11	2.07
16	4.49	3.63	3.24	3.01	2.85	2.74	2.66	2.59	2.54	2.49	2.42	2.35	2.28	2.24	2.19	2.15	2.11	2.06	2.01
17	4.45	3.59	3.20	2.96	2.81	2.70	2.61	2.55	2.49	2.45	2.38	2.31	2.23	2.19	2.15	2.10	2.06	2.01	1.96
18	4.41	3.55	3.16	2.93	2.77	2.66	2.58	2.51	2.46	2.41	2.34	2.27	2.19	2.15	2.11	2.06	2.02	1.97	1.92
19	4.38	3.52	3.13	2.90	2.74	2.63	2.54	2.48	2.42	2.38	2.31	2.23	2.16	2.11	2.07	2.03	1.98	1.93	1.88
20	4.35	3.49	3.10	2.87	2.71	2.60	2.51	2.45	2.39	2.35	2.28	2.20	2.12	2.08	2.04	1.99	1.95	1.90	1.84
21	4.32	3.47	3.07	2.84	2.68	2.57	2.49	2.42	2.37	2.32	2.25	2.18	2.10	2.05	2.01	1.96	1.92	1.87	1.81
22	4.30	3.44	3.05	2.82	2.66	2.55	2.46	2.40	2.34	2.30	2.23	2.15	2.07	2.03	1.98	1.94	1.89	1.84	1.78
23	4.28	3.42	3.03	2.80	2.64	2.53	2.44	2.37	2.32	2.27	2.20	2.13	2.05	2.01	1.96	1.91	1.86	1.81	1.76
24	4.26	3.40	3.01	2.78	2.62	2.51	2.42	2.36	2.30	2.25	2.18	2.11	2.03	1.98	1.94	1.89	1.84	1.79	1.73
25	4.24	3.39	2.99	2.76	2.60	2.49	2.40	2.34	2.28	2.24	2.16	2.09	2.01	1.96	1.92	1.87	1.82	1.77	1.71
26	4.23	3.37	2.98	2.74	2.59	2.47	2.39	2.32	2.27	2.22	2.15	2.07	1.99	1.95	1.90	1.85	1.80	1.75	1.69
27	4.21	3.35	2.96	2.73	2.57	2.46	2.37	2.31	2.25	2.20	2.13	2.06	1.97	1.93	1.88	1.84	1.79	1.73	1.67
28	4.20	3.34	2.95	2.71	2.56	2.45	2.36	2.29	2.24	2.19	2.12	2.04	1.96	1.91	1.87	1.82	1.77	1.71	1.65
29	4.18	3.33	2.93	2.70	2.55	2.43	2.35	2.28	2.22	2.18	2.10	2.03	1.94	1.90	1.85	1.81	1.75	1.70	1.64
30	4.17	3.32	2.92	2.69	2.53	2.42	2.33	2.27	2.21	2.16	2.09	2.01	1.93	1.89	1.84	1.79	1.74	1.68	1.62
40	4.08	3.23	2.84	2.61	2.45	2.34	2.25	2.18	2.12	2.08	2.00	1.92	1.84	1.79	1.74	1.69	1.64	1.58	1.51
60	4.00	3.15	2.76	2.53	2.37	2.25	2.17	2.10	2.04	1.99	1.92	1.84	1.75	1.70	1.65	1.59	1.53	1.47	1.39
120	3.92	3.07	2.68	2.45	2.29	2.17	2.09	2.02	1.96	1.91	1.83	1.75	1.66	1.61	1.55	1.50	1.43	1.35	1.25
∞	3.84	3.00	2.60	2.37	2.21	2.10	2.01	1.94	1.88	1.83	1.75	1.67	1.57	1.52	1.46	1.39	1.32	1.22	1.00

Source: From R. A. Fisher and F. Yates, *Statistical Tables for Biological, Agricultural and Medical Research*, 6e © Pearson Education, Ltd. Used by permission.

Table 6 Distribution of F: .01 Level

df_2 \ df_1	1	2	3	4	5	6	7	8	9	10	12	15	20	24	30	40	60	120	∞
1	4052	4999.5	5403	5625	5764	5859	5928	5982	6022	6056	6106	6157	6209	6235	6261	6287	6313	6339	6366
2	98.5	99.00	99.17	99.25	99.30	99.33	99.36	99.37	99.39	99.40	99.42	99.43	99.45	99.46	99.47	99.47	99.48	99.49	99.50
3	34.12	30.82	29.46	28.71	28.24	27.91	27.67	27.49	27.35	27.23	27.05	26.87	26.69	26.60	26.50	26.41	26.32	26.22	26.13
4	21.20	18.00	16.69	15.98	15.52	15.21	14.98	14.80	14.66	14.55	14.37	14.20	14.02	13.93	13.84	13.75	13.65	13.56	13.46
5	16.26	13.27	12.06	11.39	10.97	10.67	10.46	10.29	10.16	10.05	9.89	9.72	9.55	9.47	9.38	9.29	9.20	9.11	9.02
6	13.75	10.92	9.78	9.15	8.75	8.47	8.26	8.10	7.98	7.87	7.72	7.56	7.40	7.31	7.23	7.14	7.06	6.97	6.88
7	12.25	9.55	8.45	7.85	7.46	7.19	6.99	6.81	6.72	6.62	6.47	6.31	6.16	6.07	5.99	5.91	5.82	5.74	5.65
8	11.26	8.65	7.59	7.01	6.63	6.37	6.18	6.03	5.91	5.81	5.67	5.52	5.36	5.28	5.20	5.12	5.03	4.95	4.86
9	10.56	8.02	6.99	6.42	6.06	5.80	5.61	5.47	5.35	5.26	5.11	4.96	4.81	4.73	4.65	4.57	4.48	4.40	4.31
10	10.04	7.56	6.55	5.99	5.64	5.39	5.20	5.06	4.94	4.85	4.71	4.56	4.41	4.33	4.25	4.17	4.08	4.00	3.91
11	9.65	7.21	6.22	5.67	5.32	5.07	4.89	4.74	4.63	4.54	4.40	4.25	4.10	4.02	3.94	3.86	3.78	3.69	3.60
12	9.33	6.93	5.95	5.41	5.06	4.82	4.64	4.50	4.39	4.30	4.16	4.01	3.86	3.78	3.70	3.62	3.54	3.45	3.36
13	9.07	6.70	5.74	5.21	4.86	4.62	4.44	4.30	4.19	4.10	3.96	3.82	3.66	3.59	3.51	3.43	3.34	3.25	3.17
14	8.86	6.51	5.56	5.04	4.69	4.46	4.28	4.14	4.03	3.94	3.80	3.66	3.51	3.43	3.35	3.27	3.18	3.09	3.00
15	8.68	6.36	5.42	4.89	4.56	4.32	4.14	4.00	3.89	3.80	3.67	3.52	3.37	3.29	3.21	3.13	3.05	2.96	2.87
16	8.53	6.23	5.29	4.77	4.44	4.20	4.03	3.89	3.78	3.69	3.55	3.41	3.26	3.18	3.10	3.02	2.93	2.84	2.75
17	8.40	6.11	5.18	4.67	4.34	4.10	3.93	3.79	3.68	3.59	3.46	3.31	3.16	3.08	3.00	2.92	2.83	2.75	2.65
18	8.29	6.01	5.09	4.58	4.25	4.01	3.84	3.71	3.60	3.51	3.37	3.23	3.08	3.00	2.92	2.84	2.75	2.66	2.57
19	8.18	5.93	5.01	4.50	4.17	3.94	3.77	3.63	3.52	3.43	3.30	3.15	3.00	2.92	2.84	2.76	2.67	2.58	2.49

20	8.10	5.85	4.94	4.43	4.10	3.87	3.70	3.56	3.46	3.37	3.23	3.09	2.94	2.86	2.78	2.69	2.61	2.52	2.42
21	8.02	5.78	4.87	4.37	4.04	3.81	3.64	3.51	3.40	3.31	3.17	3.03	2.88	2.80	2.72	2.64	2.55	2.46	2.36
22	7.95	5.72	4.82	4.31	3.99	3.76	3.59	3.45	3.35	3.26	3.12	2.98	2.83	2.75	2.67	2.58	2.50	2.40	2.31
23	7.88	5.66	4.76	4.26	3.94	3.71	3.54	3.41	3.30	3.21	3.07	2.93	2.78	2.70	2.62	2.54	2.45	2.35	2.26
24	7.82	5.61	4.72	4.22	3.90	3.67	3.50	3.36	3.26	3.17	3.03	2.89	2.74	2.66	2.58	2.49	2.40	2.31	2.21
25	7.77	5.57	4.68	4.18	3.85	3.63	3.46	3.32	3.22	3.13	2.99	2.85	2.70	2.62	2.54	2.45	2.36	2.27	2.17
26	7.72	5.53	4.64	4.14	3.82	3.59	3.42	3.29	3.18	3.09	2.96	2.81	2.66	2.58	2.50	2.42	2.33	2.23	2.13
27	7.68	5.49	4.60	4.11	3.78	3.56	3.39	3.26	3.15	3.06	2.93	2.78	2.63	2.55	2.47	2.38	2.29	2.20	2.10
28	7.64	5.45	4.57	4.07	3.75	3.53	3.36	3.23	3.12	3.03	2.90	2.75	2.60	2.52	2.44	2.35	2.26	2.17	2.06
29	7.60	5.42	4.54	4.04	3.73	3.50	3.33	3.20	3.09	3.00	2.87	2.73	2.57	2.49	2.41	2.33	2.23	2.14	2.03
30	7.56	5.39	4.51	4.02	3.70	3.47	3.30	3.17	3.07	2.98	2.84	2.70	2.55	2.47	2.39	2.30	2.21	2.11	2.01
40	7.31	5.18	4.31	3.83	3.51	3.29	3.12	2.99	2.89	2.80	2.66	2.52	2.37	2.29	2.20	2.11	2.02	1.92	1.80
60	7.08	4.98	4.13	3.65	3.34	3.12	2.95	2.82	2.72	2.63	2.50	2.35	2.20	2.12	2.03	1.94	1.84	1.73	1.60
120	6.85	4.79	3.95	3.48	3.17	2.96	2.79	2.66	2.56	2.47	2.34	2.19	2.03	1.95	1.86	1.76	1.66	1.53	1.38
∞	6.63	4.61	3.78	3.32	3.02	2.80	2.64	2.51	2.41	2.32	2.18	2.04	1.88	1.79	1.70	1.59	1.47	1.32	1.00

Source: From R. A. Fisher and F. Yates, *Statistical Tables for Biological, Agricultural and Medical Research*, 6e © Pearson Education, Ltd. Used by permission.

Note: df_1 = rows of table (for degrees of freedom in denominator)—within
df_2 = columns of table (for degrees of freedom in numerator)—between

GLOSSARY

acceptance rate the percentage of the target sample that agrees to participate in a research project.

advertising equivalency the equivalent advertising cost of the space or time of a story placed in a newspaper or on TV or radio during a public relations campaign.

agenda setting the theory that the media provide topics of discussion and importance for consumers.

aided recall a survey technique in which the interviewer shows the respondent a copy of a newspaper, magazine, television schedule, or other item that might help him or her to remember a certain article, program, advertisement, and so on.

algorithm a statistical procedure or formula.

alpha level the probability of rejecting a null hypothesis that is in fact true.

analysis of variance (ANOVA) a statistical procedure used to decompose sources of variation into two or more independent variables.

analytical survey a survey that attempts to describe and explain why certain conditions exist (usually by testing certain hypotheses).

anonymity the researcher cannot connect the names of research participants with the information they provide.

antecedent variable (1) in survey research, the variable used to predict another variable; (2) in experimental research, the independent variable.

applied research research that attempts to solve a specific problem rather than to construct a theory.

artifact a variable that creates an alternative explanation of results (a confounding variable).

audience turnover in radio research, an estimate of the number of times the audience changes stations during a given daypart.

auditorium music testing (AMT) a testing procedure in which a group of respondents simultaneously rate music hooks.

autonomy ethical principle holding that each individual is responsible for his or her decisions and should not be exploited.

available sample a sample selected on the basis of accessibility.

average quarter-hour (AQH) the average number of persons or households tuned in to a specific channel or station for at least 5 minutes during a 15-minute time segment.

bar chart see *histogram*.

beneficence ethical principle stating that a researcher should share the positive benefits of a research project with all involved.

beta weight a mathematically derived value that represents a variable's contribution to a prediction or weighted linear combination (also called weight coefficient).

callout research a procedure used in music testing to determine the popularity of recordings; see also *hook*.

case study an empirical inquiry that uses multiple sources of data to investigate a problem.

catch-up panel members of a previous cross-sectional sample who are located again for subsequent observation.

CATI computer-assisted telephone interviewing; video display terminals used by interviewers to present questions and enter responses.

census an analysis in which the sample comprises every element of a population.

central limit theorem the sum of a large number of independent variables that has an approximate normal distribution.

central location testing (CLT) research conducted with respondents who are invited to a field service facility or other research location.

central tendency a single value that is chosen to represent a typical score in a distribution, such as the mean, the mode, or the median.

checklist question a type of question in which the respondent is given a list of items and asked to mark those that apply.

chi-square statistic a measurement of observed versus expected frequencies; often referred to as *crosstabs*.

circulation in the print media, the total number of copies of a newspaper or magazine that are delivered to subscribers plus all copies bought at newsstands or from other sellers.

circulation research (1) a market-level study of newspaper and magazine penetration; (2) a study of the delivery and pricing systems used by newspapers and magazines.

closed-ended question a question the respondent must answer by making a selection from a prepared set of options.

Cloze procedure a method for measuring readability or recall in which every *n*th word is deleted from the message and readers are asked to fill in the blanks.

cluster sample a sample placed into groups or categories.

codebook a menu or list of responses used in coding open-ended questions.

coding the placing of a unit of analysis into a particular category.

coefficient of determination in correlational statistics, the amount of variation in the criterion variable that is accounted for by the antecedent variable.

coefficient of nondetermination in correlational statistics, the amount of variation in the criterion variable that is left unexplained.

cohort analysis a study of a specific population as it changes over time.

communication audit in public relations, an examination of the internal and external means of communication used by an organization.

computer-assisted telephone interviewing (CATI) a survey method in which questionnaires are designed for the computer; interviewers enter respondents' answers directly into the computer for tabulation; and question skips and response options are controlled by the computer.

concealment withholding some information about a research project from a participant.

concept an abstract idea formed by generalization.

confidence interval an area within which there is a stated probability that the parameter will fall.

confidence level the estimated probability, usually 95% or 99%, that the population value falls within a given confidence interval. The confidence level is 1 – alpha level.

confidentiality the researcher can connect the names of research participants with the information they provide but promises to keep the connection secret.

constitutive definition a type of definition in which other words or concepts are substituted for the word being defined.

construct a combination of concepts that is created to describe a specific situation (for example, "authoritarianism").

constructive replication an analysis of a hypothesis taken from a previous study that deliberately avoids duplicating the methods used in the previous study.

continuous variable a variable that can take on any value over a range of values and can be meaningfully broken into subparts (for example, "height").

control group subjects who do not receive experimental treatment and thus serve as a basis of comparison in an experiment.

control variable a variable whose influence a researcher wishes to eliminate.

convenience sample a nonprobability sample consisting of respondents or subjects who are readily available, such as college students in a classroom.

co-op (incentive) a payment given to respondents for participating in a research project.

copy testing research used to determine the most effective way of structuring a message to achieve the desired results; also known as message research.

cost per interview (CPI) the dollar amount required to recruit or interview one respondent.

cost per thousand (CPM) the dollar cost to reach 1,000 people or households by means of a particular medium or advertising vehicle.

criterion variable (1) in survey research, the variable presumed to be the effects variable; (2) in experimental research, the dependent variable.

cross-lagged correlation a type of longitudinal study in which information about two variables is gathered from the same sample at two different times; the correlations between variables at the same point in time are compared with the correlations at different times.

cross-sectional research the collection of data from a representative sample at only one point in time.

cross-tabulation analysis (crosstabs) see *chi-square statistic*.

cross-validation a procedure in which measurement instruments or subjects' responses are compared to verify their validity or truthfulness.

cultivation analysis a research approach suggesting that heavy television viewing leads to perceptions of social reality that are consistent with the view of the world as presented on television.

cume an estimate of the number of different people who listened to or viewed a particular broadcast for at least 5 minutes during a given daypart; see also *reach*.

data archives data storage facilities where researchers can deposit data for other researchers to use.

database marketing research conducted with respondents whose names are included in databases, such as people who recently purchased a television set or members of a club or organization.

daypart a given part of the broadcast day (for example, prime time: 8:00 p.m.–11:00 p.m.).

deception deliberately misleading participants in a research project.

degrees of freedom an intentional and predetermined reduction in sample size to provide a conservative data adjustment to compensate for research error.

demand characteristic the premise that subjects' awareness of the experimental condition may affect their performance in the experiment; also known as the Hawthorne effect.

deontological describes an ethical system based on rules.

dependent variable the variable that is observed and whose value is presumed to depend on the independent variable(s).

descriptive statistics statistical methods and techniques designed to reduce data sets to allow for easier interpretation.

descriptive survey a survey that attempts to picture or document current conditions or attitudes.

design-specific results research results that are based on, or specific to, the research design used.

designated market area (DMA) a term to define a TV market area; each county in the United States belongs to only one DMA.

discrete variable a variable that can be conceptually subdivided into a finite number of indivisible parts (for example, the number of children in a family).

dispersion the amount of variability in a set of scores.

disproportionate stratified sampling overrepresentation of a specific stratum or characteristic.

distribution a collection of scores or measurements.

double-barreled question a single question that requires two separate responses (for example, "Do you like the price and style of this item?").

double-blind experiment a research study in which experimenters and others do not know whether a given subject belongs to the experimental group or to the control group.

dummy variable the variable created when a variable at the nominal level is transformed into a form more appropriate for higher-order statistics.

editor–reader comparison a readership study in which the perceptions of editors and readers are solicited.

engagement a measure used by an advertiser to gauge how involved or how connected people are with an ad or a brand.

environmental monitoring program in public relations research, a study of trends in public opinion and events in the social environment that may have a significant impact on an organization.

equivalency the internal consistency of a measure.

error variance the error created by an unknown factor.

evaluation apprehension a fear of being measured or tested, which may result in providing invalid data.

evaluation research a small-scale environmental monitoring program designed to measure an organization's social performance.

exhaustivity a state of a category system such that every unit of analysis can be placed into an existing slot.

experimental design a blueprint or set of plans for conducting laboratory research.

external validity the degree to which the results of a research study are generalizable to other situations.

eye camera a device used to track a person's gaze over some image.

factor analysis a multivariate statistical procedure used primarily for data reduction, construct development, and the investigation of variable relationships.

factor fusion a statistical procedure in which the range of ratings are artificially restricted.

factor score a composite or summary score produced by factor analysis.

factorial design a simultaneous analysis of two or more independent variables or factors.

feeling thermometer a rating scale patterned after a weather thermometer on which respondents can rate their attitudes on a scale of 0 to 100.

field observation a study of a phenomenon in a natural setting.

field service a research company that conducts interviews, recruits respondents for research projects, or both.

filter question a question designed to screen out certain individuals from participation in a study; also called a screener question.

file transfer protocol (FTP) computer language/software to upload files to a server.

Flesch reading ease formula an early readability formula based on the number of words per sentence and the number of syllables per word.

focus group an interview conducted with 6–12 subjects simultaneously and a moderator who leads a discussion about a specific topic.

Fog Index a readability scale based on sentence length and the number of syllables per word.

follow-back panel a research technique in which a current cross-sectional sample is selected and matched with archival data.

forced-choice question a question that requires a subject to choose between two specified responses.

forced exposure a test situation in which respondents are required to be exposed to a specific independent or dependent variable.

framing how the media choose to portray what they cover.

frequency in advertising, the total number of exposures to a message that a person or household receives.

frequency curve a graphical display of frequency data in a smooth, unbroken curve.

frequency distribution a collection of scores, ordered according to magnitude, and their respective frequencies.

frequency polygon a series of lines connecting points that represent the frequencies of scores.

gross incidence the percentage of qualified respondents reached of all contacts made.

gross rating points the total of audience ratings during two or more time periods, representing the size of the gross audience of a radio or television broadcast.

group administration conducting measurements with several subjects simultaneously.

histogram a bar chart that illustrates frequencies and scores.

homogeneity equality of control and experimental groups prior to an experiment; also called point of prior equivalency.

hook a short representative sample of a recording used in call-out research.

hypertext a system that links electronic documents.

hypertext markup language (HTML) a computer language used to develop web pages.

hypothesis a tentative generalization about the relationship between two or more variables that predicts an outcome.

incidence the percentage of a population that possesses the desired characteristics for a particular research study.

independent variable the variable that is systematically varied by the researcher.

informed consent an ethical guideline stating that participants in a research project should have the basic facts of the project revealed to them before they make a decision to participate in the research.

instrument decay the deterioration of a measurement instrument during the course of a study, which reduces the instrument's effectiveness and accuracy.

instrumental replication the duplication in a research study of the dependent variable of a previous study.

intensive interview an extension of the one-on-one personal interview in which in-depth information is obtained.

interaction a treatment-related effect dependent on the concomitant influence of two independent variables on a dependent variable.

intercoder reliability in content analysis, the degree of agreement between or among independent coders.

internal consistency the level of consistency of performance among items within a scale.

internal validity a property of a research study such that results are based on expected conditions rather than on extraneous variables.

internet service provider (ISP) a company that provides user connections to the Internet.

interval level a measurement system in which the intervals between adjacent points on a scale are equal (for example, a thermometer).

isomorphism similarity of form or structure.

item pretest a method of testing subjects' interest in reading magazine or newspaper articles.

item-selection study a readership study used to determine who reads specific parts of a newspaper.

justice an ethical principle holding that all people should be treated equally.

leading question a question that suggests a certain response or makes an implicit assumption (for example, "How long have you been an alcoholic?").

lifestyle segmentation research a research project that investigates and categorizes respondents' activities, interests, attitudes, and behaviors.

Likert scale a measurement scale in which respondents strongly agree, agree, are neutral, disagree, or strongly disagree with the statements.

linear regression predicting an association between two variables.

literal replication a study that is an exact duplication of a previous study.

longitudinal study the collection of data at different points in time.

magazine readership survey a survey of readers to determine which sections of the magazine were viewed, read, or both.

mail survey the mailing of self-administered questionnaires to a sample of people; the researcher must rely on the recipients to mail back their responses.

mailing list a compilation of names and addresses, sometimes prepared by a commercial firm, that is used as a sampling frame for mail surveys.

main effect the effect of the independent variable(s) on the dependent variable (no interaction is present).

manipulation check a test to determine whether the manipulation of the independent variable actually had the intended effect.

marker variable a variable that highlights or defines the construct under study.

masked recall a survey technique in which the interviewer shows respondents the front cover of a newspaper or magazine with the name of the publication blacked out to test unaided recall of the publication.

mean the arithmetic average of a set of scores.

measurement a procedure in which a researcher assigns numerals to objects, events, or properties according to certain rules.

measurement error an inconsistency produced by the instruments used in a research study.

media efficiency reaching the maximum possible audience at the least possible cost.

median the midpoint of a distribution of scores.

medium variables in a content analysis, the aspects of content that are unique to the medium under consideration (for example, typography to a newspaper or magazine).

meta-analysis a quantitative aggregation of many research findings.

method of authority a method of knowing in which something is believed because a source perceived as an authority says it is true.

method of intuition a method of knowing in which something is believed because it is "self-evident" or "stands to reason"; also called a priori reasoning.

method of tenacity a method of knowing in which something is believed because a person has always believed it to be true.

method-specific results research results based on, or specific to, the research method used.

metro survey area (MSA) a region representing one of the Consolidated Metropolitan Statistical Areas (CMSA), as defined by the U.S. Office of Management and Budget.

mode the score that occurs most often in a frequency distribution.

monotonic transformation applying the same mathematical adjustment to all data points.

mortality in panel studies and other forms of longitudinal research, the percentage of original sample members who drop out of the research project for one reason or another.

mu (μ) population mean.

multiple regression an analysis of two or more independent variables and their relationship to a single dependent variable; used to predict the dependent variable.

multistage sampling a form of cluster sampling in which individual households or persons, not groups, are selected.

multivariate analysis a statistical analysis where multiple dependent variables are measured.

mutually exclusive a category system in which a unit of analysis can be placed in one and only one category.

net incidence the number of respondents or subjects who actually participate in a research project.

neuromarketing a technique that uses brain imaging to study advertising effectiveness.

noise variables that create spurious or misleading results.

nominal level the level of measurement at which arbitrary numerals or other symbols are used to classify people, objects, or characteristics.

nonmaleficence an ethical principle stating that a researcher should do no harm.

nonparametric statistics statistical procedures used with variables measured at the nominal or ordinal level.

nonprobability sample a sample selected without regard to the laws of mathematical probability.

normal curve a symmetrical, bell-shaped curve that possesses specific mathematical characteristics.

normal distribution a mathematical model of how measurements are distributed; a graph of a normal distribution is a continuous, symmetrical, bell-shaped curve.

null hypothesis the denial or negation of a research hypothesis; the hypothesis of no difference.

objective function a mathematical formula that provides various quantitative values for a given media schedule of advertisements; used in computer simulations of advertising media schedules.

Ockham's razor the philosophy that states, "The simplest approach is always the best."

one-on-one interviews sessions in which respondents are interviewed one at a time.

open-ended question a question to which respondents are asked to generate an answer or answers with no prompting from the item itself (for example, "What is your favorite type of television program?").

operational definition a definition that specifies patterns of behavior and procedures to experience or measure a concept.

operational replication a study that duplicates only the sampling methodology and the experimental procedures of a previous study.

ordinal level the level of measurement at which items are ranked along a continuum.

overnights ratings surveys of a night's television viewing computed in five major U.S. cities by the A. C. Nielsen Company.

panel study a research technique in which the same sample of respondents is measured at different points in time.

parameter a characteristic or property of a population.

parametric statistics statistical procedures appropriate for variables measured at the interval or ratio level.

parsimony principle the premise that the simplest method is the most preferable; also known as Ockham's Razor.

partial correlation a method used to control a confounding or spurious variable that may affect the relationship between independent variables and dependent variables.

people meter an electronic television audience data-gathering device capable of recording individual viewing behavior.

periodicity any form of bias resulting from the use of a nonrandom list of subjects or items in selecting a sample.

personal interview a survey technique in which a trained interviewer visits a respondent and administers a questionnaire in a face-to-face setting.

pilot study a trial run of a study conducted on a small scale to determine whether the research design and methodology are relevant and effective.

population a group or class of objects, subjects, or units.

population distribution the frequency distribution of all the variables of interest as determined by a census of the population.

Portable People Meter (PPM) Arbitron's handheld device used to record respondent radio listening behavior.

power the probability of rejecting the null hypothesis when an alternative is true.

precision journalism a technique of inquiry in which social science research methods are used to gather the news.

precursor analysis a study assuming that leaders establish trends and that these trends ultimately trickle down to the rest of society.

predictor variable see *antecedent variable*.

prerecruits respondents who are recruited ahead of time to participate in a research project.

prestige bias the tendency of a respondent to give answers that will make him or her seem more educated, successful, financially stable, or otherwise prestigious.

private-sector research applied research designed to help decision making.

probability level a predetermined value at which researchers test their data for statistical significance.

probability sample a sample selected according to the laws of mathematical probability.

proportionate stratified sampling representing population proportions of a specific stratum or characteristic.

proposition a statement of the form "if *A*, then *B*" that links two or more concepts.

proprietary data research data gathered by a private organization that are available to the general public only if released by that organization.

prosocial having positive results for society.

protocol a document that contains the procedures to be used in a field study.

psychographics an area of research that examines why people behave and think as they do.

public relations audit a comprehensive study of the public relations position of an organization.

purposive sample a sample deliberately chosen to be representative of a population.

qualified volunteer sample probability sampling where subjects must qualify (pass) on one or more questions to be eligible for the sample but still must volunteer to participate.

qualitative research method a research method that uses flexible questioning.

quantitative research method a research method that uses standardized questioning.

quasi-experiment a research design that does not involve random assignment of subjects to experimental groups.

quota sample a sample selected to represent certain characteristics of interest.

random digit dialing (RDD) a method of selecting telephone numbers that ensures that all telephone households have an equal chance of being selected.

random error error in a research study that cannot be controlled by the researcher.

random sample a subgroup or subset of a population selected in such a way that each unit in a population has an equal chance of being selected.

range a measure of dispersion based on the difference between the highest and lowest scores in a distribution.

rating an estimate of the percentage of persons or households in a population that are tuned to a specific station or network.

ratio level a level of measurement that has all the properties of an interval level scale and also has a true zero point.

reach (advertising) the total number of persons or households exposed to a message at least once during a specific period of time; see also *cume*.

reactivity a subject's awareness of being measured or observed and its possible impact on that subject's behavior.

readability the total of all elements in a piece of printed material that affect the degree to which people understand the piece and find it interesting.

reader-nonreader study a study that contrasts nonreaders of newspapers or magazines with regular readers.

reader profile a demographic summary of the readers of a particular publication.

recall study a study in which respondents are asked to remember which advertisements they remember seeing in the medium being investigated.

recognition a measurement of readership in which respondents are shown the logo of a magazine or newspaper.

region of rejection the proportion of an area in a sampling distribution that equals the level of significance; the region of rejection represents all the values of a test statistic that are highly unlikely, provided the null hypothesis is true.

regression toward the mean tendency of very high or very low scores to move closer to the mean in subsequent measurements.

relativistic ethical system that takes into account the situation in which a decision is made.

reliability the property of a measure that consistently gives the same answer at different times.

repeated-measures design a research design in which numerous measurements are made on the same subjects.

replication an independent verification of a research study.

research question a tentative generalization about the relationship between two or more variables.

research supplier a company that provides various forms of research to clients, from data collection only to a final written analysis and summary of the data.

response set a pattern of answers given by a respondent, such as all "5" ratings on a 1–10 rating scale. These data are usually deleted from the data set.

retrospective panel a study in which each respondent is asked questions about events and attitudes in his or her lifetime.

rough cut a model or simulation of a final product.

sample a subgroup or subset of a population or universe.

sample distribution the frequency distribution of all the variables of interest as determined from a sample.

sample-specific results research results based on, or specific to, the research sample used.

sampling distribution a probability distribution of all possible values of a statistic that would occur if all possible samples of a fixed size were taken from a given population.

sampling error the degree to which measurements obtained from a sample differ from the measurements that would be obtained from the population.

sampling frame a list of the members of a particular population.

sampling interval a random interval used for selecting subjects or units in the systematic sampling method.

sampling rate the ratio of the number of people chosen in the sample to the total number in the population (for example, if 100 fraternity members were systematically chosen from a sampling frame of 1,000 fraternity members, the sampling rate would be 10%, or 1/10).

scale a form of measurement such as a 10-point scale, Likert, Guttman, or semantic differential.

scattergram a graphic technique for portraying the relationship between two variables.

scientific method a systematic, controlled, empirical, and critical investigation of hypothetical propositions about the presumed relationships among natural phenomena.

screener a short survey or a portion of a survey designed to select only appropriate respondents for a research project.

secondary analysis the use of data collected by a previous researcher or another research organization; also called data re-analysis.

semantic differential a rating scale consisting of seven spaces between two bipolar adjectives (for example, "good _ _ _ _ _ _ _ bad").

share an estimate of the percentage of persons or households tuned to a specific station, channel, or network.

shopping center interview (intercept) a nonprobability study in which respondents are recruited and interviewed in a shopping mall.

sigma (Σ) the Greek capital letter symbolizing summation.

skewness the degree of departure of a curve from the normal distribution (curves can be positively or negatively skewed).

smart media the newest mass medium, which includes smartphones, smart TVs, and tablets.

smartphone mobile phone that is essentially a handheld computer than can access the Internet and, along with the smart TV, is one of two mass media that can access all other mass media.

smart TV a TV that is essentially a computer than can access the Internet and, along with the smartphone, is one of two mass media that can access all other mass media.

social audit in public relations research, an analysis of the social performance of an organization.

split-half technique a method of determining reliability in a measure.

stability the degree of consistency of the results of a measure at different times.

staged manipulation a situation in which researchers construct events and circumstances so that they can manipulate the independent variable.

standard deviation the square root of the variance (a mathematical index of dispersion).

standard error an estimate of the amount of error present in a measurement.

standard score a measure that has been standardized in relation to a distribution's mean and standard deviation.

statistics a science that uses mathematical methods to collect, organize, summarize, and analyze data.

straightforward manipulation a situation in which materials and instructions are simply presented to respondents or subjects.

stratified sample a sample selected after the population has been divided into categories.

structured interview an interview in which standardized questions are asked in a predetermined order.

summary statistics statistics that summarize a great deal of numerical information about a distribution, such as the mean and the standard deviation.

sweeps a nationwide survey conducted by the A. C. Nielsen Company of every television market; conducted in February, May, July, and November.

systematic random sampling a procedure to select every *n*th subject for a study, such as every tenth person in a telephone directory.

systematic variance a regular increase or decrease in all scores or data in a research study by a known factor.

tablet (computer) a mobile computer that usually has a touchscreen or pen-enabled interface.

teleological describes an ethical system based on the balancing of the likely effects of a decision.

telephone coincidental a broadcasting research procedure in which random subjects or households are called and asked what they are viewing or listening to at that moment.

telephone survey a research method in which survey data are collected over the telephone by trained interviewers who ask questions and record responses.

theory a set of related propositions that presents a systematic view of phenomena by specifying relationships among concepts.

time spent listening (TSL) a quantitative statement about the average time a listener spends listening to a radio station (or several stations); stated in hours and minutes.

total observation in field observation, a situation in which the observer assumes no role in the phenomenon being observed other than that of observer.

total participation field observation in which the observer becomes a full-fledged participant in the situation under observation.

total survey area (TSA) a region in which an audience survey is conducted.

tracking study a special readership measurement technique in which respondents designate material they have read (using a different color of pencil for each reading episode).

trend study a longitudinal study in which a topic is restudied using different groups of respondents (for example, the Roper studies on the credibility of the media).

triangulation using a combined quantitative and qualitative approach to solve a problem.

trigger event an event or activity that might focus public concern on a topic or issue.

t-**test** a statistic used to determine the significance between group means.

Type I error rejection of the null hypothesis when it should be accepted.

Type II error acceptance of the null hypothesis when it should be rejected.

unaided recall question format in which respondents are asked to recall certain information without help from the researcher.

unit of analysis the smallest element of a content analysis; the thing that is counted whenever it is encountered.

unqualified volunteer sample a self-selected, non-probability sample.

unstructured interview an interview in which the interviewer asks broad and general questions but retains control over the discussion.

usability research research that examines the ease with which a person navigates a website.

uses and gratifications study a study of the motives for media usage and the rewards that are sought.

utilitarianism an ethical system that weighs the potential benefits of a decision against potential harm.

validity the degree to which a test actually measures what it purports to measure.

variable a phenomenon or event that can be measured or manipulated.

variance a mathematical index of the degree to which scores deviate from the mean.

voluntary participation an ethical guideline stating that subjects involved in a research project have a right to decline to participate or to leave the project at any time.

volunteer sample a sample consisting of respondents who consent to participate in a research project; types: qualified volunteer sample; unqualified volunteer sample.

web browser a program that searches the World Wide Web.

weighting a mathematical procedure used to adjust data from a sample to meet the characteristics of a given population; also called *sample balancing*.

World Wide Web a system of interconnected computers and electronic information sites.

NAME INDEX

Note: page numbers followed by t refer to Tables

SUBJECT INDEX

Note: page numbers followed by f or t refer to Figures or Tables